Fodor's

SOUTHERN CALIFORNIA

W9-BRZ-376

Portions of this book appear in *Fodor's California*.

WELCOME TO SOUTHERN CALIFORNIA

Balmy weather, blissful beaches, Hollywood glamour—Southern California delivers fun and relaxation year-round. Outdoor enthusiasts revel in the natural beauty and excellent outdoor activities in the dramatic Mojave Desert and iconic Big Sur coastline, and at relaxing Palm Springs resorts. Beachgoers are drawn to the seemingly endless strands that line the stunning coast. For urban culture-vultures, trendy Los Angeles and sunny San Diego hold a wealth of treasures, including movie studio tours, America's preeminent zoo, and superb restaurants.

TOP REASONS TO GO

★ **Cool Cities:** San Diego's bay, Los Angeles's movie lore, Palm Springs' spa resorts.

★ **Beaches:** For swimming, surfing, or tanning, the beaches can't be beat.

★ **Feasts:** Cutting-edge cuisine, food trucks, fusion flavors, farmers' markets.

★ **Theme Parks:** From Disneyland to LEGOLAND, SoCal has some of the biggest and best.

★ **Outdoor Adventures:** Hiking, golfing, and national park excursions are all excellent.

★ **Road Trips:** The Pacific Coast Highway offers spectacular views and thrills aplenty.

Fodor's SOUTHERN CALIFORNIA

Editorial: Douglas Stallings, *Editorial Director*; Salwa Jabado and Margaret Kelly, *Senior Editors*; Alexis Kelly, Jacinta O'Halloran, and Amanda Sadlowski, *Editors*; Teddy Minford, *Content Editor*; Rachael Roth, *Content Manager*

Design: Tina Malaney, *Art Director*

Photography: Jennifer Arnow, *Senior Photo Editor*

Maps: Rebecca Baer, *Senior Map Editor*; David Lindroth, Mark Stroud (Moon Street Cartography), *Cartographers*

Production: Jennifer DePrima, *Editorial Production Manager*; Carrie Parker, *Senior Production Editor*; Elyse Rozelle, *Production Editor*; David Satz, *Director of Content Production*

Business & Operations: Chuck Hoover, *Chief Marketing Officer*; Joy Lai, *Vice President and General Manager*; Stephen Horowitz, *Head of Business Development and Partnerships*

Public Relations: Joe Ewaskiw, *Manager*

Writers: Michele Bigley, Cheryl Crabtree, Alene Dawson, Paul Feinstein, Marlise Kast-Myers, Daniel Mangin, Kathy A. McDonald, Kai Oliver-Kurtain, Steve Pastorino, Joan Patterson, Archana Ram, Juliana Shallcross, Jeff Terich, Ashley Tibbits, Claire Deeks van der Lee, and Clarissa Wei

Editors: Salwa Jabado (lead editor), Alexis Kelly (San Diego editor), Rachael Roth (Los Angeles editor)

Production Editor: Elyse Rozelle

Production Design: Liliana Guia

15th Edition

ISBN 978-1-101-88017-3

ISSN 1543–1037

All details in this book are based on information supplied to us at press time. Always confirm information when it matters, especially if you're making a detour to visit a specific place. Fodor's expressly disclaims any liability, loss, or risk, personal or otherwise, that is incurred as a consequence of the use of any of the contents of this book.

PRINTED IN THE UNITED STATES OF AMERICA

10 9 8 7 6 5 4 3 2 1

CONTENTS

MAPS

ABOUT THIS GUIDE

Fodor's Recommendations

Everything in this guide is worth doing—we don't cover what isn't—but exceptional sights, hotels, and restaurants are recognized with additional accolades. **Fodor's**Choice★ indicates our top recommendations. Care to nominate a new place? Visit Fodors.com/contact-us.

Trip Costs

We list prices wherever possible to help you budget well. Hotel and restaurant price categories from **$** to **$$$$** are noted alongside each recommendation. For hotels, we include the lowest cost of a standard double room in high season. For restaurants, we cite the average price of a main course at dinner or, if dinner isn't served, at lunch. For attractions, we always list adult admission fees; discounts are usually available for children, students, and senior citizens.

Hotels

Our local writers vet every hotel to recommend the best overnights in each price category, from budget to expensive. Unless otherwise specified, you can expect private bath, phone, and TV in your room. *For expanded hotel reviews, visit Fodors.com.*

Top Picks

★ **Fodor's**Choice

Listings

- ✉ Address
- 📨 Branch address
- ☎ Telephone
- 📠 Fax
- 🌐 Website
- 📧 E-mail
- 🎟 Admission fee
- 🕒 Open/closed times
- [M] Subway
- ✥ Directions or Map coordinates

Hotels & Restaurants

- 🏨 Hotel
- 🛏 Number of rooms
- 🍽 Meal plans
- ✖ Restaurant
- ✍ Reservations
- 👔 Dress code
- ▭ No credit cards
- [$] Price

Other

- ⇨ See also
- ☞ Take note
- 🏌 Golf facilities

Restaurants

Unless we state otherwise, restaurants are open for lunch and dinner daily. We mention dress code only when there's a specific requirement and reservations only when they're essential or not accepted. *For expanded restaurant reviews, visit Fodors.com.*

Credit Cards

The hotels and restaurants in this guide typically accept credit cards. If not, we'll say so.

EUGENE FODOR

Hungarian-born Eugene Fodor (1905–91) began his travel career as an interpreter on a French cruise ship. The experience inspired him to write *On the Continent* (1936), the first guidebook to receive annual updates and discuss a country's way of life as well as its sights. Fodor later joined the U.S. Army and worked for the OSS in World War II. After the war, he kept up his intelligence work while expanding his guidebook series. During the Cold War, many guides were written by fellow agents who understood the value of insider information. Today's guides continue Fodor's legacy by providing travelers with timely coverage, insider tips, and cultural context.

EXPERIENCE SOUTHERN CALIFORNIA

WHAT'S NEW IN SOUTHERN CALIFORNIA

Foodie's Paradise

Great dining is a staple of the California lifestyle, and a new young generation of chefs is challenging old ideas about preparing and presenting great food. The food-truck frenzy continues to fuel movable feasts up and down the state. Esteemed chefs and urban foodies follow the trucks on Twitter as they move around cities 24/7 purveying delicious, cheap, fresh meals. You can find food-laden trucks at sports and entertainment venues, near parks and attractions, and on busy roads and boulevards.

Diners are also embracing the pop-up concept, where guest chefs offer innovative menus in unconventional settings for a limited time. These pop-up engagements are hosted anywhere from inside a warehouse to outside in a field. Often there is an air of secrecy and anticipation to them, with key details being revealed at the last moment. Visitors can look for local pop-ups listed on foodie websites such as Eater (⊕ *www.eater.com*).

Family Fun

California's theme parks work overtime to keep current and attract patrons of all ages. LEGOLAND California Resort keeps expanding with additional attractions such as the LEGOLAND Water Park and its 250-room LEGO-theme hotel.

Disneyland also continues to grow. Return visitors will notice changes around the park during the ongoing construction of the highly anticipated Star Wars Land, scheduled to open in 2019. In the meantime, visitors will enjoy the addition of new shows, parades, and attractions, such as the transformation of the Tower of Terror into the Marvel Guardians of the Galaxy ride.

Wine Discoveries

In the hillsides of San Diego County, the Ramona Valley AVA is seeing an increasing number of visitors, and Escondido-based Orfila keeps snagging awards. North of Los Angeles, the boutique wineries in the hillsides of Malibu are garnering increased attention.

All Aboard

Riding the rails can be a satisfying experience, particularly in California where the distances between destinations sometimes run into the hundreds of miles. You can save money on gas and parking, avoid freeway traffic, and see some of the best the state has to offer. California just broke ground on a high-speed rail project linking San Francisco to Los Angeles. In 2030, when the $68-billion project is complete, the train will make the run between the two cities in less than three hours.

Until then, the best trip is on the luxuriously appointed *Coast Starlight,* a long-distance train with sleeping cars that runs between Seattle and Los Angeles, passing some of California's most beautiful coastline as it hugs the beach. For the best surf-side viewing, get a seat or a room on the left side of the train and ride south to north.

State of the Arts

The Los Angeles County Museum of Art (LACMA) keeps expanding its Wilshire Boulevard campus following the 2010 opening of the Renzo Piano–designed Resnick Pavilion. It is now gearing up for a major expansion under the direction of architect Peter Zumthor, estimated to be complete in 2023.

SOUTHERN CALIFORNIA PLANNER

When to Go

Because they offer activities indoors and out, the top California cities rate as all-seasons destinations. Ditto for Southern California's coastal playgrounds.

Death Valley and Joshua Tree National Park are best in spring when desert blooms offset their austerity and temperatures are still manageable. Autumn is "crush time" in all the wine destinations.

CLIMATE

It's difficult to generalize about the state's weather beyond saying that precipitation comes in winter and summer is dry in most places. As a rule, inland regions are hotter in summer and colder in winter, compared with coastal areas, which are relatively cool year-round. Fog is a potential hazard any day of the year in coastal regions. As you climb into the mountains, seasonal variations are more apparent: winter brings snow (at elevations above 3,000 feet), autumn is crisp, spring can go either way, and summer is sunny and warm, with an occasional thundershower.

MICROCLIMATES

Mountains separate the California coastline from the state's interior, and the weather can sometimes vary dramatically within a 15-minute drive. In August, Palm Springs's thermometers can soar to 110°F at noon, and drop to 75°F at night.

Car Travel

Driving may be a way of life in California, but it isn't cheap (gas prices here are usually among the highest in the nation). It's also not for the fainthearted; you've surely heard horror stories about L.A.'s freeways, but even the state's scenic highways and byways have their own hassles. For instance, on the dramatic coastal road between San Simeon and Carmel, twists, turns, and divinely distracting vistas frequently slow traffic; in rainy season, mud slides can close the road altogether. ⚠ Never cross the double line to pass a slower car ahead of you. If you see that cars are backing up behind you, stop at the first available pullout to allow faster drivers to pass.

On California's notorious freeways, other rules apply. Nervous Nellies must resist the urge to stay in the two slow-moving lanes on the far right, used primarily by trucks. To drive at least the speed limit, get yourself in a middle lane. If you're ready to bend the rules a bit, the second lane (lanes are numbered from 1 starting at the center) moves about 5 mph faster. But avoid the far-left lane (the one next to the carpool lane), where speeds range from 75 mph to 90 mph.

Air Travel

Around Los Angeles, there are several airport options to choose from. LAX, the world's sixth-busiest airport, gets most of the attention—and not usually for good reasons. John Wayne Airport (SNA), about 25 miles south in Orange County, is a solid substitute—especially if you're planning to visit Disneyland or Orange County. You might also consider Bob Hope Airport (BUR) in Burbank (close to Hollywood and its studios) or Long Beach Airport (LGB), convenient if you're catching a cruise ship. San Diego's Lindbergh International Airport (SAN) is located minutes from the Gaslamp Quarter, Balboa Park and Zoo, and the cruise ship terminal.

WHAT'S WHERE

1 San Diego. San Diego's Gaslamp Quarter and early California–themed Old Town have a human scale—but big-ticket animal attractions like the San Diego Zoo pull in visitors.

2 Orange County. A diverse destination with premium resorts and restaurants, strollable waterfront communities, and kid-friendly attractions.

3 Los Angeles. Go for the glitz of the entertainment industry, but stay for the rich cultural attributes and communities.

4 The Central Coast. Three of the state's top stops—swanky Santa Barbara, Hearst Castle, and Big Sur—sit along the scenic 200-mile route. A quick boat trip away lies scenic Channel Islands National Park.

5 The Inland Empire. The San Bernardino Mountains provide seasonal escapes, and the Temecula Valley will challenge your ideas of "California Wine Country."

6 Palm Springs and the Desert Resorts. Golf on some of the West's most challenging courses, lounge at fabulous resorts, check out mid-20th-century-modern architectural gems, and trek through primitive desert parks.

7 Joshua Tree National Park. Proximity to major urban areas—as well as world-class rock climbing and nighttime celestial displays—help make this one of the most visited national parks.

8 Mojave Desert. Material pleasures are in short supply here, but Mother Nature's stark beauty more than compensates.

9 Death Valley National Park. America's second-largest national park is vast, beautiful, and often the hottest place in the nation.

10 Sequoia and Kings Canyon National Parks. The sight of ancient redwoods towering above jagged mountains is breathtaking.

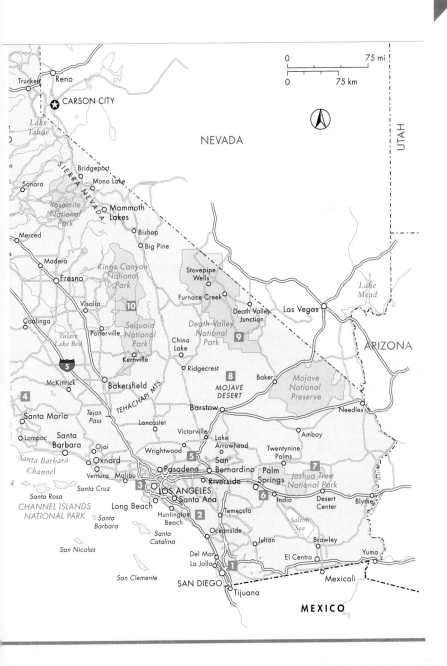

SOUTHERN CALIFORNIA TODAY

The People

California is as much a state of mind as a state in the union—a kind of perpetual promised land that has represented many things to many people. In the 18th century, Spanish missionaries came seeking converts and gold. In the 19th, miners rushed here to search for gold. And, in the years since, a long line of Dust Bowl farmers, land speculators, Haight-Ashbury hippies, migrant workers, dot-commers, real estate speculators, and would-be actors have come chasing their own dreams.

The result is a population that leans toward idealism—without necessarily being as liberal as you might think. (Remember, this is Ronald Reagan's old stomping ground.) And despite the stereotype of the blue-eyed, blond surfer, California's population is not homogeneous either. Ten million people who live here (more than 27% of Californians) are foreign born. Almost half hail from Latin American countries; another third emigrated from Asia, following the waves of Chinese workers who arrived in the 1860s to build the railroads and subsequent waves of Indochinese refugees from the Vietnam War.

The Politics

What's blue and red and green all over? California: a predominantly Democratic state with an aggressive "go green" agenda and policies that make California the greenest state in the nation, supporting more green construction, wind farms, and solar panels.

The Economy

Leading all other states in terms of the income generated by agriculture, tourism, entertainment, and industrial activity, California has the country's most diverse state economy. Moreover, with a gross state product of more than $2 trillion, California would be one of the top 10 economies *in the world* if it were an independent nation.

Despite its wealth ($61,818 median household income) and productivity, California took a large hit in the 2007 recession, but the Golden State's economic history is filled with boom and bust cycles—beginning with the mid-19th-century gold rush that started it all. Optimists already have their eyes on the next potential boom: high-tech and bioresearch, "green companies" focused on alternative energy, renewables, electric cars, and the like.

The Culture

Art and culture thrive in San Diego. Balboa Park alone holds 17 museums, opulent gardens, and three performance venues, in addition to the San Diego Zoo. The Old Globe Theater and La Jolla Playhouse routinely originate plays that capture coveted Tony Awards in New York.

But California's *real* forte is pop culture, and L.A. and its environs are the chief arbiters. Movie, TV, and video production have been centered here since the early 20th century. Capitol Records set up shop in L.A. in the 1940s, and this area has been instrumental in the music industry ever since. And while these industries continue to influence national trends, today they are only part of the pop culture equation. Websites are also a growing part of that creativity—Facebook, YouTube, and Google are California companies.

The Parks and Preserves

Cloud-spearing redwood groves, snow-tipped mountains, canyon-slashed deserts, primordial lava beds, and a seemingly endless coast: California's natural diversity is staggering—and efforts to protect it started early. Yosemite, the first national park, was established here in 1890, and the National Park Service now oversees 32 sites in California (more than in any other state). When you factor in 280 state parks—which encompass underwater preserves, historic sites, wildlife reserves, dune systems, and other sensitive habitats—the number of acres involved is almost as impressive as the topography itself.

Due to encroaching development and pollution, keeping these natural treasures in pristine condition is an ongoing challenge. For instance, Sequoia and Kings Canyon (which is plagued by pesticides and other agricultural pollutants blown in from the San Joaquin Valley) has been named America's "smoggiest park" by the National Parks Conservation Association, and the Environmental Protection Agency has designated it as an "ozone nonattainment area with levels of ozone pollution that threaten human health."

There is no question that Californians love their 280 state parks. Nearly every park has its grass-roots supporters, who volunteer to raise money, volunteer as rangers, and work other jobs to keep the parks open.

The Cuisine

California gave us McDonald's, Denny's, Carl's Jr., Taco Bell, and, of course, In-N-Out Burger. Fortunately for those of us with fast-clogging arteries, the state also kick-started the health-food movement. Back in the 1970s, California-based chefs put American cuisine on the culinary map by focusing on freshly prepared seasonal ingredients.

Today, this focus has spawned the "locavore" or sustainable food movement—followers try to consume only food produced within a 100-mile radius of where they live, since processing and refining food and transporting goods over long distances is bad for both the body and the environment. This isn't much of a restriction in California, where a huge variety of crops grow year-round. Some 350 cities and towns have certified farmers' markets—and their stalls are bursting with a variety of goods. California has been America's top agricultural producer for the last 50 years, growing more fruits and vegetables than any other state. Dairies and ranches also thrive here, and fishing fleets harvest fish and shellfish from the rich waters offshore.

SOUTHERN CALIFORNIA TOP ATTRACTIONS

Big Sur Coastline

(A) A drive along Highway 1 through the winding Big Sur Coastline is hard to beat. With towering forests on one side and rocky seaside cliffs on the other, drivers must take care not to become distracted by the spectacular ocean views. While the vistas are stunning from the road, travelers will be rewarded by short detours to visit elephant seals, relax on secluded beaches or hike through the redwoods.

Balboa Park

(B) What's not to like about San Diego's Balboa Park? A huge space in the heart of downtown where you can spend a whole day, the park is filled with open green lawns, great play areas for kids, colorful gardens, historic fountains, and beautiful Spanish-style buildings that are more than 100 years old. Fifteen museums display collections ranging from natural history to fine art and photography, from sports to classic cars to science.

Disneyland Resort

(C) A trip to Disneyland is indeed a dream come true for many. Built in 1955, Disneyland is the original Disney amusement park. Today, the Anaheim resort has grown to include Disneyland, Disney's California Adventure, Downtown Disney, and three Disney hotels. Its proximity to Los Angeles and San Diego makes it easy to incorporate a visit into almost any Southern California itinerary.

Hollywood

(D) When people think of Los Angeles, it is Hollywood that most often comes to mind. Visitors can't help but be starstruck while wandering the Hollywood Walk of Fame, standing at the epicenter of Hollywood and Vine, or gazing up at the famous Hollywood sign. A visit to one of the studios that makes the magic happen, such as Paramount Pictures, Universal Studios Hollywood, or Warner Bros. Studios, is a must.

Death Valley

(E) For well-prepared travelers, a trip to Death Valley is more awe-inspiring than ominous. Within the largest national park in the contiguous United States you'll find the brilliantly colored rock formations of Artist's Palette, the peaks of the Panamint Mountains, and the desolate salt flats of Badwater, 282 feet below sea level.

San Diego Zoo

(F) The world-renowned San Diego Zoo is a must-see for adults and kids alike. Set in 100 acres within Balboa Park, the zoo is admired for its conservation efforts. Famous for its giant panda research, the zoo's resident pandas are the stars of the show.

Mission Santa Barbara

Santa Barbara is the most beautiful of the 21 remaining settlements along California's Mission Trail. Originally built in 1786, the Mission is home to an excellent collection of Native American and Spanish and Mexican colonial art. Santa Barbara has many more attractions to warrant a visit, including its walkable downtown, and an excellent wine region.

Palm Springs and Beyond

In this improbably situated bastion of Bentleys and bling, worldly pleasures rule. Glorious golf courses, tony shops and restaurants, decadent spa resorts—they're all here. Fans of mid-century modernist architecture will love the many gems on display in Palm Springs. Solitude seekers can still slip away to nearby Joshua Tree National Park or Anza-Borrego Desert State Park.

SOUTHERN CALIFORNIA'S TOP EXPERIENCES

Ride a Wave
Surfing—which has influenced everything from fashion to moviemaking to music—is a quintessential California activity. You can find great surf breaks in many places along the coast, but one of the best places to try it is Huntington Beach. Lessons are widely available. If you're not ready to hang 10, you can hang out at "Surf City's" International Surfing Museum or stroll the Surfing Walk of Fame.

Think Globally, Eat Locally
Over the years California cuisine has evolved from a mere trend into a respected gastronomic tradition: one that pairs local, often organic or sustainable, ingredients with techniques inspired by European, Asian, and, increasingly, Indian and Middle Eastern cookery.

See Eccentric Architecture
California has always drawn creative and, well, eccentric people. And all that quirkiness has left its mark in the form of oddball architecture that makes for some fun sightseeing. Begin by touring Hearst Castle—the beautifully bizarre estate William Randolph Hearst built above San Simeon. In Death Valley, the late Marta Becket's Amargosa Opera House offers a variation on the theme.

Get Behind the Scenes
In L.A. it's almost obligatory to do some Hollywood-style stargazing. Cue the action with a behind-the-scenes tour of one of the dream factories. (Warner Bros. Studios' five-hour deluxe version, which includes lunch in the commissary, is just the ticket for cinephiles.) Other must-sees include the Dolby Theatre, home to the Academy Awards; Grauman's Chinese Theatre, where celebs press feet and hands into cement for posterity's sake; Hollywood Boulevard's star-paved Walk of Fame; and the still-iconic Hollywood sign.

People-Watch
Opportunities for world-class people-watching abound in California. Hang around L.A.'s Venice Boardwalk, where chain-saw jugglers, surfers, fortune-tellers, and well-oiled bodybuilders take beachfront exhibitionism to a new high (or low, depending on your point of view). The result is pure eye candy.

Go Wild
California communities host hundreds of annual events, but some of the best are organized by Mother Nature. The most famous is the "miracle migration" that sees swallows flock back to Mission San Juan Capistrano in Orange County each March.

IF YOU LIKE

One-of-a-Kind Accommodations

Hoteliers statewide have done their utmost to create accommodations that match the glories of the region's landscape, in the process creating lodgings that boast character as well as comfort. Some are unconventional, while others are genuine old-school gems.

Hotel Del Coronado, Coronado. A turreted beauty and veritable Victorian extravaganza, this spot inspired L. Frank Baum's description of Oz. Iconic architecture aside, Hotel Del Coronado is also famous as the filming locale for *Some Like It Hot,* and has hosted most of the U.S. presidents in the last century. Today it caters more to tour groups than Tinseltown stars, but fans remain loyal.

Mission Inn, Riverside. This sprawling Spanish colonial revival estate has welcomed a who's who of politicos. Ronald and Nancy Reagan spent their wedding night here, Richard and Pat Nixon were married in its chapel, and eight U.S. heads of state have patronized its Presidential Lounge.

Movie Colony Hotel, Palm Springs. Hollywood's 1930s heyday comes alive at this glamorous boutique hotel designed by Albert Frey, who created mid-century minimalism in Palm Springs. It now attracts a lively clientele and has a cool vibe.

Off-the-Beaten-Path Adventures

Mother Nature has truly outdone herself in California. But at the state's most popular sites, it can be hard to approach her handiwork with a sense of awe when you're encircled by souvenir hawkers and camera-wielding tourists. Step off the beaten path, though, and all you'll be able to hear will be the echo of your own voice saying "wow."

Climbing. Joshua Tree National Park is California's epicenter for rock climbing; within the park there are hundreds of formations and thousands of routes to choose from. No experience? No problem. J-Tree Outfitters offers crash courses for beginners.

Kayaking. Paddling around the lichen-covered sea caves of Channel Islands National Park, you'll feel as if you're on another planet. But kayaking in La Jolla proves you can still find peace close to the big city.

Ballooning. Hot-air ballooning—whether over Temecula or Palm Desert—lets you sightsee from a totally new perspective.

Amusement Parks

You're on vacation, so why not enjoy some carefree pleasures? For concentrated doses of old-fashioned fun, indulge in creaky waterfront amusements—like the antique carousel at Santa Monica Pier. Or opt for a full day at an over-the-top theme park.

Disneyland, Anaheim. Walt Disney set the gold standard for theme parks, and his original "magic kingdom" (the only one built during his lifetime) remains at the top of its class due to innovative rides, animatronics, and a liberal sprinkling of pixie dust.

LEGOLAND California, Carlsbad. Dedicated to the plastic bricks that have been a playtime staple for more than 60 years, this park has more than 60 LEGO-inspired attractions (including the popular Driving School, Fun Town Fire Academy, plus get-all-wet Splash Battle and Pirate Reef) and some 15,000 LEGO models ranging from teeny working taxis to a 9-foot-tall dinosaur.

San Diego Zoo Safari Park, Escondido. Get up close and personal with lions and tigers at this huge park where animals appear to be roaming free. You can feed a giraffe, talk to the gorillas, and track herds of elk as they cross the plain. Cheetahs bound, hippos huff, and zebras zip.

Spas

Ancient Romans coined the word "spa" as an acronym for *solus per aqua* (or "health by water"). There's plenty of the wet stuff in the Golden State, yet California spas—like California kitchens—are known for making the most of any indigenous ingredient. The resulting treatments are at once distinctive, decadent, and most important, relaxing.

The Golden Door, Escondido. Relax and renew at this destination spa tucked into a secluded canyon north of San Diego. Serenity and simplicity rule here, where every moment reflects its Zen-like ambience.

Glen Ivy Hot Springs Spa, Corona. The outdoor bath at this historic day spa couples red clay from Temescal Canyon with naturally heated, mineral-rich water from its own thermal springs.

Post Ranch Inn & Spa, Big Sur. Like its organic architecture, this luxe retreat's spa treatments are designed to capture the tone of Big Sur—case in point, the Crystal and Gemstone Therapy. It combines Native American tradition (a ceremonial burning of sage) with an aromatherapy massage that employs jade collected from nearby beaches and essences of local wildflowers.

SOUTHERN CALIFORNIA'S BEST ROAD TRIPS

GREAT ITINERARIES

BIG SUR, 2 DAYS

In a nutshell, this drive is all about the jaw-dropping scenery of the Pacific Coast. Visitors pressed for time often make the drive through Big Sur in one day. However, those who linger will be rewarded with more time to venture off the road and to enjoy the solitude of Big Sur once the day-trippers have gone.

⚠ Heavy rainfall in early 2017 caused a series of mud slides and the destabilization of the Pfeiffer Canyon Bridge along Highway 1 in Big Sur, and at this writing several sections of the highway remain closed with no alternate routes through Big Sur. Before planning a drive in the area, check the latest reconstruction updates on the Caltrans website at www.dot.ca.gov.

Day 1: Big Sur
(30 mins by car.)

The coastal drive through **Big Sur** is justifiably one of the most famous stretches of road in the world. The winding curves, endless views, and scenic waypoints are the stuff of road-trip legend. Keep your camera handy, fill up the tank, and prepare to be wowed. Traffic can easily back up along the route and drivers should take caution navigating the road's twists and turns. While you will only drive about 30 miles today, allow several hours for hikes and stops.

Heading into Big Sur you will first come upon the extremely photogenic **Bixby Creek Bridge.** Pull over in the turnout on the north side of the bridge to get that perfect shot. About 10 miles down the road look for a small cluster of services known as Big Sur Village just before the entrance to **Pfeiffer Big Sur State Park,** the perfect place to stop for a hike.

One mile south of the park, watch carefully for the sharp turnout and unmarked road leading to **Pfeiffer Beach.** Following the unpaved road 2 miles toward the sea you may question whether you are lost, but your perseverance will be rewarded when you reach the secluded beach with its signature rocky arch just offshore. Don't miss it!

There are several lodging options around this portion of Big Sur, ranging from rustic to luxurious. If room rates at the legendary **Post Ranch Inn** are not in your budget, consider splurging on the nine-course tasting menu at its spectacular cliff-side **Sierra Mar** restaurant instead. Alternatively, the terrace at **Nepenthe** offers decent food and gorgeous views at a lower price point. Be sure to check the time for sunset when making your dinner reservation.

Day 2: Big Sur to Cambria
(About 2 hrs by car. Allow ample time for hiking and 2 hrs to tour Hearst Castle.)

Start the morning off with a hike in **Julia Pfeiffer Burns State Park,** popular for its waterfall tumbling dramatically into the sea. Back on the road, several scenic overlooks will beckon as you head through the southern stretch of Big Sur. Treasure hunters should consider a stop at **Jade Cove.**

As you enter **San Simeon,** don't miss the **Piedras Blancas Elephant Seal Rookery.** Depending on your timing, you might catch a late afternoon tour at **Hearst Castle.** If not, you can make a reservation for a tour early the following morning. End the day with a walk at **Moonstone Beach** in the town of **Cambria,** 10 miles south of the castle, and overnight in one of the reasonably priced lodgings here.

From here, you can continue your travels south through the central coast to **Santa Barbara.** Or head inland to visit the **Paso Robles** wine region.

SANTA BARBARA WINE COUNTRY, 3 DAYS

It has been well over a decade since the popular movie *Sideways* brought the Santa Barbara Wine Country to the world's attention, and interest in this wine-growing area continues to grow. On this trip you will explore one of the most beautiful cities in the West, enjoy time along the gorgeous coast, and then head inland for a delightful wine-tasting adventure. This itinerary makes a perfect add-on to a trip to Los Angeles, or for those driving the coastal route between Los Angeles and San Francisco.

Day 1: Santa Barbara
(2 hrs by car from LAX to Santa Barbara without traffic.)

Santa Barbara is a gem, combining elegance with a laid-back coastal vibe. It provides a tranquil escape from the congestion of Los Angeles, and a dose of sophistication to the largely rural central coast.

Start your day at the beautiful **Old Mission Santa Barbara,** known as the "Queen" of the 21 missions that comprise the California Mission Trail. Plan to spend some time here; if your visit doesn't coincide with one of the 60-minute docent-led tours, self-guided tours are also available. From here, head to the waterfront and spend some time enjoying the wide stretch of sand at **East Beach** and a seafood lunch at one of the restaurants on **Stearns Wharf.**

Next stop is a tour of the **Santa Barbara County Courthouse** and the beautiful red-tile-roofed buildings of the surrounding downtown. Don't miss the murals in the ceremonial chambers or the incredible views from the top of the courthouse tower.

Back on the ground, enjoy superb shopping along **State Street** and consider kicking off your wine tour early with some tastings along the **Urban Wine Trail,** a collection of tasting rooms spread over a few blocks between downtown and the beach. Enjoy the lively dining and nightlife scene downtown, or head towards tony **Montecito** for an elegant dinner or overnight stay at the ultraexclusive (and expensive) **San Ysidro Ranch.**

PACIFIC
OCEAN

Day 2: Santa Rita Hills, Lompoc, and Los Olivos

(Without stops, this route takes about 2 hrs by car. Plan to linger and to detour down side roads to reach the wineries.)

Take the scenic drive along the coast on Highway 101 before heading inland towards Buellton. Exit onto Santa Rosa Road to begin your loop through the Santa Rita Hills. This area's cooler climate produces top-notch Chardonnay and Pinot Noir. Vineyards line the loop as you head out on Santa Rosa Road and return on Highway 246 towards Buellton. **Lafond Winery and Vineyards, Alma Rosa Winery,** and **Ken Brown Wines** are just a few of the wineries found along this route. Don't miss a stop at the so-called **Lompoc Wine Ghetto,** located midway around the route. Don't let the industrial-park setting deter you—several tasting rooms are clustered together, including well-regarded producers such as **Stolpman** and **Longoria,** making it a convenient and worthwhile stop.

Back on Highway 101, head north about 6 miles before exiting towards **Los Olivos.** Here you can park the car and spend the rest of the day exploring on foot. Tasting rooms, galleries, boutiques, and restaurants have made this former stagecoach town quite wine-country chic. **Carhartt Vineyard** and **Daniel Gehrs** are just two of the producers with tasting rooms in town. Los Olivos is a good base to overnight in, or stay just outside town at the lovely **Ballard Inn.** Or, dine at the chic locavore **Root 246** restaurant and stay at the **Hotel Corque** in nearby **Solvang.**

Day 3: Solvang, Foxen Canyon, and the Santa Ynez Valley

(The drive from Santa Ynez to Santa Barbara is about 45 mins by car via Hwy. 154.)

Start the next morning with pastries at the Danish town of **Solvang,** 10 minutes south of Los Olivos. The collection of windmills and distinct half-timber architecture of this village is charming, even if it is touristy. Spend some time exploring the town before hitting the road.

The towns of Los Olivos, Santa Ynez, and Solvang are located just a few minutes apart, with wineries spread between them in an area known as the Santa Ynez Valley. Heading north from Los Olivos, the Foxen Canyon wine trail extends all the way to Santa Maria and is home to excellent producers such as **Zaca Mesa** and the aptly named **Foxen Vineyards.** Expect some backtracking along your route today as you wind between the towns and venture into Foxen Canyon. The tour at **Firestone Vineyard** is worthwhile, but very popular. The tasting rooms throughout the Santa Ynez region can get crowded, but there are plenty to choose from—if you see a tour bus parked outside one winery, just keep driving to the next one. Don't blink or you might miss the tiny town of **Santa Ynez**; it is worth a wander or a stop for lunch.

When you've had your fill of the wine region, take scenic Highway 154 over the San Marcos Pass and back to Santa Barbara. Wind down the day with a stroll along the beach, and perhaps one last glass of wine at sunset.

ROUTE 66 AND THE MOJAVE DESERT, 4 DAYS

Route 66 was the original road trip and California the ultimate destination. The Mother Road travels west from the Arizona border, skirting the Mojave Desert before passing through Los Angeles and ending at the Pacific Ocean. What makes this journey so compelling is actually what it lacks. Desolate stretches of road through windswept towns are reminders of the tough conditions faced by dust-bowl pioneers, while faded neon signs and abandoned motels offer nostalgic glimpses of Route 66's heyday. Nearby, the solitary beauty of the Mojave National Preserve beckons with its volcanic rock formations, Joshua trees, and seemingly endless sand dunes.

Day 1: Santa Monica
By reversing the typical Route 66 journey and traveling from west to east you can hit the road upon arrival at LAX, or spend a few days exploring Los Angeles first. Starting your journey off in **Santa Monica** may feel a bit like eating your dessert first. For road-trippers on Route 66, reaching the Pacific Ocean after a long dusty drive through the desert was certainly a treat. The official end of Route 66 is marked with a plaque in **Palisades Park**, on a bluff overlooking **Santa Monica State Beach**. Soak in the quintessential SoCal beach scene on the wide expanse of sand below before heading to the famous **Santa Monica Pier**. From here, you can rent a bike and cruise south to **Venice Beach** for the ultimate people-watching experience.

In the evening, stroll the pedestrian-only **Third Street Promenade** and neighboring **Santa Monica Place** mall for a good selection of shopping, dining, and entertainment. Relax in luxury at the legendary **Shutters on the Beach.** Or, in keeping with the true Route 66 spirit, opt for the more modest motor-lodge vibe of the **Sea Shore Motel.**

Day 2: Hollywood and Pasadena
(1½ hrs by car from Santa Monica to Pasadena and another 1½–2 hrs by car to Victorville.)

Heading inland through **Beverly Hills** and **Hollywood**, the remnants of Route 66 are easily overshadowed by the surrounding glitz and glamour. A stop at the **Hollywood Museum** or the **Hollywood Walk of Fame** will help transport you back in time to Tinseltown's golden age.

The route continues through **Pasadena**, with its stately homes and spacious gardens. Fans of Craftsman architecture won't want to miss a tour of the **Gamble House**, while a stroll around **Old Town Pasadena** is a great way to stretch your legs and grab a bite to eat.

Depending on your interests and how much sightseeing you've done, you might

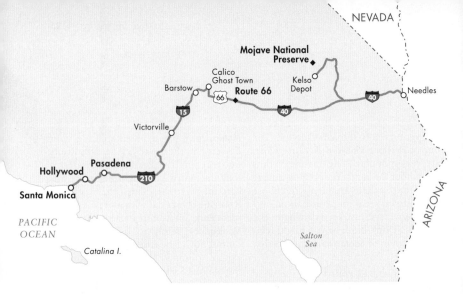

choose to stay in Pasadena for the night to enjoy a wider choice of dining and lodging options. Or, head to **Victorville** to maximize time on Route 66 tomorrow.

Day 3: Route 66

(Barstow to Needles is 2 hrs by car along I-40. However, add several more hrs to trace Route 66. Plan on spending 1–2 hrs at the Calico Ghost Town.)

Today is all about the drive. Hit the road early if you didn't spend the night in Victorville. First stop is the **California Route 66 Museum** in **Victorville**, where you'll learn all about the history of the Mother Road. Be sure to pick up a copy of their self-guided tour book and consult one of the many Route 66–related websites, such as ⊕ *www.historic66. com*, to help you navigate the old road as it crosses back and forth alongside Interstate 40 between Barstow and Needles. Abandoned service stations, shuttered motels, and faded signs dot the desert landscape in various states of alluring decay. Grab a meal at the famous **Baghdad Café** in Barstow. For a non–Route 66–related diversion spend a few hours exploring **Calico Ghost Town**, a restored old mining town just north of Barstow. In the evening, catch a flick at the **Skyline Drive-In Theatre**.

Accommodations in this area are mostly of the chain-motel variety. Victorville, Barstow, and Needles are your best bets for lodging.

Day 4: Mojave National Preserve

(There are several access points to the park along I-15 and I-40. Kelso Dunes Visitor Center is about 1½ hrs by car from either Barstow or Needles. Stick to the major roads in the park, which are either paved or gravel—others require four-wheel drive.)

In the morning, head north from Route 66 into the beautiful and remote landscape of the **Mojave National Preserve**. Reaching the top of the stunning golden **Kelso Dunes** requires some athleticism, but your efforts will be rewarded with incredible scenery and the eerie sounds of "singing" sand. If you spent the night in Needles, explore the volcanic gas formations of **Hole-in-the-Wall** first. Farther north in the park, the Cima Road will bring you to the Teutonia Peak Trailhead and the largest concentration of Joshua trees in the world. Visitor centers at **Kelso Depot** and **Hole-in-the-Wall** provide information on additional sights, hiking trails, and campgrounds in the park.

There are several options for the next leg of your journey. You can drive back to Los Angeles in about three hours or drive onward to **Las Vegas** even faster. If you have more time, you can continue north and spend a few days in **Death Valley National Park**, or head south towards **Joshua Tree** and **Palm Springs** before making your way back to **Los Angeles.**

PALM SPRINGS AND THE DESERT, 5 DAYS

The Palm Springs area is paradise for many. Most go for more than a good tan or to play golf on championship courses. Expect fabulous and funky spas, a dog-friendly atmosphere, and sparkling stars at night.

Day 1: Palm Springs
(Just over 2 hrs by car from LAX, without traffic.)

Somehow in harmony with the harsh environment, mid-century-modern homes and businesses with clean, low-slung lines define the **Palm Springs** style. Although the desert cities comprise a trendy destination with beautiful hotels, fabulous multicultural food, abundant nightlife, and plenty of culture, a quiet atmosphere prevails. Fans of Palm Springs's legendary architecture and style won't want to miss the home tours, lectures, and other events at the annual Modernism Week held each February, or the smaller fall preview event in October. If your visit doesn't coincide with these events, swing by the Palm Springs Visitor's Center for information on self-guided architecture tours. The city seems far away when you hike in hushed **Tahquitz** or **Indian Canyon**; cliffs and palm trees shelter rock art, irrigation works, and other remnants of Agua Caliente culture. If your boots aren't made for

walking, you can always practice your golf game or indulge in some sublime or funky spa treatments at an area resort instead. Embrace the Palm Springs vibe and park yourself at the retro **Orbit In Hotel** or the legendary **Parker Palm Springs.** Alternatively, base yourself at the desert oasis, **La Quinta Resort**, about 40 minutes outside downtown Palm Springs.

Day 2: Explore Palm Springs
(The Aerial Tram is 15 mins by car from central Palm Springs. Plan at least a half day for the excursion.)

If riding a tram up an 8,516-foot mountain for a stroll or even a snowball fight above the desert sounds like fun to you, then show up at the **Palm Springs Aerial Tramway** before the first morning tram leaves (later, the line can get discouragingly long). Just don't forget to dress in layers and wear decent footwear as it can be significantly colder when you reach the top. Afterward stroll through the **Palm Springs Art Museum** where you can see a shimmering display of contemporary studio glass, an array of enormous Native American baskets, and significant works of 20th-century sculpture by Henry Moore and others. After all that walking you may be ready for an early dinner. Nearly every restaurant in Palm Springs offers a happy hour, when you can sip a cocktail and nosh on a light entrée, usually for half price. Using your hotel as a base, take a few day trips to discover the natural beauty of the desert.

Day 3: Joshua Tree National Park
(1 hr by car from Palm Springs.)

Due to its proximity to Los Angeles and the highway between Las Vegas and coastal cities, **Joshua Tree** is one of the most popular and accessible of the national parks. You can see most of it in

a day, entering the park at the town of Joshua Tree, exploring sites along **Park Boulevard,** and exiting at **Twentynine Palms.** With its signature trees, piles of rocks, glorious spring wildflowers, starlit skies, and colorful pioneer history, the experience is a bit more like the Wild West than Sahara sand dunes. Whether planning to take a day hike or a scenic drive, be sure to load up on plenty of drinking water prior to entering the park.

Day 4: Anza-Borrego Desert State Park and the Salton Sea
(About 2 hrs by car from Palm Springs.)

The **Salton Sea,** about 60 miles south of Palm Springs via Interstate 10 and Highway 86S, is one of the largest inland seas on Earth. A new sea, formed by the flooding of the Colorado River in 1905, it attracts thousands of migrating birds and bird-watchers every fall. **Anza-Borrego Desert State Park** is the largest state park in California, with 600,000 acres of mostly untouched wilderness; it offers one of the best spring-wildflower displays in California and also displays a large collection of life-size bronze sculptures of animals that roamed this space millions of years ago. **Borrego Springs,** a tiny hamlet, lies in the center of it all. The desert is home to

an archaeological site, where scientists continue to uncover remnants of prehistoric animals ranging from mastodons to horses. If you have four-wheel drive, a detour down the sandy track to **Font's Point** rewards the intrepid with spectacular views of the Borrego badlands. However, do not take the challenging road conditions lightly—inquire with park rangers before setting out.

Day 5: Return to L.A.
(LAX is just over 2 hrs by car from Palm Springs without traffic, but the drive often takes significantly more time. Allow plenty of extra time if catching a flight.)

If you intend to depart from LAX, plan for a full day of driving from the desert to the airport. Be prepared for heavy traffic at any time of day or night. If possible, opt to fly out of Palm Springs International or LA/Ontario International Airport instead.

SOUTHERN CALIFORNIA WITH KIDS, 7 DAYS

SoCal offers many opportunities to entertain the kids beyond the Magic Kingdom. LEGOLAND is a blast for kids 12 and under, and families can't beat the San Diego Zoo and San Diego's historic Old Town.

2

Days 1–2: Disneyland
(45 mins by car from LAX to Disneyland.)

Get out of Los Angeles International Airport as fast as you can. Pick up your rental car and head south on the Interstate 405 freeway, which can be congested day or night, toward Orange County and **Disneyland.** Skirt the lines at the box office with advance-purchased tickets in hand and storm the gates of the Magic Kingdom. You can cram the highlights into a single day, but if you get a two-day ticket and stay the night you can see the parade and visit **Downtown Disney** before heading south. The **Grand Californian Hotel** is a top choice for lodging within the Disney Resort. If tackling Disneyland after a long flight is too much, head south from LAX to the surfer's haven at **Huntington Beach**, where you can relax at the beach and spend the night in one of several beachfront hotels before heading inland to Anaheim the next morning.

Day 3: LEGOLAND
(1–1½ hrs by car from Huntington Beach or Anaheim, depending on traffic.)

Get an early start for your next roller-coaster ride at **LEGOLAND**, about an hour's drive south of Huntington Beach via the Pacific Coast Highway. Check into the **LEGOLAND Hotel** or the **Sheraton Carlsbad Resort & Spa**; both offer direct access to the park. LEGOLAND has a water park and aquarium in addition to the LEGO-based rides, shows, and roller coasters. The little ones can live out their fairy-tale fantasies and bigger ones can spend all day on waterslides, shooting water pistols, driving boats, or water fighting with pirates.

TIPS

No matter how carefully you plan your movements to avoid busy routes at peak hours, you will inevitably encounter heavy traffic in L.A., Orange County, and San Diego. If your plans include a trip from L.A. to San Diego or O.C., you can save time (and maybe money) by booking your flight to L.A. and returning from San Diego, O.C., Palm Springs, or LA/Ontario.

Allow yourself twice as much time as you think you'll need to negotiate LAX.

Day 4: La Jolla and San Diego
(La Jolla is just over an hour's drive from Carlsbad along scenic S21, or 40 mins on the I-5 freeway; Downtown San Diego is a 20-min drive from La Jolla.)

Take a leisurely drive south to San Diego by using the "old road," the original Pacific Coast Highway that hugs the shore all the way. It's a slow drive through Leucadia, Encinitas, Solana Beach, and Del Mar, all of which are popular surfing beaches. When you get to **La Jolla**, swing around the cove to see one of the area's most beautiful beaches. Look, but don't go in the water at the Children's Pool, as it's likely to be filled with barking seals. The **Birch Aquarium at Scripps** here offers a look at how scientists study the oceans.

Hop onto Interstate 5 and head for Downtown **San Diego.** Go straight for the city's nautical heart by exploring the restored ships of the **Maritime Museum** at the waterfront in Downtown. Victorian buildings—and plenty of other tourists—surround you on a stroll through the **Gaslamp Quarter.** Plant yourself at a Downtown hotel and graze your way through the neighborhood's many restaurants.

Day 5: San Diego Zoo
(10 mins by car from Downtown San Diego.)

Malayan tapirs in a faux-Asian rain forest, polar bears in an imitation Arctic, and pandas frolicking in the trees—the **San Diego Zoo** maintains a vast and varied collection of creatures in a world-renowned facility comprised of meticulously designed habitats. Come early, wear comfy shoes, and stay as long as you like.

Day 6: SeaWorld and Old Town
(From Downtown San Diego, both Sea-World and Old Town are 10 mins by car.)

Two commercial and touristy sights are on the agenda today. **SeaWorld,** with its walk-through shark tanks, can be a lot of fun if you surrender to the experience. Also touristy, but with genuine historical significance, **Old Town** drips with Mexican and early Californian heritage. Soak it up in the plaza at **Old Town San Diego State Historic Park,** then browse the stalls and shops at **Fiesta de Reyes** and along San Diego Avenue. Unwind after a long day with dinner and margaritas at one of Old Town's many Mexican restaurants.

Day 7: Departure from San Diego or Los Angeles
(San Diego Airport is 10 mins by car from Downtown. Depending on traffic, allow 2½–4 hrs to drive from Downtown San Diego to LAX.)

Pack up your Mouseketeer gear and give yourself ample time to reach the airport. San Diego International Airport lies within a 10-minute drive from Old Town. Although you'll be driving on freeways the entire way to LAX, traffic is always heavy and you should allot at least a half day to get there.

THE SOUTHERN PACIFIC COAST HIGHWAY: SAND, SURF, AND SUN, 3 DAYS

This tour along the southern section of the Pacific Coast Highway (PCH) is a beach vacation on wheels, taking in the highlights of the Southern California coast and its world-famous surfer-chic vibe. If at any point the drive feels like something out of a movie, that's because it likely is—this is the California of Hollywood legend. The itinerary is easily combined with the Big Sur and Northern Coast itineraries to do a full run of the legendary coastal route. Roll the top down on the convertible and let the adventure begin.

Day 1: Santa Barbara to Santa Monica

(About 2 hrs by car via the 101 and Hwy. 1. Allow plenty of time for beach stops and be aware of rush-hour traffic as you approach Santa Monica.)

Don't leave **Santa Barbara** without exploring the highlights of this Mediterranean-inspired city. Take a stroll along State Street, through the red-tile-roofed buildings of downtown to the gorgeous **Santa Barbara County Courthouse** and take in the views from its tower. Before leaving town, make a stop at the **Mission Santa Barbara,** widely considered one of the finest of all the California missions.

Heading south out of town the 101 runs along the coast past the low-key beach communities of Carpinteria and Mussel Shoals. Approaching **Ventura** on a clear day, the Channel Islands are visible in the distance. Stretch your legs on the **Ventura Oceanfront** with a walk on San Buenaventura State Beach, or around the picturesque Ventura Harbor. There are several spots to grab lunch at the harbor, too, including an outpost of Santa Barbara's famous **Brophy Bros.** seafood restaurant.

Leaving Ventura, trade the 101 for Highway 1 and continue south through miles of protected, largely unpopulated coastline. Hike the trails at **Point Mugu State Park,** scout for offshore whales at **Point Dume State Beach,** or ride a wave at **Zuma Beach.** The PCH follows the curve of Santa Monica Bay from Point Mugu through Malibu and on to Santa Monica. Chances are you'll experience déjà vu driving this stretch of road: mountains on one side, ocean on the other, opulent

homes perched on hillsides; you've seen this piece of coast countless times on TV and film. As you approach Malibu proper, affectionately known as "the 'bu," be sure to walk out on the **Malibu Pier** for a great photo op, then check out **Surfrider Beach,** with three famous points where perfect waves ignited a worldwide surfing rage in the 1960s.

If you plan to visit the **Getty Villa Malibu,** with its impressive antiquities collection and jaw-dropping setting overlooking the Pacific, you will need to obtain free timed-entry tickets online prior to your arrival. Otherwise, continue the drive to Santa Monica where you can overnight near the **Santa Monica Pier** and grab dinner along the **Third Street Promenade** or at Santa Monica Place.

Day 2: Santa Monica to Newport Beach

(About 2 hrs by car without traffic, but plan for traffic.)

Start the day with a morning walk along **Santa Monica State Beach** and, if you didn't visit it the night before, the **Santa Monica Pier.** Rent some beach cruisers and pedal your way south along the bike path to **Venice Beach** (about 3 miles each way) to take in the action along the boardwalk. Once you tire of the skateboarders, body builders, and street performers, head inland a few blocks to Abbott Kinney Boulevard for lunch at **Gjelina** and a browse in the local boutiques.

Pedal back to Santa Monica and trade two wheels for four to continue the drive toward Newport Beach. If time permits, you can follow Highway 1 through Marina del Ray and the trio of beach towns well known among beach-volleyball enthusiasts: Manhattan, Hermosa, and Redondo Beach. From here

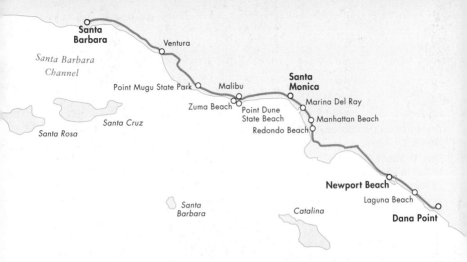

Highway 1 skirts through Long Beach and continues into Orange County. If time is short, this section of the PCH can be skipped in favor of the 405 freeway. However, as is always advisable near L.A., check current traffic reports before choosing your route.

The affluent coastal cities of Orange County, or the O.C., are familiar to many thanks to several popular television shows. However, the dazzling yachts and multimillion-dollar mansions of Newport Beach still may take you by surprise after the more laid-back brand of luxe found elsewhere on the coast.

Choose from among the many excellent restaurants and overnight at **The Island Hotel**.

Day 3: Newport Beach to Dana Point
(1 hr by car.)

The next morning, pick out your dream yacht or estate, and then head to Balboa Island in the middle of Newport Harbor. This far quainter (but equally expensive) community is a popular getaway for locals and tourists alike. Browse the boutiques along Marine Avenue before hopping in a Duffy (electric boat) for a tour around the harbor. Back on land, don't leave without enjoying a Balboa Bar—the ice-cream treat is essentially mandatory for all Balboa Island visitors. Leaving Newport Beach on the PCH, your next stop is Crystal Cove State Park just past Corona Del Mar. If the tide is low, this is a great spot for tide pooling. Otherwise, don't miss the collection of historic beach cottages dating as far back as 1935.

Back on the road, **Laguna Beach** is the final stop of this journey. In an area not often noted for its cultural offerings, Laguna Beach is the exception. Browse the art galleries and enjoy a meal in the charming downtown before taking in one last walk along the Pacific. The PCH terminates 10 miles south of Laguna Beach near Dana Point, a town famous for its harbor and whale-watching excursions. From here, you can continue towards San Diego, or return north to Anaheim or Los Angeles via Interstate 5.

HOORAY FOR HOLLYWOOD, 4 DAYS

If you are a movie fan, there's no better place to see it all than L.A. Always keep your eyes out for a familiar face: you never know when you might spot a celebrity.

Day 1: Los Angeles

As soon as you land at LAX, make like a local and hit the freeway. Even if L.A.'s top-notch art, history, and science museums don't tempt you, the hodgepodge of art deco, Beaux Arts, and futuristic architecture begs at least a drive-by. Heading east from Santa Monica, Wilshire Boulevard cuts through a historical and cultural cross section of the city. Two stellar sights on its Miracle Mile are the encyclopedic **Los Angeles County Museum of Art** and the fossil-filled **La Brea Tar Pits.** Come evening, the open-air **Farmers Market** and its many eateries hum. Hotels in Beverly Hills or West Hollywood beckon, just a few minutes away.

Day 2: Hollywood and the Movie Studios

(Avoid driving to the studios during rush hour. Studio tours vary in length—plan at least a half day for the excursion.)

Every L.A. tourist should devote at least one day to the movies and take at least one studio tour in the San Fernando Valley. For fun, choose the special-effects theme park at **Universal Studios Hollywood;** for the nitty-gritty, choose **Warner Bros. Studios.** Nostalgic musts in Hollywood include the **Walk of Fame** along **Hollywood Boulevard** and the celebrity footprints cast in concrete outside **Grauman's Chinese Theatre** (now known as the TCL Chinese Theater). When evening arrives, the Hollywood scene boasts a bevy of trendy restaurants and nightclubs.

Days 3 and 4: Beverly Hills and Santa Monica

(15–20 mins by car between destinations, but considerably longer in traffic.)

Even without that extensive art collection, the **Getty Center**'s pavilion architecture, hilltop gardens, and frame-worthy L.A. views make it a dazzling destination. Descend to the sea via Santa Monica Boulevard for lunch along **Third Street Promenade,** followed by a ride on the historic carousel on the pier. The buff and the bizarre meet at **Venice Beach Oceanfront Walk** (strap on some Rollerblades if you want to join them!). **Rodeo Drive** in Beverly Hills specializes in exhibitionism with a heftier price tag, but voyeurs are still welcome.

Splurge on breakfast or brunch at a posh café in the **Farmers Market,** then stroll through aisles and aisles of gorgeous produce and specialty food before you take a last look at the Pacific Ocean through the camera obscura at **Palisades Park** in Santa Monica.

SAN DIEGO

Visit Fodors.com for advice, updates, and bookings

WELCOME TO SAN DIEGO

TOP REASONS TO GO

★ **Beautiful beaches:** San Diego's shore shimmers with crystalline Pacific waters rolling up to some of the prettiest stretches of sand on the West Coast.

★ **Good eats:** Taking full advantage of the region's bountiful vegetables, fruits, herbs, and seafood, San Diego's chefs dazzle and delight diners with inventive California-colorful cuisine.

★ **History lessons:** The well-preserved and reconstructed historic sites in California's first European settlement help you imagine what the area was like when explorers first arrived.

★ **Stellar shopping:** The Gaslamp Quarter, Seaport Village, Coronado, Old Town, La Jolla … no matter where you go in San Diego, you'll find great places to do a little browsing.

★ **Urban oasis:** Balboa Park's 1,200 acres contain world-class museums and the San Diego Zoo, but also well-groomed lawns and gardens and wild, undeveloped canyons.

1 Downtown. San Diego's Downtown area is delightfully urban and accessible, filled with walkable A-list attractions like the Gaslamp Quarter and the waterfront.

2 Balboa Park. San Diego's cultural heart is where you'll find most of the city's museums and its world-famous zoo.

3 Old Town and Uptown. California's first permanent European settlement is now preserved as a state historic park in Old Town. Uptown is composed of several smaller neighborhoods that showcase a unique blend of historical charm and modern urban community.

4 Mission Bay and Beaches. Home to 27 miles of shoreline, this 4,600 acre aquatic park is San Diego's monument to sports and fitness. SeaWorld lies south of the bay.

5 La Jolla. This luxe, blufftop enclave fittingly means "the jewel" in Spanish. Come here for fantastic upscale shopping and unspoiled stretches of the coast.

6 Point Loma and Coronado. Home to the Hotel Del, Coronado's island-like isthmus is a favorite celebrity haunt. Visit the site of the first European landfall on Point Loma.

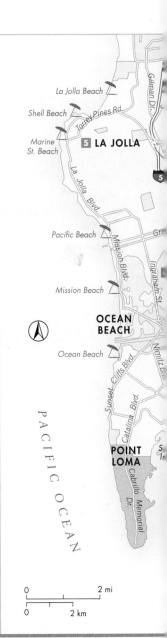

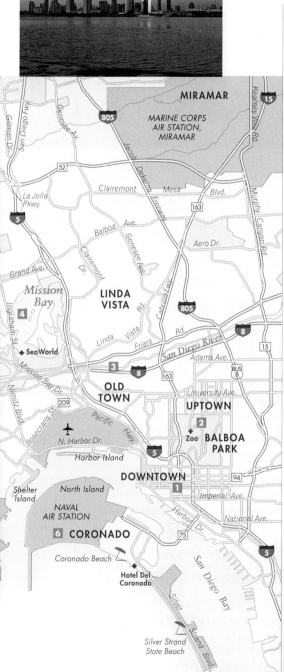

GETTING ORIENTED

Exploring San Diego may be an endless adventure, but there are limitations, especially if you don't have a car. San Diego is more a chain of separate communities than a cohesive city, and many of the major attractions are miles apart. Walking is good for getting an up close look at neighborhoods like the Gaslamp Quarter, but true Southern Californians use the freeways that criss-cross the county. Interstate 5 runs a direct north–south route through the coastal communities from Orange County in the north to the Mexican border. Interstates 805 and 15 do much the same inland. Interstate 8 is the main east–west route. Routes 163, 52, and 94 serve as connectors.

Updated by Marlise Kast-Myers, Kai Oliver-Kurtain, Archana Ram, Juliana Shallcross, Jeff Terich, and Claire Deeks Van Der Lee

San Diego is a vacationer's paradise, complete with idyllic year-round temperatures and 70 miles of pristine coastline. Recognized as one of the nation's leading family destinations, with LEGOLAND and the San Diego Zoo, San Diego is equally attractive to those in search of art, history, world-class shopping, and culinary exploration. San Diego's beaches are legendary, offering family-friendly sands, killer surf breaks, and spectacular scenery. San Diego's cultural sophistication often surprises visitors, as the city is better known for its laid-back vibe. Tourists come for some fun in the sun, only to discover a city with much greater depth.

San Diego is a big California city—second only to Los Angeles in population—with a small-town feel. San Diego's many neighborhoods offer diverse adventures: from the tony boutiques in La Jolla to the yoga and surf shops of Encinitas; from the subtle sophistication of Little Italy to the flashy nightlife of the Downtown Gaslamp Quarter, each community adds flavor and flair to San Diego's personality.

San Diego County also covers a lot of territory, roughly 400 square miles of land and sea. To the north and south of the city are its famed beaches. Inland, a succession of chaparral-covered mesas is punctuated with deep-cut canyons that step up to forested mountains.

Known as the birthplace of California, San Diego was claimed for Spain by explorer Juan Rodríguez Cabrillo in 1542 and eventually came under Mexican rule. You'll find reminders of San Diego's Spanish and Mexican heritage throughout the region—in architecture and place-names, in distinctive Mexican cuisine, and in the historic buildings of Old Town.

In 1867 developer Alonzo Horton, who called the town's bay front "the prettiest place for a city I ever saw," began building a hotel, a plaza, and prefab homes on 960 Downtown acres. A remarkable number of these buildings are preserved in San Diego's historic Gaslamp Quarter today. The city's fate was sealed in the 1920s when the U.S. Navy, impressed by the city's excellent harbor and temperate climate, decided to build a destroyer base on San Diego Bay. Today, the military operates many bases and installations throughout the county (which, added together, form the largest military base in the world) and continues to be a major contributor to the local economy.

PLANNING

WHEN TO GO

San Diego's weather is so ideal that most locals shrug off the high cost of living and relatively lower wages as a "sunshine tax." Along the coast, average temperatures range from the mid-60s to the high 70s, with clear skies and low humidity. Annual rainfall is minimal, less than 10 inches per year.

The peak season for sun seekers is July through October. In July and August, the mercury spikes and everyone spills outside. From mid-December to mid-March, whale-watchers can glimpse migrating gray whales frolicking in the Pacific. In spring and early summer, a marine layer hugs the coastline for much or all of the day (locals call it "June Gloom"), which can be dreary and disappointing for those who were expecting to bask in Southern California sunshine.

GETTING HERE AND AROUND

AIR TRAVEL

The major airport is San Diego International Airport (SAN), called Lindbergh Field locally. Major airlines depart and arrive at Terminal 1 and Terminal 2. A red shuttle bus provides free transportation between terminals.

Airport San Diego International Airport. ⊠ *3225 N. Harbor Dr., off I–5* ☏ *619/400–2400* ⊕ *www.san.org.*

Airport Transfers SuperShuttle. ⊠ *123 Caminio de la Riena* ☏ *800/974–8885* ⊕ *www.supershuttle.com.* **San Diego Transit.** ☏ *619/233–3004* ⊕ *transit.511sd.com.*

BUS AND TROLLEY TRAVEL

Under the umbrella of the Metropolitan Transit System, there are two major transit agencies in the area: San Diego Transit and North County Transit District (NCTD). The bright-red trolleys of the San Diego Trolley light-rail system operate on three lines that serve Downtown San Diego, Mission Valley, Old Town, South Bay, the U.S. border, and East County. The trolley system connects with San Diego Transit bus routes—connections are posted at each trolley station.

San Diego Transit bus fares range from $2.25 to $5; North County Transit District bus fares are $4. You must have exact change in coins and/or bills. Pay upon boarding. Transfers are not included; the $5 day pass is the best option for most bus travel and can be purchased on board.

San Diego Trolley tickets cost $2.50 and are good for two hours, but for one-way travel only. For a round-trip journey or longer, day passes are available for $5.

Bus and Trolley Information **North County Transit District.** ☎ 760/966–6500 ⊕ www.gonctd.com. **San Diego Transit.** ☎ 619/233–3004 ⊕ transit.511sd.com. **Transit Store.** ✉ 102 Broadway ☎ 619/234–1060 ⊕ www.sdmts.com.

CAR TRAVEL

A car is necessary for getting around greater San Diego on the sprawling freeway system and for visiting the North County beaches, mountains, and desert. Driving around San Diego County is pretty simple: most major attractions are within a few miles of the Pacific Ocean. Interstate 5, which stretches north–south from Oregon to the Mexican border, bisects San Diego. Interstate 8 provides access from Yuma, Arizona, and points east. Drivers coming from the Los Angeles area, Nevada, and the mountain regions beyond can reach San Diego on I–15. During rush hours there are jams on I–5 and on I–15 between I–805 and Escondido.

There are a few border inspection stations along major highways in San Diego County, the largest just north of Oceanside on I–5 near San Clemente. Travel with your driver's license, and passport if you're an international traveler.

TAXI TRAVEL

Fares vary among companies. If you're heading to the airport from a hotel, ask about the flat rate, which varies according to destination; otherwise you'll be charged by the mile (which works out to $20 or so from any Downtown location). Taxi stands are at shopping centers and hotels; otherwise you must call and reserve a cab. For on-demand private transportation, Uber is readily available throughout San Diego County with competitive rates up to 40% less than that of a taxi. The companies listed *below* don't serve all areas of San Diego County. If you're going somewhere other than Downtown, ask if the company serves that area.

Taxi Companies **Orange Cab.** ☎ 619/223–5555 ⊕ www.orangecabsandiego.net. **Silver Cabs.** ☎ 619/280–5555 ⊕ www.sandiegosilvercab.com. **Yellow Cab.** ☎ 619/444–4444 ⊕ www.driveu.com.

TRAIN TRAVEL

Amtrak serves Downtown San Diego's Santa Fe Depot with daily trains to and from Los Angeles, Santa Barbara, and San Luis Obispo. Amtrak trains stop in San Diego North County at Solana Beach and Oceanside. Coaster commuter trains, which run between Oceanside and San Diego Monday through Saturday, stop at the same stations as Amtrak as well as others. The frequency is about every half hour during the weekday rush hour, with four trains on Saturday. One-way fares are $4 to $5.50, depending on the distance traveled. The Sprinter runs between Oceanside and Escondido, with many stops along the way.

Metrolink operates high-speed rail service ($17) between the Oceanside Transit Center and Union Station in Los Angeles.

Information **Coaster.** ☎ 760/966–6500 ⊕ www.gonctd.com/coaster. **Metrolink.** ☎ 800/371–5465 ⊕ www.metrolinktrains.com.

TOURS

BIKE TOURS

Biking is popular in San Diego. You can find trails along the beach, in Mission Bay, and throughout the mountains.

Where You Want to Be Tours (*Secret San Diego*). Taking in spectacular views of the beach, bay, and skyline, these bike rides cover everything from historic neighborhoods to historic Highway 101. The walking tours, urban scavenger hunts, and Rent-a-Local custom tours are popular options as well. ✉ *611 K St., #B224* ☎ *619/917–6037* ⊕ *www.wheretours.com* ✆ *From $45.*

BOAT TOURS

Visitors to San Diego can get a great overview of the city from the water. Tour companies offer a range of harbor cruises, from one-hour jaunts to dinner and dancing cruises. In season, whale-watching voyages are another popular option.

Flagship Cruises and Events. One- and two-hour tours of the San Diego harbor loop north or south from the Broadway Pier throughout the day. Other offerings include dinner and dance cruises, brunch cruises, and winter whale-watching tours December–mid-April. ✉ *990 N. Harbor Dr., Embarcadero* ☎ *619/234–4111* ⊕ *www.flagshipsd.com* ✆ *From $23.*

H&M Landing. From mid-December to March, this outfitter offers three-hour tours to spot migrating gray whales just off the San Diego coast. From June to October—during slow fishing seasons only—six-hour cruises search for the gigantic blue whales that visit the California coast in summer. Winter gray whale cruises are offered December–March; summer blue whale tours are available Thursday, Saturday, and Sunday. ✉ *2803 Emerson St.* ☎ *619/222–1144* ⊕ *www.whalewatchingathmlanding.com* ✆ *From $45.*

Hornblower Cruises & Events. One- and two-hour cruises around San Diego harbor depart from the Embarcadero several times a day and alternate between the northern and southern portion of the bay. If you're hoping to spot some sea lions, take the North Bay route. Dinner and brunch cruises are also offered, as well as whale-watching tours in winter. ✉ *970 N. Harbor Dr.* ☎ *619/234–8687, 800/668–4322* ⊕ *www.hornblower.com* ✆ *From $25.*

San Diego SEAL Tours. This amphibious tour drives along the Embarcadero before splashing into the San Diego Harbor for a cruise. The 90-minute tours depart from Seaport Village year-round, and from outside the Maritime Museum seasonally. Call for daily departure times and locations. ✉ *500 Kettner Blvd., Embarcadero* ☎ *619/298–8687* ⊕ *www.sealtours.com* ✆ *$42.*

Seaforth Boat Rentals. For those seeking a private tour on the water, this company can provide a skipper along with your boat rental. Options include harbor cruises, whale-watching, and sunset sails. Seaforth has four locations and a diverse fleet of sail and motorboats to choose from. ✉ *1641 Quivira Rd., Mission Bay* ☎ *888/834–2628* ⊕ *www.seaforthboatrental.com* ✆ *From $225.*

BUS AND TROLLEY TOURS

For those looking to cover a lot of ground in a limited time, narrated trolley tours include everything from Balboa Park to Coronado. To venture farther afield, consider a coach tour to the desert, Los Angeles, or even Baja, Mexico.

DayTripper Tours. Single- and multiday trips throughout Southern California, the Southwest, and Baja depart from San Diego year-round. Popular day trips include the Getty Museum, and theater performances in Los Angeles. Call or check the website for pickup locations. ☎ *619/299–5777, 800/679–8747* ⊕ *www.daytripper.com* ✉ *From $75.*

Five Star Tours. Private and group sightseeing bus tour options around San Diego and beyond include everything from the San Diego Zoo to Brewery tours and trips to Baja, Mexico. ✉ *1050 Kettner Blvd.* ☎ *619/232–5040* ⊕ *www.fivestartours.com* ✉ *From $48.*

Old Town Trolley Tours. Combining points of interest with local history, trivia, and fun anecdotes, this hop-on, hop-off trolley tour provides an entertaining overview of the city and offers easy access to all the highlights. The tour is narrated, and you can get on and off as you please. Stops include Old Town, Seaport Village, the Gaslamp Quarter, Coronado, Little Italy, and Balboa Park. The trolley leaves every 30 minutes, operates daily, and takes two hours to make a full loop. ✉ *San Diego* ☎ *619/298–8687* ⊕ *www.trolleytours.com/san-diego* ✉ *From $40.*

San Diego Scenic Tours. Half- and full-day bus tours of San Diego and Tijuana depart daily, and some include a harbor cruise. Tours depart from several hotels around town. ✉ *San Diego* ☎ *858/273–8687* ⊕ *www.sandiegoscenictours.com* ✉ *From $38.*

WALKING TOURS

Several fine walking tours are available on weekdays or weekends; upcoming walks are usually listed in the *San Diego Reader*.

Balboa Park Offshoot Tours. On Saturday at 10 am, free, hour-long walks start from the Balboa Park Visitor Center. The tour's focus rotates weekly, covering topics such as the park's history, palm trees, and desert vegetation. Reservations are not required, but no tours are scheduled between Thanksgiving and the New Year. ✉ *Balboa Park Visitor Center, 1549 El Prado, Balboa Park* ☎ *619/239–0512* ⊕ *www. balboapark.org* ✉ *Free.*

Coronado Walking Tours. Departing from the Glorietta Bay Inn at 11 am Tuesday, Thursday, and Saturday, this 90-minute stroll through Coronado's historic district takes in the island's mansions, old Tent City, the Hotel del Coronado, and the castles and cottages that line the beautiful beach. Reservations are recommended. ✉ *1630 Glorietta Blvd.* ☎ *619/435–5993* ⊕ *coronadowalkingtour.com* ✉ *$12* ☞ *Cash only.*

Gaslamp Quarter Historical Foundation. Two-hour walking tours of the Downtown historic district depart from the William Heath Davis House at 11 am on Saturday. ✉ *410 Island Ave.* ☎ *619/233–4692* ⊕ *www. gaslampquarter.org* ✉ *$20.*

Urban Safaris. Led by longtime San Diego resident Patty Fares, these two-hour Saturday walks through diverse neighborhoods like Hillcrest,

Ocean Beach, and Point Loma are popular with tourists and locals alike. The tours, which always depart from a neighborhood coffeehouse, focus on art, history, and ethnic eateries, among other topics. Reservations are required, and private walks can be arranged during the week. ☎ *619/944–9255* ⊕ *www.walkingtoursofsandiego.com* 🎟 *$10.*

VISITOR INFORMATION
For general information and brochures before you go, contact the San Diego Tourism Authority, which publishes the helpful *San Diego Visitors Planning Guide*. When you arrive, stop by one of the local visitor centers for general information.

Citywide Contacts San Diego Tourism Authority. ✉ *750 B St., Suite 1500* ☎ *619/232-3101* ⊕ *www.sandiego.org.* **San Diego Visitor Information Center.** ✉ *996 N. Harbor Dr., Downtown* ☎ *619/236-1242* ⊕ *www.sandiego.org.*

EXPLORING SAN DIEGO

DOWNTOWN

Nearly written off in the 1970s, today Downtown San Diego is a testament to conservation and urban renewal. Once derelict Victorian storefronts now house the hottest restaurants, and the *Star of India,* the world's oldest active sailing ship, almost lost to scrap, floats regally along the Embarcadero. Like many modern U.S. cities, Downtown San Diego's story is as much about its rebirth as its history. Although many consider Downtown to be the 16½-block Gaslamp Quarter, it's actually comprised of eight neighborhoods, including East Village, Little Italy, and Embarcadero.

GASLAMP QUARTER
Considered the liveliest of the Downtown neighborhoods, the Gaslamp Quarter's 4th and 5th avenues are peppered with trendy nightclubs, swanky lounge bars, chic restaurants, and boisterous sports pubs. The Gaslamp has the largest collection of commercial Victorian-style buildings in the country. Despite this, when the move for Downtown redevelopment gained momentum in the 1970s, there was talk of bulldozing them and starting from scratch. In response, concerned history buffs, developers, architects, and artists formed the Gaslamp Quarter Council to clean up and preserve the quarter. The majority of the quarter's landmark buildings are on 4th and 5th avenues, between Island Avenue and Broadway.

WORTH NOTING
Gaslamp Museum at the Davis-Horton House. The oldest wooden house in San Diego houses the Gaslamp Quarter Historical Foundation, the district's curator. Before developer Alonzo Horton came to town, Davis, a prominent San Franciscan, had made an unsuccessful attempt to develop the waterfront area. In 1850 he had this prefab saltbox-style house, built in Maine, shipped around Cape Horn and assembled in San Diego (it originally stood at State and Market streets). Ninety-minute walking tours ($20) of the historic district leave from the house on

Thursday at 1 pm (summer only) and Saturday at 11 am (year-round). If you can't time your visit with the tour, a self-guided tour map ($2) is available. ⊠ *410 Island Ave., at 4th Ave., Gaslamp Quarter* ☎ *619/233–4692* ⊕ *www.gaslampfoundation.org* ✉ *$5 self-guided, $10 with audio tour* ⊘ *Closed Mon.*

EMBARCADERO

The Embarcadero cuts a scenic swath along the harbor front and connects today's Downtown San Diego to its maritime routes. The bustle of Embarcadero comes less these days from the activities of fishing folk than from the throngs of tourists, but this waterfront walkway, stretching from the Convention Center to the Maritime Museum, remains the nautical soul of the city. There are several seafood restaurants here, as well as sea vessels of every variety—cruise ships, ferries, tour boats, and navy destroyers.

A huge revitalization project is under way along the northern Embarcadero. The overhaul seeks to transform the area with large mixed-use development projects, inviting parks, walkways, and public art installations. The redevelopment will eventually head south along the waterfront, with plans under way for a major overhaul of the entire Central Embarcadero and Seaport Village.

TOP ATTRACTIONS

FAMILY
Fodor's Choice
★

Maritime Museum. From sailing ships to submarines, the Maritime Museum is a must for anyone with an interest in nautical history. This collection of restored and replica ships affords a fascinating glimpse of San Diego during its heyday as a commercial seaport. The jewel of the collection, the *Star of India,* was built in 1863 and made 21 trips around the world in the late 1800s. Saved from the scrap yard and painstakingly restored, the windjammer is the oldest active iron sailing ship in the world. The newly constructed *San Salvador* is a detailed historic replica of the original ship first sailed into San Diego Bay by explorer Juan Rodriguez Cabrillo back in 1542. And, the popular *HMS Surprise* is a replica of an 18th-century British Royal Navy frigate. The museum's headquarters are on the *Berkeley,* an 1898 steam-driven ferryboat, which served the Southern Pacific Railroad in San Francisco until 1958.

Numerous cruises of San Diego Bay are offered, including a daily 45-minute narrated tour aboard a 1914 pilot boat and 3-hour weekend sails aboard the topsail schooner the *Californian,* the state's official tall ship, and 75-minute tours aboard a historic swift boat, which highlights the city's military connection. Partnering with the museum, the renowned yacht *America* also offers sails on the bay, and whale-watching excursions are available in winter. ⊠ *1492 N. Harbor Dr., Embarcadero* ☎ *619/234–9153* ⊕ *www.sdmaritime.org* ✉ *$16, $5 more for Pilot Boat Bay Cruise.*

Fodor's Choice
★

Museum of Contemporary Art San Diego (MCASD). At the Downtown branch of the city's contemporary art museum, explore the works of international and regional artists in a modern, urban space. The Jacobs Building—formerly the baggage building at the historic Santa Fe Depot—features large gallery spaces, high ceilings, and natural lighting, giving artists the flexibility to create large-scale installations. MCASD's collection includes many Pop Art, minimalist, and conceptual works from the 1950s to the present. The museum showcases both established and emerging artists in temporary exhibitions, and has permanent, site-specific commissions by Jenny Holzer and Richard Serra. ✉ *1100 and 1001 Kettner Blvd., Downtown* ☎ *858/454–3541* ⊕ *www.mcasd.org* ✑ *$10; free 3rd Thurs. of the month 5–7* ☾ *Closed Wed.*

FAMILY
Fodor's Choice
★
The New Children's Museum (NCM). The NCM blends contemporary art with unstructured play to create an environment that appeals to children as well as adults. The 50,000-square-foot structure was constructed from recycled building materials, operates on solar energy, and is convection-cooled by an elevator shaft. It also features a nutritious and eco-conscious café. Interactive exhibits include designated areas for toddlers and teens, as well as plenty of activities for the entire family. Several art workshops are offered each day, as well as hands-on studios where visitors are encouraged to create their own art. The studio projects change frequently and the entire museum changes exhibits every 18 to 24 months, so there is always something new to explore. The adjoining 1-acre park and playground is across from the convention center trolley stop. ✉ *200 W. Island Ave., Embarcadero* ☎ *619/233–8792* ⊕ *www.thinkplaycreate.org* ✑ *$13; 2nd Sun. each month $3* ☾ *Closed Tues.*

FAMILY
Seaport Village. You'll find some of the best views of the harbor at Seaport Village, three bustling shopping plazas designed to reflect the New England clapboard, and Spanish Mission architectural styles of early California. On a prime stretch of waterfront the dining, shopping, and entertainment complex connects the harbor with hotel towers and the convention center. Specialty shops offer everything from a kite store and swing emporium to a shop devoted to hot sauces. You can dine at snack bars and restaurants, many with harbor views.

Live music can be heard daily from noon to 4 at the main food court. Additional free concerts take place every Sunday from 1 to 4 at the East Plaza Gazebo. The **Seaport Village Carousel** (rides $3) has 54 animals, hand-carved and hand-painted by Charles Looff in 1895. Across the street, the **Headquarters at Seaport Village** converted the historic police headquarters into several trendsetting shops and restaurants. ✉ *849 W. Harbor Dr., Downtown* ☎ *619/235–4014 office and events hotline* ⊕ *www.seaportvillage.com.*

FAMILY
Fodor's Choice
★
USS Midway Museum. After 47 years of worldwide service, the retired USS *Midway* began a new tour of duty on the south side of the Navy pier in 2004. Launched in 1945, the 1,001-foot-long ship was the largest in the world for the first 10 years of its existence. The most visible landmark on the north Embarcadero, it now serves as a floating interactive museum—an appropriate addition to the town that is home to one-third of the Pacific fleet and the birthplace of naval aviation. A free audio tour guides you through the massive ship while offering insight from former sailors. As you clamber through passageways and up and down ladder wells, you'll get a feel for how the *Midway*'s 4,500 crew members lived and worked on this "city at sea."

Though the entire tour is impressive, you'll really be wowed when you step out onto the 4-acre flight deck—not only the best place to get an idea of the ship's scale, but also one of the most interesting vantage points for bay and city skyline views. An F-14 Tomcat jet fighter is just one of many vintage aircraft on display. Free guided tours of the bridge and primary flight control, known as "the Island," depart every 10 minutes from the flight deck. Many of the docents stationed throughout the ship served in the Navy, some even on the *Midway*, and they are eager to answer questions or share stories. The museum also offers multiple flight simulators for an additional fee, climb-aboard cockpits, and interactive exhibits focusing on naval aviation. There is a gift shop and a café with pleasant outdoor seating. This is a wildly popular stop, with most visits lasting several hours. ⚠ Despite efforts **to provide accessibility throughout the ship, some areas can only be reached via fairly steep steps; a video tour of these areas is available on the hangar deck.** ✉ *910 N. Harbor Dr., Embarcadero* ☎ *619/544–9600* ⊕ *www.midway.org* 🎫 *$20.*

EAST VILLAGE

The most ambitious of the Downtown projects is East Village, not far from the Gaslamp Quarter, and encompassing 130 blocks between the railroad tracks up to J Street, and from 6th Avenue east to around 10th Street. Sparking the rebirth of this former warehouse district was the 2004 construction of the San Diego Padres' baseball stadium, PETCO Park. The Urban Art Trail has added pizzazz to drab city thoroughfares by transforming such things as trash cans and traffic controller boxes into works of art. As the city's largest Downtown neighborhood, East Village is continually broadening its boundaries with its urban design of redbrick cafés, spacious galleries, rooftop bars, sleek hotels, and warehouse restaurants.

LITTLE ITALY

Home to many in San Diego's design community, Little Italy exudes a sense of urban cool while remaining authentic to its roots and marked by old-country charms: church bells ring on the half hour, and Italians gather daily to play bocce in Amici Park. The main thoroughfare, India Street, is filled with lively cafés, chic shops, and many of the city's trendiest restaurants. Little Italy is one of San Diego's most walkable neighborhoods, and a great spot to wander. Art lovers can browse gallery showrooms, while shoppers adore the Fir Street cottages. The neighborhood bustles each Saturday during the wildly popular Mercato farmers' market.

BALBOA PARK AND SAN DIEGO ZOO

Overlooking Downtown and the Pacific Ocean, 1,200-acre Balboa Park is the cultural heart of San Diego. Ranked as one of the world's best parks by the Project for Public Spaces, it's also where you can find most of the city's museums, art galleries, the Tony Award–winning Old Globe Theatre, and the world-famous San Diego Zoo. Often referred to as the "Smithsonian of the West" for its concentration of museums, Balboa Park is also a series of botanical gardens, performance spaces, and outdoor playrooms endeared to the hearts of residents and visitors alike.

In addition, the captivating architecture of Balboa's buildings, fountains, and courtyards gives the park an enchanted feel. Historic buildings dating from San Diego's 1915 Panama–California International Exposition are strung along the park's main east–west thoroughfare, El Prado. The parkland across the Cabrillo Bridge, at the west end of El Prado, is set aside for picnics and athletics. East of Plaza de Panama, El Prado becomes a pedestrian mall and ends at a footbridge that crosses over Park Boulevard, to rose and desert gardens.

Bankers Hill is a small neighborhood west of Balboa Park, with gorgeous views ranging from Balboa Park's greenery in the east to the San Diego Bay in the west. It's become one of San Diego's hottest restaurant destinations.

TOP ATTRACTIONS

Bea Evenson Fountain. A favorite of barefoot children, this fountain shoots cool jets of water upwards of 50 feet. Built in 1972 between the Fleet Center and Natural History Museum, the fountain offers plenty of room to sit and watch the crowds go by. ⊠ *Balboa Park ✛ East end of El Prado* ⊕ *www.balboapark.org.*

Fodor's Choice ★ **Botanical Building.** The graceful redwood-lath structure, built for the 1915 Panama–California International Exposition, now houses more than 2,000 types of tropical and subtropical plants plus changing seasonal flower displays. Ceiling-high tree ferns shade fragile orchids and feathery bamboo. There are benches beside miniature waterfalls for resting in the shade. The rectangular pond outside, filled with lotuses and water lilies that bloom in spring and fall, is popular with photographers. ⊠ *1549 El Prado, Balboa Park* ☏ *619/239–0512* ⊕ *www.balboapark.org* ⌑ *Free* ☾ *Closed Thurs.*

Cabrillo Bridge. The official gateway into Balboa Park soars 120 feet above a canyon floor. Pedestrian-friendly, the 1,500-foot bridge provides inspiring views of the California Tower and El Prado beyond. ▪ **TIP➔** This is a great spot for photo-capturing a classic image of the park. ⊠ *Balboa Park ✛ On El Prado, at 6th Ave. park entrance* ⊕ *www.balboapark.org.*

FAMILY
Fodor's Choice ★ **Carousel.** Suspended an arm's length away on this antique merry-go-round is the brass ring that could earn you an extra free ride (it's one of the few carousels in the world that continue this bonus tradition). Hand-carved in 1910, the carousel features colorful murals, big-band music, and bobbing animals including zebras, giraffes, and dragons; real horsehair was used for the tails. ⊠ *1889 Zoo Pl., behind zoo parking lot, Balboa Park* ☏ *619/239–0512* ⊕ *www.balboapark.org* ⌑ *$2.75* ☾ *Closed weekdays Labor Day–mid-June.*

Fodor's Choice ★ **Inez Grant Parker Memorial Rose Garden and Desert Garden.** These neighboring gardens sit just across the Park Boulevard pedestrian bridge and offer gorgeous views over Florida Canyon. The formal rose garden contains 2,500 roses representing nearly 200 varieties; peak bloom is usually in April and May. The adjacent Desert Garden provides a striking contrast, with 2.5 acres of succulents and desert plants seeming to blend into the landscape of the canyon below. ⊠ *2525 Park Blvd., Balboa Park* ⊕ *www.balboapark.org.*

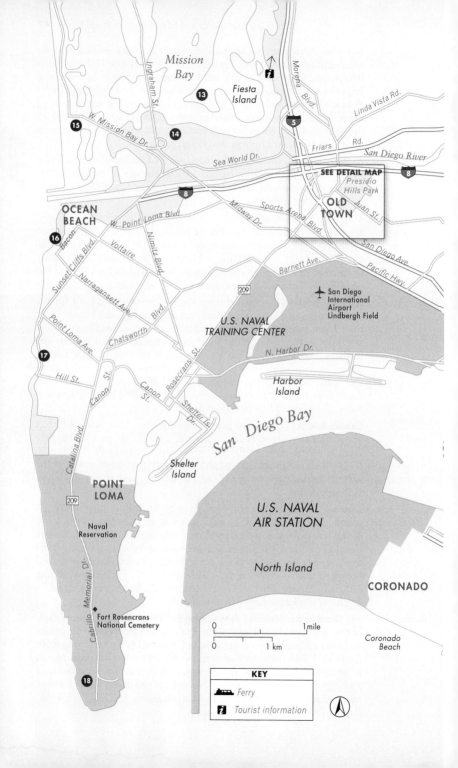

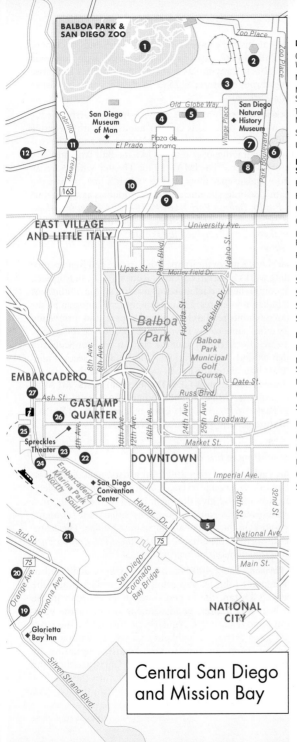

Palm Canyon. Enjoy an instant escape from the buildings and concrete of urban life in this Balboa Park oasis. Lush and tropical, with hundreds of palm trees, the 2-acre canyon has a shaded path perfect for those who love walking through nature. ✉ *1549 El Prado, south of House of Charm, Balboa Park.*

FAMILY **Reuben H. Fleet Science Center.** Interactive exhibits here are artfully educational and for all ages: older kids can get hands-on with inventive projects in the Tinkering Studio, while the five-and-under set can be easily entertained with interactive play stations like the Ball Wall and Fire Truck in the center's Kid City. The IMAX Dome Theater, which screens exhilarating nature and science films, was the world's first, as was the Fleet's "NanoSeam" (seamless) dome ceiling that doubles as a planetarium. ✉ *1875 El Prado, Balboa Park* ☎ *619/238–1233* ⊕ *www.rhfleet. org* ✉ *The Fleet experience includes gallery exhibits and 1 IMAX film $19.95; additional cost for special exhibits or add-on 2nd IMAX film or planetarium show.*

Fodor'sChoice **San Diego Museum of Art.** Known for its Spanish baroque and Renaissance
★ paintings, including works by El Greco, Goya, Rubens, and van Ruisdael, San Diego's most comprehensive art museum also has strong holdings of South Asian art, Indian miniatures, and contemporary California paintings. The museum's exhibits tend to have broad appeal, and if traveling shows from other cities come to town, you can expect to see them here. Free docent tours are offered throughout the day. An outdoor Sculpture Court and Garden exhibits both traditional and modern pieces. Enjoy the view over a craft beer and some locally sourced food in the adjacent Panama 66 courtyard restaurant. ■**TIP→ The museum hosts "Art After Hours" most Friday nights, with discounted admission 5–8 pm.** ✉ *1450 El Prado, Balboa Park* ☎ *619/232–7931* ⊕ *www.sdmart.org* ✉ *$15; $5 Fri. 5–8 pm; sculpture garden free* ☉ *Closed Wed.*

Fodor'sChoice **San Diego Zoo.**
★ *See the highlighted listing in this chapter.*

Fodor'sChoice **Spanish Village Art Center.** More than 200 local artists, including glass-
★ blowers, enamel workers, woodcarvers, sculptors, painters, jewelers, and photographers work and give demonstrations of their craft on a rotating basis in these red tile–roof studio-galleries that were set up for the 1935–36 exposition in the style of an old Spanish village. The center is a great source for memorable gifts. ✉ *1770 Village Pl., Balboa Park* ☎ *619/233–9050* ⊕ *www.spanishvillageart.com* ✉ *Free.*

Fodor'sChoice **Spreckels Organ Pavilion.** The 2,400-bench-seat pavilion, dedicated in
★ 1915 by sugar magnates John D. and Adolph B. Spreckels, holds the 4,518-pipe Spreckels Organ, the largest outdoor pipe organ in the world. You can hear this impressive instrument at one of the year-round, free, 2 pm Sunday concerts, regularly performed by the city's civic organist and guest artists—a highlight of a visit to Balboa Park. On Monday evenings from late June to mid-August, internationally renowned organists play evening concerts. At Christmastime the park's Christmas tree and life-size Nativity display turn the pavilion into a seasonal wonderland. ✉ *2211 Pan American Rd., Balboa Park* ☎ *619/702–8138* ⊕ *spreckelsorgan.org.*

Continued on page 56

Polar bear, San Diego Zoo

LIONS AND TIGERS AND PANDAS:
The World-Famous San Diego Zoo

From cuddly pandas and diving polar bears to 6-ton elephants and swinging great apes, San Diego's most famous attraction has it all. Nearly 4,000 animals representing 800 species roam the 100-acre zoo in expertly crafted habitats that replicate the animals' natural environments. While the pandas get top billing, there are plenty of other cool creatures to see here, from teeny-tiny mantella frogs to two-story-tall giraffes. But it's not all just fun and games. Known for its exemplary conservation programs, the zoo educates visitors on how to go green and explains its efforts to protect endangered species.

SAN DIEGO ZOO TOP ATTRACTIONS

Underwater viewing area at the Hippo Trail

❶ Children's Zoo (Discovery Outpost). Goats and sheep beg to be petted, and there is a viewer-friendly nursery where you may see baby animals bottle-feed and sleep peacefully in large cribs.

❷ Monkey Trails and Forest Tales (Lost Forest). Follow an elevated trail at treetop level and trek through the forest floor observing African mandrill monkeys, Asia's clouded leopard, the rare pygmy hippopotamus, and Visayan warty pigs.

❸ Orangutan and Siamang Exhibit (Lost Forest). Orangutans and siamangs climb and swing in this lush, tropical environment lined with 110-foot-long and 12-foot-high viewing windows.

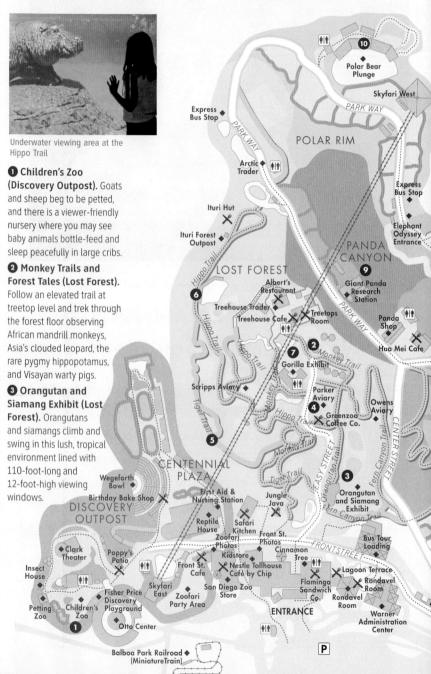

Express Bus Stop

PARK WAY

❿ Polar Bear Plunge

Skyfari West

PARK WAY

POLAR RIM

Arctic Trader

Express Bus Stop

Ituri Hut

Elephant Odyssey Entrance

Ituri Forest Outpost

PANDA CANYON

LOST FOREST

Albert's Restaurant

❾ Giant Panda Research Station

Hippo Trail

❻

Treehouse Trader

Treehouse Cafe

Treetops Room

PARK WAY

Panda Shop

Hua Mei Cafe

Hippo Trail

❼ Gorilla Exhibit

❷

Monkey Trail

Scripps Aviary

Hippo Trail

Parker Aviary

Owens Aviary

❹

Greenzoo Coffee Co.

❺

Tiger Trail

Monkey Trail

Monkey Trail

Hippo Trail

EAST STREET

Orangutan Trail

CENTER STREET

Fern Canyon Trail

CENTENNIAL PLAZA

Wegeforth Bowl

Tiger Trail

First Aid & Nursing Station

Jungle Java

❸ Orangutan and Siamang Exhibit

Birthday Bake Shop

DISCOVERY OUTPOST

Reptile House

Safari Kitchen

Front St.

Fern Canyon Trail

Bus Tour Loading

Zoofari Photos

Photos

Cinnamon Tree

Clark Theater

Poppy's Patio

Kidstore

FRONT STREET

Lagoon Terrace

Insect House

Front St. Cafe

Nestle Tollhouse Café by Chip

Flamingo Sandwich Co.

Rondavel Room

Petting Zoo

Fisher Price Discovery Playground

Skyfari East

San Diego Zoo Store

Rondavel Room

Children's Zoo

Zoofari Party Area

ENTRANCE

Warner Administration Center

❶

Otto Center

Balboa Park Railroad (MiniatureTrain)

P

4 Scripps, Parker, and Owens Aviaries (Lost Forest). Wandering paths climb through the enclosed aviaries where brightly colored tropical birds swoop between branches inches from your face.

5 Tiger Trail (Lost Forest). The mist-shrouded trails of this simulated rainforest wind down a canyon. Tigers, Malayan tapirs, and Argus pheasants wander among the exotic trees and plants.

6 Hippo Trail (Lost Forest). Glimpse huge but surprisingly graceful hippos frolicking in the water through an underwater viewing window and buffalo cavorting with monkeys on dry land.

7 Gorilla Exhibit (Lost Forest). The gorillas live in one of the zoo's bioclimatic zone exhibits modeled on their native habitat with waterfalls, climbing areas, and an open meadow. The sounds of the tropical rain forest emerge from a 144-speaker sound system that plays CDs recorded in Africa.

8 Sun Bear Forest (Asian Passage). Playful beasts claw apart the trees and shrubs that serve as a natural playground for climbing, jumping, and general merrymaking.

9 Giant Panda Research Station (Panda Canyon). An elevated pathway provides visitors with great access

Lories at Owen's Aviary

to the zoo's most famous residents in their side-by-side viewing areas. The adjacent discovery center features lots of information about these endangered animals and the zoo's efforts to protect them.

10 Polar Bear Plunge (Polar Rim). Watch polar bears take a chilly dive from the underwater viewing room. There are also Siberian reindeer, white foxes, and other Arctic creatures here. Kids can learn about the Arctic and climate change through interactive exhibits.

11 Elephant Odyssey. Get a glimpse of the animals that roamed Southern California 12,000 years ago and meet their living counterparts. The 7.5-acre, multispecies habitat features elephants, California condors, jaguars, and more.

12 Koala Exhibit (Outback). The San Diego Zoo houses the largest number of koalas outside Australia. Walk through the exhibit for photo ops of these marsupials from Down-Under curled up on their perches or dining on eucalyptus branches.

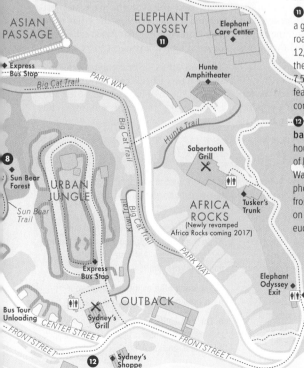

ASIAN PASSAGE

ELEPHANT ODYSSEY
11

Elephant Care Center

Express Bus Stop

Big Cat Trail

PARK WAY

Hunte Amphitheater

Big Cat Trail

Hunte Trail

8

Sun Bear Forest

Sabertooth Grill

URBAN JUNGLE

Big Cat Trail

AFRICA ROCKS
(Newly revamped Africa Rocks coming 2017)

Tusker's Trunk

Sun Bear Trail

PARK WAY

Express Bus Stop

Elephant Odyssey Exit

Express Bus Stop

Bus Tour Unloading

Sydney's Grill

OUTBACK

CENTER STREET

FRONT STREET

FRONT STREET

Sydney's Shoppe

12

Koala Exhibit

PLANNING YOUR DAY AT THE ZOO

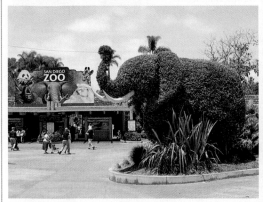 

Left: Main entrance of the San Diego Zoo. Right: Sunbear

PLANNING YOUR TIME

Plan to devote at least a half-day to exploring the zoo, but with so much to see it is easy to stay a full day or more.

If you're on a tight schedule, opt for the guided **35 minute bus tour** that lets you zip through three-quarters of the exhibits. However, lines to board the busses can be long, and you won't get as close to the animals.

Another option is to take the **Skyfari Aerial Tram** to the far end of the park, choose a route, and meander back to the entrance. The Skyfari trip gives a good overview of the zoo's layout and a spectacular view.

The **Elephant Odyssey**, while accessible from two sides of the park, is best entered from just below the Polar Rim. The extremely popular **Panda exhibit** can develop long lines, so get there early.

The zoo offers several entertaining **live shows** daily. Check the website or the back of the map handed out at the zoo entrance for the day's offerings and showtimes.

BEFORE YOU GO

■ To avoid ticket lines, purchase and print tickets online using the zoo's Web site.

■ To avoid excessive backtracking or a potential meltdown, plan your route along the zoo map before setting out. Try not to get too frustrated if you lose your way, as there are exciting exhibits around every turn and many paths intersect at several points.

■ The zoo offers a variety of program extras, including behind-the-scenes tours, backstage pass animal encounters, and sleepover events. Call in advance for pricing and reservations.

AT THE ZOO

■ Don't forget to explore at least some of the exhibits on foot—a favorite is the lush Tiger Trail.

■ If you visit on the weekend, find out when the Giraffe Experience is taking place. You can purchase leaf-eater biscuits to hand feed the giraffes!

■ Splurge a little at the gift shop: your purchases help support zoo programs.

■ The zoo rents strollers, wheelchairs, and lockers; it also has a first-aid office, a lost and found, and an ATM.

Fern Canyon, San Diego Zoo

GETTING HERE AND AROUND
The zoo is easy to get to, whether by bus or car.

Bus Travel: Take Bus No. 7 and exit at Park Boulevard and Zoo Place.

Car Travel: From Downtown, take Route 163 north through Balboa Park. Exit at Zoo/Museums (Richmond Street) and follow signs.

Several options help you get around the massive park: express buses loop through the zoo and the Skyfari Aerial Tram will take you from one end to the other. The zoo's topography is fairly hilly, but moving sidewalks lead up the slopes between some exhibits.

QUICK BITES
There is a wide variety of food available for purchase at the zoo from food carts to ethnic restaurants such as the Pan-Asian **Hua Mei Cafe.**

One of the best restaurants is **Albert's,** near the Gorilla exhibit, which features grilled fish, homemade pizza, and fresh pasta along with a full bar.

SERVICE INFORMATION	SAN DIEGO ZOO SAFARI PARK
✉ 2920 Zoo Dr., Balboa Park ☎ 619/234–3153 ⊕ www.sandiegozoo.org	About 45 minutes north of the zoo in Escondido, the 1,800-acre San Diego Zoo Safari Park is an extensive wildlife sanctuary where animals roam free—and guests can get close in escorted caravans and on backcountry trails. This park and the zoo operate under the auspices of the San Diego Zoo's nonprofit organization; joint tickets are available.

Gorilla

OLD TOWN AND UPTOWN

San Diego's Spanish and Mexican roots are most evident in Old Town and the surrounding hillside of Presidio Park. Visitors can experience settlement life in San Diego from Spanish and Mexican rule to the early days of U.S. statehood. Nearby Uptown is composed of several smaller neighborhoods near Downtown and around Balboa Park: the vibrant neighborhoods of Hillcrest, Mission Hills, North Park, and South Park showcase their unique blend of historical charm and modern urban community.

OLD TOWN

As the first European settlement in Southern California, Old Town began to develop in the 1820s. But its true beginnings took place on a nearby hillside in 1769 with the establishment of a Spanish military outpost and the first of California's missions, San Diego de Alcalá. In 1774 the hilltop was declared a *presidio reál*, a fortress built by the Spanish Empire, and the mission was relocated along the San Diego River. Over time, settlers moved down from the presidio to establish Old Town. A central plaza was laid out, surrounded by adobe and, later, wooden structures. San Diego became an incorporated U.S. city in 1850, with Old Town as its center. In the 1860s, however, the advent of Alonzo Horton's New Town to the southeast caused Old Town to wither. Efforts to preserve the area began early in the 20th century, and Old Town became a state historic park in 1968.

Today Old Town is a lively celebration of history and culture. The Old Town San Diego State Historic Park re-creates life during the early settlement, while San Diego Avenue buzzes with art galleries, gift shops, festive restaurants, and open-air stands selling inexpensive Mexican handicrafts.

TOP ATTRACTIONS

FAMILY
Fodor's Choice
★

Fiesta de Reyes. North of San Diego's Old Town Plaza lies the area's unofficial center, built to represent a colonial Mexican plaza. The collection of more than a dozen shops and restaurants around a central courtyard in blossom with magenta bougainvillea, scarlet hibiscus, and other flowers in season reflects what early California might have looked like from 1821 to 1872. Shops are even stocked with items reminiscent of that era. Mariachi bands and folklorico dance groups frequently perform on the plaza stage—check the website for times and upcoming special events. ■ TIP→ Casa de Reyes is a great stop for a margarita and some chips and guacamole. ⊠ 4016 Wallace St., Old Town ☎ 619/297–3100 ⊕ www.fiestadereyes.com.

FAMILY
Fodor's Choice
★

Old Town San Diego State Historic Park. The six square blocks on the site of San Diego's original pueblo are the heart of Old Town. Most of the 20 historic buildings preserved or re-created by the park cluster around **Old Town Plaza,** bounded by Wallace Street on the west, Calhoun Street on the north, Mason Street on the east, and San Diego Avenue on the south. The plaza is a pleasant place to rest, plan your tour of the park, and watch passers-by. San Diego Avenue is closed to vehicle traffic here.

Some of Old Town's buildings were destroyed in a fire in 1872, but after the site became a state historic park in 1968, reconstruction and restoration of the remaining structures began. Five of the original adobes are still intact.

Facing Old Town Plaza, the **Robinson-Rose House** was the original commercial center of Old San Diego, housing railroad offices, law offices, and the first newspaper press. The largest and most elaborate of the original adobe homes, the **Casa de Estudillo** was occupied by members of the Estudillo family until 1887 and later gained popularity for its billing as "Ramona's Marriage Place" based on a popular novel of the time. Albert Seeley, a stagecoach entrepreneur, opened the **Cosmopolitan Hotel** in 1869 as a way station for travelers on the daylong trip south from Los Angeles. Next door to the Cosmopolitan Hotel, the **Seeley Stable** served as San Diego's stagecoach stop in 1867 and was the transportation hub of Old Town until 1887, when trains became the favored mode of travel.

Several reconstructed buildings serve as restaurants or as shops purveying wares reminiscent of those that might have been available in the original Old Town. **Racine & Laramie**, a painstakingly reproduced version of San Diego's first cigar store in 1868, is especially interesting.

Pamphlets available at the Robinson-Rose House give details about all the historic houses on the plaza and in its vicinity. Tours of the historic park are offered daily at 11:30, 1, and 2; purchase tickets at the Robinson-Rose House. A free history program is also offered daily in the Seely Stable Theater. ■TIP→ **The covered wagon located near the intersection of Mason and Calhoun streets provides a great photo op.** ✉ *Visitor center (Robinson-Rose House), 4002 Wallace St., Old Town* ☎ *619/220–5422* ⊕ *www.parks.ca.gov* ✉ *Free; walking tour $10.*

Thomas Whaley House Museum. A New York entrepreneur, Thomas Whaley came to California during the gold rush. He wanted to provide his East Coast wife with all the comforts of home, so in 1857 he had Southern California's first two-story brick structure built, making it the oldest double-story brick building on the West Coast. The house, which served as the county courthouse and government seat during the 1870s, stands in strong contrast to the Spanish-style adobe residences that surround the nearby historic plaza and marks an early stage of San Diego's "Americanization." A garden out back includes many varieties of prehybrid roses from before 1867. The place is perhaps most famed, however, for the ghosts that are said to inhabit it. You can tour on your own during the day, but must visit by guided tour starting at 5 pm. The evening tours are geared toward the supernatural aspects of the house. They are offered every half hour, with the last tour departing at 9:30 pm, and last about 45 minutes. ✉ *2476 San Diego Ave., Old Town* ☎ *619/297–7511* ⊕ *www.whaleyhouse.org* ✉ *$8 before 5 pm; $13 after 5 pm* ☽ *Closed Sept.–May, Wed.*

HILLCREST

The large retro Hillcrest sign over the intersection of University and 5th avenues makes an excellent landmark at the epicenter of this vibrant section of Uptown. Strolling along University Avenue between 4th and 6th avenues from Washington Street to Robinson Avenue will reveal a mixture of retail shops and restaurants. A few blocks east, another interesting stretch of stores and restaurants runs along University Avenue to Normal Street. Long established as the center of San Diego's gay community, the neighborhood bustles both day and night with a mixed crowd of shoppers, diners, and partygoers. If you are visiting Hillcrest on Sunday between 9 and 2 be sure to explore the Hillcrest Farmers Market.

MISSION VALLEY

Although Mission Valley's charms may not be immediately apparent, it offers many conveniences to visitors and residents alike. One of the area's main attractions is the Fashion Valley mall, with its mix of high-end and mid-range retail stores and dining options, and movie theater. The Mission Basilica San Diego de Alcalá provides a tranquil refuge from the surrounding suburban sprawl.

TOP ATTRACTIONS

Fodor's Choice
★
Mission Basilica San Diego de Alcalá. It's hard to imagine how remote California's earliest mission must have once been; these days, however, it's accessible by major freeways (I–15 and I–8) and via the San Diego Trolley. The first of a chain of 21 missions stretching northward along the

coast, Mission San Diego de Alcalá was established by Father Junípero Serra on Presidio Hill in 1769 and moved to this location in 1774. In 1775, it proved vulnerable to enemy attack, and Padre Luis Jayme, a young friar from Spain, was clubbed to death by the Kumeyaay Indians he had been trying to convert. He was the first of more than a dozen Christians martyred in California. The present church, reconstructed in 1931 following the outline of the 1813 church, is the fifth built on the site. It measures 150 feet long but only 35 feet wide because, without easy means of joining beams, the mission buildings were only as wide as the trees that served as their ceiling supports were tall. Father Jayme is buried in the sanctuary; a small museum named for him documents mission history and exhibits tools and artifacts from the early days; there is also a gift shop. From the peaceful, palm-bedecked gardens out back you can gaze at the 46-foot-high *campanario* (bell tower), the mission's most distinctive feature, with five bells. Mass is celebrated on the weekends. ⊠ *10818 San Diego Mission Rd., Mission Valley* ✛ *From I–8 east, exit and turn left on Mission Gorge Rd., then left on Twain Rd.; mission is on right* ☎ *619/281–8449* ⊕ *www.missionsandiego.com* ✉ *$5.*

NORTH PARK

Named for its location north of Balboa Park, this evolving neighborhood is home to an exciting array of restaurants, bars, and shops. High-end condominiums and local merchants are often cleverly disguised behind historic signage from barbershops, bowling alleys, and theater marquees. The stretch of Ray Street near University Avenue is home to several small galleries. With a steady stream of new openings in the neighborhood, North Park is one of San Diego's top dining and nightlife destinations. Beer enthusiasts won't want to miss the breweries and tasting rooms along the 30th St. Beer Corridor for a chance to sample San Diego's famous ales.

MISSION BAY AND THE BEACHES

Mission Bay and the surrounding beaches are the aquatic playground of San Diego. The choice of activities available is astonishing, and the perfect weather makes you want to get out there and play. If you're craving downtime after all the activity, there are plenty of peaceful spots to relax and simply soak up the sunshine.

Mission Bay welcomes visitors with its protected waters and countless opportunities for fun. The 4,600-acre **Mission Bay Park** is the place for water sports like sailing, stand-up paddleboarding, and waterskiing. With 19 miles of beaches and grassy areas, it's also a great place for a picnic. And if you have kids, don't miss **SeaWorld,** one of San Diego's most popular attractions.

Mission Beach is a famous and lively fun zone for families and young people; if it isn't party time at the moment, it will be five minutes from now. The pathways in this area are lined with vacation homes, many for rent by the week or month.

North of Mission Beach is the college-packed party town of Pacific Beach, or "PB" as locals call it. The laid-back vibe of this surfer's mecca draws in free-spirited locals who roam the streets on skateboards and beach cruisers. The energy level peaks during happy hour, when PB's cluster of nightclubs, bars, and 150 restaurants open their doors to those ready to party.

TOP ATTRACTIONS

FAMILY

Fodor'sChoice

★

Belmont Park. The once-abandoned amusement park between the bay and Mission Beach Boardwalk is now a shopping, dining, and recreation complex. Twinkling lights outline the **Giant Dipper,** an antique wooden roller coaster on which screaming thrill-seekers ride more than 2,600 feet of track and 13 hills (riders must be at least 4 feet, 2 inches tall). Created in 1925 and listed on the National Register of Historic Places, this is one of the few old-time roller coasters left in the United States.

Other Belmont Park attractions include miniature golf, laser tag, a video arcade, bumper cars, a tilt-a-whirl, and an antique carousel. The zip line thrills as it soars over the crowds below, while the rock wall challenges both junior climbers and their elders. Belmont Park also has the most consistent wave in the county at the **Wave House,** where the FlowRider provides surfers and bodyboarders a near-perfect simulated wave on which to practice their skills. ⊠ *3146 Mission Blvd., Mission Bay* ☎ *858/488–1549 for rides* ⊕ *www.belmontpark.com* ⊠ *Unlimited ride day package $30 for 48 inches and taller, $20 for under 48 inches, some attractions not included in price; individual ride tickets and other ride/attraction combo packages are also available.*

Fodor'sChoice

★

Mission Bay Park. San Diego's monument to sports and fitness, this 4,600-acre aquatic park has 27 miles of shoreline including 19 miles of sandy beaches. Playgrounds and picnic areas abound on the beaches and low, grassy hills. On weekday evenings, joggers, bikers, and skaters take over. In the daytime, swimmers, water-skiers, paddleboarders, anglers, and boaters—some in single-person kayaks, others in crowded powerboats—vie for space in the water. ⊠ *2688 E. Mission Bay Dr., Mission Bay* ⊹ *Off I–5 at Exit 22 E. Mission Bay Dr.* ☎ *858/581–7602 park ranger's office* ⊕ *www.sandiego.gov/park-and-recreation* ⊠ *Free.*

FAMILY

SeaWorld San Diego. Spread over 189 tropically landscaped bayfront acres, SeaWorld is one of the world's largest marine-life amusement parks. The majority of its exhibits are walk-through marine environments like **Shark Encounter,** where guests walk through a 57-foot acrylic tube and come face-to-face with a variety of sharks that call the 280,000-gallon habitat home. **Turtle Reef** offers an incredible up-close encounter with the green sea turtle, while the moving sidewalk at **Penguin Encounter** whisks you through a colony of nearly 300 penguins. The park also wows with its adventure rides like **Journey to Atlantis**, with a heart-stopping 60-foot plunge, and **Manta**, a thrilling double-launch coaster. Younger children will enjoy the rides, climbing structures and splash pads at the **Sesame Street Bay of Play.**

SeaWorld is most famous for its large-arena entertainments, but this is an area in transition. A new orca experience debuted in the summer of 2017 that features a nature-inspired backdrop and demonstrates orca behaviors in the wild. This change is part of SeaWorld's efforts to refocus it's orca program toward education and conservation. Other live-entertainment shows feature dolphins, sea otters, and even household pets. Several upgraded animal encounters are available including the Dolphin Interaction Program, which gives guests the chance to interact with SeaWorld's bottlenose dolphins in the water. The hour-long program (20 minutes in the water), during which visitors can feed, touch, and give behavior signals, costs $215. ⊠ *500 SeaWorld Dr., near west end of I–8, Mission Bay* ☎ *800/257–4268* ⊕ *www. seaworldparks.com* ⊑ *$90 ages 3 and older; advanced purchase discounts available online; parking $17.*

3

LA JOLLA

La Jollans have long considered their village to be the Monte Carlo of California, and with good cause. Its coastline curves into natural coves backed by verdant hillsides covered with homes worth millions. La Jolla is both a natural and cultural treasure trove. The upscale shops, galleries, and restaurants of La Jolla Village satisfy the glitterati, while secluded trails, scenic overlooks, and abundant marine life provide balance and refuge.

Although La Jolla is a neighborhood of the city of San Diego, it has its own postal zone and a coveted sense of class; the ultrarich from around the globe own second homes here—the seaside zone between the neighborhood's bustling Downtown and the cliffs above the Pacific has a distinctly European flavor—and old-money residents maintain friendships with the visiting film stars and royalty who frequent the area's exclusive luxury hotels and private clubs.

Native Americans called the site Woholle, or "hole in the mountains," referring to the grottoes that dot the shoreline. The Spaniards changed the name to La Jolla (same pronunciation as La Hoya), "the jewel," which led to the nickname "Jewel City."

TOP ATTRACTIONS

Fodor's Choice
★

Torrey Pines State Natural Reserve. *Pinus torreyana,* the rarest native pine tree in the United States, enjoys a 1,700-acre sanctuary at the northern edge of La Jolla. About 6,000 of these unusual trees, some as tall as 60 feet, grow on the cliffs here. The park is one of only two places in the world (the other is Santa Rosa Island, off Santa Barbara) where the Torrey pine grows naturally. The reserve has several hiking trails leading to the cliffs, 300 feet above the ocean; trail maps are available at the park station. Wildflowers grow profusely in spring, and the ocean panoramas are always spectacular. When in this upper part of the park, respect the restrictions. Not permitted: picnicking, smoking, leaving the trails, dogs, alcohol, or collecting plant specimens.

You can unwrap your sandwiches, however, at Torrey Pines State Beach, just below the reserve. When the tide is out, it's possible to walk south all the way past the lifeguard towers to Black's Beach over rocky promontories carved by the waves (avoid the bluffs, however; they're unstable). **Los Peñasquitos Lagoon** at the north end of the reserve is one of the many natural estuaries that flow inland between Del Mar and Oceanside. It's a good place to watch shorebirds. Volunteers lead

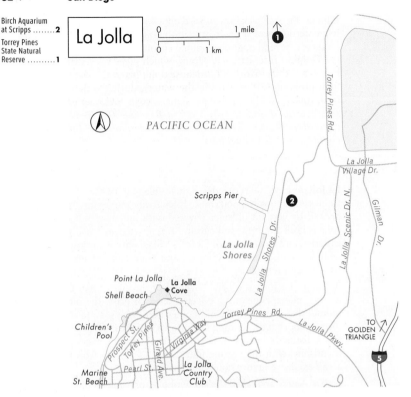

guided nature walks at 10 and 2 on most weekends. ✉ *12600 N. Torrey Pines Rd., La Jolla* ✛ *N. Torrey Pines Rd. exit off I–5 onto Carmel Valley Rd. going west, then turn left (south) on Coast Hwy. 101* ☎ *858/755–2063* ⊕ *www.torreypine.org* 🅿 *Parking $10–$20, varies by day of week and by season.*

WORTH NOTING

FAMILY **Birch Aquarium at Scripps.** Affiliated with the world-renowned Scripps Institution of Oceanography, this excellent aquarium sits at the end of a signposted drive leading off North Torrey Pines Road and has sweeping views of La Jolla coast below. More than 60 tanks are filled with colorful saltwater fish, and a 70,000-gallon tank simulates a La Jolla kelp forest. A special exhibit on sea horses features several examples of the species, plus mesmerizing sea dragons and a sea horse nursery. Besides the fish themselves, attractions include interactive educational exhibits based on the institution's ocean-related research and a variety of environmental issues. ✉ *2300 Expedition Way, La Jolla* ☎ *858/534–3474* ⊕ *www.aquarium.ucsd.edu* 🅿 *$18.50.*

POINT LOMA AND CORONADO WITH HARBOR AND SHELTER ISLANDS, AND OCEAN BEACH

Although Coronado is actually an isthmus, easily reached from the mainland if you head north from Imperial Beach, it has always seemed like an island and is often referred to as such. To the west, Point Loma protects the San Diego Bay from the Pacific's tides and waves. Both Coronado and Point Loma have stately homes, sandy beaches, private marinas, and prominent military installations. Nestled between the two, Harbor and Shelter islands owe their existence to dredging in the bay.

POINT LOMA

The hilly peninsula of Point Loma curves west and south into the Pacific and provides protection for San Diego Bay. Its high elevations and sandy cliffs provide incredible views, and make Point Loma a visible local landmark. Its maritime roots are evident, from its longtime ties to the U.S. Navy to its bustling sport fishing and sailing marinas. The funky community of Ocean Beach coexists alongside the stately homes of Sunset Cliffs and the honored graves at Fort Rosecrans National Cemetery.

TOP ATTRACTIONS

FAMILY
Fodor's Choice
★

Cabrillo National Monument. This 160-acre preserve marks the site of the first European visit to San Diego, made by 16th-century explorer Juan Rodríguez Cabrillo when he landed at this spot on September 15, 1542. Today the site, with its rugged cliffs and shores and outstanding overlooks, is one of the most frequently visited of all the national monuments.

The **visitor center** presents films and lectures about Cabrillo's voyage, the sea-level tide pools, and migrating gray whales. **Interpretive stations** have been installed along the walkways that edge the cliffs. The moderately steep **Bayside Trail**, 2½ miles round-trip, winds through coastal sage scrub, curving under the cliff-top lookouts and taking you ever closer to the bay-front scenery. You cannot reach the beach from this trail; you must stick to the path to protect the cliffs from erosion and yourself from thorny plants and snakes—including rattlers. The climb back is long but gradual, leading up to the **Old Point Loma Lighthouse.** The restored lighthouse dates to 1855 and is open to visitors. An exhibit in the Assistant Keepers Quarters next door tells the story of the Old Lighthouse and the daily lives of its keepers.

The western and southern cliffs of Cabrillo National Monument are prime whale-watching territory. A sheltered **viewing station** has wayside exhibits describing the great gray whales' yearly migration from Baja California to Alaska. High-powered telescopes help you focus on the whales' waterspouts. Whales are visible on clear days from late December through early March, with the highest concentration in January and February. More-accessible sea creatures (starfish, crabs, anemones) can be seen in the **tide pools** at the foot of the monument's western cliffs. Tide pooling is best when the tide is at its lowest, so call ahead or check tide charts online before your visit. Exercise caution on the slippery rocks. Drive north from the visitor center to Cabrillo Road, which winds down to the Coast Guard station and the shore. ⊠ *1800 Cabrillo Memorial Dr., Point Loma* ☏ *619/557–5450* ⊕ *www.nps.gov/cabr* ☏ *$10 per car, $5 per person on foot/bicycle, entry good for 7 days.*

A surfer prepares to head out before sunset at La Jolla's Torrey Pines State Beach and Reserve.

Fodor's Choice ★ **Sunset Cliffs.** As the name suggests, the 60-foot-high bluffs on the western side of Point Loma south of Ocean Beach are a perfect place to watch the sun set over the sea. To view the tide pools along the shore, use the staircase off Sunset Cliffs Boulevard at the foot of Ladera Street.

The dramatic coastline here seems to have been carved out of ancient rock. The impact of the waves is very clear: each year more sections of the cliffs are posted with caution signs. Don't ignore these warnings—it's easy to slip in the crumbling sandstone, and the surf can be extremely rough. The small coves and beaches that dot the coastline are popular with surfers drawn to the pounding waves. The homes along the boulevard—pink stucco mansions beside shingled Cape Cod–style cottages—are fine examples of Southern California luxury. ✉ *Sunset Cliffs Blvd., Point Loma.*

OCEAN BEACH

At the northern end of Point Loma lies the chilled-out, hippyesque town of Ocean Beach, commonly referred to as "OB." The main thoroughfare of this funky neighborhood is dotted with dive bars, coffeehouses, surf shops, and 1960s diners. OB is a magnet for everyone from surfers to musicians and artists. Fans of OB applaud its resistance to "selling out" to upscale development, whereas detractors lament its somewhat scruffy edges.

Ocean Beach Pier. This T-shape pier is a popular fishing spot and home to the Ocean Beach Pier Café and a small tackle shop. Constructed in 1966, it is the longest concrete pier on the West Coast and a perfect place to take in views of the harbor, ocean, and Point Loma Peninsula. Surfers flock to the waves that break just below. ✉ *1950 Abbott St., Ocean Beach.*

SHELTER ISLAND

In 1950 San Diego's port director decided to raise the shoal that lay off the eastern shore of Point Loma above sea level with the sand and mud dredged up during the course of deepening a ship channel in the 1930s and '40s. The resulting peninsula, **Shelter Island,** became home to several marinas and resorts, many with Polynesian details that still exist today, giving them a retro flair. This reclaimed peninsula now supports towering palms and resorts, restaurants, and side-by-side marinas. A long sidewalk runs past boat brokerages to the hotels and marinas that line the inner shore, facing Point Loma. On the bay side, fishermen launch their boats and families relax at picnic tables along the grass, where there are fire rings and permanent barbeque grills.

HARBOR ISLAND

Following the successful creation of Shelter Island, in 1961 the U.S. Navy used the residue from digging berths deep enough to accommodate aircraft carriers to build **Harbor Island**. Restaurants and high-rise hotels dot the inner shore of this 1½-mile-long man-made peninsula adjacent to the airport. The bay's shore is lined with pathways, gardens, and scenic picnic spots. The east-end point has killer views of the Downtown skyline.

CORONADO

As if freeze-framed in the 1950s, Coronado's quaint appeal is captured in its old-fashioned storefronts, well-manicured gardens, and charming **Ferry Landing Marketplace.** The streets of Coronado are wide, quiet, and friendly, and many of today's residents live in grand Victorian homes handed down for generations. Naval Air Station North Island was established in 1911 on Coronado's north end, across from Point Loma, and was the site of Charles Lindbergh's departure on the transcontinental flight that preceded his famous solo flight across the Atlantic. Coronado's long relationship with the U.S. Navy and its desirable real estate have made it an enclave for military personnel; it's said to have more retired admirals per capita than anywhere else in the United States.

Coronado is accessible via the arching blue 2.2-mile-long San Diego–Coronado Bay Bridge, which offers breathtaking views of the harbor and downtown. Alternatively, pedestrians and bikes can reach Coronado via the popular ferry service. Bus 904 meets the ferry and travels as far as Silver Strand State Beach. Bus 901 runs daily between the Gaslamp Quarter and Coronado.

TOP ATTRACTIONS

FAMILY **Coronado Ferry Landing.** This collection of shops at Ferry Landing is on a smaller scale than the Embarcadero's Seaport Village, but you do get a great view of the Downtown San Diego skyline. The little bayside shops and restaurants resemble the gingerbread domes of the Hotel Del Coronado. **Bikes and Beyond** (*619/435–7180, www.bikes-and-beyond.com*) rents bikes and surreys, perfect for riding through town and along Coronado's scenic bike path. ⊠ *1201 1st St., at B Ave., Coronado* ⊕ *www.coronadoferrylandingshops.com.*

Fodor's Choice
★
Hotel Del Coronado. The Del's distinctive red-tile roofs and Victorian gingerbread architecture have served as a set for many movies, political meetings, and extravagant social happenings. It's speculated that the Duke of Windsor may have first met the Duchess of Windsor Wallis Simpson here. Eleven presidents have been guests of the Del, and the film *Some Like It Hot*—starring Marilyn Monroe, Jack Lemmon, and Tony Curtis—used the hotel as a backdrop.

The Hotel Del, as locals call it, was the brainchild of financiers Elisha Spurr Babcock Jr. and H. L. Story, who saw the potential of Coronado's virgin beaches and its view of San Diego's emerging harbor. It opened in 1888 and has been a National Historic Landmark since 1977. The History Gallery displays photos from the Del's early days, and books elaborating on its history are sold, along with logo apparel and gifts, in the hotel's 15-plus shops.

Although the pool area is reserved for hotel guests, several surrounding dining patios make great places to sit back and imagine the scene during the 1920s, when the hotel rocked with good times. Behind the pool area, an attractive shopping arcade features a classic candy shop as well as several fine clothing and accessories stores. A lavish Sunday brunch is served in the Crown Room. During the holidays, the hotel hosts Skating by the Sea, an outdoor beachfront ice-skating rink open to the public. ■TIP➔ Whether or not you're staying at the Del, enjoy a drink at the Sun Deck Bar and Grill in order to gaze out over the ocean—it makes for a great escape.

Tours of the Del are $20 per person and take place on Monday, Wednesday, and Friday at 10:30, and weekends at 2; reservations are required. ✉ *1500 Orange Ave., at Glorietta Blvd., Coronado* ☎ *619/435–6611, 619/434–7242 tour reservations (through the Coronado Historical Association)* ⊕ *www.hoteldel.com.*

Fodor's Choice
★
Orange Avenue. Comprising Coronado's business district and its village-like heart, this avenue is surely one of the most charming spots in Southern California. Slow-paced and very "local" (the city fights against chain stores), it's a blast from the past, although entirely up to date in other respects. The military presence—Coronado is home to the U.S. Navy Sea, Air and Land (SEAL) forces—is reflected in shops selling military gear and places like **McP's Irish Pub,** at No. 1107. A family-friendly stop for a good, all-American meal, it's the unofficial SEALs headquarters. Many clothing boutiques, home-furnishings stores, and upscale restaurants cater to visitors with deep pockets, but you can buy plumbing supplies, too, or get a genuine military haircut at **Crown Barber Shop,** at No. 947. If you need a break, stop for a latte at the sidewalk café of **Bay Books,** San Diego's largest independent bookstore, at No. 1029. ✉ *Orange Ave., near 9th St., Coronado.*

BEACHES

San Diego's beaches have a different vibe from their northern counterparts in neighboring Orange County and glitzy Los Angeles farther up the coast. San Diego is more laid-back and less of a scene. Cyclists on cruiser bikes whiz by as surfers saunter toward the waves and sunbathers bronze under the sun, be it July or November.

Even at summer's hottest peak, San Diego's beaches are cool and breezy. Ocean waves are large, and the water will be colder than what you experience at tropical beaches—temperatures range from 55°F to 65°F from October through June, and 65°F to 73°F from July through September.

Finding a parking spot near the ocean can be hard in summer. Del Mar has a pay lot and metered street parking around the 15th Street Beach. La Jolla Shores has free street parking up to two hours. Mission Beach, and other large beaches have unmetered parking lots, but space can be limited. Your best bet is to arrive early.

Pay attention to signs listing illegal activities; undercover police often patrol the beaches. Smoking and alcoholic beverages are completely banned on city beaches. Drinking in beach parking lots, on boardwalks, and in landscaped areas is also illegal. Glass containers are not permitted on beaches, cliffs, and walkways, or in park areas and adjacent parking lots. Littering is not tolerated, and skateboarding is prohibited at some beaches. Fires are allowed only in fire rings or elevated barbecue grills. Although it may be tempting to take a sea creature from a tide pool as a souvenir, it may upset the delicate ecological balance, and it's illegal, too.

Year-round, lifeguards are stationed at nine permanent stations from Sunset Cliffs to Black's Beach. All other beaches are covered by roving patrols in the winter, and seasonal towers in the summer. When swimming in the ocean be aware of rip currents, which are common in California shores. For a surf and weather report, call San Diego's Lifeguard Services at *619/221–8824*. Visit ⊕ *www.surfline.com.* for live webcams on surf conditions and water temperature forecasts.

CORONADO

FAMILY **Silver Strand State Beach.** This quiet beach on a narrow sand-spit allows visitors a unique opportunity to experience both the Pacific Ocean and the San Diego Bay. The 2½ miles of ocean side is great for surfing and other water sports while the bay side, accessible via foot tunnel under Highway 75, has calmer, warmer water and great views of the San Diego skyline. Lifeguards and rangers are on duty year-round, and there are places for biking, volleyball, and fishing. Picnic tables, grills, and fire pits are available in summer, and the Silver Strand Beach Cafe is open Memorial Day through Labor Day. The beach is close to Loews Coronado Bay Resort and the Coronado Cays, an exclusive community popular with yacht owners. You can reserve RV sites ($65 beach; $50 inland) online (*www.reserveamerica.com*). Three day-use parking lots provide room for 800 cars. **Amenities:** food and drink, lifeguards, parking (fee), showers, toilets. **Best for:** walking, swimming, surfing. ⊠ *5000 Hwy. 75, Coronado ✛ 4½ miles south of city of Coronado* 🕾 *619/435–5184* ⊕ *www.parks.ca.gov/silverstrand* 🖼 *Parking $10, motorhome $30.*

FAMILY
Fodor's Choice
★

Coronado Beach. This wide beach is one of San Diego's most picturesque thanks to its soft white sand and sparkly blue water. The historic Hotel Del Coronado serves as a backdrop, and it's perfect for sunbathing, people-watching, and Frisbee tossing. The beach has limited surf, but it's great for bodyboarding and swimming. Exercisers might include Navy SEAL teams or other military units that conduct training runs on beaches in and around Coronado. There are picnic tables, grills, and popular fire rings, but don't bring lacquered wood or pallets. Only natural wood is allowed for burning. There's also a dog beach on the north end. There's free parking along Ocean Boulevard, though it's often hard to snag a space. **Amenities:** food and drink, lifeguards, showers, toilets. **Best for:** walking, swimming. ⊠ *Ocean Blvd., between S. O St. and Orange Ave., Coronado ✛ From the San Diego–Coronado bridge, turn left on Orange Ave. and follow signs.*

MISSION BAY, LA JOLLA, AND POINT LOMA

MISSION BAY

FAMILY
Mission Beach. With a roller coaster, artificial wave park, and hot dog stands, this 2-mile-long beach has a carnival vibe and is the closest thing you'll find to Coney Island on the West Coast. It's lively year-round but draws a huge crowd on hot summer days. A wide boardwalk paralleling the beach is popular with walkers, joggers, skateboarders, and bicyclists. To escape the crowds, head to South Mission Beach. It attracts surfers, swimmers, and scantily clad volleyball players, who often play competitive pickup games on the courts near the north jetty. The water near the Belmont Park roller coaster can be a bit rough but makes for good bodyboarding and bodysurfing. For free parking, you can try for a spot on the street, but your best bets are the two big lots at Belmont Park. **Amenities:** lifeguards, parking (no fee), showers, toilets. **Best for:** swimming, surfing, walking. ⊠ *3000 Mission Blvd., Mission Bay ✛ Parking near roller coaster at West Mission Bay Dr.* ⊕ *www.sandiego.gov/lifeguards/beaches/mb.shtml.*

Pacific Beach/North Pacific Beach. This beach, known for attracting a young college-age crowd and surfers, runs from the northern end of Mission Beach to Crystal Pier. The scene here is lively on weekends, with nearby restaurants, beach bars, and nightclubs providing a party atmosphere. In P.B. (as the locals call it) Sundays are known as "Sunday Funday," and pub crawls can last all day. So although drinking is no longer allowed on the beach, it's still likely you'll see people who have had one too many. The mood changes just north of the pier at North Pacific Beach, which attracts families and surfers. Although not quite pillowy, the sand at both beaches is nice and soft, which makes for great sunbathing and sand-castle building. ■ TIP➔ **Kelp and flies can be a problem on this stretch, so choose your spot wisely.** Parking at Pacific Beach can also be a challenge. A few coveted free angle parking spaces are available along the boardwalk, but you'll most likely have to look for spots in the surrounding neighborhood. If you're staying at nearby Pacific Terrace Hotel, you can simply walk to the beach. **Amenities:** food and drink, lifeguards, parking (no fee), showers, toilets. **Best for:** partiers, swimming, surfing. ✉ *4500 Ocean Blvd., Pacific Beach* ⊕ *www.sandiego.gov/lifeguards/beaches/pb.shtml.*

Tourmaline Surfing Park. Offering slow waves and frequent winds, this is one of the most popular beaches for surfers. For windsurfing and kiteboarding, it's only sailable with northwest winds. The 175-space parking lot at the foot of Tourmaline Street normally fills to capacity by midday. Just like Pacific Beach, Tourmaline has soft, tawny-colored sand, but when the tide is in the beach becomes quite narrow, making finding a good sunbathing spot a bit of a challenge. **Amenities:** seasonal lifeguards, parking (no fee), showers, toilets. **Best for:** windsurfing, surfing. ✉ *600 Tourmaline St., Pacific Beach.*

LA JOLLA

Fodor's Choice
★

Windansea Beach. With its rocky shoreline and strong shore break, Windansea stands out among San Diego beaches for its dramatic natural beauty. It's one of the best surf spots in San Diego County. Professional surfers love the unusual A-frame waves the reef break creates. Although the large sandstone rocks that dot the beach might sound like a hindrance, they actually serve as protective barriers from the wind, making this one of the best beaches in San Diego for sunbathing. The beach's palm-covered surf shack is a protected historical landmark, and a seat here at sunset may just be one of the most romantic spots on the West Coast. The name Windansea comes from a hotel that burned down in the late 1940s. You can usually find nearby street parking. **Amenities:** seasonal lifeguards, toilets. **Best for:** sunset, surfing, solitude. ✉ *Neptune Pl. at Nautilus St., La Jolla* ⊕ *www.sandiego.gov/lifeguards/beaches/windan.shtml.*

FAMILY
Fodor's Choice
★

La Jolla Cove. This shimmering blue-green inlet surrounded by cliffs is what first attracted everyone to La Jolla, from Native Americans to the glitterati. "The Cove," as locals refer to it, beyond where Girard Avenue dead-ends into Coast Boulevard, is marked by towering palms that line a promenade where people strolling in designer clothes are as common as Frisbee throwers. Ellen Browning Scripps Park sits atop cliffs formed by the incessant pounding of the waves and offers a great spot for picnics with a view. The Cove has beautiful white sand that is a bit course near the water's edge, but the beach is still a great place for sunbathing and lounging. At low tide, the pools and cliff caves are a destination for explorers. With visibility at 30-plus feet, this is the best place in San Diego for snorkeling, where bright-orange Garibaldi fish and other marine life populate the waters of the **San Diego–La Jolla Underwater Park Ecological Reserve.** From above water, it's not uncommon to spot sea lions and birds basking on the rocks, or dolphin fins just offshore. The cove is also a favorite of rough-water swimmers, while the area just north is best for kayakers wanting to explore the Seven La Jolla Sea Caves. **Amenities:** lifeguards, showers, toilets. **Best for:** snorkeling, swimming, walking. ✉ *1100 Coast Blvd., east of Ellen Browning Scripps Park, La Jolla* ⊕ *www.sandiego.gov/lifeguards/beaches/cove.shtml.*

FAMILY **La Jolla Shores.** This is one of San Diego's most popular beaches due to its wide sandy shore, gentle waves, and incredible views of La Jolla Peninsula. There's also a large grassy park, and adjacent to La Jolla Shores lies the **San Diego La Jolla Underwater Park Ecological Reserve,** 6,000 acres of protected ocean bottom and tide lands. The white powdery sand at La Jolla Sands is some of San Diego's best, and several surf and scuba schools teach here. Kayaks can also be rented nearby. A concrete boardwalk parallels the beach, and a boat launch for small vessels lies 300 yards south of the lifeguard station at Avenida de Playa. Arrive early to get a parking spot in the lot near Kellogg Park at the foot of Calle Frescota. Street parking is limited to one or two hours. **Amenities:** lifeguards, parking (no fee), showers, toilets. **Best for:** surfing, swimming, walking. ⊠ *8200 Camino del Oro, in front of Kellogg Park, La Jolla ✛ 2 miles north of downtown La Jolla ⊕ www.sandiego. gov/lifeguards/beaches/shores.shtml.*

Fodor'sChoice **Torrey Pines State Beach and Reserve.** With sandstone cliffs and hiking ★ trails adjacent to the beach rather than urban development, Torrey Pines State Beach feels far away from the SoCal sprawl. The beach and reserve encompass 1,600 acres of sandstone cliffs and deep ravines, and a network of meandering trails lead to the wide, pristine beach below. Along the way enjoy the rare Torrey pine trees, found only here and on Santa Rosa Island, offshore. Guides conduct free tours of the nature preserve on weekends. Torrey Pines tends to get crowded in summer, but you'll find more isolated spots heading south under the cliffs leading to Black's Beach. Smooth rocks often wash up on stretches of the beach making it a challenge, at times, to go barefoot. If you can find a patch that is clear of debris, you'll encounter the nice soft, golden sand San Diego is known for. There is a paid parking lot at the entrance to the park but also look for free angle parking along N. Torrey Pines Road. **Amenities:** lifeguards, parking (fee), showers, toilets. **Best for:** swimming, surfing, walking. ⊠ *12600 N. Torrey Pines Rd.* ☎ *858/755–2063* ⊕ *www.torreypine.org* ◻ *Parking $15 per vehicle.*

POINT LOMA

Sunset Cliffs. As the name would suggest this natural park near Point Loma Nazerene University is one of the best places in San Diego to watch the sunset thanks to its cliff-top location and expansive ocean views. Some limited beach access is accessible via an extremely steep stairway at the foot of Ladera Street. Beware of the treacherous cliff trails and pay attention to warning signs. The cliffs are very unstable and several fatalities have occurred over the last few years. If you're going to make your way to the narrow beach below, it's best to go at low tide when the southern end, near Cabrillo Point, reveals tide pools teeming with small sea creatures. Farther north the waves lure surfers, and Osprey Point offers good fishing off the rocks. Keep your eyes peeled for migrating California gray whales during the winter months. Check WaveCast (*www.wavecast.com/tides*) for tide schedules. **Amenities:** parking (no fee). **Best for:** solitude, sunset, surfing. ⊠ *Sunset Cliffs Blvd., between Ladera St. and Adair St., Point Loma* ⊕ *www.sunsetcliffs.info.*

NORTH COUNTY BEACHES

DEL MAR

FAMILY **Del Mar Beach.** This famously clean 2-mile-long beach is the perfect place for long barefoot walks and sunbathing due to its extremely fine, soft sand and lack of seaweed and other debris. Del Mar Beach is also a great place for families. It has year-round lifeguards and areas clearly marked for swimming and surfing. Depending on the swell, you may see surfers at the 15th Street surf break, right below two coastal parks, Powerhouse and Seagrove; volleyball players love the courts at the beach's far North end. The section of beach south of 15th is lined with cliffs and tends to be less crowded than Main Beach, which extends from 15th north to 29th. Leashed dogs are permitted on most sections of the beach, except Main Beach, where they are prohibited from June 15 through the Tuesday after Labor Day. For the rest of the year, dogs may run under voice control at North Beach, just north of the River Mouth, also known locally as Dog Beach. Food, shopping, and hotels including L'Auberge Del Mar, are near Del Mar Beach. Parking costs from $1.50 to $3 per hour at meters and pay lots on Coast Boulevard and along Camino Del Mar. **Amenities:** food and drink, lifeguards, parking (fee), showers, toilets. **Best for:** swimming, walking. ⊠ *Main Beach, 1700 Coast Blvd., North Beach 3200–3300 Camino Del Mar, Del Mar* ☎ *858/755–1556* ⊕ *www.delmar.ca.us/203/Beaches-Parks.*

ENCINITAS

Swami's. The palms and the golden lotus-flower domes of the nearby Self-Realization Fellowship temple and ashram earned this picturesque beach, also a top surfing spot, its name. Extreme low tides expose tide pools that harbor anemones, starfish, and other sea life. The only access is by a long stairway leading down from the cliff-top Swami's Seaside Park, where there's free parking. A shower is at the base of the steps. On big winter swells, the bluffs are lined with gawkers watching the area's best surfers take on—and be taken down by—some of the county's best big waves. The beach has flat, packed sand and can accumulate seaweed and some flies, so if laying out is your main objective you might want to head north to Moonlight Beach. Offshore, divers do their thing at North County's underwater park, Encinitas Marine Life Refuge. The small park next to the Swami's parking lot offers shade trees, picnic tables, barbecues, and clean bathrooms. Across the street is the cheerful Swami's Cafe, where surfers refuel postsurf. **Amenities:** lifeguards, parking (no fee), showers, toilets. **Best for:** snorkeling, surfing, swimming. ⊠ *1298 S. Coast Hwy. 101 (Rte. S21), Encinitas* ✛ *1 mile north of Cardiff.*

WHERE TO EAT

San Diego is an up-and-coming culinary destination, thanks to its stunning Pacific Ocean setting, proximity to Mexico, diverse population, and the area's extraordinary farming community. Increasingly the city's veteran top chefs are being joined by a new generation of talented chefs and restaurateurs who are adding stylish restaurants with innovative food and drink programs to the dining scene at a record pace. Yes, visitors still are drawn to the San Diego Zoo and miles of beaches, but now they come for memorable dining experiences as well.

The city's culinary scene got a significant boost when San Diego emerged as one of the world's top craft beer destinations, with artisan breweries and gastropubs now in almost every neighborhood. These neighborhoods are also ethnically diverse with modest eateries offering affordable authentic international cuisines that add spice to the dining mix.

The trendy Gaslamp Quarter delights visitors looking for a broad range of innovative and international dining and nightlife, while bustling Little Italy offers a mix of affordable Italian fare and posh new eateries. Modern restaurants and cafés thrive in East Village, amid the luxury condos near PETCO Park. The Uptown neighborhoods centered on Hillcrest—an urbane district with San Francisco flavor—are a mix of bars and independent restaurants, many of which specialize in ethnic cuisine. North Park, in particular, has a happening restaurant and craft beer scene, with just about every kind of cuisine you can think of, and laid-back prices to boot. And scenic La Jolla offers some of the best fine dining in the city with dramatic water views as an added bonus.

Use the coordinate (✛ A1) at the end of each listing to locate a site on the corresponding map.

PRICES

Meals in San Diego popular dining spots can be pricey, especially in areas like La Jolla, the Gaslamp Quarter, and Coronado. Many other restaurants are very affordable or offer extra value with fixed-price menus, early-dining specials and early and late happy hours.

Restaurant reviews have been shortened. For full information, visit Fodors.com.

WHAT IT COSTS				
	$	**$$**	**$$$**	**$$$$**
Restaurants	under $18	$18–$27	$28–$35	over $35

Prices in the reviews are the average cost of a main course at dinner or, if dinner is not served, at lunch.

DOWNTOWN

GASLAMP QUARTER

$$$
AMERICAN

✕ **Searsucker.** Since opened by celebrity chef Brian Malarkey a few years ago, this high-energy flagship restaurant has become the Gaslamp's best for food and energetic atmosphere. Foodies from near and far savor Malarkey's upscale down-home fare like small plates of biscuits with spicy honey, duck fat fries, and shrimp and grits. **Known for:** detailed, home-inspired decor; crispy duck fat fries; late-night menu on Fridays and Saturdays from 11 pm–1 am. $ *Average main: $30* ✉ *611 5th Ave., Gaslamp Quarter* ☎ *619/233-7327* ⊕ *www.searsucker.com* ✛ *H2.*

$$
JAPANESE

✕ **Taka.** Pristine fish imported from around the world and presented creatively attracts crowds nightly to this intimate Gaslamp restaurant. Take a seat at the bar and watch one of the sushi chefs preparing appetizers, perhaps the monkfish liver with ponzu or spicy tuna tartar. **Known for:** uni sushi topped with wasabi; omakase tasting menu; upscale sake offerings. $ *Average main: $18* ✉ *555 5th Ave., Gaslamp Quarter* ☎ *619/338-0555* ⊕ *www.takasushi.com* ⊗ No *lunch* ✛ *H2.*

EAST VILLAGE

$$
MODERN
MEXICAN
FAMILY

✕ **The Blind Burro.** East Village families, baseball fans heading to or from PETCO Park and happy-hour bound singles flock to this airy restaurant with Baja-inspired food and drink. Traditional margaritas get a fresh kick from fruit juices or jalapeno peppers; other libations include sangrias and Mexican beers, all perfect pairings for house-made guacamole, ceviche, or salsas with chips. **Known for:** house margarita with fruit infusions; surf-and-turf Baja-style tacos; gluten-free menu. $ *Average main: $18* ✉ *639 J St., East Village* ☎ *619/795-7880* ⊕ *www.theblindburro.com* ✛ *H3.*

LITTLE ITALY

$$$
MODERN
AMERICAN

✕ **Juniper and Ivy.** Celebrity chef Richard Blais's addition to San Diego's restaurant scene fills an open-beamed space with seating for 250 and an open stainless-steel dream kitchen where diners can watch the chef and team in action. Blais sources local farm fresh ingredients for his "left coast cookery" with a molecular gastronomy twist. **Known for:** a California-Baja-inspired Carne Crudo Asada topped with quail eggs; an off-menu "In & Haute" burger; very shareable Yodel chocolate dessert. $ *Average main: $35* ✉ *2228 Kettner Blvd., Little Italy* ☎ *619/269-9036* ⊕ *www.juniperandivy.com* ⊗ *Closed for lunch* ✛ *E5.*

$$
MODERN
AMERICAN
Fodor's Choice
★

✕ **Prepkitchen Little Italy.** Urbanites craving a hip casual setting and gourmet menu pack architectural salvage-styled Prepkitchen Little Italy, tucked upstairs above a busy corner in this thriving neighborhood. With first-date cocktails, after-work brews or birthday champagne, diners relish familiar choices like meatball sandwiches, chops, and pork belly with kimchi brussels. **Known for:** weekend brunch featuring popular chilaquiles dish; bacon-wrapped dates. $ *Average main: $23* ✉ *1660 India St., Little Italy* ☎ *619/398-8383* ⊕ *www.prepkitchenlittleitaly.com* ✛ *E5.*

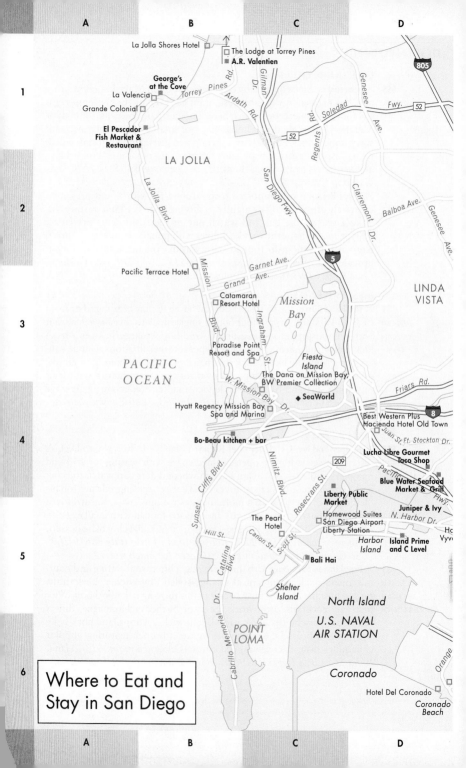

Where to Eat and Stay in San Diego

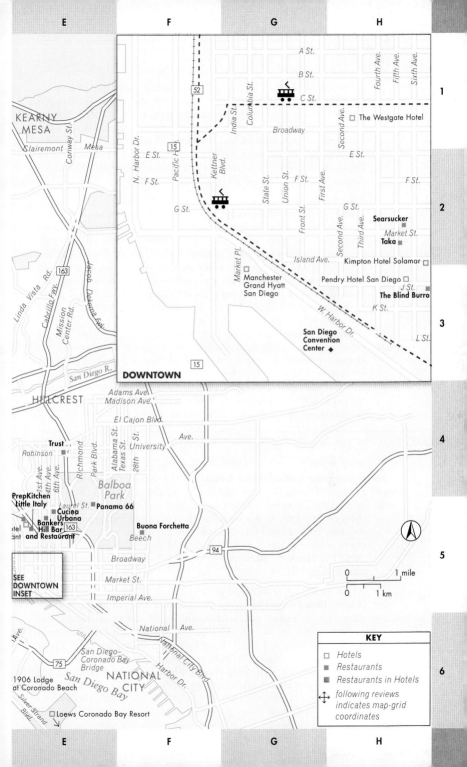

BALBOA PARK AND BANKERS HILL

BALBOA PARK

$ AMERICAN 🍴 **Panama 66.** Adding a dose of hip to Balboa Park, this gastropub, located adjacent to the San Diego Museum of Art, offers a stylish pit-stop pre-theater or between museum-hopping. Decor is contemporary, with café-style seating, sculptures in the garden, and a view of the California Tower. **Known for:** rotating cocktails pegged to museum exhibits; live music most nights. [$] *Average main: $11* ✉ *1450 El Prado, Balboa Park* ☎ *619/696–1966* 🌐 *www.panama66.com* 🕒 *No dinner Mon. and Tues.* ✥ *E5.*

BANKERS HILL

$$ MODERN AMERICAN Fodor's Choice ★ 🍴 **Bankers Hill Bar and Restaurant.** The living wall of succulents, hip warehouse interior, and wine bottle chandeliers suit this vibrant restaurant where good times and great eats meet. An after-work crowd joins residents of this quiet stretch of Bankers Hill for happy hour cocktails, craft beers, and well-curated wines served from the zinc bar. **Known for:** popular burger with truffle fries; soft-shell crab lettuce wraps with a vodka-infused batter; living plant wall on the sun-drenched patio. [$] *Average main: $21* ✉ *2202 4th Ave., Bankers Hill* ☎ *619/231–0222* 🌐 *www.bankershillsd.com* 🕒 *No lunch* ✥ *E5.*

$$ ITALIAN Fodor's Choice ★ 🍴 **Cucina Urbana.** Twentysomethings mingle with boomers in this convivial Bankers Hill dining room and bar, one of the most popular restaurants in town. Country-farmhouse decor that mixes rolling pins with modern art looks and feels festive. **Known for:** vasi appetizer platters; seasonal polenta with ragu; ricotta-stuffed zucchini blossoms. [$] *Average main: $20* ✉ *505 Laurel St., Bankers Hill* ☎ *619/239–2222* 🌐 *www.cucinaurbana.com* 🕒 *No lunch Sat.–Mon.* ✥ *E5.*

OLD TOWN AND UPTOWN

OLD TOWN

$ SEAFOOD FAMILY 🍴 **Blue Water Seafood Market & Grill.** Blame a television segment by Guy Fieri on "Diners, Drive-ins and Dives" for the long lines of fans from around the globe. But it's the fresh seafood cooked to order that keeps them coming back to this no-frills fish market and restaurant. **Known for:** beer-battered cod tacos; classic cioppino plate with mussels and clams, scallops, shrimp, and red snapper. [$] *Average main: $15* ✉ *3667 India St., Mission Hills* ☎ *619/497–0914* 🌐 *www.bluewaterseafoodsandiego.com* ✥ *D4.*

HILLCREST AND MISSION HILLS

$ MEXICAN 🍴 **Lucha Libre Gourmet Taco Shop.** Named for a form of Mexican wrestling, this taco shop with its hot-pink walls and shiny booths was famous mostly for its lack of parking until it appeared on the Travel Channel's "Man v. Food." Then long lines of burrito-crazed fans began forming outside the walk-up window for lunch. **Known for:** Tap Me Out taco with fried cheese; Champion nachos with french fries; lively and festive interior seating. [$] *Average main: $7* ✉ *1810 W. Washington St., Mission Hills* ☎ *619/296–8226* 🌐 *www.tacosmackdown.com* ✥ *D4.*

$$ ✕ **Trust.** Old-school wood-fire techniques meet modern architecture in
MODERN   this busy bistro where comic book–style art covers the concrete walls
AMERICAN and the bottle-lined bar beckons locals and visitors alike. Dishes feature
Fodor'sChoice popular items like the braised oxtail raviolini with horseradish and
★   whipped ricotta, and wood-grilled cauliflower dressed in a curry vin-
          aigrette. **Known for:** five-hour braised oxtail raviolini; roomy outdoor
          patio. $ *Average main: $20* ✉ *3752 Park Blvd., Hillcrest* ☎ *619/795–*
          6901 ⊕ *www.trustrestaurantsd.com* ✛ *E4.*

SOUTH PARK

$ ✕ **Buona Forchetta.** A golden-domed pizza oven, named Sofia after the
ITALIAN   owner's daughter, delivers authentic Neapolitan-style pizza to fans who
FAMILY   often line up for patio tables at this dog- and kid-friendly Italian res-
Fodor'sChoice taurant in South Park. Slices of classic margherita or truffle-flavored
★   mozzarella and mushroom pizzas make a meal or can be shared, but
          don't miss the equally delicious appetizers like the tender calamari or
          succulent artichokes, heaping salads, or fresh pastas, including a hearty
          lasagna, delicate ravioli, or gnocchi with pesto. **Known for:** house red
          wine; bubbly Neapolitan-style pizzas; bustling patio. $ *Average main:*
          $14 ✉ *3001 Beech St., South Park* ☎ *619/381–4844* ⊕ *www.buonafor-*
          chettasd.com ☾ *No lunch Mon. and Tues.* ✛ *F5.*

LA JOLLA

$$$$ ✕ **A.R. Valentien.** Champions of in-season, fresh-today produce and sea-
AMERICAN food, executive chef Jeff Jackson and chef de cuisine Kelli Crosson have
Fodor'sChoice made this cozy room in the luxurious, Craftsman-style Lodge at Torrey
★   Pines one of San Diego's top fine dining destinations. Their food combina-
          tions are simultaneously simple and delightfully inventive—duck breast
          with celery root risotto; ahi tuna with grapefruit and crispy quinoa; or
          swordfish with chorizo and charred scallion salsa verde. **Known for:** red-
          wine braised short rib; creamy chicken liver pâté; patio that overlooks
          the resort pool and the famed 18th green at Torrey Pines South Course.
          $ *Average main: $38* ✉ *The Lodge at Torrey Pines, 11480 N. Torrey*
          Pines Rd., La Jolla ☎ *858/777–6635* ⊕ *www.arvalentien.com* ✛ *B1.*

$ ✕ **El Pescador Fish Market & Restaurant.** This bustling fish market and
SEAFOOD   café in the heart of La Jolla Village has been popular with locals for its
          superfresh fish for more than 30 years. Order the char-grilled, locally
          caught halibut, swordfish, or yellowtail on a toasted torta roll to enjoy
          in-house or to-go for an oceanfront picnic at nearby La Jolla Cove.
          Known for: superfresh fish; bustling on-site fish market. $ *Average*
          main: $15 ✉ *634 Pearl St., La Jolla* ☎ *858/456–2526* ⊕ *www.elpesca-*
          dorfishmarket.com ✛ *B1.*

$$$$ ✕ **George's at the Cove.** La Jolla's ocean-view destination restaurant
AMERICAN includes three dining areas: California Modern on the bottom floor, the
Fodor'sChoice Level2 bar in the middle, and Ocean Terrace on the roof. The sleek main
★   dining room presents elegant preparations of seafood, beef, and venison,
          which star-chef Trey Foshee enlivens with amazing local produce. **Known**
          for: beef tartare with 67-degree egg; excellent ocean views; attention to
          detail for special occasion dinners. $ *Average main: $37* ✉ *1250 Pros-*
          pect St., La Jolla ☎ *858/454–4244* ⊕ *www.georgesatthecove.com* ✛ *B1.*

3

POINT LOMA, SHELTER ISLAND, AND HARBOR ISLAND

POINT LOMA

$$ BISTRO 🍴 **Bo-Beau kitchen + bar.** Ocean Beach is a slightly eccentric beach town, not a place diners would expect to find this warm, romantic bistro that evokes a French farmhouse. The satisfying French-inspired menu of soups, woodstone-oven flatbreads, mussels, and other bistro classics is served in cozy dining rooms and a rustic outdoor patio. **Known for:** popular crispy Brussels sprouts with pancetta; Tuesday date night special. [$] *Average main: $22* ✉ *4996 W. Point Loma Blvd., Ocean Beach* ☎ *619/224–2884* 🌐 *www.cohnrestaurants.com/bobeaukitchen-bar* ⏲ *No lunch* ✣ *B4.*

$ INTERNATIONAL FAMILY Fodor's Choice ★ 🍴 **Liberty Public Market.** The city's former Naval Training Center is now home to nearly 30 vendors so even the pickiest of diners will be pleased. Options include tacos and quesadillas at Cecilia's Taqueria; fried rice, pad Thai, and curries at Mama Made Thai; gumbo, fried chicken, jambalaya, and other Southern specialties at Cane Patch Kitchen; smoothies and cold-pressed juices at Fully Loaded; and croissants, eclairs, and macarons at Le Parfait Paris. **Known for:** colossal burgers with creative fillings at Stuffed!; lively kid- and dog-friendly patio. [$] *Average main: $10* ✉ *2820 Historic Decatur Rd., Liberty Station* ☎ *619/487–9346* 🌐 *www.libertypublicmarket.com* ✣ *C4.*

SHELTER ISLAND

$$ HAWAIIAN 🍴 **Bali Hai.** For more than 50 years, generations of San Diegans and visitors have enjoyed this Polynesian-theme icon with its stunning bay and city skyline views. Much of the kitsch has been replaced by contemporary decor, but you'll still spot tikis here and there. **Known for:** potent Bali Hai mai tais; Sunday brunch buffet with a DIY sundae bar. [$] *Average main: $25* ✉ *2230 Shelter Island Dr., Shelter Island* ☎ *619/222–1181* 🌐 *www.balihairestaurant.com* ⏲ *No lunch Sun.* ✣ *C5.*

HARBOR ISLAND

$$$$ MODERN AMERICAN 🍴 **Island Prime and C Level.** Two restaurants in one share this enviable spot on the shore of Harbor Island: the splurge-worthy Island Prime steak house and the relaxed C Level with a choice terrace. Both venues tempt with unrivaled views of downtown San Diego's skyline. **Known for:** sunset views; popover bread served with jalapeño jelly butter. [$] *Average main: $39* ✉ *880 Harbor Island Dr., Harbor Island* ☎ *619/298–6802* 🌐 *www.cohnrestaurants.com/islandprime* ⏲ *No lunch at Island Prime* ✣ *D5.*

WHERE TO STAY

Sharing the city's postcard-perfect sunny skies are neighborhoods and coastal communities that offer great diversity; San Diego is no longer the sleepy beach town it once was. In action-packed Downtown, luxury hotels cater to solo business travelers and young couples with trendy restaurants and cabana-encircled pools. Budget-friendly options can be found in smaller neighborhoods just outside the Gaslamp Quarter such as Little Italy and Uptown.

You'll need a car if you stay outside Downtown, but the beach communities are rich with lodging options. Across the bridge, Coronado's hotels and resorts offer access to a stretch of glistening white sand that's often recognized as one of the best beaches in the country. La Jolla offers many romantic, upscale ocean-view hotels and some of the area's best restaurants and specialty shopping. But it's easy to find a water view in any price range: surfers make themselves at home at the casual inns and budget stays of Pacific Beach and Mission Bay. If you're planning to fish, check out hotels located near the marinas in Shelter Island, Point Loma, or Coronado.

For families, Uptown, Mission Valley, and Old Town are close to SeaWorld and the San Diego Zoo, offering good-value accommodations with extras like sleeper sofas and video games. Mission Valley is ideal for business travelers; there are plenty of well-known chain hotels with conference space, modern business centers, and kitchenettes for extended stays.

When you make reservations, book well in advance and ask about specials. Several properties in the Hotel Circle area of Mission Valley offer reduced rates and even free tickets to the San Diego Zoo and other attractions. You can save on hotels and attractions by visiting the San Diego Tourism Authority website (🌐 *www.sandiego.org*) for special seasonal offers.

Use the coordinate (✣ A1) at the end of each listing to locate a site on the corresponding map.

PRICES

Note that even in the most expensive areas, you can find affordable rooms. High season is summer, and rates are lowest in fall. If an ocean view is important, request it when booking, but it will cost you.

Hotel reviews have been shortened. For full information, visit Fodors.com.

WHAT IT COSTS

	$	$$	$$$	$$$$
Hotels	under $150	$150–$225	$226–$300	over $300

Hotel prices are the cost of a standard double room in high season, excluding 10.5% tax.

DOWNTOWN

GASLAMP QUARTER

$$$ HOTEL FAMILY Fodor's Choice ★ 🏨 **Kimpton Hotel Solamar.** Best known for Upper East Bar, its pool-side rooftop bar, and stylish lobby decor, Solamar's recently refreshed guest rooms reflect this urban escape's mixture of luxury and fun, with prints galore and subtle nods to San Diego's happy beach culture. **Pros:** great restaurant; attentive service; upscale rooms. **Cons:** busy valet parking; daily facility fee. [$] *Rooms from: $279* ✉ *435 6th Ave., Gaslamp Quarter* ☎ *619/819–9500, 877/230–0300* 🌐 *www.hotelsolamar.com* 🛏 *235 rooms* 🍴 *No meals* ✣ *H2.*

$$$$

HOTEL

Fodor'sChoice

★

Pendry San Diego. Opened in early 2017, the Pendry San Diego is the Gaslamp's newest stunner. **Pros:** well-situated in Gaslamp Quarter; excellent dining options; complimentary coffee in the mornings. **Cons:** pricey room rates; meals are expensive. $ *Rooms from: $480 ⊠ 550 J St., Gaslamp Quarter* ☎ *619/738–7000* ⊕ *www.pendryhotels.com* ⤵ *317 rooms* ⦿ *No meals* ✛ *H3.*

$$$

HOTEL

The Westgate Hotel. A modern high-rise near Horton Plaza hides San Diego's most opulent old world–style hotel, featuring a lobby outfitted with bronze sculptures and Baccarat chandeliers. **Pros:** affordable luxury; serene rooftop pool deck. **Cons:** dated guest rooms; mandatory facility fee. $ *Rooms from: $299 ⊠ 1055 2nd Ave., Gaslamp Quarter* ☎ *619/238–1818, 800/522–1564* ⊕ *www.westgatehotel.com* ⤵ *223 rooms* ⦿ *No meals* ✛ *H1.*

LITTLE ITALY

$

B&B/INN

Hotel Vyvant. You'll find more amenities at other Downtown hotels but it's hard to beat this property's value and charm. **Pros:** good location; historic property; welcoming staff. **Cons:** some shared baths; no parking. $ *Rooms from: $139 ⊠ 505 W. Grape St., Little Italy* ☎ *619/230–1600, 800/518–9930* ⊕ *www.hotelvyvant.com* ⤵ *23 rooms* ⦿ *Breakfast* ✛ *E5.*

EMBARCADERO

$$$

HOTEL

FAMILY

Manchester Grand Hyatt San Diego. Primarily a draw for business travelers, this hotel between Seaport Village and the convention center also works well for leisure and family travelers. **Pros:** great views; conference facilities; good location; spacious rooms. **Cons:** lots of convention-goers; some trolley noise. $ *Rooms from: $259 ⊠ 1 Market Pl., Embarcadero* ☎ *619/232–1234, 800/233–1234* ⊕ *www.manchester. grand.hyatt.com* ⤵ *1628 rooms* ⦿ *No meals* ✛ *G3.*

OLD TOWN, MISSION VALLEY

OLD TOWN

$$

HOTEL

FAMILY

Best Western Plus Hacienda Hotel Old Town. Perched on a hill in the heart of Old Town, this hotel is known for its expansive courtyards, outdoor fountains, and maze of stairs that connect eight buildings of guest rooms. **Pros:** airport shuttle; well-maintained outdoor areas. **Cons:** some rooms need renovating; complicated layout. $ *Rooms from: $210 ⊠ 4041 Harney St., Old Town* ☎ *619/298–4707* ⊕ *www. haciendahotel-oldtown.com* ⤵ *198 rooms* ⦿ *No meals* ✛ *D4.*

MISSION BAY AND BEACHES

MISSION BAY

$$

RESORT

FAMILY

The Dana on Mission Bay, BW Premier Collection. A part of Best Western's BW Premier Collection, this waterfront resort, just down the road from SeaWorld, has an ideal location for active leisure travelers. **Pros:** water views; many outdoor activities. **Cons:** expensive resort fee. $ *Rooms from: $209 ⊠ 1710 W. Mission Bay Dr., Mission Bay* ☎ *619/222–6440, 800/445–3339* ⊕ *www.thedana.com* ⤵ *271 rooms* ⦿ *No meals* ✛ *C4.*

$$$ RESORT FAMILY **Hyatt Regency Mission Bay Spa and Marina.** This modern property has many desirable amenities, including balconies with excellent views of the garden, bay, ocean, or swimming pool courtyard. **Pros:** proximity to water sports; 120-foot waterslides in pools, plus kiddie slide. **Cons:** daily resort fee; not centrally located. [$] *Rooms from: $299* ✉ *1441 Quivira Rd., Mission Bay* ☎ *619/224–1234, 800/233–1234* 🌐 *www.missionbay.regency.hyatt.com* 🛏 *429 rooms* 🍴 *No meals* ✣ *C4.*

$$$ RESORT FAMILY **Paradise Point Resort and Spa.** Minutes from SeaWorld but hidden in a quiet part of Mission Bay, the beautiful landscape of this 44-acre resort offers plenty of space for families to play and relax. **Pros:** water views; five pools; good service. **Cons:** not centrally located; motel-thin walls; parking and resort fees. [$] *Rooms from: $289* ✉ *1404 Vacation Rd., Mission Bay* ☎ *858/274–4630, 800/344–2626* 🌐 *www.paradisepoint.com* 🛏 *462 rooms* 🍴 *No meals* ✣ *C3.*

PACIFIC BEACH

$$$$ RESORT **Pacific Terrace Hotel.** Travelers love this terrific beachfront hotel and the ocean views from most rooms; it's a perfect place for watching sunsets over the Pacific. **Pros:** beach views; large rooms; friendly service. **Cons:** busy and sometimes noisy area; expensive in peak season. [$] *Rooms from: $549* ✉ *610 Diamond St., Pacific Beach* ☎ *858/581–3500, 800/344–3370* 🌐 *www.pacificterrace.com* 🛏 *73 rooms* 🍴 *No meals* ✣ *B3.*

LA JOLLA

$$$$ HOTEL Fodor's Choice ★ **Grande Colonial.** This white wedding cake–style hotel in the heart of La Jolla village has ocean views and charming European details that include chandeliers, mahogany railings, and French doors. **Pros:** great location; superb restaurant. **Cons:** somewhat busy street; no fitness center; valet parking only. [$] *Rooms from: $369* ✉ *910 Prospect St., La Jolla* ☎ *888/828–5498* 🌐 *www.thegrandecolonial.com* 🛏 *93 rooms* 🍴 *No meals* ✣ *B1.*

$$$$ HOTEL FAMILY **La Jolla Shores Hotel.** One of San Diego's few hotels actually on the beach, this property is part of La Jolla Beach and Tennis Club. **Pros:** on beach; great views. **Cons:** not centrally located; pool can be noisy; three-night minimum in summer. [$] *Rooms from: $319* ✉ *8110 Camino del Oro, La Jolla* ☎ *858/923–8058, 877/346–6714* 🌐 *www.ljshoreshotel.com* 🛏 *128 rooms* 🍴 *No meals* ✣ *B1.*

$$$$ HOTEL **La Valencia.** This pink Spanish-Mediterranean confection drew Hollywood film stars in the 1930s and '40s with its setting and views of La Jolla Cove; now it draws the Kardashians. **Pros:** upscale rooms; views; near beach. **Cons:** standard rooms are tiny; lots of traffic outside. [$] *Rooms from: $449* ✉ *1132 Prospect St., La Jolla* ☎ *858/454–0771* 🌐 *www.lavalencia.com* 🛏 *114 rooms* 🍴 *No meals* ✣ *B1.*

$$$$ RESORT Fodor's Choice ★ **The Lodge at Torrey Pines.** This beautiful Craftsman-style lodge sits on a bluff between La Jolla and Del Mar and commands a coastal view. **Pros:** spacious upscale rooms; good service; adjacent the famed Torrey Pines Golf Course. **Cons:** not centrally located; expensive. [$] *Rooms from: $379* ✉ *11480 N. Torrey Pines Rd., La Jolla* ☎ *858/453–4420, 888/826–0224* 🌐 *www.lodgetorreypines.com* ⛳ *Two 18-hole championship golf courses* 🛏 *170 rooms* 🍴 *No meals* ✣ *B1.*

3

POINT LOMA AND CORONADO WITH HARBOR AND SHELTER ISLANDS

POINT LOMA

$$$$ HOTEL FAMILY Fodor'sChoice ★ **Homewood Suites San Diego Airport Liberty Station.** Families and business travelers will benefit from the space and amenities at this all-suites hotel. **Pros:** complimentary grocery shopping service; close to paths for joggers and bikers. **Cons:** no pets allowed; far from nightlife. [$] *Rooms from: $349* ✉ *2576 Laning Rd., Point Loma* ☎ *619/222–0500* 🌐 *www.homewoodsuites.com* 🛏 *150 suites* 🍴 *Breakfast* ✥ *C5.*

$$$ HOTEL Fodor'sChoice ★ **The Pearl Hotel.** This previously vintage motel received a makeover, turning it into a retro-chic hangout decorated with kitschy lamps and original, in-room art by local children. **Pros:** near marina; hip bar/restaurant on-site (dinner only, except for seasonal specials). **Cons:** not centrally located; one bed in rooms. [$] *Rooms from: $233* ✉ *1410 Rosecrans St., Point Loma* ☎ *619/226–6100* 🌐 *www.thepearlsd.com* 🛏 *23 rooms* 🍴 *No meals* ✥ *C5.*

CORONADO

$$$$ RESORT FAMILY Fodor'sChoice ★ **Hotel Del Coronado.** As much of a draw today as it was when it opened in 1888, the Victorian-style "Hotel Del" is always alive with activity, as guests—including U.S. presidents and celebrities—and tourists marvel at the fanciful architecture and ocean views. **Pros:** 17 on-site shops; on the beach; well-rounded spa. **Cons:** some rooms are small; expensive dining; hectic public areas. [$] *Rooms from: $425* ✉ *1500 Orange Ave., Coronado* ☎ *800/468–3533, 619/435–6611* 🌐 *www.hoteldel.com* 🛏 *757 rooms* 🍴 *No meals* ✥ *D6.*

$$$$ RESORT FAMILY **Loews Coronado Bay Resort.** You can park your boat at the 80-slip marina of this romantic retreat set on a secluded 15-acre peninsula on the Silver Strand. **Pros:** great restaurants; lots of activities; all rooms have furnished balconies with water views. **Cons:** far from anything; confusing layout. [$] *Rooms from: $349* ✉ *4000 Coronado Bay Rd., Coronado* ☎ *619/424–4000, 800/815–6397* 🌐 *www.loewshotels.com/CoronadoBay* 🛏 *439 rooms* 🍴 *No meals* ✥ *E6.*

$$$$ B&B/INN Fodor'sChoice ★ **1906 Lodge at Coronado Beach.** Smaller but no less luxurious than the sprawling beach resorts of Coronado, this lodge—whose name alludes to the main building's former life as a boardinghouse built in 1906—welcomes couples for romantic retreats two blocks from the ocean. **Pros:** most suites feature Jacuzzi tubs, fireplaces, and porches; historic property; free underground parking. **Cons:** too quiet for families; no pool. [$] *Rooms from: $329* ✉ *1060 Adella Ave., Coronado* ☎ *619/437–1900, 866/435–1906* 🌐 *www.1906lodge.com* 🛏 *17 rooms* 🍴 *Breakfast* ✥ *D6.*

NIGHTLIFE

A couple of decades ago, San Diego scraped by on its superb daytime offerings. Those sleepy-after-dark days are over; San Diego now sizzles when the sun goes down. Of particular interest to beer lovers, the city has become internationally acclaimed for dozens of breweries, beer pubs, and festivals.

The Gaslamp Quarter is still one of the most popular areas to go for a night on the town. Named for actual gaslights that once provided illumination along its once-seedy streets (it housed a number of gambling halls and brothels), the neighborhood bears only a trace of its debauched roots. Between the Gaslamp and nearby East Village, Downtown San Diego mostly comprises chic nightclubs, tourist-heavy pubs, and a handful of live music venues. Even most of the hotels Downtown have a street-level or rooftop bar—so plan on making it a late night if that's where you intend to bunk. On weekends, parking can be tricky; most lots run about $20, and though there is metered parking (free after 6 pm and all day Sunday), motorists don't give up those coveted spots so easily. Some restaurants and clubs offer valet, though that can get pricey.

Hillcrest is a popular area for LGBT nightlife and culture, whereas just a little bit east of Hillcrest, ever-expanding North Park features a diverse range of bars and lounges that cater to a twenty- and thirtysomething crowd, bolstering its reputation as the city's hipster capital. Nearby Normal Heights is a slightly less pretentious alternative, though whichever of these neighborhoods strikes your fancy, a cab from Downtown will run about the same price: $15.

Nightlife along the beaches is more of a mixed bag. Where the scene in Pacific Beach might feel like every week is Spring Break, La Jolla veers toward being more cost-prohibitive. And although Point Loma is often seen as a sleeper neighborhood in terms of nightlife, it's coming into its own with some select destinations.

If your drink involves caffeine and not alcohol, there's no shortage of coffeehouses in San Diego, and some of the better ones in Hillcrest and North Park stay open past midnight. Many of them also serve beer and wine, if the caffeine buzz isn't enough.

DOWNTOWN

GASLAMP QUARTER

BARS

Fluxx. Arguably the hottest club in the Gaslamp, this Vegas-style, multitheme space is packed to the gills on weekends with pretty people dancing to house and electro music and dropping major cash at the bar. ■TIP➡ **Get here early for a lower cover and to avoid the epic lines that snake around the block.** ✉ *500 4th Ave., Gaslamp Quarter* ☎ *619/232–8100* ⊕ *www.fluxxsd.com.*

Fodor'sChoice ★ **Rooftop600 @Andaz.** At this rooftop bar and lounge atop the Andaz hotel, a fashionable crowd sips cocktails poolside while gazing at gorgeous views of the city. Thursday through Saturday, the scene heats up with a DJ spinning dance music, while velvet ropes and VIP bottle service please the A-listers (like Prince Harry) in the crowd. ✉ *600 F St., Gaslamp Quarter* ☎ *619/814–2060* ⊕ *sandiego.andaz.hyatt.com.*

MUSIC CLUBS

House of Blues. The local branch of the renowned music chain is decorated floor to ceiling with colorful folk art and features three different areas to hear music. There's something going on here just about every night of the week, and the gospel brunch on select Sundays is one of the most praiseworthy events in town. Can we get a hallelujah? ⊠ *1055 5th Ave., Gaslamp Quarter* ☎ *619/299–2583* ⊕ *www.houseofblues.com.*

EAST VILLAGE

BARS

Cat Eye Club. Separated from the hectic hustle of East Village by just a short and dimly lit foyer, Cat Eye Club might as well be in an entirely different world. More specifically, it's a trip back to the 1960s, with mid-century modern furnishings, a Wurlitzer jukebox and Rat Pack flicks on regular rotation. Their menu of tiki cocktails ranges from simple sips to punch bowls, or for those who prefer their drinks flashier, the Cradle of Life, garnished with a flaming lime wedge. ⊠ *370 7th Ave., East Village* ⊕ *cateyeclubsd.com.*

LITTLE ITALY

BARS

Fodor'sChoice ★ **The Waterfront Bar & Grill.** It isn't really *on* the waterfront, but San Diego's oldest bar was once the hangout of Italian fishermen. Most of the collars are now white, and patrons enjoy an excellent selection of beers, along with chili, burgers, fish-and-chips, and other great-tasting grub, including fish tacos. Get here early, as there's almost always a crowd. ⊠ *2044 Kettner Blvd., Little Italy* ☎ *619/232–9656* ⊕ *www.waterfrontbarandgrill.com.*

OLD TOWN AND UPTOWN

HILLCREST

GAY NIGHTLIFE

Fodor'sChoice ★ **Baja Betty's.** Although it draws plenty of gay customers, the festive and friendly atmosphere is popular with just about everyone in the Hillcrest area (and their pets are welcome, too). The bar staff stocks more than 100 brands of tequila and mixes plenty of fancy cocktails. ⊠ *1421 University Ave., Hillcrest* ☎ *619/269–8510* ⊕ *www.bajabettyssd.com.*

Urban Mo's Bar and Grill. Cowboys gather for line dancing and two-stepping on the wooden dance floor—but be forewarned, yee-hawers, it can get pretty wild on Western nights. There are also Latin, hip-hop, and drag revues but the real allure is in the creative drinks ("Gone Fishing"—served in a fishbowl, for example) and the breezy patio where love (or something like it) is usually in the air. ⊠ *308 University Ave., Hillcrest* ☎ *619/491–0400* ⊕ *www.urbanmos.com.*

MISSION HILLS

BARS

Fodor'sChoice ★ **Starlite.** Bar-goers are dazzled by Starlite's award-winning interior design, which includes rock walls, luxe leather booths, and a massive mirror-mounted chandelier. A hexagonal wood-plank entryway leads to a sunken white bar, where sexy tattooed guys and girls mix creative cocktails, such as the signature Starlite Mule, served in a copper mug. An iPod plays eclectic playlists ranging from old-timey jazz and blues to obscure vintage rock (and DJs are on hand on certain evenings). During warmer months, procuring a spot on the outside wood-decked patio is an art form. ⊠ *3175 India St., Mission Hills* ☎ *619/358–9766* ⊕ *www.starlitesandiego.com.*

San Diego On Tap

The secret is out: San Diego is the nation's best beer town. In addition to more than 60 local breweries, San Diego has a stretch of beer-nerd heaven nicknamed the Belgian Corridor (30th Street in North/South Park). You can find all styles of beer in San Diego, from the meek to the mighty, but many local brewers contend that the specialty is the big, bold Double IPA (also called an Imperial IPA). It's an India Pale Ale with attitude—and lots of hops. Nearly every local brewery has its own version.

Bars with the best microbrew selection: Blind Lady Ale House, Hamilton's Tavern, Live Wire, O'Brien's, Toronado.

Best fests: Want one location and a seemingly endless supply of beer? Try the San Diego Festival of Beers (September ⊕ www.sdbeerfest.org), San Diego Beer Week (November ⊕ www.sdbw.org), and the Strong Ale Fest (December). Find more listings at ⊕ www.sandiegobrewersguild.org.

Best way to sample it all: Sign up for Brewery Tours of San Diego (⊕ www.brewerytoursofsandiego.com) to sample the best craft beers without a second thought about directions or designated drivers.

SAN DIEGO'S BEST BREWERIES

You can also head to the source, where beer is brewed. These are outside the city center, but worth the trek for beer aficionados.

Alpine Brewing Co. Well worth the mountain drive, this family-owned operation may be itty-bitty, but it's also a big champ: brewmaster Pat

McIlhenney, a former fire captain, has won national and international kudos for his hopped-up creations and took the title of the fifth-best brewery in the nation from *Beer Advocate*. Tasters are only a buck each, or fill a growler, which holds a half gallon, for future imbibing. If they're on tap, don't pass up Duet, Pure Hoppiness, or Exponential Hoppiness. Alpine recently opened a pub a few doors down where you can taste flights of their various beers. ⊠ *2363 Alpine Blvd., Alpine* ☎ *619/445–2337* ⊕ *www.alpinebeerco.com.*

Ballast Point Brewing Co. Until recently, you had to head to the Miramar/Scripps Ranch area for a tasting at Ballast Point, but now there's a local taproom in Little Italy (2215 India Street). There are also plenty of opportunities to sample the beers at local pubs—the Sculpin IPA is outstanding, and for more adventurous drinkers, the much hotter Habanero sculpin is brewed with Habanero peppers. ⊠ *10051 Old Grove Rd., Scripps Ranch* ☎ *858/695–2739* ⊕ *www.ballastpoint.com.*

Stone Brewing World Gardens and Bistro. The Big Daddy of San Diego craft brewing was founded by a couple of basement beer tinkerers in 1996; the company now exports its aggressively hoppy beers—instantly identifiable by their leering gargoyle labels—across the nation. Stone's monumental HQ is out of the way, but worth a visit for its tours ($3 includes a souvenir glass), vast on-tap selection (not just Stone beers), and hard-to-beat bistro eats. ⊠ *1999 Citracado Pkwy., Escondido* ☎ *760/294–7899* ⊕ *www.stonebrewing.com.*

NORTH PARK

BARS

Fodor'sChoice ★ **Seven Grand.** This whiskey lounge is a swanky addition to an already thriving North Park nightlife scene and a welcome alternative to the neighboring dives and dance clubs. Live jazz, a tranquil atmosphere, and a bourbon-loving craft cocktail list keep locals flocking. ✉ *3054 University Ave., North Park* ☎ *619/269–8820* ⊕ *213hospitality.com.*

BREWPUBS

Tiger! Tiger! A communal vibe prevails at this wood, metal, and brick gastropub, where patrons sit at picnic tables to schmooze and sip from one of the dozens of carefully selected craft and microbrews on tap. ✉ *3025 El Cajon Blvd., North Park* ☎ *619/487–0401* ⊕ *www.tigertigertavern.com.*

MISSION BAY AND THE BEACHES

PACIFIC BEACH

BARS

JRDN. This contemporary lounge (pronounced "Jordan") occupies the ground floor of Pacific Beach's chicest boutique hotel, Tower23, and offers a more sophisticated vibe in what is a very party-happy neighborhood. Sleek walls of windows and an expansive patio overlook the boardwalk. ✉ *723 Felspar St., Pacific Beach* ☎ *858/270–2323* ⊕ *www.t23hotel.com.*

PERFORMING ARTS

DANCE

California Ballet Company. The company performs high-quality contemporary and classical works September–May at the **Civic Theatre.** The *Nutcracker* is staged annually around the holiday season. ✉ *San Diego Civic Theatre, 1100 3rd Ave., Downtown* ☎ *619/560–5676* ⊕ *www.californiaballet.org.*

MUSIC

Fodor'sChoice ★ **Copley Symphony Hall.** The great acoustics here are surpassed only by the incredible Spanish baroque interior. Not just the home of the San Diego Symphony Orchestra, the renovated 2,200-seat 1920s-era theater has also hosted major stars like Elvis Costello, Leonard Cohen, and Sting. ✉ *750 B St., Downtown* ☎ *619/235–0804* ⊕ *www.sandiegosymphony.org.*

San Diego Symphony Orchestra. The orchestra's events include classical concerts and summer and winter pops, nearly all of them at Copley Symphony Hall. The outdoor Summer Pops series is held on the Embarcadero, on North Harbor Drive beyond the convention center. ✉ *Box office, 750 B St., Downtown* ☎ *619/235–0804* ⊕ *www.sandiegosymphony.org.*

THEATER

Fodor'sChoice **La Jolla Playhouse.** Under the artistic direction of Christopher Ashley, the
★ playhouse presents exciting and innovative plays and musicals on three
stages. Many Broadway shows—among them *Memphis, Tommy,* and
Jersey Boys—have previewed here before their East Coast premieres.
Its Without Walls program also ensures that the productions aren't
limited to the playhouse, having put on site-specific shows in places like
outdoor art spaces, cars, and even the ocean. ⊠ *University of California
at San Diego, 2910 La Jolla Village Dr., La Jolla* ☎ *858/550–1010*
⊕ *www.lajollaplayhouse.org.*

Fodor'sChoice **The Old Globe.** This complex, comprising the Sheryl and Harvey White
★ Theatre, the Lowell Davies Festival Theatre, and the Old Globe Theatre,
offers some of the finest theatrical productions in Southern California.
Theater classics such as *The Full Monty* and *Dirty Rotten Scoundrels,*
both of which went on to Broadway, premiered on these famed stages.
The Old Globe presents the family-friendly *How the Grinch Stole
Christmas* around the holidays, as well as a renowned summer Shake-
speare Festival with three to four plays in repertory. ⊠ *1363 Old Globe
Way, Balboa Park* ☎ *619/234–5623* ⊕ *www.oldglobe.org.*

SPORTS AND THE OUTDOORS

BASEBALL

Long a favorite spectator sport in San Diego, where games are rarely
rained out, baseball gained even more popularity in 2004 with the
opening of PETCO Park, a stunning 42,000-seat facility in the heart
of Downtown.

Fodor'sChoice **San Diego Padres.** From April into October, the Padres slug it out for
★ bragging rights in the National League West. Home games are played
at PETCO Park. Tickets are usually available on game day, but rival
matchups against the Los Angeles Dodgers and the San Francisco Giants
often sell out quickly. For an inexpensive day at the ballpark, go for
"The Park at the Park" tickets ($10 and up, depending on demand;
available for purchase at the park only) and have a picnic on the grass
while watching the game on one of several giant-screen TVs. You also
get access to the full concourse. Head to the fifth floor to find a Stone
Brewing outdoor beer garden with sweeping views of Downtown and
the San Diego Bay. ⊠ *100 Park Blvd., East Village* ☎ *619/795–5000,
877/374–2784* ⊕ *sandiego.padres.mlb.com* 🎫 *From $10.*

BIKING

San Diego offers bountiful opportunities for bikers, from casual boardwalk cruises to strenuous rides into the hills. The mild climate makes
biking in San Diego a year-round delight. Bike culture is respected here,
and visitors are often impressed with the miles of designated bike lanes
running alongside city streets and coastal roads throughout the county.

Cheap Rentals. One block from the boardwalk, this place has good daily and weekly prices for surfboards, paddleboards, kayaks, snorkel gear, skateboards, ice chests, umbrellas, chairs, and bike rentals, including beach cruisers, tandems, hybrids, and two-wheeled baby carriers. Kids bikes are also available. Demand is high during the busy season (May through September), so call to reserve equipment ahead of time. ⊠ *3689 Mission Blvd., Mission Beach* ☎ *858/488–9070, 800/941–7761* ⊕ *www.cheap-rentals.com* ✉ *From $12.*

Holland's Bicycles. This is a great bike rental source on Coronado Island, so you can ride the Silver Strand Bike Path on an electric bike, beach cruiser, road bike, or tandem. ⊠ *977 Orange Ave., Coronado* ☎ *619/435–3153* ⊕ *www.hollandsbicycles.com* ✉ *From $25.*

Route S21 (*Coast Highway 101*). On many summer days, Route S21, aka Old Highway 101, from La Jolla to Oceanside looks like a freeway for cyclists. About 24 miles long, it's easily the most popular and scenic bike route around, never straying far from the beach. Although the terrain is fairly easy, the long, steep Torrey Pines grade is famous for weeding out the weak. Another Darwinian challenge is dodging slow-moving pedestrians and cars pulling over to park in towns like Encinitas and Del Mar. ⊠ *La Jolla.*

DIVING

Ocean Enterprises Scuba Diving. Stop in for everything you need to plan a diving adventure, including equipment, advice, and instruction. ⊠ *7710 Balboa Ave., Suite 101, Clairemont* ☎ *858/565–6054* ⊕ *www.ocean-enterprises.com.*

Scuba San Diego. This center is well regarded for its top-notch instruction and certification programs, as well as for guided dive tours. Trips include dives to kelp reefs in La Jolla Cove, and night diving at La Jolla Canyon. They also have snorkeling tours to La Jolla's Sea Caves, plus evening kayaking tours under the firework-lit sky on Mission Bay (in summer only). ⊠ *San Diego Hilton Hotel, 1775 E. Mission Bay Dr., Mission Bay* ☎ *619/260–1880* ⊕ *www.scubasandiego.com* ✉ *From $70.*

FISHING

Fisherman's Landing. You can book space on a fleet of luxury vessels from 57 feet to 124 feet long and embark on multiday trips in search of yellowfin tuna, yellowtail, and other deep-water fish. Half-day fishing and whale-watching trips are also available. ⊠ *2838 Garrison St., Point Loma* ☎ *619/221–8500* ⊕ *www.fishermanslanding.com* ✉ *From $45.*

H&M Landing. Join one of the West's oldest sportfishing companies for year-round fishing trips plus whale-watching excursions from December through March. ⊠ *2803 Emerson St., Point Loma* ☎ *619/222–1144* ⊕ *www.hmlanding.com* ✉ *From $24.*

GOLF

Balboa Park Golf Course. San Diego's oldest public course is 5 minutes from Downtown in the heart of Balboa Park and offers impressive views of the city and the bay. The course includes a 9-hole executive course and a challenging 18-hole course that weaves among the park's canyons with some tricky drop-offs. Finish off your round with biscuits and gravy and a mimosa at Tobey's 19th Hole Cafe, a greasy spoon that's also Balboa Park's best-kept secret. ⊠ *2600 Golf Course Dr., Balboa Park* ☎ *619/235–1184* ⊕ *www.sandiego.gov* ⊠ *$40 weekdays, $50 weekends* ⚑ *27 holes, 6339 yards, par 72.*

Fodor's Choice ★ **Coronado Municipal Golf Course.** Spectacular views of Downtown San Diego and the Coronado Bridge as well as affordable prices make this public course one of the busiest in the world. Bordered by the bay, the trick is to keep your ball out of the water. Wind can add some difficulty, but otherwise this is a leisurely course and a good one to walk. It's difficult to get on unless you reserve a tee time 3 to 14 days in advance. The course's Bayside Grill restaurant is well-known for its Thursday and Sunday night prime rib dinner. Reservations are recommended. ⊠ *2000 Visalia Row, Coronado* ☎ *619/522–6590* ⊕ *www.golfcoronado.com* ⊠ *$37 weekdays, $42 weekends* ⚑ *18 holes, 6590 yards, par 72.*

Omni La Costa Resort and Spa. One of the premier golf resorts in Southern California, La Costa over the years has hosted many of the best professional golfers in the world as well as prominent politicians and Hollywood celebrities. The Dick Wilson–designed Champions course has Bermuda fairways and bunkers. The more spacious Legends Course received a complete makeover in 2013 including a redesign of all 18 greens, as well as new bunkers and turfgrass plantings. After a day on the links you can wind down with a massage, steam bath, and dinner at the resort. ⊠ *2100 Costa del Mar Rd., Carlsbad* ☎ *760/438–9111* ⊕ *www.omnihotels.com* ⊠ *$210 Mon.–Thurs., $230 Fri.–Sun.* ⚑ *Champions: 18 holes, 6747 yards, par 72. Legends: 18 holes, 6587 yards, par 72.*

Fodor's Choice ★ **Park Hyatt Aviara Golf Club.** This golf course consistently ranks as one of the best in California and is the only course in San Diego designed by Arnold Palmer. The course features gently rolling hills dotted with native wildflowers and views of the protected adjacent Batiquitos Lagoon and the Pacific Ocean. There are plenty of bunkers and water features for those looking for a challenge, and the golf carts, included in the cost, come fitted with GPS systems that tell you the distance to the pin. The two-story Spanish colonial clubhouse has full-size lockers, lounge areas, a bar, and a steak house. ⊠ *7447 Batiquitos Dr., Carlsbad* ☎ *760/603–6900* ⊕ *www.golfaviara.com* ⊠ *$235 Mon.–Thurs., $255 Fri.–Sun.* ⚑ *18 holes, 7007 yards, par 72.*

Fodor's Choice ★ **Torrey Pines Golf Course.** Due to its clifftop location overlooking the Pacific and its classic championship holes, Torrey Pines is one of the best public golf courses in the United States. The course was the site of the 2008 U.S. Open and has been the home of the Farmers Insurance Open since 1968. The par-72 South Course, redesigned by Rees Jones in 2001, receives rave reviews from touring pros; it is longer, more challenging, and more expensive than the North Course. Tee times may be booked from 8 to 90 days in advance (858/522–1662) and are subject to an advance booking fee ($45). ✉ *11480 N. Torrey Pines Rd., La Jolla* ☎ *858/452–3226, 800/985–4653* ⊕ *www.torreypinesgolfcourse. com* ✉ *South: $192 weekdays, $240 weekends. North: $105 weekdays, $131 weekends; $40 for golf cart* ⚡ *South: 18 holes, 7227 yards, par 72. North: 18 holes, 6874 yards, par 72.*

HIKING AND NATURE TRAILS

Fodor'sChoice **Bayside Trail at Cabrillo National Monument.** Driving here is a treat in itself, as
★ a vast view of the Pacific unfolds before you. The view is equally enjoyable on Bayside Trail (2 miles round-trip), which is home to the same coastal sagebrush that Juan Rodriguez Cabrillo saw when he first discovered the California coast in the 16th century. After the hike, you can explore nearby tide pools, the monument statue, and the Old Point Loma Lighthouse. Don't worry if you don't see everything on your first visit; your entrance receipt ($10 per car) is good for 7 days. ✉ *1800 Cabrillo Memorial Dr., Point Loma* ⊕ *From I–5, take Rosecrans exit and turn right on Canon St. then left on Catalina Blvd. (also known as Cabrillo Memorial Dr.); follow until end* ☎ *619/557–5450* ⊕ *www.nps.gov/cabr* ✉ *Parking $10.*

Torrey Pines State Reserve. Hikers and runners will appreciate this park's many winning features: switch-back trails that descend to the sea, an unparalleled view of the Pacific, and a chance to see the Torrey pine tree, one of the rarest pine breeds in the United States. The reserve hosts guided nature walks as well. All food is prohibited at the reserve, so save the picnic until you reach the beach below. Parking is $12–$15, depending on day and season. ✉ *12600 N. Torrey Pines Rd., La Jolla* ⊕ *Exit I–5 at Carmel Valley Rd. and head west toward Coast Hwy. 101 until you reach N. Torrey Pines Rd.; turn left.* ☎ *858/755–2063* ⊕ *www.torreypines.org* ✉ *Parking $12–$15.*

KAYAKING, SAILING, AND BOATING

Hike Bike Kayak Adventures. This shop offers several kayak tours, from easy excursions in Mission Bay that are well suited to families and beginners to more advanced jaunts. Tours include kayaking the caves off La Jolla coast, whale-watching (from a safe distance) December through March, moonlight and sunset trips, and a cruise into the bay to see SeaWorld's impressive fireworks shows over the water in the summer. Tours last two to three hours and require a minimum of four people. ✉ *2222 Ave. de la Playa, La Jolla* ☎ *858/551–9510* ⊕ *www. hikebikekayak.com* ✉ *From $65.*

SURFING

If you're a beginner, consider paddling in the waves off Mission Beach, Pacific Beach, Tourmaline Surfing Park, La Jolla Shores, Del Mar, or Oceanside. More experienced surfers usually head for Sunset Cliffs, La Jolla reef breaks, Black's Beach, or Swami's in Encinitas. All necessary equipment is included in the cost of all surfing schools. Beach-area Y's offer surf lessons and surf camp in the summer months and during spring break.

Cheap Rentals. Many local surf shops rent both surf and bodyboards. Cheap Rentals is right off the boardwalk, just steps from the waves. It rents wet suits, bodyboards, and skimboards in addition to soft surfboards and long and short fiberglass rides. It also has good hourly to weekly pricing on paddleboards and accessories. ⊠ *3689 Mission Blvd., Mission Beach* ☎ *858/488–9070, 800/941–7761* ⊕ *www.cheap-rentals. com* ⊠ *From $5/hour.*

SHOPPING

San Diego's retail landscape has changed radically in recent years with the opening of several new shopping centers—some in historic buildings—that are focused more on locally owned boutiques than national retailers. Where once the Gaslamp was the place to go for urban apparel and unique home decor, many independently owned boutiques have decided to set up shop in the charming neighborhoods east of Balboa Park known as North Park and South Park. Although Downtown is still thriving, any shopping trip to San Diego should include venturing out to the city's diverse and vibrant neighborhoods. Not far from Downtown, Little Italy is the place to find contemporary art, modern furniture, and home accessories.

Old Town is a must for pottery, ceramics, jewelry, and handcrafted baskets. Uptown is known for its mélange of funky bookstores, offbeat gift shops, and nostalgic collectibles and vintage stores. The beach towns offer the best swimwear and sandals. La Jolla's chic boutiques offer a more intimate shopping experience, along with some of the classiest clothes, jewelry, and shoes in the county. The new La Plaza La Jolla is an open-air shopping center with boutiques and galleries in a Spanish-style building overlooking the cove. Point Loma's Liberty Station shopping area in the former Naval Training Center has art galleries, restaurants, and home stores. Trendsetters will have no trouble finding must-have handbags and designer apparel at the world-class Fashion Valley mall in Mission Valley, a haven for luxury brands such as Hermès, Gucci, and Jimmy Choo.

Enjoy near-perfect weather year-round as you explore shops along the scenic waterfront. The Headquarters at Seaport is a new open-air shopping and dining center in the city's former Police Headquarters building. Here there are some big names, but mostly locally owned boutiques selling everything from gourmet cheese to coastal-inspired home accessories. Just next door, Seaport Village is still the place to go for trinkets and souvenirs. If you don't discover what you're looking for in the boutiques, head to Westfield Horton Plaza, the Downtown mall with more than 120 stores. The sprawling mall completed a major restoration project in 2016 to include a new public plaza, amphitheater, and fountains.

Most malls have free parking in a lot or garage, and parking is not usually a problem. Some of the shops in the Gaslamp Quarter offer validated parking or valet parking.

OLD TOWN AND UPTOWN

OLD TOWN

MARKET

Fodor's Choice ★ **Bazaar del Mundo Shops.** With a Mexican villa theme, the Bazaar hosts riotously colorful gift shops such as **Ariana,** for ethnic and artsy women's fashions; **Artes de Mexico,** which sells handmade Latin American crafts and Guatemalan weavings; and **The Gallery,** which carries handmade jewelry, Native American crafts, collectible glass, and original silk-screen prints. The **Laurel Burch Gallerita** carries the complete collection of its namesake artist's signature jewelry, accessories, and totes. ⊠ *4133 Taylor St., at Juan St., Old Town* ☎ *619/296–3161* ⊕ *www. bazaardelmundo.com.*

MISSION VALLEY

MALL

Fodor's Choice ★ **Fashion Valley.** More than 18 million shoppers visit Fashion Valley each year. That's more than the combined attendance of SeaWorld San Diego, LEGOLAND California, the San Diego Padres, the San Diego Chargers, and the San Diego Zoo. San Diego's best and most upscale mall has a contemporary Mission theme, lush landscaping, and more than 200 shops and restaurants. Acclaimed retailers like Nordstrom, Neiman Marcus, Bloomingdale's, and Tiffany & Co. are here, along with boutiques from fashion darlings like Michael Kors, Jimmy Choo, Tory Burch, and James Perse. H&M is a favorite of fashionistas in search of edgy and affordable styles. Free wireless Internet service is available throughout the mall. Select "Simon WiFi" from any Wi-Fi–enabled device to log onto the network. ■**TIP→ If you're visiting from out of state, are a member of the military, or have a AAA membership, you can pick up a complimentary Style Pass at Simon Guest Services (located on the lower level beneath AMC Theaters near Banana Republic), which can get you savings at more than 70 of Fashion Valley's stores and restaurants.** ⊠ *7007 Friars Rd., Mission Valley* ☎ *619/688–9113* ⊕ *www. simon.com/mall/fashion-valley.*

NORTH PARK

CLOTHING AND ACCESSORIES

Fodor's Choice ★ **Aloha Sunday Supply Co.** This carefully curated boutique with high ceilings and blonde-wood accents carries no Billabong or Quiksilver, but make no mistake, this is a surf shop. The store sells only handcrafted pieces like Matuse wet suits, Thorogood leather boots, and the store's own brand of tailored men's clothing designed by co-owner and former pro surfer Kahana Kalama. ⊠ *3039 University Ave., North Park* ☎ *619/269–9838* ⊕ *www.alohasunday.com.*

CORONADO

SHOPPING CENTER

Fodor's Choice ★ **Hotel Del Coronado.** At the gift shops within the peninsula's main historic attraction, you can purchase sportswear, designer handbags, jewelry, and antiques. **Babcock & Story Emporium** carries an amazing selection of home decor items, garden accessories, and classy gifts. **Blue Octopus** is a children's store featuring creative toys, gifts, and apparel. **Spreckels Sweets & Treats** offers old-time candies, freshly made fudge, and decadent truffles. **Kate's** has designer fashions and accessories, while **Brady's for Men,** with its shirts and sport coats, caters to well-dressed men. **Crown Jewels Coronado** features fine jewelry, some inspired by the sea. ✉ *1500 Orange Ave., Coronado* ☎ *619/435–6611* 🌐 *www.hoteldel.com/coronado-shopping.*

3

SIDE TRIPS TO NORTH COUNTY

A whole world of scenic grandeur, fascinating history, and scientific wonder lies just beyond San Diego's city limits. If you travel north along the coast, you'll encounter the great beaches for which the region is famous, along with some sophisticated towns holding fine restaurants, great galleries, and museums.

DEL MAR

23 miles north of Downtown San Diego on I–5, 9 miles north of La Jolla on Rte. S21.

Del Mar is best known for its quaint old section west of Interstate 5 marked with a glamorous racetrack, half-timber buildings, chic shops, tony restaurants, celebrity visitors, and wide beaches.

EXPLORING

FAMILY **Del Mar Fairgrounds.** The Spanish Mission–style fairground is the home of the **Del Mar Thoroughbred Club** (*www.dmtc.com*). Crooner Bing Crosby and his Hollywood buddies—Pat O'Brien, Gary Cooper, and Oliver Hardy, among others—organized the club in the 1930s, and the racing here (usually July through September, Wednesday through Monday, posttime 2 pm) remains a fashionable affair. Del Mar Fairgrounds hosts more than 100 different events each year, including the San Diego County Fair, the Del Mar National Horse Show in April and May, and the fall Scream Zone that's popular with local families. ✉ *2260 Jimmy Durante Blvd.* ☎ *858/755–1161* 🌐 *www.delmarfairgrounds.com.*

WHERE TO EAT

$$$$ FRENCH Fodor's Choice ★ 🍴 **Addison.** Indulge in the finer things in life at this AAA 5-Diamond restaurant by acclaimed chef William Bradley who serves up haute French flavors in his 4- and 10-course prix-fixe dinners. Beyond the swanky bar and wine cave is a sophisticated Tuscan-style dining room with intricately carved dark-woods, marble pillars, and arched windows draped in red velvet. **Known for:** decadent tasting menus; the ultimate fine-dining experience; impeccable service. [$] *Average main: $110* ✉ *5200 Grand Del Mar Way* ☎ *858/314–1900* 🌐 *www.addisondelmar.com* 🕘 *Closed Sun. and Mon. No lunch.*

$$$ AMERICAN Fodor's Choice ★ 🍴 **Market Restaurant + Bar.** Carl Schroeder, one of California's hottest young chefs, draws well-heeled foodies to his creative and locally sourced California fare, much of it with an Asian influence from his time in Japan. The menu changes regularly depending upon what's fresh, but might include carrot-ginger soup or crispy duck confit with

candied kumquats. **Known for:** succulent short ribs; award-winning chef; seasonal menu. $ *Average main: $30* ⊠ *3702 Via de la Valle* ☎ *858/523–0007* ⊕ *www.marketdelmar.com* ⊗ *No lunch.*

WHERE TO STAY

$$$$
RESORT
FAMILY
Fodor'sChoice
★

Fairmont Grand Del Mar. Mind-blowing indulgence in serene surroundings, from drop-dead gorgeous guest accommodations to myriad outdoor adventures, sets the opulent Mediterranean-style Fairmont Grand Del Mar apart from any other luxury hotel in San Diego. **Pros:** ultimate luxury; secluded, on-site golf course; enormous rooms; has most acclaimed fine-dining restaurant in San Diego. **Cons:** floor plan may be confusing; hotel is not on the beach. $ *Rooms from: $415* ⊠ *5200 Grand Del Mar Ct., San Diego* ☎ *858/314–2000, 855/314–2030* ⊕ *www.fairmont.com/san-diego* ⅄ *Greens fees $250; 18 holes, 7160 yards, par 72* ⇆ *249 rooms* ⊙| *No meals.*

CARLSBAD

6 miles north of Encinitas on Rte. S21, 36 miles north of Downtown San Diego on I–5.

Once-sleepy Carlsbad long been popular with beachgoers and sun seekers. On a clear day in this village, you can take in sweeping ocean views that stretch from La Jolla to Oceanside by walking the 2-mile-long sea walk running between the Encina power plant and Pine Street. En route, you'll find several stairways leading to the beach and quite a few benches. Inland are LEGOLAND California and other attractions in its vicinity.

EXPLORING

FAMILY
Fodor'sChoice
★

Flower Fields at Carlsbad Ranch. The largest bulb production farm in Southern California has hillsides abloom here each spring, when thousands of Giant Tecolote ranunculus produce a stunning 50-acre display of color against the backdrop of the blue Pacific Ocean. Other knockouts include the rose gardens—with examples of every All-American Rose Selection award-winner since 1940—and a historical display of Paul Ecke poinsettias. Open to the public during this time, the farm offers family activities that include wagon rides, panning for gold, and a kids' playground. ⊠ *5704 Paseo del Norte, east of I–5* ☎ *760/431–0352* ⊕ *www.theflowerfields.com* ⊠ *$14* ⊗ *Closed mid-May–Feb.*

FAMILY
Fodor'sChoice
★

LEGOLAND California Resort. The centerpiece of a development that includes resort hotels, a designer discount shopping mall, an aquarium, and a water park, LEGOLAND has rides and diversions geared to kids ages 2 to 12. Fans of *Star Wars*, and building Legos in general, should head straight to *Star Wars* **Miniland**, where you can follow the exploits of Yoda, Princess Leia, Obi-Wan, Anakin, R2, Luke, and the denizens of the *Star Wars* films. There's also **Miniland U.S.A.**, which features a miniature, animated, interactive collection of U.S. icons that were constructed out of 34 million LEGO bricks! **LEGO Heartlake City,** features LEGO Friends and Elves, and you can test your ninja skills in **LEGO NINJAGO WORLD.**

A LEGOLAND model worker puts the finishing touches on the San Francisco portion of Miniland U.S.A.

If you're looking for rides, **NINJAGO The Ride** uses hand gesture technology to throw fireballs, shock waves, ice, and lightning to defeat villains in this interactive 4-D experience. Journey through ancient Egyptian ruins in a desert roadster, scoring points as you hit targets with a laser blaster at **Lost Kingdom Adventure.** Or, jump on the **Dragon Coaster,** an indoor/outdoor steel roller coaster that goes through a castle. Don't let the name frighten you—the motif is more humorous than scary. Kids ages 6 to 13 can stop by the **Driving School** to drive speed-controlled cars (not on rails) on a miniature road; driver's licenses are awarded after the course. Junior Driving School is the pint-size version for kids 3 to 5.

Bring bathing suits—there are lockers at the entrance and at Pirate Shores—if you plan to go to **Soak-N-Sail,** which has 60 interactive features, including a pirate shipwreck–theme area. You'll also need your swimsuit for **LEGOLAND Water Park,** where an additional $30 gives you access to slides, rides, rafts, and the CHIMA Water Park, as well as Surfer's Bay with competitive water raceways and a "spray ground" with water jets.

Be sure to try Granny's Apple Fries, Castle Burgers, and Pizza Mania for pizzas and salads. The Market near the entrance has excellent coffee, fresh fruit, and yogurt. The LEGOLAND Hotel is worth a visit even if you're not staying overnight. There are activities and a LEGO pit in the lobby that will entertain kids while parents recover with a cocktail. ■TIP→ The best value is one of the Hopper Tickets that give you one admission to LEGOLAND plus Sea Life Aquarium and/or the LEGOLAND Water Park for $119. These can be used on the same day or on different days. Purchase tickets online for discounted pricing. Go midweek to avoid the crowds. ⊠ *1 Legoland Dr.* ⊕ *Exit I–5 at Cannon Rd. and follow signs east ¼ mile* ☎ *760/918–5346* ⊕ *www.legoland.com/california* 🎫 *LEGOLAND $95 adults, $89 children; parking $15; water park additional $30; hopper ticket $119* ⊗ *Closed Tues. and Wed. Sept.–Feb.*

WHERE TO EAT

$$
BARBECUE
Fodor's Choice
★

✕ **Campfire.** Paying tribute to community around the campfire, it's all about connecting here, both with the cool crowd and with the distinctive cocktail and dinner menus. Throughout the restaurant, subtle hints of the camping theme—canvas-backed booths, servers in flannels, leather menus branded with the Campfire log—are visible, but it's the food that will leave you setting up camp, as chefs work their magic behind glass walls grilling, roasting, and smoking almost every dish including the shrimp with pumpkin chili butter. **Known for:** smoky cocktails; wood-fired American fare. $ *Average main: $23* ⊠ *2725 State St.* ☎ *760/637–5121* ⊕ *www.thisiscampfire.com* ⊗ *No lunch Mon.*

WHERE TO STAY

$$$$
RESORT
FAMILY

🏨 **Omni La Costa Resort & Spa.** This chic Spanish colonial oasis on 400 tree-shaded acres has ample guest rooms, two golf courses, and is known for being family-friendly, with plenty of kids' activities (including a kids' club, a game room, eight swimming pools, three waterslides, and a water play zone). **Pros:** adult-only pool; excellent kids' facilities; spa under the stars. **Cons:** very spread out, making long walks necessary; lots of kids; $30 daily resort fee. $ *Rooms from: $349* ⊠ *2100 Costa del Mar Rd.* ☎ *760/438–9111, 800/439–9111* ⊕ *www.lacosta.com* ⇄ *748 rooms* ⊗ *No meals.*

$$$$
RESORT
FAMILY
Fodor's Choice
★

🏨 **Park Hyatt Aviara Resort.** This former Four Seasons hilltop retreat is one of the most luxurious hotels in San Diego, boasting an Arnold Palmer–designed golf course, a tennis club, two pools, six restaurants, and views overlooking Batiquitos Lagoon and the Pacific among it's 250 acres. **Pros:** unbeatable location; best golf course in San Diego; surrounding nature trails. **Cons:** $25 resort fee and $35 parking; expensive; breakfast not included. $ *Rooms from: $309* ⊠ *7100 Aviara Resort Dr.* ☎ *800/233–1234, 760/448–1234* ⊕ *www.parkhyattaviara.com* ⊗ *Greens fees $255; 18 holes, 7007 yards, par 72* ⇄ *327 rooms* ⊗ *No meals.*

ESCONDIDO

8 miles north of Rancho Bernardo on I–15, 31 miles northeast of Downtown San Diego on I–15.

Escondido and the lovely rolling hills around it were originally a land grant bestowed by the governor of Mexico on Juan Bautista Alvarado in 1843. For a century and a half, these hills supported citrus and avocado trees, plus large vineyards. The rural character of the area began to change when the San Diego Zoo established its Safari Park in the San Pasqual Valley east of town in the 1970s. Despite its urbanization, Escondido still supports several pristine open-space preserves that attract nature lovers, hikers, and mountain bikers. And, the area's abundant farms are slowly luring award-winning chefs who are taking the lead on opening farm-to-fork establishments.

DID YOU KNOW?

"Ranunculus flowers explode into color every spring at the Flower Fields in Carlsbad. While taking a detour from the freeway, I caught these two sisters admiring the view." —photo by mlgb, Fodors.com member

EXPLORING

FAMILY

Fodor's Choice

★

San Diego Zoo Safari Park. A branch of the San Diego Zoo, 35 miles to the north, the 1,800-acre preserve in the San Pasqual Valley is designed to protect endangered species from around the world. Exhibit areas have been carved out of the dry, dusty canyons and mesas to represent the animals' natural habitats in various parts of Africa and Asia.

The best way to see these preserves is to take the 25-minute, 2½-mile Africa tram safari, included with admission. More than 3,500 animals of more than 400 species roam or fly above the expansive grounds. Predators are separated from prey by deep moats, but only the elephants, tigers, lions, and cheetahs are kept in enclosures. Good viewpoints are at the Elephant Viewing Patio, African Plains Outlook, and Kilmia Point. The park's newest project is the **Tull Family Tiger Trail**, a Sumatran tiger habitat opened in 2014, where you can get face-to-face (with a glass between) with the gorgeous cats. The 5-acre exhibit features a waterfall and swimming hole, and addresses poaching and other environmental threats to the species. ■ **TIP➜ In summer, when the park stays open late, the trip is especially enjoyable in the early evening, when the heat has subsided and the animals are active and feeding. When the tram travels through the park after dark, sodium-vapor lamps illuminate the active animals. Photographers with zoom lenses can get spectacular shots of zebras, gazelles, and rhinos.**

For a more focused view of the park, you can take one of several other safaris that are well worth the additional charge. You can choose from several behind-the-scenes safaris, fly above it all via the zip-line safari, or get up close to giraffes and rhinos on a Caravan safari.

The park is as much a botanical garden as a zoo, serving as a "rescue center" for rare and endangered plants. Unique gardens include cacti and succulents from Baja California, a bonsai collection, a fuchsia display, native plants, and protea.

The gift shops are well worth a visit for their limited-edition items. There are lots of restaurants, snack bars, and some picnic areas. Rental lockers, strollers, and wheelchairs are available. You can also arrange to stay overnight in the park in summer on a Roar and Snore Sleepover ($140 and up, plus admission).

✉ *15500 San Pasqual Valley Rd.* ✛ *Take I–15 north to Via Rancho Pkwy. and follow signs for 6 miles* ☎ *760/747–8702* ⊕ *www.sdzsafaripark.org* 🎫 *$52 one-day pass including Africa tram ride; multipark and multiday passes are available; special safaris are extra starting at $50 per person; parking $12.*

4

ORANGE COUNTY AND CATALINA ISLAND

with Disneyland and Knott's Berry Farm

WELCOME TO ORANGE COUNTY AND CATALINA ISLAND

TOP REASONS TO GO

★ **Disney Magic:** Walking down Main Street, U.S.A., with Cinderella's Castle straight ahead, you really will feel that you're in one of the happiest places on Earth.

★ **Beautiful Beaches:** Surf, swim, paddleboard, or just relax on one of the state's most breathtaking stretches of coastline. Keep in mind, the water may be colder than you expect.

★ **Island Getaways:** Just a short high-speed catamaran ride away, Catalina Island feels 1,000 miles from the mainland. Wander around charming Avalon, or explore the unspoiled beauty of the island's wild interior.

★ **The Fine Life:** Some of the state's wealthiest communities are in coastal Orange County, so spend at least part of your stay here experiencing how the other half lives.

★ **Family Fun:** Spend some quality time with the kids riding roller coasters, eating ice cream, fishing off ocean piers, and bodysurfing.

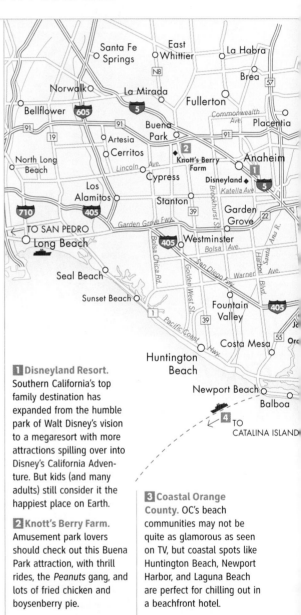

1 **Disneyland Resort.** Southern California's top family destination has expanded from the humble park of Walt Disney's vision to a megaresort with more attractions spilling over into Disney's California Adventure. But kids (and many adults) still consider it the happiest place on Earth.

2 **Knott's Berry Farm.** Amusement park lovers should check out this Buena Park attraction, with thrill rides, the *Peanuts* gang, and lots of fried chicken and boysenberry pie.

3 **Coastal Orange County.** OC's beach communities may not be quite as glamorous as seen on TV, but coastal spots like Huntington Beach, Newport Harbor, and Laguna Beach are perfect for chilling out in a beachfront hotel.

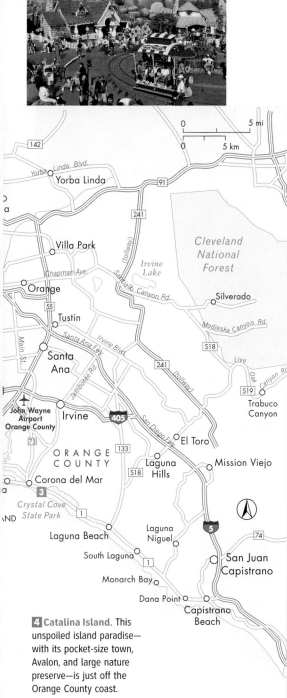

GETTING ORIENTED

Like Los Angeles, Orange County stretches over a large area, lacks a singular focal point, and has limited public transportation. You'll need a car and a sensible game plan to make the most of your visit. Anaheim, home of Disneyland, has every style of hotel imaginable, from family-friendly motels to luxurious high-rises. The coastal cities are more expensive but have cooler weather in summer, and marvelous beaches that you can enjoy throughout the year.

4

0   5 mi
0   5 km

142

Yorba Linda Blvd.
Yorba Linda   91

241

Villa Park

Irvine
Lake

Cleveland
National
Forest

Chapman Ave.

Orange
55

Tustin

Santa Fe

Santa
Ana

John Wayne
Airport
Orange County   Irvine   405

73

ORANGE
COUNTY   133

Corona del Mar

Crystal Cove
State Park   1

Laguna Beach

South Laguna   1

Monarch Bay

Dana Point

Silverado

Modjeska Canyon Rd.

S18

Live   Oak   Canyon Rd

S19

Trabuco
Canyon

El Toro

Laguna
Hills   S18

Laguna
Niguel

Mission Viejo

5

74

San Juan
Capistrano

Capistrano
Beach

4 **Catalina Island.** This unspoiled island paradise—with its pocket-size town, Avalon, and large nature preserve—is just off the Orange County coast.

Updated
by Kathy A.
McDonald

With its tropical flowers and palm trees, the stretch of coast between Seal Beach and San Clemente is often called the California Riviera. Exclusive Newport Beach and artsy Laguna are the stars. Offshore, meanwhile, lies gorgeous Catalina Island, a terrific spot for diving, snorkeling, and hiking.

Few of the citrus groves that gave Orange County its name remain. This region south and east of Los Angeles is now ruled by tourism and high-tech business rather than agriculture. Despite a building boom that began in the 1990s, the area is still a place to find wilderness trails, canyons, greenbelts, and natural environs. Just offshore is a deep-water wilderness that's possible to explore via daily whale-watching excursions.

PLANNING

GETTING HERE AND AROUND

AIR TRAVEL

Orange County's main facility is John Wayne Airport Orange County (SNA), which is served by eight major domestic airlines and a commuter line. Long Beach Airport (LGB) is served by three airlines, including its major player, JetBlue. It's roughly 20 to 30 minutes by car from Anaheim.

Super Shuttle and Prime Time Airport Shuttle provide transportation from John Wayne and LAX to the Disneyland area of Anaheim. Round-trip fares average about $25 per person from John Wayne and $16 to $42 from LAX.

BUS TRAVEL

The Orange County Transportation Authority will take you virtually anywhere in the county, but it will take time; OCTA buses go from Knott's Berry Farm and Disneyland to Huntington Beach and Newport Beach. Bus 1 travels along the coast; buses 701 and 721 provide express service to Los Angeles.

Bus Contacts Orange County Transportation Authority. ☎ 714/636-7433 ⊕ www.octa.net.

CAR TRAVEL

The San Diego Freeway (Interstate 405), the coastal route, and the Santa Ana Freeway (Interstate 5), the inland route, run north–south through Orange County. South of Laguna, Interstate 405 merges into Interstate 5 (called the San Diego Freeway south from this point). A toll road, Highway 73, runs 15 miles from Newport Beach to San Juan Capistrano; it costs $6.65–$7.35 (lower rates are for weekends and off-peak hours) and is usually less jammed than the regular freeways. Keep in mind, however, there are no toll booths on OC toll roads; payment is required via a FastTrak transponder (available at AAA, Costco, and Albertson's). Some car-rental companies (like Avis) provide them for a daily service fee; Hertz does not. You can always pay the toll fee online (⊕ *thetollroads.com*). Do your best to avoid all Orange County freeways during rush hours (6–9 am and 3:30–6:30 pm). Highway 55 leads to Newport Beach. The Pacific Coast Highway (Highway 1) allows easy access to beach communities, and is the most scenic route, but expect it to be crowded, especially on summer weekends and holidays.

FERRY TRAVEL

There are two ferries that service Catalina Island; Catalina Express runs from Long Beach (about 90 minutes) and from Newport Beach (about 75 minutes). Reservations are strongly advised for summers and weekends. During the winter months, ferry crossings are not as frequent as in the summer high season.

TRAIN TRAVEL

Amtrak makes daily stops in Orange County at all major towns. Metro-link is a weekday commuter train that runs to and from Los Angeles and Orange County.

Train Contacts Amtrak. ☎ 800/872-7245 ⊕ www.amtrak.com. **Metrolink.** ☎ 800/371-5465 ⊕ www.metrolinktrains.com.

RESTAURANTS

Much like those of L.A., restaurants in Orange County are generally casual, and you'll rarely see suits and ties. Nevertheless, at top resort hotel dining rooms, many guests choose to dress up.

Of course, there's also a swath of casual places along the beachfronts—seafood takeout, taquerias, burger joints—that won't mind if you wear flip-flops. Reservations are recommended for the nicest restaurants.

Many places don't serve past 11 pm, and locals tend to eat early. Remember that according to California law, smoking is prohibited in all enclosed areas. *Restaurant reviews have been shortened. For full information, visit Fodors.com.*

HOTELS

Along the coast there are remarkable luxury resorts; if you can't afford a stay, pop in for the view at Laguna Beach's Montage or the always-welcoming Ritz-Carlton at Dana Point. For a taste of the OC glam life, have lunch overlooking the yachts of Newport Bay at the Balboa Bay Resort.

As a rule, lodging prices tend to rise the closer the hotels are to the beach. If you're looking for value, consider a hotel that is inland along the Interstate 405 freeway corridor.

In most cases, you can take advantage of some of the facilities of the high-end resorts, such as restaurants and spas, even if you aren't an overnight guest. *Hotel reviews have been shortened. For full information, visit Fodors.com.*

WHAT IT COSTS			
$	**$$**	**$$$**	**$$$$**
RESTAURANTS under $16	$16–$22	$23–$30	over $30
HOTELS under $120	$120–$175	$176–$250	over $250

Restaurant prices are the average cost of a main course at dinner or, if dinner is not served, at lunch, excluding sales tax. Hotel prices are the lowest cost of a standard double room in high season, excluding service charges and tax.

VISITOR INFORMATION

The Anaheim/Orange County Visitor and Convention Bureau on the main floor of the Anaheim Convention Center is an excellent resource for both leisure and business travelers.

The Orange County Tourism Council's website is also a useful source of information.

Information Visit Anaheim. ⊠ *Anaheim Convention Center, 800 W. Katella Ave., Anaheim* ☎ *714/765-8888* ⊕ *www.visitanaheim.org.* **Orange County Visitors Association.** ⊕ *www.visittheoc.com.*

DISNEYLAND RESORT

26 miles southeast of Los Angeles, via I-5.

The snowcapped Matterhorn, the centerpiece of the Magic Kingdom, punctuates the skyline of Anaheim. Since 1955, when Walt Disney chose this once-quiet farming community for the site of his first amusement park, Disneyland has attracted more than 616 million visitors and tens of thousands of workers, and Anaheim has been their host.

To understand the symbiotic relationship between Disneyland and Anaheim, you need only look at the $4.2 billion spent in a combined effort to revitalize Anaheim's tourist center and run-down areas, and to expand and renovate the Disney properties into what is known now as Disneyland Resort.

The resort is a sprawling complex that includes Disney's two amusement parks, three hotels, and Downtown Disney, a shopping, dining, and entertainment promenade. Anaheim's tourist center includes Angel Stadium of Anaheim, home of baseball's 2002 World Series Champions Los Angeles Angels of Anaheim; the Honda Center (formerly the Arrowhead Pond), which hosts concerts and the Anaheim Ducks hockey team; and the enormous Anaheim Convention Center.

GETTING HERE

Disney is about a 30-mile drive from either LAX or Downtown. From LAX, follow Sepulveda Boulevard south to the Interstate 105 freeway and drive east 16 miles to the Interstate 605 north exit. Exit at the Santa Ana Freeway (Interstate 5) and continue south for 12 miles to the Disneyland Drive exit. Follow signs to the resort. From Downtown, follow Interstate 5 south 28 miles and exit at Disneyland Drive. **Disneyland Resort Express** (*800/828* ☎ *–6699 graylineanaheim.com*) offers daily nonstop bus service between LAX, John Wayne Airport, and Anaheim. Reservations are not required. The cost is $30 one-way from LAX, and $20 from John Wayne Airport.

SAVING TIME AND MONEY

If you plan to visit for more than a day, you can save money by buying two- three-, four-, and five-day Park Hopper tickets that grant same-day "hopping" privileges between Disneyland and Disney's California Adventure. You get a discount on the multiple-day passes if you buy online through the Disneyland website.

A one-day Park Hopper pass costs $155–$169 for anyone 10 or older, and $149–$163 for kids ages 3–9 depending on what day you go. Admission to either park (but not both) is $97–$124 or $89–$119 for kids ages 3–9; kids 2 and under are free.

In addition to tickets, parking is $18–$35 (unless your hotel has a shuttle or is within walking distance), and meals in the parks and at Downtown Disney range from $10 to $50 per person.

DISNEY'S TOP ATTRACTIONS

Indiana Jones: You're at the wheel for this thrilling ride through a cursed temple. Watch out for boulders!

Matterhorn Bobsleds: This ride is modeled after the Matterhorn mountain in Switzerland; beware the Abominable Snowman.

Pirates of the Caribbean: Watch buccaneers wreak havoc as you float along in a rowboat.

Space Mountain: This scary and thrilling roller coaster is mostly in the dark.

Star Tours 3D: Fly through a 3-D galaxy with your favorite Star Wars characters.

4

DISNEYLAND

FAMILY

Fodor's Choice

★

Disneyland. One of the biggest misconceptions people have about Disneyland is that it's the same as Florida's mammoth Walt Disney World, or one of the Disney parks overseas. But Disneyland, which opened in 1955 and is the only one of the parks to have been overseen by Walt himself, has a genuine historic feel and occupies a unique place in the Disney legend. Expertly run, perfectly maintained, with polite and helpful staff ("cast members" in the Disney lexicon), the park has plenty that you won't find anywhere else—such as the Indiana Jones Adventure ride and Storybook Land, with its miniature replicas of animated Disney scenes from classics such as *Pinocchio* and *Alice in Wonderland*. Characters appear for autographs and photos throughout the day; times and places are posted at the entrances. Live shows, parades, strolling musicians, fireworks on weekends, and endless snack choices add to the carnival atmosphere. You can also meet some of the animated icons at one of the character meals served at the three Disney hotels (open to the public). Belongings can be stored in lockers just off Main Street; stroller rentals at the entrance gate are a convenient option for families with small tykes. ✉ *1313 S. Disneyland Dr., between Ball Rd. and Katella Ave., Anaheim* ☎ *714/781–4636 guest information* ⊕ *www.disneyland.com* ✉ *$95–$119; parking $18.*

PARK NEIGHBORHOODS

Neighborhoods for Disneyland are arranged in geographic order.

MAIN STREET, U.S.A.

Walt's hometown of Marceline, Missouri, was the inspiration behind this romanticized image of small-town America, circa 1900. The sidewalks are lined with a penny arcade, an endless supply of sugar confections, shops that sell everything from tradable pins to Disney-theme clothing, and a photo shop that offers souvenirs created via Disney's PhotoPass (on-site photographers capture memorable moments digitally—you can access in person or online). Main Street opens a half hour before the rest of the park, so it's a good place to explore if you're getting an early start to beat the crowds (it's also open an hour after the other attractions close, so you may want to save your shopping for the end of the day). **Main Street Cinema** offers a cool respite from the crowds, and six classic Disney animated shorts, including *Steamboat Willie*. There's rarely a wait to enter. Grab a cappuccino and fresh-made pastry at the Jolly Holiday bakery to jump-start your visit. Board the **Disneyland Railroad** here to save on walking; it tours all the lands plus offers unique views of Splash Mountain and the Grand Canyon and Primeval World dioramas.

NEW ORLEANS SQUARE

This mini–French Quarter, with narrow streets, hidden courtyards, and live street performances, is home to two iconic attractions and the Cajun-inspired Blue Bayou restaurant. **Pirates of the Caribbean** now features Jack Sparrow and the cursed Captain Barbossa, in a nod to the blockbuster movies of the same name, plus enhanced special effects and battle scenes (complete with cannonball explosions). Nearby, the **Haunted Mansion** continues to spook guests with its stretching room and "doombuggy" rides (plus there's now an expanded storyline for the beating-heart bride). Its *Nightmare Before Christmas* holiday overlay is

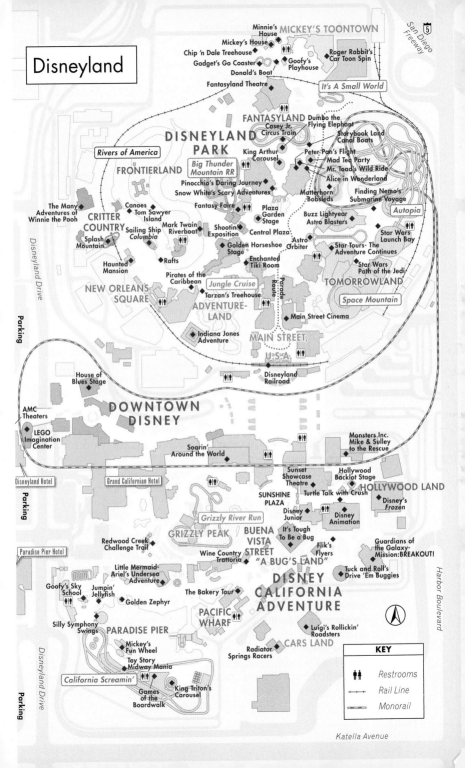

Disneyland

MICKEY'S TOONTOWN

Minnie's House
Mickey's House
Chip 'n Dale Treehouse
Gadget's Go Coaster
Donald's Boat
Goofy's Playhouse
Roger Rabbit's Car Toon Spin
Fantasyland Theatre
It's A Small World

FANTASYLAND
Dumbo the Flying Elephant
Casey Jr. Circus Train
Starbook Land Canal Boats

DISNEYLAND PARK
King Arthur Carousel
Peter Pan's Flight
Mad Tea Party
Mr. Toad's Wild Ride
Alice in Wonderland

Rivers of America
Big Thunder Mountain RR

FRONTIERLAND
Pinocchio's Daring Journey
Snow White's Scary Adventures
Finding Nemo's Submarine Voyage
Autopia

Matterhorn Bobsleds

The Many Adventures of Winnie the Pooh
Canoes
Tom Sawyer Island
Fantasy Faire
Plaza Garden Stage
Buzz Lightyear Astro Blasters
Star Wars Launch Bay

CRITTER COUNTRY
Sailing Ship Columbia
Mark Twain Riverboat
Shootin' Exposition
Central Plaza
Astro Orbiter
Star Tours- The Adventure Continues

Splash Mountain
Rafts
Golden Horseshoe Stage
Enchanted Tiki Room
Star Wars Path of the Jedi

Haunted Mansion
Pirates of the Caribbean
Jungle Cruise
Tarzan's Treehouse
TOMORROWLAND

NEW ORLEANS SQUARE
ADVENTURE-LAND
Space Mountain

Indiana Jones Adventure
Main Street Cinema

MAIN STREET, U.S.A.

Disneyland Railroad

House of Blues Stage

AMC Theaters

LEGO Imagination Center

DOWNTOWN DISNEY

Soarin' Around the World

Monsters Inc. Mike & Sulley to the Rescue

Disneyland Hotel
Grand Californian Hotel

Sunset Showcase Theatre
Hollywood Backlot Stage
HOLLYWOOD LAND

Turtle Talk with Crush

SUNSHINE PLAZA
Disney's Frozen

Paradise Pier Hotel
Grizzly River Run

Disney Junior
Disney Animation

GRIZZLY PEAK
BUENA VISTA STREET
It's Tough To Be a Bug
Flik's Flyers
Guardians of the Galaxy- Mission:BREAKOUT!

Redwood Creek Challenge Trail
Wine Country Trattoria
"A BUG'S LAND"
Tuck and Roll's Drive 'Em Buggies

Little Mermaid- Ariel's Undersea Adventure
The Bakery Tour
DISNEY CALIFORNIA ADVENTURE

Goofy's Sky School
Jumpin' Jellyfish
Golden Zephyr

Silly Symphony Swings
PACIFIC WHARF
Luigi's Rollickin' Roadsters

Mickey's Fun Wheel
Radiator Springs Racers
CARS LAND

PARADISE PIER
Toy Story Midway Mania
California Screamin'
Games of the Boardwalk
King Triton's Carousel

San Diego Freeway
[5]

Disneyland Drive
Parking
Parking
Parking

Harbor Boulevard
Katella Avenue

KEY

👫 Restrooms
╂ Rail Line
▭ Monorail

an annual tradition. This is a good area to get a casual bite to eat; the clam chowder in sourdough bread bowls, sold at the French Market Restaurant and Royal Street Veranda, is a popular choice. Food carts offer everything from just-popped popcorn to churros, and even fresh fruit.

FRONTIERLAND

Between Adventureland and Fantasyland, Frontierland transports you to the Wild, Wild West with its rustic buildings, shooting gallery, mountain range, and foot-stompin' dance hall. The marquee attraction, **Big Thunder Mountain Railroad,** is a relatively tame roller-coaster ride (no steep descents) that takes the form of a runaway mine car as it rumbles past desert canyons and an old mining town. Tour the Rivers of America on the **Mark Twain Riverboat,** in the company of a grizzled old river pilot, or circumnavigate the globe on the **Sailing Ship Columbia,** though its operating hours are usually limited to weekends. From here you can raft over to Pirate's Lair on **Tom Sawyer Island,** which now features pirate-theme caves, treasure hunts, and music, along with plenty of caves and hills to climb and explore. If you don't mind tight seating, have a snack at the Golden Horseshoe Restaurant while enjoying the always-entertaining comedy and bluegrass show of Billy Hill and the Hillybillies. Children won't want to miss **Big Thunder Ranch,** a small petting zoo featuring pigs, goats, and cows, beyond Big Thunder Mountain.

CRITTER COUNTRY

Down-home country is the theme in this shady corner of the park, where Winnie the Pooh and Davy Crockett make their homes. Here you can find **Splash Mountain,** a classic flume ride accompanied by music and appearances by Brer Rabbit and other characters from *Song of the South*. Don't forget to check out your photo (the camera snaps close-ups of each car just before it plunges into the water) on the way out. The patio of the popular Hungry Bear Restaurant has great views of Tom Sawyer's Island and Davy Crockett's Explorer Canoes.

ADVENTURELAND

Modeled after the lands of Africa, Polynesia, and Arabia, this tiny tropical paradise is worth braving the crowds that flock here for the ambience and better-than-average food. Sing along with the animatronic birds and tiki gods in the **Enchanted Tiki Room,** sail the rivers of the world with joke-cracking skippers on **Jungle Cruise,** and climb the *Disneyodendron semperflorens* (aka always-blooming Disney tree) to **Tarzan's Treehouse,** where you can walk through scenes, some interactive, from the 1999 animated film. Cap off the visit with a wild Jeep ride at **Indiana Jones Adventure,** where the special effects and decipherable hieroglyphics distract you while you're waiting in line. The skewers (some vegetarian options available) at Bengal Barbecue and pineapple whip at Tiki Juice Bar are some of the best options for quick bites in the park.

FANTASYLAND

Sleeping Beauty Castle marks the entrance to Fantasyland, a visual wonderland of princesses, spinning teacups, flying elephants, and other classic storybook characters. Rides and shops (such as the princess-theme Once Upon a Time and Gepetto's Toys and Gifts) take precedence over restaurants in this area of the park, but outdoor carts sell everything from

BEST TIPS FOR DISNEYLAND

■TIP→ As of 2017, all visitors must pass through metal detectors, and bags are searched before entering the Disneyland Resort. Allot 10–15 extra minutes for passing through the security line.

Buy entry tickets in advance. Many nearby hotels sell park admission tickets; you can also buy them through the Disney website. If you book a package deal, such as those offered through AAA, tickets are included, too.

The lines at the ticket booths can take more than an hour on busy days, so you'll definitely save time by buying in advance, especially if you're committed to going on a certain day regardless of the weather.

Come midweek. Weekends, especially in summer, are a mob scene. Holidays are crowded, too. A rainy winter weekday is often the least crowded time to visit.

Plan your times to hit the most popular rides. Fodorites recommend getting to the park as early as possible and staying as late as possible. If you're at the park when the gates open, make a beeline for the top rides before the crowds reach a critical mass. Another good time is the late evening, when the hordes thin out, and, if planned right, during a parade or other show. Save the quieter attractions for midafternoon.

Use FASTPASS. These passes allow you to reserve your place in line at some of the most crowded attractions (only one at a time). Distribution machines are posted near the entrances of each attraction. Feed in your park admission ticket, and you'll receive a pass with a printed time frame (generally up to 1–1½ hours later) during which you can return to wait in a much shorter line.

Plan your meals to avoid peak mealtime crowds. Start the day with a big breakfast, so you won't be too hungry at noon, when restaurants and vendors get swarmed. Wait to have lunch until after 1 pm.

If you want to eat at the **Blue Bayou** in New Orleans Square, you can make a reservation up to six months in advance online. Another (cheaper) option is to bring your own food. There are areas just outside the park gates with picnic tables set up for this. It's always a good idea to bring water.

Check the daily events schedule online or at the park entrance. During parades, fireworks, and other special events, sections of the parks clog with crowds. This can work for you or against you. An event could make it difficult to get around a park—but if you plan ahead, you can take advantage of the distraction to hit popular rides.

Send the teens next door. Disneyland's newer sister park, California Adventure, features more intense rides suitable for older kids (Park Hopper passes include admission to both parks).

4

churros to turkey legs. Tots love the **King Arthur Carousel, Casey Jr. Circus Train,** and **Storybook Land Canal Boats.** This is also home to **Mr. Toad's Wild Ride, Peter Pan's Flight,** and **Pinocchio's Daring Journey—** classic, movie-theater-dark rides that immerse riders in Disney fairy tales and appeal to adults and kids alike. The Abominable Snowman pops up on the **Matterhorn Bobsleds,** a roller coaster that twists and turns up and around on a made-to-scale model of the real Swiss mountain. Anchoring the east end of Fantasyland is **It's a Small World,** a smorgasbord of dancing animatronic dolls, cuckoo clock–covered walls, and variations of the song everyone knows, or soon *will* know, by heart. Beloved Disney characters like Ariel from *Under the Sea* are also part of the mix. Fantasy Faire is a fairy tale–style village that collects all the Disney princesses together. Each has her own reception nook in the Royal Hall. Condensed retellings of *Tangled* and *Beauty and the Beast* take place at the Royal Theatre.

MICKEY'S TOONTOWN

Geared toward small fries, this lopsided cartoonlike downtown, complete with cars and trolleys that invite exploring, is where Mickey, Donald, Goofy, and other classic Disney characters hang their hats. One of the most popular attractions is **Roger Rabbit's Car Toon Spin,** a twisting, turning cab ride through the Toontown of *Who Framed Roger Rabbit?* You can also walk through **Mickey's House** to meet and be photographed with the famous mouse, take a low-key ride on **Gadget's Go Coaster,** or bounce around the fenced-in playground in front of **Goofy's House.**

TOMORROWLAND

This popular section of the park continues to tinker with its future, adding and enhancing rides regularly. *Star Wars*–themed attractions can't be missed, like the immersive, 3-D **Star Tours – The Adventures Continue,** where you can join the Rebellion in a galaxy far, far away. **Finding Nemo's Submarine Voyage** updates the old Submarine Voyage ride with the exploits of Nemo, Dory, Marlin, and other characters from the Disney-Pixar film. Try to visit this popular ride early in the day if you can, and be prepared for a wait. The interactive **Buzz Lightyear Astro Blasters** lets you zap your neighbors with laser beams and compete for the highest score. Hurtle through the cosmos on **Space Mountain** or check out mainstays like the futuristic **Astro Orbiter** rockets, **Star Wars Launch Bay,** which showcases costumes, models, and props from the franchise, and **Star Wars, Path of the Jedi,** which catches viewers up on all the movies with a quick 12-minute film. Disneyland Monorail and Disneyland Railroad both have stations here. There's also a video arcade and dancing water fountain that makes a perfect playground for kids on hot summer days. The Jedi Training Academy spotlights future Luke Skywalkers in the crowd.

Besides the eight lands, the daily live-action shows and parades are always crowd-pleasers. Among these is **Fantasmic!** a musical, fireworks, and laser show in which Mickey and friends wage a spellbinding battle against Disneyland's darker characters. ■TIP→ **Arrive early to secure a good view; if there are two shows scheduled for the day, the second one tends to be less crowded. A fireworks display illuminates the sky weekends and most summer evenings.** Brochures with maps, available at the entrance, list show and parade times.

Sleeping Beauty Castle was actually built before the movie Sleeping Beauty came out, because it took so long to produce animated feature films.

DISNEY CALIFORNIA ADVENTURE

FAMILY

Fodor's Choice

★

Disney California Adventure. The sprawling Disney California Adventure, adjacent to Disneyland (their entrances face each other), pays tribute to the Golden State with eight theme areas that re-create vintage architectural styles and embrace several hit Pixar films via engaging attractions. Visitors enter through the art deco–style Buena Vista Street, past shops and a helpful information booth that advises wait times on attractions. The 12-acre Cars Land features Radiator Springs Racers, a speedy trip in six-passenger speedsters through scenes featured in the blockbuster hit. (FASTPASS tickets for the ride run out early most days.) Other popular attractions include World of Color, a nighttime water-effects show, and Toy Story Mania!, an interactive adventure ride hosted by Woody and Buzz Lightyear. At night the park takes on neon hues as glowing signs light up Route 66 in Cars Land and Mickey's Fun Wheel, a giant Ferris wheel on the Paradise Pier. Unlike at Disneyland, cocktails, beer, and wine are available; craft beers and premium wines from California are poured. Live nightly entertainment also features a 1930s jazz troupe that arrives in a vintage jalopy. ⊠ *1313 S. Disneyland Dr., between Ball Rd. and Katella Ave., Anaheim* ☎ *714/781–4636* ⊕ *www.disneyland. com* ⊠ *$95–$119; parking $18.*

PARK NEIGHBORHOODS

Neighborhoods for Disney California Adventure are arranged in geographic order.

BUENA VISTA STREET

California Adventure's grand entryway re-creates the lost 1920s of Los Angeles that Walt Disney encountered when he moved to the Golden State. There's a **Red Car trolley** (modeled after Los Angeles's bygone streetcar line); hop on for the brief ride to Hollywood Land. Buena Vista Street is also home to a Starbucks outlet—within the Fiddler, Fifer & Practical Café—and the upscale Carthay Circle Restaurant and Lounge, which serves modern craft cocktails and beer.

GRIZZLY PEAK

This woodsy land celebrates the great outdoors. Test your skills on the **Redwood Creek Challenge Trail,** a challenging trek across net ladders and suspension bridges. **Grizzly River Run** mimics the river rapids of the Sierra Nevadas; be prepared to get soaked.

Soarin' Around the world is a spectacular simulated hang-gliding ride over internationally known landmarks like Switzerland's Matterhorn and India's Taj Mahal.

HOLLYWOOD LAND

With a main street modeled after Hollywood Boulevard, a fake sky backdrop, and real soundstages, this area celebrates California's film industry. **Disney Animation** gives you an insider's look at how animators create characters. **Turtle Talk with Crush** lets kids have an unscripted chat with a computer-animated Crush, the sea turtle from *Finding Nemo.* The Hyperion Theater hosts **Frozen,** a 45-minute live performance from a Broadway-sized cast with terrific visual effects. ■TIP➔ Plan on getting in line about half an hour in advance; the show is worth the wait. On the film-inspired ride, **Monsters, Inc. Mike & Sulley to the Rescue,** visitors climb into taxis and travel the streets of Monstropolis on a mission to safely return Boo to her bedroom. **Guardians of the Galaxy – Mission: BREAKOUT!** which opened in summer 2017, replaced the now-closed Twilight Zone Tower of Terror.

A BUG'S LAND

Inspired by the 1998 film *A Bug's Life,* this section skews its attractions to an insect's point of view. Kids can spin around in giant takeout Chinese food boxes on **Flik's Flyers,** and hit the bug-shaped bumper cars on **Tuck and Roll's Drive 'Em Buggies.** The short show *It's Tough to Be a Bug!* gives a 3-D look at insect life.

CARS LAND

Amble down Route 66, the main thoroughfare of Cars Land, a pitch-perfect re-creation of the vintage highway. Quick eats are found at the Cozy Cone Motel (in a teepee-shape motor court), while Flo's V8 café serves hearty comfort food. Start your day at Radiator Springs Racers, the park's most popular attraction, where waits can be two hours or longer. Strap into a nifty sports car and meet the characters of Pixar's *Cars*; the ride ends in a speedy auto race through the red rocks and desert of Radiator Springs.

PACIFIC WHARF

The Wine Country Trattoria is a great place for Italian specialties paired with California wine; relax outside on the restaurant's terrace for a casual bite. Mexican cuisine and potent margaritas are available at the Cocina Cucamonga Mexican Grill and Rita's Baja Blenders.

PARADISE PIER

This section re-creates the glory days of California's seaside piers. If you're looking for thrills, the **California Screamin'** roller coaster takes its riders from 0 to 55 mph in about four seconds and proceeds through scream tunnels, steeply angled drops, and a 360-degree loop. **Goofy's Sky School** is a rollicking roller-coaster ride that goes up three stories and covers more than 1,200 feet of track. **Mickey's Fun Wheel,** a giant Ferris wheel, provides a good view of the grounds, though some cars spin and sway for more kicks. There are also carnival games, an aquatic-themed carousel, and Ariel's Grotto, where future princesses can dine with the mermaid and her friends (reservations are a must). Get a close-up look at Ariel's world on **Little Mermaid—Ariel's Undersea Adventure.** The best views of the nighttime music, water, and light show, **World of Color,** are from the paths along Paradise Bay. FASTPASS tickets are available. Or for a guaranteed spot, book dinner at the Wine Country Trattoria that includes a ticket to a viewing area to catch all the show's stunning visuals.

OTHER ATTRACTIONS

FAMILY **Downtown Disney District.** The Downtown Disney District is a 20-acre promenade of dining, shopping, and entertainment that connects the resort's hotels and theme parks. At **Ralph Brennan's Jazz Kitchen** you can dig into New Orleans–style food and music. Sports fans gravitate to **ESPN Zone,** which serves American food from the grill, and lets visitors play video games or watch worldwide sports events telecast through 120 HDTVs. An **AMC** multiplex movie theater with stadium-style seating plays the latest blockbusters and, naturally, a couple of kid flicks. Shops sell everything from Disney goods to antique jewelry—don't miss **Disney Vault 28,** a hip boutique that sells designer-made Disney wear and couture clothing and accessories. At the mega-sized **Lego Store** there are hands-on demonstrations and space to play with the latest Lego creations. Anna & Elsa's Store speedily makes over kids into their favorite character from the hit film *Frozen.* Parking is a deal: the first two hours are free, or four hours with validation. All visitors must pass through a security checkpoint and metal detectors before entering. ⊠ *1580 Disneyland Dr., Anaheim* ☎ *714/300–7800* ⊕ *disneyland. disney.go.com/downtown-disney* ◻ *Free.*

WHERE TO EAT

$$$ ✕ **Catal Restaurant & Uva Bar.** Famed chef Joachim Splichal and his staff
MEDITERRANEAN take a relaxed approach at this bi-level Mediterranean spot where 40 wines by the glass, craft beers, and craft cocktails pair well with Spanish-influenced dishes. Upstairs, Catal's menu has tapas, a variety of flavorful paellas (lobster is worth the splurge), and charcuterie. **Known for:** people-watching; gourmet burgers; paella. Ⓢ *Average main: $30* ⊠ *Downtown Disney District, 1580 S. Disneyland Dr., Suite 103, Anaheim* ☎ *714/774–4442* ⊕ *www.patinagroup.com.*

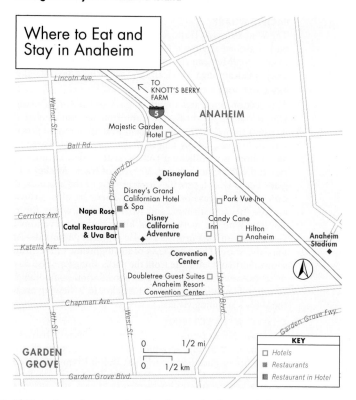

Where to Eat and Stay in Anaheim

$$$$ ✕ **Napa Rose.** Done up in a handsome Craftsman style, Napa Rose's
AMERICAN rich seasonal cuisine is matched with an extensive wine list, with 1,000
labels and 80 available by the glass. For a look into the open kitchen,
sit at the counter and watch the chefs as they whip up such signature
dishes as grilled diver scallops and chanterelles, and roasted lamp
chops topped with pomegranate. **Known for:** excellent wine list; kid-
friendly options; grilled diver scallops. ⑤ *Average main: $45 ✉ Dis-
ney's Grand Californian Hotel, 1600 S. Disneyland Dr., Anaheim*
☎ *714/300–7170, 714/781–3463 reservations* ⊕ *disneyland.disney.
go.com/grand-californian-hotel/napa-rose.*

WHERE TO STAY

$$ ⚏ **Candy Cane Inn.** One of the Disneyland area's first hotels, the Candy
HOTEL Cane is one of Anaheim's most relaxing properties, with spacious
FAMILY and understated rooms and an inviting palm-fringed pool. **Pros:**
proximity to everything Disney; friendly service; well-lighted prop-
erty. **Cons:** rooms and lobby are on the small side; all rooms face
parking lot. ⑤ *Rooms from: $158 ✉ 1747 S. Harbor Blvd., Anaheim*
☎ *714/774–5284, 800/345–7057* ⊕ *www.candycaneinn.net* ⮑ *171
rooms* ⦿ *Breakfast.*

$$$$ 🏨 **Disney's Grand Californian Hotel & Spa.** The most opulent of Disneyland's three hotels, the Craftsman-style Grand Californian offers views
RESORT   of Disney California Adventure and Downtown Disney. **Pros:** gorgeous
FAMILY   lobby; family friendly; direct access to California Adventure. **Cons:**
Fodor's Choice the self-parking lot is across the street; standard rooms are on the
★   small side. $ *Rooms from: $461* ✉ *1600 S. Disneyland Dr., Anaheim*
☎ *714/635-2300* ⊕ *disneyland.disney.go.com/grand-californian-hotel*
↩ *998 rooms* ⦶ *No meals.*

$$ 🏨 **Doubletree Guest Suites Anaheim Resort-Convention Center.** This busy
HOTEL   hotel near the Anaheim Convention Center and a 20-minute walk from
Disneyland caters to business travelers and vacationers alike. **Pros:** huge
suites; walking distance to a variety of restaurants. **Cons:** a bit far
from Disneyland; pool area is small. $ *Rooms from: $129* ✉ *2085 S.
Harbor Blvd., Anaheim* ☎ *714/750-3000, 800/215-7316* ⊕ *double-treeanaheim.com* ↩ *252 rooms* ⦶ *No meals.*

$$ 🏨 **Hilton Anaheim.** Next to the Anaheim Convention Center, this busy
HOTEL   Hilton is one of the largest hotels in Southern California, with a restau-
FAMILY   rant and food court, cocktail lounges, a full-service gym, and its own
Starbucks. **Pros:** efficient service; great children's programs; some rooms
have views of the park fireworks. **Cons:** huge size can be daunting;
fee to use health club. $ *Rooms from: $159* ✉ *777 Convention Way,
Anaheim* ☎ *714/750-4321, 800/445-8667* ⊕ *www.anaheim.hilton.com*
↩ *1,572 rooms* ⦶ *No meals.*

$$ 🏨 **Park Vue Inn.** Watch the frequent fireworks from the rooftop sundeck
HOTEL   at this bougainvillea-covered Spanish-style inn, one of the closest lodgings
FAMILY   to Disneyland's main gate. **Pros:** easy walk to Disneyland, Downtown
Disney, and Disney California Adventure; free parking until midnight
on checkout day; some rooms have bunk beds. **Cons:** all rooms face the
parking lot; rooms near the breakfast room can be noisy. $ *Rooms from:
$159* ✉ *1570 S. Harbor Blvd., Anaheim* ☎ *714/772-3691, 800/334-
7021* ⊕ *www.parkvueinn.com* ↩ *86 rooms* ⦶ *Breakfast.*

$$ 🏨 **Majestic Garden Hotel.** If you're hoping to escape from the commercial
HOTEL   atmosphere of the hotels near Disneyland and California Adventure,
FAMILY   consider this sprawling replica of a Tudor castle. **Pros:** large, attractive lobby; game room; spacious rooms with comfortable beds. **Cons:**
confusing layout; hotel sits close to a busy freeway; small bathrooms.
$ *Rooms from: $144* ✉ *900 S. Disneyland Dr., Anaheim* ☎ *714/778-
1700, 844/326-7122* ⊕ *www.majesticgardenhotel.com* ↩ *489 rooms*
⦶ *No meals.*

SPORTS AND THE OUTDOORS

Anaheim Ducks. The National Hockey League's Anaheim Ducks, winners
of the 2007 Stanley Cup, play at Honda Center. ✉ *Honda Center, 2695
E. Katella Ave., Anaheim* ☎ *877/945-3946* ⊕ *nhl.com/ducks.*

Los Angeles Angels of Anaheim. Professional baseball's Los Angeles Angels
of Anaheim play at Angel Stadium. An "Outfield Extravaganza" celebrates great plays on the field, with fireworks and a geyser exploding
over a model evoking the California coast. ✉ *Angel Stadium, 2000
E. Gene Autry Way, Anaheim* ☎ *714/426-4357* ⊕ *www.angels.com*
Ⓜ *Metrolink Angels Express.*

KNOTT'S BERRY FARM

25 miles south of Los Angeles, via I-5, in Buena Park.

FAMILY **Knott's Berry Farm.** The land where the boysenberry was invented (by crossing raspberry, blackberry, and loganberry bushes) is now occupied by Knott's Berry Farm. In 1934 Cordelia Knott began serving chicken dinners on her wedding china to supplement her family's income. The dinners and her boysenberry pies proved more profitable than husband Walter's farm, so the two moved first into the restaurant business and then into the entertainment business. The park is now a 160-acre complex with 40 rides, dozens of restaurants and shops, arcade games, live shows, a brick-by-brick replica of Philadelphia's Independence Hall, and loads of Americana. Although it has plenty to keep small children occupied, the park is best known for its awesome rides. The Boardwalk area is home to several coasters, including the stomach-churning Rip Tide that turns thrill-seekers upside down and around several times, plus water features to cool things off on hot days, and a lighted promenade. And, yes, you can still get that boysenberry pie (and jam, juice—you name it). ⊠ *8039 Beach Blvd., Buena Park* ✢ *Between La Palma Ave. and Crescent St., 2 blocks south of Hwy. 91* ☎ *714/220–5200* ⊕ *www.knotts.com* ◷ *$75.*

PARK NEIGHBORHOODS

Neighborhoods for Knott's Berry Farm are arranged in geographic order.

CAMP SNOOPY

It can be gridlocked on weekends, but small fries love this miniature High Sierra wonderland where the *Peanuts* gang hangs out. Tykes can push and pump their own mini–mining cars on **Huff and Puff,** zip around a pint-size racetrack on **Charlie Brown Speedway,** and hop aboard **Woodstock's Airmail,** a kids' version of the park's Supreme Scream ride. Most of the rides here are geared toward kids only, leaving parents to cheer them on from the sidelines. **Sierra Sidewinder,** a roller coaster near the entrance of Camp Snoopy, is aimed at older children, with spinning saucer–type vehicles that go a maximum speed of 37 mph.

FIESTA VILLAGE

Over in **Fiesta Village** are two more musts for adrenaline junkies: **Montezooma's Revenge,** a roller coaster that goes from 0 to 55 mph in less than five seconds, and **Jaguar!,** which simulates the motions of a cat stalking its prey, twisting, spiraling, and speeding up and slowing down as it takes you on its stomach-dropping course. There's also **Hat Dance,** a version of the spinning teacups but with sombreros, and a 100-year-old **Dentzel carousel,** complete with an antique organ and menagerie of hand-carved animals. In a nod to history, there are restored scale models of the California Missions at Fiesta Village's southern entrance.

THE BOARDWALK

Not-for-the-squeamish thrill rides and skill-based games dominate the scene at the **boardwalk.** New roller coasters—Coast Rider, Surfside Glider, and Pacific Scrambler—were added in 2013 and surround a pond that keeps things cooler on hot days. Go head over heels on the **Boomerang** roller coaster, then do it again—backward. The boardwalk is also home to a string of test-your-skill games that are fun to watch whether you're playing or not, and Johnny Rockets, the park's newest restaurant.

GHOST TOWN

Clusters of authentic old buildings relocated from their original mining-town sites mark this section of the park. You can stroll down the street, stop and chat with a blacksmith, pan for gold (for a fee), crack open a geode, check out the chalkboard of a circa-1875 schoolhouse, and ride an original Butterfield stagecoach. Looming over it all is **GhostRider,** Orange County's first wooden roller coaster. Traveling up to 56 mph and reaching 118 feet at its highest point, the park's biggest attraction is riddled with sudden dips and curves, subjecting riders to forces up to three times of gravity. On the Western-theme **Silver Bullet,** riders are sent to a height of 146 feet and then back down 109 feet. Riders spiral, corkscrew, fly into a cobra roll, and experience overbanked curves. The **Calico Mine** ride descends into a replica of a working gold mine. The **Timber Mountain Log Ride** is a visitor favorite—the flume ride underwent a complete renovation in 2013. Also found here is the park's newest thrill ride, the **Pony Express,** a roller coaster that lets riders saddle up on packs of "horses" tethered to platforms that take off on a series of hairpin turns and travel up to 38 mph. Don't miss the **Western Trails Museum,** a dusty old gem full of Old West memorabilia and rural Americana, plus menus from the original chicken restaurant, and an impressive antique button collection. **Calico Railroad** departs regularly from Ghost Town station for a round-trip tour of the park (bandit holdups notwithstanding).

This section is also home to **Big Foot Rapids,** a splash-fest of whitewater river rafting over towering cliffs, cascading waterfalls, and wild rapids. Don't miss the visually stunning show at **Mystery Lodge,** which tells the story of Native Americans in the Pacific Northwest with lights, music, and beautiful images.

KNOTT'S SOAK CITY WATERPARK

Knott's Soak City Waterpark is directly across from the main park on 13 acres next to Independence Hall. It has a dozen major water rides; **Pacific Spin** is an oversize waterslide that drops riders 75 feet into a catch pool. There's also a children's pool; a 750,000-gallon wave pool; and a funhouse. Soak City's season runs mid-May to mid-September. It's open daily after Memorial Day, weekends only after Labor Day, and then closes for the season.

WHERE TO EAT AND STAY

$$ ✕ **Mrs. Knott's Chicken Dinner Restaurant.** Cordelia Knott's fried chicken
AMERICAN and boysenberry pies drew crowds so big that Knott's Berry Farm
FAMILY was built to keep the hungry customers occupied while they waited.
The restaurant's current incarnation (outside the park's entrance)
still serves crispy fried chicken, along with fluffy handmade biscuits,
mashed potatoes, and Mrs. Knott's signature chilled cherry-rhubarb
compote. **Known for:** fried chicken; family friendly; outdoor din-
ing. $ *Average main: $22* ⊠ *Knott's Berry Farm Marketplace, 8039
Beach Blvd., Buena Park* ☎ *714/220–5055* ⊕ *www.knotts.com/
california-marketplace/mrs-knott-s-chicken-dinner-restaurant.*

$ 🏨 **Knott's Berry Farm Hotel.** This convenient high-rise hotel is run by
RESORT the park and sits right on park grounds surrounded by graceful palm
FAMILY trees. **Pros:** easy access to Knott's Berry Farm; plenty of family activi-
ties; basketball court. **Cons:** lobby and hallways can be noisy; public
areas show significant wear and tear. $ *Rooms from: $99* ⊠ *7675
Crescent Ave., Buena Park* ☎ *714/995–1111, 866/752–2444* ⊕ *www.
knottshotel.com* 🛏 *320 rooms* ⵔ *No meals.*

THE COAST

Running along the Orange County coastline is scenic Pacific Coast High-
way (Highway 1, known locally as the PCH). Older beachfront settle-
ments, with their modest bungalow-style homes, are joined by posh gated
communities. The pricey land between Newport Beach and Laguna Beach
is where ex-Laker Kobe Bryant, novelist Dean Koontz, those infamous
Real Housewives of Bravo, and a slew of finance moguls live.

Though the coastline is rapidly being filled in, there are still a few
stretches of beautiful, protected open land. And at many places along
the way you can catch an idealized glimpse of the Southern California
lifestyle: surfers hitting the beach, boards under their arms.

LONG BEACH

About 25 miles southeast of Los Angeles, via I-110 south.

Long Beach is L.A.'s gateway to the Pacific with ferries to Catalina
Island and fishing charters. Long Beach also welcomes cruise ships,
offers whale-watching excursions, and is home to the now retired
grande dame of trans-Atlantic crossings, *The Queen Mary.*

EXPLORING

FAMILY **Aquarium of the Pacific.** Sea lions, nurse sharks, and penguins, oh my!—
this aquarium focuses on creatures of the Pacific Ocean. The main
exhibits include large tanks of sharks, sting rays, and ethereal sea
dragons, which the aquarium has successfully bred in captivity. The
Great Hall features the multimedia attraction *Penguins,* a panoramic
film that captures the world of this endangered species. Be sure to say
hello to Betty, a rescue at the engaging sea otter exhibit. For a non-
aquatic experience, head to Lorikeet Forest, a walk-in aviary full of
the friendliest parrots from Australia. Buy a cup of nectar and smile as

you become a human bird perch. If you're a true animal lover, book an up-close-and-personal Animal Encounters Tour ($109) to learn about and assist in the care and feeding of the animals; or find out how the aquarium functions with the extensive Behind the Scenes Tour ($42.95 for adults, including admission). Certified divers can book a supervised dive in the aquarium's Tropical Reef Habitat ($299). Twice daily whale-watching trips on the *Harbor Breeze* depart from the dock adjacent to the aquarium; summer sightings of blue whales are an unforgettable thrill. ✉ *100 Aquarium Way, Long Beach* ☎ *562/590–3100* 🌐 *www.aquariumofpacific.org* 🎟 *$29.95.*

WHERE TO STAY

$$ HOTEL FAMILY 🏨 **Queen Mary Hotel.** Experience the golden age of transatlantic travel without the seasickness: a 1936–art deco style reigns on *The Queen Mary,* from the ship's mahogany paneling to its nickel-plated doors to the majestic Grand Salon. **Pros:** a walkable historic Promenade deck; views from Long Beach out to the Pacific; art deco details. **Cons:** spotty service; vintage soundproofing makes for a challenging night's sleep; mandatory Wi-Fi fee. [$] *Rooms from: $149* ✉ *1126 Queens Hwy., Long Beach* ☎ *562/435–3511, 877/342–0742* 🌐 *www.queenmary.com* 🛏 *346 staterooms* 🍴 *No meals.*

$$ B&B/INN 🏨 **The Varden.** Constructed in 1929 to house Bixby Knolls Sr.'s mistress, Dolly Varden, this small, historic, European-style hotel, on the metro line in downtown Long Beach, now caters to worldly budget travelers. Compact rooms are mostly white and blend modern touches like flat-screen TVs and geometric silver fixtures with period details like exposed beams, Dakota Jackson periwinkle chairs, and round penny-tile baths. **Pros:** great value for downtown location; discount passes to Gold's Gym across the street; complimentary Continental breakfast. **Cons:** no resort services; small rooms. [$] *Rooms from: $159* ✉ *335 Pacific Ave., Long Beach* ☎ *562/432–8950* 🌐 *www.thevardenhotel.com* 🛏 *35 rooms.*

NEWPORT BEACH

6 miles south of Huntington Beach via the Pacific Coast Highway.

Newport Beach has evolved from a simple seaside village to an icon of chic coastal living. Its ritzy reputation comes from mega-yachts bobbing in the harbor, boutiques that rival those in Beverly Hills, and spectacular homes overlooking the ocean.

The city boasts some of the cleanest beaches in Southern California; inland Newport Beach's concentration of high-rise office buildings, shopping centers, and luxury hotels drive the economy. But on the city's Balboa Peninsula, you can still catch a glimpse of a more humble, down-to-earth town scattered with taco spots, tackle shops, and sailor bars.

ESSENTIALS

Visitor Information Visit Newport Beach. ✉ *Atrium Court at Fashion Island, 401 Newport Center Dr.* ☎ *855/563–9767* 🌐 *www.visitnewportbeach.com.*

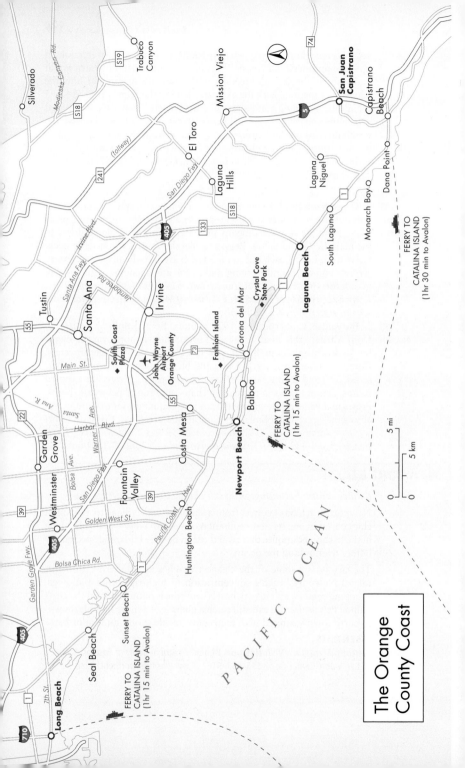

The Orange County Coast

EXPLORING

Balboa Island. This sliver of terra firma in Newport Harbor boasts quaint streets tightly packed with impossibly charming multimillion-dollar cottages. The island's main drag, Marine Avenue, is lined with equally picturesque cafés and shops.

NEED A BREAK

Sugar 'N Spice. Stop by ice cream parlor Sugar 'N Spice for a Balboa Bar—a slab of vanilla ice cream dipped first in chocolate and then in a topping of your choice such as hard candy or Oreo crumbs. Other parlors serve the concoction, but Sugar 'N Spice claims to have invented it back in 1945. ✉ *310 Marine Ave., Balboa Island* ☎ *949/673–8907.*

4

FAMILY **Balboa Peninsula.** Newport's best beaches are on Balboa Peninsula, where many jetties pave the way to ideal swimming areas. The most intense spot for bodysurfing in Orange County, and arguably on the West Coast, known as the **Wedge,** is at the south end of the peninsula. It was created by accident in the 1930s when the Federal Works Progress Administration built a jetty to protect Newport Harbor. **■ TIP→ Rip currents mean it's strictly for the pros—but it sure is fun to watch an experienced local ride it.** 🌐 *www.visitnewportbeach.com/vacations/balboa-peninsula.*

FAMILY **Discovery Cube's Ocean Quest.** This family-friendly destination has exhibits on the history of the harbor, ocean explorers, and scientific aspects of the Pacific Ocean. There's a fleet of ship models: some date to 1798, and one is made entirely of gold and silver. Other fun features include a touch tank holding local sea creatures and a lab for kids that encourages innovation. ✉ *600 E. Bay Ave.* ☎ *949/675–8915* 🌐 *www.oceanquestoc.org* 🎟 *$3* 🕒 *Closed Mon.–Thurs.*

Newport Harbor. Sheltering nearly 16,000 small boats, Newport Harbor may seduce even those who don't own a yacht. Spend an afternoon exploring the charming avenues and surrounding alleys; take California's longest running auto ferry across to Balboa Island. The fare is $2 for car and driver for the scenic crossing. Several grassy areas on the primarily residential Lido Isle have views of the water. ✉ *Pacific Coast Hwy.* 🌐 *www.balboaislandferry.com.*

FAMILY **Newport Pier.** Jutting out into the ocean near 20th Street, Newport Pier is a popular fishing spot. Street parking is difficult, so grab the first space you find and be prepared to walk. Early on Wednesday–Sunday mornings you're likely to encounter dory fishermen hawking their predawn catches, as they've done for generations. On weekends the area is alive with kids of all ages on in-line skates, skateboards, and bikes dodging pedestrians and whizzing past fast-food joints and classic dive bars. ✉ *72 McFadden Pl.*

WHERE TO EAT

$$$$ BRASSERIE 🍴 **Basilic.** This intimate French-Swiss bistro adds a touch of old-world elegance to the island with its white linen and flower-topped tables. Chef Bernard Althaus grows the herbs used in his classic French dishes. **Known for:** French classics; fine wine; old-school ambience. [$] *Average main: $32* ✉ *217 Marine Ave., Balboa Island* ☎ *949/673–0570* 🌐 *www.basilicrestaurant.com* 🕒 *Closed Sun. No lunch Mon.*

Riding the waves at Newport Beach

$ 🍴 **Bear Flag Fish Co.** Expect long lines in summer at this indoor/outdoor dining spot serving up the freshest local fish (swordfish, sea bass, halibut, and tuna) and a wide range of creative seafood dishes (the Hawaiian-style *poke* salad with ahi tuna is a local favorite). Order at the counter, which doubles as a seafood market, and sit inside the airy dining room or outside on a grand patio. **Known for:** freshest seafood; fish tacos; craft beers. [$] *Average main: $12* ✉ *Newport Peninsula, 3421 Via Lido* ☎ *949/673–3474* 🌐 *www.bearflagfishco.com.*
SEAFOOD
FAMILY

$$$$ 🍴 **The Cannery.** This 1920s cannery building still teems with fish, but now they go into dishes on the eclectic Pacific Rim menu rather than being packed into crates. Settle in at the sushi bar, in the dining room, or on the patio before choosing between sashimi, seafood platters, or the upscale surf-and-turf with filet mignon and grilled Maine lobsters. **Known for:** waterfront views; seafood specialties; craft cocktails. [$] *Average main: $35* ✉ *3010 Lafayette Rd.* ☎ *949/566–0060* 🌐 *www.cannerynewport.com.*
SEAFOOD

$$$ 🍴 **Gulfstream.** This on-trend restaurant has an open kitchen, comfortable booths, and outdoor seating. The patio is a fantastic place to hang out. **Known for:** oysters on the half shell; local hangout; outdoor patio. [$] *Average main: $30* ✉ *850 Avocado Ave.* ☎ *949/718–0188* 🌐 *www.hillstone.com.*
SEAFOOD

$$$ 🍴 **3-Thirty-3.** This stylish eatery attracts a convivial crowd—both young and old—for midday, sunset, and late-night dining. A long list of small, shareable plates heightens the camaraderie. **Known for:** happy hour; brunch burritos; generous portions. [$] *Average main: $26* ✉ *333 Bayside Dr.* ☎ *949/673–8464* 🌐 *www.3thirty3nb.com.*
AMERICAN

WHERE TO STAY

$$$$ RESORT FAMILY **Balboa Bay Resort.** Sharing the same frontage as the private Balboa Bay Club that long ago hosted Humphrey Bogart, Lauren Bacall, and the Reagans, this waterfront resort has one of the best bay views around. **Pros:** exquisite bay-front views; comfortable beds; a raked beach for guests. **Cons:** not much within walking distance; $25 nightly hospitality fee. [$] *Rooms from: $309* ✉ *1221 W. Coast Hwy.* ☎ *949/645–5000* 🌐 *www.balboabayresort.com* 🛏 *159 rooms* 🍴 *No meals.*

$$$$ HOTEL **The Island Hotel.** Across a palm tree-lined boulevard from stylish Fashion Island, this 20-story tower caters to business types during the week and luxury seekers on weekends. **Pros:** lively lounge scene; first-class spa; great location. **Cons:** steep valet parking prices; some rooms have views of mall parking. [$] *Rooms from: $259* ✉ *690 Newport Center Dr.* ☎ *949/759–0808, 877/591–9145* 🌐 *www.islandhotel.com* 🛏 *378 rooms* 🍴 *No meals.*

$$$ RESORT **Newport Beach Marriott Hotel and Spa.** Here you'll be smack in the moneyed part of town: across from Fashion Island, next to a country club, and with a view toward Newport Harbor. **Pros:** four concierge floors offer enhanced amenities; fantastic spa; complimentary bike rentals. **Cons:** sprawling floor plan; small bathrooms; car is essential for exploring beyond Fashion Island. [$] *Rooms from: $229* ✉ *900 Newport Center Dr.* ☎ *949/640–4000* 🌐 *www.marriott.com* 🛏 *532 rooms.*

SPORTS AND THE OUTDOORS

BOAT RENTALS

FAMILY **Balboa Boat Rentals.** You can tour Lido and Balboa isles with kayaks ($18 an hour), stand-up paddleboards ($25 an hour), small motorboats ($75 an hour), and electric boats ($80 to $95 an hour) at Balboa Boat Rentals. ✉ *510 E. Edgewater Ave.* ☎ *949/673–7200* 🌐 *www.boats4rent.com.*

BOAT TOURS

FAMILY **Catalina Flyer.** At Balboa Pavilion, the Catalina Flyer operates a 90-minute daily round-trip passage to Catalina Island for $70. Reservations are required; check the schedule in January and February, as crossings may be canceled due to annual maintenance. ✉ *400 Main St.* ☎ *949/673–5245* 🌐 *www.catalinainfo.com.*

Hornblower Cruises & Events. This operator books three-hour weekend dinner cruises with dancing for $87. The two-hour Sunday brunch cruise starts at $68. Cruises traverse the mostly placid and scenic waters of Newport Harbor. ✉ *2431 W. Coast Hwy.* ☎ *888/467–6256* 🌐 *www.hornblower.com.*

FISHING

FAMILY **Davey's Locker.** In addition to a complete tackle shop, Davey's Locker offers half-day sportfishing trips starting at $41.50. Whale-watching excursions begin at $26 for weekdays. ✉ *Balboa Pavilion, 400 Main St.* ☎ *949/673–1434* 🌐 *www.daveyslocker.com.*

4

SHOPPING

Fodor'sChoice **Fashion Island.** Shake the sand out of your shoes to head inland to the
★ ritzy Fashion Island outdoor mall, a cluster of arcades and courtyards
complete with koi pond, fountains, and a family-friendly trolley—plus
some awesome ocean views. It has the luxe department stores Neiman
Marcus and Bloomingdale's, plus expensive spots like Jonathan Adler,
Kate Spade, and Michael Stars. ⊠ *401 Newport Center Dr., between
Jamboree and MacArthur Blvds., off PCH* ☎ *949/721–2000, 855/658–
8527* ⊕ *www.shopfashionisland.com.*

LAGUNA BEACH

*10 miles south of Newport Beach on PCH, 60 miles south of Los
Angeles on I-5 south to Hwy. 133, which turns into Laguna Canyon Rd.*

Fodor'sChoice Driving in along Laguna Canyon Road from the I-405 freeway gives
★ you the chance to cruise through a gorgeous coastal canyon, large
stretches of which remain undeveloped, before arriving at a glistening
wedge of ocean.

Laguna's welcome mat is legendary. On the corner of Forest and Park
avenues is a gate proclaiming, "This gate hangs well and hinders none,
refresh and rest, then travel on." A gay community has long been established here; art galleries dot the village streets, and there's usually someone daubing up in Heisler Park. Along the Pacific Coast Highway you'll
find dozens of clothing boutiques, jewelry stores, and cafés.

ESSENTIALS

Visitor Information Visit Laguna Beach Visitors Center. ⊠ *381 Forest Ave.*
☎ *949/497–9229, 800/877–1115* ⊕ *www.visitlagunabeach.com.*

EXPLORING

Laguna Art Museum. This museum displays American art, with an
emphasis on California artists from all periods. Special exhibits
change quarterly. ⊠ *307 Cliff Dr.* ☎ *949/494–8971* ⊕ *www.lagunaart-
museum.org* ▨ *$7* ⊙ *Closed Wed.*

Festival of Arts and Pageant of the Masters. An outdoor amphitheater near
the mouth of the canyon hosts the annual Pageant of the Masters,
Laguna's most impressive event. Local participants arrange tableaux
vivants, in which live models and carefully orchestrated backgrounds
merge in striking mimicry of classical and contemporary paintings.
The pageant is part of the **Festival of Arts,** held in July and August;
tickets are in high demand, so plan ahead. ⊠ *650 Laguna Canyon Rd.*
☎ *949/497–6582, 800/487–3378* ⊕ *www.foapom.com.*

BEACHES

FAMILY **1,000 Steps Beach.** Off South Coast Highway at 9th Street, 1,000 Steps
Beach is a hard-to-find spot tucked away in a neighborhood with
great waves and hard-packed, white sand. There aren't really 1,000
steps down (but when you hike back up, it'll certainly feel like it).
Sea caves and tide pools enhance this already beautiful natural spot.
Amenities: parking. **Best for:** sunset; surfing; swimming. ⊠ *S. Coast
Hwy., at 9th St.*

FAMILY Fodor's Choice ★ **Main Beach Park.** A stocky 1920s lifeguard tower marks Main Beach Park, where a wooden boardwalk separates the sand from a strip of lawn. Walk along this soft-sand beach, or grab a bench and watch people bodysurfing, playing volleyball, or scrambling around two half-basketball courts. The beach also has children's play equipment. Most of Laguna's hotels are within a short (but hilly) walk. **Amenities:** lifeguards; showers; toilets. **Best for:** sunset; swimming; walking. ✉ *Broadway at S. Coast Hwy.* 🌐 *www.visitlagunabeach.com.*

FAMILY **Wood's Cove.** Off South Coast Highway, Wood's Cove is especially quiet during the week. Big rock formations hide lurking crabs. This is a prime scuba-diving spot, and at high tide much of the beach is underwater. Climbing the steps to leave, you can see a Tudor-style mansion that was once home to Bette Davis. Street parking is limited. **Amenities:** none. **Best for:** snorkeling; scuba diving; sunset. ✉ *Diamond St. and Ocean Way* 🌐 *www.visitlagunabeach.com.*

WHERE TO EAT

$$$ INTERNATIONAL 🍴 **Sapphire Laguna.** This Laguna Beach establishment set in a historic Craftsman is part gourmet pantry (a must-stop for your every picnic need) and part global dining adventure. Iranian-born chef Azmin Ghahreman takes you on a journey through Europe and Asia with dishes ranging from a summer vegetable gazpacho to banana-curried black cod. **Known for:** cheese selection; weekend brunch; pet-friendly patio. [$] *Average main: $27* ✉ *The Old Pottery Place, 1200 S. Coast Hwy.* ☎ *949/715–9888* 🌐 *www.sapphirelaguna.com.*

$$$$ MODERN AMERICAN Fodor's Choice ★ 🍴 **Studio.** In a nod to Laguna's art history, Studio has house-made specialties that entice the eye as well as the palate. The restaurant occupies its own Craftsman-style bungalow, atop a 50-foot bluff overlooking the Pacific. **Known for:** attentive service; chef's tasting menu; great for special occasions. [$] *Average main: $55* ✉ *Montage Laguna Beach, 30801 S. Coast Hwy.* ☎ *949/715–6420* 🌐 *www.studiolagunabeach.com* 🕒 *Closed Mon. No lunch.*

$ MEXICAN 🍴 **Taco Loco.** This may look like a fast-food taco stand, and the hemp brownies on the menu may make you think the kitchen's *really* laid-back, but the quality of the food here equals that in many higher-price restaurants. Some Mexican standards get a Louisiana twist, like Cajun-spiced seafood tacos. **Known for:** vegetarian tacos; sidewalk seating; surfer clientele. [$] *Average main: $9* ✉ *640 S. Coast Hwy.* ☎ *949/497–1635* 🌐 *www.tacoloco.net.*

$ VEGETARIAN FAMILY 🍴 **Zinc Café & Market.** Families flock to this small Laguna Beach institution for reasonably priced breakfast and lunch options. Try the signature quiches or poached egg dishes in the morning, or swing by later in the day for healthy salads, house-made soups, quesadillas, or pizzettes. **Known for:** gourmet goodies; avocado toast; busy outdoor patio. [$] *Average main: $15* ✉ *350 Ocean Ave.* ☎ *949/494–6302* 🌐 *www.zinccafe.com* 🕒 *No dinner Nov.–Apr.*

WHERE TO STAY

$$$$ HOTEL FAMILY 🏨 **Inn at Laguna Beach.** On a bluff overlooking the ocean, this inn is steps from the surf. **Pros:** large rooms; oceanfront location; sustainable design. **Cons:** ocean-view rooms are pricey; rooms on highway can be

noisy. $ *Rooms from: $379* ⊠ *211 N. Coast Hwy.* ☎ *949/497–9722, 800/544–4479* ⊕ *www.innatlagunabeach.com* ⮎ *70 rooms.*

$$$
HOTEL

⊡ **La Casa del Camino.** The look is Old California at the 1929-built La Casa del Camino, with dark woods, arched doors, and wrought iron in the lobby. **Pros:** breathtaking views from rooftop lounge; personable service; close to beach. **Cons:** some rooms face the highway; frequent events can make hotel noisy; some rooms are very small. $ *Rooms from: $229* ⊠ *1289 S. Coast Hwy.* ☎ *949/497–2446, 855/634–5736* ⊕ *www.lacasadelcamino.com* ⮎ *36 rooms* ⦅◎⦆ *No meals.*

$$$$
RESORT
FAMILY
Fodor's Choice
★

⊡ **Montage Laguna Beach.** Laguna's connection to the Californian plein-air artists is mined for inspiration at this head-turning, lavish hotel. **Pros:** top-notch, enthusiastic service; idyllic coastal location; numerous sporty pursuits available offshore. **Cons:** multi-night stays required on weekends and holidays; $40 valet parking; $38 daily resort fee. $ *Rooms from: $695* ⊠ *30801 S. Coast Hwy.* ☎ *949/715–6000, 866/271–6953* ⊕ *www.montagehotels.com/lagunabeach* ⮎ *248 rooms* ⦅◎⦆ *No meals.*

$$$$
RESORT

⊡ **Surf & Sand Resort.** One mile south of downtown, on an exquisite stretch of beach with thundering waves and gorgeous rocks, this is a getaway for those who want a boutique hotel experience without all the formalities. **Pros:** easy beach access; intimate property; slightly removed from Main Street crowds. **Cons:** pricey valet parking; surf can be quite loud. $ *Rooms from: $575* ⊠ *1555 S. Coast Hwy.* ☎ *949/497–4477, 877/741–5908* ⊕ *www.surfandsandresort. com* ⮎ *167 rooms* ⦅◎⦆ *No meals.*

NIGHTLIFE AND PERFORMING ARTS

Laguna Playhouse. Dating back to the 1920s, the Laguna Playhouse mounts a variety of productions, from classics to youth-oriented plays. ⊠ *606 Laguna Canyon Rd.* ☎ *949/497–2787* ⊕ *www.lagunaplayhouse.com.*

Sandpiper Lounge. A hole-in-the-wall joint with live music, the Sandpiper Lounge attracts an eclectic crowd. ⊠ *1183 S. Coast Hwy.* ☎ *949/494–4694.*

White House. This hip club on the main strip has nightly entertainment and dancing, which begins at 9:30 nightly. From early morning on, it's also a landmark Laguna Beach restaurant serving pasta, burgers, and brunch favorites. ⊠ *340 S. Coast Hwy.* ☎ *949/494–8088* ⊕ *www. whitehouserestaurant.com.*

SHOPPING

Coast Highway, Forest and Ocean avenues, and Glenneyre Street are full of art galleries, fine jewelry stores, and clothing boutiques.

Adam Neeley Fine Art Jewelry. Be prepared to be dazzled at Adam Neeley Fine Art Jewelry, where artisan proprietor Adam Neeley creates one-of-a-kind modern pieces. ⊠ *352 N. Coast Hwy.* ☎ *949/715–0953* ⊕ *www. adamneeley.com* ◷ *Closed Sun. and Mon.*

Art for the Soul. A riot of color, Art for the Soul has hand-painted furniture, crafts, and unusual gifts. ⊠ *272 Forest Ave.* ☎ *949/497–8700* ⊕ *www.art4thesoul.com.*

Fetneh Blake. Hit Fetneh Blake for pricey, Euro-chic clothes. The emerging designers found here lure Angelenos to make the trek south. ⊠ *427 N. Coast Hwy.* ☎ *949/494–3787* ⊕ *www.fetnehblake.com.*

La Rue du Chocolat. This shop dispenses chocolate-covered strawberries and handcrafted chocolates in seasonal flavors. ✉ *Peppertree La., 448 S. Coast Hwy., Suite B* ☎ *949/494–2372* 🌐 *www.larueduchocolat.com.*

SAN JUAN CAPISTRANO

5 miles north of Dana Point via Hwy. 74, 60 miles north of San Diego via I-5.

San Juan Capistrano is best known for its historic mission, where the swallows traditionally return each year, migrating from their winter haven in Argentina (though these days they are more likely to choose other local sites for nesting). St. Joseph's Day, March 19, launches a week of fowl festivities. Charming antiques stores, which range from pricey to cheap, line Camino Capistrano.

GETTING HERE AND AROUND

If you arrive by train, which is far more romantic and restful than battling freeway traffic, you'll be dropped off across from the mission at the San Juan Capistrano depot. With its appealing brick café and preserved Santa Fe cars, the depot retains much of the magic of early American railroads. If driving, park near Ortega and Camino Capistrano, the city's main streets.

EXPLORING

FAMILY Fodor's Choice ★ **Mission San Juan Capistrano.** Founded in 1776 by Father Junípero Serra, Mission San Juan Capistrano was one of two Roman Catholic outposts between Los Angeles and San Diego. The Great Stone Church, begun in 1797, is the largest structure created by the Spanish in California. Many of the mission's adobe buildings have been preserved to illustrate mission life, with exhibits of an olive millstone, tallow ovens, tanning vats, metalworking furnaces, and the padres' living quarters. The gardens, with their fountains, are a lovely spot in which to wander. The bougainvillea-covered Serra Chapel is believed to be the oldest church still standing in California, and is the only building remaining in which Fr. Serra actually led Mass. Mass takes place weekdays at 7 am in the chapel. Enter via a small gift shop in the gatehouse. ✉ *Camino Capistrano and Ortega Hwy.* ☎ *949/234–1300* 🌐 *www.missionsjc.com* 🎟 *$9.*

FAMILY **San Juan Capistrano Library.** Near Mission San Juan Capistrano is the San Juan Capistrano Library, a postmodern structure built in 1983. Architect Michael Graves combined classical and Mission styles to striking effect. Its courtyard has secluded places for reading. ✉ *31495 El Camino Real* ☎ *949/493–1752* 🌐 *ocpl.org/libloc/sjc* 🕒 *Closed Fri.*

WHERE TO EAT

$$$ AMERICAN FAMILY 🍴 **Cedar Creek Inn.** Just across the street from Mission San Juan Capistrano, this restaurant has a patio that's perfect for a late lunch or a romantic dinner. The menu is fairly straightforward, dishes are tasty, and portions are substantial—try the Monte Cristo or a burger at lunch, or splurge on the prime rib for dinner. **Known for:** brunch; rich desserts; comfortable seating. [$] *Average main: $30* ✉ *26860 Ortega Hwy.* ☎ *949/240–2229* 🌐 *www.cedarcreekinn.com.*

Mission San Juan Capistrano

$$$$ FRENCH 🍴 **L'Hirondelle.** Locals have romanced at cozy tables for decades at this delightful restaurant. Such classic dishes as beef bourguignonne and a New York strip in a black peppercorn and brandy sauce are the hallmark of this French and Belgian restaurant, whose name means "the little swallow." The extensive wine list is matched by an impressive selection of Belgian beers. **Known for:** Sunday brunch; traditional French cuisine; composed salads. [$] *Average main: $32* ✉ *31631 Camino Capistrano* ☎ *949/661–0425* 🌐 *www.lhirondellesjc.com* 🕒 *Closed Mon.*

$$ AMERICAN 🍴 **The Ramos House Cafe.** It may be worth hopping the Amtrak to San Juan Capistrano just for the chance to have breakfast or lunch at one of Orange County's most beloved restaurants located in an historic board-and-batten home dating back to 1881. This café sits practically on the railroad tracks across from the depot—nab a table on the patio and dig into a hearty breakfast, such as the smoked bacon scramble. **Known for:** Southern specialties; weekend brunch; historic setting. [$] *Average main: $20* ✉ *31752 Los Rios St.* ☎ *949/443–1342* 🌐 *www.ramoshouse.com* 🕒 *Closed Mon. No dinner.*

NIGHTLIFE

Swallow's Inn. Across the way from Mission San Juan Capistrano you'll spot a line of Harleys in front of the Swallow's Inn. Despite a somewhat tough look, it attracts all kinds—bikers, surfers, modern-day cowboys, grandparents—for a drink, a casual bite, karaoke nights, and some rowdy live country music. ✉ *31786 Camino Capistrano* ☎ *949/493–3188* 🌐 *www.swallowsinn.com.*

CATALINA ISLAND

Fodor's Choice
★

Just 22 miles out from the L.A. coastline, across from Newport Beach and Long Beach, Catalina has virtually unspoiled mountains, canyons, coves, and beaches; best of all, it gives you a glimpse of what undeveloped Southern California once looked like.

Water sports are a big draw, as divers and snorkelers come for the exceptionally clear water surrounding the island. Kayakers are attracted to the calm cove waters and thrill seekers have made the eco-themed zip line so popular that there are nighttime tours via flashlight in summer. The main town, Avalon, is a charming, old-fashioned beach community, where yachts and pleasure boats bob in the crescent bay. Wander beyond the main drag and find brightly painted little bungalows fronting the sidewalks; golf carts are the preferred mode of transport.

In 1919 William Wrigley Jr., the chewing-gum magnate, purchased a controlling interest in the company developing Catalina Island, whose most famous landmark, the Casino, was built in 1929 under his orders. Because he owned the Chicago Cubs baseball team, Wrigley made Catalina the team's spring training site, an arrangement that lasted until 1951.

In 1975 the Catalina Island Conservancy, a nonprofit foundation, acquired about 88% of the island to help preserve the area's natural flora and fauna, including the bald eagle and the Catalina Island fox. These days the conservancy is restoring the rugged interior country with plantings of native grasses and trees. Along the coast you might spot oddities like electric perch, saltwater goldfish, and flying fish.

GETTING HERE AND AROUND

BUS TRAVEL

Catalina Safari Shuttle Bus has regular bus service (in season) between Avalon, Two Harbors, and several campgrounds. The trip between Avalon and Two Harbors takes two hours and costs $54 one-way.

Bus Contacts Catalina Safari Shuttle Bus. ☎ *310/510–4205, 877/778–8322.*

FERRY TRAVEL

Two companies offer ferry service to Catalina Island. The boats have both indoor and outdoor seating and snack bars. Excessive baggage is not allowed, and there are extra fees for bicycles and surfboards. The waters around Santa Catalina can get rough, so if you're prone to seasickness, come prepared. Winter, holiday, and weekend schedules vary, so reservations are recommended.

Catalina Express makes an hour-long run from Long Beach or San Pedro to Avalon and a 90-minute run from Dana Point to Avalon with some stops at Two Harbors. Round-trip fares begin at $73.50, with discounts for seniors and kids. On busy days a $15 upgrade to the Commodore Lounge, when available, is worth it. Service from Newport Beach to Avalon is available through the Catalina Flyer. Boats leave from Balboa Pavilion at 9 am (in season), take 75 minutes to reach the island, and cost $70 round-trip. Return boats leave Catalina at 4:30 pm. Reservations are required for the Catalina Flyer and recommended for all weekend and summer trips. ■TIP→ **Keep an eye out for dolphins, which sometimes swim alongside the ferries.**

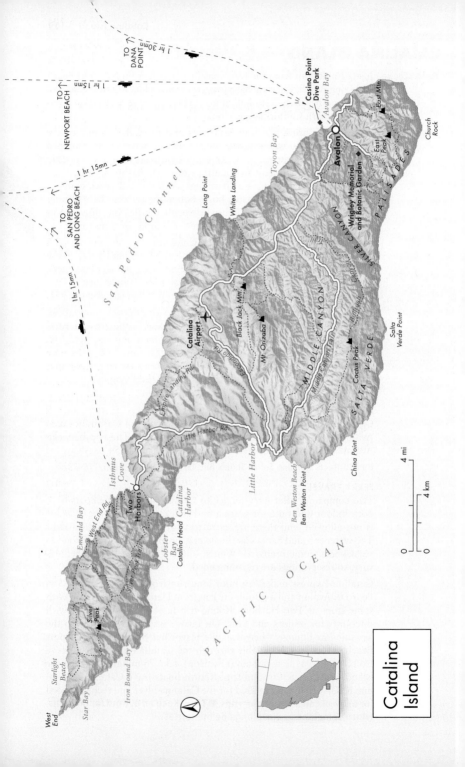

Catalina Island

Ferry Contacts **Catalina Express.** ☎ *800/481–3470, 562/485–3300* ⊕ *www. catalinaexpress.com.* **Catalina Flyer.** ☎ *949/673–5245* ⊕ *www.catalinainfo.com.*

GOLF CARTS

Golf carts constitute the island's main form of transportation for sight-seeing in the area, however some parts of town are off limits, as is the island's interior. You can rent them along Avalon's Crescent Avenue and Pebbly Beach Road for about $40 per hour with a $40 deposit, payable via cash or traveler's check only.

Golf Cart Rentals Island Rentals. ⊠ *125 Pebbly Beach Rd., Avalon* ☎ *310/510–1456* ⊕ *www.catalinagolfcartrentals.com.*

HELICOPTER TRAVEL

Island Express helicopters depart hourly from San Pedro, Santa Ana, and Long Beach next to the retired *Queen Mary* (8 am–dusk). The trip from Long Beach takes about 15 minutes and costs $125 one-way, $250 round-trip (plus tax). Winter rates are lower. Reservations a week in advance are recommended.

Helicopter Contacts Island Express. ☎ *800/228–2566* ⊕ *www.islandexpress.com.*

TIMING

Although Catalina can be seen in one very hectic day, several inviting hotels make it worth extending your stay for one or more nights. A short itinerary might include breakfast on the pier, a tour of the interior, a snorkeling excursion at Casino Point, or a beach day at the Descanso Beach Club and a romantic waterfront dinner in Avalon.

After late October, rooms are much easier to find on short notice, rates drop dramatically, and many hotels offer packages that include transportation from the mainland and/or sightseeing tours. January to March you have a good chance of spotting migrating gray whales on the ferry crossing.

TOURS

FAMILY **Catalina Adventure Tours.** Catalina Adventure Tours, which has booths at the boat landing and on the pier, arranges tours inland as well as on the water via glass-bottom boat and other crafts. ☎ *877/510–2888* ⊕ *www.catalinaadventuretours.com.*

Catalina Island Conservancy. The Catalina Island Conservancy organizes custom ecotours and hikes of the interior. Naturalist guides drive open Jeeps through some gorgeously untrammeled parts of the island. Tours start at $70 per person for a two-hour trip (two-person minimum); you can also book half- and full-day tours. The tours run year-round. ⊠ *125 Claressa Ave., Avalon* ☎ *310/510–2595* ⊕ *www.catalinaconservancy.org.*

FAMILY **Santa Catalina Island Company.** Santa Catalina Island Company runs 15 land and sea tours, including the Flying Fish boat trip (summer evenings only); a comprehensive inland motor tour; a tour of Skyline Drive; several Casino tours; a scenic tour of Avalon; a glass-bottom boat tour; an undersea tour on a semisubmersible vessel; an eco-themed zip-line tour that traverses a scenic canyon; a speedy Ocean Runner expedition that searches for all manner of sea creatures.

Reservations are highly recommended for the inland tours. Tours cost $13 to $129. There are ticket booths on the Green Pleasure Pier, at the Casino, in the plaza, and at the boat landing. ✉ *Avalon* ☎ *877/778–8322* ⊕ *www.visitcatalinaisland.com.*

VISITOR INFORMATION

Visitor Contacts Catalina Island Chamber of Commerce & Visitors Bureau. ✉ *1 Green Pleasure Pier, Avalon* ☎ *310/510–1520* ⊕ *www.catalinachamber.com.*

AVALON

A 1- to 2-hour ferry ride from Long Beach, Newport Beach, or San Pedro; a 15-minute helicopter ride from Long Beach or San Pedro, slightly longer from Santa Ana.

Avalon, Catalina's only real town, extends from the shore of its natural harbor to the surrounding hillsides. Its resident population is about 3,800, but it swells with tourists on summer weekends. Most of the city's activity, however, is centered on the pedestrian mall on Crescent Avenue, and most sights are easily reached on foot. Private cars are restricted, and rental cars aren't allowed, but taxis, trams, and shuttles can take you anywhere you need to go. Bicycles, electric bikes, and golf carts can be rented from shops along Crescent Avenue.

EXPLORING

Fodor'sChoice
★
Casino. This circular white structure is one of the finest examples of art deco architecture anywhere. Its Spanish-inspired floors and murals gleam with brilliant blue and green Catalina tiles. In this case, *casino,* the Italian word for "gathering place," has nothing to do with gambling. First-run movies are screened nightly at the Avalon Theatre, noteworthy for its classic 1929 theater pipe organ and art deco wall murals.

The Santa Catalina Island Company leads two tours of the Casino—the 30-minute basic tour ($13) and the 90-minute behind-the-scenes tour ($27), which leads visitors through the green room and into the Wrigleys' private lounge. ✉ *1 Casino Way* ☎ *310/510–0179 theater* ⊕ *www.visitcatalinaisland.com.*

Casino Point Dive Park. In front of the Casino are the crystal-clear waters of the Casino Point Dive Park, a protected marine preserve where moray eels, bat rays, spiny lobsters, harbor seals, and other sea creatures cruise around kelp forests and along the sandy bottom. It's a terrific site for scuba diving, with some shallow areas suitable for snorkeling. Equipment can be rented on and near the pier. The shallow waters of Lover's Cove, east of the boat landing, are also good for snorkeling. ✉ *Avalon.*

Wrigley Memorial and Botanic Garden. Two miles south of the bay is Wrigley Memorial and Botanic Garden, home to plants native to Southern California. Several grow only on Catalina Island—Catalina ironwood, wild tomato, and rare Catalina mahogany. The Wrigley family commissioned the garden as well as the monument, which has a grand staircase and a Spanish-style mausoleum inlaid with colorful Catalina tile. Wrigley Jr. was once buried here but his remains were moved to Pasadena during the Second World War. ✉ *Avalon Canyon Rd.* ☎ *310/510–2897* ⊕ *www.catalinaconservancy.org* ▣ *$7.*

WHERE TO EAT

$$$ ✕ **Bluewater Grill.** Overlooking the ferry landing and the entire harbor,
SEAFOOD the open-to-the-salt-air Bluewater Grill offers freshly caught fish, savory
FAMILY chowders, and all manner of shellfish. If they're on the menu, don't
miss the swordfish steak or the sand dabs. **Known for:** fresh local fish;
happy hour; harbor views. $ *Average main: $25* ✉ *306 Crescent Ave.*
☎ *310/510–3474* ⊕ *www.bluewatergrill.com.*

$$$ ✕ **The Lobster Trap.** Seafood rules at the Lobster Trap—the restaurant's
SEAFOOD owner has his own boat and fishes for the catch of the day and, in sea-
son, spiny lobster. Ceviche is a great starter, always fresh and brightly
flavored. **Known for:** locally caught seafood; convivial atmosphere;
locals' hangout. $ *Average main: $24* ✉ *128 Catalina St.* ☎ *310/510–*
8585 ⊕ *catalinalobstertrap.com.*

WHERE TO STAY

$$$ 🛏 **Aurora Hotel & Spa.** In a town dominated by historic properties, the
HOTEL Aurora is refreshingly contemporary, with a hip attitude and sleek fur-
nishings. **Pros:** trendy design; quiet location off main drag; close to res-
taurants. **Cons:** standard rooms are small, even by Catalina standards;
no elevator. $ *Rooms from: $249* ✉ *137 Marilla Ave.* ☎ *310/510–0454*
⊕ *www.auroracatalina.com* ⮐ *18 rooms* ⦿*Breakfast.*

$$$ 🛏 **Hotel Villa Portofino.** Steps from the Green Pleasure Pier, this European-
HOTEL style hotel creates an intimate feel with brick courtyards and walkways
FAMILY and suites named after Italian cities. **Pros:** romantic; close to beach;
incredible sundeck. **Cons:** ground-floor rooms can be noisy; some rooms
are on small side; no elevator. $ *Rooms from: $179* ✉ *111 Crescent*
Ave. ☎ *310/510–0555, 888/510–0555* ⊕ *www.hotelvillaportofino.com*
⮐ *35 rooms* ⦿*Breakfast.*

$$$$ 🛏 **Hotel Vista del Mar.** On the bay-facing Crescent Avenue, this third-floor
HOTEL property is steps from the beach, where complimentary towels, chairs,
FAMILY and umbrellas await guests. **Pros:** comfortable beds; central location;
modern decor. **Cons:** no restaurant or spa facilities; few rooms with
ocean views; no elevator. $ *Rooms from: $295* ✉ *417 Crescent Ave.*
☎ *310/510–1452, 800/601–3836* ⊕ *www.hotel-vistadelmar.com* ⮐ *14*
rooms ⦿*Breakfast.*

$$$$ 🛏 **Mt. Ada.** If you stay in the mansion where Wrigley Jr. once lived,
B&B/INN you can enjoy all the comforts of a millionaire's home—at a millionaire's prices. **Pros:** timeless charm; shuttle from heliport and dock;
incredible views. **Cons:** smallish rooms and bathrooms; expensive.
$ *Rooms from: $480* ✉ *398 Wrigley Rd.* ☎ *310/510–2030, 877/778–*
8322 ⊕ *www.visitcatalinaisland.com* ⦵ *Closed mid-Jan.–early Feb.*
⮐ *6 rooms* ⦿*Some meals.*

$$$$ 🛏 **Pavilion Hotel.** This mid-century-modern-style hotel is Avalon's
HOTEL most citified spot, though just a few steps from the sand. **Pros:** cen-
FAMILY trally located, steps from the beach and harbor; friendly staff; plush
bedding. **Cons:** no pool. $ *Rooms from: $265* ✉ *513 Crescent Ave.*
☎ *310/510–1788, 877/778–8322* ⊕ *www.visitcatalinaisland.com* ⮐ *71*
rooms ⦿*Breakfast.*

SPORTS AND THE OUTDOORS

BICYCLING

FAMILY **Brown's Bikes.** Look for rentals on Crescent Avenue and Pebbly Beach Road, where Brown's Bikes is located. Beach cruisers and mountain bikes start at $20 per day. Electric bikes are also on offer. ✉ *107 Pebbly Beach Rd.* ☎ *310/510–0986* ⊕ *www.catalinabiking.com.*

DIVING AND SNORKELING

The Casino Point Underwater Park, with its handful of wrecks, is best suited for diving. Lover's Cove is better for snorkeling (but you'll share the area with glass-bottom boats). Both are protected marine preserves.

Catalina Divers Supply. Head to Catalina Divers Supply to rent equipment, sign up for guided scuba and snorkel tours, and attend certification classes. It also has an outpost at the Dive Park at Casino Point. ✉ *7 Green Pleasure Pier* ☎ *310/510–0330* ⊕ *www.catalinadiverssupply.com.*

HIKING

Catalina Island Conservancy. Permits from the Catalina Island Conservancy are required for hiking into Santa Catalina Island's interior. If you plan to backpack overnight, you'll need a camping reservation. The interior is dry and desert-like; bring plenty of water, sunblock, and all necessary supplies. The permits are free and can be picked up at the main house of the conservancy or at the airport. You don't need a permit for shorter hikes, such as the one from Avalon to the Botanical Garden. The conservancy has maps of the island's east-end hikes, such as Hermit's Gulch Trail. It's possible to hike between Avalon and Two Harbors, starting at the Hogsback Gate, above Avalon, but the 28-mile journey has an elevation gain of 3,000 feet and is not for the weak. ■TIP→ For a pleasant 4-mile hike out of Avalon, take Avalon Canyon Road to the Wrigley Botanical Garden and follow the trail to Lone Pine. At the top there's an amazing view of the Palisades cliffs and, beyond them, the sea. ✉ *125 Claressa Ave.* ☎ *310/510–2595* ⊕ *www. catalinaconservancy.org.*

LOS ANGELES

WELCOME TO LOS ANGELES

TOP REASONS TO GO

★ **Stargazing:** Both through the telescope atop Griffith Park and among the residents of Beverly Hills.

★ **Eating:** From food trucks to fine dining, an unparalleled meal awaits your palate.

★ **Beaches and Boardwalks:** The dream of '80s Venice is alive in California.

★ **Shopping:** Peruse eclectic boutiques or window-shop on Rodeo Drive.

★ **Architecture:** Art deco wonders to Frank Gehry masterpieces abound.

★ **Scenic Drives:** You haven't seen the sunset until you've seen it from a winding L.A. road.

1 Downtown. Downtown L.A. shows off spectacular modern architecture with the swooping Walt Disney Concert Hall, the brand new art museum, The Broad, and the stark Cathedral of Our Lady of the Angels. The Music Center and the Museum of Contemporary Art anchor a world-class arts scene, while Olvera Street, Chinatown, and Little Tokyo reflect the city's history and diversity.

2 Hollywood and the Studios. Glitzy and tarnished, good and bad— Hollywood is just like the entertainment business itself. The Walk of Fame, TCL Chinese Theatre, Paramount Pictures, and the Hollywood Bowl keep its glamorous past alive. Universal Studios Hollywood, Warner Bros., and NBC Television Studios are in the San Fernando Valley.

3 Beverly Hills and the Westside. Go for the glamour, the restaurants, and the scene. Rodeo Drive is particularly good for a look at excess. But don't forget the Westside's cultural attractions— especially the dazzling Getty Center. West Hollywood is an area for urban indulgences—shopping, restaurants, nightlife—rather than sightseeing. Its main arteries

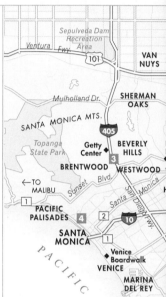

are the Sunset Strip and Melrose Avenue, lined with shops that range from punk to postmodern.

4 Santa Monica and the Beaches. These desirable beach communities move from ultrarich, ultracasual Malibu to bohemian/transitioning Venice, with liberal, Mediterranean-style Santa Monica in between.

5 Pasadena. Its own separate city, Pasadena is a quiet area with outstanding Arts and Crafts homes, good dining, and a pair of exceptional museums: Huntington Library and Norton Simon Museum.

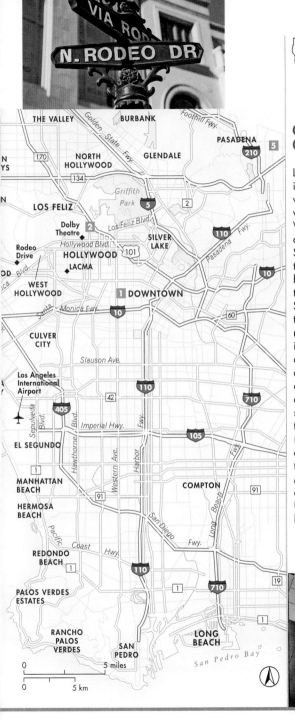

GETTING ORIENTED

Looking at a map of sprawling Los Angeles, first-time visitors are sometimes overwhelmed. Where to begin? What to see first? And what about all those freeways? Start by setting your priorities—movie and television buffs should first head to Hollywood, Universal Studios, and a taping of a television show. Beach and nature lovers might start out in Santa Monica, Venice, or Malibu, or spend an afternoon in Griffith Park, one of the country's largest city parks. Culture vultures should make a beeline for top museums: the twin Gettys (the center in Brentwood and the villa near Malibu), the Los Angeles County Museum of Art (LACMA), or Downtown's MOCA. Urban explorers might begin with Downtown L.A.

5

SOUTH-OF-THE-BORDER FLAVOR

From Cal-Mex burritos to Mexico City–style tacos, Southern California is a top stateside destination for experiencing Mexico's myriad culinary styles.

Many Americans are surprised to learn that the Mexican menu goes far beyond Tex-Mex (or Cal-Mex) favorites like burritos, chimichangas, enchiladas, fajitas, and nachos—many of which were created or popularized stateside. Indeed, Mexico has rich, regional food styles, like the complex *mole* sauces of Puebla and Oaxaca and the fresh *ceviches* of Veracruz, as well as the trademark snack of Mexico City: tacos.

In Southern California tacos are an obsession, with numerous blogs and websites dedicated to the quest for the perfect taco. They're everywhere—in ramshackle taco stands, roving trucks, and strip-mall taquerias. Whether you're looking for a cheap snack or a lunch on-the-go, SoCal's taco selection can't be beat. But be forewarned: there may not be an English menu. Here we've noted unfamiliar taco terms, along with other potentially new-to-you items from the Mexican menu.

THIRST QUENCHERS

Spanish for "fresh water," *agua fresca* is a nonalcoholic Mexican drink made from fruit, rice, or seeds that are blended with sugar and water. Fruit flavors like lemon, lime, and watermelon are common. Other varieties include *agua de Jamaica*, flavored with red hibiscus petals; *agua de horchata*, a cinnamon-scented rice milk; and *agua de tamarindo*, a bittersweet variety flavored with tamarind. For something with more of a kick, try a *Michelada*, a beer with a mixture of lime juice, chili sauce, and other savory ingredients. It's typically served in a salt-rimmed glass with ice.

DECODING THE MENU

Ceviche—Citrus-marinated raw seafood appetizer from the Gulf shores of Veracruz. Often eaten with tortilla chips.

Chile relleno—Roasted poblano pepper that is stuffed with ingredients like ground meat or cheese, then dipped in egg batter, fried, and served in tomato sauce.

Clayuda—An Oaxacan dish similar to pizza. Large corn tortillas are baked until hard, then topped with ingredients like refried beans, cheese, and salsa.

Fish taco—A specialty in Southern California, the fish taco is a soft corn tortilla stuffed with grilled or fried white fish (mahimahi, tilapia, or wahoo), pico de gallo, *crema*, and shredded cabbage.

Gordita—"Little fat one" in Spanish, this dish is like a taco, but the cornmeal shell is thicker, similar to pita bread.

Mole—A complex, sweet sauce with Aztec roots made from more than 20 ingredients, including chilies, cinnamon, cumin, anise, black pepper, sesame seeds, and Mexican chocolate. There are many types of mole using various chilies and ingredient combinations, but the most common is *mole poblano* from the Puebla region.

Quesadilla—A snack made from a fresh tortilla that is folded over and stuffed with simple fillings like cheese, then toasted on a griddle. Elevated versions

of the quesadilla may be stuffed with sautéed *flor de calabaza* (squash blossoms) or *huitlacoche* (corn mushrooms).

Salsa—A class of cooked or raw sauces made from chilies, tomatoes, and other ingredients. Popular salsas include *pico de gallo*, a fresh sauce made from chopped tomatoes, onions, chilies, cilantro, and lime; *salsa verde*, made with tomatillos instead of tomatoes; and *salsa roja*, a cooked sauce made with chilies, tomatoes, onion, garlic, and cilantro.

Sopes—A small, fried corn cake topped with ingredients like refried beans, shredded chicken, and salsa.

Taco—In Southern California, as in Mexico, tacos are made from soft, palm-sized corn tortillas folded over and filled with meat, chopped onion, cilantro, and salsa. Common taco fillings include *al pastor* (spiced pork), *barbacoa* (braised beef), *carnitas* (roasted pork), *cecina* (chili-coated pork), *carne asada* (roasted, chopped beef), *chorizo* (spicy sausage), *lengua* (beef tongue), *sesos* (cow brain), and *tasajo* (spiced, grilled beef).

Tamales—Sweet or savory corn cakes that are steamed, and may be filled with cheese, roasted chilies, shredded meat, or other fillings.

Torta—A Mexican sandwich served on a crusty sandwich roll. Fillings often include meat, refried beans, and cheese.

5

Updated
by Michele
Bigley, Alene
Dawson, Paul
Feinstein,
Ashley Tibbits,
and Clarissa
Wei

Los Angeles is a polarizing place, but those who hate it just haven't found their niche—there's truly a corner of the city for everyone. Drive for miles between towering palm trees, bodega-lined streets, and Downtown's skyscrapers, and you'll still never discover all of L.A.'s hidden gems.

Yes, you'll encounter traffic-clogged freeways, but there are also walkable pockets like Venice's Abbot Kinney. You'll drive past Beverly Hills mansions and spy palaces perched atop hills, but you'll also see the roots of midcentury modern architecture in Silver Lake. You'll soak up the sun in Santa Monica and then find yourself barhopping in the city's revitalized Downtown while enjoying scrumptious fish tacos along the way.

You might think that you'll have to spend most of your visit in a car, but that's not the case. In fact, exploring by foot is the only way to really get to know the various fringe neighborhoods and mini-cities that make up the vast L.A. area. But no single locale—whether it's Malibu, Downtown, Beverly Hills, or Burbank—fully embodies Los Angeles. It's in the mix that you'll discover the city's character.

PLANNING

WHEN TO GO

Almost any time of the year is the right time to go to Los Angeles; the climate is mild and pleasant year-round. Winter brings crisp, sunny, unusually smogless days from about November to May (expect brief rains from December to April). Los Angeles summers, which are virtually rainless, can lead to air-quality alerts. Prices skyrocket and reservations are a must when tourism peaks from July through early October.

GETTING HERE AND AROUND

AIR TRAVEL

It's generally easier to navigate the secondary airports than to get through sprawling LAX, the city's major gateway. Bob Hope Airport in Burbank is closest to Downtown, and domestic flights to it can be cheaper than those to LAX—it's definitely worth checking out. From Long Beach Airport it's equally convenient to go north to central Los Angeles or south to Orange County. Flights to Orange County's John Wayne Airport are often more expensive than those to the other secondary airports. Parking at the smaller airports is cheaper than at LAX.

At LAX, SuperShuttle allows walk-on shuttle passengers without prior reservations. FlyAway buses travel between LAX and Van Nuys, Westwood, La Brea, and Union Station in Downtown.

Airports Hollywood Burbank Airport (*BUR*). ✉ *2627 N. Hollywood Way, near I-5 and U.S. 101, Burbank* ☎ *818/840–8840* ⊕ *www.bobhopeairport.com.* **John Wayne Airport** (*SNA*). ✉ *18601 Airport Way, Santa Ana* ☎ *949/252–5200* ⊕ *www.ocair.com.* **L.A./Ontario International Airport** (*ONT*). ✉ *E. Airport Dr., off I-10, Ontario* ☎ *909/937–2700* ⊕ *www.flyontario.com.* **Long Beach Airport** (*LGB*). ✉ *4100 Donald Douglas Dr., Long Beach* ☎ *562/570–2600* ⊕ *www.lgb. org.* **Los Angeles International Airport** (*LAX*). ✉ *1 World Way, off Hwy. 1* ☎ *855/463–5252* ⊕ *www.lawa.org.*

Shuttles FlyAway. ☎ *866/435–9529* ⊕ *www.lawa.org/flyaway.* **SuperShuttle.** ☎ *323/775–6600, 800/258–3826* ⊕ *www.supershuttle.com.*

BUS TRAVEL

Inadequate public transportation has plagued L.A. for decades. That said, many local trips can be made, with time and patience, by buses run by the Los Angeles County Metropolitan Transit Authority. In certain cases—visiting the Getty Center, for instance, or Universal Studios—buses may be your best option. There's a special Dodger Stadium Express that shuttles passengers between Union Station and the ballpark for home games. It's free if you have a ticket in hand, and saves you parking-related stress.

Metro Buses cost $1.75, plus 50¢ for each transfer to another bus or to the subway. A one-day pass costs $7, and a weekly pass is $25 for unlimited travel on all buses and trains. Passes are valid from Sunday through Saturday. For the fastest service, look for the red-and-white Metro Rapid buses; these stop less frequently and are able to extend green lights. There are 25 Metro Rapid routes, including along Wilshire and Vermont boulevards.

Other bus services make it possible to explore the entire metropolitan area. DASH minibuses cover six different circular routes in Hollywood, Mid-Wilshire, and Downtown. You pay 50¢ every time you get on. The Santa Monica Municipal Bus Line, also known as the Big Blue Bus, is a pleasant and inexpensive way to move around the Westside. Trips cost $1, and transfers are free. An express bus to and from Downtown L.A., run by Culver CityBus, costs $1.

Bus Information Culver CityBus. ☎ *310/253–6510* ⊕ *www.culvercity.org.* **DASH.** ☎ *310/808–2273* ⊕ *www.ladottransit.com.* **Los Angeles County Metropolitan Transit Authority.** ☎ *323/466–3876* ⊕ *www.metro.net.* **Santa Monica Municipal Bus Line.** ☎ *310/451–5444* ⊕ *www.bigbluebus.com.*

CAR TRAVEL

If you're used to driving in a congested urban area, you shouldn't have too much trouble navigating the streets of Los Angeles. If not, L.A. can be unnerving. Nevertheless, the city evolved with drivers in mind. Streets are wide and parking garages abound, so it's more car-friendly than many older big cities.

Remember that most freeways are known by a name and a number; for example, the San Diego Freeway is Interstate 405 (or just The 405), the Hollywood Freeway is U.S. 101, the Ventura Freeway is a different stretch of U.S. 101, the Santa Monica Freeway is Interstate 10, and the Harbor Freeway is Interstate 110. It helps, too, to know which direction you're traveling; say, west toward Santa Monica or east toward Downtown Los Angeles. Distance in miles doesn't mean much, depending on the time of day you're traveling: the short 10-mile drive between the San Fernando Valley and Downtown Los Angeles might take an hour to travel during rush hour but only 20 minutes at other times.

There are plenty of identical or similarly named streets in L.A. (Beverly Boulevard and Beverly Drive, for example), so be as specific as you can when asking directions. Expect sudden changes in addresses as streets pass through neighborhoods, then incorporated cities, then back into neighborhoods. This can be most bewildering on Robertson Boulevard, an otherwise useful north–south artery that, by crossing through L.A., West Hollywood, and Beverly Hills, dips in and out of several such numbering shifts in a matter of miles.

Information Caltrans Current Highway Conditions. ☎ *800/427–7623 for road conditions* ⊕ *www.dot.ca.gov.*

Emergency Services Metro Freeway Service Patrol. ☎ *511 for breakdowns* ⊕ *www.go511.com.*

METRO RAIL TRAVEL

Metro Rail covers only a small part of L.A.'s vast expanse, but it's convenient, frequent, and inexpensive. Most popular with visitors is the underground Red Line, which runs from Downtown's Union Station through Mid-Wilshire, Hollywood, and Universal City on its way to North Hollywood, stopping at the most popular tourist destinations along the way.

The light-rail Green Line stretches from Redondo Beach to Norwalk, while the partially underground Blue Line travels from Downtown to the South Bay. The monorail-like Gold Line extends from Union Station to Pasadena and Sierra Madre. The Orange Line, a 14-mile bus corridor, connects the North Hollywood subway station with the western San Fernando Valley.

Most recently unveiled was the Expo Line, which connects Downtown to Culver City and ends in Santa Monica, two blocks from the Pacific Ocean.

There's daily service from about 4:30 am to 12:30 am, with departures every 5 to 15 minutes. On weekends trains run until 2 am. Buy tickets from station vending machines; fares are $1.75, or $7 for an all-day pass.

Metro Rail Information Los Angeles County Metropolitan Transit Authority. ☎ *323/466–3876* ⊕ *www.metro.net.*

TAXI AND LIMOUSINE TRAVEL

Instead of trying to hail a taxi on the street, phone one of the many taxi companies. The metered rate is $2.70 per mile, plus a $2.85 per-fare charge. Taxi rides from LAX have an additional $4 surcharge. Be aware that distances are greater than they might appear on the map, so fares add up quickly.

On the other end of the price spectrum, limousines come equipped with everything from full bars to nightclub-style sound-and-light systems. Most charge by the hour, with a three-hour minimum.

Limo Companies Apex Limo. ☎ 818/637–2277, 877/427–1777 for 24-hr pickup ⊕ www.apexlimola.com. **Dav El Chauffeured Transportation Network.** ☎ 800/922–0343 ⊕ www.davel.com. **First Class Limousine Service.** ☎ 800/400–9771 ⊕ www.first-classlimo.com. **Wilshire Limousine Services.** ☎ 888/813–8420 ⊕ www.wilshirelimousine.com.

Taxi Companies Beverly Hills Cab Co. ☎ 800/273–6611 ⊕ www.beverlyhills-cabco.com. **LA Checker Cab.** ☎ 800/300–5007 ⊕ www.ineedtaxi.com. **United Independent Taxi.** ☎ 800/822–8294, 323/207–8294 text to order taxi ⊕ www.unitedtaxi.com. **Yellow Cab Los Angeles.** ☎ 424/222–2222 ⊕ www.layellow-cab.com. **Independent Cab Co.** ☎ 800/521–8294 ⊕ www.taxi4u.com.

TRAIN TRAVEL

Downtown's Union Station is one of the great American railroad terminals. The interior includes comfortable seating, a restaurant, and several snack bars. As the city's rail hub, it's the place to catch an Amtrak or Metrolink commuter train. Among Amtrak's Southern California routes are 22 daily trips to San Diego and five to Santa Barbara. Amtrak's luxury *Coast Starlight* travels along the spectacular coastline from Seattle to Los Angeles in just a day and a half (though it's often a little late). The *Sunset Limited* arrives from New Orleans, and the *Southwest Chief* comes from Chicago.

Information Amtrak. ☎ 800/872–7245 ⊕ www.amtrak.com. **Metrolink.** ☎ 800/371–5465 ⊕ www.metrolinktrains.com. **Union Station.** ✉ 800 N. Alameda St. ☎ 213/683–6979 ⊕ www.unionstationla.com.

VISITOR INFORMATION

Discover Los Angeles publishes an annually updated general information packet with suggestions for entertainment, lodging, and dining, as well as a list of special events. There are two visitor information centers, both accessible to Metro stops: the Hollywood & Highland entertainment complex and Union Station.

Contacts Beverly Hills Conference and Visitors Bureau. ☎ 310/248–1015, 800/345–2210 ⊕ www.lovebeverlyhills.com. **Discover Los Angeles.** ☎ 213/624–7300, 800/228–2452 ⊕ www.discoverlosangeles.com. **Hollywood Chamber of Commerce.** ☎ 323/469–8311 ⊕ www.hollywoodchamber.net. **Long Beach Area Convention and Visitors Bureau.** ☎ 562/436–3645 ⊕ www.visitlongbeach.com. **Pasadena Convention & Visitor Bureau.** ☎ 800/307–7977 ⊕ www.visitpasadena.com. **Santa Monica Travel & Tourism.** ☎ 310/393–7593, 800/544–5319 ⊕ www.santamonica.com. **Visit California.** ☎ 916/444–4429, 800/862–2543 ⊕ www.visitcalifornia.com. **Visit West Hollywood.** ☎ 310/289–2525, 800/368–6020 ⊕ www.visitwesthollywood.com.

EXPLORING LOS ANGELES

Starstruck. Excessive. Smoggy. Superficial.... There's a modicum of truth to each of the adjectives regularly applied to L.A., but the locals dismiss their prevalence as envy from those who aren't as blessed with year-round sunshine.

Pop culture does permeate life here, its massive economy employing millions of Southern Californians, but the city where dreams are made accommodates those from all avenues of life.

DOWNTOWN

Updated by
Clarissa Wei

If there's one thing Angelenos love, it's a makeover, and city planners have put the wheels in motion for a dramatic revitalization. Downtown is both glamorous and gritty and is an example of Los Angeles's complexity as a whole. There's a dizzying variety of experiences not to be missed here if you're curious about the artistic, historic, ethnic, or sports-loving sides of L.A.

Downtown Los Angeles isn't just one neighborhood: it's a cluster of pedestrian-friendly enclaves where you can sample an eclectic mix of flavors, wander through world-class museums, and enjoy great live performances or sports events.

TOP ATTRACTIONS

Fodor's Choice ★ **The Broad Museum.** The talk of the Los Angeles art world when it opened in 2015, this museum in an intriguing, honeycomb-looking building created by philanthropists Eli and Edythe Broad (rhymes with "road") to showcase their stunning private collection of contemporary art, amassed over five decades and still growing. With upward of 2,000 pieces by more than 200 artists, the collection has in-depth representations of the work of such prominent names as Jean Michel Basquiat, Jeff Koons, Ed Ruscha, Cindy Sherman, Cy Twombly, Kara Walker, and Christopher Wool. The "veil and vault" design of the main building integrates gallery space and storage space (visitors can glimpse the latter through a window in the stairwell): the veil refers to the fiberglass, concrete, and steel exterior; the vault is the concrete base. Temporary exhibits and works from the permanent collection are arranged in the small first-floor rooms and in the more expansive third floor of the museum, so you can explore everything in a few hours. Next door to The Broad is a small plaza with olive trees and seating, as well as the museum restaurant, Otium. Admission to the museum is free, but book timed tickets in advance to guarantee entry. ✉ *221 S. Grand Ave., Downtown* 🕾 *213/232–6200* ⊕ *www.thebroad.org* ✉ *Free* ☉ *Closed Mon.*

FAMILY **California Science Center.** You're bound to see excited kids running up to the dozens of interactive exhibits here that illustrate the prevalence of science in everyday life. Clustered in different "worlds," the center keeps young guests busy for hours. They can design their own buildings and learn how to make them earthquake-proof; watch Tess, the dramatic 50-foot animatronic star of the exhibit "Body Works," demonstrate how the body's organs work together; and ride a bike across a trapeze wire three stories high in the air. One of the exhibits in the Air

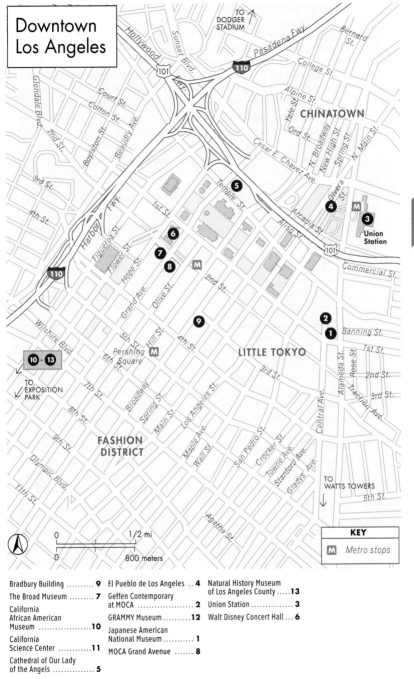

Downtown Los Angeles

& Space section shows how astronauts Pete Conrad and Dick Gordon made it to outer space in the Gemini 11 capsule in 1966; also here is NASA's massive space shuttle *Endeavor,* located in the Samuel Oschin Pavilion, for which a timed ticket is needed to visit. The IMAX theater screens science-related large-format films. ⊠ *700 Exposition Park Dr., Exposition Park* ☎ *213/744–7400, 323/724–3623* ⊕ *www.californiasciencecenter.org* ✉ *Free to permanent exhibitions; fees for some attractions, special exhibitions, and IMAX screenings vary.*

Fodor's Choice **Cathedral of Our Lady of the Angels.** A half block from Frank Gehry's cur-

★ vaceous Walt Disney Concert Hall sits the austere Cathedral of Our Lady of the Angels—a spiritual draw as well as an architectural attraction. Controversy surrounded Spanish architect José Rafael Moneo's unconventional design for the seat of the Archdiocese of Los Angeles. But judging from the swarms of visitors and the standing-room-only holiday masses, the church has carved out a niche for itself in Downtown L.A.

The plaza in front is glaringly bright on sunny days, though a children's play garden with bronze animals mitigates the starkness somewhat. Head underground to wander the mausoleum's mazelike white-marble corridors. Free guided tours start at the entrance fountain at 1 pm on weekdays. ■TIP→ **There's plenty of underground visitors parking; the vehicle entrance is on Hill Street.** ⊠ *555 W. Temple St., Downtown* ☎ *213/680–5200* ⊕ *www.olacathedral.org* ✉ *Free, parking $4 every 15 mins, $19 maximum.*

El Pueblo de Los Angeles. The oldest section of the city, known as El Pueblo de Los Angeles, represents the rich Mexican heritage of L.A. It had a close shave with disintegration in the early 20th century, but key buildings were preserved, and eventually **Olvera Street,** the district's heart, was transformed into a Mexican-American marketplace. Today vendors still sell puppets, leather goods, sandals, and woolen shawls from stalls lining the narrow street. You can find everything from salt and pepper shakers shaped like donkeys, to gorgeous glassware and pottery.

At the beginning of Olvera Street is the Plaza, a Mexican-style park with plenty of benches and walkways shaded by a huge Moreton Bay fig tree. On weekends, mariachi bands and folkloric dance groups perform. Nearby places worth investigating include the historic Avila Adobe, the Chinese American Museum, the Plaza Firehouse Museum, and the America Tropical Interpretive Center. Exhibits at the Italian American Museum of Los Angeles chronicle the area's formerly heavy Italian presence. ⊠ *Avila Adobe/Olvera Street Visitors Center, E-10 Olvera St., Downtown* ☎ *213/628–1274* ⊕ *www.elpueblo.lacity.org* ✉ *Free for Olvera St. and guided tours, fees at some museums.*

Geffen Contemporary at MOCA. The Geffen Contemporary is one of architect Frank Gehry's boldest creations. The largest of the three MOCA branches, with 40,000 square feet of exhibition space, it was once used as a police car warehouse. Works from the museum's permanent collection on display here include the artists Willem de Kooning, Franz Kline, Jackson Pollock, Mark Rothko, and Cindy Sherman. ⊠ *152 N. Central Ave., Downtown* ☎ *213/626–6222* ⊕ *www.moca.org/exhibitions* ✉ *$12; free Thurs. 5 pm–8 pm* ☉ *Closed Tues.*

Frank Gehry's Walt Disney Concert Hall became an instant L.A. icon.

GRAMMY Museum. The interactive GRAMMY Museum brings the music industry's history to life. Throughout 30,000 square feet of space, the museum shows rare footage of GRAMMY performances, plus rotating exhibits on award-winning musicians. ⊠ *800 W. Olympic Blvd., Downtown* ☎ *213/765–6800* ⊕ *www.grammymuseum.org* ✉ *$12.95.*

MOCA Grand Avenue. The main branch of the Museum of Contemporary Art, designed by Arata Isozaki, contains underground galleries and presents elegant exhibitions. A huge Nancy Rubins sculpture fashioned from used airplane parts graces the museum's front plaza. ■ TIP➔ Take advantage of the free audio tour. ⊠ *250 S. Grand Ave., Downtown* ☎ *213/626–6222* ⊕ *www.moca.org* ✉ *$12; free Thurs. 5 pm–8 pm* ☉ *Closed Tues.*

Fodor'sChoice
★

Walt Disney Concert Hall. One of the architectural wonders of Los Angeles, the 2,265-seat hall is a sculptural monument of gleaming, curved steel designed by Frank Gehry. It's part of a complex that includes a public park, gardens, shops, and two outdoor amphitheaters, one of them atop the concert hall. The acoustically superlative venue is the home of the city's premier orchestra, the Los Angeles Philharmonic, whose music director, Gustavo Dudamel, is an international celebrity in his own right. The orchestra's season runs from late September to early June, before they head to the Hollywood Bowl for the summer. The highly praised Los Angeles Master Chorale also performs here. Look for big-name acts such as Pink Martini during the off-season, and special holiday events like the Deck the Hall Holiday Sing-Along. ■ TIP➔ Free 60-minute guided tours are offered on most days, and there are self-guided audio tours. ⊠ *111 S. Grand Ave., Downtown* ☎ *323/850–2000* ⊕ *www.laphil.org* ✉ *Tours free.*

WORTH NOTING

Bradbury Building. Stunning wrought-iron railings, ornate plaster moldings, pink marble staircases, a birdcage elevator, and a skylighted atrium that rises almost 50 feet—it's easy to see why the Bradbury Building leaves visitors awestruck. Designed in 1893 by a novice architect who drew his inspiration from a science-fiction story and a conversation with his dead brother via Ouija board, the office building was originally the site of turn-of-the-20th-century sweatshops, but now it houses a variety of businesses. Scenes from *Blade Runner* and *Chinatown* were filmed here, which means there's often a barrage of tourists snapping photos. Visits are limited to the lobby and the first-floor landing. ✉ *304 S. Broadway, at 3rd St., Downtown* ☎ *213/626–1893.*

California African American Museum. With more than 3,500 historical artifacts, this museum showcases contemporary art of the African diaspora. Artists represented here include Betye Saar, Charles Haywood, and June Edmonds. The museum has a research library with more than 20,000 books available for public use. ■**TIP**➡ **If possible, visit on a Sunday, when there's almost always a diverse lineup of speakers and performances.** ✉ *600 State Dr., Exposition Park* ☎ *213/744–7432* ⊕ *www. caamuseum.org* 🖼 *Free* ⊙ *Closed Mon.*

Japanese American National Museum. What was it like to grow up on a sugar plantation in Hawaii? How difficult was life for Japanese Americans interned in concentration camps during World War II? These questions are addressed by changing exhibitions at this museum in Little Tokyo that also include fun tributes to anime and Hello Kitty. Volunteer docents are on hand to share their own stories and experiences. The museum occupies its original site in a renovated 1925 Buddhist temple and an 85,000-square-foot adjacent pavilion. ✉ *100 N. Central Ave., off E. 1st St., Downtown* ☎ *213/625–0414* ⊕ *www.janm.org* 🖼 *$10* ⊙ *Closed Mon.*

FAMILY **Natural History Museum of Los Angeles County.** The hot ticket at this beaux arts–style museum completed in 1913 is the Dinosaur Hall, whose more than 300 fossils include adult, juvenile, and baby skeletons of the fearsome Tyrannosaurus rex. The Discovery Center lets kids and curious grown-ups touch real animal pelts, and the Insect Zoo gets everyone up close and personal with the white-eyed assassin bug and other creepy crawlers. A massive hall displays dioramas of animals in their natural habitats. Also look for pre-Columbian artifacts and crafts from the South Pacific. Outdoors, the 3½-acre Nature Gardens shelter native plant and insect species and contain an expansive edible garden. ✉ *900 Exposition Blvd., off I–110, near Vermont Ave., Exposition Park* ☎ *213/763–3466* ⊕ *www.nhm.org* 🖼 *$12.*

Union Station. Even if you don't plan on traveling by train anywhere, head here to soak up the ambience of a great rail station. Envisioned by John and Donald Parkinson, the architects who also designed the grand City Hall, the 1939 masterpiece combines Spanish Colonial Revival and art deco elements that have retained their classic warmth and quality. The waiting hall's commanding scale and enormous chandeliers have provided the backdrop for countless scenes in films, TV shows, and music videos. ✉ *800 N. Alameda St., Downtown* ⊕ *www.unionstationla.com.*

HOLLYWOOD AND THE STUDIOS

Updated by
Clarissa Wei

The Tinseltown mythology of Los Angeles was born in Hollywood. Daytime attractions can be found on foot around the home of the Academy Awards at the Dolby Theatre, part of the Hollywood & Highland entertainment complex. The adjacent TCL Chinese Theatre delivers silver screen magic with its cinematic facade and ornate interiors from a bygone era. Walk the renowned Hollywood Walk of Stars to find your favorite celebrities' hand- and footprints. In summer, visit the crown jewel of Hollywood, the Hollywood Bowl, which hosts the Los Angeles Philharmonic.

To the north is Studio City, a thriving commercial strip at the base of the Hollywood Hills that's home to many smaller film companies and lunching studio execs; Universal City, where you'll find Universal Studios Hollywood; and bustling Burbank, home of several of the major studios. In Los Feliz, to the east, Griffith Park connects L.A.'s largest greenbelt with the trendy Vermont Avenue area. Beyond that you'll find Silver Lake and Echo Park.

TOP ATTRACTIONS

Dolby Theatre. The interior design of the theater that hosts the Academy Awards was inspired by European opera houses, but underneath all the trimmings the space has one of the finest technical systems in the world. A tour of the Dolby, which debuted in 2001 as the Kodak Theatre, is a worthwhile expense for movie buffs who just can't get enough insider information. Tour guides share plenty of behind-the-scenes tidbits about Oscar ceremonies as they escort you through the theater. You'll get to step into the VIP lounge where celebrities mingle on the big night and get a bird's-eye view from the balcony seating. ■ TIP➔ **If you have the Go Los Angeles Card, the tour is included.** ✉ *6801 Hollywood Blvd., Hollywood* ☎ *323/308–6300* ⊕ *www.dolbytheatre.com* ▦ *Tour $22.*

Fodor's Choice
★

Griffith Observatory. High on a hillside overlooking the city, Griffith Observatory is one of the area's most celebrated landmarks. Its interior is just as impressive as its exterior, thanks to a massive expansion and cosmic makeover completed a decade ago. Highlights of the building include the Foucault's pendulum hanging in the main lobby, the planet exhibitions on the lower level, and the playful wall display of galaxy-themed jewelry along the twisty indoor ramp.

In true L.A. style, the Leonard Nimoy Event Horizon Theater presents guest speakers and shows on space-related topics and discoveries. The Samuel Oschin Planetarium features an impressive dome, digital projection system, theatrical lighting, and a stellar sound system. Shows are $7.

Grab a meal at the Café at the End of the Universe, which serves up dishes created by celebrity chef Wolfgang Puck. ■ TIP➔ **For a fantastic view, come at sunset to watch the sky turn fiery shades of red with the city's skyline silhouetted.** ✉ *2800 E. Observatory Ave., Los Feliz* ☎ *213/473–0800* ⊕ *www.griffithobservatory.org* ⊘ *Closed Mon.* ☞ *Observatory grounds and parking are open daily.*

Griffith Park. The country's largest municipal park, the 4,210-acre Griffith Park is a must for nature lovers, the perfect spot for respite from the hustle and bustle of the surrounding urban areas. Plants and animals native to Southern California can be found within the park's borders, including deer, coyotes, and even a reclusive mountain lion. Bronson Canyon (where the Batcave from the 1960s *Batman* TV series is located) and Crystal Springs are favorite picnic spots.

The park is named after Colonel Griffith J. Griffith, a mining tycoon who donated 3,000 acres to the city in 1896. As you might expect, the park has been used as a film and television location for at least a century. Here you'll find the Griffith Observatory, the Los Angeles Zoo, the Greek Theater, two golf courses, hiking and bridle trails, a swimming pool, a merry-go-round, and an outdoor train museum. ⊠ *4730 Crystal Springs Dr., Los Feliz* ☎ *323/913–4688* ⊕ *www.laparks.org/dos/parks/griffithpk* ⊠ *Free; attractions inside park have separate admission fees.*

Fodor'sChoice   **Hollywood Museum.** Lovers of Tinseltown's glamorous past may find
★   themselves humming "Hooray for Hollywood" as they tour this gem of cinema history inside the Max Factor Building. For years, Factor's famous makeup was manufactured on the top floors, and on the ground floor was a salon. After an extensive renovation, this art deco landmark that Factor purchased in 1928 now holds this museum with more than 10,000 bits of film memorabilia.

Exhibits include sections dedicated to Marilyn Monroe, Michael Jackson, and Bob Hope, and to costumes and props from such films as *Moulin Rouge, The Silence of the Lambs,* and *Planet of the Apes.* There's also an impressive gallery of photos showing movie stars frolicking at the Brown Derby, Ciro's, the Trocadero, the Mocambo, and other fabled venues.

Hallway walls are covered with the autograph collection of ultimate fan Joe Ackerman; aspiring filmmakers may want to check out the early film equipment. The museum's showpiece is the Max Factor exhibit, where separate dressing rooms are dedicated to Factor's "color harmony," which created distinct looks for "brownettes" (Factor's term), redheads, and, of course, bombshell blondes. You can practically smell the peroxide of Marilyn Monroe getting her trademark platinum look here. Also worth a peek are makeup cases owned by Lucille Ball, Lana Turner, Ginger Rogers, Bette Davis, Rita Hayworth, and others who made Max Factor makeup popular. ⊠ *1660 N. Highland Ave., at Hollywood Blvd., Hollywood* ☎ *323/464–7776* ⊕ *www.thehollywoodmuseum.com* ⊠ *$15* ☉ *Closed Mon. and Tues.*

Hollywood Walk of Fame. Along Hollywood Boulevard (and part of Vine Street) runs a trail of affirmations for entertainment-industry overachievers. On this mile-long stretch of sidewalk, inspired by the concrete handprints in front of TLC Chinese Theatre, names are embossed in brass, each at the center of a pink star embedded in dark-gray terrazzo. They're not all screen deities; many stars commemorate people who worked in a technical field, such as sound or lighting. The first eight stars were unveiled in 1960 at the northwest corner of Highland Avenue and Hollywood Boulevard: Olive Borden, Ronald Colman, Louise Fazenda,

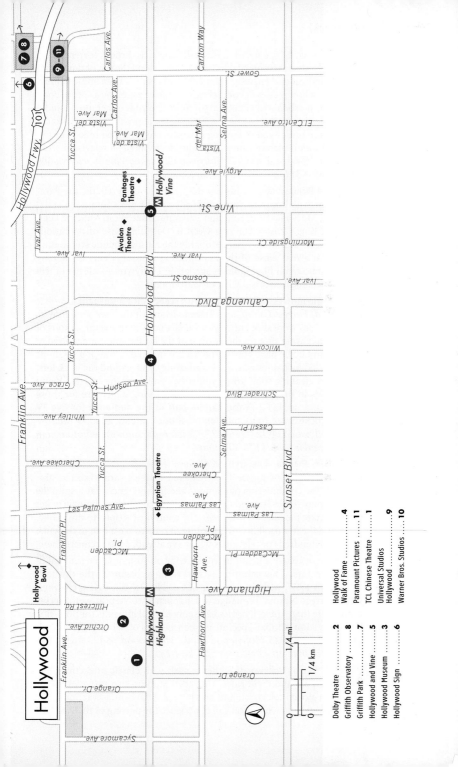

Hollywood

Dolby Theatre	2	
Griffith Observatory	8	
Griffith Park	7	
Hollywood and Vine	5	
Hollywood Museum	3	
Hollywood Sign	6	
Hollywood Walk of Fame	4	
Paramount Pictures	11	
TCL Chinese Theatre	1	
Universal Studios Hollywood	9	
Warner Bros. Studios	10	

Preston Foster, Burt Lancaster, Edward Sedgwick, Ernest Torrence, and Joanne Woodward (some of these names have stood the test of time better than others). Since then, more than 2,000 others have been immortalized, though that honor doesn't come cheap—upon selection by a special committee, the personality in question (or more likely his or her movie studio or record company) pays about $30,000 for the privilege. To aid you in spotting celebrities you're looking for, stars are identified by one of five icons: a motion-picture camera, a radio microphone, a television set, a record, or a theatrical mask. ⊠ *Hollywood Blvd. and Vine St., Hollywood* ☏ *323/469–8311* ⊕ *www.walkoffame.com.*

Fodor'sChoice **Paramount Pictures.** With a history dating to the early 1920s, the Para-
★ mount lot was home to some of Hollywood's most luminous stars, including Mary Pickford, Rudolph Valentino, Mae West, Marlene Dietrich, and Bing Crosby. Director Cecil B. DeMille's base of operations for decades, Paramount offers probably the most authentic studio tour, giving you a real sense of the film industry's history. This is the only major studio from film's golden age left in Hollywood—all the others are in Burbank, Universal City, or Culver City.

Memorable movies and TV shows with scenes shot here include *Sunset Boulevard, Forrest Gump,* and *Titanic.* Many of the *Star Trek* movies and TV series were shot entirely or in part here, and several seasons of *I Love Lucy* were shot on the portion of the lot Paramount acquired in 1967 from Lucille Ball. You can take a 2-hour studio tour or a 4½-hour VIP tour, led by guides who walk and trolley you around the back lots. As well as gleaning some gossipy history, you'll spot the sets of TV and film shoots in progress. Reserve ahead for tours, which are for those ages 10 and up. ■TIP➔ **You can be part of the audience for live TV tapings (tickets are free), but you must book ahead.** ⊠ *5555 Melrose Ave., Hollywood* ☏ *323/956–1777* ⊕ *www.paramountstudiotour.com* ☞ *$55 regular tour, $178 VIP tour.*

TCL Chinese Theatre. The stylized Chinese pagodas and temples of the former Grauman's Chinese Theatre have become a shrine both to stardom and the combination of glamour and flamboyance that inspire the phrase "only in Hollywood." Although you have to buy a movie ticket to appreciate the interior trappings, the courtyard is open to the public. The main theater itself is worth visiting, if only to see a film in the same setting as hundreds of celebrities who have attended big premieres here.

And then, of course, outside in front are the oh-so-famous cement hand- and footprints. This tradition is said to have begun at the theater's opening in 1927, with the premiere of Cecil B. DeMille's *King of Kings,* when actress Norma Talmadge just happened to step in wet cement. Now more than 160 celebrities have contributed imprints for posterity, including some oddball specimens, such as casts of Whoopi Goldberg's dreadlocks. ⊠ *6925 Hollywood Blvd., Hollywood* ☏ *323/461–3331* ⊕ *www.tclchinesetheatres.com* ☞ *Tour $15.*

FAMILY **Universal Studios Hollywood.** A theme park with classic attractions like roller coasters and thrill rides, Universal Studios also provides a tour of some beloved television and movie sets. A favorite attraction is the tram tour, during which you can experience the parting of the Red Sea;

duck from dinosaurs in *Jurassic Park*; visit Dr. Seuss's Whoville; see the airplane wreckage of *War of the Worlds*; and get chills looking at the house from *Psycho*. ■TIP→ **The tram ride is usually the best place to begin your visit, because the lines become longer as the day goes on.**

Most attractions are designed to give you a thrill in one form or another, including the spine-tingling Transformers: The Ride 3-D, or the bone-rattling roller coaster, Revenge of the Mummy. The Simpsons Ride takes you on a hair-raising animated journey through the clan's hometown of Springfield. Don't forget to indulge in magical moments at The Wizarding World of Harry Potter and try some Butterbeer in Hogsmeade. Geared more toward adults, CityWalk is a separate venue run by Universal Studios, where you'll find shops, restaurants, nightclubs, and movie theaters. ⊠ *100 Universal City Pl., Universal City* ☎ *818/622–3801* ⊕ *www.universalstudioshollywood.com* ☜ *$99.*

Warner Bros. Studios. If you're looking for an authentic behind-the-scenes look at how films and TV shows are made, head to this major studio center, one of the world's busiest. After a short film on the studio's movies and TV shows, hop aboard a tram for a ride through the sets and soundstages of such favorites as *Casablanca* and *Rebel Without a Cause*. You'll see the bungalows where Marlon Brando, Bette Davis, and other icons relaxed between shots, and the current production offices for Clint Eastwood and George Clooney. You might even spot a celeb or see a shoot in action—tours change from day to day depending on the productions taking place on the lot.

Tours are given at least every hour, more frequently from May to September, and last 2 hours and 25 minutes. Reservations are required, and advance notice is needed for people with mobility issues. Children under eight are not admitted. A five-hour deluxe tour costing $295 includes lunch, and lets you spend more time exploring the sets. ⊠ *3400 W. Riverside Dr., Burbank* ☎ *877/492–8687* ⊕ *www.wbstudiotour.com* ☜ *$62, $295 for deluxe tour.*

WORTH NOTING

Hollywood and Vine. The mere mention of this intersection inspires images of a street corner bustling with movie stars, hopefuls, and moguls arriving on foot or in a Duesenberg or a Rolls-Royce. In the old days this was the hub of the radio and movie industry: film stars like Gable and Garbo hustled in and out of their agents' office buildings (some now converted to luxury condos) at these fabled cross streets. Even the Red Line Metro station here keeps up the Hollywood theme, with a *Wizard of Oz*–style yellow brick road, vintage movie projectors, and old film reels on permanent display. Sights visible from this intersection include the Capitol Records Building, the Avalon Hollywood nightclub, Pantages Theater, and the W Hollywood Hotel. ⊠ *Hollywood Ave. and Vine St., Hollywood.*

Hollywood Sign. With letters 50 feet tall, Hollywood's trademark sign can be spotted from miles away. The icon, which originally read "Hollywoodland," was erected in the Hollywood Hills in 1923 to advertise a segregated housing development and was outfitted with 4,000 light bulbs. In 1949 the "land" portion of the sign was taken down. By 1973 the sign had earned landmark status, but since the letters were made of wood, its longevity came into question. A make-over project was launched and the letters were auctioned off (rocker Alice Cooper bought an "O" and singing cowboy Gene Autry sponsored an "L") to make way for a new sign made of sheet metal. Inevitably, the sign has drawn pranksters who have altered it over the years, albeit temporarily, to spell out "Hollyweed" (in the 1970s, to push for more lenient marijuana laws), "Go Navy" (before a Rose Bowl game), and "Perotwood" (during businessman Ross Perot's 1992 presidential bid). A fence and surveillance equipment have since been installed to deter intruders, but another vandal managed to pull the "Hollyweed" prank once again in 2017 after Californians voted to make recreational use of marijuana legal statewide. ■TIP➜ Use caution if driving up to the sign on residential streets; many cars speed around the blind corners. ✉ *Griffith Park, Mt. Lee Dr., Hollywood* ⊕ *www.hollywoodsign.org.*

BEVERLY HILLS AND THE WESTSIDE

Updated by Clarissa Wei

The rumors are true: Beverly Hills delivers on a dramatic, cinematic scale of wealth and excess. A known celebrity haunt, come here to daydream, or to live like the rich and famous for a day. In West Hollywood you'll find nightclubs, world-famous eateries, and gallery openings.

The three-block stretch of Wilshire Boulevard known as Museum Row, east of Fairfax Avenue, features intriguing museums and a prehistoric tar pit. Wilshire Boulevard itself is something of a cultural monument—it begins its grand 16-mile sweep to the sea in Downtown L.A.

West of La Cienega Boulevard, you'll find chic, attractive neighborhoods with coveted postal codes—Bel Air, Brentwood, Westwood, West Los Angeles, and Pacific Palisades. The Westside is rich in culture—and not just entertainment-industry culture: it's home to the monumental Getty Center and the engrossing Museum of Tolerance.

TOP ATTRACTIONS

FAMILY
Fodor's Choice
★

The Getty Center. With its curving walls and isolated hilltop perch, the Getty Center resembles a pristine fortified city of its own. You may have been lured here by the beautiful views of Los Angeles—on a clear day stretching all the way to the Pacific Ocean—but the amazing architecture, uncommon gardens, and fascinating art collections will be more than enough to capture and hold your attention. When the sun is out, the complex's rough-cut travertine marble skin seems to soak up the light.

Getting to the center involves a bit of anticipatory lead-up. At the base of the hill, a pavilion disguises the underground parking structure. From there you either walk or take a smooth, computer-driven tram up the steep slope, checking out the Bel Air estates across the humming 405 freeway. The five pavilions that house the museum surround a central courtyard and are bridged by walkways. From the courtyard, plazas, and walkways, you can survey the city from the San Gabriel Mountains to the ocean.

The *Urban Light* assemblage sculpture outisde of LACMA consists of 202 restored street lamps from the 1920s and 1930s.

In a ravine separating the museum and the Getty Research Institute, conceptual artist Robert Irwin created the playful Central Garden in stark contrast to Meier's mathematical architectural geometry. The garden's design is what Hollywood feuds are made of: Meier couldn't control Irwin's vision, and the two men sniped at each other during construction, with Irwin stirring the pot with every loose twist his garden path took. The result is a refreshing garden walk whose focal point is an azalea maze (some insist the Mickey Mouse shape is on purpose) in a reflecting pool.

Inside the pavilions are the galleries for the permanent collections of European paintings, drawings, sculpture, illuminated manuscripts, and decorative arts, as well as photographs gathered internationally. The Getty's collection of French furniture and decorative arts, especially from the early years of Louis XIV (1643–1715) to the end of the reign of Louis XVI (1774–92), is renowned for its quality and condition; you can see a pair of completely reconstructed salons. In the paintings galleries, a computerized system of louvered skylights allows natural light to filter in, creating a closer approximation of the conditions in which the artists painted. Notable among the paintings are Rembrandt's *The Abduction of Europa,* Van Gogh's *Irises,* Monet's *Wheatstack, Snow Effects,* and *Morning,* and James Ensor's *Christ's Entry into Brussels.*

If you want to start with a quick overview, pick up the brochure in the entrance hall that guides you to collection highlights. There's also an instructive audio tour (free, but you have to leave your ID) with commentaries by art historians and other experts. Art information rooms with multimedia computer stations contain more details about the collections. The Getty also presents lectures, films, concerts, and special programs for kids, families, and all-around culture lovers. The complex includes an upscale restaurant and downstairs cafeteria with panoramic window views. There are also outdoor coffee carts. ■TIP➜ On-site parking is subject to availability and can fill up by midday on holidays and in the summer, so try to come early in the day or after lunch. A tram takes you from the street-level entrance to the top of the hill. Public buses (Metro Rapid Line 734) also serve the center and link to the Expo Rail extension. ⊠ *1200 Getty Center Dr., Brentwood* ☎ *310/440–7300* ⊕ *www.getty.edu* ☞ *Free; parking $15* ☾ *Closed Mon.*

FAMILY **La Brea Tar Pits Museum.** Show your kids where Ice Age fossils come from by taking them to the stickiest park in town. The area formed when deposits of oil rose to the earth's surface, collected in shallow pools, and coagulated into asphalt. In the early 20th century geologists discovered that all that goo contained the largest collection of Pleistocene (Ice Age) fossils ever found at one location: more than 600 species of birds, mammals, plants, reptiles, and insects. Roughly 100 tons of fossil bones have been removed in excavations during the last 100 years, making this one of the world's most famous fossil sites. You can see most of the pits through chain-link fences, and the new Excavator Tour gets you as close as possible to the action.

Pit 91 and Project 23 are ongoing excavation projects; tours are offered, and you can volunteer to help with the excavations in the summer. Several pits are scattered around Hancock Park and the surrounding neighborhood; construction in the area has often had to accommodate them, and in nearby streets and along sidewalks, little bits of tar occasionally ooze up. The museum displays fossils from the tar pits and has a glass-walled laboratory that allows visitors to view paleontologists and volunteers as they work on specimens. ⊠ *5801 Wilshire Blvd., West Hollywood* ☎ *323/857–6300* ⊕ *www.tarpits.org* ☞ *$12; parking $12.*

Fodor'sChoice **Los Angeles County Museum of Art (LACMA).** Without a doubt, this is the
★ focal point of the museum district that runs along Wilshire Boulevard. Chris Burden's *Urban Light* sculpture, composed of 202 restored cast-iron antique street lamps, elegantly marks the location. Inside you'll find one of the country's most comprehensive art collections, with more than 120,000 objects dating from ancient times to the present. The museum, which opened in 1965, now includes numerous buildings that cover more than 20 acres.

The permanent collection's strengths include works by prominent Southern California artists; Latin American artists such as Diego Rivera and Frida Kahlo; Islamic and European art; paintings by Henri Matisse, Rene Magritte, Paul Klee, and Wassily Kandinsky; art representing the ancient civilizations of Egypt, the Near East, Greece, and Rome; and costumes and textiles dating back to the 16th century.

The Broad Contemporary Art Museum, designed by Renzo Piano, opened in 2008 and impresses with three vast floors. BCAM presents contemporary art from LACMA's collection in addition to temporary exhibitions that explore the interplay between the present and the past.

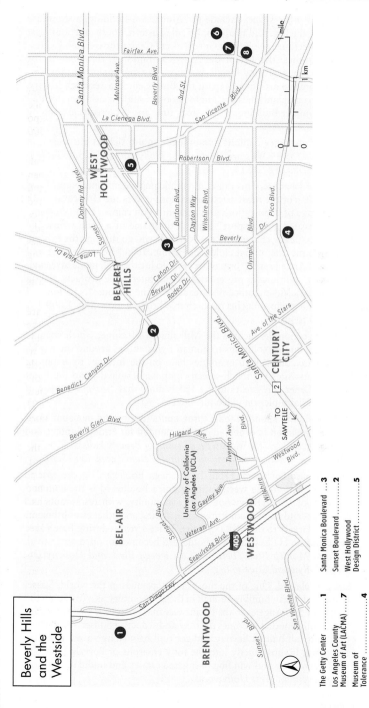

Beverly Hills and the Westside

LACMA's other spaces include the Ahmanson Building, a showcase for Art of the Pacific, European, Middle Eastern, South and Southeast Asian collections; the Robert Gore Rifkind Center for German Expressionist Studies; the Art of the Americas Building; the Pavilion for Japanese Art, featuring scrolls, screens, drawings, paintings, textiles, and decorative arts from Japan; the Bing Center, a research library, resource center, and theater; and the Boone Children's Gallery, located in the Hammer Building, where story time and art lessons are among the activities offered.

■TIP→ Temporary exhibits sometimes require tickets purchased in advance. ⊠ *5905 Wilshire Blvd., West Hollywood* ☎ *323/857–6000* ⊕ *www.lacma.org* ✉ *$15.*

FAMILY **Museum of Tolerance.** This museum unflinchingly confronts bigotry and racism. One of the most affecting sections covers the Holocaust, with film footage of deportations and concentration camps. Upon entering, you are issued a "passport" bearing the name of a child whose life was dramatically changed by the Nazis; as you go through the exhibit, you learn the fate of that child. An exhibit called "Anne: The Life and Legacy of Anne Frank," brings her story to life through immersive environments, multimedia presentations, and interesting artifacts. Simon Wiesenthal's Vienna office is set exactly as the famous "Nazi hunter" had it while performing his research that brought more than 1,000 war criminals to justice.

Interactive exhibits include the Millennium Machine, which engages visitors in finding solutions to human rights abuses around the world; Globalhate.com, which examines hate on the Internet by exposing problematic sites via touch-screen computer terminals; and the Point of View Diner, a re-creation of a 1950s diner that "serves" a menu of controversial topics on video jukeboxes.

■TIP→ Plan to spend at least three hours touring the museum; making a reservation is especially recommended for Friday, Sunday, and holiday visits. ⊠ *9786 W. Pico Blvd., south of Beverly Hills* ☎ *310/772–2505 for reservations* ⊕ *www.museumoftolerance.com* ✉ *$15.50.*

Santa Monica Boulevard. From La Cienega Boulevard in the east to Doheny Drive in the west, Santa Monica Boulevard is the commercial core of West Hollywood's gay community, with restaurants and cafés, bars and clubs, bookstores and galleries, and other establishments catering largely to the LGBTQ scene. Twice a year—during June's L.A. Pride and on Halloween—the boulevard becomes an open-air festival. ⊠ *Santa Monica Blvd., between La Cienega Blvd. and Doheny Dr., West Hollywood* ⊕ *weho.org.*

Sunset Boulevard. One of the most fabled avenues in the world, Sunset Boulevard began humbly enough in the 18th century as a route from El Pueblo de Los Angeles to the Pacific Ocean. Today, as it passes through West Hollywood, it becomes the sexy and seductive Sunset Strip, where rock and roll had its heyday and cocktail bars charge a premium for the views. It slips quietly into the tony environs of Beverly Hills and Bel Air, twisting and winding past gated estates and undulating vistas. ⊠ *Sunset Blvd., West Hollywood.*

WORTH NOTING

FAMILY **Petersen Automotive Museum.** L.A. is a mecca for car lovers, which explains the popularity of this museum with a collection of more than 300 automobiles and other motorized vehicles. But you don't have to be a gearhead to appreciate the Petersen; there's plenty of fascinating history here for all to enjoy. Learn how Los Angeles grew up around its freeways, how cars evolve from the design phase to the production line, and how automobiles have influenced film and television. To see how the vehicles, many of them quite rare, are preserved and maintained, take the 90-minute tour of the basement-level Vault (young kids aren't permitted in the Vault, but they'll find plenty to keep them occupied throughout the museum). ⊠ *6060 Wilshire Blvd., Mid-Wilshire* ☎ *323/930–2277* ⊕ *www.petersen.org* ⌨ *$15.*

West Hollywood Design District. More than 200 businesses—art galleries, antiques shops, fashion outlets (including Rag & Bone and Christian Louboutin), and interior design stores—are found in the design district. There are also about 40 restaurants, including the famous paparazzi magnet, The Ivy. All are clustered within walking distance of each other—rare for L.A. ⊠ *Melrose Ave. and Robertson and Beverly Blvds., West Hollywood* ☎ *310/289–2534* ⊕ *wehodesigndistrict.com.*

SANTA MONICA AND THE BEACHES

Updated by Clarissa Wei

Hugging the Santa Monica Bay in an arch, the desirable communities of Malibu, Santa Monica, and Venice move from ultrarich and ultracasual Malibu to bohemian, borderline-seedy Venice. What they have in common is cleaner air, mild temperatures, heavy traffic, and an emphasis on beach culture.

Fodor's Choice ★ **Getty Villa Malibu.** Feeding off the cultures of ancient Rome, Greece, and Etruria, the villa exhibits astounding antiquities, though on a first visit even they take a backseat to their environment. This megamansion sits on some of the most valuable coastal property in the world. Modeled after an Italian country home, the Villa dei Papiri in Herculaneum, the Getty Villa includes beautifully manicured gardens, reflecting pools, and statuary. The structures blend thoughtfully into the rolling terrain and significantly improve the public spaces, such as the new outdoor amphitheater, gift store, café, and entry arcade. Talks and educational programs are offered at an indoor theater. ■TIP➜ **An advance timed entry ticket is required for admission. Tickets are free and may be ordered from the museum's website or by phone.** ⊠ *17985 Pacific Coast Hwy., Pacific Palisades* ☎ *310/440–7300* ⊕ *www.getty.edu* ⌨ *Free, tickets required; parking $15* ☾ *Closed Tues.*

FAMILY **Santa Monica Pier.** Souvenir shops, carnival games, arcades, eateries, an outdoor trapeze school, a small amusement park, and an aquarium all contribute to the festive atmosphere of this truncated pier at the foot of Colorado Boulevard below Palisades Park. The pier's trademark 46-horse Looff Carousel, built in 1922, has appeared in several films, including *The Sting.* The Soda Jerks ice cream fountain (named for the motion the attendant makes when pulling the machine's arm) inside

the carousel building is a pier staple. Free concerts are held on the pier in the summer. ⊠ *Colorado Ave. and the ocean, Santa Monica* ☎ *310/458–8901* ⊕ *www.santamonicapier.org.*

Third Street Promenade. Stretch your legs along this pedestrians-only three-block stretch of 3rd Street, close to the Pacific, lined with jacaranda trees, ivy-topiary dinosaur fountains, strings of lights, and branches of nearly every major U.S. retail chain. Outdoor cafés, street vendors, movie theaters, and a rich nightlife make this a main gathering spot for locals, visitors, street musicians, and performance artists. Plan a night just to take it all in or take an afternoon for a long people-watching stroll. There's plenty of parking in city structures on the streets flanking the promenade. **Santa Monica Place,** at the south end of the promenade, is a sleek outdoor mall and foodie haven. Its three stories are home to Bloomingdale's, Louis Vuitton, Coach, and other upscale retailers. Don't miss the ocean views from the rooftop food court. ⊠ *Third St., between Colorado and Wilshire Blvds., Santa Monica* ⊕ *www.downtownsm.com.*

Venice Beach Boardwalk. The surf and sand of Venice are fine, but the main attraction here is the boardwalk scene, which is a cosmos all its own. Go on weekend afternoons for the best people-watching experience. You can also swim, fish, surf, and skateboard, or play racquetball, handball, shuffleboard, and basketball (the boardwalk is the site of hotly contested pickup games). You can rent a bike or in-line skates and hit The Strand bike path, then pull up a seat at a sidewalk café and watch the action unfold. ⊠ *1800 Ocean Front Walk, west of Pacific Ave., Venice* ☎ *310/392–4687* ⊕ *www.venicebeach.com.*

BEACHES

Malibu Lagoon State Beach. Bird-watchers, take note: in this 5-acre marshy area near Malibu Beach Inn you can spot egrets, blue herons, avocets, and gulls. (You need to stay on the boardwalks so as not to disturb their habitats.) The path leads out to a rocky stretch of Surfrider Beach, and makes for a pleasant stroll. The sand is soft, clean, and white, and you're also likely to spot a variety of marine life. Look for the signs to help identify these sometimes exotic-looking creatures. The lagoon is particularly enjoyable in the early morning and at sunset—and even more so now, thanks to a restoration effort that improved the lagoon's scent. The parking lot has limited hours, but street-side parking is usually available at off-peak times. Close by are shops and a theater. **Amenities:** lifeguards; parking (fee); showers; toilets. **Best for:** sunset; walking. ⊠ *23200 Pacific Coast Hwy., Malibu* ☎ *310/457–8143* ⊕ *www.parks.ca.gov* 🅿 *$12 parking.*

FodorsChoice
★
Robert H. Meyer Memorial State Beach. Part of Malibu's most beautiful coastal area, this beach is made up of three minibeaches—El Pescador, La Piedra, and El Matador—each with the same spectacular view. Scramble down the steps to the rocky coves via steep, steep stairways; all food and water needs to be toted in, as there are no services. Portable toilets at the trailhead are the only restrooms. "El Mat" has a series of caves, Piedra some nifty rock formations, and Pescador a secluded feel, but they're all picturesque and fairly private. ⚠ **Keep track of the incoming tide so you won't get trapped between those otherwise scenic boulders. Amenities:** parking (fee); toilets. **Best for:** snorkeling; solitude; sunset; surfing; walking; windsurfing. ⊠ *32350, 32700, and 32900 Pacific Coast Hwy., Malibu* ☎ *818/880–0363* ⊕ *www.parks.ca.gov.*

Santa Monica State Beach. The first beach you'll hit after the Santa Monica Freeway (I–10) runs into the Pacific Coast Highway, wide and sandy Santa Monica is *the* place for sunning and socializing. Be prepared for a mob scene on summer weekends, when parking becomes an expensive ordeal. Swimming is fine (with the usual post-storm pollution caveat); for surfing, go elsewhere. For a memorable view, climb up the stairway over the PCH to Palisades Park, at the top of the bluffs. Free summer-evening concerts are held on the pier on Thursday nights. **Amenities:** food and drink; lifeguards; parking; showers; toilets; water sports. **Best for:** partiers; sunset; surfing; swimming; walking. ⊠ *1642 Promenade, PCH at California Incline, Santa Monica* ☎ *310/458–8573* ⊕ *www. smgov.net/portals/beach* 🅿 *$10 parking.*

5

PASADENA AREA

Updated by
Clarissa Wei

Although seemingly absorbed into the general Los Angeles sprawl, Pasadena is a separate and distinct city. Noted for its Tournament of Roses, seen around the world each New Year's Day, the city brims with noteworthy spots, from its gorgeous Craftsman homes to its exceptional museums, particularly the Norton Simon and the Huntington Library, Art Collections, and Botanical Gardens. Where else can you see a Chaucer manuscript and rare cacti in one place?

TOP ATTRACTIONS

Gamble House. Built by Charles and Henry Greene in 1908, this American Arts and Crafts bungalow illustrates the incredible craftsmanship that went into early L.A. architecture. The term *bungalow* can be misleading, since the Gamble House is a huge three-story home. To wealthy Easterners such as the Gambles (as in Procter & Gamble), this type of vacation home seemed informal compared with their mansions back home. Admirers swoon over the teak staircase and cabinetry, the Greene and Greene–designed furniture, and an Emil Lange glass door. The dark exterior has broad eaves, with sleeping porches on the second floor. An hour-long, docent-led tour of the Gamble's interior will draw your eye to the exquisite details. For those who want to see more of the Greene and Greene homes, there are guided walks around the historic Arroyo Terrace neighborhood. Advance tickets are highly recommended. ⊠ *4 Westmoreland Pl., Pasadena* 🕾 *626/793–3334* ⊕ *www.gamblehouse.org* ⬛ *$15.*

Fodor's Choice
★

Huntington Library, Art Collections, and Botanical Gardens. If you have time for just one stop in the Pasadena area, be sure to see this sprawling estate built for railroad tycoon Henry E. Huntington in the early 1900s. Henry and his wife, Arabella (who was also his aunt by marriage), voraciously collected rare books and manuscripts, botanical specimens, and 18th-century British art. The institution they established became one of the most extraordinary cultural complexes in the world.

The library contains more than 700,000 books and 4 million manuscripts, including one of the world's biggest history of science collections.

Don't resist being lured outside into the Botanical Gardens, which extend out from the main building. The 10-acre Desert Garden has one of the world's largest groups of mature cacti and other succulents (visit on a cool morning or late afternoon). The Shakespeare Garden, meanwhile, blooms with plants mentioned in Shakespeare's works. The Japanese Garden features an authentic ceremonial teahouse built in Kyoto in the 1960s. A waterfall flows from the teahouse to the ponds below. In the Rose Garden Tea Room, afternoon tea is served (reserve in advance). The Chinese Garden, which is among the largest outside of China, sinews around waveless pools.

The Bing Children's Garden lets tiny tots explore the ancient elements of water, fire, air, and earth. A 1¼-hour guided tour of the Botanical Gardens is led by docents at posted times, and a free brochure with a map and property highlights is available in the entrance pavilion. ⊠ *1151 Oxford Rd., San Marino* 🕾 *626/405–2100* ⊕ *www.huntington. org* ⬛ *$20 weekdays, $23 weekends* ⊘ *Closed Tues.*

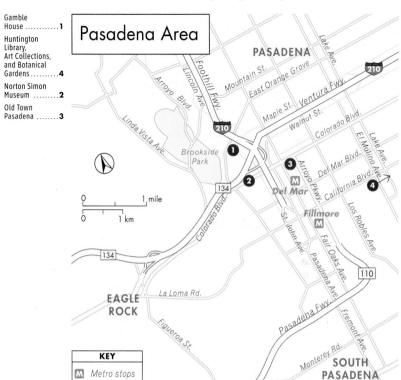

Fodor'sChoice **Norton Simon Museum.** As seen in the New Year's Day Tournament of
★ Roses Parade, this low-profile brown building is one of the finest midsize museums anywhere, with a collection that spans more than 2,000
years of Western and Asian art. It all began in the 1950s when Norton
Simon (Hunt-Wesson Foods, McCalls Corporation, and Canada Dry)
started collecting works by Degas, Renoir, Gauguin, and Cézanne. His
collection grew to include old masters, impressionists, and modern
works from Europe, as well as Indian and Southeast Asian art.

Today the Norton Simon Museum is richest in works by Rembrandt,
Picasso, and, most of all, Degas—this is one of the only two U.S. institutions (the other is New York's Metropolitan Museum of Art) to hold
nearly all of the artist's model bronzes.

Head down to the bottom floor to see temporary exhibits and phe-
nomenal Southeast Asian and Indian sculptures and artifacts, where
pieces like a Ban Chiang black ware vessel date back to well before
1000 BC. Don't miss a living artwork outdoors: the garden, conceived
by noted Southern California landscape designer Nancy Goslee Power.
The tranquil pond was inspired by Monet's gardens at Giverny. ⊠ *411
W. Colorado Blvd., Pasadena* ☎ *626/449–6840* ⊕ *www.nortonsimon.
org* ⬛ *$12, free 1st Fri. of month 5–8 pm* ۞ *Closed Tues.*

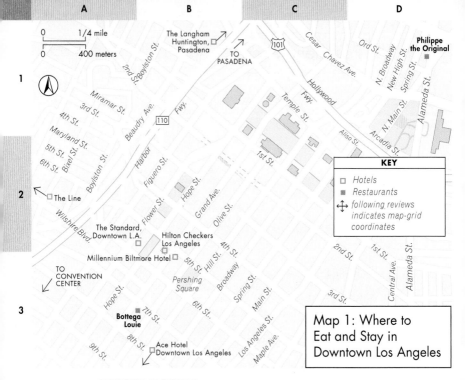

Map 1: Where to Eat and Stay in Downtown Los Angeles

WORTH NOTING

Old Town Pasadena. This 22-block historic district contains a vibrant mix of restored 19th-century brick buildings interspersed with contemporary architecture. Chain stores have muscled in, but there are still some homegrown shops, plenty of tempting cafés and restaurants, and a bustling beer scene. In recent years, a vibrant Asian food scene has popped up in the vicinity as well. In the evening and on weekends, the streets are packed with people. Old Town's main action takes place on Colorado Boulevard between Pasadena Avenue and Arroyo Parkway. ✉ *Pasadena.*

WHERE TO EAT

Updated by
Paul Feinstein

Los Angeles may be known for its beach living and celebrity-infused backdrop, but it was once a farm town. The hillsides were covered in citrus orchards and dairy farms, and agriculture was a major industry. Today, even as L.A. is urbanized, the city's culinary landscape has re-embraced a local, sustainable, and seasonal philosophy at many levels—from fine dining to street snacks.

Use the coordinate (✛ 1:A1) at the end of each listing to locate a site on the corresponding map. Restaurant reviews have been shortened. For full information, visit Fodors.com.

WHAT IT COSTS			
	$	$$	$$$	$$$$
Restaurants	under $18	$18–$24	$25–$35	over $35

Prices are the average cost of a main course at dinner or, if dinner is not served, at lunch, excluding 9.75% tax.

DOWNTOWN

$$$
ITALIAN
✗ **Bottega Louie.** A Downtown dining staple, this lively Italian restaurant and gourmet market features open spaces, stark white walls, and majestic floor-to-ceiling windows. If the wait is too long at this no-reservations eatery, you can sip on prosecco and nibble on pastries at the bar. **Known for:** mouthwatering crab beignets; one-of-a-kind portobello fries. $ *Average main: $25* ⊠ *700 S. Grand Ave., Downtown* ☎ *213/802–1470* ⊕ *www.bottegalouie.com* ✛ *1:A3.*

$
AMERICAN
FAMILY
Fodor's Choice
★
✗ **Philippe the Original.** First opened in 1908, Philippe's is one of L.A.'s oldest restaurants and claims to be the originator of the French dip sandwich. While the debate continues around the city, one thing is certain: the dips made with beef, pork, ham, lamb, or turkey on a freshly baked roll stand the test of time. **Known for:** $0.50 coffee; communal tables; post–Dodgers game eats. $ *Average main: $8* ⊠ *1001 N. Alameda St., Downtown* ☎ *213/628–3781* ⊕ *www.philippes.com* ✛ *1:D1.*

HOLLYWOOD AND THE STUDIOS

BURBANK

$
CUBAN
FAMILY
✗ **Porto's Bakery.** Waiting in line at Porto's is as much a part of the experience as is indulging in a roasted pork sandwich or a chocolate-dipped croissant. This Cuban bakery and café has been an L.A. staple for more than 50 years, often bustling during lunch. **Known for:** counter service; potato balls; roasted pork sandwiches. $ *Average main: $10* ⊠ *3614 W. Magnolia Blvd., Burbank* ☎ *818/846–9100* ⊕ *www.portosbakery.com* ✛ *2:E1.*

HOLLYWOOD

$
AMERICAN
FAMILY
✗ **Pink's Hot Dogs.** Since 1939, Angelenos and tourists alike have been lining up at this roadside hot dog joint. Open until 3 am on weekends, the chili dogs are the main draw, but don't shy away from themed and celebrity-inspired specials like the Emeril Legasse Bam Dog, the Lord of the Rings Dog, or the Giada De Laurentiis Dog. **Known for:** long lines; outside seating. $ *Average main: $6* ⊠ *709 N. La Brea Ave., Hollywood* ☎ *323/931–4223* ⊕ *www.pinkshollywood.com* ✛ *2:D2.*

$$
ITALIAN
✗ **Pizzeria Mozza.** Mario Batali and Nancy Silverton own this upscale pizza and antipasti eatery. The pies—thin-crusted delights with golden, blistered edges—are more Campania than California, and are served piping hot daily. **Known for:** affordable Italian-only wines; walk-ins welcome at bar. $ *Average main: $19* ⊠ *641 N. Highland Ave., Hollywood* ☎ *323/297–0101* ⊕ *www.pizzeriamozza.com* ✛ *2:D2.*

5

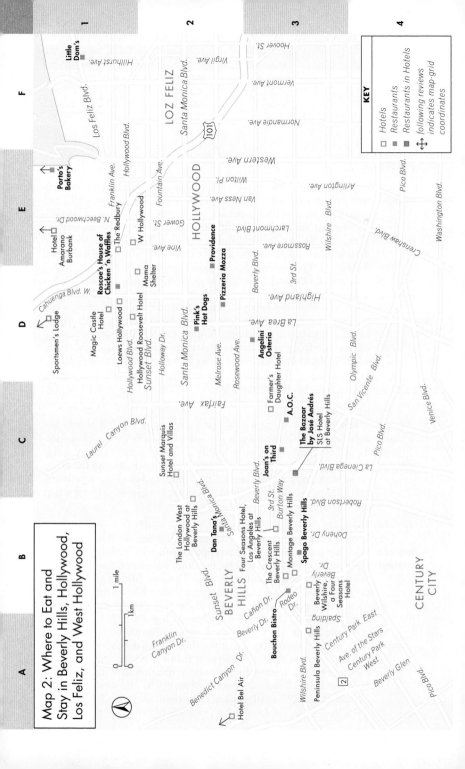

Map 2: Where to Eat and Stay in Beverly Hills, Hollywood, Los Feliz, and West Hollywood

KEY

☐ Hotels
◼ Restaurants
◼ Restaurants in Hotels
↔ following reviews indicates map-grid coordinates

$$$$ ✕ **Providence.** Widely considered one of the best seafood restaurants in the
SEAFOOD country, chef-owner Michael Cimarusti and co-owner Donato Poto ele-
Fodor's Choice vate sustainably driven fine dining to an art form. The elegant space is the
★ perfect spot to sample exquisite seafood with the chef's signature application of French technique, traditional American themes, and Asian accents.
Known for: pastries by chef Jessie Liu; Friday lunch special. $ *Average
main: $120* ✉ *5955 Melrose Ave., Hollywood* ☎ *323/460–4170* ⊕ *www.
providencela.com* ⊘ *No lunch Mon.–Thurs. and weekends* ✛ *2:E2.*

$ ✕ **Roscoe's House of Chicken 'n Waffles.** Roscoe's is *the* place for down-
SOUTHERN home Southern cooking in Southern California. Just ask the patrons
FAMILY who drive from all over L.A. for bargain-priced fried chicken and
waffles. The name of this casual eatery honors a late-night combo
popularized in Harlem jazz clubs. **Known for:** busy; late-night eats;
lemonade. $ *Average main: $15* ✉ *1514 N. Gower St., Hollywood*
☎ *323/466–7453* ⊕ *www.roscoeschickenandwaffles.com* ✛ *2:E1.*

LOS FELIZ

$$ ✕ **Little Dom's.** With a vintage bar and dapper barkeep who mixes up
ITALIAN seasonally inspired retro cocktails, an attached Italian deli where you
can pick up a pork-cheek sub, and an $18 Monday-night supper, it's not
surprising that Little Dom's is a neighborhood gem. Cozy and inviting,
with big leather booths you can sink into for the night, the restaurant
puts a modern spin on classic Italian dishes such as wild-boar meatballs,
almond-milk ricotta agnolotti, and grilled steak slathered in Parmesan.
Known for: spaghetti and meatballs; outdoor seating; brunch. $ *Av-
erage main: $20* ✉ *2128 Hillhurst Ave., Los Feliz* ☎ *323/661–0055*
⊕ *www.littledoms.com* ✛ *2:F1.*

BEVERLY HILLS AND THE WESTSIDE

BEVERLY HILLS

$$$$ ✕ **The Bazaar by José Andrés.** Celebrity Spanish chef José Andrés has con-
SPANISH quered L.A. with this colorful and opulent Beverly Hills spot, which fea-
tures a bar stocked with liquid nitrogen and a super-flashy patisserie. Pore
over a menu of items like Spanish tapas (with a twist), and "liquid" olives
(created through a technique called spherification). **Known for:** molecular
gastronomy; foie gras cotton candy. $ *Average main: $65* ✉ *SLS Hotel
at Beverly Hills, 465 S. La Cienega Blvd., Beverly Hills* ☎ *310/246–5555*
⊕ *slshotels.com/beverlyhills/bazaar* ⊘ *No lunch* ✛ *2:C3.*

$$$ ✕ **Bouchon Bistro.** Chef Thomas Keller of Napa Valley's The French
FRENCH Laundry fame is at the head of this majestic bistro in Beverly Hills. Start
FAMILY with the classic onion soup that arrives with a bubbling lid of cheese,
Fodor's Choice or the salmon rillettes, which are big enough to share. **Known for:** tasty
★ steak frites; sumptuous croque madame; sweet profiteroles for dessert.
$ *Average main: $35* ✉ *235 N. Canon Dr., Beverly Hills* ☎ *310/271–
9910* ⊕ *www.thomaskeller.com/bouchonbeverlyhills* ✛ *2:B3.*

$$$ ✕ **Spago Beverly Hills.** Wolfgang Puck's flagship restaurant is a modern
MODERN L.A. classic. Spago centers on a buzzing redbrick outdoor courtyard
AMERICAN shaded by 100-year-old olive trees, and a daily-changing menu offers
Fodor's Choice dishes like Cantonese-style striped bass, traditional Austrian specialties,
★ or pizza with white truffles. **Known for:** great people-watching; magical

CLOSE UP

Local Chains Worth Stopping For

It's said that the drive-in burger joint was invented in L.A., probably to meet the demands of an ever-mobile car culture. Burger aficionados line up at all hours outside **In-N-Out Burger** (🌐 *www.in-n-out.com, multiple locations*), still a family-owned operation whose terrific made-to-order burgers are revered by Angelenos. Visitors may recognize the chain as the infamous spot where Paris Hilton got nabbed for drunk driving, but locals are more concerned with getting their burger fix off the "secret" menu, with variations like "Animal Style" (mustard-grilled patty with grilled onions and extra spread), a "4 x 4" (four burger patties and four cheese slices, for big eaters) or the bun-less "Protein Style" that comes wrapped in a bib of lettuce. Go online for a list of every "secret" menu item.

Tommy's is best known for their delightfully sloppy chili burger. Visit their no-frills original location (✉ *2575 Beverly Blvd., Los Angeles* ☎ *213/389-9060*)—a culinary landmark. For rotisserie chicken that will make you forget the Colonel altogether, head to **Zankou Chicken** (✉ *5065 Sunset Blvd., Hollywood* ☎ *323/665-7845* 🌐 *www.zankouchicken.com*), a small chain noted for its golden crispy-skinned birds, potent garlic sauce, and Armenian specialties. One-of-a-kind-sausage lovers will appreciate **Wurstküche** (✉ *800 E. 3rd St., Downtown* ☎ *213/687-4444* 🌐 *www.jerrysfamousdeli.com*), where the menu includes items like rattlesnake and rabbit or pheasant with Herbs de Provence. With a lively bar scene, the occasional celebrity sighting, and a spot directly across from the beach, **BOA Steakhouse** (✉ *101 Santa Monica Blvd., Santa Monica* ☎ *310/899-4466* 🌐 *www.hillstone.com*) is a popular hangout, while **Lemonade** (✉ *9001 Beverly Blvd., West Hollywood* ☎ *310/247-2500* 🌐 *www.senorfish.net*) is known for its healthy seasonally driven menu, pulled straight from L.A.'s farmers' markets.

mango soufflé. [$] *Average main: $32* ✉ *176 N. Cañon Dr., Beverly Hills* ☎ *310/385-0880* 🌐 *www.wolfgangpuck.com* ⏱ *No lunch Sun.* ✣ *2:B3.*

WEST HOLLYWOOD

$$$$ ITALIAN Fodor's Choice ★ 🍴 **Angelini Osteria.** Despite its modest, rather congested dining room, this is one of L.A.'s most celebrated Italian restaurants. The key is chef-owner Gino Angelini's consistently impressive dishes, like whole branzino, tender veal kidneys, or rich oxtail stew, as well as lasagna oozing with besciamella. **Known for:** large Italian wine selection; bold flavors. [$] *Average main: $40* ✉ *7313 Beverly Blvd., West Hollywood* ☎ *323/297-0070* 🌐 *www.angeliniosteria.com* ⏱ *Closed Mon. No lunch weekends* ✣ *2:D3.*

$$$$ MEDITERRANEAN 🍴 **A.O.C.** An acronym for Appellation d'Origine Contrôlée, the regulatory system that ensures the quality of local wines and cheeses in France, A.O.C. upholds this standard of excellence from shared plates to perfect wine pairings. Try the Spanish fried chicken, diver scallops with rapini pesto, or arroz negro with squid. **Known for:** amazing bacon-wrapped dates; quaint outdoor seating; fireplaces indoors. [$] *Average main: $36*

✉ *8700 W. 3rd St., West Hollywood* ☎ *310/859–9859* 🌐 *www.aocwinebar.com* 🕐 *No lunch weekends* ⊕ *2:C3.*

$$$ ITALIAN 🍴 **Dan Tana's.** If you're looking for an Italian vibe straight out of *Goodfellas*, your search ends here. Checkered tablecloths cover the tightly packed tables as Hollywood players dine on the city's best chicken and veal Parm, and down Scotches by the finger. **Known for:** elbow-room-only bar; lively atmosphere; long lines. [$] *Average main: $35* ✉ *9071 California Rte. 2, West Hollywood* ☎ *310/275–9444* 🌐 *www.dantanasrestaurant.com* ⊕ *2:B2.*

$ CAFÉ FAMILY 🍴 **Joan's on Third.** Part restaurant, part bakery, part market, Joan's on Third has a little bit of everything. This roadside French-style café caters to families, the occasional local celebrity, and lovers of all things wholesome. **Known for:** crispy baguettes; fresh pastries; long lines. [$] *Average main: $16* ✉ *8350 W. 3rd St., West Hollywood* ☎ *323/655–2285* 🌐 *www.joansonthird.com* ⊕ *2:C3.*

WEST LOS ANGELES

$ AMERICAN Fodor's Choice ★ 🍴 **The Apple Pan.** A favorite since 1947, this unassuming joint with a horseshoe-shaped counter—no tables here—turns out one heck of a good burger. Try the cheeseburger with Tillamook cheddar, or the hickory burger with barbecue sauce. **Known for:** indulgent apple pie; perfect fries; Sanka coffee. [$] *Average main: $8* ✉ *10801 W. Pico Blvd., West L.A.* ☎ *310/475–3585* 💳 *No credit cards* 🕐 *Closed Mon.* ⊕ *3:D2.*

SANTA MONICA AND VENICE

SANTA MONICA

$ DELI 🍴 **Bay Cities Italian Deli.** Part deli, part market, Bay Cities has been home to incredible Italian subs since 1925. This renowned counter service spot is always crowded (best to order ahead), but monster subs run the gamut from the mighty meatball, to their signature "Godmother" made with prosciutto, ham, capicola, mortadella, Genoa salami, and provolone. **Known for:** market with rare imports; excellent service. [$] *Average main: $10* ✉ *1517 Lincoln Blvd., Santa Monica* ☎ *310/395–8279* 🌐 *www.baycitiesitaliandeli.com* 🕐 *Closed Mon.* ⊕ *3:B2.*

$ AMERICAN 🍴 **Father's Office.** Distinguished by its vintage neon sign, this pub is famous for handcrafted beers and a brilliant signature burger. Topped with Gruyère and Maytag blue cheeses, arugula, caramelized onions, and applewood-smoked bacon compote, the "Office Burger" is a guilty pleasure worth waiting in line for, which is usually required. **Known for:** addictive sweet-potato fries; strict no-substitutions policy. [$] *Average main: $15* ✉ *1018 Montana Ave., Santa Monica* ☎ *310/736–2224* 🌐 *www.fathersoffice.com* 🕐 *No lunch weekdays* ⊕ *3:B2.*

$$$$ FRENCH Fodor's Choice ★ 🍴 **Mélisse.** Chef-owner Josiah Citrin enhances his modern French cooking with seasonal California produce. The tasting menu might feature a white-corn ravioli in brown butter-truffle froth, lobster Bolognese, or elegant table-side presentations of Dover sole and stuffed rotisserie chicken. **Known for:** domestic and European cheese cart; contemporary/elegant decor. [$] *Average main: $135* ✉ *1104 Wilshire Blvd., Santa Monica* ☎ *310/395–0881* 🌐 *www.melisse.com* 🕐 *Closed Sun. and Mon. No lunch* ⊕ *3:B2.*

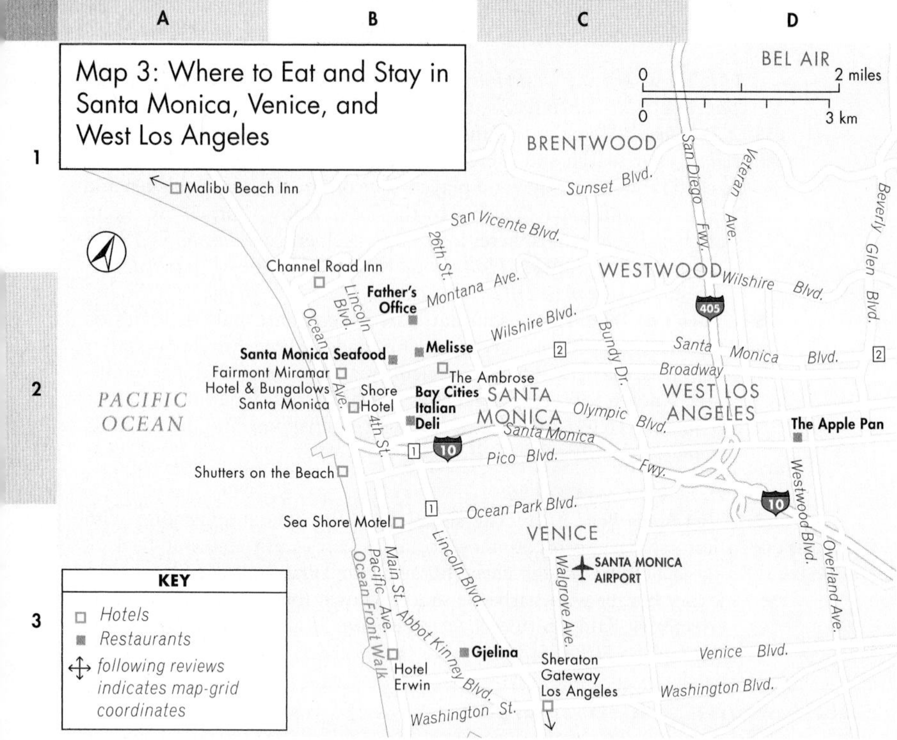

Map 3: Where to Eat and Stay in Santa Monica, Venice, and West Los Angeles

$$ SEAFOOD FAMILY 🍴 **Santa Monica Seafood.** A Southern California favorite, this Italian seafood haven has been serving up fresh fish since 1939. Come for lunch or dinner, but make sure to take time to stroll around the market, read up on the history, and enjoy free tastings of the specials. **Known for:** deliciously seasoned rainbow trout; oyster bar; kids' meals. [$] *Average main: $20* ✉ *1000 Wilshire Blvd., Santa Monica* ☎ *310/393–5244* 🌐 *www.santamonicaseafood.com* ✥ *3:B2.*

VENICE

$$ AMERICAN 🍴 **Gjelina.** Gjelina comes alive the minute you walk through the rustic wooden door and into a softly lit dining room with long communal tables. The menu is seasonal, with outstanding small plates, charcuterie, pastas, and pizza. **Known for:** lively crowd on the patio; late-night menu; wild nettle pizza. [$] *Average main: $20* ✉ *1429 Abbot Kinney Blvd., Venice* ☎ *310/450–1429* 🌐 *www.gjelina.com* ✥ *3:B3.*

WHERE TO STAY

Updated by Michele Bigley

When looking for a hotel, don't write off the pricier establishments immediately. Price categories are determined by "rack rates"—the list price of a hotel room, which is usually discounted. Specials abound, particularly Downtown on the weekends. Many hotels have packages that include breakfast, theater tickets, spa services, or exotic rental cars. Pricing is very competitive, so always check the hotel website in advance for current special offers.

Use the coordinate (⊕ 1:B2) at the end of each listing to locate a site on the corresponding map. Hotel reviews have been shortened. For full information, visit Fodors.com.

WHAT IT COSTS			
$	$$	$$$	$$$$

	$	$$	$$$	$$$$
Hotels	under $200	$200–$300	$301–$400	over $400

Hotel prices are the lowest cost of a standard double room in high season, excluding taxes (as high as 14%, depending on the region).

DOWNTOWN

$$ **Ace Hotel Downtown Los Angeles.** The L.A. edition of this bohemian-
HOTEL chic hipster haven is at once a hotel, theater, bar, and poolside lounge, housed in the gorgeous Spanish Gothic–style United Artists building in the heart of Downtown. **Pros:** lively rooftop lounge/pool area, aptly named Upstairs; gorgeous building and views; heart of Downtown. **Cons:** expensive parking rates compared to nightly rates ($36); some kinks in the service; compact rooms. $ *Rooms from: $239* ⊠ *929 S. Broadway, Downtown* ☎ *213/623–3233* ⊕ *www.acehotel.com/losangeles* ⤳ *183 rooms* ⭘*No meals* ⊕ *1:B3.*

$$ **Hilton Checkers Los Angeles.** Opened as the Mayflower Hotel in 1927,
HOTEL Checkers combines its original character and period detail with contemporary luxuries such as pillow-top mattresses and high-speed Internet, and offers views of the L.A. Library and the Downtown skyline from its rooftop deck. **Pros:** historic charm; 24-hour room service; business-friendly. **Cons:** no on-street parking and valet is over $38.50; some rooms are compact. $ *Rooms from: $229* ⊠ *535 S. Grand Ave., Downtown* ☎ *213/624–0000, 800/445–8667* ⊕ *www.hilton.com* ⤳ *193 rooms* ⭘*No meals* ⊕ *1:B2.*

$$$ **The Line.** This boutique hotel pays homage to its Koreatown address
HOTEL (about 20 minutes from Downtown) with a dynamic dining concept by superstar chef Roy Choi, and a hidden karaoke speakeasy. **Pros:** on-site bikes to explore the area; cheery staff; houses the Houston Brothers' '80s-themed bar. **Cons:** expensive parking; lobby club crowds public spaces; far from parts of the city you may want to explore. $ *Rooms from: $349* ⊠ *3515 Wilshire Blvd.* ☎ *213/381–7411* ⊕ *www.thelinehotel.com* ⤳ *384 rooms* ⭘*No meals* ⊕ *1:A2.*

$$$ **Millennium Biltmore Hotel.** As the local headquarters of John F. Ken-
HOTEL nedy's 1960 presidential campaign and the location of some of the earliest Academy Awards ceremonies, this Downtown treasure, with its gilded 1923 beaux-arts design, exudes ambience and history. **Pros:** 24-hour business center; tiled indoor pool and steam room; multimillion-dollar refurbishment in 2017. **Cons:** pricey valet parking ($45); standard rooms are compact. $ *Rooms from: $349* ⊠ *506 S. Grand Ave., Downtown* ☎ *213/624–1011, 866/866–8086* ⊕ *www.millenniumhotels.com* ⤳ *683 rooms* ⭘*No meals* ⊕ *1:B3.*

$$ HOTEL

The Standard, Downtown L.A. Built in 1955 as the headquarters of Standard Oil, the building was completely revamped in 2002 under the sharp eye of owner André Balazs, to become a sleek, cutting-edge hotel with spacious guest rooms. **Pros:** Rudy's barbershop on-site; 24/7 coffee shop; lively rooftop lounge. **Cons:** disruptive party scene on weekends and holidays; street noise; pricey valet parking ($44). [$] *Rooms from: $279* ✉ *550 S. Flower St., Downtown* ☎ *213/892–8080* 🌐 *www.standardhotels.com* 🛏 *207 rooms* 🍴 *No meals* ✥ *1:B2.*

HOLLYWOOD AND THE STUDIOS

BURBANK

$$ HOTEL

Hotel Amarano Burbank. Close to Burbank's TV and movie studios, the smartly designed Amarano feels like a Beverly Hills boutique hotel, complete with 24-hour room service, a homey on-site restaurant and lounge, and spiffy rooms. **Pros:** fireplace, cocktails, and tapas in lobby; penthouse with private gym; saltwater pool. **Cons:** street noise. [$] *Rooms from: $269* ✉ *322 N. Pass Ave., Burbank* ☎ *818/842–8887, 888/956–1900* 🌐 *www.hotelamarano.com* 🛏 *98 rooms, 34 suites* 🍴 *No meals* ✥ *2:E1.*

HOLLYWOOD

$$$$ HOTEL Fodor's Choice ★

Hollywood Roosevelt Hotel. Poolside cabana rooms are adorned with cow-skin rugs and marble bathrooms, while rooms in the main building accentuate the property's history at this party-centric hotel in the heart of Hollywood. **Pros:** Spare Room bowling alley on-site; pool is a popular weekend hangout; great burgers at the on-site 25 Degrees restaurant. **Cons:** reports of noise and staff attitude; stiff parking fees ($42). [$] *Rooms from: $419* ✉ *7000 Hollywood Blvd., Hollywood* ☎ *323/466–7000, 800/950–7667* 🌐 *www.hollywoodroosevelt.com* 🛏 *353 rooms* 🍴 *No meals* ✥ *2:D2.*

$$$ HOTEL FAMILY

Loews Hollywood. Part of the massive Hollywood and Highland shopping, dining, and entertainment complex, the 20-story Loews is at the center of Hollywood's action but manages to deliver a quiet night's sleep. **Pros:** large rooms with contemporary furniture; free Wi-Fi; Red Line Metro station adjacent. **Cons:** corporate feeling; very touristy; pricy parking ($50). [$] *Rooms from: $349* ✉ *1755 N. Highland Ave., Hollywood* ☎ *323/856–1200, 800/769–4774* 🌐 *www.loewshotels.com/en/hollywood-hotel* 🛏 *628 rooms* 🍴 *No meals* ✥ *2:D1.*

$ HOTEL FAMILY Fodor's Choice ★

Magic Castle Hotel. Guests at the hotel can secure advanced dinner reservations and attend magic shows at the Magic Castle, a private club in a 1908 mansion next door for magicians and their admirers. **Pros:** heated pool; near Hollywood and Highland; lush patio. **Cons:** strict dress code; no elevator; highly trafficked street. [$] *Rooms from: $199* ✉ *7025 Franklin Ave., Hollywood* ☎ *323/851–0800, 800/741–4915* 🌐 *magiccastlehotel.com* 🛏 *43 rooms* 🍴 *Breakfast* ✥ *2:D1.*

$ HOTEL Fodor's Choice ★

Mama Shelter. Even locals are just catching on to Hollywood's sexiest new property, complete with a rooftop bar populated with beautiful people lounging on loveseats, simple affordable rooms with quirky amenities like Bert and Ernie masks, and a down-home lobby restaurant that serves a mean Korean-style burrito. **Pros:** delicious food and cocktails on the property; affordable rooms don't skimp on style; foosball in lobby. **Cons:** spare and small rooms; creaky elevators. $ *Rooms from: $159* ✉ *6500 Selma Ave., Hollywood* ☎ *323/785–6666* ⊕ *www.mamashelter.com/en/los-angeles* ⌖ *70 rooms* ⦿ *No meals* ✛ *2:D1.*

$$$
HOTEL
Fodor's Choice
★

The Redbury. In the heart of Hollywood's nightlife, near the intersection of Hollywood and Vine, the Redbury is designed to appeal to guests' inner bohemian with paisley-patterned wallpaper, vibrant Persian rugs, and vintage rock posters. **Pros:** on-site kitchenettes and washer-dryer; excellent dining options; spacious suites. **Cons:** no pool or on-site gym; noisy on lower floors; some guests may find the Hollywood scene too chaotic. $ *Rooms from: $329* ✉ *1717 Vine St., Hollywood* ☎ *323/962–1717, 977/962–1717* ⊕ *www.theredbury.com* ⌖ *57 suites* ⦿ *No meals* ✛ *2:E1.*

$$$$
HOTEL

W Hollywood. This centrally located, ultramodern-it location is outfitted for the wired traveler, and features a rooftop pool deck and popular on-site bars, like the Station Hollywood and the mod Living Room lobby bar. **Pros:** metro stop outside the front door; comes with in-room party necessities, from ice to cocktail glasses; comfy beds with petal-soft duvets. **Cons:** small pool; pricey dining and valet parking; in noisy part of Hollywood. $ *Rooms from: $659* ✉ *6250 Hollywood Blvd., Hollywood* ☎ *323/798–1300, 888/625–4955* ⊕ *www.whotels.com/hollywood* ⌖ *305 rooms* ⦿ *No meals* ✛ *2:E1.*

STUDIO CITY

$$
HOTEL
FAMILY

Sportsmen's Lodge. This sprawling five-story hotel, a San Fernando Valley landmark just a short jaunt over the Hollywood Hills, has an updated contemporary look highlighted by the Olympic-size pool and summer patio with an outdoor bar. **Pros:** close to Ventura Boulevard restaurants; free shuttle to Universal Hollywood; quiet garden-view rooms worth asking for. **Cons:** pricey daily self-parking fee ($18); a distance from the city. $ *Rooms from: $249* ✉ *12825 Ventura Blvd., Studio City* ☎ *818/769–4700, 800/821–8511* ⊕ *www.sportsmenslodge.com* ⌖ *190 rooms* ⦿ *No meals* ✛ *2:D1.*

BEVERLY HILLS AND THE WESTSIDE

BEL AIR

$$$$
HOTEL
Fodor's Choice
★

Hotel Bel-Air. This Spanish Mission–style icon has been a discreet hillside retreat for celebrities and society types since 1946, and was given a face-lift by star designers Alexandra Champalimaud and David Rockwell. **Pros:** Bang & Olfusen TVs; fireplace and private patio in many rooms; alfresco dining at Wolfgang Puck restaurant. **Cons:** attracts society crowd; hefty price tag; a car is essential. $ *Rooms from: $525* ✉ *701 Stone Canyon Rd., Bel Air* ☎ *310/472–1211, 800/648–4097* ⊕ *www.hotelbelair.com* ⌖ *91 rooms* ⦿ *No meals* ✛ *2:A2.*

BEVERLY HILLS

$$$$
HOTEL

Beverly Wilshire, a Four Seasons Hotel. Built in 1928, this Rodeo Drive–adjacent hotel is part Italian Renaissance (with elegant details like crystal chandeliers) and part contemporary. **Pros:** complimentary car service; Wolfgang Puck restaurant on-site; first-rate spa. **Cons:** small lobby; valet parking backs up at peak times; expensive dining options.

$ *Rooms from: $845* ✉ *9500 Wilshire Blvd., Beverly Hills* ☎ *310/275–5200, 800/427–4354* ⊕ *www.fourseasons.com/beverlywilshire* ⇌ *395 rooms* ⦿ *No meals* ✛ *2:B3.*

$ ▦ **The Crescent Beverly Hills.** Built in 1926 as a dorm for silent-film actors,
HOTEL   the Crescent is now a sleek boutique hotel with a great location—within
Fodor's Choice   the Beverly Hills shopping triangle—and with an even better price. **Pros:**
★   indoor/outdoor fireplace; lively on-site restaurant Crescent Bar and Terrace;
economic room available for $148. **Cons:** gym an additional fee; no elevator. $ *Rooms from: $149* ✉ *403 N. Crescent Dr., Beverly Hills* ☎ *310/247–0505* ⊕ *www.crescentbh.com* ⇌ *35 rooms* ⦿ *No meals* ✛ *2:B3.*

$$$$ ▦ **Four Seasons Hotel, Los Angeles at Beverly Hills.** High hedges and patio
HOTEL   gardens make this hotel a secluded retreat that even the hum of traffic
can't permeate—one reason it's a favorite of Hollywood's elite, whom
you might spot at the pool and espresso bar. **Pros:** tropical terrace
with pool; high-end Italian eatery Culina on-site; great massages and
nail salon. **Cons:** Hollywood scene in bar and restaurant means rarefied prices. $ *Rooms from: $625* ✉ *300 S. Doheny Dr., Beverly Hills*
☎ *310/273–2222, 800/332–3442* ⊕ *www.fourseasons.com/losangeles*
⇌ *285 rooms* ⦿ *No meals* ✛ *2:B3.*

$$$$ ▦ **Montage Beverly Hills.** The nine-story, Mediterranean-style palazzo
HOTEL   is dedicated to welcoming those who relish luxury, providing classic
FAMILY   style and exemplary service. **Pros:** secret whiskey bar tucked upstairs;
Fodor's Choice   Gornick & Drucker Barber Shop on-site; obliging, highly trained
★   staff; families love the kids' club Paintbox. **Cons:** the hefty tab for all
this finery. $ *Rooms from: $695* ✉ *225 N. Cañon Dr., Beverly Hills*
☎ *310/860–7800, 888/860–0788* ⊕ *www.montagebeverlyhills.com/beverlyhills* ⇌ *201 rooms* ⦿ *No meals* ✛ *2:B3.*

$$$$ ▦ **Peninsula Beverly Hills.** This French Rivera–style palace overflowing
HOTEL   with antiques and art is a favorite of boldface names, but visitors consis-
Fodor's Choice   tently describe a stay here as near perfect. **Pros:** Belvedere restaurant on-
★   site is a lunchtime favorite; sunny pool area with cabanas; complimentary
Rolls-Royce takes you to nearby Beverly Hills. **Cons:** very expensive;
room decor might feel too ornate for some. $ *Rooms from: $595* ✉ *9882
S. Santa Monica Blvd., Beverly Hills* ☎ *310/551–2888, 800/462–7899*
⊕ *beverlyhills.peninsula.com* ⇌ *195 rooms* ⦿ *No meals* ✛ *2:A3.*

$$$$ ▦ **SLS Hotel at Beverly Hills.** From the sleek, Philippe Starck–designed lobby
HOTEL   and lounge with fireplaces, hidden nooks, and a communal table, to poolside cabanas with DVD players, this hotel offers a cushy, dreamlike stay.
Pros: on-property cuisine masterminded by Jose Andres; fully stocked
bar in each room; dreamy Ciel spa. **Cons:** standard rooms are compact;
pricey dining and parking; design might seem cold to some. $ *Rooms
from: $639* ✉ *465 S. La Cienega Blvd., Beverly Hills* ☎ *310/247–0400*
⊕ *www.slshotels.com* ⇌ *297 rooms* ⦿ *No meals* ✛ *2:C3.*

WEST HOLLYWOOD

$$ ▦ **Farmer's Daughter Hotel.** A favorite of *The Price Is Right* and *Danc-*
HOTEL   *ing with the Stars* hopefuls (both TV shows tape at the CBS studios
Fodor's Choice   nearby), this hotel has a tongue-in-cheek country style with a hopping
★   Sunday brunch, and a little pool accented by giant rubber duckies. **Pros:**
bikes for rent; daily yoga; book lending library. **Cons:** shaded pool; no
bathtubs; staff can be stiff. $ *Rooms from: $260* ✉ *115 S. Fairfax Ave.,*

West Hollywood ☎ *323/937–3930, 800/334–1658* 🌐 *www.farmersdaughterhotel.com* 🛏 *65 rooms* 🍴 *No meals* ✥ *2:C3.*

$$$ HOTEL 🏨 **The London West Hollywood at Beverly Hills.** Just off the Sunset Strip, cosmopolitan and chic in design, especially after the $27-million renovation in 2015, the London West Hollywood is known for its large suites, rooftop pool with citywide views, and luxury touches throughout. **Pros:** state-of-the-art fitness center; Chef Anthony Keen oversees dining program; 110-seat screening room. **Cons:** too refined for kids to be comfortable; lower floors have mundane views. [$] *Rooms from: $395* ✉ *1020 N. San Vicente Blvd., West Hollywood* ☎ *310/854–1111, 866/282–4560* 🌐 *www.thelondonwesthollywood.com* 🛏 *225 suites* 🍴 *No meals* ✥ *2:B2.*

$$$ HOTEL Fodor's Choice ★ 🏨 **Sunset Marquis Hotel & Villas.** If you're in town to cut your new hit single, you'll appreciate this near-the-Strip hidden retreat in the heart of WeHo, with two on-site recording studios. **Pros:** favorite among rock stars; 53 villas with lavish extras; exclusive Bar 1200; free passes to Equinox nearby. **Cons:** rooms can feel dark; small balconies. [$] *Rooms from: $365* ✉ *1200 N. Alta Loma Rd., West Hollywood* ☎ *310/657–1333, 800/858–9758* 🌐 *www.sunsetmarquis.com* 🛏 *154 rooms* 🍴 *No meals* ✥ *2:C2.*

5

SANTA MONICA AND THE BEACHES

LOS ANGELES INTERNATIONAL AIRPORT

$ HOTEL 🏨 **Sheraton Gateway Los Angeles.** LAX's swanky hotel just had some serious work done to its already sleek look, yet the appeal is in more than just the style; in-transit visitors love the 24-hour room service, fitness center, and airport shuttle. **Pros:** significantly lower weekend rates; free LAX shuttle; on-site restaurant, Costero California Bar and Bistro, slings craft beer. **Cons:** convenient to airport but not much else. [$] *Rooms from: $149* ✉ *6101 W. Century Blvd., Los Angeles International Airport* ☎ *310/642–1111, 800/325–3535* 🌐 *www.sheratonlosangeles.com* 🛏 *802 rooms* 🍴 *No meals* ✥ *3:C3.*

MALIBU

$$$$ B&B/INN 🏨 **Malibu Beach Inn.** Set right on exclusive Carbon Beach, Malibu's hideaway for the super-rich remains the room to nab along the coast, with an ultrachic new look thanks to designer Waldo Fernandez, and an upscale restaurant and wine bar overlooking the Pacific. **Pros:** see the ocean from your private balcony; wine list curated by sommelier Laurie Sutton. **Cons:** billionaire's travel budget required; noise of PCH; no pool, gym, or hot tub. [$] *Rooms from: $575* ✉ *22878 Pacific Coast Hwy., Malibu* ☎ *310/456–6444* 🌐 *www.malibubeachinn.com* 🛏 *47 rooms* 🍴 *No meals* ✥ *3:A1.*

SANTA MONICA

$$$ HOTEL 🏨 **The Ambrose.** An air of tranquillity pervades the beach-chic four-story Ambrose, which blends right into its mostly residential Santa Monica neighborhood. **Pros:**"green" practices: nontoxic cleaners, recycling bins; partial ocean view. **Cons:** quiet, residential area of Santa Monica; parking fee ($27). [$] *Rooms from: $345* ✉ *1255 20th St., Santa Monica* ☎ *310/315–1555, 877/262–7673* 🌐 *www.ambrosehotel.com* 🛏 *77 rooms* 🍴 *Breakfast* ✥ *3:B2.*

$$
B&B/INN
Fodor's Choice
★
🏨 **Channel Road Inn.** A quaint surprise in Southern California, the Channel Road Inn is every bit the country retreat bed-and-breakfast lovers adore, with four-poster beds, fluffy duvets, and a cozy living room with a fireplace. **Pros:** free wine and hors d'oeuvres every evening; home-cooked breakfast included; meditative rose garden on-site. **Cons:** no pool; need a car to get around. $ *Rooms from: $225* ✉ *219 W. Channel Rd., Santa Monica* ☎ *310/459–1920* ⊕ *www.channelroadinn.com* ⬎ *15 rooms* ❅ *Breakfast* ✛ *3:B2.*

$$$$
HOTEL
🏨 **Fairmont Miramar Hotel & Bungalows Santa Monica.** A mammoth Moreton Bay fig tree dwarfs the main entrance of the 5-acre beach-adjacent Santa Monica wellness retreat, and lends its name to the inviting on-site Mediterranean-inspired restaurant, FIG, which focuses on local ingredients. **Pros:** guests can play games on the heated patio; swanky open-air cocktail spot The Bungalow on-site; stay in retrofitted '20s and '40s bungalows. **Cons:** all this luxury comes at a big price. $ *Rooms from: $439* ✉ *101 Wilshire Blvd., Santa Monica* ☎ *310/576–7777, 866/540–4470* ⊕ *www.fairmont.com/santamonica* ⬎ *334 rooms* ❅ *No meals* ✛ *3:B2.*

$
HOTEL
🏨 **Sea Shore Motel.** On Santa Monica's busy Main Street, the Sea Shore is a throwback to Route 66 and to '60s-style, family-run roadside motels, and is surrounded by an ultra-trendy neighborhood. **Pros:** close to beach and restaurants; free Wi-Fi and parking; popular rooftop deck and on-site restaurant, Amelia's. **Cons:** street noise; motel-style decor and beds. $ *Rooms from: $155* ✉ *2637 Main St., Santa Monica* ☎ *310/392–2787* ⊕ *www.seashoremotel.com* ⬎ *24 rooms* ❅ *No meals* ✛ *3:B3.*

$$$$
HOTEL
Fodor's Choice
★
🏨 **Shore Hotel.** With views of the Santa Monica Pier, this hotel with a friendly staff offers eco-minded travelers stylish rooms with a modern design, just steps from the sand and sea. **Pros:** near beach and Third Street Promenade; rainfall showerheads; solar-heated pool and hot tub. **Cons:** expensive rooms and parking fees; fronting busy Ocean Avenue. $ *Rooms from: $539* ✉ *1515 Ocean Ave., Santa Monica* ☎ *310/458–1515* ⊕ *shorehotel.com* ⬎ *164 rooms* ❅ *No meals* ✛ *3:B2.*

$$$$
HOTEL
FAMILY
Fodor's Choice
★
🏨 **Shutters on the Beach.** Set right on the sand, this inn has become synonymous with staycations, and while the hotel's service gets mixed reviews from some readers, the beachfront location and show-house decor make this one of SoCal's most popular luxury hotels. **Pros:** built-in cabinets filled with art books and curios; rooms designed by Michael Smith; rooms come with whirlpool tub. **Cons:** service could improve; very expensive. $ *Rooms from: $800* ✉ *1 Pico Blvd., Santa Monica* ☎ *310/458–0030, 800/334–9000* ⊕ *www.shuttersonthebeach.com* ⬎ *198 rooms* ❅ *No meals* ✛ *3:B2.*

VENICE

$$$
HOTEL
🏨 **Hotel Erwin.** A boutique hotel a block off the Venice Beach Boardwalk, the Erwin has spacious, airy rooms and a local-favorite rooftop bar and lounge (appropriately named High). **Pros:** dining emphasizes fresh ingredients; playful design in guest rooms. **Cons:** some rooms face a noisy alley; no pool. $ *Rooms from: $319* ✉ *1697 Pacific Ave., Venice* ☎ *310/452–1111, 800/786–7789* ⊕ *www.hotelerwin.com* ⬎ *119 rooms* ❅ *No meals* ✛ *3:B3.*

PASADENA

$$$$
HOTEL
FAMILY
Fodor's Choice
★

The Langham Huntington, Pasadena. Fronted by the historic Horseshoe Garden, this 1907 grande dame spans 23 acres and includes an Italianate-style main building, Spanish Revival cottages, a lanai, an azalea-filled Japanese garden, and several dining options. **Pros:** great for a romantic escape; delicious Cal-French restaurant Royce; top-notch Chuan Spa. **Cons:** in a suburban neighborhood far from local shopping and dining. ⓢ *Rooms from: $429* ✉ *1401 S. Oak Knoll Ave., Pasadena* ☎ *626/568–3900* ⊕ *www.pasadena.langhamhotels.com* ➵ *380 rooms* ⊘ *No meals* ✛ *1:B1.*

NIGHTLIFE AND PERFORMING ARTS

Local publications *Los Angeles* magazine (⊕ *www.lamag.com*) and *LA Weekly* (⊕ *www.laweekly.com*), or sites like TimeOut (⊕ *www. timeout.com/los-angeles)*, are great places to discover what's happening in the city.

NIGHTLIFE

Updated
by Meg
Butler, Audrey
Farnsworth,
Rachael Levitt,
Rachael Roth,
Jesse Tabit,
and Jeremy
Tarr

The focus of L.A. nightlife once centered on the Sunset Strip, with its multitude of bars and rock clubs; now most corners of the city have their own distinct after-hours culture. Whether you plan to test your limits at historic establishments Downtown or take advantage of a cheap happy hour at a Hollywood dive, this city's nightlife has something for you.

Utilize a ride-share app to avoid pricey parking. Most neighborhoods near party-heavy areas like West Hollywood require residential parking permits, so if you do drive, you're often better off with a garage or valet parking. Either option costs from $5 to $20.

HOLLYWOOD

BARS

FAMILY
Fodor's Choice
★

Musso & Frank Grill. The prim and proper vibe of this old-school steak house won't appeal to those looking for a raucous night out; instead, its appeal lies in its history and sturdy drinks. Established in 1919, its dark wood decor, red tuxedo–clad waiters, and highly skilled bartenders can easily shuttle you back to its Hollywood heyday when Marilyn Monroe, F. Scott Fitzgerald, and Greta Garbo once hung around and sipped martinis. ✉ *6667 Hollywood Blvd., Hollywood* ☎ *323/467–7788* ⊕ *www. mussoandfrank.com.*

Three Clubs. Part martini lounge, part biker bar, this spot right on the corner of Santa Monica and Vine has plush leather booths and cozy bar seats. The focus is on fresh and local ingredients for all the cocktails, and they offer a daily happy hour. There's a small cover charge to watch bands, comedy, or burlesque shows on the stage in the back room. ✉ *1123 Vine St., Hollywood* ☎ *323/462–6441* ⊕ *www.threeclubs.com.*

Yamashiro Hollywood. Modeled after a mansion in Kyoto, this Japanese place with a hillside perch has spectacular koi ponds and gardens, as well as sweeping views of Hollywood's twinkling lights. Additional lures here include the tasty, if pricey, food and delicious drinks. ■**TIP→ The mandatory valet parking costs $10.** ⊠ *1999 N. Sycamore Ave., Hollywood* ☏ *323/466–5125* ⊕ *www.yamashirohollywood.com.*

CLUBS

Boardner's. This neighborhood lounge has been around for decades, and its dim lighting and leather booths give it a well-worn feel. The adjoining open-air Club 52, with an ornate tiled fountain in the center, has its own cover charge and entrance, and often hosts burlesque shows or live bands. The long-running Saturday Goth night, Bar Sinister, remains popular here after 19 years. ⊠ *1652 N. Cherokee Ave., Hollywood* ☏ *323/462–9621* ⊕ *www.boardners.com.*

COMEDY

Fodor's Choice
★

Upright Citizens Brigade. The L.A. offshoot of New York's famous troupe continues its tradition of sketch comedy and improv with weekly shows like "Facebook" (where the audience's online profiles are mined for material), and "Doug Loves Movies," where comedian Doug Benson invites three surprise guests (Zach Galifianakis and Sarah Silverman have both made appearances) to play a movie-themed game show with loose rules. Arrive early as space is limited. A second theater on Sunset Boulevard opened in 2014. ⊠ *5919 Franklin Ave., Hollywood* ☏ *323/908–8702* ⊕ *www.ucbtheatre.com.*

LIVE MUSIC

Avalon. This multitasking art deco venue offers both live music and club nights. The killer sound system, cavernous space, and multiple bars make it a perfect venue for both. The club is best known for its DJs, who often spin well past the 2 am cutoff for drinks. The crowd can be a mixed bag, depending on the night, but if you're looking to dance, you likely won't be disappointed. Upstairs is **Bardot,** which hosts a free Monday night showcase of up-and-coming artists called School Night! that's always a good time. Remember to RSVP online in advance; they'll be checking names at the door. ⊠ *1735 Vine St., Hollywood* ☏ *323/462–8900* ⊕ *www.avalonhollywood.com.*

Fodor's Choice
★

El Floridita. Although the exterior might not look like much, El Floridita is a popular live salsa music spot on Monday, Friday, and Saturday, with dancers ranging from enthusiasts to those just trying to keep up. There's a $15 cover to listen to the band, although admission is free with dinner. Reservations are recommended to guarantee a table. ⊠ *1253 N. Vine St., Hollywood* ☏ *323/871–8612* ⊕ *www.elfloridita.com.*

Largo at the Coronet. The welcoming vibe of this venue attracts big-name performers who treat its stage as their home away from home in Los Angeles. Standouts include musician and music producer Jon Brion, who often appears here with special drop-in guests (Fiona Apple and Andrew Bird have both been on the bill). Comedians Sarah Silverman and Patton Oswalt each host a monthly comedy show. Bring cash for drinks in the Little Room before the show. ⊠ *366 N. La Cienega Blvd., Hollywood* ☏ *310/855–0350* ⊕ *www.largo-la.com.*

Continued on page 183

Cole's

L.A. STORY
THE CITY'S HISTORY THROUGH ITS BARS

Los Angeles is known as a place where dreams are realized, but it is also a place where pasts are forgotten. Despite what people say about L.A.'s lack of memory, however, there are quite a few noteworthy old-school bars that pay tribute to the city's vibrant past and its famous patrons.

Collectively, these eclectic watering holes have hosted everyone from ex-presidents to rock legends to famed authors and, of course, a continual stream of countless movie stars.

The bars are located in virtually every corner of the city—from Downtown to West Hollywood to Santa Monica.

In terms of character, they run the gamut from dive to dressy and serve everything from top-shelf whisky to bargain-basement beer.

While it's their differences that have kept people coming back through the decades, they all have something in common: Each has a story to tell.

EIGHT OF L.A.'S BEST

Mixing at Cole's

Chez Jay

Cole's

Frolic Room

CHEZ JAY RESTAURANT (1959)
Noteworthy for: Located down the block from the Santa Monica Pier, this steak-and-seafood joint walks the line between celebrity hangout and dive bar.
Signature drink: Martini
Celeb clientele: Members of the Rat Pack, Leonard Nimoy, Sean Penn, Julia Roberts, Renée Zellweger, Owen Wilson, Drew Barrymore
Don't miss: The little booth in the back of the restaurant, known to insiders as Table 10, is a favorite celebrity hideout.
Filmed here: *A Single Man, Goliath*
Join the crowd: *1657 Ocean Ave., Santa Monica, 310/395–1741*

COLE'S (1908)
Noteworthy for: Found inside the Pacific Electric building, touted as Los Angeles's oldest public house, and once the epicenter of the Red Car railway network, this watering hole has its original glass lighting, penny-tile floors, and 40-foot mahogany bar.

Signature drink: Oldfashioned
Celeb clientele: The men's room boasts that Charles Bukowski and Mickey Cohen once relieved themselves here.
Don't miss: The Varnish at Cole's is an in-house speakeasy with 11 booths that can be accessed through a hidden door marked by a tiny framed picture of a cocktail glass.
Filmed here: *Forrest Gump, L.A. Confidential, Mad Men*
Join the crowd: *118 E. 6th St., Los Angeles, 213/622–4049*

CLIFTON'S REPUBLIC (1931)
Noteworthy for: This historical cafeteria/playground featuring a giant redwood tree in the center and intimidating wildlife taxidermy throughout, serves tasty comfort food and houses three lively bars: the Monarch, the Gothic, and the Pacific Seas.
Signature drink: The Mind Eraser at the Tiki bar; El Presidio at the Monarch; the Hyperion at The Gothic Bar (careful—this one's strong).
Claim to fame: Clifton's whimsical forest-themed dining area inspired Walt Disney to create Disneyland.

Chez Jay

Harvelle's

Kibitz Room

Dresden Restaurant

Don't miss: The 40's-era Tiki Bar. Located at the top of a secret stairway, it features deliciously strong drinks, dancing cigarette girls and the occasional appearance of a sequined mermaid.

FROLIC ROOM (1935)

Noteworthy for: This Hollywood favorite next door to the famed Pantages Theater has served actors and writers from Elizabeth Short to Charles Bukowski.

Signature drink: Cheap Budweiser ($2.75 during happy hour)

Celeb clientele: Kiefer Sutherland

Don't miss: A bowl of popcorn from the old-fashioned machine; the Hirschfeld mural depicting Marilyn Monroe, Charlie Chaplin, Louis Armstrong, Frank Sinatra, and others.

Filmed here: *L.A. Confidential, Southland*

Join the crowd: *6245 Hollywood Blvd., Los Angeles, 323/462–5890*

HARVELLE'S (1931)

Noteworthy for: Located one block off the Third Street Promenade, this dark and sexy jazz bar is said to be the oldest live music venue on the Westside.

Signature drink: The Deadly Sins martini menu offers house made mixes named after the seven sins, from Pride to Lust.

Don't miss: The Toledo Show is a pulse-quickening weekly burlesque-and-jazz performance on Sunday nights.

Join the crowd: *1432 4th St., Santa Monica, 310/395–1676.*

THE KIBITZ ROOM AT CANTER'S DELI (1961)

Noteworthy for: Adjacent to the famous Canter's Deli, which opened in 1948, this Fairfax District nightspot is definitely a dive bar, but that doesn't keep the A-listers away. Joni Mitchell, Jakob Dylan, and Fiona Apple have all played here.

Signature drink: Cheap beer

Celeb clientele: Jim Morrison, Frank Zappa, Juliette Lewis, Julia Roberts, Javier Bardem, Penélope Cruz

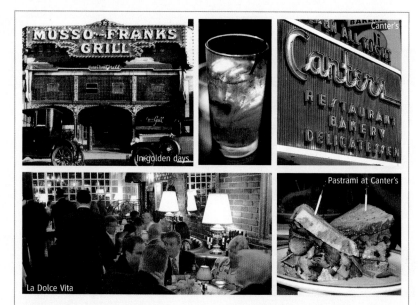

In golden days

Canter's

Pastrami at Canter's

La Dolce Vita

Don't miss: The decor is pure retro 1960s, including vinyl booths and a fall-leaf motif on the ceiling.
Filmed here: *I Ought to Be in Pictures, Entourage, Curb Your Enthusiasm, Sunset Strip, Enemy of the State, What's Eating Gilbert Grape*
Join the crowd: *419 N. Fairfax Ave., Los Angeles, 323/651–2030.*

DOLCE VITA (1966)
Noteworthy for: Located in tony Beverly Hills, this staple for northern Italian has a classy clubhouse atmosphere, round leather booths, white tablecloths, and exposed-brick walls.
Signature drink: Martini
Celeb clientele: Members of the Rat Pack; several ex-presidents, including Ronald Reagan. The place prides itself on being a safe haven from pesky paparazzi.
Don't miss: The burgundy-hued round leather booths.
Join the crowd: *9785 Santa Monica Blvd., Los Angeles, 310/278–1845*

MUSSO & FRANK GRILL (1919)
Noteworthy for: This swanky old-timer is called the oldest bar in Hollywood. While that title may spark jealousy among some of its Tinseltown counterparts, there is no doubt that this famed grill conjures Hollywood's halcyon days with its authentic '30s-era decor—and serves a mean martini.
Signature drink: The Mean Martini
Celeb clientele: Charlie Chaplin, Greta Garbo, Ernest Hemingway, F. Scott Fitzgerald, Marilyn Monroe
Don't miss: The red tuxedo-clad waiters are famous in their own right; some have been at the restaurant for more than 40 years.
Filmed here: *Ocean's Eleven, Charlie's Angels 2, Mad Men*
Join the crowd: *6667 Hollywood Blvd., Los Angeles, 323/467–7788*

The Musso & Frank Grill

THE OLDEST RESTAURANT IN HOLLYWOOD
Since 1919

WEST HOLLYWOOD

BARS

Rainbow Bar & Grill. Its location next door to a long-running music venue, the Roxy, helped cement this bar and restaurant's status as a legendary watering hole for musicians (as well as their entourages and groupies). The Who, Guns N' Roses, Poison, Kiss, and many others have all passed through the doors. Expect a $5–$10 cover, but you'll get the money back in drink tickets or a food discount. ⊠ *9015 W. Sunset Blvd., West Hollywood* ☎ *310/278–4232* ⊕ *www.rainbowbarandgrill.com.*

The Standard. Weekend pool parties in the summer are downright notorious at the Standard Hollywood. Party on the pool deck with DJs, or hear acoustic sets in the Cactus Lodge on Wednesday evenings. Check the calendar for special events like film screenings. ⊠ *The Standard Hollywood, 8300 Sunset Blvd., West Hollywood* ☎ *323/650–9090* ⊕ *www.standardhotels.com.*

CLUBS

Rage. The various events at this gay bar and dance club draw different crowds—show queens for Broadway musical sing-alongs, drag queens (and more show queens) for the Dreamgirls Revue, half-nude chiseled-bodied men for Fetch Tuesdays and Thursday Night College Night. There's lots of eye candy, even more so on weekends. ⊠ *8911 Santa Monica Blvd., West Hollywood* ☎ *310/652–7055* ⊕ *www.rage-nightclub.com.*

COMEDY

Comedy Store. Three stages give seasoned and unseasoned comedians a place to perform and try out new material, with performers such as Louis C.K. and Sarah Silverman dropping by just for fun. The front bar along Sunset Boulevard is a popular hangout after or between shows, oftentimes with that night's comedians mingling with fans. ⊠ *8433 Sunset Blvd., West Hollywood* ☎ *323/650–6268* ⊕ *www.thecomedystore.com.*

Laugh Factory. Top stand-up comics appear at this Sunset Boulevard mainstay, often working out the kinks in new material in advance of national tours. Stars such as Kevin Hart and Tim Allen sometimes drop by unannounced, and Kevin Nealon puts on a monthly show. Midnight Madness on the weekends is extremely popular, with comics performing more daring sets. ⊠ *8001 W. Sunset Blvd., West Hollywood* ☎ *323/656–1336* ⊕ *www.laughfactory.com* ⊟ *$20.*

LIVE MUSIC

The Troubadour. The intimate vibe of the Troubadour helps make this club a favorite with music fans. Around since 1957, this venue has a storied past. These days, the eclectic lineup is still attracting the crowds, with the focus mostly on rock, indie, and folk music. Those looking for drinks can imbibe to their heart's content at the adjacent bar. ⊠ *9081 Santa Monica Blvd., West Hollywood* ⊕ *www.troubadour.com.*

Viper Room. This rock club on the edge of the Sunset Strip has been around for more than 20 years and is famously known as the site of much controversial Hollywood history. Today the venue books rising alt-rock acts, and covers typically range from $5 to $10. ✉ *8852 W. Sunset Blvd., West Hollywood* ☎ *310/358–1881* ⊕ *www.viperroom.com.*

Whisky A Go Go. The hard-core metal and rock scene is alive and well at the legendary Whisky A Go Go (the full name includes the prefix "World Famous"), where Janis Joplin, Led Zeppelin, Alice Cooper, Van Halen, the Doors (they were the house band for a short stint), and Frank Zappa have all played. On the Strip for more than five decades, they book both underground acts, and huge names in rock. ✉ *8901 Sunset Blvd., West Hollywood* ☎ *310/652–4202* ⊕ *www.whiskyagogo.com.*

ECHO PARK AND SILVER LAKE
BARS
Cha Cha Lounge. This place's decor—part tiki hut, part tacky party palace—shouldn't work, but it does. An import from Seattle, its cheap drinks, foosball tables, and jovial atmosphere make it a natural party scene. ✉ *2375 Glendale Blvd., Silver Lake* ☎ *323/660–7595* ⊕ *www.chachalounge.com.*

Fodor's Choice ★ **Tiki-Ti.** The cozy feel of this Polynesian-theme bar is due in part to its small size—12 seats at the bar, plus a few tables along one side. Open since 1961, it serves strong drinks (92 to be exact), one of which will have the entire place yelling your order. Don't be surprised to find a line outside. ✉ *4427 Sunset Blvd., Silver Lake* ☎ *323/669–9381* ⊕ *www.tiki-ti.com.*

LIVE MUSIC
Fodor's Choice ★ **The Echo.** A neighborhood staple, this beloved spot showcases up-and-coming indie bands that are soon to be big names, with soul or reggae dance nights and DJ mash-up sessions rounding out the calendar. ✉ *1822 Sunset Blvd., Echo Park* ☎ *213/413–8200* ⊕ *www.theecho.com.*

Echoplex. It may surprise you that while this spot is in the basement of the Echo, you have to cross the street and walk under the bridge to access it. A larger space than its sister theater, the Echoplex books bigger national tours and events. Comedians like Marc Maron, and a slew of big names in indie rock have graced the stage. ✉ *1154 Glendale Blvd., Echo Park* ☎ *213/413–8200* ⊕ *www.attheecho.com.*

Fodor's Choice ★ **The Satellite.** This venue hosts a variety of bands, mostly indie rock acts, as well as a popular DJ night, Dance Yourself Clean (with a great range of highly danceable jams), which is held every Saturday. Monday nights are free, and feature exciting up-and-coming acts. Cover charges on other days range from $8 to $15. ✉ *1717 Silver Lake Blvd., Silver Lake* ☎ *323/661–4380* ⊕ *www.thesatellitela.com.*

Silverlake Lounge. Discover new indie, rock, and classical acts at this divey venue. Cheap beer and well drinks abound, with happy hour specials daily. Order delivery from one of the restaurants nearby and eat it at the bar. ✉ *2906 Sunset Blvd., Silver Lake* ☎ *323/663–9636* ⊕ *www.thesilverlakelounge.com.*

PERFORMING ARTS

CONCERT HALLS

Updated by
Alene Dawson

Fodor's Choice
★

Dorothy Chandler Pavilion. Though half a century old, this theater maintains the glamour of its early years, richly decorated with crystal chandeliers and classical theatrical drapes. Part of the Los Angeles Music Center, a large portion of programming is made up of dance and ballet performances, like Shen Yun Performing Arts, a large production showcasing classical Chinese dance and music. Ticket-holders can attend free talks that take place an hour before opera performances. ■TIP➔ Reservations for the talks aren't required, but it's wise to arrive early as space is limited. ✉ *135 N. Grand Ave., Downtown* ☎ *213/972–7211* ⊕ *www. musiccenter.org.*

Greek Theatre. With a robust lineup from May through November, acts such as Beck, John Legend, and Chicago have all graced the stage at this scenic outdoor venue. The 5,900-capacity amphitheater is at the base of Griffith Park, and you may want to make a day of it by hiking or stargazing beforehand. There is usually slow, preshow traffic on concert nights, but it'll give you a chance to take in the beautiful park foliage and homes in the Hollywood Hills. Paid lots are available for parking, but wear comfortable shoes and expect to walk, as some lots are fairly far from the theater. Or, park and enjoy cocktails in the trendy and chic Los Feliz neighborhood below before a show, then walk up to the venue. ✉ *2700 N. Vermont Ave., Los Feliz* ☎ *323/665–5857* ⊕ *www. greektheatrela.com.*

Fodor's Choice
★

Hollywood Bowl. For those seeking a quintessential Los Angeles experience, a concert on a summer night at the Bowl, the city's iconic outdoor venue, is unsurpassed. The Bowl has presented world-class performers since it opened in 1920. The L.A. Philharmonic plays here from June to September; its performances and other events draw large crowds. Parking is limited near the venue, but there are additional remote parking locations serviced by shuttles. You can bring food and drink to any event, which Angelenos often do, though you can only bring alcohol when the LA Phil, as the orchestra is known, is performing. (Bars sell alcohol at all events, and there are dining options.) It's wise to bring a jacket even if daytime temperatures have been warm—the Bowl can get quite chilly at night. ■TIP➔ Visitors can sometimes watch the LA Phil practice for free, usually on a weekday; call ahead for times. ✉ *2301 Highland Ave., Hollywood* ☎ *323/850–2000* ⊕ *www.hollywoodbowl.com.*

Microsoft Theatre. Formerly known as the Nokia Theatre L.A., the Microsoft Theatre is host to a variety of concerts and big-name awards shows—the Emmys, American Music Awards, BET Awards, and the ESPYs. This theater and the surrounding L.A. Live complex are a draw for those looking for a fun night out. The building's emphasis on acoustics and versatile seating arrangements means that all the seats are good, whether you're at an intimate Neil Young concert or the People's Choice Awards. Outside, the L.A. Live complex hosts restaurants and attractions, including the Grammy Museum, to keep patrons entertained before and after shows (though it's open whether or not there's a performance). ✉ *777 Chick Hearn Ct., Downtown* ☎ *213/763–6030* ⊕ *www.nokiatheatrelalive.com.*

Shrine Auditorium. Since opening in 1926, the auditorium has hosted nearly every major awards show at one point or another. Today, the venue and adjacent Expo Hall hosts performers like Radiohead, and festivals, including Tenacious D's comedy/music extravaganza, Festival Supreme, in October. The Shrine's Moorish Revival–style architecture is a spectacle all its own. ⊠ *665 W. Jefferson Blvd., Downtown* ☎ *213/748–5116* ⊕ *www.shrineauditorium.com.*

FILM

Watching movies here isn't merely an efficient way to kill time, but it's an *event*. With theaters this close to the movie studios, it's not unusual for major directors or actors to participate in a post-film discussion. Whether it's a first-run film or a revival, the show will likely be worth the trip out.

The American Cinemathèque at the Aero and Egyptian Theatres. American Cinemathèque screens classic and independent films at two theaters, the Aero and the Egyptian. Expect everything from Hitchcock thrillers, to anime by Hayao Miyazaki, plus occasional Q&A sessions with directors and actors following film screenings. The Egyptian Theatre in Hollywood has the distinction of hosting the first-ever movie premiere when it opened back in 1922. Its ornate courtyard and columns have been restored to preserve the building's history. The Aero Theatre in Santa Monica opened in 1940. ⊠ *6712 Hollywood Blvd., Hollywood* ☎ *323/466–3456* ⊕ *www.americancinematheque.com.*

Fodor'sChoice **ArcLight.** This big multiplex includes the historic Cinerama Dome, that
★ impossible-to-miss golf ball–looking structure on Sunset Boulevard, which was built in 1963. Like many L.A. theaters, the ArcLight has assigned seating (you will be asked to select seats when purchasing tickets). The complex is a one-stop shop with a parking garage, shopping area, restaurant, and in-house bar. The events calendar is worth paying attention to, as directors and actors often drop by to chat with audiences. Amy Adams and Samuel L. Jackson, for example, have both made time for post-screening Q&As. Movies here can be pricey (ranging from around $18–$25), but the theater shows just about every new release. ■TIP→ **Evening shows on the weekend feature "21+" shows, during which moviegoers can bring alcoholic beverages into the screening rooms.** ⊠ *6360 Sunset Blvd., Hollywood* ☎ *323/464–4226* ⊕ *www.arclightcinemas.com.*

Cinefamily at The Silent Movie Theatre. Although the name may imply that only silent movies are shown here, this theater also has a packed schedule of film screenings, from rare to indie to foreign. Regular events include Doug Benson's Movie Interruption, Haunted Hangovers (early matinees paired with coffee or mimosas on weekends leading up to Halloween), and The Silent Treatment—pre–sound era films that run on the second Saturday of every month (though it's best to check the calendar for changes). Also expect special guests, live music, dance parties, and potlucks. ⊠ *611 N. Fairfax Ave., Fairfax District* ☎ *323/655–2510* ⊕ *www.cinefamily.org.*

THEATER

Center Theatre Group. Celebrating their 50th anniversary, Center Theatre Group is comprised of three venues: The Ahmanson and the Taper (both at the Music Center campus Downtown), and the Kirk Douglas Theatre in Culver City. They show an array of productions, from the world premiere of newcomer Nigerian playwright Ngozi Anyanwu's *Good Grief*, to touring productions of Broadway hits like *Jersey Boys.* ⊠ *135 N. Grand Ave., Downtown* ☎ *213/972–7211* ⊕ *www.centertheatregroup.org.*

Ahmanson Theatre. The largest of L.A.'s Center Group's three theaters, Ahmanson Theatre presents larger-scale classic revivals, dramas, musicals, and comedies like *Into the Woods,* that are either going to, or coming from Broadway and the West End. The ambience is a theater-lover's delight. ⊠ *135 N. Grand Ave., Downtown* ☎ *213/628–2772* ⊕ *www.centertheatregroup.org.*

Mark Taper Forum. Both dramas and comedies dominate the stage at the Mark Taper Forum, next door to the Ahmanson Theatre in Downtown. Plenty of shows that premiered here have gone on to Broadway and off-Broadway theaters (a number of Pulitzer Prize–winning plays have also been developed here). ⊠ *135 N. Grand Ave., Downtown* ☎ *213/628–2772* ⊕ *www.centertheatregroup.org.*

Kirk Douglas Theatre. This theater, located in a walkable Culver City neighborhood (close to cocktail bars and trendy restaurants), stages modern works and world premieres. The smallest venue of the group at 317 seats, the theater also hosts intimate workshops and readings. ⊠ *9820 W. Washington Blvd., Culver City* ☎ *213/628–2772* ⊕ *www.centertheatregroup.org.*

Geffen Playhouse. Well-known actors are often on the bill at the Geffen, and plays by established playwrights, such as Neil LaBute and Lynn Nottage, happen regularly. With two stages hosting world premieres and critically acclaimed works, there's always something compelling to watch. ■ TIP→ **Free events are frequently put on for ticket holders, including Wine Down Sundays, which feature music and wine sampling before evening shows.** ⊠ *10886 Le Conte Ave., Westwood* ☎ *310/208–5454* ⊕ *www.geffenplayhouse.com.*

Ricardo Montalbán Theatre. Plays, musicals, and concerts all happen at this midsize theater, mostly focusing on Latin culture. When the weather warms up, they host the Rooftop Cinema Club, where you can watch a flick on the roof (they give out blankets on cold nights), indulge at the snack bar, and take in views of Hollywood. ⊠ *1615 N. Vine St., Hollywood* ☎ *323/871–2420* ⊕ *www.themontalban.com.*

Pantages Theatre. For the grand-scale theatrics of a Broadway show, such as *Hamilton* and *The Book of Mormon*, the 2,703-seat Pantages Theatre (the last theater built by Greek-American vaudeville producer Alexander Pantages) lights up Hollywood Boulevard on show nights, when lines of excited patrons extend down the block. ⊠ *6233 Hollywood Blvd., Hollywood* ☎ *800/982–2787* ⊕ *www.hollywoodpantages.com.*

5

SPORTS AND THE OUTDOORS

BASEBALL

Los Angeles Angels of Anaheim. The Angels often contend for the top slot in the Western Division of pro baseball's American League. ⊠ *Angel Stadium of Anaheim, 2000 E. Gene Autry Way, Anaheim* ☎ *714/940–2000* ⊕ *www.angelsbaseball.com.*

Los Angeles Dodgers. The Dodgers take on their National League rivals at one of major league baseball's most comfortable ballparks, Dodger Stadium. ⊠ *Dodger Stadium, 1000 Elysian Park Ave., exit off I–110, Pasadena Fwy.* ☎ *323/224–1507* ⊕ *www.dodgers.com.*

BASKETBALL

L.A.'s pro basketball teams play at the Staples Center.

Los Angeles Clippers. L.A.'s "other" pro basketball team, the Clippers, was formerly an easy ticket, but these days the club routinely sells out its home games. ⊠ *Staples Center, 1111 S. Figueroa St.* ☎ *213/742–7100* ⊕ *www.nba.com/clippers.*

Los Angeles Lakers. The team of pro-basketball champions Magic and Kareem, and Shaq and Kobe has slipped in recent years, but games are still intense, especially if the Lakers are playing a rival team. ⊠ *Staples Center, 1111 S. Figueroa St., Downtown* ☎ *310/426–6000* ⊕ *www. nba.com/lakers.*

Los Angeles Sparks. The women's pro basketball team has made it to the WNBA playoffs more than a dozen times in the past two decades. ⊠ *Staples Center, 1111 S. Figueroa St.* ☎ *310/426–6031* ⊕ *www.wnba.com/sparks.*

SHOPPING

DOWNTOWN

Updated by
Ashley Tibbits

Los Angeles's close association to the rich and famous has long made it a major shopping destination, but in recent years the city has grown beyond just a locale for luxe clothing and accessories—although high-end goods will always be a cornerstone of L.A.'s retail scene. With a wealth of stellar vintage spots, purveyors of affordable on-the-pulse products, and an ever-growing number of shops selling local artisanal goods, there is truly something for every type of spender here.

SHOPPING STREETS AND DISTRICTS

Fashion District. With the influx of emerging designers in this pocket of Downtown, it's become much more than just a wholesale market. Besides containing the plant paradise that is the Flower District as well as the Fabric District, the neighborhood now boasts a bevy of boutiques and cool coffee shops, thanks in part to the opening of the stylish Ace Hotel. ⊠ *Roughly between I–10 and 7th St., and S. San Pedro and S. Main Sts., Downtown* ⊕ *www.fashiondistrict.org.*

The Santa Monica Pier is packed with fun diversions and hosts free concerts in summer.

Santee Alley. Situated in the Fashion District, Santee Alley is known for back-alley deals on knockoffs of designer sunglasses, jewelry, handbags, shoes, and clothing. Be prepared to haggle, and don't lose sight of your wallet. Weekend crowds can be overwhelming, but there's plenty of street food to keep your energy up. ⊠ *Santee St. and Maple Ave. from Olympic Blvd. to 11th St., Downtown* ⊕ *www.thesanteealley.com.*

Jewelry District. Filled with bargain hunters, these crowded sidewalks resemble a slice of Manhattan. While you can save big on everything from wedding bands to sparkling belt buckles, the neighborhood also offers several more upscale vendors for those in search of super-special pieces. ⊠ *Between Olive St. and Broadway from 5th to 8th St., Downtown.*

Fodor'sChoice ★ **Olvera Street.** Historic buildings line this redbrick walkway overhung with grape vines. At dozens of clapboard stalls you can browse south-of-the-border goods—leather sandals, woven blankets, and devotional candles, as well as cheap toys and souvenirs—and sample outstanding tacos. With the musicians and cafés providing the soundtrack, the area is constantly lively. ⊠ *Between Cesar Chavez Ave. and Arcadia St., Downtown* ⊕ *www.olvera-street.com.*

HOLLYWOOD AND THE STUDIOS

Here you can find everything from records to lingerie to movie memorabilia.

BOOKS AND MUSIC

Fodor'sChoice
★
Amoeba Records. Touted as the "World's Largest Independent Record Store," Amoeba is a playground for music-lovers, with a knowledgeable staff and a focus on local artists. Catch free in-store appearances and signings by artists and bands that play sold-out shows at venues down the road. There's a rich stock of new and used CDs and DVDs, LPs, and 45s, an impressive cache of collectibles, and walls filled with concert posters. ⊠ *6400 W. Sunset Blvd., at Cahuenga Blvd., Hollywood* ☎ *323/245–6400* ⊕ *www.amoeba.com.*

CLOTHING

Lost & Found. Specializing in emerging local and indie designers, this impeccably curated retailer keeps posh housewares such as lambswool throws, Brazilian soapstone cookware, and hand-thrown ceramics regularly in stock. But while you're here, don't sleep on the men's French shirting, modern bohemian clothing by Los Angeles' own Raquel Allegra, and luxurious baby blankets; there's something chic for everyone in the family. ⊠ *6320 Yucca St., Hollywood* ☎ *323/856–5872* ⊕ *www.lostandfoundshop.com.*

MALLS AND SHOPPING CENTERS

Hollywood & Highland. Full of designer shops (BCBGMaxAzria, Louis Vuitton) and chain stores (Victoria's Secret, Fossil, and Sephora), this entertainment complex is a huge tourist magnet. The design pays tribute to the city's film legacy, with a grand staircase leading up to a pair of three-story-tall stucco elephants, a nod to the 1916 movie *Intolerance.* Pause at the entrance arch, called Babylon Court, which frames a picture-perfect view of the Hollywood sign. On the second level, next to the Dolby Theatre, is a visitor information center with maps, brochures, and a multilingual staff. The streets nearby provide the setting for Sunday's Hollywood Farmers Market, where you're likely to spot a celebrity or two picking up fresh produce or stopping to pick up breakfast from the food vendors. ⊠ *Hollywood Blvd. and Highland Ave., Hollywood* ☎ *323/817–0220* ⊕ *www.hollywoodandhighland.com.*

BEVERLY HILLS AND THE WESTSIDE

BEVERLY HILLS

The shops of Beverly Hills, particularly Rodeo Drive, are a big draw for window-shopping, and leave visitors awestruck by L.A.'s excess. In this highly walkable neighborhood you'll find big-name luxury jewelers and department stores such as Cartier and Barneys New York.

BOOKS

Taschen. Philippe Starck designed the Taschen space to evoke a cool 1920s Parisian salon—a perfect showcase for the publisher's design-forward coffee table books about architecture, travel, culture, and photography. A suspended glass cube gallery in back hosts art exhibits and features limited-edition books. ⊠ *354 N. Beverly Dr., Beverly Hills* ☎ *310/274–4300* ⊕ *www.taschen.com.*

CLOTHING

Tory Burch. Preppy, stylish, and colorful clothes appropriate for a road trip to Palm Springs or a flight to Palm Beach fill this flagship boutique. ⊠ *142 S. Robertson Blvd., Beverly Hills* ☎ *310/248–2612* ⊕ *www.toryburch.com.*

DEPARTMENT STORES

Barneys New York. This is truly an impressive one-stop shop for high fashion. Deal hunters will appreciate the co-op section, which introduces indie designers before they make it big. Shop for beauty products, shoes, and accessories on the first floor, then wind your way up the staircase for couture. Keep your eyes peeled for fabulous and/or famous folks spearing salads at Fred's on the top floor. ⊠ *9570 Wilshire Blvd., Beverly Hills* ☎ *310/276–4400* ⊕ *www.barneys.com.*

MALLS AND SHOPPING CENTERS

Beverly Center. In addition to luxury retailers like Bloomingdale's, Henri Bendel, and Dolce & Gabbana (which are always ideal for window-shopping if you don't have the means to splurge), this eight-level shopping center also offers plenty of outposts for more affordable brands including Aldo, H&M, and Uniqlo. ⊠ *8500 Beverly Blvd., West Hollywood* ☎ *310/854–0071* ⊕ *www.beverlycenter.com.*

WEST HOLLYWOOD

This is prime shopping real estate, with everything from bridal couture design shops to furnishing stores sharing sidewalk space along posh streets like Melrose Place and Robertson Boulevard. It's also worth strolling West 3rd Street, which is lined with independent but affordable boutiques and several of the city's hottest restaurants and cafés.

CLOTHING

Fodor's Choice ★ **American Rag Cie.** Half the store features new clothing from established and emerging labels, while the other side is stocked with well-preserved vintage clothing organized by color and style. You'll also find plenty of shoes and accessories being picked over by the hippest of Angelenos. ⊠ *150 S. La Brea Ave., West Hollywood* ☎ *323/935–3154* ⊕ *www.amrag.com.*

Fodor's Choice ★ **Fred Segal.** The ivy-covered building and security guards in the parking lot might tip you off that this is *the* place to be. Visit during the lunch hour to stargaze at the super-trendy café. This L.A. landmark is subdivided into smaller boutiques purveying everything from couture clothing to skateboard wear. The entertainment industry's fashion fiends are addicted to these exclusive creations, many from cult designers just beginning to excite the masses. ⊠ *8100 Melrose Ave., West Hollywood* ☎ *323/651–4129* ⊕ *www.fredsegal.com.*

Fodor's Choice ★ **Maxfield.** This modern concrete structure is one of L.A.'s most desirable destinations for ultimate high fashion. The space is stocked with sleek offerings from Chanel, Saint Laurent, Balmain, and Rick Owen, plus occasional pop-ups by fashion's labels-of-the-moment. For serious shoppers (or gawkers) only. ⊠ *8825 Melrose Ave., at Robertson Blvd., West Hollywood* ☎ *310/274–8800* ⊕ *www.maxfieldla.com.*

MALLS AND SHOPPING CENTERS

The Grove. Come to this popular (and polarizing) outdoor mall for familiar names like Anthropologie, Nike, and Nordstrom; stay for the central fountain with "dancing" water and light shows, people-watching from the trolley, and, during the holiday season, artificial snowfall and a winter wonderland. Feel-good pop blasting over the loudspeakers aims to boost your mood while you spend. The adjacent Farmers' Market offers tons of great dining options. ⊠ *189 The Grove Dr., West Hollywood* ☎ *323/900–8080* ⊕ *www.thegrovela.com.*

SANTA MONICA AND THE BEACHES

The breezy beachside communities of Santa Monica and Venice are ideal for leisurely shopping. Scads of tourists (and some locals) gravitate toward Santa Monica Place and Third Street Promenade, a popular pedestrians-only shopping area that is within walking distance of the beach and historic Santa Monica Pier. ■TIP→ **Parking in Santa Monica is next to impossible on Wednesday, when some streets are blocked off for the farmers' market, but there are several parking structures with free parking for an hour or two.**

MALLS AND SHOPPING CENTERS

Malibu Lumber Yard. Emblematic Malibu lifestyle stores in this shopping complex include James Perse, Maxfield, and a too-chic J. Crew outpost. The playground and alfresco dining area make this an ideal weekend destination for families. ⊠ *3939 Cross Creek Rd., Malibu* ⊕ *www.themalibulumberyard.com.*

PASADENA

In Pasadena the stretch of Colorado Boulevard between Pasadena Avenue and Arroyo Parkway, known as Old Town, is a popular pedestrian shopping destination, with retailers such as Crate & Barrel and H&M, and Tiffany's, which sits a block away from Forever 21.

BOOKS

Vroman's Bookstore. Southern California's oldest and largest independent bookseller is justly famous for its great service. A newsstand, café, and stationery store add to the appeal. A regular rotation of events including trivia night, kids' story time, author meet-and-greets, crafting sessions, discussions, and more get the community actively involved. ⊠ *695 E. Colorado Blvd., Pasadena* ☎ *626/449–5320* ⊕ *www.vromansbookstore.com.*

THE CENTRAL COAST

from Ventura to Big Sur with
Channel Island National Park

WELCOME TO
THE CENTRAL COAST

TOP REASONS
TO GO

★ **Incredible nature:** The wild and wonderful Central Coast is home to Channel Islands National Park, two national marine sanctuaries, state parks and beaches, and the rugged Los Padres National Forest.

★ **Edible bounty:** Land and sea provide enough fresh regional foods to satisfy the most sophisticated foodies—grapes, strawberries, seafood, olive oil, and much more. Get your fill at countless farmers' markets, wineries, and restaurants.

★ **Outdoor activities:** Kick back and revel in the California lifestyle. Surf, golf, kayak, hike, play tennis—or just hang out and enjoy the gorgeous scenery.

★ **Small-town charm, big-city culture:** With all the amazing cultural opportunities—museums, theater, music, and festivals—you might start thinking you're in L.A. or San Francisco.

★ **Wine tasting:** Central Coast wines earn high critical praise. Sample them in urban tasting rooms, dusty crossroads towns, and at high- and low-tech rural wineries.

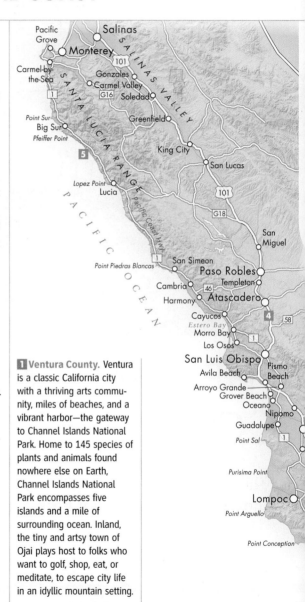

1 Ventura County. Ventura is a classic California city with a thriving arts community, miles of beaches, and a vibrant harbor—the gateway to Channel Islands National Park. Home to 145 species of plants and animals found nowhere else on Earth, Channel Islands National Park encompasses five islands and a mile of surrounding ocean. Inland, the tiny and artsy town of Ojai plays host to folks who want to golf, shop, eat, or meditate, to escape city life in an idyllic mountain setting.

2 **Santa Barbara.** Down-home surfers rub elbows with Hollywood celebrities in sunny, well-scrubbed Santa Barbara, 95 miles north of Los Angeles. Its Spanish-Mexican heritage is reflected in the architectural style of its mission, court-house, and many homes and public buildings.

3 **Northern Santa Barbara County.** Wineries, ranches, and small villages dominate the quintessentially Californian landscape here. The quaint Danish town of Solvang is worth a stop for its half-timber buildings, galleries, and bakeries.

4 **San Luis Obispo County.** Friendly college town San Luis Obispo serves as the hub of a burgeoning wine region that stretches nearly 100 miles from Pismo Beach north to Paso Robles; the 230-plus wineries here have earned reputations for high-quality vintages that rival those of Northern California.

5 **Big Sur Coastline.** Rugged cliffs meet the Pacific for more than 60 miles—one of the most scenic and dramatic drives in the world.

GETTING ORIENTED

The Central Coast region begins about 60 miles north of Los Angeles, near the seaside city of Ventura. North along the sinuous coastline from here lie the cities of Santa Barbara and San Luis Obispo, and beyond them the smaller towns of Morro Bay, Cambria, and Big Sur. The nearly 300-mile drive through this region, especially the section of Highway 1 from San Simeon to Big Sur, is one of the most scenic in the state.

6

0   20 miles

0   30 kilometers

COAST RANGES

166

Santa Maria

Orcutt

101

Los Olivos

246 **3** Santa Ynez

Buellton

Solvang 154   Los Padres National Forest

SAN RAFAEL MOUNTAINS

SANTA YNEZ MOUNTAINS

101   Goleta

Montecito

Mira Monte

Ojai

Santa Paula

2 **Santa Barbara**   Carpinteria

1 Oak View

126

TO CHANNEL ISLANDS

Ventura

Oxnard 101

Santa Barbara Channel

Updated
by Cheryl
Crabtree

Balmy weather, glorious beaches, crystal clear air, and serene landscapes have lured people to the Central Coast since prehistoric times. Today it's also known for its farm-fresh bounty, from grapes vintners crafted into world-class wines, to strawberries and other produce incorporated by chefs into distinctive cuisine. The scenic variety along the Pacific coast is equally impressive—you'll see everything from dramatic cliffs and grass-tufted bluffs to wildlife estuaries and miles of dunes. It's an ideal place to relax, slow down, and appreciate the abundant natural beauty.

Offshore, a pristine national park and a vast marine sanctuary protect the wild, wonderful underwater resources of this incredible corner of the planet. But not all of the Central Coast's top attractions are natural: Ventura, Santa Barbara, and San Luis Obispo are filled with sparkling examples of Spanish-Mediterranean architecture, bustling shopping districts, and first-rate restaurants showcasing regional foods and wines.

PLANNING

WHEN TO GO

The Central Coast climate is mild year-round. If you like to swim in warmer (if still nippy) ocean waters, July and August are the best months to visit. Be aware that this is also high season. Fog often rolls in along the coastal areas in early summer; you'll need a jacket, especially after sunset, close to the shore. It usually rains from December through March. From April to early June and early fall the weather is almost as fine as in high season, and the pace is less hectic.

GETTING HERE AND AROUND

AIR TRAVEL

Alaska Air, American, and United fly to Santa Barbara Airport (SBA), 9 miles from downtown. The same airlines provide service to San Luis Obispo County Regional Airport (SBP), 3 miles from downtown San Luis Obispo.

Santa Barbara Airbus shuttles travelers between Santa Barbara and Los Angeles for $55 one-way and $100 round-trip. The Santa Barbara Metropolitan Transit District Bus 11 ($1.75) runs every 30 minutes from the airport to the downtown transit center. A taxi between the airport and the hotel districts costs between $22 and $40.

Airport Contacts San Luis Obispo County Regional Airport. ✉ *901 Airport Dr., off Hwy. 227, San Luis Obispo* ☎ *805/781–5205* ⊕ *sloairport.com.* **Santa Barbara Airport.** ✉ *500 Fowler Rd., off U.S. 101 Exit 104B, Santa Barbara* ☎ *805/683–4011* ⊕ *flysba.com.* **Santa Barbara Airbus.** ☎ *805/964–7759, 800/423–1618* ⊕ *www.sbairbus.com.* **Santa Barbara Metropolitan Transit District.** ☎ *805/963–3366* ⊕ *sbmtd.gov.*

BUS TRAVEL

Greyhound provides service from Los Angeles and San Francisco to San Luis Obispo, Ventura, and Santa Barbara. Local transit companies serve these three cities and several smaller towns. Buses can be useful for visiting some urban sights, particularly in Santa Barbara; they're less so for rural ones.

Bus Contacts Greyhound. ☎ *800/231–2222* ⊕ *www.greyhound.com.*

CAR TRAVEL

Driving is the easiest way to experience the Central Coast. U.S. 101 and Highway 1, which run north–south, are the main routes to and through the Central Coast from Los Angeles and San Francisco. Highly scenic Highway 1 hugs the coast, and U.S. 101 runs inland. Between Ventura County and northern Santa Barbara County, the two highways are the same road. Highway 1 again separates from U.S. 101 north of Gaviota, then rejoins the highway at Pismo Beach. Along any stretch where these two highways are separate, U.S. 101 is the quicker route.

The most dramatic section of the Central Coast is the 70 miles between San Simeon and Big Sur. The road is narrow and twisting, with a single lane in each direction. In fog or rain the drive can be downright nerve-racking; in wet seasons mudslides can close portions of the road.

Other routes into the Central Coast include Highway 46 and Highway 33, which head, respectively, west and south from Interstate 5 near Bakersfield.

Road Conditions Caltrans. ☎ *800/427–7623, 888/836–0866 Hwy. 1 visitor hotline (Cambria north to Carmel)* ⊕ *www.dot.ca.gov.*

TRAIN TRAVEL

The Amtrak *Coast Starlight,* which runs between Los Angeles and Seattle via Oakland, stops in Paso Robles, San Luis Obispo, Santa Barbara, and Oxnard. Amtrak runs several *Pacific Surfliner* trains and buses daily between San Luis Obispo, Santa Barbara, Los Angeles, and

San Diego. Metrolink Regional Rail Service trains connect Ventura and Oxnard with Los Angeles and points between.

Train Contacts Amtrak. ☎ 800/872–7245 ⊕ www.amtrak.com, www.amtrakcalifornia.com, www.pacificsurfliner.com. **Metrolink.** ☎ 800/371–5465 ⊕ metrolinktrains.com.

RESTAURANTS

The cuisine in Ventura and Santa Barbara is every bit as eclectic as it is in California's bigger cities; fresh seafood is a standout. A foodie renaissance has overtaken the entire region from Ventura to Paso Robles, spawning dozens of restaurants touting locavore cuisine made with fresh organic produce and meats. Dining attire on the Central Coast is generally casual, though slightly dressy casual wear is the custom at pricier restaurants. *Restaurant reviews have been shortened. For full information, visit Fodors.com.*

HOTELS

Expect to pay top dollar for rooms along the shore, especially in summer. Moderately priced hotels and motels do exist—most just a short drive inland from their higher-price counterparts. Make your reservations as early as possible, and take advantage of midweek specials to get the best rates. It's common for lodgings to require two-day minimum stays on holidays and some weekends, especially in summer, and to double rates during festivals and other events. *Hotel reviews have been shortened. For full information, visit Fodors.com.*

WHAT IT COSTS			
$	**$$**	**$$$**	**$$$$**
Restaurants	under $16	$16–$22	$23–$30	over $30
Hotels	under $120	$120–$175	$176–$250	over $250

Restaurant prices are the average cost of a main course at dinner or, if dinner is not served, at lunch, excluding sales tax of 8%–8.25% (depending on location). Hotel prices are the lowest cost of a standard double room in high season, excluding service charges and 9%–12% occupancy tax.

TOURS

Many tour companies will pick you up at your hotel or central locations; ask about this when booking.

Central Coast Food Tours. Food and wine destinations are the focus of this outfit's walking tours of shops, restaurants, wineries, and other spots in San Luis Obispo, Paso Robles, and elsewhere. Some tours combine wine tasting with an ocean sail or a zip-line adventure. ☎ 800/656–0713 ⊕ centralcoastfoodtours.com ✉ From $69.

Cloud Climbers Jeep and Wine Tours. This outfit conducts trips in open-air, six-passenger jeeps to the Santa Barbara/Santa Ynez mountains and Wine Country. Tour options include wine tasting, mountain, sunset, and a discovery adventure for families. The company also offers a four-hour All Around Ojai Tour and arranges horseback riding and trap-shooting tours. ☎ 805/646–3200 ⊕ ccjeeps.com ✉ From $89.

Grapeline Wine Tours. Wine and vineyard picnic tours in Paso Robles and the Santa Ynez Valley are Grapeline's specialty. ☎ *888/894–6379* ⊕ *gogrape.com* ✉ *From $119.*

Santa Barbara Wine Country Cycling Tours. The company leads half- and full-day tours of the Santa Ynez wine region, conducts hiking and cycling tours, and rents out bicycles. ☎ *888/557–8687, 805/686–9490* ⊕ *winecountrycycling.com* ✉ *From $100.*

Stagecoach Wine Tours. Locally owned and operated, Stagecoach runs daily wine-tasting excursions through the Santa Ynez Valley in vans, minicoaches, and SUVs. ✉ *Solvang* ☎ *805/686–8347* ⊕ *winetourssantaynez.com* ✉ *From $171.*

Sustainable Vine Wine Tours. This green-minded company specializes in eco-friendly Santa Ynez Valley wine tours in luxury vans and Tesla SUVs. Trips include tastings at limited-production wineries committed to sustainable practices. An organic picnic lunch is served. ☎ *805/698–3911* ⊕ *sustainablevine.com* ✉ *$150.*

VISITOR INFORMATION

Contacts **Central Coast Tourism Council.** ⊕ *centralcoast-tourism.com.*

6

VENTURA COUNTY

Ventura County was first settled by the Chumash Indians. Spanish missionaries were the first Europeans to arrive, followed by Americans and other Europeans, who established towns, transportation networks, and highly productive farms. Since the 1920s, agriculture has been steadily replaced as the area's main industry—first by the oil business and more recently by tourism.

Accessible via boat or plane from Ventura and Santa Barbara, Channel Islands National Park is a series of five protected islands just 11 miles offshore where hiking, kayaking, and wildlife viewing abound.

VENTURA

60 miles north of Los Angeles.

Like Los Angeles, the city of Ventura enjoys gorgeous weather and sun-kissed beaches—but without the smog and congestion. The miles of beautiful beaches attract athletes—body-surfers and boogie boarders, runners and bikers—and those who'd rather doze beneath an umbrella all day. Ventura Harbor is home to myriad fishing boats, restaurants, and water-activity centers where you can rent boats and take harbor cruises. Foodies can get their fix all over Ventura—dozens of upscale cafés and wine and tapas bars have opened in recent years. Arts and antiques buffs have long trekked downtown to browse the galleries and shops here. One of the greatest perks of Ventura is its walkability. If you drive here, park your car in one of the free 24-hour parking lots sprinkled around the city and hoof it on foot, or board a free trolley that cruises from downtown along the waterfront (Thursday–Sunday 11 am –11 pm).

GETTING HERE AND AROUND

Amtrak and Metrolink trains serve the area from Los Angeles. Greyhound buses stop in Ventura; Gold Coast Transit serves the city and the rest of Ventura County.

U.S. 101 is the north–south main route into town, but for a scenic drive, take Highway 1 north from Santa Monica. The highway merges with U.S. 101 just south of Ventura. ■ **TIP→ Traveling north to Ventura from Los Angeles on weekdays, it's best to depart before 6 am, between 10 and 2, or after 7 pm, or you'll get caught in the extended rush-hour traffic. Coming south from Santa Barbara, depart before 1 or after 6 pm.** On weekends, traffic is generally fine except southbound on U.S. 101 between Santa Barbara and Ventura on Sunday late afternoon and early evening.

ESSENTIALS

Bus Contact Gold Coast Transit. ☎ 805/487–4222 ⊕ www.goldcoasttransit.org.

Visitor Information Ventura Visitors and Convention Bureau. ⊠ Downtown Visitor Center, 101 S. California St. ☎ 805/648–2075, 800/483–6214 ⊕ visitventuraca.com.

EXPLORING

Mission San Buenaventura. The ninth of the 21 California missions, Mission San Buenaventura was established in 1782 and the current church was rebuilt and rededicated in 1809. A self-guided tour takes you through a small museum, a quiet courtyard, and a chapel with 250-year-old paintings. ⊠ 211 E. Main St., at Figueroa St. ☎ 805/643–4318 ⊕ www.sanbuenaventuramission.org ☞ $4.

Museum of Ventura County. Exhibits in a contemporary complex of galleries and a sunny courtyard plaza tell the story of Ventura County from prehistoric times to the present. A highlight is the gallery that contains Ojai artist George Stuart's historical figures, dressed in exceptionally detailed, custom-made clothing reflecting their particular eras. In the courtyard, eight panels made with 45,000 pieces of cut glass form a history time line. ⊠ 100 E. Main St., at S. Ventura Ave. ☎ 805/653–0323 ⊕ www.venturamuseum.org ☞ $5, free 1st Sun. of month.

Fodor's Choice
★

Ventura Oceanfront. Four miles of gorgeous coastline stretch from the county fairgrounds at the northern border of the city of San Buenaventura, through San Buenaventura State Beach, down to Ventura Harbor in the south. The main attraction here is the San Buenaventura City Pier, a landmark built in 1872 and restored in 1993. Surfers rip the waves just north of the pier, and sunbathers relax on white-sand beaches on either side. The mile-long promenade and the Omer Rains Bike Trail north of the pier attract scores of joggers, surrey cyclers, and bikers throughout the year. ⊠ California St., at ocean's edge.

WHERE TO EAT

$$$
SEAFOOD

✕ **Brophy Bros.** The Ventura outpost of the wildly popular Santa Barbara restaurant provides the same fresh seafood-oriented meals in a spacious second-story setting overlooking the harbor. Feast on everything from fish-and-chips and crab cakes to chowder and delectable

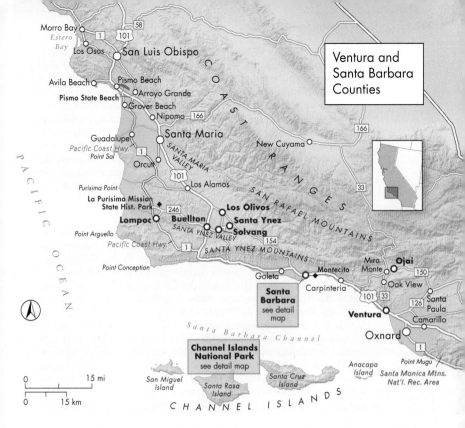

Santa Barbara see detail map

Channel Islands National Park see detail map

Ventura and Santa Barbara Counties

fish—often straight from the boats moored below. **Known for:** lively atmosphere; harbor views; killer clam bar. $ *Average main: $25* ✉ *1559 Spinnaker Dr., in Ventura Harbor Village* ☎ *805/639–0865* ⊕ *brophybros.com.*

$$$
AMERICAN
Fodor's Choice
★

✕ **Café Zack.** A local favorite for anniversaries and other celebrations, Zack's serves classic European dishes in an intimate, two-room 1930s cottage adorned with local art. Entrées of note include seafood specials (depending on the local catch), slow-roasted boar shank and filet mignon, the latter typically crusted in peppercorns or topped with porcini mushrooms. **Known for:** personal service; house-made desserts; excellent California wines. $ *Average main: $30* ✉ *1095 E. Thompson Blvd., at S. Ann St.* ☎ *805/643–9445* ⊕ *cafezack.com* ☾ *Closed Sun. No lunch Sat.*

$$
SEAFOOD

✕ **Lure Fish House.** Fresh, sustainably caught seafood charbroiled over a mesquite grill, a well-stocked oyster bar, specialty cocktails, and a wine list heavy on local vintages lure diners into this slick, nautical-themed spot downtown. The menu centers on the mostly local catch and organic vegetables, and includes tacos, sandwiches, and salads. **Known for:** shrimp-and-chips; cioppino; citrus crab-cake salad. $ *Average main: $22* ✉ *60 S. California St.* ☎ *805/567–4400* ⊕ *lurefishhouse.com.*

$$$ CARIBBEAN 🍴 **Rumfish y Vino.** The sibling of a popular namesake restaurant in Placencia, Belize, Rumfish y Vino serves up zesty Caribbean fare with a California wine country twist in a courtyard venue just off Main Street near the mission. Dine in the beach-chic dining room or in the heated patio with a roaring fireplace, where live music plays several nights a week, The seafood-heavy menu changes depending on the local catch, but you might start with Peruvian ceviche conch fritters with rumfish sauce or zesty local yellowtail carpaccio, then dig into Caribbean seafood stew or a hangar steak with crispy avocado. **Known for:** delectable fish tacos and flatbreads; happy hour and creative cocktails; chile-braised beef lasagne. [$] *Average main: $26* ✉ *434 N. Palm St.* ☎ *805/667–9288* 🌐 *www.rumfishyvinoventura.com.*

WHERE TO STAY

$$$ RESORT 🏨 **Four Points by Sheraton Ventura Harbor Resort.** An on-site restaurant, spacious rooms, and a slew of amenities make this 17-acre property—which includes sister hotel Holiday Inn Express—a popular and practical choice for Channel Islands visitors. **Pros:** close to island transportation; quiet location; short drive to historic downtown. **Cons:** not in the heart of downtown; noisy seagulls sometimes congregate nearby. [$] *Rooms from: $179* ✉ *1050 Schooner Dr.* ☎ *805/658–1212, 800/368–7764* 🌐 *fourpoints.com/ventura* 🛏 *106 rooms* 🍽 *No meals.*

$$$ HOTEL 🏨 **Holiday Inn Express Ventura Harbor.** A favorite among Channel Islands visitors, this quiet, comfortable, lodge-inspired property sits right at the Ventura Harbor entrance. **Pros:** quiet at night; easy access to harbor restaurants and activities; five-minute drive to downtown. **Cons:** busy area on weekends; complaints of erratic service. [$] *Rooms from: $179* ✉ *1080 Navigator Dr.* ☎ *805/856–9533, 888/233–9450* 🌐 *holidayinnexpress.com/venturaca* 🛏 *69 rooms* 🍽 *Breakfast.*

$$$ HOTEL 🏨 **Ventura Beach Marriott.** Spacious, contemporary rooms, a peaceful location just steps from San Buenaventura State Beach, and easy access to downtown arts and culture make the Marriott a popular choice. **Pros:** walk to beach and biking/jogging trails; a block from historic pier; great value for location. **Cons:** close to highway; near busy intersection. [$] *Rooms from: $195* ✉ *2055 E. Harbor Blvd.* ☎ *805/643–6000, 888/236–2427* 🌐 *marriottventurabeach.com* 🛏 *285 rooms* 🍽 *No meals.*

SPORTS AND THE OUTDOORS

The most popular outdoor activities in Ventura are beach-going and whale-watching. California gray whales migrate offshore through the Santa Barbara Channel from late December through March; giant blue and humpback whales feed here from mid-June through September. The channel teems with marine life year-round, so tours, which depart from Ventura Harbor, include more than just whale sightings.

Island Packers Cruises. A cruise through the Santa Barbara Channel with Island Packers will give you the chance to spot dolphins, seals, and sometimes even whales. ✉ *Ventura Harbor, 1691 Spinnaker Dr.* ☎ *805/642–1393* 🌐 *islandpackers.com.*

CHANNEL ISLANDS NATIONAL PARK

11 miles southwest of Ventura Harbor via boat.

On crystal clear days the craggy peaks of the Channel Islands are easy to see from the mainland, jutting from the Pacific in such sharp detail it seems you could reach out and touch them. The islands are not too far away—a high-speed boat will whisk you to the closest ones in less than an hour—yet very few people ever visit them. Those who do venture out to the islands will experience one of the most splendid land-and-sea wilderness areas on the planet. Camping is your only lodging choice on the islands, but it's a fantastic way to experience the natural beauty and isolation of the park. Campsites are primitive, with no water (except on Santa Rosa and Santa Cruz) or electricity. Campsites are $15 per night; you must arrange your transportation before you reserve your site (☎ *(800) 444–6777*) or online (⊕ *www.recreation.gov*) up to five months in advance.

Channel Islands National Park includes five of the eight Channel Islands and the one nautical mile of ocean that surrounds them. Six nautical miles of surrounding channel waters are designated a National Marine Sanctuary, and are teeming with life, including giant kelp forests, 345 fish species, dolphins, whales, seals, sea lions, and seabirds. To maintain the integrity of their habitats, pets are not allowed in the park.

GETTING HERE AND AROUND

Most visitors access the Channel Islands via an Island Packers boat from Ventura Harbor. To reach the harbor by car, exit U.S. 101 in Ventura at Seaward Boulevard or Victoria Avenue and follow the signs to Ventura Harbor/Spinnaker Drive. An Island Packers boat heads to Anacapa Island from Oxnard's Channel Islands Harbor, which you can reach from Ventura Harbor by following Harbor Boulevard south about 6 miles and continuing south on Victoria Avenue. Private vehicles are not permitted on the islands.

BOAT TOURS

Island Packers. Sailing on high-speed catamarans from Ventura or a mono-hull vessel from Oxnard, Island Packers goes to Santa Cruz Island daily most of the year, weather permitting. The boats also go to Anacapa several days a week, and to the outer islands from April through November. They also cruise along Anacapa's north shore on three-hour wildlife tours (no disembarking) several times a week. ✉ *3550 Harbor Blvd., Oxnard* ☎ *805/642–1393* ⊕ *islandpackers.com.*

EXPLORING

TOP ATTRACTIONS

Channel Islands National Park Visitor Center. The park's Robert J. Lagomarsino Visitor Center has a museum, a bookstore, and a three-story observation tower with telescopes. The museum's exhibits and a 24-minute film, *Treasure in the Sea,* provide an engaging overview of the islands. In the marine life exhibit, sea stars cling to rocks, and a brilliant orange Garibaldi darts around. Also on display are full-size reproductions of a male northern elephant seal and the pygmy mammoth skeleton unearthed on Santa Rosa Island in 1994.

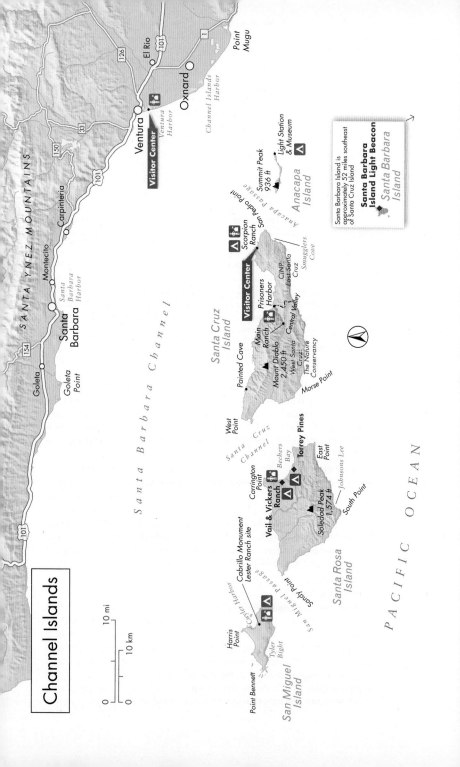

Channel Islands

Santa Barbara Island is approximately 52 miles southeast of Santa Cruz Island

Santa Barbara Island Light Beacon

Santa Barbara Island

Santa Cruz Island

Visitor Center

Scorpion Ranch

San Pedro Point

Anacapa Passage

Summit Peak 936 ft

Light Station & Museum

Anacapa Island

CINP: East Santa Cruz

Smugglers Cove

Prisoners Harbor

Main Ranch

Central Valley

Painted Cave

Mount Diablo 2,450 ft

West Santa Cruz: The Nature Conservancy

Morse Point

West Point

Santa Cruz Channel

Torrey Pines

East Point

Johnsons Lee

Bechers Bay

Carrington Point

Vail & Vickers Ranch

Soledad Peak 1,574 ft

South Point

Santa Rosa Island

Cabrillo Monument
Lester Ranch site

Harris Point

Cuyler Harbor

Tyler Bight

Sandy Point

San Miguel Passage

San Miguel Island

Point Bennett

Mainland

Point Mugu

El Rio

Oxnard

Channel Islands Harbor

Ventura

Visitor Center

Ventura Harbor

Carpinteria

Montecito

Santa Barbara

Santa Barbara Harbor

Goleta

Goleta Point

SANTA YNEZ MOUNTAINS

Santa Barbara Channel

PACIFIC OCEAN

0 — 10 mi

0 — 10 km

On weekends and holidays at 11 am and 3 pm, rangers lead various free public programs describing park resources, and from Wednesday through Saturday in summer the center screens live ranger broadcasts of hikes and dives on Anacapa Island. Webcam images of bald eagles and other land and sea creatures are shown at the center and on the park's website. ⊠ *1901 Spinnaker Dr., Ventura* ☎ *805/658–5730* ⊕ *www.nps.gov/chis.*

Fodor's Choice **Santa Cruz Island.** Five miles west of Anacapa, 96-square-mile Santa Cruz
★ Island is the largest of the Channel Islands. The National Park Service manages the easternmost 24% of the island; the rest is owned by the Nature Conservancy, which requires a permit to land. When your boat drops you off on a portion of the 70 miles of craggy coastline, you see two rugged mountain ranges with peaks soaring to 2,500 feet and deep canyons traversed by streams. This landscape is the habitat of a remarkable variety of flora and fauna—more than 600 types of plants, 140 kinds of land birds, 11 mammal species, five varieties of reptiles, and three amphibian species live here. Bird-watchers may want to look for the endemic island scrub jay, which is found nowhere else in the world.

One of the largest and deepest sea caves in the world, **Painted Cave** lies along the northwest coast of Santa Cruz. Named for the colorful lichen and algae that cover its walls, Painted Cave is nearly ¼ mile long and 100 feet wide. In spring a waterfall cascades over the entrance. Kayakers may encounter seals or sea lions cruising alongside their boats inside the cave. The Channel Islands hold some of the richest archaeological resources in North America; all artifacts are protected within the park. Remnants of a dozen Chumash villages can be seen on the island. The largest of these villages, at the eastern end, occupied the area now called **Scorpion Ranch.** The Chumash mined extensive chert deposits on the island for tools to produce shell-bead money, which they traded with people on the mainland. You can learn about Chumash history and view artifacts, tools, and exhibits on native plant and wildlife at the interpretive visitor center near the landing dock. Visitors can also explore remnants of the early-1900s ranching era in the restored historic adobe and outbuildings. ⊠ *Channel Islands National Park.*

WORTH NOTING

Anacapa Island. Most people think of Anacapa as an island, but it's actually comprised of three narrow islets. Although the tips of these volcanic formations nearly touch, the islets are inaccessible from one another except by boat. All three have towering cliffs, isolated sea caves, and natural bridges; Arch Rock, on East Anacapa, is one of the best-known symbols of Channel Islands National Park.

Wildlife viewing is the main activity on East Anacapa, particularly in summer when seagull chicks are newly hatched and sea lions and seals lounge on the beaches. Exhibits at East Anacapa's compact **museum** include the original lead-crystal Fresnel lens from the 1932 lighthouse.

On West Anacapa, depending on the season and the number of desirable species lurking about here, boats travel to **Frenchy's Cove.** On a voyage here you might see anemones, limpets, barnacles, mussel beds, and colorful marine algae in the pristine tide pools. The rest of West Anacapa is closed to protect nesting brown pelicans. ⊠ *Channel Islands National Park.*

San Miguel Island. The westernmost of the Channel Islands, San Miguel Island is frequently battered by storms sweeping across the North Pacific. The 15-square-mile island's wild windswept landscape is lush with vegetation. Point Bennett, at the western tip, offers one of the world's most spectacular wildlife displays when more than 100,000 pinnipeds hit its beach. Explorer Juan Rodríguez Cabrillo was the first European to visit this island; he claimed it for Spain in 1542. Legend holds that Cabrillo died on one of the Channel Islands—no one knows where he's buried, but there's a memorial to him on a bluff above Cuyler Harbor. ⊠ *Channel Islands National Park.*

Santa Barbara Island. At about 1 square mile, Santa Barbara Island is the smallest of the Channel Islands and nearly 35 miles south of the others. Triangular in shape, Santa Barbara's steep cliffs—which offer a perfect nesting spot for the Scripps's murrelet, a rare seabird—are topped by twin peaks. In spring you can enjoy a brilliant display of yellow coreopsis. Learn about the wildlife on and around the islands at the island's small museum. ⊠ *Channel Islands National Park.*

Santa Rosa Island. Between Santa Cruz and San Miguel, Santa Rosa is the second largest of the Channel Islands. The terrain along the coast varies from broad, sandy beaches to sheer cliffs—a central mountain range, rising to 1,589 feet, breaks the island's relatively low profile. Santa Rosa is home to about 500 species of plants, including the rare Torrey pine, and three unusual mammals, the island fox, the spotted skunk, and the deer mouse. They hardly compare, though, to their predecessors: a nearly complete skeleton of a 6-foot-tall pygmy mammoth was unearthed in 1994.

From 1901 to 1998, cattle were raised at the island's **Vail & Vickers Ranch.** The route from Santa Rosa's landing dock to the campground passes by the historic ranch buildings, barns, equipment, and the wooden pier where cattle were brought onto the island. ⊠ *Channel Islands National Park.*

SPORTS AND THE OUTDOORS

Channel Islands Adventure Company (owned and operated by Santa Barbara Adventure Company) *(see Santa Barbara Sports and the Outdoors)* arranges paddling, kayaking, and other Channel Islands excursions out of Ventura, and various concessionaires at Ventura Harbor Village (☎ 805/477–0470 ⊕ *www.venturaharborvillage.com*) arrange diving, kayaking, and other rentals and tours. Island Packers conducts whale-watching cruises.

DIVING

Some of the best snorkeling and diving in the world can be found in the cool waters surrounding the Channel Islands. In the relatively warm water around Anacapa and eastern Santa Cruz, photographers can get great shots of rarely seen giant black bass swimming among the kelp forests. Here you also find a reef covered with red brittle starfish. If you're an experienced diver, you might swim among five species of seals and sea lions, or try your hand at spearing rockfish or halibut near San Miguel and Santa Rosa. The best time to scuba dive is in summer and fall, when the water is often clear up to a 100-foot depth.

KAYAKING

The most remote parts of the Channel Islands are accessible only by a sea kayak. Some of the best kayaking in the park can be found on Anacapa, Santa Barbara, and the eastern tip of Santa Cruz. It's too far to kayak from the mainland out to the islands, but outfitters have tours that take you to the islands. Tours are offered year-round, but high seas may cause trip cancellations between December and March. ⚠ Channel waters can be unpredictable and challenging. Guided trips are highly recommended.

WHALE-WATCHING

About a third of the world's cetacean species (27 to be exact) can be seen in the Santa Barbara Channel. In July and August, humpback and blue whales feed off the north shore of Santa Rosa. From late December through March, up to 10,000 gray whales pass through the Santa Barbara Channel on their way from Alaska to Mexico and back again; if you go on a whale-watching trip during this time frame you're likely to spot one or more of them. Other types of whales, but fewer in number, swim the channel from June through August.

OJAI

6

15 miles north of Ventura.

The Ojai Valley, which director Frank Capra used as a backdrop for his 1936 film *Lost Horizon,* sizzles in the summer when temperatures routinely reach 90°F. The acres of orange and avocado groves here evoke postcard images of long-ago agricultural Southern California. Many artists and celebrities have sought refuge from life in the fast lane in lush Ojai.

GETTING HERE AND AROUND

From northern Ventura, Highway 33 veers east from U.S. 101 and climbs inland to Ojai. From Santa Barbara, exit U.S. 101 at Highway 150 in Carpinteria, then travel east 20 miles on a twisting, two-lane road that is not recommended at night or during poor weather. You can also access Ojai by heading west from Interstate 5 on Highway 126. Exit at Santa Paula and follow Highway 150 north for 16 miles to Ojai. Gold Coast Transit provides service to Ojai from Ventura.

Ojai can be easily explored on foot; you can also hop on the Ojai Trolley ($1, or $2 day pass), which until about 5 pm follows two routes around Ojai and neighboring Miramonte on weekdays and one route on weekends. Tell the driver you're visiting and you'll get an informal guided tour.

ESSENTIALS

Bus Contacts Gold Coast Transit. ☎ *805/487–4222* ⊕ *goldcoasttransit.org.* **Ojai Trolley.** ☎ *805/646–5581* ⊕ *ojaitrolley.com.*

Visitor Information Ojai Visitors Bureau. ✉ *109 N. Blanche St., Suite 103, at W. Matilija St.* ☎ *888/652–4669* ⊕ *ojaivisitors.com.*

EXPLORING

Meditation Mount. Enter through a Peace Portal hewn from reclaimed 1,200-year-old Douglas Fir to walk through the International Garden of Peace and sit in a beautiful meditation room at this nonprofit meditation center, open to the public from 8 am to sunset. ⊠ *10340 Reeves Rd.* ✛ *5 miles east of downtown Ojai* ☎ *805/646–5508* ⊕ *meditationmount.org* ☉ *Closed Mon. and Tues.*

Ojai Art Center. California's oldest nonprofit, multipurpose arts center exhibits visual art from various disciplines and presents theater, dance, and other performances. ⊠ *113 S. Montgomery St., near E. Ojai Ave.* ☎ *805/646–0117* ⊕ *www.ojaiartcenter.org.*

Ojai Avenue. The work of local artists is displayed in the Spanish-style shopping arcade along the avenue downtown. On Sunday between 9 and 1, organic and specialty growers sell their produce at the outdoor market behind the arcade.

Ojai Valley Museum. The museum collects, preserves, and presents exhibits about the art, history, and culture of Ojai and Ojai Valley. Walking tours of Ojai depart from here. ⊠ *130 W. Ojai Ave.* ☎ *805/640–1390* ⊕ *ojaivalleymuseum.org* ⌦ *Museum $5, walking tour $7 ($15 family)* ☉ *Closed Mon.*

Ojai Valley Trail. The 18-mile trail is open to pedestrians, joggers, equestrians, bikers, and others on nonmotorized vehicles. You can access it anywhere along its route. ⊠ *Parallel to Hwy. 33 from Soule Park in Ojai to ocean in Ventura* ☎ *888/652–4669* ⊕ *ojaivisitors.com.*

WHERE TO EAT

$$$
MEDITERRANEAN
✕**Azu.** Slick furnishings, piped-in jazz, craft cocktails, and local beers and wines draw diners to this artsy Mediterranean bistro known for tapas made from organic ingredients. You can also order soups, salads, and bistro fare such as steak frites and paella. **Known for:** many vegan and gluten-free options; amazing homemade gelato; more than 30 wines by the glass. $ *Average main: $25* ⊠ *457 E. Ojai Ave.* ☎ *805/640–7987* ⊕ *azuojai.com.*

$
ITALIAN
✕**Boccali's.** Edging a ranch, citrus groves, and a seasonal garden that provides produce for menu items, the modest but cheery Boccali's attracts many loyal fans. When it's warm, you can dine alfresco in the oak-shaded patio and lawn area and sometimes listen to live music. **Known for:** family-run operation; handrolled pizzas and home-style pastas; seasonal strawberry shortcake. $ *Average main: $15* ⊠ *3277 Ojai Ave., about 2 miles east of downtown* ☎ *805/646–6116* ⊕ *boccalis. com* ☉ *No lunch Mon. and Tues.*

$
AMERICAN
✕**Farmer and the Cook.** An organic farmer and his chef-wife run this funky café/bakery/market in Meiners Oaks, just a few miles west of downtown Ojai. Fill up at the soup and salad bar, order a wood-fired pizza, bento box, sandwich, or a daily special, then grab a table indoors or out on the patio, Vegans have ample choices from the Mexican-inspired menu. **Known for:** many veggie and gluten-free options; grab-and-go meals; weekend breakfasts. $ *Average main: $12* ⊠ *339 W. El Roblar* ☎ *805/640–9608* ⊕ *www.farmerandcook.com.*

$$$ ✕**Nocciola.** Authentic northern Italian dishes with a California twist, a
ITALIAN cozy fireplace dining room in a century-old Craftsman-style house, and a
Fodor'sChoice covered patio amid the oaks draw locals and visitors alike to this popular
★ eatery, owned by an Italian chef and his American wife (the family lives
upstairs). The menu changes seasonally, but regular stars include seared
sea scallops with Parmesan fondue and truffle shavings, homemade pas-
tas made with organic egg yolks, and *pappardelle* with slow-roasted
wild boar. **Known for:** great wild fish and game; Moment Pink signature
cocktail; five-course tasting menu. $ *Average main: $29* ✉ *314 El Paseo
Rd.* ☎ *805/640–1648* ⊕ *nocciolaojai.com* ⊘ *Closed Mon.*

$$$$ ✕**Suzanne's Cuisine.** Peppered filet mignon, linguine with steamed clams,
EUROPEAN and pan-roasted salmon with a roasted mango sauce are among the
offerings at this European-style restaurant. Seafood, roasted meats, and
poultry, as well as vegetarian dishes dominate the dinner menu, and
salads and soups star at lunchtime. **Known for:** professional service;
cozy dining room with fireplace; all desserts made on the premises.
$ *Average main: $32* ✉ *502 W. Ojai Ave.* ☎ *805/640–1961* ⊕ *suzan-
nescuisine.com* ⊘ *Closed Tues.*

WHERE TO STAY

$$ ⌂**The Iguana Inns of Ojai.** Artists own and operate these two bohemian-
B&B/INN chic inns: The Blue Iguana, a cozy Southwestern-style hotel about
2 miles west of downtown, and the Emerald Iguana, which has art
nouveau rooms, suites, and cottages in a secluded residential setting
near downtown Ojai. **Pros:** colorful art everywhere; secluded. **Cons:**
2 miles from downtown; on a highway; small. $ *Rooms from: $139*
✉ *11794 N. Ventura Ave.* ☎ *805/646–5277* ⊕ *iguanainnsofojai.com*
⇦ *12 rooms, 8 cottages* ⦿| *Breakfast.*

$$$$ ⌂**Oaks at Ojai.** Rejuvenation is the name of the game at this destina-
RESORT tion spa where you can work out all day or just lounge by the pool.
Pros: all-inclusive fitness package available; hikes and fitness classes;
healthful meals. **Cons:** some rooms are basic; on main road through
town. $ *Rooms from: $265* ✉ *122 E. Ojai Ave.* ☎ *805/646–5573,
800/753–6257* ⊕ *oaksspa.com* ⇦ *46 rooms* ⦿| *All meals* ⌕ *2-night
minimum stay.*

$$ ⌂**Ojai Rancho Inn.** A collection of one-story buildings and cottages
HOTEL tucked between Ojai Avenue and the bike trail, this ranch-style motel
attracts hipsters and those who appreciate a rustic getaway with mod-
ern comforts and a laid-back vintage vibe. **Pros:** free loaner cruiser
bikes; small on-site bar; nice pool area with lounge chairs. **Cons:** not
fancy or luxurious; rooms could use soundproofing; some road noise
in rooms close to the road. $ *Rooms from: $150* ✉ *615 W. Ojai Ave.*
☎ *805/646–1434* ⊕ *ojairanchoinn.com* ⇦ *17 rooms* ⦿| *No meals.*

$$$$ ⌂**Ojai Valley Inn & Spa.** This outdoorsy, golf-oriented resort and spa
RESORT is set on beautifully landscaped grounds, with hillside views in nearly
Fodor'sChoice all directions. **Pros:** Spanish-colonial architecture; exceptional outdoor
★ activities; seven on-site restaurants serving regional cuisine. **Cons:**
expensive; areas near restaurants can be noisy. $ *Rooms from: $349*
✉ *905 Country Club Rd.* ☎ *805/646–1111, 855/697–8780* ⊕ *ojairesort.
com* ⇦ *303 rooms* ⦿| *No meals.*

6

$$$ 　Ⓟ **Su Nido Inn.** A short walk from downtown Ojai sights and restau-
B&B/INN 　rants, this posh Mission Revival–style inn sits in a quiet neighborhood
a few blocks from Libbey Park. **Pros:** walking distance from down-
town; homey feel. **Cons:** no pool; can get hot during summer. Ⓢ *Rooms
from: $199* ⊠ *301 N. Montgomery St.* ☎ *805/646–7080, 866/646–7080*
⊕ *www.sunidoinn.com* ➴ *12 rooms* ⦿ *No meals* ↻ *2-night minimum
stay on weekends.*

SANTA BARBARA

27 miles northwest of Ventura and 29 miles west of Ojai.

Santa Barbara has long been an oasis for Los Angelenos seeking respite
from big-city life. The attractions begin at the ocean and end in the
foothills of the Santa Ynez Mountains. A few miles up the coast east and
west—but still very much a part of Santa Barbara—are the exclusive
residential districts of Montecito and Hope Ranch. Santa Barbara is on
a jog in the coastline, so the ocean is actually to the south, instead of
the west. "Up" the coast toward San Francisco is west, "down" toward
Los Angeles is east, and the mountains are north.

GETTING HERE AND AROUND

U.S. 101 is the main route into Santa Barbara. If you're staying in
town, a car is handy but not essential; the beaches and downtown are
easily explored by bicycle or on foot. Visit the Santa Barbara Car Free
website for bike-route and walking-tour maps, suggestions for car-free
vacations, and transportation discounts.

Santa Barbara Metropolitan Transit District's Line 22 bus serves major
tourist sights. Several bus lines connect with the very convenient elec-
tric shuttles that cruise the downtown and waterfront every 10 to 15
minutes (50¢ each way).

Santa Barbara Trolley Co. operates a motorized San Francisco–style
cable car that loops past major hotels, shopping areas, and attractions
from 10 am to 4 pm. Get off whenever you like, and pick up another
trolley (they come every hour) when you're ready to move on. The fare
is $22 for the day.

TOURS

Land and Sea Tours. This outfit conducts 90-minute narrated tours in
an amphibious 49-passenger vehicle nicknamed the Land Shark. The
adventure begins with a drive through the city, followed by a plunge
into the harbor for a cruise along the coast. ⊠ *10 E. Cabrillo Blvd., at
Stearns Wharf* ☎ *805/683–7600* ⊕ *out2seesb.com* ⊠ *From $30.*

Segway Tours of Santa Barbara. After a brief training session, a guide leads
you around town on electric-powered personal balancing transporters.
Tour options include the waterfront (1¼ hours), Butterfly Beach and
Montecito (2 hours), historic downtown Santa Barbara (2½ hours), and
through town to the mission (3 hours). ⊠ *16 Helena Ave., at Cabrillo
Blvd.* ☎ *805/963–7672* ⊕ *segwayofsb.com* ⊠ *$75–$115.*

ESSENTIALS

Transportation Contacts Santa Barbara Car Free. ☎ 805/696–1100 ⊕ *santabarbaracarfree.org.* **Santa Barbara Metropolitan Transit District.** ☎ *805/963–3366* ⊕ *sbmtd. gov.* **Santa Barbara Trolley Co.** ☎ *805/965–0353* ⊕ *www.sbtrolley.com.*

Visitor Information Santa Barbara Visitor Center. ✉ *1 Garden St., at Cabrillo Blvd.* ☎ *805/965–3021* ⊕ *www.sbchamber.org.* **Visit Santa Barbara.** ✉ *500 E. Montecito St.* ☎ *805/966–9222* ⊕ *santabarbaraca.com.*

BEST VIEWS

Drive along Alameda Padre Serra, a hillside road that begins near the mission and continues to Montecito, to feast your eyes on spectacular views of the city and the Santa Barbara Channel.

EXPLORING

Santa Barbara's waterfront is beautiful, with palm-studded promenades and plenty of sand. In the few miles between the beaches and the hills are downtown, Mission Santa Barbara, and the Santa Barbara Botanic Garden.

TOP ATTRACTIONS

El Presidio State Historic Park. Founded in 1782, El Presidio was one of four military strongholds established by the Spanish along the coast of California. The park encompasses much of the original site in the heart of downtown. El Cuartel, the adobe guardhouse, is the oldest building in Santa Barbara and the second oldest in California. ■TIP➜ **Admission is free for children 16 and under.** ✉ *123 E. Canon Perdido St., at Anacapa St.* ☎ *805/965–0093* ⊕ *www.sbthp.org* 🎫 *$5.*

FAMILY
Fodor's Choice
★
Lotusland. The 37-acre estate called Lotusland once belonged to the Polish opera singer Ganna Walska, who purchased it in the late 1940s and lived here until her death in 1984. Many of the exotic trees and other subtropical flora were planted in 1882 by horticulturist R. Kinton Stevens. On the two-hour guided tour—the only option for visiting unless you're a member (reserve well ahead in summer)—you'll see an outdoor theater, a topiary garden, a lotus pond, and a huge collection of rare cycads, an unusual plant genus that has been around since the time of the dinosaurs. ■TIP➜ **Child-friendly family tours are available for groups with children under the age of 10; contact Lotusland for scheduling.** ✉ *695 Ashley Rd., off Sycamore Canyon Rd. (Hwy. 192), Montecito* ☎ *805/969–9990* ⊕ *lotusland.org* 🎫 *$48* ⊗ *Closed mid-Nov.–mid-Feb. No tours Sun.–Tues.*

Fodor's Choice
★
Mission Santa Barbara. Widely referred to as the "Queen of Missions," this is one of the most beautiful and frequently photographed buildings in coastal California. Dating to 1786, the architecture evolved from adobe-brick buildings with thatch roofs to more permanent edifices as the mission's population burgeoned. An earthquake in 1812 destroyed the third church built on the site. Its replacement, the present structure, is still a functioning Catholic church. Mission Santa Barbara has a splendid Spanish/Mexican colonial art collection, as well as Chumash sculptures and the only Native American–made altar and tabernacle left

CALIFORNIA'S MISSIONS

California history changed forever in the 18th century when Spanish explorers founded a series of missions along the Pacific coast. Believing they were following God's will, they wanted to spread the gospel and convert as many natives as possible. The process produced a collision between the Hispanic and California Indian cultures, resulting in one of the most striking legacies of Old California: the Spanish mission churches. Rising like mirages in the middle of desert plains and rolling hills, these historic sites transport you back to the days of the Spanish colonial period.

missions. In 1848, the Americans assumed control of the territory, and California became part of the United States. Today, all 21 of these missions stand as extraordinary monuments to their colorful past. Many are found on or near the "King's Road"—El Camino Real—which linked these mission outposts. At the height of the mission system the trail was approximately 600 miles long, eventually extending from San Diego to Sonoma. Today the road is commemorated on portions of routes 101 and 82 in the form of roadside bell markers erected by CalTrans every 1 to 2 miles between San Diego and San Francisco.

FATHER OF THE MISSIONS

Father Junípero Serra is an icon of the Spanish colonial period. At the behest of the Spanish government, the diminutive padre—then well into his fifties, and despite a chronic leg infection—started out on foot from Baja California to search for suitable mission sites, with a goal of reaching Monterey. In 1769 he helped establish Alta California's first mission in San Diego and continued his travels until his death in 1784, by which time he had founded eight more missions.

EL CAMINO REAL

The system ended about a decade after the Mexican government took control of Alta California in the early 1820s and began to secularize the

MISSION ARCHITECTURE

Mission architecture reflects a gorgeous blend of European and New World influences. While naves followed the simple forms of Franciscan Gothic, cloisters (with beautiful arcades) adopted aspects of the Romanesque style, and ornamental touches of the Spanish Renaissance—including red-tiled roofs and wrought-iron grilles—added even more elegance. In the 20th century, the Mission Revival Style had a huge impact on architecture and design in California, as seen in examples ranging from San Diego's Union Station to Stanford University's main quadrangle. For information on California's missions, see ⊕ *californiamissionsfoundation.org.*

in the California missions. Docents lead 60-minute tours ($13 adult) Thursday and Friday at 11 am, and Saturday at 10:30 am. ⊠ *2201 Laguna St., at E. Los Olivos St.* ☎ *805/682–4149 gift shop, 805/682–4713 tours* ⊕ *www.santabarbaramission.org* ⊠ *$9 self-guided tour.*

FAMILY
Fodor'sChoice
★

MOXI–The Wolf Museum of Exploration and Innovation. It took more than two decades of unrelenting community advocacy to plan and build this exceptional science hub, which opened in early 2017 in a gorgeous three-story Spanish-Mediterranean building next to the train station and a block from Stearns Wharf and the beach. MOXI ignites learning through interactive activities in science and creativity for curious minds of all ages, from pre-K to gray. The 70-plus interactive exhibits—devoted to science, technology, engineering, arts, and mathematics (STEAM)—are integrated so visitors can explore seven themed areas (called tracks) in concert with one another and discover connections between them, for example, the relationship between music and electricity. In the Speed and Motion track you can build a model car and challenge two others to a race on a Tesla track—then use the collected data to reconfigure your car for improved performance. In the Fantastic Forces space, build a contraption to send on a test flight in a wind column. Other sections include Light and Color, The Tech Track, Innovation Lab, Sound Track, and interactive media spaces. Up on the rooftop "sky, which has some of the best panoramic views in downtown, you can listen to an orchestra of wind and solar-powered instruments and peer down through glass floor-windows to view the happy faces of explorers on the floors below. ✉ *125 State St.* ☎ *805/770–5000* ⊕ *moxi.org* ✉ *$14.*

Santa Barbara Botanic Garden. Five miles of scenic trails meander through the garden's 78 acres of native plants. The Mission Dam, built in 1806, stands just beyond the redwood grove and above the restored aqueduct that once carried water to Mission Santa Barbara. More than a thousand plant species thrive in various themed sections, including mountains, deserts, meadows, redwoods, and Channel Islands. ■**TIP**➔ **A conservation center dedicated to rare and endangered plant species opened in 2016 and presents rotating exhibitions.** ✉ *1212 Mission Canyon Rd., north of Foothill Rd. (Hwy. 192)* ☎ *805/682–4726* ⊕ *www. sbbg.org* ✉ *$12.*

Fodor's Choice ★ **Santa Barbara County Courthouse.** Hand-painted tiles and a spiral staircase infuse the courthouse, a national historic landmark, with the grandeur of a Moorish palace. This magnificent building was completed in 1929. An elevator rises to an arched observation area in the tower that provides a panoramic view of the city. Before or after you take in the view, you can (if it's open) visit an engaging gallery devoted to the workings of the tower's original, still operational Seth Thomas clock. The murals in the ceremonial chambers on the courthouse's second floor were painted by an artist who did backdrops for some of Cecil B. DeMille's films. ■**TIP**➔ **Join a free guided tour weekdays at 10:30, daily at 2** ✉ *1100 Anacapa St., at E. Anapamu St.* ☎ *805/962–6464* ⊕ *sbcourthouse.org.*

QUICK BITES

Jeannine's. Take a break from shopping at Jeannine's, revered locally for its wholesome sandwiches, salads, and baked goods, made from scratch with organic and natural ingredients. Pick up a turkey cranberry or chicken pesto sandwich to go, and picnic in the courthouse gardens a block away. **Known for: fantastic pastries; hearty, healthful breakfasts; turkey roasted or smoked in house.** ✉ *La Arcada, 15 E. Figueroa St., at State St.* ☎ *805/966–1717* ⊕ *jeannines.com/restaurants.*

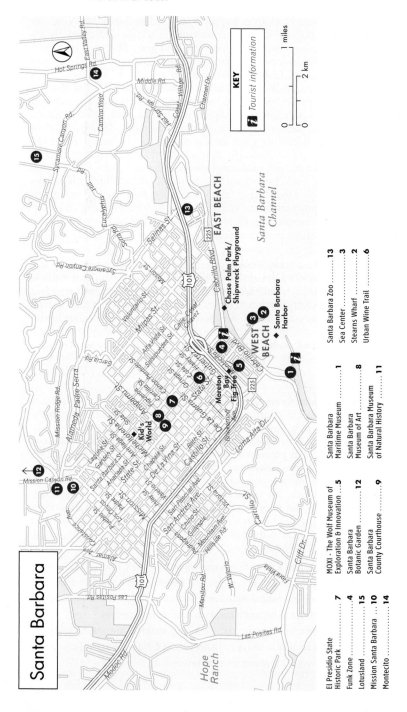

Santa Barbara

KEY

ⅈ Tourist information

Santa Barbara Museum of Art. The highlights of this museum's permanent collection include ancient sculpture, Asian art, impressionist paintings, contemporary art, photography, and American works in several mediums. ⊠ *1130 State St., at E. Anapamu St.* ☎ *805/963–4364* ⊕ *sbma.net* ☎ *$10, free Thurs. 5–8* ⊙ *Closed Mon.*

FAMILY **Santa Barbara Museum of Natural History.** The gigantic blue whale skeleton greets you at the entrance to this complex whose major draws include its planetarium, space lab, and gem and mineral display. Startlingly alive-looking stuffed specimens, complete with nests and eggs, roost in the bird hall, and a room of dioramas illustrates Chumash Indian history and culture. Outdoors, nature trails wind through the serene oak-studded grounds. A Nature Pass, available at the museum and the associated Sea Center, is good for discounted admission to both facilities. ⊠ *2559 Puesta del Sol Rd., off Mission Canyon Rd.* ☎ *805/682–4711* ⊕ *sbnature.org* ☎ *$12; free 3rd Sun. of month Sept.–Apr.*

FAMILY **Santa Barbara Zoo.** This compact zoo's gorgeous grounds shelter elephants, gorillas, exotic birds, and big cats. For small children, there's a scenic railroad and barnyard petting zoo. Three high-tech dinosaurs and an eight-foot-tall grizzly bear puppet perform in live stage shows (free with admission), daily in summer and on weekends the rest of the year. Kids especially love feeding the giraffes from a view deck overlooking the beach. ▪TIP➔ The palm-studded lawns on a hilltop overlooking the beach are perfect spots for family picnics. ⊠ *500 Niños Dr., off El Cabrillo Blvd.* ☎ *805/962–5339 main line* ⊕ *santabarbarazoo.org* ☎ *Zoo $17, parking $7.*

FAMILY **Sea Center.** A branch of the Santa Barbara Museum of Natural History, the center specializes in Santa Barbara Channel marine life and conservation. Though small compared to aquariums in Monterey and Long Beach, this is a fascinating, hands-on marine science laboratory that lets you participate in experiments, projects, and exhibits, including touch pools. The two-story glass walls here open to stunning ocean, mountain, and city views. ▪TIP➔ Purchase a Nature Pass, available here, for discounted admission to the center and the natural history museum. ⊠ *211 Stearns Wharf* ☎ *805/962–2526* ⊕ *sbnature.org* ☎ *$8.50.*

Stearns Wharf. Built in 1872, Stearns Wharf is Santa Barbara's most visited landmark. Expansive views of the mountains, cityscape, and harbor unfold from every vantage point on the three-block-long pier. Although it's a nice walk from the Cabrillo Boulevard parking areas, you can also park on the pier and then wander through the shops or stop for a meal at one of the wharf's restaurants. ⊠ *Cabrillo Blvd. and State St.* ⊕ *stearnswharf.org.*

Be sure to visit Santa Barbara's beautiful—and usually uncrowded—beaches.

WORTH NOTING

Funk Zone. A formerly run-down industrial neighborhood near the waterfront and train station, the Funk Zone has evolved into a hip hangout filled with wine-tasting rooms, arts-and-crafts studios, murals, breweries, restaurants, and small shops. It's fun to poke around the three-square-block district. ■TIP→ **Street parking is limited, so leave your car in a nearby city lot and cruise up and down the alleys on foot.** ✉ *Between State and Garden Sts. and Cabrillo Blvd. and U.S. 101* ⊕ *funkzone.net.*

Montecito. Since the late 1800s the tree-studded hills and valleys of this town have attracted the rich and famous: Hollywood icons, business tycoons, tech moguls, and old-money families who installed themselves years ago. Shady roads wind through the community, which consists mostly of gated estates. Swank boutiques line **Coast Village Road,** where well-heeled residents such as Oprah Winfrey sometimes browse for truffle oil, picture frames, and designer jeans. Residents also hang out in the Upper Village, a chic shopping area with restaurants and cafés at the intersection of San Ysidro and East Valley roads.

FAMILY **Santa Barbara Maritime Museum.** California's seafaring history is the focus here. High-tech, hands-on exhibits, such as a virtual sportfishing activity that lets participants haul in a "big one" and a local surfing history retrospective, make this a fun stop for families. The museum's shining star is a rare, 17-foot-tall Fresnel lens from the historic Point Conception Lighthouse. Ride the elevator to the fourth-floor observation area for great harbor views. ✉ *113 Harbor Way, off Shoreline Dr.* ☎ *805/962–8404* ⊕ *sbmm.org* ✆ *$8* ☉ *Closed Wed.*

Urban Wine Trail. Nearly two dozen winery tasting rooms form the Urban Wine Trail; most are within walking distance of the waterfront and the lower State Street shopping and restaurant district. **Santa Barbara Winery,** at 202 Anacapa Street, and **Au Bon Climat,** at 813 Anacapa Street, are good places to start your oenological trek. ✉ *Santa Barbara* 🌐 *urbanwinetrailsb.com.*

BEACHES

FAMILY **Arroyo Burro Beach.** The beach's usually gentle surf makes it ideal for families with young children. It's a local favorite because you can walk for miles in both directions when tides are low. Leashed dogs are allowed on the main stretch of beach and westward; they are allowed to romp off-leash east of the slough at the beach entrance. The parking lots fill early on weekends and throughout the summer, but the park is relatively quiet at other times. Walk along the beach just a few hundreds yards away from the main steps at the entrance to escape crowds on warm-weather days. Surfers, swimmers, stand-up paddlers, and boogie boarders regularly ply the waves, and photographers come often to catch the vivid sunsets. **Amenities:** food and drink; lifeguard in summer; parking, showers, toilets. **Best for:** sunset; surfing; swimming; walking. ✉ *Cliff Dr. and Las Positas Rd.* 🌐 *countyofsb.org/parks.*

6

FAMILY
Fodor's Choice ★ **East Beach.** The wide swath of sand at the east end of Cabrillo Boulevard is a great spot for people-watching. East Beach has sand volleyball courts, summertime lifeguard and sports competitions, and arts-and-crafts shows on Sundays and holidays. You can use showers, a weight room, and lockers (bring your own towel) and rent umbrellas and boogie boards at the Cabrillo Bathhouse. Next door, there's an elaborate jungle-gym play area for kids. Hotels line the boulevard across from the beach. **Amenities:** food and drink; lifeguards in summer; parking (fee); showers; toilets; water sports. **Best for:** walking; swimming; surfing. ✉ *1118 Cabrillo Blvd., at Ninos Dr.* ☎ *805/897–2680.*

WHERE TO EAT

$$$
JAPANESE
🍴 **Arigato Sushi.** You might have to wait for a table at this two-story restaurant and sushi bar—locals line up early for the wildly creative combination rolls and other delectables (first come, first served). Fans of authentic Japanese food sometimes disagree about the quality of the seafood, but all dishes are fresh and artfully presented. **Known for:** innovative creations; lively atmosphere; patio and second-floor balcony seating. [$] *Average main: $30* ✉ *1225 State St., near W. Victoria St.* ☎ *805/965–6074* 🌐 *www.arigatosb.com* 🕒 *No lunch.*

$$
MODERN AMERICAN
🍴 **Barbareño.** Determined to push the boundaries of farm-to-table, three college friends who worked at the same Los Angeles eatery banded together in 2014 to launch Barbareño. The three churn their own butter, bake their own breads, make condiments from scratch, and forage mushrooms, eucalyptus leaves, and other ingredients from the wild. **Known for:** youthful, sophisticated vibe; chef's sampler plate; monthly seasonal menu. [$] *Average main: $22* ✉ *205 W. Canon Perdido St., at De La Vina St.* ☎ *805/963–9591* 🌐 *barbareno.com* 🕒 *No lunch weekdays.*

$$$ SEAFOOD ✕ **Brophy Bros.** The outdoor tables at this casual harborside restaurant have perfect views of the marina and mountains. Staffers serve enormous, exceptionally fresh fish dishes and provide guests with a pager so you can stroll along the waterfront until the beep lets you know your table is ready. **Known for:** seafood salad and chowder; stellar clam bar; long wait times. [$] *Average main: $25* ✉ *119 Harbor Way, off Shoreline Dr.* ☎ *805/966–4418* 🌐 *brophybros.com.*

$ MEXICAN ✕ **La Super-Rica.** This food stand on the east side of town serves some of the spiciest and most authentic Mexican dishes between Los Angeles and San Francisco. Fans (the late chef Julia Child was one) fill up on the soft tacos served with yummy spicy or mild sauces and legendary beans. **Known for:** house-made tortillas; daily specials such as chilaquiles; vegetarian and gluten-free dishes. [$] *Average main: $12* ✉ *622 N. Milpas St., at Alphonse St.* ☎ *805/963–4940* 💳 *No credit cards* 🕒 *Closed Tues. and Wed.*

$$$ MODERN AMERICAN Fodor'sChoice ★ ✕ **The Lark.** Shared dining—small plates and larger—and a seasonal menu showcasing local ingredients are the focus at this urban-chic restaurant named for an overnight all-Pullman train that chugged into the nearby railroad station for six decades. Sit at the 24-seat communal table set atop vintage radiators, or at tables and booths crafted from antique Spanish church pews and other repurposed or recycled materials. **Known for:** social environment; wines curated by a master sommelier; handcrafted locavore cocktails. [$] *Average main: $28* ✉ *131 Anacapa St., at E. Yanonali St.* ☎ *805/284–0370* 🌐 *www.thelarksb.com* 🕒 *No lunch.*

$$$ SPANISH ✕ **Loquita.** In a cozy space in a prime corner at the gateway to the Funk Zone near Stearns Wharf, Loquita honors Santa Barbara's Spanish heritage by serving up authentic Spanish dishes, wines, and cocktails made with fresh, sustainably sourced local ingredients. The menu covers all bases, from tapas, to wood-fired seafood, and grilled meats, to Spanish wines, vermouth, gin and tonics, and sangria. **Known for:** multiple types of paella; counter and takeaway items; great gin and tonic. [$] *Average main: $28* ✉ *202 State St.* 🌐 *www.loquitasb.com.*

$$$$ ITALIAN ✕ **Olio e Limone.** Sophisticated Italian cuisine with an emphasis on Sicily is served at this restaurant near the Arlington. The juicy veal chop is popular, but surprises abound here; be sure to try unusual dishes such as ribbon pasta with quail and sausage in a mushroom ragout, or the duck ravioli. **Known for:** grilled veal and lamb chops; cozy white-tablecloth dining room; adjacent raw bar and casual pizzeria. [$] *Average main: $31* ✉ *17 W. Victoria St., at State St.* ☎ *805/899–2699* 🌐 *www.olioelimone.com* 🕒 *No lunch Sun.*

TAKE THE KIDS

Two fun playgrounds provide welcome interludes for the young set. Children love tooling around **Kids' World** (✉ *Garden and Micheltorena Sts.*), a public playground with a castle-shaped maze of climbing structures, slides, and tunnels. At **Shipwreck Playground** (✉ *Chase Palm Park, E. Cabrillo Blvd., east of Garden St.*), parents take as much pleasure in the waterfront views as the kids do in the nautical-themed diversions and the antique carousel.

$$$
SOUTHERN

✕ **Palace Grill.** Mardi Gras energy, team-style service, lively music, and great Cajun, creole, and Caribbean food have made the Palace a Santa Barbara icon. Be prepared to wait for a table on Friday and Saturday nights (when reservations are taken for a 5:30 seating only), though the live entertainment and free appetizers, sent out front when the line is long, will whet your appetite for the feast to come. **Known for:** blackened fish and meats; Louisiana bread pudding soufflé; Cajun martini served in a mason jar. $ *Average main: $30* ✉ *8 E. Cota St., at State St.* ☏ *805/963–5000* ⊕ *palacegrill.com.*

$$$$
AMERICAN
Fodor's Choice
★

✕ **Somerset.** A romantic courtyard shaded by century-old olive trees, an elegant interior that reflects European Grand Café style (marble walls, candles on zinc-topped tables), and cuisine that aims to please the most discerning of foodies quickly launched Somerset to the pinnacle of swank Santa Barbara dining when it opened in early 2017. Just a few steps away from The Granada and Arlington theaters in the arts and culture district, Somerset is an ideal upscale choice for pre- or postperformance dining. **Known for:** California cuisine with Mediterranean/European influences; full bar with craft cocktails; prime arts district location. $ *Average main: $34* ✉ *7 E. Anapamu St.* ☏ *805/845–7112* ⊕ *somersetsb.com.*

$$$$
AMERICAN
Fodor's Choice
★

✕ **The Stonehouse.** The elegant Stonehouse—consistently lauded as one of the nation's top restaurants—is inside a century-old granite former farmhouse at the San Ysidro Ranch resort. The menu changes constantly, but might include pan-seared abalone or classic steak Diane flambéed table-side. **Known for:** ingredients from on-site garden; heated oceanview deck with fireplace; elegant dining room. $ *Average main: $49* ✉ *900 San Ysidro La., off San Ysidro Rd., Montecito* ☏ *805/565–1700* ⊕ *www.sanysidroranch.com.*

$$$
ITALIAN
Fodor's Choice
★

✕ **Toma.** Seasonal, locally sourced ingredients and softly lit muted-yellow walls evoke the flavors and charms of Tuscany and the Mediterranean at this rustic-romantic restaurant across from the harbor and West Beach. Ahi sashimi tucked in a crisp sesame cone is a popular appetizer, after which you can proceed to a house-made pasta dish or rock shrimp gnocchi. **Known for:** house-made pastas and gnocchi; wines from Italy and California's Central Coast; romantic waterfront setting. $ *Average main: $29* ✉ *324 W. Cabrillo Blvd., near Castillo St.* ☏ *805/962–0777* ⊕ *www.tomarestaurant.com* ☾ *No lunch.*

$$$$
AMERICAN

✕ **Wine Cask.** The Wine Cask serves bistro-style meals in a comfortable and classy dining room with a huge fireplace and wood-beam ceiling decorated with gold leaf. The more casual bar-café, Intermezzo, across the courtyard, serves pizzas, salads, small plates, wines, and cocktails and is open late. **Known for:** extensive wine list and pairing suggestions; historic courtyard patio; late hours. $ *Average main: $31* ✉ *El Paseo, 813 Anacapa St., at E. De La Guerra St.* ☏ *805/966–9463* ⊕ *winecask. com* ☾ *Closed Sun. and Mon.*

6

WHERE TO STAY

$$$$ ⬛ **Bacara Resort & Spa.** A luxury resort with four restaurants and a
RESORT 42,000-square-foot spa and fitness center with 36 treatment rooms, the
Fodor'sChoice Bacara provides a gorgeous setting for relaxing retreats. **Pros:** serene
★ natural setting; three zero-edge pools; three golf courses nearby. **Cons:**
pricey; not close to downtown; sand on beach not pristine enough for
some. $ *Rooms from: $450* ✉ *8301 Hollister Ave., Goleta* ☎ *844/610–
9688* ⊕ *bacararesort.com* ↝ *358 rooms* ⦿ *No meals.*

$$$$ ⬛ **Belmond El Encanto.** Following nearly seven years and more than $100
HOTEL million of extensive renovations, this Santa Barbara icon lives on to
Fodor'sChoice thrill a new generation of guests with its relaxed-luxe bungalow rooms,
★ lush gardens, and personalized service. **Pros:** revitalized historic landmark; stellar spa facility; has hosted luminaries including Franklin D.
Roosevelt. **Cons:** long walk to downtown; pricey; guests staying for
more than a few days may find the restaurant menus limited. $ *Rooms
from: $404* ✉ *800 Alvarado Pl.* ☎ *805/845–5800, 800/393–5315*
⊕ *www.belmond.com/elencanto* ↝ *92 rooms* ⦿ *No meals.*

$$$$ ⬛ **Canary Hotel.** The only full-service hotel in the heart of downtown,
HOTEL this Kimpton property blends a casual, beach-getaway feel with urban
sophistication. **Pros:** upscale local cuisine at Finch & Fork; rooms come
with candles, yoga mats, and binoculars (for touring); adjacent fitness center. **Cons:** across from transit center; a mile from the beach.
$ *Rooms from: $415* ✉ *31 W. Carrillo St.* ☎ *805/884–0300, 866/999–
5401* ⊕ *www.canarysantabarbara.com* ↝ *97 rooms* ⦿ *No meals.*

$$$$ ⬛ **The Fess Parker, A DoubleTree by Hilton Resort.** A full-scale resort with
RESORT seven buildings spread over 24 landscaped acres across from East Beach,
the hotel was founded by the late TV actor Fess Parker, best known for
playing Davy Crockett and Daniel Boone. **Pros:** numerous amenities;
right across from the beach; free shuttle to train station and airport.
Cons: train noise filters into some rooms; too spread out for some.
$ *Rooms from: $269* ✉ *633 East Cabrillo Blvd.* ☎ *800/879–2929,
805/564–4333* ⊕ *www.fessparkersantabarbarahotel.com* ↝ *360 rooms*
⦿ *No meals.*

$$$$ ⬛ **Four Seasons Resort The Biltmore Santa Barbara.** Surrounded by lush,
RESORT perfectly manicured gardens and across from the beach, Santa Barbara's
Fodor'sChoice grande dame has long been a favorite for quiet, California-style luxury.
★ **Pros:** spa with 11 treatment rooms; access to members-only clubs and
restaurant on site; steps from the beach. **Cons:** back rooms are close
to train tracks; expensive. $ *Rooms from: $795* ✉ *1260 Channel Dr.*
☎ *805/969–2261, 805/332–3442 for reservations only* ⊕ *www.foursea-
sons.com/santabarbara* ↝ *207 rooms* ⦿ *No meals.*

$$$$ ⬛ **The Goodland.** A vintage Woody car, a silver Airstream trailer, and
HOTEL a digital photo booth are among the elements that bring 1960s California surf culture to life at this Kimpton hotel in Goleta. **Pros:** cool
and casual vibe; short walk to shops and services; a short drive to
the beach. **Cons:** not close to downtown Santa Barbara; some rooms
on the small side. $ *Rooms from: $284* ✉ *5650 Calle Real, Goleta*
☎ *877/480–1465, 805/964–6241* ⊕ *www.thegoodland.com* ↝ *158
rooms* ⦿ *No meals.*

$$$$
HOTEL
Fodor'sChoice
★

Hotel Californian. A sprawling collection of Spanish-Moorish buildings that opened in summer 2017 at the site of the historic 1925 Hotel Californian, this sophisticated hotel with a hip youthful vibe occupies nearly three full blocks on State Street just steps from Stearns Wharf, MOXI, the Funk Zone, beaches, and the harbor. **Pros:** steps from the waterfront, Funk Zone, and beaches; resort-style amenities; on-site parking. **Cons:** pricey; must walk or ride the shuttle to downtown attractions; train whistle noise in rooms close to station. $ *Rooms from: $550* ⊠ *36 State St.* ☎ *805/882–0100* ⊕ *www.thehotelcalifornian.com* ⤺ *121 rooms.*

$$$
HOTEL

Hotel Indigo. The closest hotel to the train station and across the street from the Funk Zone, artsy Hotel Indigo is a fine choice for travelers who appreciate contemporary art and want easy access to dining, nightlife, and the beach. **Pros:** multilingual staff; a block from Stearns Wharf; great value for location. **Cons:** showers only (no bathtubs); rooms on small side; train whistles early morning. $ *Rooms from: $189* ⊠ *121 State St.* ☎ *805/966–6586* ⊕ *www.indigosantabarbara. com* ⤺ *41 rooms* ⏻ *No meals.*

$$$$
HOTEL

Hyatt Santa Barbara. A complex of four buildings on three landscaped acres, the Hyatt provides an appealing lodging option in a prime location right across from East Beach. **Pros:** steps from the beach; many room types and rates; walk to the zoo and waterfront shuttle. **Cons:** motel feel; busy area in summer. $ *Rooms from: $289* ⊠ *1111 E. Cabrillo Blvd.* ☎ *805/882–1234, 800/643–1994* ⊕ *santabarbara.centric.hyatt.com* ⤺ *174 rooms* ⏻ *No meals.*

$$
HOTEL

Motel 6 Santa Barbara Beach. A half block from East Beach amid fancier hotels sits this basic but comfortable motel—the first Motel 6 in existence, and the first in the chain to transform into a contemporary Euro-style abode. **Pros:** very close to zoo and beach; friendly staff; clean. **Cons:** no frills; motel-style rooms; no breakfast. $ *Rooms from: $146* ⊠ *443 Corona Del Mar Dr.* ☎ *805/564–1392, 800/466–8356* ⊕ *motel6. com* ⤺ *51 rooms* ⏻ *No meals.*

$$$$
RESORT
Fodor'sChoice
★

San Ysidro Ranch. At this romantic hideaway on a historic property in the Montecito foothills—where John and Jackie Kennedy spent their honeymoon and Oprah sends her out-of-town visitors—guest cottages are scattered among groves of orange trees and flower beds. **Pros:** rooms come with private outdoor spas; 17 miles of hiking trails nearby; Plow & Angel Bistro and Stonehouse restaurants on site are Santa Barbara institutions. **Cons:** very expensive; too remote for some. $ *Rooms from: $845* ⊠ *900 San Ysidro La., Montecito* ☎ *805/565–1700, 800/368–6788* ⊕ *www.sanysidroranch.com* ⤺ *41 rooms and cottages* ⏻ *No meals* ⏱ *2-day minimum stay on weekends, 3 days on holiday weekends.*

$$$$
HOTEL
Fodor'sChoice
★

Santa Barbara Inn. After a two-year closure to undergo a massive remodel and expansion, this full-service family-owned hotel reopened in summer 2016 in sparkling Spanish-Mediterranean style in a prime waterfront corner across from East Beach. **Pros:** more than half the rooms have ocean views; suites come with whirlpool tubs; delicious on-site restaurant Convivo. **Cons:** on a busy boulevard; limited street parking. $ *Rooms from: $280* ⊠ *901 E. Cabrillo Blvd.* ✛ *At Milpas St.* ☎ *805/966–3636* ⊕ *www.santabarbarainn.com* ⤺ *70 rooms* ⏻ *Breakfast.*

$$$$ B&B/INN Fodor's Choice ★ 🏨 **Simpson House Inn.** If you're a fan of traditional bed-and-breakfast inns, this property, with its beautifully appointed Victorian main house and acre of lush gardens, is for you. **Pros:** elegant; impeccable landscaping; within walking distance of downtown. **Cons:** some rooms in main building are small; two-night minimum stay on weekends May–October. [$] *Rooms from: $325* ✉ *121 E. Arrellaga St.* ☎ *805/963–7067, 800/676–1280* 🌐 *www.simpsonhouseinn.com* 🛏 *15 rooms* 🍴 *Breakfast.*

$$$$ B&B/INN 🏨 **Spanish Garden Inn.** A half block from the Presidio in the heart of downtown, this Spanish-Mediterranean retreat celebrates Santa Barbara style, from the tile floors, wrought-iron balconies, and exotic plants to the original art by local plein-air artists. **Pros:** walking distance from downtown; classic Spanish-Mediterranean style; free parking. **Cons:** no restaurant. [$] *Rooms from: $399* ✉ *915 Garden St.* ☎ *805/564–4700* 🌐 *www.spanishgardeninn.com* 🛏 *24 rooms* 🍴 *Breakfast.*

$$$$ B&B/INN 🏨 **The Upham.** Built in 1871, this downtown Victorian in the arts and culture district has been restored as a full-service hotel. **Pros:** 1-acre garden; easy walk to theaters; excellent on-site restaurant. **Cons:** some rooms are small; not near beach or waterfront. [$] *Rooms from: $285* ✉ *1404 De la Vina St.* ☎ *805/962–0058, 800/727–0876* 🌐 *www.uphamhotel.com* 🛏 *50 rooms* 🍴 *Breakfast* ☞ *2-night minimum stay on weekends.*

$$$ HOTEL 🏨 **The Wayfarer.** One of the nicest international hostels you'll ever come across, the hip and stylish Wayfarer opened in 2014 in a prime Funk Zone location, three blocks from Stearns Wharf and the beach, and across the street from the train station. **Pros:** outdoor heated pool; breakfast included; free parking. **Cons:** some rooms on the small side; freeway and train noise bothers some guests; pricey during high season. [$] *Rooms from: $239* ✉ *12 E. Montecito St.* ☎ *805/845–1000* 🌐 *wayfarersb.com* 🛏 *31 rooms* 🍴 *Breakfast.*

NIGHTLIFE AND PERFORMING ARTS

The bar, club, and live music scene centers on lower State Street, between the 300 and 800 blocks. The arts district, with theaters, restaurants, and cafés, starts around the 900 block of State and continues north to the 1300 block. To see what's scheduled around town, pick up the free weekly *Santa Barbara Independent* newspaper or visit its website, 🌐 *www.independent.com.*

NIGHTLIFE

Dargan's. Lively Dargan's pub has pool tables, great draft beers and Irish whiskies, and serves a full menu of traditional Irish dishes. ✉ *18 E. Ortega St., at Anacapa St.* ☎ *805/568–0702* 🌐 *darganssb.com.*

The Good Lion. The cocktail menu at this intimate neighborhood bar near The Granada Theatre changes weekly, depending on the fresh organic bounty available at the markets. All juices are organic and squeezed fresh daily, and all syrups are made in house with organic produce and sweeteners. ✉ *1212 State St.* ☎ *805/845–8754* 🌐 *www.goodlioncocktails.com.*

James Joyce. A good place to have a few beers and while away an evening; the James Joyce hosts rock, blues, jazz, and other performers six nights a week. ✉ *513 State St., at W. Haley St.* ☎ *805/962–2688* 🌐 *sbjamesjoyce.com.*

Joe's Cafe. Steins of beer and stiff cocktails accompany hearty bar food at Joe's. It's a fun, if occasionally rowdy, collegiate scene. ⊠ *536 State St., at E. Cota St.* ☎ *805/966–4638* ⊕ *joescafesb.com.*

Les Marchands. Brian McClintic, one of four real-life candidates trying to achieve master sommelier status in the 2013 film *Somm* (he succeeded), co-owns and operates this combination wine bar, store, and eatery in the Funk Zone. ⊠ *131 Anacapa St., at Yananoli St.* ☎ *805/284–0380* ⊕ *www.lesmarchandswine.com.*

Lucky's. A slick sports bar attached to an upscale steak house owned by the maker of Lucky Brand dungarees, this place attracts hip patrons hoping to see and be seen. ⊠ *1279 Coast Village Rd., near Olive Mill Rd., Montecito* ☎ *805/565–7540* ⊕ *luckys-steakhouse.com.*

Milk & Honey. Artfully prepared tapas, mango mojitos, and exotic cocktails lure trendy crowds to swank M&H, despite high prices and a reputation for inattentive service. ⊠ *30 W. Anapamu St., at State St.* ☎ *805/275–4232* ⊕ *www.milknhoneytapas.com.*

SOhO. A lively restaurant, bar, and music venue, SOhO books all kinds of musical acts, from jazz to blues to rock. ⊠ *1221 State St., at W. Victoria St.* ☎ *805/962–7776* ⊕ *www.sohosb.com.*

PERFORMING ARTS

Arlington Theatre. This Moorish-style auditorium presents touring performers and films throughout the year. ⊠ *1317 State St., at Arlington Ave.* ☎ *805/963–4408* ⊕ *thearlingtontheatre.com.*

Center Stage Theatre. This venue hosts plays, music, dance, and readings. ⊠ *Paseo Nuevo Center, Chapala and De la Guerra Sts., 2nd fl.* ☎ *805/963–0408* ⊕ *www.centerstagetheater.org.*

Ensemble Theatre Company (ETC). The company stages classic and contemporary comedies, musicals, and dramas. ⊠ *33 W. Victoria St., at Chapala St.* ☎ *805/965–5400* ⊕ *www.etcsb.org.*

The Granada Theatre. A restored, modernized landmark that dates from 1924, the Granada hosts Broadway touring shows and dance, music, and other cultural events. ⊠ *1214 State St., at E. Anapamu St.* ☎ *805/899–2222* ⊕ *granadasb.org.*

Lobero Theatre. A state landmark, the Lobero hosts community theater groups and touring professionals. ⊠ *33 E. Canon Perdido St., at Anacapa St.* ☎ *805/963–0761* ⊕ *www.lobero.com.*

Santa Barbara Bowl. Built in 1936 and recently renovated to meet the highest standards of visiting musicians, the 4,500-seat Bowl attracts world-class entertainers (past acts include Radiohead, The Who, John Legend, and Natalie Merchant), from April through October. ⊠ *1122 N. Milpas St. ✛ At Anapamu St.* ☎ *805/962–7411* ⊕ *www. sbbowl.com.*

Fodor'sChoice **Old Spanish Days Fiesta.** The city celebrates its Spanish, Mexican, and ★ Chumash heritage in early August with events that include music, dancing, an all-equestrian parade, a carnival, and a rodeo. ⊠ *Santa Barbara* ⊕ *oldspanishdays-fiesta.org.*

Fodor's Choice ★ **Santa Barbara International Film Festival.** The 12-day festival in late January and early February attracts film enthusiasts and major stars to downtown venues for screenings, panels, and tributes. ✉ *Santa Barbara* ⊕ *www.sbiff.org.*

Summer Solstice Celebration. More than 100,000 revelers celebrate the arts at this mid-June event whose highlight is a huge parade of costumed participants who dance, drum, and ride people-powered floats up State Street. ✉ *Santa Barbara* ☎ *805/965–3396* ⊕ *www.solsticeparade.com.*

> **EARTH DAY**
>
> In 1969, 200,000 gallons of crude oil spilled into the Santa Barbara Channel, causing an immediate outcry from residents. The day after the spill, Get Oil Out (GOO) was established; the group helped lead the successful fight for legislation to limit and regulate offshore drilling in California. The Santa Barbara spill also spawned Earth Day, which is still celebrated across the nation today.

SPORTS AND THE OUTDOORS

BIKING

Cabrillo Bike Lane. The level, two-lane, 3-mile Cabrillo Bike Lane passes the Santa Barbara Zoo, the Andree Clark Bird Refuge, beaches, and the harbor. Stop for a meal at one of the restaurants along the way, or for a picnic along the palm-lined path looking out on the Pacific.

Wheel Fun Rentals. You can rent bikes, quadricycles, and skates here. ✉ *23 E. Cabrillo Blvd.* ☎ *805/966–2282* ⊕ *wheelfunrentalssb.com.*

BOATS AND CHARTERS

Fodor's Choice ★ **Condor Express.** From SEA Landing, the *Condor Express*, a 75-foot high-speed catamaran, whisks up to 149 passengers toward the Channel Islands on whale-watching excursions and sunset and dinner cruises. ✉ *301 W. Cabrillo Blvd.* ☎ *805/882–0088, 888/779–4253* ⊕ *condorexpress.com.*

Paddle Sports Center. A full-service paddle-sports center in the harbor, this outfit rents kayaks, stand-up paddleboards, surfboards, boogie boards, and water-sports gear. ✉ *117 B Harbor Way, off Shoreline Dr.* ☎ *805/617–3425 rentals* ⊕ *www.paddlesportsca.com.*

Santa Barbara Sailing Center. The center offers sailing instruction, rents and charters sailboats, kayaks, and stand-up paddleboards, and organizes dinner and sunset champagne cruises, island excursions, and whale-watching trips. ✉ *Santa Barbara Harbor launching ramp* ☎ *805/962–2826* ⊕ *sbsail.com.*

Truth Aquatics. Truth runs kayaking, paddleboarding, hiking, snorkeling, and scuba excursions to the National Marine Sanctuary and Channel Islands National Park. ✉ *Departures from SEA Landing, Santa Barbara Harbor* ☎ *805/962–1127* ⊕ *truthaquatics.com* ⌁ *From $120.*

SHOPPING

CLOTHING

DIANI. This upscale, European-style women's boutique dresses clients in designer clothing from around the world. Sibling shoe and home-and-garden shops are nearby. ✉ *1324 State St., at Arlington Ave.* ☎ *805/966–3114, 805/966–7175 shoe shop* ⊕ *dianiboutique.com.*

Surf N Wear's Beach House. This shop carries surf clothing, gear, and collectibles; it's also the home of Santa Barbara Surf Shop and the exclusive local dealer of Surfboards by Yater. ✉ *10 State St., at Cabrillo Blvd.* ☎ *805/963–1281* ⊕ *www.surfnwear.com.*

Wendy Foster. This store sells casual-chic women's fashions. ✉ *833 State St., at W. Canon Perdido St.* ☎ *805/966–2276* ⊕ *wendyfoster.com.*

FOOD AND WINE

Santa Barbara Public Market. A dozen food and beverage vendors occupy this spacious arts district galleria. Stock up on olive oils, vinegars, and other gourmet goodies; sip on handcrafted wines and beers while watching sports events; and nosh on noodle bowls, sushi and baked goods. ✉ *38 W. Victoria St., at Chapala St.* ☎ *805/770–7702* ⊕ *sb-publicmarket.com.*

SHOPPING AREAS

Fodor'sChoice ★ **El Paseo.** Wine-tasting rooms, shops, art galleries, and studios share the courtyard and gardens of this historic arcade. ✉ *Canon Perdido St., between State and Anacapa Sts.*

Fodor'sChoice ★ **State Street.** Between Cabrillo Boulevard and Sola Street, State Street is a shopper's paradise. Chic malls, quirky storefronts, antiques emporia, elegant boutiques, and funky thrift shops abound. You can shop on foot or ride a battery-powered trolley (50¢) that runs between the waterfront and the 1300 block. Nordstrom and Macy's anchor **Paseo Nuevo** , an open-air mall in the 700 block. Shops, restaurants, galleries, and fountains line the tiled walkways of **La Arcada,** a small complex of landscaped courtyards in the 1100 block designed by architect Myron Hunt in 1926.

NORTHERN SANTA BARBARA COUNTY

The Santa Ynez Mountains divide Santa Barbara County geographically; U.S. 101 passes through a mountain tunnel leading inland. Northern Santa Barbara County used to be known for sprawling ranches and strawberry and broccoli fields. Today its 200-plus wineries and 22,000 acres of vineyards dominate the landscape from the Santa Ynez Valley in the south to Santa Maria in the north. Though more than 50 grape varietals are grown in the county, more than half the vineyards are planted to Chardonnay, Pinot Noir, and Syrah.

GETTING HERE AND AROUND

Two-lane Highway 154 over San Marcos Pass is the shortest and most scenic route from Santa Barbara into the Santa Ynez Valley. You can also drive along U.S. 101 north 43 miles to Buellton, then 7 miles east through Solvang to Santa Ynez. Santa Ynez Valley Transit shuttle buses serve Santa Ynez, Los Olivos, Ballard, Solvang, and Buellton. COLT Wine Country Express buses connect Lompoc, Buellton, and Solvang on weekdays except holidays.

ESSENTIALS

Bus Contacts **COLT Wine Country Express.** ☎ *805/736–7666* 🌐 *www.cityoflompoc.com/transit.* **Santa Ynez Valley Transit.** ☎ *805/688–5452* 🌐 *www.syvt.com.*

Visitor Information **Santa Barbara Vintners.** ☎ *805/688–0881* 🌐 *www.sbcountywines.com.* **Visit Santa Barbara.** 🌐 *www.santabarbaraca.com.* **Visit the Santa Ynez Valley.** 🌐 *www.visitsyv.com.*

SANTA YNEZ

31 miles north of Goleta.

Founded in 1882, the tiny town of Santa Ynez still has many of its original frontier buildings. You can walk through the three-block downtown area in a few minutes, shop for antiques, and hang around the old-time saloon. At some of the Santa Ynez Valley's best restaurants, you just might bump into one of the celebrities who own nearby ranches.

GETTING HERE AND AROUND

Take Highway 154 over San Marcos Pass or U.S. 101 north 43 miles to Buellton, then 7 miles east.

EXPLORING

Gainey Vineyard. The 1,800-acre Gainey Ranch, straddling the banks of the Santa Ynez River, includes about 100 acres of organic vineyards: Sauvignon Blanc, Merlot, Cabernet Sauvignon, and Cabernet Franc. The winery also makes wines from Chardonnay, Pinot Noir, and Syrah grapes from the Santa Rita Hills. You can taste the latest releases—the estate Pinot Noir is especially good—in a Spanish-style hacienda overlooking the ranch. Barrel tasting is also available through the week (except in winter). ✉ *3950 E. Hwy. 246* ☎ *805/688–0558* 🌐 *www.gaineyvineyard.com* 🎟 *Tasting $15–$45.*

WHERE TO EAT AND STAY

$$$ ITALIAN 🍴 **Santa Ynez Kitchen.** The owners of Toscana, a popular eatery in L.A.'s Brentwood neighborhood, run this rustic-chic restaurant with an Italy-meets-California Wine Country vibe. Chef and co-owner Luca Crestanelli, a native of Verona, Italy, typically offers about 10 seasonal daily specials. **Known for:** wood-fired pizzas and oak-grilled entrées; creative craft cocktails; gelatos and "not-so-classic" tiramisu. [$] *Average main: $25* ✉ *1110 Faraday St., at Sagunto St.* ☎ *805/691–9794* 🌐 *www.sykitchen.com* 🕑 *No lunch Mon.–Thurs.*

$$$ ITALIAN 🍴 **Trattoria Grappolo.** Authentic Italian fare, an open kitchen, and festive, family-style seating make this trattoria equally popular with celebrities from Hollywood and ranchers from the Santa Ynez Valley. The noise level tends to rise in the evening, so this isn't the best spot for a romantic getaway. **Known for:** thin-crust wood-fired pizzas; risottos and homemade pastas; carpaccio. [$] *Average main: $25* ✉ *3687–C Sagunto St.* ☎ *805/688–6899* 🌐 *trattoriagrappolo.com* 🕑 *No lunch Mon.*

$$$$ **B&B/INN** 🏨 **ForFriends Inn.** Four close friends—Jim and Debbie Campbell and Dave and Katie Pollock—own and operate this luxury bed-and-breakfast, designed as a social place where friends gather to enjoy good wine, food, and music in a casual backyard setting. **Pros:** three-course breakfast, evening wine and appetizers included; friendly innkeepers; "Friendship Pass" provides perks and savings at restaurants and wineries. **Cons:** not suitable for children; no pets allowed. [$] *Rooms from: $295* ✉ *1121 Edison St.* ☎ *805/693–0303* 🌐 *www.forfriendsinn.com* 🛏 *5 rooms, 2 cottages* 🍴 *Breakfast.*

$$$$ **B&B/INN** 🏨 **Santa Ynez Inn.** This posh two-story Victorian inn in downtown Santa Ynez was built from scratch in 2002, and the owners have furnished all the rooms with authentic historical pieces. **Pros:** near restaurants; unusual antiques; spacious rooms. **Cons:** high price for location; building not historic. [$] *Rooms from: $339* ✉ *3627 Sagunto St.* ☎ *805/688–5588, 800/643–5774* 🌐 *www.santaynezinn.com* 🛏 *20 rooms* 🍴 *Breakfast.*

SPORTS AND THE OUTDOORS

Santa Barbara Soaring. The outfit's scenic glider rides last from 10 to 50 minutes. Tour options include the Santa Ynez Valley, coastal mountains and the Channel Islands, and celebrity homes. ✉ *Santa Ynez Airport, 900 Airport Rd.* ☎ *805/688–2517* 🌐 *www.sbsoaring.com* 🎟 *$185–$475.*

6

LOS OLIVOS

4 miles north of Santa Ynez.

This pretty village was once on Spanish-built El Camino Real (Royal Road) and later a stop on major stagecoach and rail routes. Tasting rooms, art galleries, antiques stores, and country markets line Grand Avenue and intersecting streets for several blocks.

GETTING HERE AND AROUND

From U.S. 101 north or south, exit at Highway 154 and drive east about 8 miles. From Santa Barbara, travel 30 miles northwest on Highway 154.

EXPLORING

Blair Fox Cellars. Blair Fox, a Santa Barbara native, crafts small-lot Rhône-style wines made from organic grapes. The bar in his rustic Los Olivos tasting room, where you can sample exceptional vineyard-designated Syrahs and other wines, was hewn from Australian white oak reclaimed from an old Tasmanian schoolhouse. ✉ *2902–B San Marcos Ave.* ☎ *805/691–1678* 🌐 *www.blairfoxcellars.com* 🎟 *Tasting $15* 🕒 *Closed Tues. and Wed.*

Coquelicot Estate Vineyard. Named for the vivid red poppy flowers that blanket the French countryside and appear on all its labels, this limited-production winery focuses on handcrafted Bordeaux wines made from grapes at its certified organic 58-acre Santa Ynez Valley vineyard. Don't miss samples of the flagship wines: Sixer (a Syrah and Viogner blend), Mon Amour (a Bordeaux blend), and the estate Sauvignon Blanc and Rosé. ✉ *2884 Grand Ave.* ☎ *805/688–1500* 🌐 *www.coquelicotwines.com* 🎟 *Tastings $15–$20.*

Firestone Vineyard. Heirs to the Firestone tire fortune developed (but no longer own) this winery known for Chardonnay, Gewürztraminer, Cabernet Sauvignon, and Syrah—and for the fantastic valley views from its tasting room and picnic area. The tour here is highly informative. ✉ *5017 Zaca Station Rd., off U.S. 101* ☎ *805/688–3940* 🌐 *www.firestonewine.com* 🎫 *Tastings $10–$15.*

WHERE TO EAT AND STAY

$$$ AMERICAN 🍴 **Los Olivos Wine Merchant Cafe.** Part wine store and part social hub, this café focuses on wine-friendly fish, pasta, and meat dishes, plus salads, pizzas, and burgers. Don't miss the homemade muffuletta and olive tapenade spreads, or the French toast soufflé for breakfast (weekends only). **Known for:** nearly everything made in-house; ingredients from own organic café farm; wines from own estate winery. [$] *Average main: $23* ✉ *2879 Grand Ave.* ☎ *805/688–7265* 🌐 *www.winemerchantcafe.com* 🕒 *No breakfast weekdays.*

$$$ AMERICAN 🍴 **Sides Hardware & Shoes: A Brothers Restaurant.** Inside a historic storefront they renovated, brothers Matt and Jeff Nichols serve comfort food prepared with panache. The Kobe-style burgers, especially the one with bacon and white cheddar, make a great lunch, and the dinner favorites include za'atar chicken, Scottish salmon, and lamb sirloin with goat cheese gnocchi. **Known for:** in-house cured and smoked bacon; juicy burgers; jalapeño margaritas. [$] *Average main: $30* ✉ *2375 Alamo Pintado Ave.* ☎ *805/688–4820* 🌐 *brothersrestaurant.com.*

$$$$ B&B/INN Fodor's Choice ★ 🏨 **The Ballard Inn.** Set among orchards and vineyards in the tiny town of Ballard, 2 miles south of Los Olivos, this inn makes an elegant wine-country escape. **Pros:** exceptional food; attentive staff; secluded. **Cons:** some baths could use updating. [$] *Rooms from: $315* ✉ *2436 Baseline Ave., Ballard* ☎ *805/688–7770, 800/638–2466* 🌐 *ballardinn.com* 🛏 *15 rooms* 🍽 *Breakfast.*

$$$$ B&B/INN 🏨 **Fess Parker's Wine Country Inn and Spa.** This luxury inn includes an elegant, tree-shaded French country–style main building and an equally attractive annex across the street with a pool and day spa. **Pros:** convenient wine-touring base; walking distance from restaurants and galleries; rate includes full breakfast at The Bear and Star on site. **Cons:** pricey; not pet-friendly. [$] *Rooms from: $395* ✉ *2860 Grand Ave.* ☎ *805/688–7788, 800/446–2455* 🌐 *www.fessparkerinn.com* 🛏 *19 rooms* 🍽 *Breakfast.*

SOLVANG

5 miles south of Los Olivos.

You'll know you've reached the town of Solvang when the architecture suddenly changes to half-timber buildings and windmills. Danish educators settled the town in 1911—the flatlands and rolling green hills reminded them of home. Solvang has attracted tourists for decades, but it's lately become more sophisticated, with smorgasbords giving way to galleries, upscale restaurants, and wine-tasting rooms by day and wine bars by night. The visitor center on Copenhagen Drive has walking-tour maps (also available online). The Sweet Treats tour covers the town's Danish bakeries, confectionary stores, and ice-cream parlors. The Olsen's and Solvang bakeries and Ingeborg's Danish Chocolates are worth investigating.

GETTING HERE AND AROUND

Highway 246 West (Mission Drive) traverses Solvang, connecting with U.S. 101 to the west and Highway 154 to the east. Alamo Pintado Road connects Solvang with Ballard and Los Olivos to the north. Park your car in one of the free public lots and stroll the town. Or take the bus: Santa Ynez Valley Transit shuttles run between Solvang and nearby towns.

ESSENTIALS

Visitor Information Solvang Conference & Visitors Bureau. ✉ *1639 Copenhagen Dr., at 2nd St.* ☎ *805/688–6144* ⊕ *www.solvangusa.com.*

EXPLORING

Mission Santa Inés. The mission holds an impressive collection of paintings, statuary, vestments, and Chumash and Spanish artifacts in a serene bluff-top setting. You can tour the museum, sanctuary, and gardens. ✉ *1760 Mission Dr., at Alisal Rd.* ☎ *805/688–4815* ⊕ *missionsantaines. org* ◔ *$5.*

Rideau Vineyard. This winery celebrates its locale's rich history—the King of Spain himself once owned this land, and the tasting room occupies a former guest ranch inn—but fully embraces the area's wine-making present. Wines made from the Rhône varietals Mourvèdre, Roussanne, Syrah, and Viognier are the specialty here. ✉ *1562 Alamo Pintado Rd., 2 miles north of Hwy. 246* ☎ *805/688–0717* ⊕ *rideauvineyard.com* ◔ *Tastings $12–$16.*

Sevtap. Winemaker Art Sevtap, an Istanbul native, is often on hand to pour samples of his limited-production wines—mostly from Bordeaux varietals—in this artsy wine bar that's decked out with Tibetan prayer flags and chalkboard walls and has a stage where guests can pick up a guitar and strum away. ✉ *1622 Copenhagen Dr., at 2nd St.* ☎ *805/693–9200* ⊕ *www.sevtapwinery.com* ◔ *Tasting $15.*

WHERE TO EAT

$$$$
AMERICAN
Fodor's Choice
★

✕ **First & Oak.** Create your own custom tasting menu by choosing among five different groups of eclectic California-French dishes paired with local wines at this elegant farm-to-table restaurant inside the Mirabelle Inn. The seasonal menu changes constantly, but regulars include smoked sweet-and-spicy duck wings, truffle-roasted cauliflower, local spot prawns, short rib bourguignonne, and pears poached in red wine from the sommelier-owner's organic Coceliquot Estate Vineyard, **Known for:** intimate fine-dining setting; sommelier-owner selected wine list; complex dishes and presentation. Ⓢ *Average main: $34* ✉ *409 1st St.* ✛ *at Oak St.* ☎ *805/688–1703* ⊕ *www.firstandoak.com.*

$$$$
AMERICAN
Fodor's Choice
★

✕ **Root 246.** This chic restaurant's chefs tap local purveyors and shop for organic ingredients at farmers' markets before deciding on the day's menu. Depending on the season, you might feast on Dungeness crab, a savory cassoulet, Santa Maria–style tri-tip grilled over an oak fire, or seaweed-crusted steelhead trout in a smoky red wine broth. **Known for:** gorgeous contemporary Native American-influenced design; 1,800-bottle wine selection; popular happy hour with craft cocktails. Ⓢ *Average main: $33* ✉ *Hotel Corque, 420 Alisal Rd., at Molle Way* ☎ *805/686–8681* ⊕ *www.root-246.com* ☽ *Closed Mon. No lunch. No breakfast weekdays.*

$$$
AMERICAN

✕**Succulent Café.** Locals flock to this cozy café for its comfort cuisine and regional wines and craft beers. Order at the counter, and staffers will deliver your meal to the interior dining areas or the sunny outdoor patio. **Known for:** artisanal charcuterie plates; pet-friendly patio; homemade biscuits and gravy, house-roasted turkey. $ *Average main: $26* ⊠ *1555 Mission Dr., at 4th Pl.* ☎ *805/691–9444* ⊕ *succulentcafe.com* ⊙ *Closed Tues.*

WHERE TO STAY

$$$$
RESORT
Fodor'sChoice
★

Alisal Guest Ranch and Resort. Since 1946 this 10,000-acre ranch has been popular with celebrities and plain folk alike. **Pros:** Old West atmosphere; many activities; ultraprivate. **Cons:** isolated; not close to downtown. $ *Rooms from: $600* ⊠ *1054 Alisal Rd.* ☎ *805/688–6411, 800/425–4725* ⊕ *alisal.com* ⤳ *73 rooms* ⫶⃘ *Some meals.*

$$$
HOTEL
Fodor'sChoice
★

Hotel Corque. Owned by the Santa Ynez Band of Chumash Indians, the stunning three-story "Corque" provides a full slate of upscale amenities. **Pros:** friendly, professional staff; short walk to shops, tasting rooms and restaurants; free Wi-Fi. **Cons:** no kitchenettes or laundry facilities; pricey. $ *Rooms from: $239* ⊠ *400 Alisal Rd.* ☎ *805/688–8000, 800/624–5572* ⊕ *hotelcorque.com* ⤳ *132 rooms* ⫶⃘ *No meals.*

$$$
B&B/INN
Fodor'sChoice
★

Mirabelle Inn. French, Danish, and American flags at the entrance crystal chandeliers, soaring ceilings, and skylights in the lobby set the tone from the get-go in this elegant four-story inn a few blocks from the main tourist hub. **Pros:** excellent farm-to-table restaurant (dinner only); full cook-to-order breakfast included; away from noisy crowds. **Cons:** some rooms on the small side; not in the heart of town. $ *Rooms from: $250* ⊠ *409 1st St.* ✛ *at Oak St.* ☎ *805/688–1703, 800/786–7925* ⤳ *12 rooms* ⫶⃘ *Breakfast.*

PERFORMING ARTS

Solvang Festival Theater. Pacific Conservatory of the Performing Arts presents crowd-pleasing musicals like *Lend Me a Tenor* and *Beauty and the Beast*, as well as Shakespeare's *Twelfth Night*, and contemporary plays at this 700-seat outdoor amphitheater. ⊠ *420 2nd St., at Molle Way* ☎ *805/922–8313* ⊕ *pcpa.org* ☞ *Performances June–Oct.*

BUELLTON

3 miles west of Solvang.

A crossroads town at the intersection of U.S. 101 and Highway 246, Buellton has evolved from a sleepy gas and coffee stop into an enclave of wine-tasting rooms, beer gardens, and restaurants. It's also a gateway to Lompoc and the Santa Rita Hills Wine Trail to the west, and to Solvang, Santa Ynez, and Los Olivos to the east.

GETTING HERE AND AROUND

Driving is the easiest way to get to Buellton. From Santa Barbara, follow U.S. 101 north to the Highway 246 exit. Santa Ynez Valley Transit serves Buellton with shuttle buses from Solvang and nearby towns.

ESSENTIALS

Visitor Information Buellton Visitors Bureau. ⊠ *597 Ave. of the Flags, No. 101* ☎ *805/688–7829, 800/324–3800* ⊕ *visitbuellton.com.* **Santa Rita Hills Wine Trail.** ⊕ *santaritahillswinetrail.com.*

EXPLORING

Alma Rosa Winery. Winemaker Richard Sanford helped put Santa Barbara County on the international wine map with a 1989 Pinot Noir. For Alma Rosa, started in 2005, he crafts wines from grapes grown on 100-plus acres of certified organic vineyards in the Santa Rita Hills. The Pinot Noirs and Chardonnays are exceptional. Vineyard tours and tastings are available by appointment. ✉ *181 C Industrial Way, off Hwy. 246, west of U.S. 101* ☎ *805/688–9090* 🌐 *almarosawinery.com* 🎫 *Tastings $15* 🕒 *Sun.–Thurs., daily 11–4:30; Fri. and Sat., daily 11–6:30.*

Industrial Way. A half-mile west of U.S. 101, head south from Highway 246 on Industrial Way to explore a hip and happening collection of food and drink destinations. Top stops include **Industrial Eats** (a craft butcher shop and restaurant), **Figueroa Mountain Brewing Co.,** the **Alma Rosa Winery** tasting room, **Terravant, Tesora Sweets,** and the **Ascendant Spirits Distillery.** ✉ *Industrial Way, off Hwy. 246.*

Lafond Winery and Vineyards. A rich, concentrated Pinot Noir is the main attention-getter at this winery that also produces noteworthy Chardonnays and Syrahs. Bottles with Lafond's SRH (Santa Rita Hills) label are an especially good value. The winery also has a tasting room at 111 East Yanonali Street in Santa Barbara's Funk Zone. ✉ *6855 Santa Rosa Rd., west off U.S. 101 Exit 139* ☎ *805/688–7921* 🌐 *lafondwinery.com* 🎫 *Tasting $12 (includes logo glass).*

6

WHERE TO EAT

$$$$ AMERICAN

🍴 **The Hitching Post II.** You'll find everything from grilled artichokes to quail at this casual eatery, but most people come for the smoky Santa Maria–style barbecue. Be sure to try a glass of owner-chef-winemaker Frank Ostini's signature Highliner Pinot Noir, a star in the film *Sideways.* **Known for:** entrées grilled over local red oak; chef-owner makes his own wines. [$] *Average main: $32* ✉ *406 E. Hwy. 246, off U.S. 101* ☎ *805/688–0676* 🌐 *www.hitchingpost2.com* 🕒 *No lunch.*

LOMPOC

20 miles west of Solvang.

Known as the flower-seed capital of the world, Lompoc is blanketed with vast fields of brightly colored flowers that bloom from May through August. Also home to a starkly beautiful mission, Lompoc has emerged as a major Pinot Noir and Chardonnay grape-growing region. Overlapping the Santa Rita Hills Wine Trail in parts, the Lompoc Wine Trail includes wineries in the Wine Ghetto, a downtown industrial park, and along Highway 246 and (to the south) Santa Rosa Road, which form a loop between Lompoc and Buellton.

GETTING HERE AND AROUND

Driving is the easiest way to get to Lompoc. From Santa Barbara, follow U.S. 101 north to Highway 1 exit off Gaviota Pass, or Highway 246 west at Buellton.

ESSENTIALS

Visitor Information **Lompoc Valley Chamber of Commerce & Visitors Bureau.** ✉ *111 S. I St., at Hwy. 246* ☎ *805/736–4567, 800/240–0999* 🌐 *lompoc.com.*

EXPLORING

FAMILY **La Purísima Mission State Historic Park.** The state's most fully restored mission, founded in 1787, stands in a stark and still remote location that powerfully evokes the lives and isolation of California's Spanish settlers. Docents lead tours every afternoon, and vivid displays illustrate the secular and religious activities that formed mission life. ✉ *2295 Purisima Rd., off Hwy. 246* ☎ *805/733–3713* ⊕ *www.lapurisimamission.org* 🎫 *$6 per vehicle.*

Lompoc Wine Ghetto. Laid-back tasting rooms can be found in a downtown industrial park. Taste of Sta. Rita Hills and Flying Goat are two rooms worth checking out here. ✉ *200 N. 9th St.* ⊕ *lompoctrail.com* 🎫 *Tasting fees vary, some free* ☉ *Many tasting rooms closed Mon.–Wed.*

SAN LUIS OBISPO COUNTY

San Luis Obispo County's pristine landscapes and abundant wildlife areas, especially those around Morro Bay, have long attracted nature lovers. In the south, Pismo Beach and other coastal towns have great sand and surf; inland, a booming wine region stretches from the Edna, Arroyo Grande, and Avila valleys and Nipomo in the south, to Paso Robles in the north. A good way to explore the county is to follow the Highway 1 Discovery Route, a 101-mile road trip that takes you off the beaten track through 10 small towns and cities, from Ragged Point, San Simeon, Cambria, and Cayucos in the north to Los Osos/Baywood Park, Avila Beach, Edna Valley, Arroyo Grande, and Oceano/Nipomo in the south (⊕ *www.highway1discoveryroute.com*).

GETTING HERE AND AROUND

San Luis Obispo Regional Transit Authority operates buses in San Luis Obispo and serves Paso Robles as well as Pismo Beach and other coastal towns.

ESSENTIALS

Transportation Contact San Luis Obispo Regional Transit Authority. ☎ *805/541–2228* ⊕ *www.slorta.org.*

Visitor Information California Highway 1 Discovery Route. ⊕ *highway1discoveryroute.com.* **SLO Wine Country.** ☎ *805/541–5868* ⊕ *www.slowine.com.* **Visit SLO CAL.** ✉ *1334 Marsh St., San Luis Obispo* ☎ *805/541–8000* ⊕ *slocal.com.*

PISMO BEACH

40 miles north of Lompoc.

About 20 miles of sandy shoreline—nicknamed the Bakersfield Riviera for the throngs of vacationers who come here from the Central Valley—begins at the town of Pismo Beach. The southern end of town runs along sand dunes, some of which are open to cars and off-road vehicles. Sheltered by the dunes, a grove of eucalyptus trees attracts thousands of migrating monarch butterflies from November through February. A long, broad beach fronts the center of town, where a municipal pier extends into the sea at the foot of shop-lined Pomeroy Street. To the north, hotels and homes perch atop chalky oceanfront cliffs. Fewer than 10,000 people live in this quintessential surfer haven, but Pismo Beach has a slew of hotels and restaurants with great views of the Pacific Ocean.

GETTING HERE AND AROUND

Pismo Beach straddles both sides of U.S. 101. If you're coming from the south and have time for a scenic drive, exit U.S. 101 in Santa Maria and take Highway 166 west for 8 miles to Guadalupe and follow Highway 1 north 16 miles to Pismo Beach. South County Area Transit (SCAT; ⊕ *www.slorta.org*) buses run throughout San Luis Obispo and connect the city with nearby towns. On summer weekends, the free Avila Trolley extends service to Pismo Beach.

VOLCANOES?

Those eye-catching sawed-off peaks along the drive from Pismo Beach to Morro Bay are called the Nine Sisters—a series of ancient volcanic plugs. Morro Rock, the northernmost sibling and a state historic monument, is the most famous and photographed of the clan.

ESSENTIALS

Visitor Information California Welcome Center. ⊠ *333 Five Cities Dr.* ☎ *805/773-7924.* **Pismo Beach Visitors Information Center.** ⊠ *Dolliver St./ Hwy. 1, at Hinds Ave.* ☎ *800/443-7778, 805/773-4382* ⊕ *classiccalifornia.com.*

BEACHES

Fodor's Choice ★ **Oceano Dunes State Vehicular Recreation Area.** Part of the spectacular Guadalupe-Nipomo Dunes, this 3,600-acre coastal playground is one of the few places in California where you can drive or ride off-highway vehicles on the beach and sand dunes. Hike, ride horses, kiteboard, join a Hummer tour, or rent an ATV or a dune buggy and cruise up the white-sand peaks for spectacular views. At **Oso Flaco Lake Nature Area**—3 miles west of Highway 1 on Oso Flaco Road—a 1½-mile boardwalk over the lake leads to a platform with views up and down the coast. Leashed dogs are allowed in much of the park except Oso Flaco and Pismo Dunes Natural Reserve. **Amenities:** food and drink; lifeguards (seasonal); parking (fee); showers; toilets; water sports. **Best for:** sunset; surfing; swimming; walking. ⊠ *West end of Pier Ave., off Hwy. 1, Oceano* ☎ *805/473-7220* ⊕ *www.parks.ca.gov* 🖫 *$5 per vehicle.*

Pismo State Beach. Hike, surf, ride horses, swim, fish in a lagoon or off the pier, and dig for Pismo clams at this busy state beach. One of the day-use parking areas is off Highway 1 near the **Monarch Butterfly Grove,** where from November through February monarch butterflies nest in eucalyptus and Monterey pines. The other parking area is about 1½ miles south at Pier Avenue. **Amenities:** food and drink; lifeguards (seasonal); parking (fee); showers; toilets; water sports. **Best for:** surfing; swimming; walking. ⊠ *555 Pier Ave., off Hwy. 1, 3 miles south of downtown Pismo Beach, Oceano* ☎ *805/489-1869* ⊕ *www.parks. ca.gov* 🖫 *Day use $5 per vehicle if parking at the beach.*

6

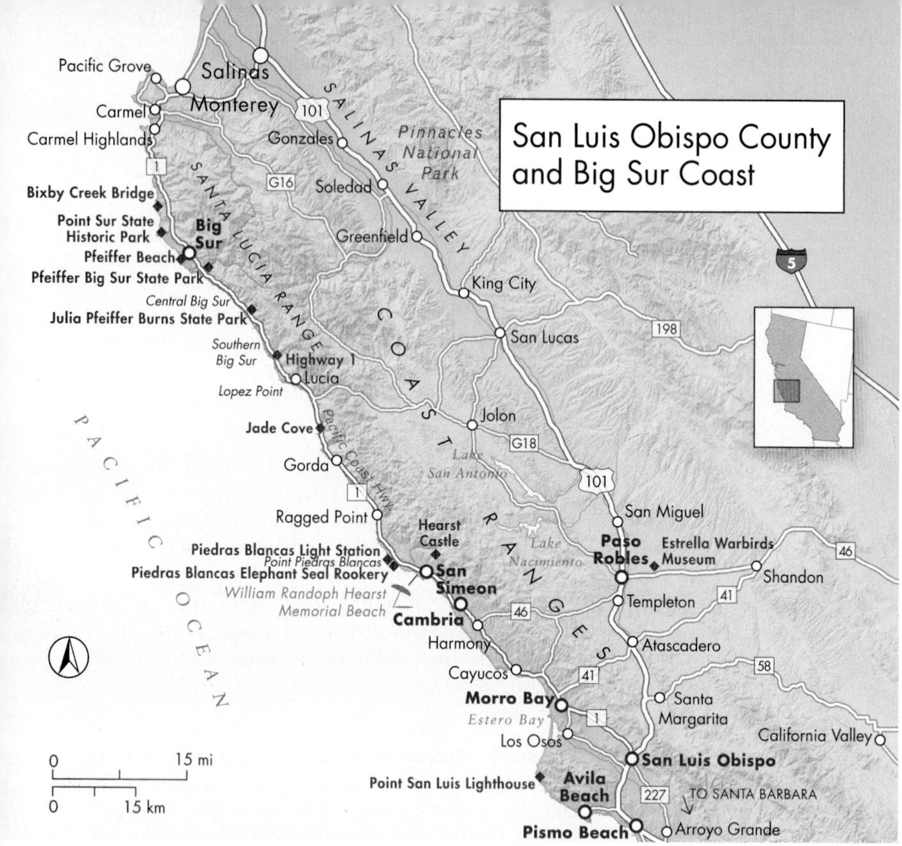
San Luis Obispo County and Big Sur Coast
Pacific Grove
Salinas
Monterey
Carmel
Carmel Highlands
101
SALINAS VALLEY
Gonzales
Pinnacles National Park
1
G16
Soledad
SANTA LUCIA RANGE
Bixby Creek Bridge
Point Sur State Historic Park
Big Sur
Greenfield
Pfeiffer Beach
Pfeiffer Big Sur State Park
5
King City
Central Big Sur
Julia Pfeiffer Burns State Park
COAST RANGES
198
San Lucas
Southern Big Sur
Highway 1
Lucia
Lopez Point
PACIFIC OCEAN
Jolon
Jade Cove
Pacific Coast Hwy.
G18
Lake San Antonio
Gorda
101
1
San Miguel
Ragged Point
Hearst Castle
Lake Nacimiento
Paso Robles
Estrella Warbirds Museum
46
Piedras Blancas Light Station
Point Piedras Blancas
Piedras Blancas Elephant Seal Rookery
San Simeon
Shandon
William Randoph Hearst Memorial Beach
41
Templeton
46
Cambria
Harmony
Atascadero
58
Cayucos
41
Morro Bay
Santa Margarita
Estero Bay
1
Los Osos
California Valley
0
15 mi
San Luis Obispo
0
15 km
Point San Luis Lighthouse
Avila Beach
227
TO SANTA BARBARA
Pismo Beach
Arroyo Grande

WHERE TO EAT

$$$ SEAFOOD 🍴 **Cracked Crab.** This traditional New England–style crab shack imports fresh seafood daily from Australia, Alaska, and the East Coast. Fish is line-caught, much of the produce is organic, and everything is made from scratch. **Known for:** shellfish meals in a bucket, dumped on the table; casual setting; menu changes daily. [$] *Average main: $30* ✉ *751 Price St., near Main St.* ☎ *805/773–2722* 🌐 *www.crackedcrab.com.*

$ AMERICAN FAMILY 🍴 **Doc Burnstein's Ice Cream Lab.** The delectable ice creams are churned on site at this beloved old-fashioned parlor east of Pismo Beach. Top-selling flavors include the Elvis Special (banana and peanut butter) and Motor Oil, a blend of dark chocolate and Kahlua with a fudge swirl. [$] *Average main: $7* ✉ *114 W. Branch St., at Nevada St., east off U.S. 101, Arroyo Grande* ☎ *805/474–4068* 🌐 *docburnsteins.com.*

$$ MODERN AMERICAN Fodor's Choice ★ 🍴 **Ember.** A barn-style restaurant with high ceilings and an open kitchen, Ember enjoys a red-hot reputation for Italian-inflected dishes prepared in an authentic Tuscan fireplace or a wood-burning oven. Chef-owner Brian Collins, a native of Arroyo Grande, the town bordering Pismo Beach, honed his culinary skills at Berkeley's legendary Chez Panisse Restaurant. **Known for:** seasonal menu changes monthly; wood-fired flatbread pizzas; long lines during prime time (no reservations). [$] *Average main: $22* ✉ *1200 E. Grand Ave., at Brisco Rd., Arroyo Grande* ☎ *805/474–7700* 🌐 *www.emberwoodfire.com* ⏲ *Closed Mon. and Tues. No lunch.*

$ ✕ **Splash Café.** Folks stand in line down the block for clam chowder
SEAFOOD   served in a sourdough bread bowl at this wildly popular seafood stand.
You can also order beach food such as fresh steamed clams, burgers,
and fried calamari at the counter (no table service). **Known for:** famous
clam chowder; sourdough bread bowls baked in house; cheery hole-
in-the-wall. $ *Average main: $9* ⊠ *197 Pomeroy St., at Cypress St.*
☎ *805/773–4653* ⊕ *splashcafe.com.*

$$$ ✕ **Ventana Grill.** Perched on a bluff at the northern edge of Pismo Beach,
FUSION   Ventana Grill offers ocean views from nearly every table, unusual sea-
food-centered Latin American-California fusion dishes, and more than
50 tequilas plus craft cocktails at the bar. Reservations are essential—
this place is almost always packed, especially during the weekday happy
hour. **Known for:** happy hour with sunset views; salsas and sauces made
from scratch; more than 50 tequila selections. $ *Average main: $25*
⊠ *2575 Price St.* ☎ *805/773–0000.*

WHERE TO STAY

$$$ ⬚ **The Cliffs Resort.** Lawns and palm trees surround this full-service resort
RESORT   that perches dramatically on an oceanfront cliff. **Pros:** beach access
via short downhill path; oceanfront restaurant and lounge; bluff-top
walking trail. **Cons:** not close to downtown; rooms near service areas
and elevator can be noisy. $ *Rooms from: $195* ⊠ *2757 Shell Beach
Rd.* ☎ *805/773–5000, 800/826–7827* ⊕ *www.cliffsresort.com* ⤶ *160
rooms* ❙❘❙ *No meals.*

$$$$ ⬚ **Dolphin Bay Resort & Spa.** On grass-covered bluffs overlooking Shell
RESORT   Beach, this luxury resort looks and feels like an exclusive community of
villas; choose among sprawling one- or two-bedroom suites, each with
a gourmet kitchen, laundry room with washer and dryer, and contemporary furnishings. **Pros:** lavish apartment units; killer views; walking
distance from the beach. **Cons:** hefty price tag; vibe too upper-crust for
some. $ *Rooms from: $419* ⊠ *2727 Shell Beach Rd.* ☎ *805/773–4300,
800/516–0112 reservations, 805/773–8900 restaurant* ⊕ *www.thedol-
phinbay.com* ⤶ *60 suites* ❙❘❙ *No meals.*

$$$ ⬚ **Hilton Garden Inn.** A slew of on-site amenities, easy access to the
HOTEL   freeway and state beaches, and reasonable rates for the location make
this chain hotel a good choice at the southern edge of Pismo Beach.
Pros: newly renovated rooms with adjustable beds; on-site restau-
rant, bar and lounge; free parking and Wi-Fi. **Cons:** chain hotel; some
rooms overlook freeway; not pet-friendly. $ *Rooms from: $179* ⊠ *601
James Way* ☎ *805/773–6020* ⊕ *www.sanluisobispopismobeach.hgi.
com* ⤶ *120 rooms* ❙❘❙ *Breakfast.*

$$$$ ⬚ **Pismo Lighthouse Suites.** Each of the well-appointed two-room, two-
HOTEL   bath suites at this oceanfront resort has a private balcony or patio.
Pros: sport court features life-size chess game; nautical-style furnish-
ings; nice pool area. **Cons:** not easy to walk to main attractions; some
units are next to busy road. $ *Rooms from: $259* ⊠ *2411 Price St.*
☎ *805/773–2411, 800/245–2411* ⊕ *www.pismolighthousesuites.com*
⤶ *70 suites* ❙❘❙ *Breakfast.*

$$$ ⬚ **SeaVenture Beachfront Hotel & Restaurant.** The bright, homey rooms
HOTEL   at this hotel all have fireplaces and featherbeds; most have balconies
with private hot tubs, and some have beautiful ocean views. **Pros:**

on the beach; excellent food; romantic rooms. **Cons:** touristy area; some rooms and facilities dated; dark hallways. [$] *Rooms from: $235* ✉ *100 Ocean View Ave.* ☎ *805/773–4994* 🌐 *www.seaventure.com* 🛏 *50 rooms* 🍴 *No meals.*

$ HOTEL 🏨 **Shell Beach Inn.** Just 2½ blocks from the beach, this basic but cozy motor court is a great bargain for the area. **Pros:** walking distance from the beach; free parking; friendly and dependable service. **Cons:** sits on a busy road; small rooms; tiny pool. [$] *Rooms from: $100* ✉ *653 Shell Beach Rd.* ☎ *805/773–4373, 800/549–4727* 🌐 *shellbeachinn.com* 🛏 *10 rooms* 🍴 *No meals.*

AVILA BEACH

4 miles north of Pismo Beach.

Because the village of Avila Beach and the sandy, cove-front shoreline for which it's named face south into the Pacific Ocean, they get more sun and less fog than any other stretch of coast in the area. With its fortuitous climate and protected waters, Avila's public beach draws sunbathers and families; summer weekends are very busy. Downtown Avila Beach has a lively seaside promenade and some shops and hotels, but for real local color, head to the far end of the cove and watch the commercial fishers offload their catch on the old Port San Luis wharf. On Friday from mid-April through mid-September, a fish and farmers' market livens up the beach area with music, fresh local produce and seafood, and children's activities.

GETTING HERE AND AROUND

Exit U.S. 101 at Avila Beach Drive and head 3 miles west to reach the beach. The free Avila Trolley operates weekends year-round, plus Friday afternoon and evening from April to September. The minibuses connect Avila Beach and Port San Luis to Shell Beach, with multiple stops along the way. Service extends to Pismo Beach in summer.

ESSENTIALS

Visitor Information Avila Beach Tourism Alliance. 🌐 *visitavilabeach.com.*

EXPLORING

FAMILY **Avila Valley Barn.** An old-fashioned, family-friendly country store jam-packed with local fruits and vegetables, prepared foods, and gifts, Avila Valley Barn also gives visitors a chance to experience rural American traditions. You can pet farm animals and savor homemade ice cream and pies daily, and on weekends ride a hay wagon out to the fields to pick your own produce. ✉ *560 Avila Beach Dr., San Luis Obispo* ☎ *805/595–2816* 🌐 *www.avilavalleybarn.com.*

Central Coast Aquarium. You'll learn all about local marine plants and animals from the hands-on exhibits at this science center next to the main beach. ✉ *50 San Juan St., at 1st St., off Avila Beach Dr.* ☎ *805/595–7280* 🌐 *www.centralcoastaquarium.com* 🎫 *$8* 🕐 *Closed Tues.–Fri. Sept.–May.*

FAMILY **Point San Luis Lighthouse.** Docents lead hikes along scenic Pecho Coast Trail (3½ miles round-trip) to see the historic 1890 lighthouse and its rare Fresnel lens. ■ **TIP→ If you'd prefer a lift out to the lighthouse,**

join a trolley tour. Hikes and tours require reservations. ✉ *Point San Luis, 1¾ miles west of Harford Pier, Port San Luis* ☎ *805/540–5771, 805/528–8758 hikes reservations* 🌐 *www.pointsanluislighthouse.org* 🎫 *Trolley tours $20; hikes free ($5 to enter lighthouse).*

BEACHES

FAMILY **Avila State Beach.** At the edge of a sunny cove next to downtown shops and restaurants, Avila's ½-mile stretch of white sand is especially family-friendly, with a playground, barbecue and picnic tables, volleyball and basketball courts, and lifeguards on watch in summer and on many holiday weekends. The free beachfront parking fills up fast, but there's a nearby pay lot ($6 for the day, $2 after 4 pm). Dogs aren't allowed on the beach from 10 to 5. **Amenities:** food and drink; lifeguards (seasonal); parking; showers; toilets; water sports. **Best for:** sunset; surfing; swimming; walking. ✉ *Avila Beach Dr., at 1st St.* 🌐 *www.visitavilabeach.com* 🎫 *Free.*

WHERE TO EAT AND STAY

$ SEAFOOD 🍴 **Mersea's.** Walk down the pier to this casual crabshack where you can order at the counter, grab a drink at the bar, and find a seat on the deck or in the casual indoor dining area to gaze at spectacular Avila Bay views while you dine. The menu includes chowder bowls, burgers, sandwiches, seafood, and salads, plus bowls of fish, shrimp, or chicken served over rice pilaf and veggies. **Known for:** clam chowder in sourdough bread bowls; fish tacos; fresh local ingredients. [$] *Average main: $13* ✉ *3985 Port San Luis Pier* ✣ *At Port San Luis* ☎ *805/548–2290* 🌐 *www.merseas.com.*

$$$ SEAFOOD 🍴 **Ocean Grill.** Across from the promenade, beach, and pier, Ocean Grill serves up fresh seafood to diners who typically arrive before sunset to enjoy the views. Boats anchored in the bay provide much of the seafood, which pairs well with the mostly regional wines on the list. **Known for:** fantastic ocean views; wood-fired pizzas; gluten-free and vegetarian options. [$] *Average main: $29* ✉ *268 Front St.* ☎ *805/595–4050* 🌐 *www.oceangrillavila.com* ⏲ *No lunch Mon.–Thurs.*

$$$$ HOTEL 🏨 **Avila La Fonda.** Modeled after a village in early California's Mexican period, Avila La Fonda surrounds guests with rich jewel tones, fountains, and upscale comfort; its facade replicates eight different casitas, including several famous historic homes in Mexico. **Pros:** one-of-a-kind theme and artwork; flexible room combinations; a block from the beach. **Cons:** pricey; most rooms don't have an ocean view. [$] *Rooms from: $329* ✉ *101 San Miguel St.* ☎ *805/595–1700* 🌐 *www.avilalafondahotel.com* 🛏 *29 rooms* 🍽 *No meals.*

$$$$ HOTEL 🏨 **Avila Lighthouse Suites.** Families, honeymooners, and business travelers all find respite at this two-story, all-suites luxury hotel. **Pros:** directly across from beach; easy walk to restaurants and shops; on-site activities like golf course and life-size checkerboard. **Cons:** noise from passersby can be heard in room; some ocean-view rooms have limited vistas. [$] *Rooms from: $359* ✉ *550 Front St.* ☎ *805/627–1900, 800/372–8452* 🌐 *www.avilalighthousesuites.com* 🛏 *54 suites* 🍽 *Breakfast.*

6

$$$　　⬚ **Avila Village Inn.** This intimate hotel embraces Craftsman style in its
HOTEL　wood-and-stone architecture and in custom furnishings such as faux-
Tiffany lampshades. **Pros:** in a residential community; access to great
fitness center with pool; gorgeous lobby. **Cons:** some rooms are small
and dark; several miles from the beach. $ *Rooms from: $200 ⊠ 6655
Bay Laurel Dr.* ☎ *800/454–0840, 805/627–1810* ⊕ *www.avilavillage-
inn.com* ⟿ *30 rooms* ⍾ *Breakfast.*

$$　　⬚ **Sycamore Mineral Springs Resort.** This wellness resort's hot mineral
RESORT　springs bubble up into private outdoor tubs on an oak-and-sycamore-
forest hillside. **Pros:** great place to rejuvenate; nice hiking nearby;
incredible spa services. **Cons:** rooms vary in quality; 2½ miles from
the beach. $ *Rooms from: $169 ⊠ 1215 Avila Beach Dr., San Luis
Obispo* ☎ *805/595–7302* ⊕ *www.sycamoresprings.com* ⟿ *72 rooms*
⍾ *No meals.*

SAN LUIS OBISPO

8 miles north of Avila Beach.

About halfway between San Francisco and Los Angeles, San Luis
Obispo spreads out below gentle hills and rocky extinct volcanoes.
Its main appeal lies in its architecturally diverse, pedestrian-friendly
downtown, which bustles with shoppers, restaurant goers, and students from California Polytechnic State University, known as Cal
Poly. On Thursday evening from 6 to 9 the city's famed farmers'
market fills Higuera Street with local produce, entertainment, and
food stalls.

GETTING HERE AND AROUND

U.S. 101/Highway 1 traverses the city for several miles. From the north,
Highway 1 merges with U.S. 101 when it reaches the city limits. The
wineries of the Edna Valley and Arroyo Grande Valley wine regions lie
south of town off Highway 227, the parallel (to the east) Orcutt Road,
and connecting roads.

SLO City Transit buses operate daily; Regional Transit Authority
(SLORTA) buses connect with north county towns. The Downtown
Trolley provides evening service to the city's hub every Thursday,
on Friday from June to early September, and Saturday from April
through October.

ESSENTIALS

Visitor Information San Luis Obispo Chamber of Commerce. ⊠ *895
Monterey St.* ☎ *805/781–2777* ⊕ *www.visitslo.com.* **San Luis Obispo City
Visitor Information.** ☎ *877/756–8698* ⊕ *www.sanluisobispovacations.com.*

EXPLORING
TOP ATTRACTIONS

Mission San Luis Obispo de Tolosa. Sun-dappled Mission Plaza fronts the
fifth mission established in 1772 by Franciscan friars. A small museum
exhibits artifacts of the Chumash Indians and early Spanish settlers.
⊠ *751 Palm St., at Chorro St.* ☎ *805/543–6850* ⊕ *www.missionsan-
luisobispo.org* ⊟ *$3.*

Fodor'sChoice ★ **Talley Vineyards.** Acres of Chardonnay and Pinot Noir, plus smaller parcels of Sauvignon Blanc, Syrah, and other varietals blanket Talley's mountain-ringed dell in the Arroyo Grande Valley. The estate tour ($40), worth a splurge, includes wine and cheese, a visit to an 1860s adobe, and barrel-room tastings of upcoming releases. ⊠ *3031 Lopez Dr., off Orcutt Rd., Arroyo Grande* ☏ *805/489–0446* ⊕ *www. talleyvineyards.com* ☏ *Tastings $12–$18; tours $20–$40.*

> **DEEP ROOTS**
>
> Way back in the 1700s, the Spanish padres who accompanied Father Junípero Serra planted grapevines from Mexico along California's Central Coast, and began using European wine-making techniques to turn the grapes into delectable vintages.

WORTH NOTING

Biddle Ranch Vineyard. Glass doors and walls in a converted dairy barn fill the Biddle Ranch Vineyard tasting room with light and sweeping valley, mountain, and vineyard views. The small-production winery focuses on estate Chardonnay (the adjacent 17-acre vineyard is planted exclusively to the grape), plus Pinot Noir and sparkling wines. The winery also crafts Sangiovese and Cabernet and Syrah blends. ⊠ *2050 Biddle Ranch Rd.* ✛ *At Hwy. 227* ☏ *805/543–2399* ⊕ *www.biddleranch.com* ☏ *Tasting $15* ☽ *Closed Tues. and Wed.*

Claiborne & Churchill. An eco-friendly winery built from straw bales, C&C makes small lots of aromatic Alsatian-style wines such as dry Riesling and Gewürztraminer, plus Pinot Noir blends, Syrah and Chardonnay. ⊠ *2649 Carpenter Canyon Rd., at Price Canyon Rd.* ☏ *805/544–4066* ⊕ *www.claibornechurchill.com* ☏ *Tasting $15.*

Edna Valley Vineyard. For sweeping valley views and crisp Sauvignon Blancs and Chardonnays, head to the modern tasting bar here. ■TIP→ The reserve tasting ($20) is the best option. ⊠ *2585 Biddle Ranch Rd., off Edna Rd.* ☏ *805/544–5855* ⊕ *www.ednavalleyvineyard. com* ☏ *Tastings $15–$20.*

Madonna Inn Trail Rides. Experts and novices enjoy the Madonna Inn concession's one-hour rides on dirt trails fringed by sagebrush, cacti, and lava rock. After a brief lesson in rein control, a congenial guide leads participants partway up 1,292-foot-high Cerro San Luis, one of the flattop volcanic peaks that stretch from San Luis Obispo to Morro Bay. In addition to viewing plant life, the city, and rocky terrain that recalls the Old West, riders often spot hawks and woodpeckers, and occasionally a roadrunner or two. ⊠ *Madonna Inn, 100 Madonna Rd., off U.S. 101* ☏ *805/305–5470* ⊕ *www.madonnainn.com* ☏ *$65 1 hr ride, $80 ride plus wine and cheese tasting.*

Niven Family Wine Estates. A refurbished 1909 schoolhouse serves as tasting room for six Niven Family wineries: Baileyana, Cadre, Tangent, Trenza, True Myth, and Zocker. The winemaker for all these labels is Christian Roguenant, whose Cadre Pinot Noirs are worth checking out. ⊠ *5828 Orcutt Rd., at Righetti Rd.* ☏ *805/269–8200* ⊕ *www.nivenfamilywines.com* ☏ *Tasting $15.*

6

Old Edna. This peaceful, 2-acre site once *was* the town of Edna. Nowadays you can peek at the vintage 1897 and 1908 farmhouse cottages, taste Sextant wines, pick up sandwiches at the gourmet deli, and stroll along Old Edna Lane. ✉ *1655 Old Price Canyon Rd., at Hwy. 227* ☎ *805/710–3701 Old Edna Townsite, 805/542–0133 tasting room and deli* 🌐 *oldedna.com.*

FAMILY **San Luis Obispo Children's Museum.** Activities at this facility geared to kids under age eight include an "imagination-powered" elevator that transports visitors to a series of underground caverns. Elsewhere, simulated lava and steam sputter from an active volcano. Kids can pick rubber fruit at a farmers' market and race in a fire engine to fight a fire. ✉ *1010 Nipomo St., at Monterey St.* ☎ *805/544–5437* 🌐 *www.slocm.org* 🎟 *$8* 🕒 *Closed nonholiday Mon. Sept.–Apr.*

Wolff Vineyards. Syrah, Petite Sirah, and Riesling join the expected Pinot Noir and Chardonnay as the stars at this family-run winery 6 miles south of downtown. The pourers are friendly, and you'll often meet one of the owners or their children in the tasting room. With its hillside views, the outdoor patio is a great place to enjoy an afternoon picnic. ✉ *6238 Orcutt Rd., near Biddle Ranch Rd.* ☎ *805/781–0448* 🌐 *www.wolffvineyards.com* 🎟 *Tasting $10.*

WHERE TO EAT

$$ ECLECTIC 🍴 **Big Sky Café.** Family-friendly Big Sky turns local and organically grown ingredients into global dishes, starting with breakfast. Just pick your continent: Brazilian churrasco chicken breast, Thai catfish, North African vegetable stew, Maryland crab cakes. **Known for:** artsy, creative vibe; ample choices for vegetarians; locavore pioneer. [$] *Average main: $19* ✉ *1121 Broad St., at Higuera St.* ☎ *805/545–5401* 🌐 *bigskycafe.com.*

$$ ITALIAN 🍴 **Buona Tavola.** Northern Italian dishes are this casual spot's specialty. You might find homemade pumpkin-stuffed tortellini in a creamy mascarpone sauce on the menu, or porcini-mushroom risotto with river shrimp. **Known for:** daily fresh fish and salad specials; impressive wine list; gluten-free menus. [$] *Average main: $22* ✉ *1037 Monterey St., near Osos St.* ☎ *805/545–8000* 🌐 *btslo.com* 🕒 *No lunch weekends.*

$$ NORTHERN ITALIAN 🍴 **Café Roma.** At this Railroad Square restaurant you can dine on authentic northern Italian cuisine in the warmly lit dining room or out on the covered patio. Menu favorites include ricotta-filled squash blossoms, and beef tenderloin glistening with porcini butter and a Pinot Noir reduction. **Known for:** classic Italian dining room and bar; well-selected international wine list with more than 200 choices; attentive service. [$] *Average main: $22* ✉ *1020 Railroad Ave., at Osos St.* ☎ *805/541–6800* 🌐 *www.caferomaslo.com* 🕒 *No lunch weekends.*

$$$ MODERN AMERICAN 🍴 **Foremost Wine Company.** A hip combination restaurant, wine bar, lounge, and wine shop in the Creamery building, a former dairy, Foremost focuses on community-linked food and wine and sustainable practices. The bar, dining areas, and wine store occupy a huge interior space with copper-topped tables and other furnishings made with repurposed materials. **Known for:** seasonal menu with many dishes to share; plentiful vegan and vegetarian options; delicious burrata and charcuterie. [$] *Average main: $29* ✉ *570 Higuera St., near Nipomo St.* ☎ *805/439–3410* 🌐 *www.foremostwineco.com* 🕒 *Closed Mon.*

$$$ INTERNATIONAL 🍴 **Luna Red.** A spacious, contemporary space with a festive outdoor patio, this restaurant near Mission Plaza serves creative tapas and cocktails. The small plates include lamb sausage flatbread, avocado-tuna ceviche, and *piquillo* peppers stuffed with goat cheese. **Known for:** excellent traditional Valencian paellas; craft cocktails; lively music scene. [$] *Average main: $25* ✉ *1023 Chorro St., at Monterey St.* ☎ *805/540–5243* 🌐 *www.lunaredslo.com.*

$$ ECLECTIC 🍴 **Novo Restaurant & Lounge.** In the colorful dining room or on the large creek-side deck, this animated downtown eatery will take you on a culinary world tour. The salads, small plates, and entrées come from nearly every continent. **Known for:** value-laden happy hour from 3 to 6; savory curry and noodle dishes; local farmers' market ingredients. [$] *Average main: $22* ✉ *726 Higuera St., at Broad St.* ☎ *805/543–3986* 🌐 *www.novorestaurant.com.*

$$ MODERN AMERICAN 🍴 **Sidecar.** Sidecar serves farm-fresh meals and small plates along with inventive cocktails and 16 beers on tap, most of them local. Burger patties made from grass-fed beef and free-range chicken are served on a brioche bun with inventive sauces such as bacon-maple ketchup. **Known for:** comfort food and artisanal cocktails made with local ingredients; many vegetarian and vegan options; daily happy hour and Sunday brunch. [$] *Average main: $22* ✉ *1127 Broad St., at Marsh St.* ☎ *805/540–5340* 🌐 *sidecarslo.com.*

6

$$$ FUSION Fodor's Choice ★ 🍴 **Thomas Hill Organic Kitchen.** This hip eatery—the chic sibling of a much-lauded restaurant in Paso Robles—opened on the second story of a downtown building near the mission in early 2017. Organic locavore dishes take center stage here, spiced up with international flavors and paired with an extensive list of local wines. **Known for:** signature wood-fired pizzas; global cuisine; excellent craft cocktails and spirits. [$] *Average main: $27* ✉ *858 Monterey St., Santa Barbara* ☎ *805/457–1616* 🌐 *www.thomashillorganics.com.*

WHERE TO STAY

$$$ HOTEL 🏨 **Apple Farm.** Decorated to the hilt with floral bedspreads and watercolors by local artists, this Wine Country–theme hotel is highly popular. **Pros:** flowers everywhere; convenient to Cal Poly and U.S. 101; creekside setting. **Cons:** hordes of tourists during the day; some rooms too floral for some people's tastes. [$] *Rooms from: $219* ✉ *2015 Monterey St.* ☎ *800/255–2040, 805/544-2040* 🌐 *www.applefarm.com* 🛏 *104 rooms* 🍽 *No meals.*

$$$ B&B/INN 🏨 **Garden Street Inn.** From this restored 1887 Italianate Queen Anne downtown, you can walk to many restaurants and attractions; uniquely decorated rooms, each with private bath, are filled with antiques, and some rooms have stained-glass windows, fireplaces, and decks. **Pros:** lavish homemade breakfast; convenient location; complementary wine-and-cheese reception. **Cons:** city noise filters into some rooms; not great for families. [$] *Rooms from: $199* ✉ *1212 Garden St.* ☎ *805/545–9802, 800/488–2045* 🌐 *www.gardenstreetinn.com* 🛏 *13 rooms* 🍽 *Breakfast.*

$$$ HOTEL 🏨 **Granada Hotel & Bistro.** Built in 1922 and sparkling again after renovations completed in 2012, the Granada is one of the few full-service hotels in the heart of downtown. **Pros:** vintage style retreat; easy walk

to downtown; popular farm-to-table hangout Granada Bistro on site. **Cons:** some rooms are tiny; sometimes noisy near restaurant kitchen. [$] *Rooms from: $249* ✉ *1126 Morro St.* ☎ *805/544–9100* 🌐 *www.granadahotelandbistro.com* 🛏 *17 rooms* 🍴 *No meals.*

$$$ HOTEL 🏨 **Madonna Inn.** From its rococo bathrooms to its pink-on-pink froufrou steak house, the Madonna Inn is fabulous or tacky, depending on your taste. **Pros:** fun, one-of-a-kind experience; on-site horseback riding for all levels; each room has its own distinct identity, for example, Safari Room. **Cons:** rooms vary widely; must appreciate kitsch. [$] *Rooms from: $209* ✉ *100 Madonna Rd.* ☎ *805/543–3000, 800/543–9666* 🌐 *www.madonnainn.com* 🛏 *110 rooms* 🍴 *No meals.*

$ HOTEL 🏨 **Peach Tree Inn.** Extra touches such as rose gardens, a porch with rockers, and flower-filled vases turn this modest, family-run motel into a relaxing creek-side haven. **Pros:** bargain rates; cozy rooms; picnic area. **Cons:** near a busy intersection; basic amenities. [$] *Rooms from: $99* ✉ *2001 Monterey St.* ☎ *805/543–3170, 800/227–6396* 🌐 *www.peachtreeinn.com* 🛏 *37 rooms* 🍴 *Breakfast.*

$$$ B&B/INN 🏨 **Petit Soleil.** A cobblestone courtyard, country-French custom furnishings, and Gallic music piped through the halls evoke a Provençal mood at this cheery inn. **Pros:** includes wine and appetizers at cocktail hour; includes scrumptious breakfasts; cozy rooms with luxury touches. **Cons:** sits on a busy avenue; cramped parking. [$] *Rooms from: $179* ✉ *1473 Monterey St.* ☎ *805/549–0321, 800/676–1588* 🌐 *www.psslo.com* 🛏 *16 rooms* 🍴 *Breakfast.*

$$$$ HOTEL 🏨 **SLO Brew Lofts.** If you want to be in the heart of the downtown nightlife action, you can't get much closer than this contemporary collection of apartment-stye rooms on the second floor of the historic brick SLO Brew building. **Pros:** in the heart of downtown; upscale amenities; residential vibe. **Cons:** live music plays on the first floor Thursday–Monday; no on-site desk staff after business hours; parking is in a city lot several blocks away. [$] *Rooms from: $350* ✉ *738 Higuera St,* ☎ *805/543–1843* 🌐 *www.slobrew.com/the-lofts* 🛏 *5 suites* 🍴 *No meals.*

NIGHTLIFE AND PERFORMING ARTS

SLO's club scene is centered on Higuera Street, off Monterey Street.

Koberl at Blue. A trendy crowd hangs out at this upscale restaurant's slick bar to sip on exotic martinis and the many local and imported beers and wines. ✉ *998 Monterey St., at Osos St.* ☎ *805/783–1135* 🌐 *www.epkoberl.com.*

The Libertine Brewing Company. Come to Libertine to savor 76 craft beers and wines on tap, housemade brews of kombucha and cold brew coffee, and pub food infused with the brewery's own wild ales. ✉ *1234 Broad St.* ☎ *805/548–2337* 🌐 *www.libertinebrewing.com/san-luis-obispo.*

Linnaea's. A mellow java joint, Linnaea's hosts poetry readings, as well as blues, jazz, and folk music performances. ✉ *1110 Garden St., at Higuera St.* ☎ *805/541–5888* 🌐 *linnaeas.com* ☞ *No events Mon.*

MoTav. Chicago-style MoTav draws crowds with good pub food and live entertainment in a turn-of-the-20th-century setting, complete with antique U.S. flags and a wall-mounted moose head. ✉ *725 Higuera St., at Broad St.* ☎ *805/541–8733* 🌐 *motherstavern.com.*

Performing Arts Center, San Luis Obispo. A truly great performance space, the center hosts live theater, dance, and music. ⊠ *Cal Poly, 1 Grand Ave., off U.S. 101* ☎ *805/756–4849* ⊕ *www.calpolyarts.org.*

San Luis Obispo Repertory Theatre. SLO County's only nonprofit, fully professional theater group presents dramas, musicals, readings, and other performances year-round. ⊠ *888 Morro St.* ☎ *805/786–2440 box office* ⊕ *www.slolittletheatre.org.*

SLO Brew. Handcrafted microbrews and live music most nights make for a winning combination at this downtown watering hole and restaurant in a restored historic brick building. In 2017 SLO Brew opened The Rock, a satellite brewing and tasting facility near the airport with a beer garden, restaurant, and regular live music performances. ⊠ *736 Higuera St.* ☎ *805/543–1843* ⊕ *www.slobrewingco.com.*

MORRO BAY

14 miles north of San Luis Obispo.

Commercial fishermen slog around Morro Bay in galoshes, and beat-up fishing boats bob in the bay's protected waters. Nature-oriented activities take center stage here: kayaking, hiking, biking, fishing, and wildlife-watching around the bay and national marine estuary and along the state beach.

GETTING HERE AND AROUND

From U.S. 101 south or north, exit at Highway 1 in San Luis Obispo and head west. Scenic Highway 1 passes through the eastern edge of town. From Atascadero, two-lane Highway 41 West treks over the mountains to Morro Bay. San Luis Obispo RTA Route 12 buses travel year-round between Morro Bay, San Luis Obispo, Cayucos, Cambria, San Simeon, and Hearst Castle. The Morro Bay Shuttle picks up riders throughout the town from Friday through Monday in summer ($1.25 one-way, $3 day pass).

ESSENTIALS

Visitor Information Morro Bay Visitors Center. ⊠ *695 Harbor St., at Napa Ave.* ☎ *805/225–1570* ⊕ *www.morrobay.org.*

EXPLORING

Embarcadero. The center of Morro Bay action on land is the Embarcadero, where vacationers pour in and out of souvenir shops and seafood restaurants and stroll or bike along the scenic half-mile Harborwalk to Morro Rock. From here, you can get out on the bay in a kayak or tour boat. ⊠ *On waterfront from Beach St. to Tidelands Park.*

FAMILY **Morro Bay State Park Museum of Natural History.** The museum's entertaining interactive exhibits explain the natural environment and how to preserve it—in the bay and estuary and on the rest of the planet. ■TIP➔ **Kids age 16 and under are admitted free.** ⊠ *20 State Park Rd., south of downtown* ☎ *805/772–2694* ⊕ *centralcoastparks.org* 💲*$3.*

Morro Rock. At the mouth of Morro Bay stands 576-foot-high Morro Rock, one of nine small volcanic peaks, or morros, in the area. A short walk leads to a breakwater, with the harbor on one side and crashing ocean waves on the other. You may not climb the rock, where endangered falcons and other birds nest. Sea lions and otters often play in the water below the rock. ✉ *Northern end of Embarcadero.*

WHERE TO EAT

$$ SEAFOOD
🍴 **Dorn's Original Breakers Cafe.** This restaurant overlooking the harbor has satisfied local appetites since 1942. In addition to straight-ahead dishes such as cod or shrimp fish-and-chips or calamari tubes sautéed in butter and wine, Dorn's serves breakfast. **Known for:** sweeping views of Morro Rock and the bay; fresh local seafood; friendly, efficient service. [$] *Average main: $22* ✉ *801 Market Ave., at Morro Bay Blvd.* ☎ *805/772–4415* 🌐 *www.dornscafe.com.*

$ SOUTHWESTERN
🍴 **Taco Temple.** This family-run diner serves some of the freshest food around. The seafood-heavy menu includes salmon burritos, superb fish tacos with mango salsa, and other dishes hailing from somewhere between California and Mexico. **Known for:** fresh seafood and salsa bar; hefty portions; daily specials. [$] *Average main: $15* ✉ *2680 Main St., at Elena St., just north of Hwy. 1/Hwy. 41 junction* ☎ *805/772–4965.*

$$ SEAFOOD
Fodor's Choice ★
🍴 **Tognazzini's Dockside.** Captain Mark Tognazzini catches seasonal seafood and delivers the bounty to his family's collection of down-home, no frills enterprises in the harbor: a fish market with patio dining and up-close views of Morro Rock (Dockside Too), the original Dockside restaurant, and a combination smokehouse, oyster bar, and pub (Dockside 3). Local musicians play live music nearly every day at the outdoor patio at Dockside Too, and Dockside 3 serves more than 50 brews on tap and in the bottle. **Known for:** fresh-as-it-gets local seafood; live music nearly every day year-round; front-row seats to Morro Rock views. [$] *Average main: $18* ✉ *1245 Embarcadero* ☎ *805/772–8100 restaurant, 805/772–8120 fish market and patio dining, 805/772–8130 smokehouse, oyster bar, and pub.*

$$$$ SEAFOOD
🍴 **Windows on the Water.** Diners at this second-floor restaurant view the sunset through giant picture windows. Meanwhile, fresh fish and other dishes based on local ingredients emerge from the wood-fired oven in the open kitchen, and oysters on the half shell beckon from the raw bar. **Known for:** sustainably farmed seafood; 20-plus wines by the glass; menu changes nightly. [$] *Average main: $33* ✉ *699 Embarcadero, at Pacific St.* ☎ *805/772–0677* 🌐 *www.windowsmb.com* ⏲ *No lunch.*

WHERE TO STAY

$$$$ B&B/INN
Fodor's Choice ★
🏨 **Anderson Inn.** Friendly, personalized service and an oceanfront setting keep loyal patrons returning to this Embarcadero inn, which was built from scratch in 2008, and features well-appointed rooms with state-of-the-art tiled bathrooms and cozy comforters atop queen beds. **Pros:** walk to restaurants and sights; spacious rooms; oceanfront rooms have fireplaces and private balconies. **Cons:** not low-budget; waterfront area can get crowded. [$] *Rooms from: $269* ✉ *897 Embarcadero* ☎ *805/772–3434, 866/950–3434 toll-free reservations* 🌐 *andersoninnmorrobay.com* 🛏 *8 rooms* 🍽 *No meals.*

$$$$ B&B/INN
🏨 **Cass House.** In tiny Cayucos, 4 miles north of Morro Bay, a shipping pioneer's 1867 home is now a luxurious bed-and-breakfast surrounded by rose and other gardens. **Pros:** historic property; some ocean views; delicious lobster roll at The Grill. **Cons:** away from nightlife

and attractions; not good for families. Ⓢ *Rooms from: $265* ✉ *222 N. Ocean Ave., Cayucos* ☎ *805/995–3669* ⊕ *casshouseinn.com* ⤳ *5 rooms* ⦿*l Breakfast.*

$$$ ⛤ **456 Embarcadero.** The rooms at this waterfront hotel are cheery and
HOTEL welcoming, and many have fireplaces. **Pros:** across from waterfront.
Cons: tiny lobby; no pool. Ⓢ *Rooms from: $189* ✉ *456 Embarcadero*
☎ *805/772–2700, 800/292–7625* ⊕ *www.embarcaderoinn.com* ⤳ *33 rooms* ⦿*l Breakfast.*

$$$ ⛤ **The Inn at Morro Bay.** Surrounded by eucalyptus trees, this inn abuts a
RESORT heron rookery and Morro Bay State Park. **Pros:** great for wildlife lov-
ers; stellar views from restaurant and some rooms; nearby golf course,
wellness center on-site. **Cons:** some rooms on the small side; birds and
seals can wake you early. Ⓢ *Rooms from: $229* ✉ *60 State Park Rd.*
☎ *805/772–5651* ⊕ *innatmorrobay.com* ⤳ *98 rooms* ⦿*l No meals.*

$$ ⛤ **Pleasant Inn.** A friendly staff, bright flower boxes, and comfy, clean
HOTEL rooms are the hallmarks of this basic but cheery lodge less than two
blocks from the waterfront. **Pros:** great value for the location; friendly
staff; cozy and clean. **Cons:** small rooms; few amenities. Ⓢ *Rooms from:
$169* ✉ *235 Harbor St.* ☎ *805/772–8521, 888/772–8521* ⊕ *www.pleas-
antinnmotel.com* ⤳ *11 rooms* ⦿*l No meals.*

SPORTS AND THE OUTDOORS

Kayak Horizons. This outfit rents kayaks and paddleboards and gives
lessons and guided tours. ✉ *551 Embarcadero, near Marina St.*
☎ *805/772–6444* ⊕ *kayakhorizons.com.*

The Paddleboard Co. Come to this waterfront shop to rent stand-up
paddleboards and to take paddleboard lessons and yoga and fitness
classes (for all ages and skill levels), and stock up on outdoor wear
and paddling gear. You can sign up for classes online as well. ✉ *575
Embarcadero* ☎ *805/225–5555* ⊕ *www.thepaddleboardcompany.com*
⛵*board rentals $25 per hr, $10 additional ½ hr, lessons from $85.*

Sub-Sea Tours & Kayaks. You can view sea life aboard this outfit's glass-
bottom boat, watch whales from its catamaran, or rent a kayak,
canoe, or stand-up paddleboard. ✉ *699 Embarcadero* ☎ *805/772–
9463* ⊕ *subseatours.com.*

Virg's Landing. Virg's conducts deep-sea-fishing and whale-watching
trips. ✉ *1169 Market Ave.* ☎ *805/772–1222* ⊕ *virgslanding.com.*

PASO ROBLES

30 miles north of San Luis Obispo, 25 miles northwest of Morro Bay.

In the 1860s, tourists began flocking to this ranching outpost to "take
the cure" in a bathhouse fed by underground mineral hot springs. An
Old West town emerged, and grand Victorian homes went up, followed
in the 20th century by Craftsman bungalows. These days, the wooded
hills of Paso Robles west of U.S. 101 and the flatter, more open land
to the freeway's east hold more than 250 wineries, many with tasting
rooms. Hot summer days, cool nights, and varied soils and microclimates
allow growers to cultivate an impressive array of Bordeaux, Rhône, and
other grape types. Cabernet Sauvignon grows well in the Paso Robles

6

AVA—32,000 of its 600,000-plus acres are planted to grapes—as do Petit Verdot, Grenache, Syrah, Viognier, and Zinfandel. In recognition of the diverse growing conditions, the AVA was divided into 11 subappellations in 2014. Pick up a wine-touring map at lodgings, wineries, and attractions around town. The fee at most tasting rooms is between $10 and $25; many lodgings pass out discount coupons.

Upmarket restaurants, bars, antiques stores, and little shops fill the streets around oak-shaded City Park, where special events of all kinds—custom car shows, an olive festival, Friday-night summer concerts—take place on many weekends. Despite its increasing sophistication, Paso (as the locals call it) retains a small-town vibe. The city celebrates its cowboy roots in late July and early August with the two-week California Mid-State Fair, complete with livestock auctions, carnival rides, and corn dogs.

GETTING HERE AND AROUND

U.S. 101 runs north–south through Paso Robles. Highway 46 West links Paso Robles to Highway 1 and Cambria on the coast. Highway 46 East connects Paso Robles with Interstate 5 and the San Joaquin Valley. Public transit is not convenient for wine touring and sightseeing.

Visitor Information Paso Robles CAB Collective. ☎ 805/543–2288 ⊕ pasoroblescab.com. **Paso Robles Wine Country Alliance.** ☎ 805/239–8463 ⊕ pasowine.com. **Paso Robles Visitor Center.** ✉ 1225 Park St., near 12th St. ☎ 805/238–0506 ⊕ travelpaso.com. **Rhone Rangers/Paso Robles.** ⊕ rhonerangers.org/pasorobles.

EXPLORING

TOP ATTRACTIONS

Fodor's Choice ★ **Calcareous Vineyard.** Elegant wines, a stylish tasting room, and knockout hilltop views make for a winning experience at this winery along winding Peachy Canyon Road. Cabernet Sauvignon, Syrah, and Zinfandel grapes thrive in the summer heat and limestone soils of the two vineyards near the tasting room; and a third vineyard on cooler York Mountain produces Pinot Noir, Chardonnay, and a Cabernet with a completely different character from the Peachy Canyon edition. ■ TIP→ The picnic area's expansive eastward views invite lingering. ✉ 3430 Peachy Canyon Rd. ☎ 805/239–0289 ⊕ calcareous.com ☐ Tasting $10; tour and tasting (reservations required) $15–$35.

FAMILY **Estrella Warbirds Museum.** An entertaining homage to fighter planes, flyboys, and flygirls, this museum maintains indoor exhibits about wartime aviation and displays retired aircraft outdoors and in repair shops. Bonus attraction: a huge building with spruced-up autos, drag racers, and "funny cars." ✉ 4251 Dry Creek Rd., off Airport Rd., north off Hwy. 46E ☎ 805/238–9317 ⊕ ewarbirds.org ☐ $10 ⊙ Closed Mon.– Wed. except legal holidays.

Firestone Walker Brewing Company. At this working craft brewery you can sample medal-winners such as the Double Barrel Ale and learn about the beer-making process on 30-minute guided tours of the brew house and cellar. ✉ 1400 Ramada Dr., east side of U.S. 101; exit at Hwy. 46 W/Cambria, but head east ☎ 805/225–5911 ⊕ www.firestonebeer.com ☐ Tastings $1.50–$3 per sample, tour free.

Halter Ranch Vineyard. A good place to learn about contemporary Paso Robles wine making, this ultramodern operation produces high-quality wines from estate-grown Bordeaux and Rhône grapes grown in sustainably farmed vineyards. The gravity-flow winery, which you can view on tours, is a marvel of efficiency. Ancestor, the flagship wine, a potent Bordeaux-style blend of Cabernet Sauvignon, Petit Verdot, and Malbec, is named for the ranch's huge centuries-old coast oak tree. ⊠ *8910 Adelaida Rd., at Vineyard Dr.* ☎ *888/367–9977* ⊕ *www.halterranch. com* 🖻 *Tasting $10.*

Fodor's Choice ★ **HammerSky Vineyards.** Owner Doug Hauck bucks a few trends by focusing on Merlot and Zinfandel, two varietals of variable popularity in recent years. Hauck makes excellent small lots of each, along with a Merlot-heavy Bordeaux-style blend; on the lighter side are Sauvignon Blanc and a Rosé of Zinfandel. Set amid rolling hills of vineyards punctuated by a huge oak, HammerSky's bright-white contemporary structure houses both the tasting and barrel-aging rooms; an outdoor patio has views of the estate vines. ⊠ *7725 Vineyard Dr., at Jensen Rd.* ☎ *805/239–0930* ⊕ *www.hammersky.com* 🖻 *Tasting $10* ☉ *Closed Wed.*

Fodor's Choice ★ **Jada Vineyard & Winery.** Winemaker David Galzignato, formerly of the Napa Valley's Charles Krug Winery, crafts Jada's nuanced, highly structured wines. Two worth checking out are Jack of Hearts, starring Petit Verdot, and Passing By, a Cabernet-heavy blend. Galzignato also shines with Tannat and with Rhône-style wines, particularly Grenache. At tastings, the wines are paired with gourmet cheeses. ⊠ *5620 Vineyard Dr., north of Hwy. 46 W* ☎ *805/226–4200* ⊕ *jadavineyard.com* 🖻 *Tastings $15.*

JUSTIN Vineyards & Winery. This suave winery built its reputation on Isosceles, a hearty Bordeaux blend, usually of Cabernet Sauvignon, Cabernet Franc, and Merlot. JUSTIN's Cabernet Sauvignon is also well regarded, as is the Right Angle blend of Cab and three other varietals. Tastings here take place in an expansive room whose equally expansive windows provide views of the hillside vineyards. ⊠ *11680 Chimney Rock Rd., 15 miles west of U.S. 101's Hwy 46 E exit; take 24th St. west and follow road (name changes along the way) to Chimney Rock Rd.* ☎ *805/238–6932* ⊕ *justinwine.com* 🖻 *Tasting $20, tour and tasting $25* ☞ *Tours 10 and 2:30 (reservations recommended).*

Fodor's Choice ★ **Pasolivo.** While touring the idyllic west side of Paso Robles, take a break from wine tasting by stopping at Pasolivo. Find out how the artisans here make their Tuscan-style olive oils on a high-tech Italian press, and test the acclaimed results. ⊠ *8530 Vineyard Dr., west off U.S. 101 (Exit 224) or Hwy. 46 W (Exit 228)* ☎ *805/227–0186* ⊕ *www.pasolivo. com* 🖻 *Free.*

Tablas Creek Vineyard. Tucked in the western hills of Paso Robles, Tablas Creek is known for its blends of organically grown, hand-harvested Rhône varietals. Roussanne and Viognier are the standout whites; the Mourvèdre-heavy blend called Panoplie (it also includes Grenache and Syrah) has received high praise in recent years. ■**TIP**➔ **There's a fine picnic area here.** ⊠ *9339 Adelaida Rd., west of Vineyard Dr.* ☎ *805/237–1231* ⊕ *www.tablascreek.com* 🖻 *Tasting $15 (reserve $40 by appointment), tour free.*

6

WORTH NOTING

Eberle Winery. Even if you don't drink wine, stop here for a tour of the huge wine caves beneath the vineyards (departs every half hour all day). Eberle produces wines from Bordeaux, Rhône, and Italian varietals and makes intriguing blends including Grenache Blanc–Viognier and Cabernet Sauvignon–Syrah. ⊠ *3810 Hwy. 46 E, 3½ miles east of U.S. 101* ☎ *805/238–9607* ⊕ *www.eberlewinery.com* ⊠ *Basic tasting and tour free, weekend reserve tasting $25, private tour and tasting $35 by appointment.*

Paso Robles Pioneer Museum. The delightful museum's one-room schoolhouse and its displays of ranching paraphernalia, horse-drawn vehicles, hot-springs artifacts, and photos evoke Paso's rural heritage. ⊠ *2010 Riverside Ave., at 21st St.* ☎ *805/239–4556* ⊕ *www.pasoroblespioneermuseum.org* ⊠ *Free.*

FAMILY **Pomar Junction Vineyard & Winery.** A vintage railroad boxcar and a caboose provide a visual change of pace at Pomar Junction. Its flagship wine, Train Wreck, is a daring but usually winning blend of Cabernet Sauvignon, Zinfandel, Mourvèdre, Syrah, and Petite Sirah. With sparkling wine, a Grenache Blanc, Pinot Noir, a smooth Merlot, and several white and red blends, there's something for pretty much everyone here. ■TIP➔ Picnic areas shaded by elms, oaks, and other trees—not to mention old farm equipment and those train cars—make this a popular stop for wine tasters with kids. ⊠ *5036 S. El Pomar Rd., at El Pomar Dr.* ☎ *805/238–9940* ⊕ *pomarjunction.com* ⊠ *Tastings $10–$15.*

River Oaks Hot Springs & Spa. The lakeside spa, on 240 hilly acres near the intersection of U.S. 101 and Highway 46 East, is a great place to relax after wine tasting or festival-going. Soak in a private indoor or outdoor hot tub fed by natural mineral springs, or indulge in a massage or facial. ⊠ *800 Clubhouse Dr., off River Oaks Dr., just north of River Oaks Golf Course* ☎ *805/238–4600* ⊕ *riveroakshotsprings.com* ⊠ *$12–$15 per hr.*

Robert Hall Winery. The late Robert Hall's winery made its reputation on a well-made, reasonably priced Cabernet Sauvignon from Paso Robles AVA grapes, but at the high-ceilinged tasting room you can sample less widely distributed wines. These include a reserve Cabernet, a Merlot, a Malbec, a Bordeaux-style Meritage blend, and a Port made from Portuguese grapes. Whites of note include Roussanne, Sauvignon Blanc, and Viognier. ■TIP➔ Ask for a 30-minute tour if you'd like to see the production facilities. ⊠ *3443 Mill Rd., at Hwy. 46E, 3 miles east of U.S. 101* ☎ *805/239–1616* ⊕ *roberthallwinery.com* ⊠ *Tastings $10; tour free.*

SIP CERTIFICATION

Many wineries in Paso Robles take pride in being SIP (Sustainability in Practice) Certified, for which they undergo a rigorous third-party audit of their entire operations. Water and energy conservation practices are reviewed, along with pest management and other aspects of farming. Also considered are the wages, benefits, and working conditions of the employees, and the steps taken to mitigate the impact of grape growing and wine production on area habitats.

SummerWood Winery. Rhône varietals do well in the Paso Robles AVA, where many wineries, including this one, produce "GSM" (Grenache, Syrah, Mourvèdre) red blends, along with whites such as Viognier, Marsanne, and Grenache Blanc. Winemaker Mauricio Marchant displays a subtle touch with Rhône whites and reds, as well as Sentio, a Petit Verdot–heavy Bordeaux red blend. Tastings here are relaxed and informal, and there's a patio from which you can enjoy the vineyard views. ✉ *2175 Arbor Rd., off Hwy. 46W* ☎ *805/227–1365* 🌐 *summerwoodwine.com* 🎫 *Tasting $15.*

Villa San-Juliette Vineyard & Winery. Nigel Lithgoe (co-creator of *So You Think You Can Dance* is one of his many titles), and Ken Warwick (executive producer of *American Idol,* among other programs) established this winery northeast of Paso Robles. With a cast that includes Petit Verdot, a fine Grenache, and a perky Albariño (a Spanish white varietal), their stylish operation is no flash in the pan. From 11 to 4 you can order snacks, panini, pizzas, soup and salad, and cheese and charcuterie plates to enjoy with your wine in the tasting room or on the view-filled outdoor terrace. ✉ *6385 Cross Canyons Rd., at Ranchita Canyon Rd., San Miguel* ☎ *805/467–0014* 🌐 *www.villasanjuliette.com* 🎫 *Tasting $10* 🕒 *Closed Tues. and Wed. except by appointment.*

Wild Horse Winery & Vineyards. High-profile Wild Horse, these days part of the Constellation Brands lineup, is known for its Central Coast Pinot Noir and other widely distributed wines. The draws at its winery, though, are smaller-production, vineyard-designated Pinot Noirs, several made from grapes grown in Santa Barbara County's Santa Maria Valley and Sta. Rita Hills AVAs. ✉ *1437 Wild Horse Winery Ct., off Templeton Rd., Templeton* ☎ *805/788–6300* 🌐 *www.wildhorsewinery.com* 🎫 *Tasting $10–$15, tour $15.*

WHERE TO EAT

$$$$ FRENCH

🍴 **Bistro Laurent.** Owner-chef Laurent Grangien's handsome, welcoming French bistro occupies an 1890s brick building across from City Park. He focuses on traditional dishes such as duck confit, rack of lamb, and onion soup, but always prepares a few au courant daily specials as well. **Known for:** classic French dishes made with local ingredients; good selection of local and international wines; four- or five-course tasting menus. [$] *Average main: $32* ✉ *1202 Pine St., at 12th St.* ☎ *805/226–8191* 🌐 *www.bistrolaurent.com* 🕒 *Closed Sun. and Mon.*

$$$ MODERN ITALIAN Fodor's Choice ★

🍴 **Il Cortile.** One of two Paso establishments owned by chef Santos MacDonal and his wife, Carole, this Italian restaurant entices diners with complex flavors and a contemporary space with art deco overtones. Consistent crowd-pleasers often on the menu include beef carpaccio with white truffle cream sauce and shaved black truffles, pappardelle with wild boar ragu, and pork osso buco, perhaps served with Parmesan herb risotto. **Known for:** house-made pastas; excellent wine pairings; ingredients from chef's garden. [$] *Average main: $30* ✉ *608 12th St., near Spring St.* ☎ *805/226–0300* 🌐 *www.ilcortileristorante.com* 🕒 *Closed Tues. No lunch.*

$$$ SOUTH AMERICAN

🍴 **La Cosecha.** At barlike, tin-ceilinged La Cosecha (Spanish for "the harvest"), Honduran-born chef Santos MacDonal faithfully re-creates dishes from Spain and South America. Noteworthy starters include *pastelitos catracho,* Honduran-style empanadas in a light tomato sauce served with *queso fresco* (fresh cheese) and micro cilantro. **Known for:** fusion of Latin spices and fresh local fare; daily paella special; artisanal cocktails. $ *Average main: $29* ⊠ *835 12th St., near Pine St.* ☎ *805/237–0019* ⊕ *www.lacosechabr.com* ◷ *Closed Mon.*

$$$$ ╳ **McPhee's Grill.** Just south of Paso Robles in tiny Templeton, this casual

AMERICAN chophouse in an 1860s wood-frame storefront serves sophisticated, contemporary versions of traditional Western fare such as oak-grilled filet mignon and fresh seafood tostadas. The house-label wines, made especially for the restaurant, are quite good. **Known for:** meats grilled over red oak; local seasonal menu; excellent wine selections. $ *Average main: $32* ⊠ *416 S. Main St., at 5th St., Templeton* ☎ *805/434–3204* ⊕ *mcpheesgrill.com* ◷ *No lunch Sun.*

$$$ ╳ **Panolivo Family Bistro.** Affordable French fare draws patrons to this

FRENCH café north of the town square. For breakfast, try a fresh pastry or quiche, or build your own omelet. **Known for:** vegan and gluten-free menus; three-course prix-fixe dinner option; all-day breakfast (until 4). $ *Average main: $26* ⊠ *1344 Park St., at 14th St.* ☎ *805/239–3366* ⊕ *www.panolivo.com.*

$$$$ ╳ **Thomas Hill Organics.** The Central Coast's abundance of organic and

MODERN sustainably sourced bounty—veggies, seafood, meats, and breads—are

AMERICAN creatively woven into innovative dishes at this brick-walled down-

Fodor'sChoice town favorite. The wine list celebrates local wines; with many by the

★ half-glass, you can sample a good cross-section. **Known for:** organic sustainable menu; local-centric wine list; regional locavore pioneer. $ *Average main: $31* ⊠ *1313 Park St., at 13th St.* ☎ *805/226–5888* ⊕ *thomashillorganics.com.*

$$$ ╳ **Villa Creek.** Within a spacious brick-and-wood building at the north-

SOUTHWESTERN east corner of the main square, chef Tim Veatch Fundaro conjures rustic wine country cuisine with sustainably sourced ingredients from small Californian farms and ranches. The seasonal menu changes often, and might include Sicilian fried cauliflower with caper mayo and Calabrian chilies, and Liberty Farms duck with crispy potatoes, house-fermented sauerkraut, and caraway onions. **Known for:** popular bar with small plates; potent margaritas; lively vibe. $ *Average main: $26* ⊠ *1144 Pine St., at 12th St.* ☎ *805/238–3000* ⊕ *www.villacreek.com* ◷ *No lunch.*

WHERE TO STAY

$ ⌁ **Adelaide Inn.** Family-owned and -managed, this clean oasis with

HOTEL meticulous landscaping offers spacious rooms and everything you

FAMILY need: coffeemaker, iron, hair dryer, and peace and quiet. **Pros:** good bargain; attractive pool area; ideal for families. **Cons:** not a romantic retreat; near a busy intersection. $ *Rooms from: $104* ⊠ *1215 Ysabel Ave.* ☎ *805/238–2770, 800/549–7276* ⊕ *adelaideinn.com* ⟿ *108 rooms* ｜◎｜ *Breakfast.*

$$$$ ⌁ **Allegretto.** This swank, 20-acre Tuscan-style resort amid estate vine-

RESORT yards is also a private museum where owner Doug Ayres displays hun-

Fodor'sChoice dreds of artworks and artifacts collected on his world travels: ancient

★ Indian river stones and statues; a massive cross section from a giant Sequoia; Russian and California impressionist paintings; mandalas, and more (nonguests are welcome to walk around). **Pros:** yoga in medieval alley; full-service restaurant Cello and spa; bocce ball, fire pit, and other diversions. **Cons:** not close to downtown square; pricey; some rooms close to courtyard music. ⓢ *Rooms from: $349* ✉ *2700 Buena Vista Dr.* ☎ *805/369–2500* ⊕ *www.allegrettoresort.com* ⤺ *171 rooms.*

$$$$
HOTEL
Fodor'sChoice
★

⊡ **Hotel Cheval.** Equestrian themes surface throughout this intimate European-style boutique hotel a half-block from the main square and near some of Paso's best restaurants. **Pros:** most rooms have fireplaces; sip wine and champagne at the on-site Pony Club and zinc bar; extremely personalized service. **Cons:** views aren't great; no pool or hot tub. ⓢ *Rooms from: $330* ✉ *1021 Pine St.* ☎ *805/226–9995, 866/522–6999* ⊕ *www.hotelcheval.com* ⤺ *16 rooms* ⦿*Breakfast.*

$$$$
B&B/INN

⊡ **JUST Inn.** Fine wines, a destination restaurant, and a vineyard's-edge setting make a stay at Justin winery's on-site inn an exercise in sophisticated seclusion. **Pros:** secluded; vineyard views; destination restaurant. **Cons:** half-hour drive to town; location may be too secluded for some. ⓢ *Rooms from: $400* ✉ *11680 Chimney Rock Rd.* ☎ *805/238–6932, 800/726–0049* ⊕ *www.justinwine.com* ⤺ *4 suites* ⦿*Breakfast.*

$$$
HOTEL

⊡ **La Bellasera Hotel & Suites.** A full-service hotel just off Highway 101 at the Highway 46 exit, La Bellasera caters to those looking for high-tech amenities and easy access to major Central Coast roadways. **Pros:** oversize rooms; Romanesque architectural features; close to freeways. **Cons:** far from downtown; at a major intersection. ⓢ *Rooms from: $199* ✉ *206 Alexa Ct.* ☎ *805/238–2834, 866/782–9669* ⊕ *labellasera. com* ⤺ *35 rooms, 25 suites* ⦿*No meals.*

$$$
HOTEL

⊡ **La Quinta Inn & Suites.** A good value for Paso Robles, this three-story chain property attracts heavy repeat business with its upbeat staff and slew of perks. **Pros:** apartment-style suites in separate building; free happy hour with local wines and appetizers; good for leisure or business travelers. **Cons:** conventional decor; not downtown. ⓢ *Rooms from: $189* ✉ *2615 Buena Vista Dr.* ☎ *805/239–3004, 800/753–3757* ⊕ *www.laquintapasorobles.com* ⤺ *101 rooms* ⦿*Breakfast.*

$$
HOTEL

⊡ **Paso Robles Inn.** On the site of an old spa hotel of the same name, the inn is built around a lush, shaded garden with a pool (the water is still the reason to stay here), and each of the 18 deluxe rooms has a spring-fed hot tub in its bathroom or on its balcony. **Pros:** private spring-fed hot tubs; special touches like unique photography in each room; across from town square. **Cons:** fronts a busy street; rooms vary in size and amenities. ⓢ *Rooms from: $149* ✉ *1103 Spring St.* ☎ *805/238–2660, 800/676–1713* ⊕ *www.pasoroblesinn.com* ⤺ *92 rooms, 6 suites* ⦿*No meals.*

$$$$
B&B/INN
Fodor'sChoice
★

⊡ **SummerWood Inn.** Easygoing hospitality, vineyard-view rooms, and elaborate breakfasts make this inn a mile west of U.S. 101 worth seeking out. **Pros:** convenient wine-touring base; elaborate breakfasts; complimentary tastings at associated winery. **Cons:** some noise from nearby highway during the day. ⓢ *Rooms from: $275* ✉ *2130 Arbor Rd., 1 mile west of U.S. 101, at Hwy. 46W* ☎ *805/227–1111* ⊕ *www.summerwoodwine.com/inn* ⤺ *9 rooms* ⦿*Breakfast.*

PERFORMING ARTS

Vina Robles Amphitheatre. At this 3,300-seat, Mission-style venue with good food, wine, and sight lines, you can enjoy acclaimed musicians in concert. ✉ *Vina Robles winery, 3800 Mill Rd., off Hwy. 46* ☎ *805/286–3680* ⊕ *www.vinaroblesamphitheatre.com* ☞ *Performances Apr.–Nov.*

CAMBRIA

28 miles west of Paso Robles, 20 miles north of Morro Bay.

Cambria, set on piney hills above the sea, was settled by Welsh miners in the 1890s. In the 1970s the isolated setting attracted artists and other independent types; the town now caters to tourists, but it still bears the imprint of its bohemian past. Both of Cambria's downtowns, the original East Village and the newer West Village, are packed with art and crafts galleries, antiques shops, cafés, restaurants, and bed-and-breakfasts.

Two diverting detours lie between Morro Bay and Cambria. In the laid-back beach town of **Cayucos,** 4 miles north of Morro Bay, you can stroll the long pier, feast on chowder (at Duckie's), and sample the namesake delicacies of the Brown Butter Cookie Co. Over in **Harmony,** a quaint former dairy town 7 miles south of Cambria (population 18), you can take in the glassworks, pottery, and other artsy enterprises.

GETTING HERE AND AROUND

Highway 1 leads to Cambria from the north and south. Highway 246 West curves from U.S. 101 through the mountains to Cambria. San Luis Obispo RTA Route 12 buses stop in Cambria (and Hearst Castle).

ESSENTIALS

Visitor Information Cambria Chamber of Commerce. ⊠ *767 Main St.* ☎ *805/927–3624* ⊕ *www.cambriachamber.org.*

EXPLORING

Covells California Clydesdales. Come to the vast 2,000-acre Covell Ranch to see one of the world's largest private stands of endangered Monterey pines and witness herds of gentle Clydesdales roaming the range. Much of the ranch is in a conservation easement that will never be developed. The two-hour guided tours include a 3-mile ride that takes you through an historic picnic grove amid the pines to the barn. The ranch also offers trail rides and Saturday night barbecue dinners at the barn, where you can take a hayride on a custom-built "people mover" wagon. ⊠ *5694 Bridge St.* ☎ *805/927–3398* ⊕ *www.covellscaliforniaclydesdales.com* ✉ *Tours $100 per person, Sat. night barbecues $100 per person* ☉ *Tours, trail rides, and barbecues by appointment only.*

Fiscalini Ranch Preserve. Walk down a mile-long coastal bluff trail to spot migrating whales, otters, and shore birds at this 450-acre public space. Miles of additional scenic trails crisscross the protected habitats of rare and endangered species of flora and fauna, including a Monterey pine forest, western pond turtles, monarch butterflies, and burrowing owls. Dogs are permitted on-leash everywhere and off-leash on all trails except the bluff. ⊠ *Hwy. 1, between Cambria Rd. and Main St. to the north, and Burton Dr. and Warren Rd. to the south; access either end of bluff trail off Windsor Blvd.* ☎ *805/927–2856* ⊕ *www.ffrpcambria.org.*

Leffingwell Landing. A state picnic ground, the landing is a good place for examining tidal pools and watching otters as they frolic in the surf. ⊠ *North end of Moonstone Beach Dr.* ☎ *805/927–2070.*

Moonstone Beach Drive. The drive runs along a bluff above the ocean, paralleled by a 3-mile boardwalk that winds along the beach. On this photogenic walk you might glimpse sea lions and sea otters, and perhaps a gray whale during winter and spring. Year-round, birds fly about, and tiny creatures scurry amid the tidepools. ⊠ *Off Hwy. 1.*

Nit Wit Ridge. Arthur Beal (aka Captain Nit Wit, Der Tinkerpaw) spent 51 years building a home above Cambria's West Village out of collected junk: beer cans, rocks, abalone shells, car parts, TV antennas—you name it. The site, sometimes signed as Nitt Witt Ridge, is a state landmark. ■TIP→ **You can drive by and peek in—from the 700 block of Main Street, head southeast on Cornwall Street and east on Hillcrest Drive. Or, schedule a guided tour.** ⊠ *881 Hillcrest Dr.* ☎ *805/927–2690* ⊠ *$10.*

WHERE TO EAT

$$

MODERN AMERICAN

✗ **Centrally Grown at Off the Grid.** A collection of sustainably conscious spaces fashioned from repurposed materials, Centrally Grown encompasses a coffee shop, market, wine tasting, exotic gardens, and a second-floor restaurant with fantastic views of San Simeon Bay and the Big Sur Coast. The restaurant, decorated in a "planet-friendly chic" style that includes a driftwood archway, serves classic California cuisine with global influences. **Known for:** all day dining; great place to stop before or after driving the Big Sur Coast; exotic gardens with meandering paths. Ⓢ *Average main: $22* ⊠ *7432 Exotic Garden Dr., off Hwy. 1* ☎ *800/927–3563* ⊕ *www.centrallygrown.com.*

$$$

AMERICAN FAMILY

✗ **Linn's Restaurant.** Homemade olallieberry pies, soups, potpies, and other farmhouse comfort foods share the menu at this spacious East Village restaurant with fancier farm-to-table dishes such as organic, free-range chicken topped with raspberry-orange-cranberry sauce. Also on-site are a bakery, a café serving more casual fare (take-out available), and a gift shop that sells gourmet foods. **Known for:** olallieberry pie; numerous gluten-free and vegan options; family owned and operated for decades. Ⓢ *Average main: $23* ⊠ *2277 Main St., at Wall St.* ☎ *805/927–0371* ⊕ *www.linnsfruitbin.com.*

$$

ECLECTIC

✗ **Robin's.** A multiethnic, vegetarian-friendly dining experience awaits you at this cozy East Village cottage. Dinner choices include wild prawn enchiladas, grilled Skuna Bay salmon, Japanese scallops, and short ribs. **Known for:** savory curries; top-notch salmon bisque; secluded (heated) garden patio. Ⓢ *Average main: $22* ⊠ *4095 Burton Dr., at Center St.* ☎ *805/927–5007* ⊕ *robinsrestaurant.com.*

$$$

SEAFOOD

Fodor's Choice

★

✗ **Sea Chest Oyster Bar and Restaurant.** Cambria's best place for seafood fills up soon after it opens at 5:30 (no reservations taken). Those in the know grab seats at the oyster bar and take in spectacular sunsets while watching the chefs broil fresh halibut, steam garlicky clams, and fry crispy calamari steaks. **Known for:** New England chowder house vibe; savory cioppino; waiting areas in wine bar, game room, and patio with fire pit. Ⓢ *Average main: $30* ⊠ *6216 Moonstone Beach Dr., near Weymouth St.* ☎ *805/927–4514* ⊕ *www.seachestrestaurant.com* ⊟ *No credit cards* ☉ *Closed Tues. mid-Sept.–May. No lunch.*

6

WHERE TO STAY

$$
HOTEL

Bluebird Inn. This sweet motel in Cambria's East Village sits amid beautiful gardens along Santa Rosa Creek. **Pros:** excellent value; well-kept gardens; friendly staff. **Cons:** few frills; basic rooms; not on beach. $ *Rooms from: $125* ✉ *1880 Main St.* ☎ *805/927–4634, 800/552–5434* ⊕ *bluebirdmotel.com* ⬩ *37 rooms* ⦿ *Breakfast.*

$$
RESORT

Cambria Pines Lodge. This 25-acre retreat up the hill from the East Village is a good choice for families; accommodations range from basic fireplace cabins to motel-style standard rooms to large fireplace suites and deluxe suites with spa tubs. **Pros:** short walk from downtown; live music nightly in the lounge; verdant gardens. **Cons:** service and housekeeping not always top-quality; some units need updating. $ *Rooms from: $149* ✉ *2905 Burton Dr.* ☎ *805/927–4200, 800/966–6490* ⊕ *www.cambriapineslodge.com* ⬩ *152 rooms* ⦿ *Breakfast.*

$$$
B&B/INN

J. Patrick House. Monterey pines and flower gardens surround this Irish-themed inn, which sits on a hilltop above Cambria's East Village. **Pros:** fantastic breakfasts; friendly innkeepers; quiet neighborhood. **Cons:** few rooms; fills up quickly. $ *Rooms from: $195* ✉ *2990 Burton Dr.* ☎ *805/927–3812, 800/341–5258* ⊕ *jpatrickhouse.com* ⬩ *7 rooms* ⦿ *Breakfast.*

$$$
HOTEL

Moonstone Landing. This up-to-date motel's amenities, reasonable rates, and accommodating staff make it a Moonstone Beach winner. **Pros:** sleek furnishings; across from the beach; cheery lounge. **Cons:** narrow property; some rooms overlook a parking lot. $ *Rooms from: $189* ✉ *6240 Moonstone Beach Dr.* ☎ *805/927–0012, 800/830–4540* ⊕ *www.moonstonelanding.com* ⬩ *29 rooms* ⦿ *Breakfast.*

SAN SIMEON

9 miles north of Cambria, 65 miles south of Big Sur.

Whalers founded San Simeon in the 1850s, but had virtually abandoned it by 1865, when Senator George Hearst began purchasing most of the surrounding ranch land. Hearst turned San Simeon into a bustling port, and his son, William Randolph Hearst, further developed the area while erecting Hearst Castle (one of the many remarkable stops you'll encounter when driving along Highway 1). Today San Simeon is basically a strip of unremarkable gift shops and so-so motels that straddle Highway 1 about 4 miles south of the castle's entrance, but **Old San Simeon,** right across from the entrance, is worth a peek. Julia Morgan, William Randolph Hearst's architect, designed some of the village's Mission Revival–style buildings.

GETTING HERE AND AROUND

Highway 1 is the only way to reach San Simeon. Connect with the highway off U.S. 101 directly or via rural routes such as Highway 41 West (Atascadero to Morro Bay) and Highway 46 West (Paso Robles to Cambria).

San Simeon Chamber of Commerce Visitor Center. ✉ *250 San Simeon Ave.* ☎ *805/927–3500* ⊕ *www.sansimeonchamber.org.*

EXPLORING
TOP ATTRACTIONS

Fodor's Choice ★ **Hearst Castle.** Officially known as "Hearst San Simeon State Historical Monument," Hearst Castle sits in solitary splendor atop La Cuesta Encantada (the Enchanted Hill). Its buildings and gardens spread over 127 acres that were the heart of newspaper magnate William Randolph Hearst's 250,000-acre ranch. Hearst commissioned renowned California architect Julia Morgan to design the estate, but he was very much involved with the final product, a blend of Italian, Spanish, and Moorish styles. The 115-room main structure and three huge "cottages" are connected by terraces and staircases and surrounded by pools, gardens, and statuary. In its heyday the castle, whose buildings hold about 22,000 works of fine and decorative art, was a playground for Hearst and his guests—Hollywood celebrities, political leaders, scientists, and other well-known figures. Construction began in 1919 and was never officially completed. Work was halted in 1947 when Hearst had to leave San Simeon because of failing health. The Hearst Corporation donated the property to the State of California in 1958, and it is now part of the state park system.

Access to the castle is through the visitor center at the foot of the hill, where you can view educational exhibits and a 40-minute film about Hearst's life and the castle's construction. Buses from the center zigzag up to the hilltop estate, where guides conduct four daytime tours, each with a different focus: Grand Rooms, Upstairs Suites, Designing the Dream, and Cottages and Kitchen. These tours take about three hours and include a movie screening, and time at the end to explore the castle's exterior and gardens. In spring and fall, docents in period costume portray Hearst's guests and staff for the Evening Tour, which begins around sunset. Reservations are recommended for all tours, which include a ½-mile walk and between 150 and 400 stairs. ⊠ *San Simeon State Park, 750 Hearst Castle Rd.* ☎ *800/444–4445, 518/218–5078 international reservations* ⊕ *www.hearstcastle.org* ⌛ *Daytime tours $25–$30, evening tours $36.*

FAMILY **Piedras Blancas Elephant Seal Rookery.** A large colony of elephant seals (at last count 22,000) gathers every year at Piedras Blancas Elephant Seal Rookery, on the beaches near Piedras Blancas Lighthouse. The huge males with their pendulous, trunklike noses typically start appearing on shore in late November, and the females begin to arrive in December to give birth—most babies are born in the last two weeks of January. The newborn pups spend about four weeks nursing before their mothers head out to sea, leaving them on their own; the "weaners" leave the rookery when they are about 3½ months old. The seals return in the spring and summer months to molt or rest, but not en masse as in winter. You can watch them from a boardwalk along the bluffs just a few feet above the beach; do not attempt to approach them as they are wild animals. The nonprofit Friends of the Elephant Seal runs a small visitor center and gift shop (*250 San Simeon Avenue*) in San Simeon. ⊠ *Off Hwy. 1, 4½ miles north of Hearst Castle, just south of Piedras Blancas Lighthouse* ☎ *805/924–1628* ⊕ *www.elephantseal.org.*

Piedras Blancas Light Station. If you think traversing craggy, twisting Highway 1 is tough, imagine trying to navigate a boat up the rocky coastline (*piedras blancas* means "white rocks" in Spanish) near San Simeon before lighthouses were built. Captains must have cheered wildly when the beam began to shine here in 1875. Try to time a visit to include a morning tour (reservations not required). Tours are at 9:45 am on Tuesday, Thursday, and Saturday year-round (except for on major holidays). **■ TIP→ Do not meet at the gate to the lighthouse—you'll miss the tour. Meet your guide instead at the former Piedras Blancas Motel, a mile and a half north of the light station.** ✉ *San Simeon* ☎ *805/927–7361,* 🌐 *www.piedrasblancas.org* 🎟 *$10* ☞ *No pets allowed.*

WORTH NOTING

Hearst Ranch Winery. Old whaling equipment and Hearst Ranch and Hearst Castle memorabilia decorate this winery's casual Old San Simeon outpost. The tasting room occupies part of Sebastian's, a former whaling store built in 1852 and moved by oxen to its present location in 1878. The flagship wines include a Bordeaux-style red blend with Petite Sirah added to round out the flavor, and Rhône-style white and red blends. Malbec and Tempranillo are two other strong suits. **■ TIP→ Templeton chef Ian McPhee serves burgers and other lunch items at the adjacent deli, whose outdoor patio is a delight in good weather.** ✉ *442 SLO San Simeon Rd., off Hwy. 1* ☎ *805/927–4100* 🌐 *www.hearstranchwinery.com* 🎟 *Tasting $10–$15.*

6

BEACHES

William Randolph Hearst Memorial Beach. This wide, sandy beach edges a protected cove on both sides of San Simeon Pier. Fish from the pier or from a charter boat, picnic and barbecue on the bluffs, or boogie board or bodysurf the relatively gentle waves. In summer you can rent a kayak and paddle out into the bay for close encounters with marine life and sea caves. The NOAA Coastal Discovery Center, next to the parking lot, has interactive exhibits and hosts educational activities and events. **Amenities:** food and drink; parking; toilets; water sports. **Best for:** sunset; swimming; walking. ✉ *750 Hearst Castle Rd., off Hwy. 1, west of Hearst Castle entrance* ☎ *805/927–2020, 805/927–6575 Coastal Discovery Center* 🌐 *www.slostateparks.com* 🎟 *Free.*

WHERE TO STAY

$$$ HOTEL 🏨 **Cavalier Oceanfront Resort.** Reasonable rates, an oceanfront location, evening bonfires, and well-equipped rooms—some with wood-burning fireplaces and private patios—make this motel a great choice. **Pros:** on the bluffs; fantastic views; close to Hearst Castle. **Cons:** room amenities and sizes vary; pools are small and sometimes crowded. [$] *Rooms from: $229* ✉ *9415 Hearst Dr.* ☎ *805/927–4688, 800/826–8168* 🌐 *www.cavalierresort.com* 🛏 *90 rooms* 🍴 *No meals.*

$$ HOTEL 🏨 **The Morgan San Simeon.** On Highway 1's ocean side, the Morgan offers motel-style rooming options in two buildings designed to reflect the life and style of Hearst Castle architect, Julia Morgan. **Pros:** fascinating artwork; easy access to Hearst Castle; some ocean views. **Cons:** not right on beach; no fitness room or laundry facilities. [$] *Rooms from: $149* ✉ *9135 Hearst Dr.* ☎ *805/927–3878, 800/451–9900* 🌐 *www.hotel-morgan.com* 🛏 *55 rooms* 🍴 *Breakfast.*

BIG SUR COASTLINE

Long a retreat of artists and writers, Big Sur is a place of ancient forests and rugged shoreline, stretching 90 miles from San Simeon to Carmel. Residents have protected it from overdevelopment, and much of the region lies within several state parks and the more than 165,000-acre Ventana Wilderness, itself part of the Los Padres National Forest.

ESSENTIALS

Visitor Information Big Sur Chamber of Commerce. ☎ *831/667–2100* ⊕ *bigsurcalifornia.org.*

SOUTHERN BIG SUR

Hwy. 1 from San Simeon to Julia Pfeiffer Burns State Park.

This especially rugged stretch of oceanfront is a rocky world of mountains, cliffs, and beaches.

GETTING HERE AND AROUND

Highway 1 is the only major access route from north or south. From the south, access Highway 1 from U.S. 101 in San Luis Obispo. From the north, take rural route Highway 46 West (Paso Robles to Cambria) or Highway 41 West (Atascadero to Morro Bay). Nacimiento-Fergusson Road snakes through mountains and forest from U.S. 101 at Jolon about 25 miles to Highway 1 at Kirk Creek, about 4 miles south of Lucia; this curving, at times precipitous road is a motorcyclist favorite, not recommended for the faint of heart or during inclement weather.

EXPLORING

Fodor's Choice ★ **Highway 1.** One of California's most spectacular drives, Highway 1 snakes up the coast north of San Simeon. Numerous pullouts along the way offer tremendous views and photo ops. On some of the beaches huge elephant seals lounge nonchalantly, seemingly oblivious to the attention of rubberneckers. Heavy rain sometimes causes mudslides that block the highway north and south of Big Sur. ⚠ Sections of Highway 1 are sometimes closed for general maintenance or to repair damage from natural incidents such as mudslides. It's wise to visit bigsurcalifornia.org and click on the Highway 1 Conditions and Information link for the latest news before you travel. ⊕ *www.dot.ca.gov.*

Jade Cove. In Los Padres National Forest just north of the town of Gorda is Jade Cove, a well-known jade-hunting spot. Rock hunting is allowed on the beach, but you may not remove anything from the walls of the cliffs. ⊠ *Hwy. 1, 34 miles north of San Simeon.*

Julia Pfeiffer Burns State Park. The park provides fine hiking, from an easy ½-mile stroll with marvelous coastal views to a strenuous 6-mile trek through redwoods. The big draw here, an 80-foot waterfall that drops into the ocean, gets crowded in summer; still, it's an astounding place to contemplate nature. Migrating whales, harbor seals, and sea lions can sometimes be spotted just offshore. ⊠ *Hwy. 1, 15 miles north of Lucia* ☎ *831/667–2315* ⊕ *www.parks.ca.gov* ⊠ *$10.*

WHERE TO STAY

$$$ HOTEL 🏨 **Ragged Point Inn.** At this cliff-top resort—the only inn and restaurant for miles around—glass walls in most rooms open to awesome ocean views. **Pros:** on the cliffs; good burgers and locally made ice cream; idyllic views. **Cons:** busy road stop during the day; often booked for weekend weddings. [$] *Rooms from: $199* ✉ *19019 Hwy. 1, 20 miles north of San Simeon, Ragged Point* ☎ *805/927–4502, 805/927–5708 restaurant* 🌐 *www.raggedpointinn.com* 🛏 *39 rooms* 🍴 *No meals.*

$$$$ RESORT 🏨 **Treebones Resort.** Perched on a hilltop surrounded by national forest and stunning, unobstructed ocean views, this yurt resort provides a stellar back-to-nature experience along with creature comforts. **Pros:** luxury yurts with cozy beds; lodge with fireplace and games; local food at Wild Coast Restaurant and decked sushi bar. **Cons:** steep paths; no private bathrooms; not good for families with young children. [$] *Rooms from: $320* ✉ *71895 Hwy. 1, Willow Creek Rd., 32 miles north of San Simeon, 1 mile north of Gorda* ☎ *805/927–2390, 877/424–4787* 🌐 *www.treebonesresort.com* 🛏 *16 yurts, 5 campsites, 1 human nest w/ campsite* 🍴 *Breakfast* ☞ *2-night minimum.*

6

CENTRAL BIG SUR

Hwy. 1, from Partington Cove to Bixby Bridge.

The countercultural spirit of Big Sur—which instead of a conventional town is a loose string of coast-hugging properties along Highway 1—is alive and well today. Its few residents include the very wealthy, the enthusiastically outdoorsy, and the thoroughly evolved: since the 1960s the Esalen Institute, a center for alternative education and East–West philosophical study, has attracted seekers of higher consciousness and devotees of the property's hot springs. Today posh and rustic resorts hidden among the redwoods cater to visitors drawn from near and far by the extraordinary scenery and serene isolation.

GETTING HERE AND AROUND

From the north, follow Highway 1 south from Carmel. From the south, continue the drive north from Julia Pfeiffer Burns State Park on Highway 1. Monterey-Salinas Transit operates the Line 22 Big Sur bus from Monterey and Carmel to Central Big Sur (the last stop is Nepenthe), daily from late May to early September and weekends only the rest of the year.

Bus Contact Monterey-Salinas Transit. ☎ *888/678–2871* 🌐 *www.mst.org.*

EXPLORING

Bixby Creek Bridge. The graceful arc of Bixby Creek Bridge is a photographer's dream. Built in 1932, the bridge spans a deep canyon, more than 100 feet wide at the bottom. From the north-side parking area you can admire the view or walk the 550-foot structure. ✉ *Hwy. 1, 6 miles north of Point Sur State Historic Park, 13 miles south of Carmel, Big Sur.*

Pfeiffer Big Sur State Park. Among the many hiking trails at Pfeiffer Big Sur, a short route through a redwood-filled valley leads to a waterfall. You can double back or continue on the more difficult trail along the valley wall for views over miles of treetops to the sea. ✉ *47225 Hwy. 1, Big Sur* ☎ *831/667–2315* 🌐 *www.parks.ca.gov* 🎟 *$10 per vehicle.*

Point Sur State Historic Park. An 1889 lighthouse at this state park still stands watch from atop a large volcanic rock. Four lighthouse keepers lived here with their families until 1974, when the light station became automated. Their homes and working spaces are open to the public only on 2½- to 3-hour ranger-led tours. Considerable walking, including up two stairways, is involved. Strollers are not allowed. ✉ *Hwy. 1, 7 miles north of Pfeiffer Big Sur State Park, Big Sur* ☎ *831/625–4419* 🌐 *www.pointsur.org* 🎫 *$12* ☞ *Call or visit website for current tour schedule.*

BEACHES

Pfeiffer Beach. Through a hole in one of the gigantic boulders at secluded Pfeiffer Beach, you can watch the waves break first on the seaside and then on the beach side. Keep a sharp eye out for the unsigned, nongated road to the beach: it branches west of Highway 1 between the post office and Pfeiffer Big Sur State Park. The 2-mile, one-lane road descends sharply. **Amenities:** parking (fee); toilets. **Best for:** solitude; sunset. ✉ *Off Hwy. 1, 1 mile south of Pfeiffer Big Sur State Park, Big Sur* 🎫 *$10 per vehicle.*

WHERE TO EAT

$$$ AMERICAN Fodor'sChoice ★

🍴 **Deetjen's Big Sur Inn.** The candle-lighted, creaky-floor restaurant in the main house at the historic inn of the same name is a Big Sur institution. It serves spicy seafood paella, grass-fed filet mignon, and rack of lamb for dinner and flavorful eggs Benedict for breakfast. **Known for:** rustic, romantic setting; ingredients from sustainable purveyors; stellar weekend brunch. [$] *Average main: $30* ✉ *Hwy. 1, 3½ miles south of Pfeiffer Big Sur State Park, Big Sur* ☎ *831/667–2378* 🌐 *www.deetjens.com* ⏲ *No lunch.*

$$$$ AMERICAN Fodor'sChoice ★

🍴 **Nepenthe.** It may be that no other restaurant between San Francisco and Los Angeles has a better coastal view than Nepenthe, named for an opiate mentioned in Greek literature that would induce a state of "no sorrow." For the real show, settle on the terraced deck in the late afternoon, order a glass from the extensive wine list, and watch the sun slip into the Pacific Ocean. The food and drink are overpriced but good; there are burgers, sandwiches, and salads for lunch, and fresh fish and hormone-free steaks for dinner. **Known for:** ambrosia burger, fresh fish, hormone-free steaks; multiple view decks; brunch and lunch at casual outdoor Café Kevah. [$] *Average main: $32* ✉ *48510 Hwy. 1, 2½ miles south of Big Sur Station, Big Sur* ☎ *831/667–2345* 🌐 *nepenthebigsur.com.*

$$$$ AMERICAN Fodor'sChoice ★

🍴 **The Restaurant at Ventana.** The Ventana Inn's restaurant sits high on a ridge, and magnificent terraces offer stunning ocean views and a full-service outdoor bar. Regional and international wines on a comprehensive list pair well with the California-inspired dishes, many of whose ingredients are sourced from local purveyors, and the bar serves seasonal specialty cocktails and California craft beers. **Known for:** stunning views; local ingredients; excellent wine list. [$] *Average main: $40* ✉ *48123 Hwy. 1, 1½ miles south of Pfeiffer Big Sur State Park, Big Sur* ☎ *831/667–4242* 🌐 *www.ventanainn.com.*

$$$$ ✕ **Sierra Mar.** At cliff's edge 1,200 feet above the Pacific at the ultra-
AMERICAN chic Post Ranch Inn, Sierra Mar serves cutting-edge American cuisine
Fodor'sChoice made from mostly organic, seasonal ingredients, some from the on-
★ site chef's garden. The four-course prix-fixe option always shines,
and the nine-course Taste of Big Sur menu centers on ingredients
grown or foraged on the property or sourced locally. **Known for:**
stunning panoramic ocean views; one of the nation's most extensive
wine lists; iconic Big Sur farm-to-table experience. $ *Average main:*
$125 ✉ *Hwy. 1, 1½ miles south of Pfeiffer Big Sur State Park, Big Sur*
☎ *831/667–2800* ⊕ *www.postranchinn.com/dining.*

WHERE TO STAY

$$$$ ⬚ **Big Sur Lodge.** The lodge's modern, motel-style cottages with Mission-
HOTEL style furnishings and vaulted ceilings sit in a meadow surrounded by
redwood trees and flowering shrubbery. **Pros:** secluded setting near trailheads; good camping alternative; rates include state parks pass. **Cons:**
basic rooms; walk to main lodge. $ *Rooms from: $309* ✉ *Pfeiffer Big*
Sur State Park, 47225 Hwy. 1, Big Sur ☎ *831/667–3100, 800/424–4787*
⊕ *www.bigsurlodge.com* ⇆ *62 rooms* ⦶*No meals.*

$$$ ⬚ **Big Sur River Inn.** During summer at this rustic property you can
B&B/INN sip drinks beside—or in—the Big Sur River fronted by the inn's
wooded grounds; if you're here on a Sunday afternoon between
May and September you can enjoy live music on the restaurant's
deck. **Pros:** riverside setting; next to a restaurant and small market;
outdoor pool; recently renovated baths. **Cons:** standard rooms across
the road; no phone in rooms. $ *Rooms from: $250* ✉ *Hwy. 1, 2*
miles north of Pfeiffer Big Sur State Park, Big Sur ☎ *831/667–2700,*
831/667–2743, 800/548–3610 ⊕ *www.bigsurriverinn.com* ⇆ *22*
rooms ⦶*No meals.*

$$ ⬚ **Deetjen's Big Sur Inn.** This historic 1930s Norwegian-style property is
B&B/INN endearingly rustic, with its village of cabins nestled in the redwoods;
many of the very individual rooms have their own fireplaces. **Pros:** tons
of character; wooded grounds. **Cons:** thin walls; some rooms don't have
private baths; no TVs or Wi-Fi, limited cell service. $ *Rooms from:*
$170 ✉ *Hwy. 1, 3½ miles south of Pfeiffer Big Sur State Park, Big*
Sur ☎ *831/667–2377* ⊕ *www.deetjens.com* ⇆ *20 rooms, 15 with bath*
⦶*No meals* ⌆ *2-night minimum stay on weekends.*

$$$$ ⬚ **Glen Oaks Big Sur.** At this rustic-modern cluster of adobe-and-
HOTEL redwood buildings, you can choose between motel-style rooms, cabins, and cottages in the woods. **Pros:** in the heart of town; natural
river-rock radiant-heated tiles; gas fireplaces in each room. **Cons:**
near busy road and parking lot; no TVs. $ *Rooms from: $300*
✉ *Hwy. 1, 1 mile north of Pfeiffer Big Sur State Park, Big Sur*
☎ *831/667–2105* ⊕ *www.glenoaksbigsur.com* ⇆ *16 rooms, 2 cot-*
tages, 7 cabins ⦶*No meals.*

$$$$ ⬚ **Post Ranch Inn.** This luxurious retreat is perfect for getaways; the
RESORT redwood guesthouses, all of which have views of the sea or the moun-
Fodor'sChoice tains, blend almost invisibly into a wooded cliff 1,200 feet above the
★ ocean. **Pros:** units come with fireplaces and private decks; on-site
activities like yoga and stargazing; gorgeous property with hiking
trails and spectacular views. **Cons:** expensive; austere design; not a

6

good choice if you're afraid of heights. [$] *Rooms from: $925* ✉ *Hwy. 1, 1½ miles south of Pfeiffer Big Sur State Park, Big Sur* ☎ *831/667–2200, 800/527–2200* 🌐 *www.postranchinn.com* 🛏 *39 rooms, 2 houses* 🍴 *Breakfast.*

$$$$ HOTEL Fodor's Choice ★ 🏨 **Ventana.** Hundreds of celebrities, from Oprah Winfrey to Sir Anthony Hopkins, have escaped to Ventana, a romantic resort on 243 tranquil acres 1,200 feet above the Pacific. **Pros:** secluded; nature trails everywhere; rates include daily guided hike, yoga, wine and cheese hour. **Cons:** expensive; some rooms lack an ocean view; not family-friendly. [$] *Rooms from: $650* ✉ *Hwy. 1, almost 1 mile south of Pfeiffer Big Sur State Park, Big Sur* ☎ *831/667–2331, 800/628–6500* 🌐 *www.ventanainn.com* 🛏 *59 rooms* 🍴 *Breakfast.*

THE INLAND EMPIRE

East of Los Angeles to Temecula

WELCOME TO
THE INLAND EMPIRE

TOP REASONS
TO GO

★ **Wine Country:** The idyllic, ever-expanding Temecula Valley is home to family-owned and resort-style wineries cooled by faint ocean breezes.

★ **The Mission Inn:** One of the most unusual hotels in America, Riverside's rambling, eclectic Mission Inn feels like an urban Hearst Castle.

★ **Apple country:** In the Oak Glen apple-growing region, you can attend an old-fashioned hoedown, take a wagon ride, and sample apple pies and homemade ciders.

★ **Soothing spas:** The lushly landscaped grounds, bubbling hot springs, and playful mud baths of Glen Ivy are ideal spots to unwind; Kelly's Spa at the historic Mission Inn provides a cozy Tuscan-style retreat.

★ **Alpine escapes:** Breathe in the clean mountain air or get cozy at a bed-and-breakfast at great mountain hideaways like Lake Arrowhead and Big Bear.

1 **The Western Inland Empire.** At the foot of 10,064-foot-high Mt. Baldy in the San Gabriel Mountains, the community of Claremont is known for the prestigious seven-school Claremont Colleges complex. A classic tree-shaded, lively, sophisticated college town, Claremont resembles trendy sections of Los Angeles more than the laid-back Inland Empire.

2 **Riverside Area.** In the late 1700s, Mexican settlers called this now-suburban region Valle de Paraiso. Citrus-growing here began in 1873, when homesteader Eliza Tibbets planted two navel-orange trees in her yard. The area's biggest draws are the majestic Mission Inn, with its fine restaurants and unique history and architecture, and Glen Ivy Hot Springs in nearby Corona.

GETTING ORIENTED

Several freeways provide access to the Inland Empire from Los Angeles and San Diego. Temecula lines up along interstates 10 and 215; and Corona, Riverside, and San Bernardino lie along Highway 91. As a Los Angeles bedroom community, the area sees nasty freeway congestion on Highway 60 and interstates 10 and 15, so try to avoid driving during rush hour, usually from 6 to 9 am and 3:30 to 7 pm.

3 San Bernardino Mountains. Lake Arrowhead and always-sunny Big Bear are the recreational centers of this area. Though the two are geographically close, they're distinct in appeal. Lake Arrowhead, with its cool mountain air, trail-threaded woods, and brilliant lake, draws a summertime crowd. Big Bear's ski and snowboarding slopes, cross-country trails, and cheerful lodges come alive in winter and provide a quiet retreat in summer. Even if you're not interested in visiting the resorts themselves, the Rim of the World Scenic Byway (Highway 18), which connects Big Bear Lake and Lake Arrowhead at an elevation up to 8,000 feet, is a magnificent drive. On a clear day, you'll feel that you can see forever.

4 The Temecula Valley. Life is quieter in the southern portion of the Inland Empire than it is to the north. In this corner of Riverside County, the town of Temecula is an oasis of the good life for locals and visitors alike.

Updated by
Daniel Mangin

Threaded with rolling vineyards, homey agricultural towns, and mountain retreats, the Inland Empire has a humble allure. Often bypassed because of its freeway maze and suburban sprawl, this historically rich region offers visitors a quiet and quirky alternative to metropolitan Los Angeles and San Diego. You can hurtle down a 7,000-foot ski slope perched above a clear blue lake, hike or snowshoe in serene forests, and taste wines wrought by Temecula's misty mornings and subtle ocean breezes.

For fresh California flavors, explore apple country in Oak Glen, and trace the roots of the state's navel orange industry in Riverside, while the San Bernardino Mountains offer Big Bear Lake, Lake Arrowhead, and plentiful recreational opportunities.

PLANNING

WHEN TO GO
The climate varies greatly, depending on what part of the Inland Empire you're visiting. Summer temperatures in the mountains and in Temecula, 20 miles from the coast, usually hover around 80°F, though it's not uncommon for Riverside to reach temperatures of 100°F or higher. From September to March this area is subject to Santa Ana winds, sometimes strong enough to overturn trucks on the freeway. In winter, temperatures in the mountains and in Temecula usually range from 30°F to 55°F, and in the Riverside area from 40°F to 60°F. Most of the ski areas open when the first natural snow falls (usually in November) and close in mid-March.

GETTING HERE AND AROUND
AIR TRAVEL
Ontario International Airport (ONT) is the local airport. Aeromexico, Alaska, American, Delta, Southwest, United, and Volaris fly here.

Airport Contacts **Ontario International Airport.** ⊠ *2500 E. Airport Dr., Archibald Ave. exit off I–10, Ontario* ☎ *909/937–2700* ⊕ *www.flyontario.com.*

CAR TRAVEL

Avoid Highway 91 if possible; it's almost always backed up from Corona through Orange County. Check with Caltrans for information about highway conditions, or dial 511 or log onto the IE511 website, which also has bus–train trip planners.

Contacts **Caltrans.** ☎ *800/427–7623* ⊕ *www.dot.ca.gov.* **IE511.** ☎ *877/694–3511* ⊕ *www.ie511.org.*

TRAIN TRAVEL

■**TIP→** Many locals get around on Metrolink, which is clean and quick, and generally a much nicer way to travel than by bus. Metrolink trains stop at several stations on the Inter-County, San Bernardino, and Riverside lines. You can buy tickets and passes at station vending machines, or by telephone. The IE511 website *(Car Travel, above)* has bus–train trip planners; dial 511 for recorded train-schedule information.

Train Contacts **Metrolink.** ☎ *800/371–5465* ⊕ *www.metrolinktrains.com.*

RESTAURANTS

Downtown Riverside is home to a few ambitious restaurants, along with the familiar chains. The college town of Claremont has creative contemporary and ethnic fare. Innovative cuisine has become the norm in Temecula, especially at winery restaurants, some of whose chefs specialize in farm-to-table cuisine. The options are more limited in the smaller mountain communities; typically, each town supports a single upscale restaurant, along with fast-food outlets, steak-and-potatoes family spots, and perhaps an Italian or Mexican eatery. Universally, dining out is casual. *Restaurant reviews have been shortened. For full information, visit Fodors.com.*

HOTELS

In the San Bernardino Mountains many accommodations are bed-and-breakfasts or rustic cabins, though Lake Arrowhead and Big Bear offer more luxurious resort lodging. Rates for Big Bear lodgings fluctuate widely, depending on the season. When winter snow brings droves of Angelenos to the mountains for skiing, expect to pay sky-high prices for any kind of room. Most establishments require a two-night stay on weekends. In Riverside the landmark Mission Inn is the marquee accommodation. In the Wine Country, lodgings can be found at wineries, golf resorts, and chain hotels. *Hotel reviews have been shortened. For full information, visit Fodors.com.*

WHAT IT COSTS			
$	$$	$$$	$$$$
Restaurants	under $16	$16–$22	$23–$30	over $30
Hotels	under $120	$120–$175	$176–$250	over $250

Restaurant prices are the average cost of a main course at dinner or, if dinner is not served, at lunch, excluding sales tax of 7¾%–9¼%. Hotel prices are the lowest cost of a standard double room in high season, excluding service charges and 7¾%–13% tax.

THE WESTERN INLAND EMPIRE

Straddling the line between Los Angeles and San Bernardino counties, the western section of the Inland Empire is home to some of California's oldest vineyards and original citrus orchards. Now a busy suburban community, it holds the closest ski slopes to metro Los Angeles. Claremont, home to a collection of high-ranking colleges, is also here.

GETTING HERE AND AROUND

To reach this area from Los Angeles, take Interstate 10, which bisects the Western Inland Empire west to east; from Pasadena, take Interstate 210, which runs parallel to the north. Take Highway 57 from Anaheim. Some areas are quite walkable, especially the Claremont Colleges, where you can stroll through parks from one school building to another.

The Foothill Transit Bus Line serves Claremont. Metrolink serves the area from Los Angeles and elsewhere.

ESSENTIALS

Bus Contacts Foothill Transit. ☎ 800/743–3463 ⊕ www.foothilltransit.org.

CLAREMONT

26 miles north of Anaheim, 27 miles east of Pasadena.

The seven Claremont Colleges are among the most prestigious in the nation, lending the town an ambitious and creative energy. The campuses are all laid out cheek-by-jowl; as you wander from one leafy street to the next, you won't be able to tell where one college ends and the next begins.

Claremont was originally the home of the Sunkist citrus growers cooperative movement. Today Claremont Village, home to descendants of those early farmers, is bright and lively—a beautifully restored lemon-packing house, built in 1922, now hosts numerous shops and cafés in College Heights. The business district village, with streets named for prestigious eastern colleges, is walkable and appealing with a collection of boutiques, fancy food emporiums, cafés, and lounges. The downtown district is a beautiful place to visit, with Victorian, Craftsman, and Spanish Colonial buildings.

GETTING HERE AND AROUND

If you're driving, exit Interstate 10 at Indian Hill Boulevard, and drive north to Claremont. Parking can be difficult, although there are metered spots. Overnight parking is prohibited within the village; however there is a parking structure adjacent to the College Heights Packing House that is also north of the freeway; exit Garey and drive toward the mountains. You can reach this area by public transportation, but you'll need a car to get around unless you plan to spend all your time in the Claremont Village.

ESSENTIALS

Visitor Information Claremont Chamber of Commerce. ✉ 205 Yale Ave. ☎ 909/624–1681 ⊕ www.claremontchamber.org.

EXPLORING

Claremont Heritage. College walking tours, historic home tours, and nature tours are conducted throughout the year by Claremont Heritage. On the first Saturday of each month the organization gives guided walking tours ($5) of the village. Self-guided tour maps can be found on the group's website. ✉ *840 N. Indian Hill Blvd.* ☎ *909/621–0848* 🌐 *www.claremontheritage.org* 🎫 *$5.*

Pomona College Museum of Art. This small campus museum exhibits contemporary art, works by old masters, and Native American art and artifacts. Highlights include a mural by Mexican artist Jose Clemente Orozco, first-edition Goya etchings, and 15th- and 16th-century Italian panel paintings. Thursday-night Art After Hours events often include music by local bands. *Skyspace: Dividing the Light,* alumnus James Turrell's stunning light installation in Draper Courtyard, is best experienced before sunrise or sunset. ✉ *333 N. College Ave.* ✥ *Skyscape: Draper Courtyard, 6th St. and College Way* ☎ *909/621–8283* 🌐 *www.pomona.edu/museum* 🎫 *Free* 🕒 *Museum closed Mon.; Skyspace closed Tues.–Fri. Sept.–May.*

QUICK BITES

Bert & Rocky's Cream Company. The sinfully innovative concoctions at this local ice cream store include mint Oreo, blueberry-cheesecake, and the Elvis special with bananas and peanut butter. The vanilla's delightful, too. Known for: 200-plus ice cream flavors; homemade waffle cones; caramel-covered apples. ✉ ***242 Yale Ave.*** ☎ ***909/625–1852*** 🌐 ***www.bertandrockys.com.***

Fodor's Choice ★

Rancho Santa Ana Botanic Garden. Founded in 1927 by Susanna Bixby Bryant, a wealthy landowner and conservationist, the garden is dedicated to the preservation of native California plant species. You can meander here for hours enjoying the shade of an oak tree canopy or take a guided tour of the grounds, whose 86 acres of ponds and greenery shelter California wild lilacs, big berry manzanitas, four-needled piñons, and other specimens. Countless bird species also live here. **■ TIP→ Guided tram tours are offered the third Sunday of the month (reserve by the 15th of the preceding month).** ✉ *1500 N. College Ave.* ☎ *909/625–8767* 🌐 *www.rsabg.org* 🎫 *Garden $8, tram tour $10 (includes garden admission).*

WHERE TO EAT

$$ ITALIAN

🍴 **Il Mattone Trattoria Italiana.** Locals line up on weekends for a table at this busy spot where waiters zip through small rooms to deliver fresh and beautifully seasoned fare from an extensive Italian menu. Popular dishes include pappardelle with Bolognese ragout and cioppino Livornese (seafood stew). **Known for:** cheerful family-run operation; many ingredients from Inland Empire suppliers; bread pudding made with ciabatta and crème anglaise. [$] *Average main: $19* ✉ *201 N. Indian Hill Blvd.* ☎ *909/624–1516* 🌐 *www.ilmattoneusa.com.*

$$ ECLECTIC

🍴 **Packing House Wines.** At this shop, bar, and restaurant inside a former orange-packing house, you can purchase wines from around the world and enjoy them on-site. Throughout the day pair your selection with seasonal small plates and specialty cheeses and, for dinner, entrées like poke tostadas with sushi-grade ahi tuna and an organic beef burger with smoked bacon, aged cheddar, and spicy tomato aioli. **Known for:** admirable by-the-glass wine selection; reasonable corkage fee; fine stop for wine and nibbles but also for dinner. $ *Average main: $16* ☒ *540 W. 1st St.* ☎ *909/445–9463* ⊕ *www.packinghousewines.com* ☾ *Closed Mon.*

$$$$ ✕ **Tutti Mangia Italian Grill.** A favorite of college students and their visiting parents, this storefront dining room has a warm and cozy feel and menu choices that include long-bone pork chops, osso buco, and pan-roasted salmon with blood-orange rosemary sauce. Bruschetta, fried calamari, zucchini flowers stuffed with goat cheese, and other small plates, some seasonal, always entice. **Known for:** wide selection of first and second courses and sides; martini and wine bar happy hour except Sunday; heart-healthy low-calorie menu items. $ *Average main: $40* ☒ *102 Harvard Ave.* ☎ *909/625–4669* ⊕ *www.tuttimangia.com* ☾ *No lunch weekends.*

ITALIAN

$$$ ✕ **Walter's Restaurant.** With a menu that samples cuisines from Europe to India, Walter's is where locals dine, sip wine, and chat—outside on the sidewalk, on the lively patio, or in a cozy setting inside. The diverse possibilities include omelets, sausages and eggs, and burritos for breakfast; salads, soups, pastas, and kebabs for lunch; and everything from fried chicken to tandoori shrimp for dinner. **Known for:** Afghan battered fries with hot sauce; happy hour weekdays 4–7, weekends 8 am–closing. $ *Average main: $24* ☒ *310 N. Yale Ave.* ☎ *909/624–4914* ⊕ *www.waltersrestaurant.com.*

ECLECTIC

WHERE TO STAY

$$$ 🛏 **Casa 425.** This boutique inn on a corner opposite the College Heights Lemon Packing House entertainment and shopping complex is the most attractive lodging option in Claremont Village. **Pros:** within walking distance of attractions and restaurants; bicycles available; most rooms have soaking tubs. **Cons:** occasional noise. $ *Rooms from: $195* ☒ *425 W. 1st St.* ☎ *866/450–0425* ⊕ *www.foursisters.com* ⇨ *28 rooms* ⦿ *Some meals.*

B&B/INN
Fodor's Choice
★

$$ 🛏 **DoubleTree by Hilton Hotel Claremont.** The hotel of choice for parents visiting children attending local colleges has spacious rooms clustered in three Spanish-style buildings that surround a flower-decked central courtyard. **Pros:** convenient to colleges; swimming pool; chocolate chip cookies. **Cons:** small bathrooms. $ *Rooms from: $169* ☒ *555 W. Foothill Blvd.* ☎ *909/626–2411* ⊕ *www.doubletreeclaremont.com* ⇨ *190 rooms* ⦿ *No meals.*

HOTEL
FAMILY

NIGHTLIFE

Being a college town, Claremont has many bars and cafés, some of which showcase bands.

Flappers Comedy Club. A typical stand-up venue that sometimes hosts celebrity comics, Flappers is a branch of a Burbank club. ☒ *532 W. 1st St., at N. Oberlin Ave.* ☎ *818/845–9721* ⊕ *www.flapperscomedy.com* 🎟 *$10–$22, some shows free* ☾ *Closed Mon.–Wed.*

SPORTS AND THE OUTDOORS
SKIING

Mt. Baldy Ski Resort. The 10,064-foot mountain's real name is Mt. San Antonio, but Mt. Baldy Ski Resort—the oldest ski area in Southern California—takes its name from the treeless slopes. The Mt. Baldy base lies at 6,500 feet, and four chairlifts ascend to 8,600 feet. The resort is known for its steep triple-diamond runs; the longest of the 26 runs here is 2,100 vertical feet. The resort also operates a ski and snowboard park. Backcountry skiing is available via shuttle in the spring, and there's a school on weekends for kids ages 5 to 12. ■**TIP**➔ **Winter or summer, you can take a scenic chairlift ride ($29) to the Top of the Notch restaurant and hiking and mountain-biking trails.** ⊠ *8401 Mt. Baldy Rd., Mt. Baldy* ☎ *909/982–0800* ⊕ *www.mtbaldyskilifts.com* ⊠ *$69 full-day lift ticket* ☞ *Closed weekdays May–Oct. (days and hrs may vary yr-round, so check to confirm).*

WATER PARK

FAMILY **Raging Waters.** This tropical-theme water park 10 miles west of Claremont is the largest water park in Southern California. It has numerous chutes and slides with such names as Neptune's Fury, Thunder Rapids, Dragon's Den, and the scary dark Tunnel of Terror. When you're ready for a break, head over to the sandy beach lagoon and relax, or go to the Snack Shack. Complimentary life jackets are provided for youngsters. Locker rentals run from $12 to $20; inner tube rental is free. For a special treat, rent a cabana (from $119 to $300) and order lunch. Check the website for online coupons. ⊠ *111 Raging Waters Dr., San Dimas Ave., off Hwy. 57, San Dimas* ☎ *909/802–2200* ⊕ *www.ragingwaters. com* ⊠ *$43–$46; parking (cash only) $15* ☞ *Closed Oct.–late May and sometimes (days vary, so call ahead) late May–Sept.*

RIVERSIDE AREA

Historic Riverside lies at the heart of the Inland Empire. Major highways linking it to other regional destinations spoke out from this city to the north, south, and east.

GETTING HERE AND AROUND

The most direct route from Los Angeles to Riverside is by Highway 60 (Pomona Freeway). From San Diego take Interstate 15 northeast to the junction with Highway 60. From North Orange County, Highway 91 is the best route.

ESSENTIALS

Bus Contacts Omnitrans. ☎ *800/966–6428* ⊕ *www.omnitrans.org.*
Riverside Transit Authority. ☎ *951/565–5000* ⊕ *www.riversidetransit.com.*

CORONA

25 miles southeast of Claremont.

Corona's Temescal Canyon is named for the dome-shaped mud saunas that the Luiseño Indians built around the area's artesian hot springs in the early 19th century. Starting in 1860, weary Butterfield Overland Stage Company passengers stopped here to relax in the soothing mineral springs. In 1890 Mr. and Mrs. W.G. Steers turned the springs into Glen Ivy Hot Springs, whose popularity has yet to fade.

GETTING HERE AND AROUND

Corona lies at the intersection of Interstate 15 and Highway 91. The many roadside malls make it a convenient stop for food or gas.

EXPLORING

FAMILY   **Tom's Farms.** Opened as a produce stand along Interstate 15 in 1974, Tom's Farms has grown to include a locally popular hamburger stand, a furniture showroom, and a sweets shop. You can still buy produce here, but the big draws are various weekend attractions for children: tractor driving, Tom's mining company, a petting zoo, a children's train, a pony ride, free magic shows, face painting, and an old-style carousel. Most cost a modest fee. Of interest for adults is the wine-and-cheese shop, which has more than 600 varieties of wine, including some from the nearby Temecula Valley. ⊠ *23900 Temescal Canyon Rd.* ☎ *951/277–4422* ⊕ *www.tomsfarms.com* ✉ *Free, attraction fees vary; wine tasting $5.*

SPAS

Glen Ivy Hot Springs Spa. Colorful bougainvillea and birds-of-paradise surround the secluded Glen Ivy, which offers a full range of facials, manicures, pedicures, body wraps, and massages. Some treatments are performed in underground granite chambers known collectively as the Grotto. The Under the Oaks treatment center holds eight open-air massage rooms surrounded by waterfalls and ancient oak trees. Don't bring your best bikini if you plan to dive into the red clay of Club Mud. Paying the admission fee entitles you to lounge here all day. Make reservations for treatments, which cost extra. ⊠ *25000 Glen Ivy Rd.* ☎ *888/453–6489* ⊕ *www.glenivy.com* ✉ *Admission Tues.–Thurs. $46, Fri.–Mon. $64; treatments $25–$175.*

RIVERSIDE

14 miles northeast of Corona, 34 miles northeast of Anaheim.

By 1882 Riverside was home to more than half of California's citrus groves, making it the state's wealthiest city per capita in 1895. The prosperity produced a downtown area of opulent architecture, which is well preserved today. Main Street's pedestrian strip is lined with antiques and gift stores, art galleries, salons, and the UCR/California Museum of Photography.

GETTING HERE AND AROUND

Downtown Riverside lies north of Highway 91 at the University Avenue exit. The Mission Inn is at the corner of Mission Inn Avenue and Orange Street, and key museums, shops, and restaurants are nearby. You can park around here and walk to them.

EXPLORING

Mission Inn Museum. The crown jewel of Riverside is the Mission Inn, a Spanish-Revival hotel whose elaborate turrets, clock tower, mission bells, and flying buttresses rise above downtown. Docents of the Mission Inn Foundation, whose museum contains displays depicting the building's illustrious history, lead guided tours. Taking his cues from the Spanish missions in San Gabriel and Carmel, architect Arthur B. Benton designed the initial wing, which opened in 1903. Locals G. Stanley Wilson and Peter Weber are credited with the grand fourth section, the Rotunda Wing, completed in 1931. You can climb to the

CLOSE UP

Navel Oranges in California: Good as Gold

In 1873 a woman named Eliza Tibbets changed the course of California history when she planted two Brazilian navel-orange trees in her Riverside garden.

The trees flourished in the area's warm climate and rich soil—and before long Tibbett's garden was producing the sweetest seedless oranges anyone had ever tasted. After winning awards at several major exhibitions, Tibbets realized she could make a profit from her trees. She sold buds to the increasing droves of citrus farmers flocking to the Inland Empire, and by 1882,

almost 250,000 citrus trees had been planted in Riverside alone. California's citrus industry had been born.

Today Riverside still celebrates its citrus-growing heritage. The downtown Marketplace district contains several restored packing houses, and the Riverside Metropolitan Museum is home to a permanent exhibit of historic tools and machinery once used in the industry. The University of California at Riverside still remains at the forefront of citrus research; its Citrus Variety Collection includes specimens of 1,000 different fruit trees from around the world.

top of its five-story spiral stairway, or linger in the Courtyard of the Birds, where a tinkling fountain and shady trees invite meditation. You can also peek inside the St. Francis Chapel, where celebrities such as Bette Davis, Humphrey Bogart, and Richard and Pat Nixon tied the knot before the Mexican cedar altar. Ten U.S. presidents have patronized the Presidential Lounge, a bright, wood-panel bar. ✉ *3696 Main St.* ☎ *951/788–9556* ⊕ *www.missioninnmuseum.org* ✉ *Admission $2, tour $13.*

Riverside Art Museum. Hearst Castle architect Julia Morgan designed this museum that houses a significant collection of paintings by Southern California landscape artists, including William Keith, Robert Wood, and Ralph Love. Major temporary exhibitions are mounted year-round. ✉ *3425 Mission Inn Ave., at Lime St.* ☎ *951/684–7111* ⊕ *www.riversideartmuseum.org* ✉ *$5; free 1st Thurs. of month 6–9* ⊗ *Closed Mon.*

Fodor's Choice
★

UCR/California Museum of Photography. With a collection that includes thousands of Kodak Brownie and Zeiss Ikon cameras, this museum—the centerpiece of UCR ARTSblock—surveys the history of photography *and* the devices that produced it. Exhibitions, some of contemporary images, others historically oriented, are always top-notch and often incorporate photographs from the permanent collection of works by Ansel Adams, Imogen Cunningham, and other greats. ✉ *3824 Main St.* ☎ *951/827–4787* ⊕ *artsblock.ucr.edu/Exhibition* ✉ *$3 (includes same-day admission to two other facilities)* ⊗ *Closed Sun. and Mon.*

WHERE TO EAT AND STAY

$$$
ITALIAN

✕ **Mario's Place.** The clientele is as beautiful as the food at this intimate jazz and supper club across the street from the Mission Inn. The northern Italian cuisine is first-rate—try the pear-and-Gorgonzola wood-fired pizza, followed by the star-anise panna cotta for dessert. Jazz groups play on Friday and Saturday night in the restaurant's lounge. **Known for:** classy setting; live jazz on Friday and Saturday; first-rate northern Italian cuisine. ⓢ *Average main: $27* ✉ *3646 Mission Inn Ave.* ☏ *951/684–7755* ⊕ *www.mariosplace.com* ⊘ *Closed Sun.*

$
AMERICAN

✕ **Simple Simon's Bakery & Bistro.** Expect to wait in line at this popular little sandwich shop on the pedestrian-only shopping strip outside the Mission Inn. At lunchtime, salads, soups, and sandwiches on house-baked breads are served; standouts include the chicken-apple sausage sandwich and the roast lamb sandwich topped with grilled eggplant, roasted red pepper, and tomato-fennel sauce. **Known for:** specialty sandwiches for lunch; pastries, eggs dishes, and French toast for breakfast; vegetarian and vegan items. ⓢ *Average main: $11* ✉ *3639 Main St., near 6th St.* ☏ *951/369–6030* ⊘ *Closed Sun. No dinner.*

$$$
HOTEL
FAMILY
Fodor'sChoice
★

⛅ **Mission Inn and Spa.** One of California's most historic hotels, the inn grew from a modest adobe lodge in 1876 to the grand Spanish-Revival structure it is today. **Pros:** fascinating historic site; luxurious rooms; family friendly. **Cons:** train noise can be deafening at night; old style not for everyone; expensive rates. ⓢ *Rooms from: $219* ✉ *3649 Mission Inn Ave.* ☏ *951/784–0300, 800/843–7755* ⊕ *www.missioninn.com* ⇥ *265 rooms* ❑ *No meals.*

OAK GLEN

33 miles northeast of Riverside.

More than 60 varieties of apples are grown in Oak Glen. This rustic village in the foothills above Yucaipa is home to acres of farms, produce stands, country shops, and homey cafés. The town really comes alive during the fall harvest (from September through December), which is celebrated with piglet races, live entertainment, and other events. Many farms also grow berries and stone fruit, which are available in summer. Most of the apple farms lie along Oak Glen Road.

GETTING HERE AND AROUND

Oak Glen is tucked into a mountainside about halfway up the San Bernardinos. Exit Interstate 10 at Yucaipa Boulevard, heading east to the intersection with Oak Glen Road, a 5-mile loop along which you'll find most of the shops, cafés, and apple orchards.

ESSENTIALS

Visitor Information Oak Glen Apple Growers Association. ⊕ *www.oakglen.net.*

EXPLORING

Mom's Country Orchards. Oak Glen's informal information center is at Mom's, where you can head to the samples bar and learn about the nuances of apple tasting, or warm up with a hot cider heated on an antique stove. Organic produce, local honey, apple butter, and jams are also specialties here. ✉ *38695 Oak Glen Rd.* ☎ *909/797–4249* ⊕ *momsoakglen.com.*

FAMILY **Oak Tree Village.** This 14-acre children's park has miniature train rides, trout fishing, gold panning, exotic animal exhibits, shops, and a petting zoo and several eateries. Some activities don't take place year-round. ✉ *38480 Oak Glen Rd.* ☎ *909/797–4420* ⊕ *www.oaktreevillageoakglen.net* 🖼 *$5.*

BEFORE YOU GO PICKING

Be sure to call before visiting the farms, most of which are family run. Unpasteurized cider—sold at some farms—should not be consumed by children, the elderly, or those with weakened immune systems.

Rileys at Los Rios Rancho. The fantastic country store at this 100-acre apple farm sells jams, syrups, and candied apples. Drop by the bakery for a hot tri-tip sandwich before heading outside to the picnic grounds for lunch. During the fall you can pick your own apples and pumpkins, take a hayride, or enjoy live bluegrass music. On the rancho grounds, the **Oak Glen Preserve** contains 400 acres of nature trails. The diverting Hummingbird Garden of native plants is near the entrance; just beyond the garden is an outdoor display of plows and other farm machinery. ✉ *39611 Oak Glen Rd.* ☎ *909/797–1005* ⊕ *www.losriosrancho.com* ✆ *Closed Mon. and Tues. Dec.–Sept.*

FAMILY **Riley's Farm.** Employees dress in period costumes at this interactive, kid-friendly ranch. Riley's hosts school groups from September to June, and individuals can join the groups by reservation. You can hop on a hayride, take part in a barn dance, pick your own apples, press some cider, or throw a tomahawk while enjoying living-history performances. The farm is also home to Colonial Chesterfield, a replica New England–style estate where costumed 18th-century reenactors offer lessons in cider pressing, candle dipping, colonial games, and etiquette. ✉ *12261 S. Oak Glen Rd.* ☎ *909/797–7534* ⊕ *www.rileysfarm.com* 🖼 *Free to visit ranch, fees vary for activities* ✆ *Closed Mon. and Tues.*

WHERE TO EAT

$ ✕ **Apple Annie's Restaurant and Bakery.** You won't leave hungry from this
AMERICAN country-western diner, popular with locals for its family-style seven-course dinners. Perennial favorites include the Annie deluxe burger and the beefeater melt. **Known for:** hefty meals; 5-pound apple pies; comfortable, rustic decor. $ *Average main: $12* ✉ *38480 Oak Glen Rd.* ☎ *909/797–2311.*

$ ✕ **Law's Oak Glen Coffee Shop.** Since 1953, this old-fashioned coffee
AMERICAN shop has been serving up hot java, hearty breakfasts and lunches, and famous apple pies. Menu stalwarts include meat loaf, country-fried steak, and Reuben sandwiches. **Known for:** apple pie; classic American diner grub; hearty breakfast. $ *Average main: $9* ✉ *38392 Oak Glen Rd.* ☎ *909/797–1642* ⊕ *www.lawsoakglen.com* ✆ *No dinner.*

SAN BERNARDINO MOUNTAINS

One of three transverse mountain ranges that lie in the Inland Empire, the San Bernardino range holds the tallest peak in Southern California, San Gorgonio Mountain, at 11,503 feet. It's frequently snowcapped in winter, providing the region's only challenging ski slopes. In summer the forested hillsides and lakes provide a cool retreat from the city for many locals.

LAKE ARROWHEAD

37 miles northeast of Riverside.

Lake Arrowhead Village is an alpine community with lodgings, shops, outlet stores, and eateries that descend a hill to the lake. Outside the village, access to the lake and its beaches is limited to area residents and their guests.

GETTING HERE AND AROUND

Lake Arrowhead is most easily accessed via Highway 18 off Highway 210's Exit 76. Also called the Rim of the World, Highway 18 straddles a mountainside ledge at elevation 5,000 feet, revealing fabulous views. At the Lake Arrowhead turnoff, Highway 173, you'll descend into a wooded bowl surrounding the lake. The village itself is walkable, but hilly. Highway 173 winding along the east side of the lake offers scenic blue water views through the forest.

ESSENTIALS

Visitor Information Lake Arrowhead Communities Chamber of Commerce. ✉ *28200 Hwy. 189, Suite 207* ☎ *909/337–3715* 🌐 *lakearrowhead.net.*

EXPLORING

Lake Arrowhead Queen. One of the few ways visitors can access Lake Arrowhead is on a 50-minute *Lake Arrowhead Queen* cruise, operated daily from the Lake Arrowhead Village marina. ✉ *28200 Hwy. 189, Bldg. C-100* ☎ *909/336–6992* 🌐 *lakearrowheadqueen.com* 🎫 *$17* ☞ *Purchase tickets at nearby Leroy's Boardshop.*

WHERE TO EAT AND STAY

$ CAFÉ FAMILY

🍴 **Belgian Waffle Works.** This dockside eatery steps from the *Lake Arrowhead Queen* is quaint and homey, with country decor and beautiful lake views. Dive into a mud-pie Belgian waffle with chocolate fudge sauce or try a Belgian s'more with a marshmallow-and-chocolate sauce—burgers, pulled pork sandwiches, tuna melts, chili, meat loaf, chicken dishes, and salads are among the other fare. **Known for:** 17 different waffles; Inland Empire microbrews and Belgian beers; great Lake Arrowhead views from outdoor patio. [$] *Average main: $9* ✉ *28200 Hwy. 189, Suite 150* ☎ *909/337–5222* 🌐 *belgianwaffle.com* ⏲ *No dinner from early Sept.–late May.*

$$$ RESORT FAMILY Fodor's Choice ★

🏨 **Lake Arrowhead Resort and Spa.** This lakeside lodge offers water or forest views from private patios or balconies, and there's a warm and comfy atmosphere throughout thanks to the many fireplaces. **Pros:** beautiful views from most rooms; on-site spa; delicious dining. **Cons:** some rooms have thin walls; some rooms overlook parking lot; some rooms lack balconies. [$] *Rooms from: $189* ✉ *27984 Hwy. 189* ☎ *909/336–1511* 🌐 *www.lakearrowheadresort.com* 🛏 *173 rooms* 🍽 *No meals.*

SPORTS AND THE OUTDOORS
WATERSKIING
McKenzie Waterski School. Summer ski-boat rides and waterskiing and wakeboarding lessons are available through this school in summer. ✉ *28200 Hwy. 189* ☎ *909/337–3814* ⊕ *www.mckenziewaterskischool. com* 🖃 *From $50.*

BIG BEAR LAKE

24 miles east of Lake Arrowhead.

When Angelenos say they're going to the mountains, they usually mean Big Bear, where alpine-style villages surround the 7-mile-long lake. The south shore has ski slopes, the Big Bear Alpine Zoo, water-sports opportunities, restaurants, and lodgings that include Apples Bed & Breakfast Inn. The more serene north shore offers easy to moderate hiking and biking trails, splendid alpine scenery, a fascinating nature center, and the gorgeous Windy Point Inn.

GETTING HERE AND AROUND
Driving is the best way to get to and explore the Big Bear area. But there are alternatives. The Mountain Area Regional Transit Authority (MARTA) provides bus service to and in San Bernardino Mountain communities and connects with Metrolink and Omnitrans.

ESSENTIALS
Bus Contacts Mountain Transit. ☎ *909/878–5200* ⊕ www.mountaintransit.org.

Visitor Information Big Bear Lake Visitors Bureau. ✉ *630 Bartlett Rd., near Big Bear Blvd.* ☎ *800/424–4232* ⊕ www.bigbear.com.

EXPLORING
FAMILY **Alpine Slide at Magic Mountain.** Take a ride down a twisting Olympic-style bobsled course in winter, or beat the summer heat on a dual waterslide at Alpine Slide, which also has an 18-hole miniature golf course and go-karts. ■TIP→ In winter, when snow makes high-elevation roads impassable, taking the lift here affords the best lake views. ✉ *800 Wildrose La., at Big Bear Blvd.* ☎ *909/866–4626* ⊕ *www.alpineslidebigbear.com* 🖃 *$6 single rides, $25 5-ride pass, $30 all-day snow-play pass.*

FAMILY **Big Bear Alpine Zoo.** This rescue and rehabilitation center specializes in animals native to the San Bernardino Mountains. Its residents may include black and (non-native) grizzly bears, bald eagles, coyotes, mountain lions, wolves, and bobcats. A presentation at which guests learn about an individual animal takes place daily at noon, with shorter sessions at 1, 2, and 3. ■TIP→ The zoo is scheduled to move to a nearby location in 2019. Phone or check website for details. ✉ *43285 Goldmine Dr., at Moonridge Rd.* ☎ *909/584–1299* ⊕ *www. bigbearzoo.com* 🖃 *$12.*

FAMILY
Fodor'sChoice
★
Big Bear Discovery Center. At this nature center you can sign up for canoe and kayak tours of Big Bear Lake, a naturalist-led tour of the Baldwin Lake Ecological Reserve in the spring and summer, and winter snowshoe tours. Exhibits here explain the area's flora and fauna, and staffers provide maps and camping and hiking information. ✉ *40971 N. Shore*

7

At 7 miles long, Big Bear Lake is a favorite for Angelenos seeking respite from the city.

Dr. (Hwy. 38), 2½ miles east of town center, Fawnskin ☎ *909/382–2790* ⊕ *www.mountainsfoundation.org/big-bear-discovery-center* 🎫 *Free* ⊘ *Closed Tues. and Wed.*

Big Bear Marina. The paddle wheeler *Big Bear Queen* departs from the marina for 90-minute lake tours. The marina also rents fishing boats, jet skis, kayaks, and canoes. ✉ *500 Paine Ct.* ☎ *909/866–3218* ⊕ *www. bigbearmarina.com* 🎫 *$20* ⊘ *Closed early Sept.–May.*

FAMILY **Time Bandit Pirate Ship.** Featured in the 1981 movie *Time Bandits*, this small-scale replica of a 17th-century English galleon cruises Big Bear Lake. The ship travels along the southern lakeshore to 6,743-foot-high Big Bear Dam; along the way you'll pass big bayfront mansions, some owned by celebrities. A sightseeing excursion with the crew dressed up like pirates, the cruise is popular with kids and adults. There's a bar, but no dining, on board. ✉ *Holloway's Marina and RV Park, 398 Edgemoor Rd.* ☎ *909/878–4040* ⊕ *www.bigbearboating.com/lake-cruise.html* 🎫 *$22* ⊘ *Closed Nov.–Mar.*

WHERE TO EAT

$$$ ✗ **Black Kat Fine Dining & Wine Room.** Floor-to-ceiling murals of vineyards
MODERN and wine cellars decorate this 2017 newcomer whose international wine
AMERICAN selection impresses as much as its seasonal menu. You can stop in for just wine, pair it with a cheese plate or an ahi poke or other small appetizer, or order a full entrée—perhaps delicate Dover sole or a massive rib eye. **Known for:** impressive wine selection; small plates, full meals; upscale casual vibe. 💲 *Average main: $25* ✉ *560 Pine Knot Ave.* ☎ *909/878–0401* ⊕ *www.theblackkat.com.*

$ NEPALESE FAMILY Fodor's Choice ★ 🍴 **Himalayan Restaurant.** It's best to order family style at this no-frills storefront restaurant so that everyone gets a taste of the many Nepalese and Indian delicacies offered. Customer favorites include the spicy *mo-mo* (pot stickers), *daal* (green lentils), lamb and shrimp-curry vindaloo, fish and chicken masala, and clay-oven-roasted tandoori meats and seafood. **Known for:** family-style dining; lamb and shrimp-curry vindaloo; aromatic teas and lemonades. [$] *Average main: $14* ✉ *672 Pine Knot Ave.* ☎ *909/878–3068* 🌐 *www.himalayanbigbear.com.*

$$ AMERICAN 🍴 **Peppercorn Grille.** Filling pizzas, pastas, and steak and fish dishes make this clubby-looking restaurant a fine choice after a long day of skiing in winter or hiking in summer. Start with the signature New England clam chowder (bacon bits add a smoky touch) and follow it up with a salad with the zesty house Peppercorn Ranch dressing before moving on to a flat-iron steak or scallop and shrimp pasta entrée. **Known for:** heated outdoor patio; New England clam chowder; root-beer float desserts. [$] *Average main: $22* ✉ *553 Pine Knot Ave.* ☎ *909/ 866–5405* 🌐 *www.peppercorngrille.com.*

WHERE TO STAY

$$$ B&B/INN 🏨 **Apples Bed & Breakfast Inn.** Despite its location on a busy road to the ski lifts, the inn feels remote and peaceful, thanks to the surrounding pines. **Pros:** large rooms; free snacks and movies; delicious big breakfast. **Cons:** some traffic noise; fussy decor; sometimes feels busy. [$] *Rooms from: $198* ✉ *42430 Moonridge Rd.* ☎ *909/866–0903* 🌐 *www.apples-bigbear.com* 🛏 *21 rooms* 🍽 *Breakfast.*

$$$ B&B/INN Fodor's Choice ★ 🏨 **Gold Mountain Manor.** Each room at this restored 1928 log mansion has its own theme based on a rich Hollywood history: the Clark Gable room, for example, contains the Franklin stove that once warmed the honeymoon suite Gable and actress Carole Lombard shared. **Pros:** romantic setting; gracious hosts; snowshoes and kayaks available. **Cons:** somewhat thin walls; narrow corridors; many stairs. [$] *Rooms from: $179* ✉ *1117 Anita Ave., Big Bear City* ☎ *909/585–6997* 🌐 *www.goldmountainmanor.com* 🛏 *7 rooms* 🍽 *Breakfast; Some meals.*

$$$ HOTEL 🏨 **Lodge at Big Bear Lake.** Resembling a giant log cabin, the four-story Lodge, formerly Northwoods and now run by Holiday Inn's resort division, pays homage to Big Bear's mountain roots with the lobby's antler chandelier and stone fireplace. **Pros:** pool heated in winter; ski packages available; game room for kids. **Cons:** some rooms lack balconies or patios; some noise at night ; rate increases when it snows. [$] *Rooms from: $249* ✉ *40650 Village Dr.* ☎ *909/866–3121, 800/866–3121* 🌐 *www.northwoodsresort.com* 🛏 *140 rooms, 7 suites* 🍽 *No meals.*

SPORTS AND THE OUTDOORS

BOATS AND CHARTERS

Pine Knot Landing Marina. This full-service marina rents fishing boats, pontoon boats, and kayaks and sells bait, ice, and snacks. You can take water skiing lessons here or pick up some Jet Skis and parasailing equipment. On weekends from late April through September, the paddle wheeler *Miss Liberty* leaves from the landing for a 90-minute tour ($22) of Big Bear Lake. Refreshments are available on board. ✉ *439 Pine Knot Blvd.* ☎ *909/866–7766* 🌐 *pineknotmarina.com.*

7

HORSEBACK RIDING

Baldwin Lake Stables. Explore the forested mountain on horseback on a group or private guided trail ride (from an hour to half a day) arranged by this outfit that in summer has a petting zoo for kids and offers pony rides on weekends. ✉ *46475 Pioneertown Rd., Big Bear City* ☎ *909/585–6482* ⊕ *www.baldwinlakestables.com* ☑ *From $50 per hr.*

SKIING

Big Bear Mountain Resorts. Two distinct resorts, Bear Mountain and Snow Summit, comprise Southern California's largest winter playground, one of the few that challenge skilled skiers. The complex offers 438 skiable acres, 55 runs, and 26 chairlifts, including four high-speed quads. The vibe is youthful at Bear, which has beginner slopes (training available) and the after-ski hangout The Scene. Snow Summit holds challenging runs and is open for night skiing. Although lift tickets are valid on both mountains and a shuttle connects the two mountains so you don't have to drive, on weekends and holidays, when the resort is often crowded, it's best to stay on one mountain. Bear rents skis and boards.

The resorts are open in summer for mountain biking, hiking, golfing, and some special events. The Snow Summit Scenic Sky Chair zips to the mountain's 8,200-foot peak, where the Skyline Taphouse ($), a casual outdoor barbecue restaurant, has breathtaking views of the lake and San Gorgonio Mountain. ✉ *Big Bear, 880 Summit Blvd., off Moonridge Rd.* ☎ *844/462–2327* ⊕ *www.bigbearmountainresorts.com* ☑ *$89–$99.*

THE TEMECULA VALLEY

The southern end of the Inland Empire is devoted to the good life. Its most visited destination, Temecula, lying at the base of Mt. San Jacinto, is a popular wine region where you'll find vineyards, tasting rooms, fine dining, and cozy lodgings.

TEMECULA

43 miles south of Riverside, 60 miles north of San Diego, 90 miles southeast of Los Angeles.

Fodor's Choice ★ Temecula, with its rolling green vineyards, country inns, and first-rate restaurants, bills itself as "Southern California Wine Country." The region is home to about four dozen wineries, several of which offer spas, fine dining, or luxury lodging and shopping. Not to be missed are the small, family-run vineyards whose devotion to showcasing Temecula's unique combination of climates and soils—the terroir, as the French call it—results in some impressive wines.

The name Temecula comes from a word Luiseño Indians translate from their native tongue as "place of the sun." The city goes with "where the sun shines through the mist," which also describes ideal conditions for growing wine grapes. Intense afternoon sun and cool nighttime temperatures, complemented by ocean breezes that flow through the Rainbow and Santa Margarita gaps in the coastal range, help grapevines flourish in the area's granite soil. Once best known for Chardonnay, Temecula Valley winemakers are moving in new directions, producing

Rhône varietals like Viognier and Syrah along with Cabernet Sauvignon, Malbec, and other Bordeaux reds.

Most wineries charge from $15 to $25 for a tasting that includes several wines. On its website the Temecula Valley Winegrowers Association offers suggestions for self-guided winery tours and has coupons good for tasting discounts.

GETTING HERE AND AROUND

Interstate 15 cuts right through Temecula. Many wineries can be found on the east side of the freeway along Rancho California Road; with another large grouping on the eastern portion of De Portola Road. Old Town Temecula lies west of the freeway along Front Street.

TOURS

Destination Temecula. Full-day winery tours run by Destination Temecula include stops at three wineries, lunch, and time to explore Old Town Temecula. The company picks up participants in Old Town Temecula and at San Diego and Anaheim hotels. ☎ *951/695–1232* ⊕ *www.destem.com* ✉ *From $129.*

Grapeline Wine Country Shuttle. Enthusiastic local experts lead lively tours of Temecula Valley wineries, including excursions that incorporate insider visits with vintners and catered picnic lunches. Full- and half-day tours (from $95) are offered, with private or shared transportation by luxury SUV, limousine, or coach bus. Participants are picked up at area hotels, in Old Town Temecula, and elsewhere in Southern California. ☎ *951/693–5755, 888/894–6379* ⊕ *www.gogrape.com* ✉ *From $95.*

VISITOR INFORMATION

Temecula Valley Winegrowers Association. ☎ *951/699–3626* ⊕ *www.temeculawines.org.*

Visit Temecula Valley. ✉ *28690 Mercedes St.* ☎ *951/491–6085, 888/363–2852* ⊕ *www.visittemeculavalley.com.*

EXPLORING

TOP ATTRACTIONS

Doffo Winery. This Italian-Argentine wine-making family with a 30-acre property at the Temecula Valley's northeastern edge takes a passionate and quirky approach. Winemaker Damian Doffo and his father, Marcelo, play music for their vines, whose grapes go into small-lot wines, among them a rich Syrah and the signature Malbec, from estate grapes. Tastings of these and other wines take place inside a refurbished garage. The family's racing and vintage motorcycles, which guests can view on free self-guided walking tours, are displayed in an open-air showroom nearby. ✉ *36083 Summitville St.* ☎ *951/676–6989* ⊕ *www.doffowines.com* ✉ *Tastings $20–$30, tour $65.*

Fodor's Choice ★ **Hart Family Winery.** A perennial crowd-pleaser, this winery specializes in well-crafted red wines made by Jim Hart, whose father and mother, Joe and Nancy, started the winery in the 1970s. Syrah, Cabernet Franc, and Cabernet Sauvignon are among the stars, but Hart Family also works with little known varietals like Aleatico, used in a marvelous dessert wine. ✉ *41300 Ave. Biona, off Rancho California Rd.* ☎ *951/676–6300* ⊕ *www.hartfamilywinery.com* ✉ *Tasting $12.*

Miramonte Winery. Temecula's hippest winery sits high on a hilltop. Rhône-style whites (including the Four Torch Blanc blend of Grenache Blanc) and reds like the estate Syrah and Opulente blend of Grenache, Syrah, and Mourvèdre are the strong suits, though the Tempranillo and rosé have their partisans. Taste inside at the casual bar, outside on the deck, perhaps with an artisanal cheese plate. On Friday and Saturday night from 7 to 10, the winery goes into party mode with tastings of wine and beer, live music, and dancing that spills into the vineyards. ✉ *33410 Rancho California Rd.* ☎ *951/506–5500* ⊕ *www.miramontewinery.com* 🍷 *Tastings $17–$20, tours $75 (reservations required).*

Old Town Temecula. For a bit of old-fashioned fun, head to Old Town Temecula, where turn-of-the-20th-century-style storefronts and boardwalks extend for 12 blocks. Along with dozens of restaurants and boutiques, there are antiques stores, tasting rooms, hip brewpubs, a performing arts center and jazz club, and art galleries. ✉ *Front St., between Rancho California Rd. and Hwy. 79* ☎ *888/363–2852* ⊕ *www.visittemeculavalley.com.*

FAMILY **Pennypickle's Workshop — Temecula Children's Museum.** If you have the kids along, check out the fictional 7,500-square-foot workshop of Professor Phineas T. Pennypickle, PhD. This elaborately decorated children's museum is filled with secret passageways, machines, wacky contraptions, and time-travel inventions. ■**TIP**→ Take one of the two-hour tours offered daily to get the most out of your visit. ✉ *42081 Main St.* ☎ *951/308–6376* ⊕ *www.pennypickles.org* 🍷 *$5* ☉ *Closed Mon.*

Ponte Family Estates. Lush gardens and more than 300 acres of vineyards provide a rustic, elegant setting at Ponte, whose small-lot bottlings range from sparkling wines and light whites to very fine Cabernet Sauvignon and Malbec reds. Another favorite in the light-filled tasting room is the flagship Super T wine, a Cabernet Sauvignon–Sangiovese blend. To find out how the wines are made, take the Premium Tour ($85) by electric bus of the vineyards and production facility. The tour (reservation required) concludes with a wine and cheese tasting. The shaded outdoor Restaurant at Ponte serves salads, wood-fired pizzas, and seafood daily for lunch, and on Friday and Saturday for dinner. ✉ *35053 Rancho California Rd.* ☎ *951/694–8855* ⊕ *www.pontewinery.com* 🍷 *Tasting $20, tours $40–$85* ☉ *No dinner Sun.–Thurs.*

WORTH NOTING

Callaway Vineyard and Winery. One of Temecula's oldest wineries is centered on a stunning steel-and-glass cube with vineyard views all around. Callaway made its reputation with Chardonnay, but these days is also known for Roussanne, Viognier, Cabernet Sauvignon, and Syrah. The winery's Meritage Restaurant specializes in tapas, salads, and sandwiches. ✉ *32720 Rancho California Rd.* ☎ *951/676–4001* ⊕ *www.callawaywinery.com* 🍷 *Tasting $20; tour and tasting $25.*

Europa Village. Though all of this luxury wine resort's dining, lodging, winery, and other components won't be completed for a few years, a pleasant tasting room here serves wines made from French, Spanish, and Italian varietals. The selections range from Vermentino, Albariño, and other light whites to reds like Syrah and Primitivo. Winemaker dinners take place in the village, which also presents live music on some weekend nights. ✉ *33475 La Serena Way, off Rancho California Rd.* ☎ *888/383–8767* ⊕ *www.europavillage.com* 🍷 *Tasting $15.*

Leoness Cellars. Bordeaux and Rhône blends are the specialties of this 20-acre hilltop estate with magnificent views of Cabernet Sauvignon vines. If it's available, try the winemaker's pride and joy, the Mélange de Reves (Blend of Dreams), made from the traditional Rhône combo of Grenache, Syrah, and Mourvèdre. Winery tours take in the vineyards and the wine-making areas. The tours require a reservation, as do wine-and-food pairing sessions that might include fruits and cheeses or, in the case of dessert wines, chocolates. Leoness's popular French-inspired restaurant is open from Friday through Sunday. ✉ *38311 De Portola Rd.* ☎ *951/302–7601* ⊕ *www.leonesscellars.com* 🍷 *Tasting $16–$20; tours with tasting $30–$125.*

Mount Palomar Winery. One of the original Temecula Valley wineries, opened in 1969, Mount Palomar introduced Sangiovese, a varietal that has proven perfectly suited to the region's soil and climate. New owners have transformed the homey winery into a grand Mediterranean villa with acres of gardens and trees. The Sangiovese is worth a try, as are the Solera Cream Sherry (ask how it's made) and the popular Cloudbreak, an inky red blend with a Petit Verdot base. Annata Bistro/Bar, open daily for lunch and dinner, presents live entertainment on Friday night. ✉ *33820 Rancho California Rd.* ☎ *951/676–5047* ⊕ *www.mountpalomar.com* 🍷 *Tastings $16 Mon.–Thurs., $20 Fri.– Sun.*

Temecula Valley Museum. A good introduction to Temecula, this two-story museum on the edge of Old Town focuses on the valley's role in California's history, from the early days of the Luiseño Indians and the mission and cattle-ranching periods to the present era of wine making and tourism. A permanent second-floor exhibit is devoted to Erle Stanley Gardner, the prolific author of the Perry Mason mysteries and a longtime Temecula resident. ✉ *28314 Mercedes St.* ☎ *951/694–6450* ⊕ *temeculavalleymuseum.org* 🍷 *$5* ⊘ *Closed Sun. and Mon.*

Wiens Family Cellars. A winery on the rise, Wiens promotes its "Big Reds"—among them the Reserve Primitivo and a Tempranillo–Petite Sirah blend—but many visitors often wind up taking home a bottle of the perky-fruity Amour De L'Orange sparkling wine. Other wines of note include the Ruby Port and the Dulce Maria, made from Chardonnay and Muscat Canelli grapes. The ambience at Wiens is informal, but the cordial tasting-room staffers are well informed about the wines they enthusiastically pour. ✉ *35055 Via Del Ponte* ☎ *951/694–9892* ⊕ *www.wienscellars.com* 🍷 *Tasting $20.*

Wilson Creek Winery & Vineyards. One of Temecula's busiest tasting rooms sits amid inviting, parklike grounds. Wilson is known for its Almond Champagne, but the winery also produces appealing still wines. Among these the Petite Sirah, Viognier, reserve Syrah, reserve Zinfandel, and late-harvest Zinfandel all merit a taste. The on-site gluten-free Creekside Grill Restaurant serves sandwiches, salads, vegetable potpie, and seasonal entrées such as Mexican white sea bass. Dine inside or select a picnic spot, and the servers will deliver your meal to you. Nine guest rooms are available for overnight stays. ✉ *35960 Rancho California Rd.* ☎ *951/699–9463* 🌐 *www.wilsoncreekwinery.com* 🎫 *Tasting $20.*

WHERE TO EAT AND STAY

$$$ CONTEMPORARY 🍴 **Café Champagne.** With its bubbling fountain, flowering trellises, and vineyard views, the spacious patio at Thornton Winery's café is the perfect place to lunch on a sunny day. The kitchen, which faces the French-country–style dining room, turns out pan-seared New York steak, chicken with pesto risotto, sandwiches, and other hearty fare. **Known for:** bacon cheeseburger and New York steak sandwich; Sunday brunch; live music on Friday night. [$] *Average main: $24* ✉ *Thornton Winery, 32575 Rancho California Rd.* ☎ *951/699–0099* 🌐 *www.thorntonwine.com.*

$$$ MEDITERRANEAN 🍴 **Meritage Restaurant at Callaway Vineyards.** Impressively prepared cuisine and stunning Temecula Valley views from a shaded terrace make a visit to the restaurant at Callaway winery a memorable occasion. Pomegranate *pico de gallo* (salsa), radish and ginger vinaigrette, and other inventive flourishes add piquancy and pep to the mostly Mediterranean dishes, which include tapas made from slow-roasted meats and fresh seafood. **Known for:** stunning valley views; tapas from slow-roasted meats and fresh seafood; wines and craft beers. [$] *Average main: $25* ✉ *32720 Rancho California Rd., east of Butterfield Stage Rd.* ☎ *951/587–8889* 🌐 *www.callawaywinery.com* 🕒 *No dinner Mon.–Thurs.*

$$ MODERN AMERICAN 🍴 **1909.** Superb cocktails and craft-beer samplers, a something-for-everyone menu, and the always swingin' streetside patio have made this gastropub one of Old Town's jolliest hangouts. Starters like blue corn Kobe beef hot dogs, smoked chicken wings, and crab and shrimp empanadas pair well with the drinks; standout mains include the 1909 burger (love the bacon-onion jam) and braised lamb shank. **Known for:** superb cocktails; streetside patio; popular weekend brunch. [$] *Average main: $19* ✉ *28656 Front St.* ☎ *951/619–1909* 🌐 *www.1909temecula.com.*

$$ MODERN AMERICAN FAMILY 🍴 **Public House.** A low-key gastropub inside a restored 1950s home, this Old Town spot with a sunlit patio hosts live music on weekends. A roasted 16-ounce New York steak over mashed potatoes satisfies carnivores; and the mixed arugula and quinoa with roasted red beet and goat cheese is a hit with those seeking more healthful fare. **Known for:** low-key vibe; diverse menu items; Southern California craft beers. [$] *Average main: $21* ✉ *41971 Main St.* ☎ *951/676–7305* 🌐 *www.publicrestaurants.com/public-house-temecula.*

$$$ HOTEL 🏨 **Ponte Vineyard Inn.** Slow down in old Californio Rancho style at this hotel on the grounds of the Ponte Family Estate winery. **Pros:** huge rooms; excellent winery on-site; gracious service. **Cons:** many weddings; can feel remote; pets not allowed. [$] *Rooms from: $200* ✉ *35001 Rancho California Rd.* ☎ *951/587–6688* 🌐 *www.pontevineyardinn.com* 🛏 *60 rooms* 🍽 *No meals.*

$$$ RESORT 🏨 **South Coast Winery Resort and Spa.** Spacious vineyard villas, an all-suites hotel, an excellent restaurant, a spa with a saltwater pool, and a working winery—South Coast blends these elements into one luxurious, harmonious location. **Pros:** good wine-country location; quiet, private

villas; beautiful grounds. **Cons:** can be very busy; many weddings; two-night minimum much of the year. [$] *Rooms from: $199* ✉ *34843 Rancho California Rd.* ☎ *951/587–9463* 🌐 *www.wineresort.com* 🛏 *132 rooms* 🍴 *No meals.*

$$$ RESORT 🏨 **Temecula Creek Inn.** Most of the rooms at this property that sprawls over 360 acres have private patios or balconies overlooking the championship golf course. **Pros:** beautiful grounds; top golf course; course views from most rooms. **Cons:** nongolfers may feel out of place; often busy; location away from Old Town and wineries. [$] *Rooms from: $209* ✉ *44501 Rainbow Canyon Rd.* ☎ *951/694–1000, 888/976–3404* 🌐 *www.temeculacreekinn.com* ⛳ *Green fees $80–$100, 27 holes, 6800 yards, par 36* 🛏 *130 rooms* 🍴 *No meals.*

NIGHTLIFE

Old Town Temecula Community Theater. An entertainment complex that holds two venues, the Old Town Theater offers a full season of performances ranging from classical ballet and symphonies to jazz. The Temecula Valley Players offer Broadway musicals through June. At the adjacent, intimate Merc theater you can hear small jazz and country groups. ✉ *42051 Main St.* ☎ *866/653–8696* 🌐 *www.temeculatheater.org.*

Pechanga Resort and Casino. Casino gambling is the main attraction here, and there are several entertainment venues. Headliners such as Paul Anka, Jill Scott, and Jerry Seinfeld have appeared at the Pechanga Theater; the intimate Comedy Club books up-and-coming talent. HBO and Fox Sports championship boxing matches draw thousands of fans. The largest Indian casino in California, Pechanga has a 517-room hotel, a golf course, a spa, and an RV park. ✉ *45000 Pechanga Pkwy.* ☎ *888/732–4264, 951/770–1819* 🌐 *www.pechanga.com.*

SPORTS AND THE OUTDOORS

GOLF

Temecula has several championship golf courses cooled by the valley's ocean breezes.

The Legends Golf Club. The tiered greens, five lakes, and many blind spots make for challenging rounds at this club's Ted Robinson–designed championship course. ✉ *41687 Temeku Dr.* ☎ *951/694–9998* 🌐 *thelegendsgc.com* 🎟 *$49–$65* ⛳ *18 holes, 6636 yards, par 72.*

Redhawk Golf Club. Considered one of the best 18-hole public golf courses in California, the Ron Fream–designed championship golf course is designed to take advantage of Temecula's tree-studded rolling hills set against craggy mountains. Watch out for wind, doglegs, skinny sand traps, and tiered greens. Rico's Cantina here offers Mexican and Southwestern items for breakfast and lunch. ✉ *45100 Redhawk Pkwy.* ☎ *951/302–3850* 🌐 *www.redhawkgolfcourse.com* 🎟 *$44–$62* ⛳ *18 holes, 7110 yards, par 72.*

Temecula Creek Inn Golf Resort. Ted Robinson and Dick Rossen designed this Wine Country resort's three picturesque nine-hole courses. Stonehouse, the most challenging one, demands precise tee shots. ✉ *44501 Rainbow Canyon Rd.* ☎ *951/676–2405* 🌐 *www.temeculacreekinn.com* 🎟 *$80 weekdays; $100 weekends* ⛳ *Creek: 9 holes, 3348 yards, par 36; Oaks: 9 holes, 3436 yards, par 36; Stonehouse: 9 holes, 3257 yards, par 36.*

7

HOT-AIR BALLOONING

California Dreamin'. Float serenely above Temecula's vineyards and country estates on an early-morning balloon adventure. The ride includes champagne, coffee, a pastry breakfast, and a souvenir photo. ✉ *Flights depart from La Vindemia Vineyard, 33133 Vista Del Monte Rd.* ☎ *800/373–3359* ⊕ *www.californiadreamin.com* ✉ *$148 weekdays and Sun., Sat. $178.*

FAMILY **Balloon and Wine Festival.** This festival at Lake Skinner each June consists of three days of partying, wine and food tastings, live entertainment, vendors, and early-morning balloon ascensions. Many kids' activities are scheduled. Camping is popular; there are 400 sites at the lake, including RV sites nearby. ✉ *37701 Warren Rd.* ☎ *951/676–6713* ⊕ *www.tvbwf. com* ✉ *$23–$33 1-day pass, $60 3-day pass; tasting extra.*

SHOPPING

Rancho Fruit Market. This cheerful little shop sells honey, "uglies" (shrivel-skinned but deliciously sweet tangerines), and other locally sourced produce. Much of it is organic, and the prices are reasonable. Sweet tooths head straight for the chocolate-dipped fruit and caramel apples. ✉ *28670 Old Town Front St.* ☎ *951/676–5519.*

Temecula Lavender Co. Owner Jan Schneider offers an inspiring collection of the herb that fosters peace, purification, sleep, and longevity. Bath salts, hand soaps, essential oil, even dryer bags to freshen up the laundry—she's got it all. ✉ *28561 Old Town Front St.* ☎ *951/676–1931* ⊕ *www.temeculalavenderco.com.*

Temecula Olive Oil Company. While you're shopping in Old Town, stop by the cool tasting room here for a sample of extra-virgin olive oils, flavored balsamic vinegars and sea salts, bath products, and Mission, Ascalano, and Italian olives. Guided tours of the ranch where the olives are grown are available. ✉ *28653 Old Town Front St., Suite H* ☎ *951/693–4029* ⊕ *www.temeculaoliveoil.com.*

PALM SPRINGS

WELCOME TO PALM SPRINGS

TOP REASONS TO GO

★ **Year-round sunshine:** The Palm Springs area has 350 days of sun each year, and the weather is usually ideal for playing one of the area's more than 100 golf courses.

★ **Spa under the stars:** Many resorts and small hotels now offer after-dark spa services, including outdoor soaks and treatments you can savor while sipping wine under the clear, starry sky.

★ **Personal pampering:** The resorts here have it all, beautifully appointed rooms packed with amenities, professional staffs, sublime spas, and delicious dining options.

★ **Divine desert scenery:** You'll probably spend a lot of time taking in the gorgeous 360-degree natural panorama, a flat desert floor surrounded by 10,000-foot mountains rising into a brilliant blue sky.

★ **The Hollywood connection:** The Palm Springs area has more celebrity ties than any other resort community. So keep your eyes open for your favorite star.

1 Palm Springs. A hideaway for celebrities, artists, politicians, and sports personalities since the mid-century, Palm Springs retains the luster of its golden era. Most visitors spend their days lounging poolside at a posh resort or an artsy inn, enjoying a well-crafted meal at an upscale restaurant, or shopping for treasures at the Uptown Design District before heading back to sip martinis under the stars.

2 The Desert Resorts. East of Palm Springs on Highway 111 lie several towns, each containing strip malls, gated communities, and huge resort complexes. Palm Desert is the Coachella Valley's answer to Rodeo Drive in Beverly Hills, with walkable downtown dining options aplenty. The golfing havens of Rancho Mirage, Indian Wells, and La Quinta cater to moneyed outdoor types.

3 Along Twentynine Palms Highway. The towns of Yucca Valley, Joshua Tree, and Twentynine Palms punctuate Twentynine Palms Highway (Highway 62)—the northern highway from the desert resorts to Joshua Tree National Park—and provide visitor information, lodging, and other services to park visitors.

4 Anza-Borrego Desert. If you're looking for a break from the action, you'll find solitude and solace in this 600,000-acre desert landscape.

GETTING ORIENTED

The Palm Springs resort area lies within the Colorado Desert, on the western edge of the Coachella Valley. The area holds seven cities that are strung out along Highway 111, with Palm Springs at the northwestern end of the strip and Indio at the southeastern end. North of Palm Springs, between Interstate 10 and Highway 62, is Desert Hot Springs. Northeast of Palm Springs, the towns of the Morongo Valley lie along Twentynine Palms Highway (Highway 62), which leads to Joshua Tree National Park. Head south on Highway 86 from Indio to reach Anza-Borrego Desert State Park and the Salton Sea. All of the area's attractions are easy day trips from Palm Springs.

8

Updated
by Cheryl
Crabtree

With the Palm Springs area's year-round sunshine, luxurious spas, chef-driven restaurants, and see-and-be-seen pool parties, it's no wonder that Hollywood A-listers and weekend warriors make the desert a getaway. Stretching south and east of the city along Highway 111, the desert resort towns—Cathedral City, Rancho Mirage, Palm Desert, Indian Wells, La Quinta, and Indio, along with Desert Hot Springs to the north—teem with resorts, golf courses, and shopping centers. Yucca Valley, Joshua Tree, and other artistic communities lie farther north and northeast. To the south, the wildflowers of Anza-Borrego Desert State Park herald the arrival of spring.

The Palm Springs area has long been a playground for the celebrity elite. In the 1920s Al Capone opened the Two Bunch Palms Hotel in Desert Hot Springs (with multiple tunnels to help him avoid the police); Marilyn Monroe was discovered poolside in the late 1940s at a downtown Palm Springs tennis club; Elvis and Priscilla Presley honeymooned here—the list goes on.

Over the years the desert arts scene has blossomed as spectacularly as the wildflowers of Anza-Borrego. Downtown Palm Springs is laden with urban-chic contemporary artwork (check out the Backstreet Arts District), but the surrounding rural areas are also artist enclaves: Yucca Valley, Joshua Tree, Pioneertown, and Twentynine Palms all have noteworthy galleries, art installations, and natural scenic views. Each April attention centers on Indio, where the Coachella Valley Music and Arts Festival, California's largest outdoor concert, culls droves of Angelenos, and music lovers from all over the world.

PLANNING

WHEN TO GO

Desert weather is best between January and April, the height of the visitor season. The fall months are nearly as lovely, but less crowded and less expensive (although autumn draws many conventions and business travelers). In summer, a popular time with European visitors, daytime temperatures may rise above 110°F (though evenings cool to the mid-70s); some attractions and restaurants close or reduce their hours during this time.

GETTING HERE AND AROUND

AIR TRAVEL

Palm Springs International Airport serves California's desert communities. Air Canada, Alaska, Allegiant, American, Delta, JetBlue, Sun Country, United, Virgin America, and WestJet all fly to Palm Springs, some only seasonally. Yellow Cab of the Desert serves the airport, which is about 3 miles from downtown. The fare is $3 to enter the cab and about $3.12 per mile.

Airport Information Palm Springs International Airport. ✉ *3200 E. Tahquitz Canyon Way, Palm Springs* ☎ *760/320–3882 info line, 760/318–3800* ⊕ *www.palmspringsairport.com.*

Airport Transfers Yellow Cab of the Desert. ✉ *75150 St. Charles Pl., Palm Desert* ☎ *760/340–8294* ⊕ *www.yellowcabofthedesert.com.*

BUS TRAVEL

Greyhound provides service to Palm Springs from many cities. SunBus, operated by the SunLine Transit Agency, serves the entire Coachella Valley, from Desert Hot Springs to Mecca.

Bus Contacts Greyhound. ☎ *800/231–2222* ⊕ *www.greyhound.com.*
SunLine Transit Agency. ☎ *800/347–8628* ⊕ *www.sunline.org.*

CAR TRAVEL

The desert resort communities occupy a 20-mile stretch between Interstate 10 to the east, and Palm Canyon Drive (Highway 111), to the west. The region is about a two-hour drive east of the Los Angeles area and a three-hour drive northeast of San Diego. It can take twice as long to make the trip from Los Angeles to the desert on winter and spring weekends because of heavy traffic. From Los Angeles take the San Bernardino Freeway (Interstate 10) east to Highway 111. From San Diego, Interstate 15 heading north connects with the Pomona Freeway (Highway 60), leading to the San Bernardino Freeway east.

To reach Borrego Springs from Los Angeles, take Interstate 10 east past the desert resorts area to Highway 86 south to the Borrego Salton Seaway (Highway S22) west. You can reach the Borrego area from San Diego via Interstate 8 to Highway 79 through Cuyamaca State Park. This will take you to Highway 78 in Julian, which you follow east to Yaqui Pass Road (S3) into Borrego Springs.

TAXI TRAVEL

Yellow Cab of the Desert serves the entire Coachella Valley. The fare is $3 to enter a cab and about $3 per mile.

TRAIN TRAVEL

The Amtrak Sunset Limited, which runs between Florida and Los Angeles, stops in Palm Springs.

Train Contact Amtrak. ☎ 800/872–7245 ⊕ www.amtrakcalifornia.com.

HEALTH AND SAFETY

Never travel alone in the desert. Let someone know your trip route, destination, and estimated time and date of return. Before setting out, make sure your vehicle is in good condition. Stay on main roads, and watch out for horses and range cattle.

Drink at least a gallon of water a day (three gallons if you're hiking or otherwise exerting yourself). Dress in layered clothing and wear comfortable, sturdy shoes and a hat. Keep snacks, sunscreen, and a first-aid kit on hand. If you suddenly have a headache or feel dizzy or nauseous, you could be suffering from dehydration. Get out of the sun immediately and drink plenty of water. Dampen your clothing to lower your body temperature.

Do not enter mine tunnels or shafts. Avoid canyons during rainstorms. Never place your hands or feet where you can't see them: rattlesnakes, scorpions, and black widow spiders may be hiding there.

TOURS

Art in Public Places. Several self-guided tours cover the works in Palm Desert's 150-piece Art in Public Places collection. Each tour is walkable or drivable. Maps and information about guided tours (one Saturday each month) are available at the city's visitor center and online. ⊠ *Palm Desert Visitor Center, 73510 Fred Waring Dr., Palm Desert* ☎ *760/568– 1441* ⊕ *www.palm-desert.org/arts-entertainment/public-art* ⊠ *Free.*

Best of the Best Tours. One of the valley's largest outfits leads tours into Andreas Canyon, along the celebrity circuit, or to view windmills up close. ☎ *760/320–1365* ⊕ *www.thebestofthebesttours.com* ⊠ *From $40.*

Big Wheel Bike Tours. This outfit delivers rental mountain, three-speed, and tandem bikes to area hotels. The company also conducts full- and half-day escorted on- and off-road bike tours, and also offers hiking and jeep tours to Joshua Tree National Park and the San Andreas Fault. Guides are first-rate. ⊠ *Palm Springs* ☎ *760/779–1837* ⊕ *www.bwb-tours.com* ⊠ *$105 per person.*

Desert Adventures. This outfit's two- to four-hour jeep, SUV, or van tours explore Joshua Tree National Park, Indian Canyon, Mecca Hills Painted Canyons, and the San Andreas Fault. The groups are small and the guides are knowledgeable. Departures are from Palm Springs and/or La Quinta; hotel pickups are available. ☎ *760/324–5337* ⊕ *www.red-jeep. com* ⊠ *From $79.*

Trail Discovery Hiking Tours. For more than two decades, this outfit has been guiding hikers of all abilities through the desert canyons of the Palm Springs area. Tours include Joshua Tree National Park, Indian Canyons, San Jacinto State Park, and sections of the Pacific Crest Trail. ☎ *760/413–1575* ⊕ *www.palmspringshiking.com* ⊠ *From $75.*

RESTAURANTS

An influx of talented chefs has expanded the dining possibilities of a formerly staid scene. The meat-and-potatoes crowd still has plenty of options, but you'll also find fresh seafood superbly prepared and contemporary Californian, Asian, Indian, and vegetarian cuisine, and Mexican food abounds. Most restaurants have early-evening happy hours, with discounted drinks and small-plate menus. Restaurants that remain open in July and August frequently discount deeply; others close in July and August or offer limited service. *Restaurant reviews have been shortened. For full information, visit Fodors.com.*

HOTELS

In general you can find the widest choice of lodgings in Palm Springs, from tiny bed-and-breakfasts and chain motels to business and resort hotels. Massive resort properties predominate in down-valley communities, such as Palm Desert and Rancho Mirage. You can stay in the desert for as little as $100, or splurge for luxury digs at more than $1,000 a night. Rates vary widely by season and expected occupancy—a $200 room midweek can jump in price to $450 on Saturday.

Hotel and resort prices are frequently 50% cheaper in summer and fall than in winter and early spring. From January through May prices soar, and lodgings book up far in advance. You should book well ahead for stays during events such as Modernism Week or the Coachella and Stagecoach music festivals.

Most resort hotels charge a daily fee of up to $40 that is not included in the room rate; be sure to ask about extra fees when you book. Many hotels are pet-friendly and offer special services, though these also come with additional fees. Small boutique hotels and bed-and-breakfasts have plenty of character and are popular with hipsters and artsy types; discounts are sometimes given for extended stays. Casino hotels often offer good deals on lodging. Take care, though, when considering budget lodgings; other than reliable chains, they may not be up to par. *Hotel reviews have been shortened. For full information, visit Fodors.com.*

WHAT IT COSTS				
	$	$$	$$$	$$$$
Restaurants	under $16	$16–$22	$23–$30	over $30
Hotels	under $120	$120–$175	$176–$250	over $250

Restaurant prices are the average cost of a main course at dinner or, if dinner is not served, at lunch. Hotel prices are the lowest cost of a standard double room in high season.

NIGHTLIFE

Desert nightlife is concentrated and abundant in Palm Springs, with plenty of bars and clubs, but the action centers on hotel bars and lively pool parties. Arts festivals occur on a regular basis, especially in winter and spring. *Palm Springs Life* magazine (⊕ *www.palmspringslife.com*), available at hotels and visitor centers, has nightlife listings, as does the *Desert Sun* newspaper (⊕ *www.mydesert.com*).

PALM SPRINGS

A tourist destination since the late 19th century, Palm Springs evolved into an ideal hideaway for early Hollywood celebrities who slipped into town to play tennis, lounge poolside, attend a party or two, and unless things got out of hand, steer clear of gossip columnists. But the area blossomed in the 1930s after actors Charlie Farrell and Ralph Bellamy bought 200 acres of land for $30 an acre and opened the Palm Springs Racquet Club, which soon listed Ginger Rogers, Humphrey Bogart, and Clark Gable among its members.

Today, Palm Springs is embracing its glory days. Owners of resorts, bed-and-breakfasts, and galleries have renovated mid-century modern buildings, luring a new crop of celebs and high-powered executives. LGBTQ travelers, twentysomethings, and families also sojourn here. Pleasantly touristy Palm Canyon Drive is packed with alfresco restaurants, many with views of the bustling sidewalk, along with indoor cafés and semi-chic shops. Farther west is the Uptown Design District, the area's shopping and dining destination. Continuing east on Palm Canyon Drive just outside downtown lie resorts and boutique hotels that host lively pool parties and house exclusive dining establishments and trendy bars.

GETTING HERE AND AROUND

Palm Springs is 90 miles southeast of Los Angeles on Interstate 10. Most visitors arrive in the Palm Springs area by car from the Los Angeles or San Diego area via this freeway, which intersects with Highway 111 north of Palm Springs. Tahquitz Canyon Way marks the division between north and south on major streets (e.g., North and South Palm Canyon Drive). Once in Palm Springs, take advantage of the free Palm Springs Buzz, an air-conditioned pet-friendly trolley that loops around town Thursday through Sunday every 15 minutes from Via Escuela to Smoketree (⊕ *buzzps.com*).

ESSENTIALS

Visitor Information Greater Palm Springs Convention and Visitors Bureau. ⊠ *Visitor Center, 70–100 Hwy. 111, at Via Florencia, Rancho Mirage* ☎ *760/770–9000, 800/967–3767* ⊕ *www.visitgreaterpalmsprings.com.* **Palm Springs Visitors Center Downtown.** ⊠ *100 S. Palm Canyon Dr.* ✛ *In Welwood Murray Memorial Library* ☎ *760/323–8296* ⊕ *www.visitpalmsprings.com.* **Palm Springs Visitors Center North.** ⊠ *2901 N. Palm Canyon Dr.* ☎ *760/778–8418, 800/347–7746* ⊕ *www.visitpalmsprings.com.*

EXPLORING

TOP ATTRACTIONS

Elvis's Honeymoon Hideaway. The hideaway of the King of rock 'n' roll and his young bride, Priscilla, during their first year of marriage, this house perches on a hilltop abutting the San Jacinto Mountains. A stunning example of local mid-century modern architecture, it is rich in Elvis lore, photos, and furnishings. Docents describe the fabulous parties that took place here, attended by celebrities and local legends. Built in 1962 by Robert Alexander, one of Palm Spring's largest developers,

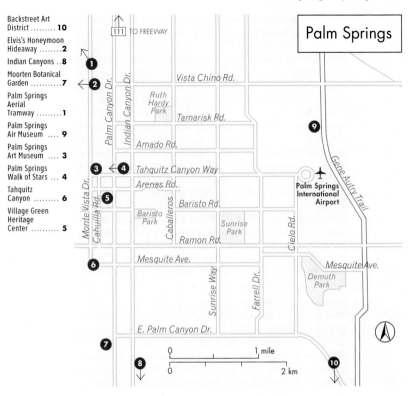

Palm Springs

the house consists of four perfect circles, each set on a different level. At the time, *Look* magazine described the structure as the "house of tomorrow," and indeed many of its features are standard in the homes of today. ✉ *1350 Ladera Circle* ☎ *760/322–1192* ⊕ *www.elvishoney-moon.com* ✉ *$30.*

FAMILY

Fodor's Choice
★

Indian Canyons. The Indian Canyons are the ancestral home of the Agua Caliente, part of the Cahuilla people. You can see remnants of their ancient life, including rock art, house pits and foundations, irrigation ditches, bedrock mortars, pictographs, and stone houses and shelters atop cliff walls. Short easy walks through the canyons reveal palm oases, waterfalls, and, in spring, wildflowers. Tree-shaded picnic areas are abundant. The attraction includes three canyons open for touring: Palm Canyon, noted for its stand of Washingtonia palms; Murray Canyon, home of Peninsula bighorn sheep and a herd of wild ponies; and Andreas Canyon, where a stand of fan palms contrasts with sharp rock formations. Ranger-led hikes to Palm and Andreas canyons are offered daily for an additional charge. The trading post at the entrance to Palm Canyon has hiking maps and refreshments, as well as Native American art, jewelry, and weaving. ✉ *38520 S. Palm Canyon Dr., south of Acanto Dr.* ☎ *760/323–6018* ⊕ *www.indian-canyons.com* ✉ *$9, ranger hikes $3* ⊙ *Closed Mon.–Thurs. July–Sept.*

FAMILY
Fodor's Choice
★
Palm Springs Aerial Tramway. A trip on the tramway provides a 360-degree view of the desert through the picture windows of rotating cars. The 2½-mile ascent through Chino Canyon, the steepest vertical cable ride in the United States, brings you to an elevation of 8,516 feet in less than 20 minutes. On clear days, which are common, the view stretches 75 miles—from the peak of Mt. San Gorgonio in the north to the Salton Sea in the southeast. Stepping out into the snow at the summit is a winter treat. At the top, a bit below the summit of Mt. San Jacinto, are several diversions. Mountain Station has an observation deck, two restaurants, a cocktail lounge, apparel and gift shops, picnic facilities, a small wildlife exhibit, and a theater that screens movies on the history of the tramway and the adjacent Mount San Jacinto State Park and Wilderness. Take advantage of free guided and self-guided nature walks through the state park, or if there's snow on the ground, rent skis, snowshoes, or snow tubes. The tramway generally closes for maintenance in mid-September. ■TIP→ Ride-and-dine packages are available in late afternoon. The tram is a popular attraction; to avoid a two-hour or longer wait, arrive before the first car leaves in the morning. ⊠ *1 Tramway Rd., off N. Palm Canyon Dr. (Hwy. 111)* ☎ *888/515–8726* ⊕ *www. pstramway.com* ⊠ *$25.95, ride-and-dine package $36* ۞ *Closed 2 wks in Sept. for maintenance.*

FAMILY
Fodor's Choice
★
Palm Springs Air Museum. This museum's impressive collection of World War II aircraft includes a B-17 Flying Fortress bomber, a P-51 Mustang, a Lockheed P-38, and a Grumman TBF Avenger. Among the cool exhibits are model warships, a Pearl Harbor diorama, and a Grumman Goose into which kids can crawl. Photos, artifacts, memorabilia, and uniforms are also on display, and educational programs take place on Saturday. Flight demonstrations are scheduled regularly. Biplane rides are offered on Saturday. ⊠ *745 N. Gene Autry Trail* ☎ *760/778–6262* ⊕ *palmspringsairmuseum.org* ⊠ *$16.50.*

Palm Springs Art Museum. This world-class art museum focuses on photography, modern architecture, and the traditional arts of the Americas. Galleries are bright and open. The permanent collection includes shimmering works in glass by Dale Chihuly, Ginny Ruffner, and William Morris. You'll also find handcrafted furniture by the late actor George Montgomery, mid-century modern architectural photos by Julius Shulman, enormous Native American baskets, and works by artists like Allen Houser, Arlo Namingha, and Fritz Scholder. The museum also displays significant works of 20th-century sculpture by Henry Moore, Marino Marina, Deborah Butterfield, and Mark Di Suvero. The Annenberg Theater presents plays, concerts, lectures, operas, and other cultural events. ⊠ *101 Museum Dr., off W. Tahquitz Canyon Dr.* ☎ *760/322–4800* ⊕ *www.psmuseum.org* ⊠ *$12.50, free Thurs. 4–8 during Villagefest* ۞ *Closed Wed.*

Tahquitz Canyon. On ranger-led tours of this secluded canyon on the Agua Caliente Reservation you can view a spectacular 60-foot waterfall, rock art, ancient irrigation systems, and native wildlife and plants. Tours are conducted several times daily; participants must be able to navigate 100 steep rock steps. (You can also take a self-guided tour of the 1.8-mile trail.) At the visitor center at the canyon entrance, watch a short video, look at artifacts, and pick up a map. ✉ *500 W. Mesquite Ave., west of S. Palm Canyon Dr.* ☎ *760/416–7044* 🌐 *www.tahquitzcanyon.com* 🎟 *$12.50* 🕒 *Closed Mon.–Thurs. July–Sept.*

WORTH NOTING

Backstreet Art District. Galleries and live-work studios just off East Canyon Drive showcase the works of a number of highly acclaimed artists. Painter and ceramicist Linda Maxson, fine artist Chris Hoffman at Fusion Art Gallery, and new and emerging artists at Rebel Art Space are among the stars here. **■ TIP→ On the first Wednesday evening of the month, the galleries are open from 5 to 8.** ✉ *2600 S. Cherokee Way* 🌐 *www.backstreetartdistrict.com* 🎟 *Free* 🕒 *Most galleries closed Mon. and Tues.*

Moorten Botanical Garden. In the 1920s, Chester "Cactus Slim" Moorten and his wife Patricia opened this showpiece for desert plants—now numbering in the thousands—that include an ocotillo, a massive elephant tree, a boojum tree, and vine cacti. Their son Clark now operates the garden. **■ TIP→ Take a stroll through the Cactarium to spot rare finds such as the welwitschia, which originated in the Namib Desert in southwestern Africa.** ✉ *1701 S. Palm Canyon Dr.* ☎ *760/327–6555* 🌐 *www.moortengarden.com* 🎟 *$5* 🕒 *Closed Wed.*

Palm Springs Walk of Stars. Along the walk, more than 300 bronze stars are embedded in the sidewalk (à la Hollywood Walk of Fame) to honor celebrities with a Palm Springs connection. Frank, Elvis, Marilyn, Dinah, Lucy, Ginger, Liz, and Liberace have all received their due. Those still around to walk the Walk and see their stars include Nancy Sinatra and Kathy Griffin. ✉ *Palm Canyon Dr., around Tahquitz Canyon Way, and Tahquitz Canyon Way, between Palm Canyon and Indian Canyon Drs.* ☎ *760/320–3129* 🌐 *www.palmsprings.com/stars.*

Village Green Heritage Center. Three small museums at the Village Green Heritage Center illustrate early life in Palm Springs. The centerpiece, the **Agua Caliente Cultural Museum,** traces the culture and history of the Cahuilla tribe with several exhibits. The **McCallum Adobe** and the **Cornelia White House** hold the collection of the Palm Springs Historical Society. **Rudy's General Store Museum** is a re-creation of a 1930s general store. ✉ *219–221 S. Palm Canyon Dr.* ☎ *760/323–8297* 🌐 *www.pshistoricalsociety.org* 🎟 *Agua Caliente free, McCallum $2, Rudy's $1* 🕒 *Closed Tues.*

8

WHERE TO EAT

$$ MEDITERRANEAN

🍴 **Alicante.** This sidewalk café near the Plaza Theatre is one of the best people-watching spots in Palm Springs. Pasta, pizza, and veal scaloppine are among the hearty items on the lunch and dinner menus. **Known for:** separate tapas menu; paella; cioppino. [$] *Average main: $20* ✉ *140 S. Palm Canyon Dr., at La Plaza* ☎ *760/325–9464* 🌐 *www.alicanteps.com.*

$ AMERICAN Fodor's Choice ★

🍴 **Cheeky's.** The artisanal bacon bar and hangover-halting mimosas attract legions to this breakfast and lunch joint, but brioche French toast and other favorites also contribute to the epic wait on weekends (no reservations accepted). Huevos rancheros, a gem salad with green goddess dressing, and other farm-centric dishes entice the foodie crowd. **Known for:** homemade pastries and sausages; local organic ingredients; grass-fed burger topped with house bacon. $ *Average main: $12* ⊠ *622 N. Palm Canyon Dr., at E. Granvia Valmonte* ☎ *760/327–7595* ⊕ *www.cheekysps.com* ⊘ *Closed Tues. No dinner.*

$$$ ╳ **Copley's on Palm Canyon.** Chef Manion Copley prepares innovative cuisine in a setting that's straight out of Hollywood—a hacienda once owned
MODERN
AMERICAN by Cary Grant. Dine in the clubby house or under the stars in the garden. **Known for:** romantic patio dining; fresh seafood and meats with innovative flavors; sweet and savory herb ice creams. $ *Average main: $28* ⊠ *621 N. Palm Canyon Dr., at E. Granvia Valmonte* ☎ *760/327–9555* ⊕ *www.copleyspalmsprings.com* ⊘ *No lunch. Closed July and Aug.*

$$$ ╳ **EIGHT4NINE.** The dazzling interior design and eclectic Pacific Coast
AMERICAN dishes made from scratch lure locals and visitors alike to this swank
Fodor's Choice yet casual restaurant and lounge in the Uptown Design District. Sink
★ into white patent leather chairs or comfy sofas in the lounge where you can gaze at historic celebrity photos, or choose a table in a grand corridor with a collection of private rooms, or in the outdoor patio with mountain views. **Known for:** nearly everything made from scratch; four-course chef's menu; all-day happy hour in lounge. $ *Average main: $28* ⊠ *849 N. Palm Canyon Dr.* ☎ *760/325–8490* ⊕ *eight4nine.com.*

$$ ╳ **El Mirasol at Los Arboles.** Chef Felipe Castañeda owns two Mexican
MODERN restaurants in Palm Springs—this one, part of Los Arboles Hotel, is
MEXICAN outside on a charming patio set amid flower gardens and shaded by red umbrellas. Castañeda prepares classic combinations of tacos, tamales, and enchiladas, along with specialties such as double-cooked pork and *pollo en pipián* (chicken with a pre-Columbian sauce made of ground roasted pumpkin seeds and dry chilies). **Known for:** classic Mexican dishes; great vegetarian options; garden setting. $ *Average main: $20* ⊠ *266 Via Altamira, off N. Indian Canyon Dr.* ☎ *760/459–3136,* ⊕ *www.elmirasolrestaurants.com.*

$$$$ ╳ **Le Vallauris.** A longtime favorite that occupies the historic Roberson
FRENCH House, Le Vallauris is popular with ladies who lunch, all of whom get a hug from the maître d'. The Belgian-French-inspired menu changes daily, and each day it's handwritten on a white board. **Known for:** prix-fixe menus for lunch and dinner; lovely tree-shaded garden; romantic setting. $ *Average main: $35* ⊠ *385 W. Tahquitz Canyon Way, west of Palm Canyon Dr.* ☎ *760/325–5059* ⊕ *www.levallauris.com* ⊘ *Closed July and Aug.*

$$$$ ╳ **Purple Palm.** The hottest tables in Palm Springs are those that surround
MODERN the pool at the Colony Palms Hotel, where the hip and elite pay homage
AMERICAN to Purple Gang mobster Al Wertheimer, who reportedly built the hotel in the mid-1930s. Now it's a casual, convivial place where you can dine alfresco surrounded by a tropical garden near the pool. **Known for:** craft cocktails; happy hour and weekend brunch; extensive international wine list. $ *Average main: $31* ⊠ *572 N. Indian Canyon Dr., at E. Granvia Valmonte* ☎ *800/557–2187* ⊕ *www.colonypalmshotel.com.*

$$$$ ╳ **Spencer's Restaurant.** The swank dining space inside the Palm Springs
MODERN Tennis Club Resort occupies a historic mid-century modern structure,
AMERICAN but the cuisine of chef Eric Wadlund, a local star with a national reputation, is the main attraction. Crab cakes, kung pao calamari, and crispy

flash-fried oysters are favorite starters. **Known for:** French–Pacific Rim influences; romantic patio; elegant dining room. $ *Average main: $35* ✉ *701 W. Baristo Rd.* ☎ *760/327–3446* ⊕ *www.spencersrestaurant.com.*

$$
MODERN
AMERICAN
✕ **Trio.** The owners of this high-energy Uptown Design District restaurant claim that it's "where Palm Springs eats," and it certainly seems so on nights when the lines to get in run deep. The menu includes home-style staples such as Yankee pot roast, crawfish pie, and other dishes, along with veggie burgers and other vegetarian and gluten-free items. **Known for:** local artwork; inventive desserts; ample vegetarian and gluten-free options. $ *Average main: $22* ✉ *707 N. Palm Canyon Dr.* ☎ *760/864–8746* ⊕ *www.triopalmsprings.com.*

$$$
INTERNATIONAL
✕ **The Tropicale.** Tucked onto a side-street corner, the Tropicale is a mid-century-style watering hole with a contemporary vibe. The bar and main dining room hold cozy leather booths; flowers and water features brighten the outdoor area. **Known for:** globe-trotting menu; happy hour (all night on Wednesday); weekly specials. $ *Average main: $30* ✉ *330 E. Amado Rd., at N. Calle Encilia* ☎ *760/866–1952* ⊕ *www.thetropicale.com* ⊗ *No lunch.*

$
AMERICAN
FAMILY
Fodor's Choice
★
✕ **Tyler's Burgers.** Families, singles, and couples head to Tyler's for simple lunch fare that appeals to carnivores and vegetarians alike. Expect mid-20th-century America's greatest hits: heaping burgers, stacks of fries, root beer floats, milk shakes; on weekends, be prepared to wait with the masses. **Known for:** house-made cole slaw; excellent burgers and fries; delicious shakes. $ *Average main: $9* ✉ *149 S. Indian Canyon Dr., at La Plaza* ☎ *760/325–2990* ⊕ *www.tylersburgers.com* ⊗ *Closed Sun. late May–mid-Feb. Closed mid-July–early Sept.*

$$$$
AMERICAN
✕ **Workshop Kitchen + Bar.** Chef Michael Beckman's Uptown Design District hot spot pairs high-quality California cuisine with creative cocktails in a sleek, almost utilitarian setting. The outdoor patio lures the oversize sunglasses Sunday brunch crowd, who slurp cava mimosas and artisanal cocktails; inside, the sleek concrete booths are topped with black leather cushions. **Known for:** most ingredients sourced from within a 100-mile radius; artisanal cocktails; own charcuterie and cheese shop in same complex. $ *Average main: $32* ✉ *800 N. Palm Canyon Dr., at E. Tamarisk Rd.* ☎ *760/459–3451* ⊕ *www.workshoppalmsprings.com* ⊗ *No lunch Mon.–Sat.*

8

WHERE TO STAY

$$$
RESORT
🏨 **Ace Hotel and Swim Club.** With the hotel's vintage feel and hippie-chic decor, it would be no surprise to find guests gathered around cozy communal fire pits enjoying feel-good '60s music. **Pros:** Amigo Room has late-night dining; poolside stargazing deck; weekend DJ scene at the pool. **Cons:** party atmosphere not for everyone; limited amenities; casual staff and service. $ *Rooms from: $189* ✉ *701 E. Palm Canyon Dr.* ☎ *760/325–9900* ⊕ *www.acehotel.com/palmsprings* ⤴ *188 rooms* ⌾ *No meals.*

$$
HOTEL
🏨 **Alcazar Palm Springs.** Amid an area known as the Movie Colony, Alcazar features ample, blazing-white guestrooms that wrap around a sparkling pool; some rooms have Jacuzzis, and many have private patios or fireplaces. **Pros:** walking distance of downtown; parking on-site;

bikes available. **Cons:** limited service; wall air-conditioners; resort fee. $ *Rooms from: $159* ⊠ *622 N. Indian Canyon Dr.* ☎ *760/318–9850* ⊕ *www.alcazarpalmsprings.com* ↝ *34 rooms* ⧉ *No meals.*

$$$$
HOTEL
Fodor's Choice
★

⊡ **ARRIVE.** During the day, sip cocktails from the indoor outdoor bar (which doubles as the reception desk), and lounge in the pool on an inflatable seahorse, or dance to a live DJ; at night, relax outside in the hot tub and socialize around the communal fire pits (half of the rooms also come with a private patio and fireplace), or cozy up in your king-size bed among tasteful modern furnishings, and wake to sunny mountain views. **Pros:** private cabanas with misting systems; great restaurant, artisanal ice-cream shop, and local coffee shop on-site; free valet. **Cons:** only king rooms available; shower offers little privacy; party scene may not suit everyone. $ *Rooms from: $329* ⊠ *1551 N. Palm Canyon Dr.* ☎ *760/507–1650* ⊕ *www.arrivehotels.com* ↝ *32 rooms* ⧉ *No meals.*

$$$$
RESORT

⊡ **Avalon Hotel Palm Springs.** A visit to the Avalon, formerly the Viceroy, is like entering a tableau of bright white and yellow, reminiscent of a sun-filled desert day; guest rooms for two and villas for three or more, some with fireplaces and private patios, are spread out over four tree-shaded acres. **Pros:** poolside cabanas; complimentary fitness classes; luxurious on-site Estrella Spa and stylish restaurant Chi Chi. **Cons:** popular wedding site. $ *Rooms from: $400* ⊠ *415 S. Belardo Rd.* ☎ *844/328–2566* ⊕ *www.avalonpalmsprings.com* ↝ *79 rooms* ⧉ *No meals.*

$
B&B/INN

⊡ **Casa Cody.** The service is personal and gracious at this historic bed-and-breakfast near the Palm Springs Art Museum; spacious studios and one- and two-bedroom suites hold Santa Fe–style rustic furnishings. **Pros:** former hangout of Charlie Chaplin; friendly ambience; some rooms come with fireplaces, patios, and/or kitchens. **Cons:** old buildings; limited amenities. $ *Rooms from: $99* ⊠ *175 S. Cahuilla Rd.* ☎ *760/320–9346, 800/231–2639* ⊕ *www.casacody.com* ↝ *29 rooms* ⧉ *Breakfast.*

$$$$
HOTEL

⊡ **Colony Palms Hotel.** This hotel has been a hip place to stay since the 1930s, when gangster Al Wertheimer built it to front his casino, bar, and brothel; it later became the Howard Hotel, owned by local luminaries Robert Stewart Howard (his dad owned the fabled racehorse Seabiscuit) and actress Andrea Leeds (the couple hosted a young Frank Sinatra, Elizabeth Taylor, and Liberace), and today it still attracts a younger crowd. **Pros:** rooms open to pool in the central courtyard; attentive staff; fireplaces and whirlpool tubs in many rooms. **Cons:** high noise level outside; not for families with young children. $ *Rooms from: $299* ⊠ *572 N. Indian Canyon Dr.* ☎ *760/969–1800, 800/577–2187* ⊕ *www. colonypalmshotel.com* ↝ *57 rooms* ⧉ *No meals.*

$$$
B&B/INN

⊡ **East Canyon Hotel & Spa.** The vibe is social and the rooms are spacious at this classy resort whose gracious hosts serve a primarily gay clientele. **Pros:** elegant but laid-back feel; attentive service; complimentary poolside cocktails. **Cons:** some guests may find decor too masculine. $ *Rooms from: $189* ⊠ *288 E. Camino Monte Vista* ☎ *760/320–1928, 877/324–6835* ⊕ *www.eastcanyonps.com* ↝ *15 rooms* ⧉ *Breakfast.*

$$
HOTEL
Fodor's Choice
★

⊡ **Hotel California.** Expect homey accommodations for all budgets at this delightful hotel that's decked out in rustic Mexican furniture. **Pros:** comfortable design; friendly hosts; free limo service in the evenings. **Cons:** away from downtown. $ *Rooms from: $175* ⊠ *424 E. Palm*

Canyon Dr. ☎ *760/322–8855* 🌐 *www.palmspringshotelcalifornia.com* 🛏 *14 rooms* 🍴 *No meals.*

$$ HOTEL 🏨 **The Hyatt Palm Springs.** The best-situated downtown hotel in Palm Springs, the Hyatt has spacious suites where you can watch the sun rise over the city, or set behind the mountains from your bedroom's balcony. **Pros:** underground parking; restaurant plus two outdoor bar-lounges; daily sunset hour with free wine, beer, and appetizers. **Cons:** lots of business travelers; some street noise. [$] *Rooms from: $159* ✉ *285 N. Palm Canyon Dr.* ☎ *760/322–9000* 🌐 *palmsprings.hyatt.com* 🛏 *197 suites* 🍴 *No meals.*

$$$ B&B/INN Fodor's Choice ★ 🏨 **Korakia Pensione.** The painter Gordon Coutts, best known for desert landscapes, constructed this Moroccan villa in 1924 as an artist's studio, and these days creative types gather in the main house and the adjacent Mediterranean-style villa to soak up the spirit of that era. **Pros:** design-minded decor; complimentary breakfast; yoga on weekends. **Cons:** might not appeal to those who prefer standard resorts; no TVs or phones in rooms. [$] *Rooms from: $239* ✉ *257 S. Patencio Rd.* ☎ *760/864–6411* 🌐 *www.korakia.com* 🛏 *20 rooms, 8 rental units* 🍴 *No meals.*

$$$ B&B/INN 🏨 **La Maison.** Offering all the comforts of home, this small bed-and-breakfast contains large rooms that surround the terra-cotta–tiled and very comfortable pool area, where you can spend quiet time soaking up the sun or taking a dip. **Pros:** restaurants nearby; quiet; genial hosts. **Cons:** on busy Highway 111; rooms open directly onto pool deck. [$] *Rooms from: $220* ✉ *1600 E. Palm Canyon Dr.* ☎ *760/325–1600* 🌐 *www.lamaisonpalmsprings.com* 🛏 *13 rooms* 🍴 *Breakfast.*

$$ B&B/INN Fodor's Choice ★ 🏨 **Orbit In Hotel.** The architectural style of this hip inn on a quiet backstreet dates back to the late 1940s and '50s—nearly flat roofs, wide overhangs, glass everywhere—and the period feel continues inside. **Pros:** saltwater pool; in-room spa services; Orbitini cocktail hour. **Cons:** best for couples; style not to everyone's taste; staff not available 24 hours. [$] *Rooms from: $169* ✉ *562 W. Arenas Rd.* ☎ *760/323–3585, 877/996–7248* 🌐 *www.orbitin.com* 🛏 *9 rooms* 🍴 *Breakfast.*

$$$$ RESORT Fodor's Choice ★ 🏨 **The Parker Palm Springs.** A cacophony of color and over-the-top contemporary art assembled by New York City–based designer Jonathan Adler mixes well with the brilliant desert garden, three pools (two outdoor), fire pits, and expansive spa of this hip hotel that attracts a stylish, worldly clientele. **Pros:** fun in the sun; celebrity clientele; on-site Palm Springs Yacht Club Spa; design-centric. **Cons:** pricey drinks and wine; a bit of a drive from downtown; resort fee ($35). [$] *Rooms from: $325* ✉ *4200 E. Palm Canyon Dr.* ☎ *760/770–5000, 800/543–4300* 🌐 *www.theparkerpalmsprings.com* 🛏 *144 rooms* 🍴 *No meals.*

$$$$ RESORT 🏨 **Riviera Resort & Spa.** A party place built in 1958 and renovated in 2008, the Riviera attracts young, well-heeled, bikini-clad guests who hang out around the pool by day, and at the Bikini Bar by night. **Pros:** personal fire pits throughout the property; hip vibe; excellent spa. **Cons:** high noise level outdoors; party atmosphere; location at north end of Palm Springs. [$] *Rooms from: $300* ✉ *1600 N. Indian Canyon Dr.* ☎ *760/327–8311* 🌐 *rivierapalmsprings.com* 🛏 *449 rooms* 🍴 *No meals.*

$$ HOTEL Fodor's Choice ★ **The Saguaro.** A startling, rainbow-hued oasis—the brainchild of Manhattan-based architects Peter Stamberg and Paul Aferiat—the Saguaro caters to pet-toting partygoers who appreciate its lively pool and casual- and fine-dining options. **Pros:** excellent on-site dining; daily yoga; shuttle service to downtown. **Cons:** a few miles from downtown. [$] *Rooms from: $169* ✉ *1800 E. Palm Canyon Dr.* ☎ *760/323–1711* 🌐 *thesaguaro.com* 🛏 *244 rooms* 🍴 *No meals.*

$$$$ RESORT FAMILY **Smoke Tree Ranch.** A world apart from Palm Springs' pulsating urban village, the area's most under-the-radar resort complex occupies 400 pristine desert acres surrounded by mountains and unspoiled vistas. **Pros:** priceless privacy; simple luxury; recreational activities like horseback riding and more. **Cons:** no glitz; limited entertainment options; family atmosphere not for everyone. [$] *Rooms from: $400* ✉ *1850 Smoke Tree La.* ☎ *760/327–1221, 800/787–3922* 🌐 *www.smoketreeranch.com* 🕓 *Closed Apr.–late Oct.* 🛏 *49 cottages, includes 18 suites* 🍴 *All-inclusive; Some meals.*

$$$ B&B/INN **Sparrows Lodge.** Rustic earthiness meets haute design at the adult-centered Sparrows, just off Palm Springs' main drag. **Pros:** unique design; intimate property; private patios. **Cons:** rooms feel a little dark; some guests might deem them charmless; no TVs or phones in rooms. [$] *Rooms from: $249* ✉ *1330 E. Palm Canyon Dr.* ☎ *760/327–2300* 🌐 *www.sparrowshotel.com* 🛏 *20 rooms* 🍴 *Breakfast.*

$$$$ B&B/INN Fodor's Choice ★ **Willows Historic Palm Springs Inn.** An opulent Mediterranean-style mansion built in the 1920s to host the rich and famous, this luxurious hillside bed-and-breakfast has gleaming hardwood and slate floors, stone fireplaces, frescoed ceilings, hand-painted tiles, iron balconies, antiques throughout, and a 50-foot waterfall that splashes into a pool outside the dining room. **Pros:** luxurious; sublime service; expansive breakfast. **Cons:** closed from June to September; pricey. [$] *Rooms from: $395* ✉ *412 W. Tahquitz Canyon Way* ☎ *760/320–0771, 800/966–9597* 🌐 *www.thewillowspalmsprings.com* 🛏 *8 rooms* 🍴 *Breakfast.*

NIGHTLIFE AND PERFORMING ARTS

NIGHTLIFE

BARS AND PUBS

Bootlegger Tiki. Palm Springs tiki-drink traditions, especially during the daily happy hour, draw loyal patrons to Bootlegger, which occupies the same space as Don the Beachcomber in the 1950s. ✉ *1101 N. Palm Canyon Dr.* ☎ *760/318-4154.*

Fodor's Choice ★ **Draughtsman.** In the Uptown Design District and part of the ARRIVE hotel, this upscale pub focuses on Palm Springs and SoCal craft beers, classic cocktails, and modern comfort food, as well as classics like chicken pot pie and short rib poutine. Hang out in the contemporary indoor space with soaring ceilings and watch sports, or chill on the patio where you can play cornhole or foosball. ✉ *1501 N. Palm Canyon Dr.* ☎ *760/507–1644* 🌐 *draughtsmanpalmsprings.com.*

Purple Room Supper Club. In an elegant venue within the Club Trinidad Hotel, this swinging '60s-era supper club offers live entertainment six nights a week. Come for drinks, dinner, and dancing Tuesday through

Palm Springs Modernism

Some of the world's most forward-looking architects designed and constructed buildings around Palm Springs between 1940 and 1970; and modernism, also popular elsewhere in California in the years after World War II, became an ideal fit for desert living, because it minimizes the separation between indoors and outdoors. See-through houses with glass exterior walls are common. Oversize flat roofs provide shade from the sun, and many buildings' sculptural forms reflect nearby landforms. The style is notable for elegant informality, clean lines, and simple landscaping.

Most obvious to visitors are three buildings that are part of the Palm Springs Aerial Tramway complex, built in the 1960s. Albert Frey, a Swiss-born architect, designed the soaring A-frame Tramway Gas Station, visually echoing the pointed peaks behind it. Frey also created the glass-walled Valley Station, from which you get your initial view of the Coachella Valley before you board the tram to the Mountain Station, designed by E. Stewart Williams.

Frey, a Palm Springs resident for more than 60 years, also designed the indoor-outdoor City Hall, Fire Station No. 1, and numerous houses. His

second home, perched atop stilts on the hillside above the Palm Springs Art Museum, affords a sweeping view of the Coachella Valley through glass walls. The classy Movie Colony Hotel, one of the first buildings Frey designed in the desert, may seem like a typical 1950s motel with rooms surrounding a swimming pool now, but when it was built in 1935, it was years ahead of its time.

Donald Wexler, who honed his vision with Los Angeles architect Richard Neutra, brought new ideas about the use of materials to the desert, where he teamed up with William Cody on a number of projects, including the terminal at the Palm Springs Airport. Many of Wexler's buildings have soaring overhanging roofs, designed to provide shade from the blazing desert sun. Wexler also experimented with steel framing back in 1961, but the metal proved too expensive. Seven of his steel-frame houses can be seen in a neighborhood off Indian Canyon and Frances drives.

The Palm Springs Modern Committee sponsors Modernism Week in mid-February, when you can visit some of the most remarkable buildings in the area. Visit ⊕ *www.psmodcom.org* for an app that guides you to the most interesting buildings.

Thursday night (no cover charge, but reservations are recommended). On Friday and Saturday night, dine at 6 pm and watch a scheduled show at 8 pm (reserve tickets in advance). Try to time your visit to catch *The Judy Show*, actor/owner Michael Holmes's Sunday evening comical tribute to Judy Garland, Bette Davis, Katharine Hepburn, and other stars (tickets required). ⊠ *1900 E. Palm Canyon Dr.* ☏ *760/322–4422* ⊕ *www.purpleroompalmsprings.com.*

Tonga Hut. The sibling of L.A.'s oldest tiki hut (opened in 1958 in North Hollywood), Tonga Hut Palm Springs transports guests to Polynesia with an authentic tiki vibe, pupu platters, and tropical drinks. It's on the second floor of a building in the heart of the downtown strip—try to nab a table on the lanai where you can experience the action from above. The bar and dining area are also fun and lively spaces; ask about the telephone booth that leads to a secret room, available for private parties. ⊠ *254 N. Palm Canyon Dr.* ☎ *760/322–4449* ⊕ *www. tongahut.com.*

Fodor'sChoice
★ **Village Pub.** With live entertainment, DJs, and friendly service, this popular bar caters to a young crowd. Happy hour is fantastic. On weekend days there is live music as well. ⊠ *266 S. Palm Canyon Dr., at Baristo Rd.* ☎ *760/323–3265* ⊕ *www.palmspringsvillagepub.com.*

CASINOS

Casino Morongo. A 20-minute drive west of Palm Springs, this casino has 2,600 slot machines, video games, the Vibe nightclub, plus Vegas-style shows. ⊠ *49500 Seminole Dr., off I–10, Cabazon* ☎ *800/252–4499, 951/849–3080* ⊕ *www.morongocasinoresort.com.*

Spa Resort Casino. This resort holds 1,000 slot machines, blackjack tables, a high-limit room, four restaurants, two bars, and the Cascade Lounge for entertainment. ⊠ *401 E. Amado Rd., at N. Calle Encilia* ☎ *888/999–1995* ⊕ *www.sparesortcasino.com.*

DANCE CLUBS

Zelda's Nightclub. At this Palm Springs institution, the high-energy DJs, dancing, and drinking are still going strong and the dance floor is still thumping with Latin, hip-hop, and sounds from the '60s, '70s, and '80s. Zelda's offers bottle service in the VIP Sky Box. ⊠ *611 S. Palm Canyon Dr., at E. Camino Parocela* ☎ *760/325–2375* ⊕ *www.zeldasnightclub. com* ☉ *Closed Mon.*

GAY AND LESBIAN

The Dinah. In late March, when the world's finest female golfers hit the links for the Annual LPGA ANA Inspiration Championship in Rancho Mirage, thousands of lesbians converge on Palm Springs for a four-day party popularly known as The Dinah. ☎ *888/923–4624* ⊕ *thedinah.com.*

Hunter's Video Bar. Drawing a young gay and straight crowd, Hunter's is a club-scene mainstay. ⊠ *302 E. Arenas Rd., at Calle Encilia* ☎ *760/323–0700* ⊕ *huntersnightclubs.com.*

Fodor'sChoice
★ **Toucans Tiki Lounge.** A friendly place with a tropical–rain forest setting, Toucans serves festive drinks and hosts live entertainment and theme nights. On Sunday it seems as though all of Palm Springs has turned out for drag night. ⊠ *2100 N. Palm Canyon Dr., at W. Via Escuela* ☎ *760/416–7584* ⊕ *www.toucanstikilounge.com.*

White Party Palm Springs. Held during spring break, the White Party draws tens of thousands of gay men from around the world for four days of parties and events. ⊠ *Palm Springs* ⊕ *jeffreysanker.com.*

THEMED ENTERTAINMENT

Fodor'sChoice
★ **Ace Hotel and Swim Club.** Events are held here nearly every night, including film screenings, full moon parties, live concerts, DJs, and dancing. Many are free, and some are family friendly. The poolside venue makes most events fun and casual. ⊠ *701 E. Palm Canyon Dr., at Calle Palo Fierro* ☎ *760/325–9900* ⊕ *www.acehotel.com.*

PERFORMING ARTS

ARTS CENTERS

Annenberg Theater. Broadway shows, operas, lectures, Sunday-afternoon chamber concerts, and other events take place at the Palm Springs Art Museum's handsome theater. ⊠ *101 N. Museum Dr., at W. Tahquitz Canyon Way* ☎ *760/325–4490* ⊕ *www.psmuseum.org.*

FESTIVALS

Modernism Week. Each February the desert communities celebrate the work of the architects and designers who created the Palm Springs "look" in the '40s, '50s, and '60s. Described these days as mid-century modern—you'll also see the term "desert modernism" used—these structures were created by Albert Frey, Richard Neutra, William F. Cody, John Lautner, and other notables. The 11-day event features lectures, a modernism show, films, vintage car and trailer shows, galas, and home and garden tours. A shorter preview week happens in October. ⊠ *Palm Springs* ⊕ *www.modernismweek.com.*

FILM

Palm Springs International Film Festival. In mid-January this 12-day festival brings stars and nearly 200 feature films from several dozen countries, plus panel discussions, short films, and documentaries, to various venues. The weeklong "Shortfest," celebrating more than 300 short films, takes place in June. ⊠ *Palm Springs* ☎ *760/322–2930, 800/898–7256* ⊕ *www.psfilmfest.org.*

SHOPPING

8

BOUTIQUES

Fodor'sChoice ★ **Just Fabulous.** Find everything from original photography and art, coffee table books, greeting cards, designer home decor, candles, and many other eclectic items at this fun gift shop that celebrates the area's retro-modern lifestyle and desert dolce vita. ⊠ *515 N. Palm Canyon Dr.* ☎ *760/864–1300* ⊕ *bjustfabulous.com.*

Fodor'sChoice ★ **Trina Turk Boutique.** Celebrity designer Trina Turk's empire takes up a city block in the Uptown Design District. Turk, famous for men's and women's outdoor wear, reached out to another celebrity, interior designer Kelly Wearstler, to create adjoining clothing and residential boutiques. Lively fabrics brighten up the many chairs and couches for sale at the residential store, which also carries bowls, paintings, and other fun pieces to spiff up your home. ⊠ *891 N. Palm Canyon Dr.* ☎ *760/416–2856* ⊕ *www.trinaturk.com.*

OUTLET MALLS

Fodor'sChoice ★ **Desert Hills Premium Outlets.** About 20 miles west of Palm Springs lies one of California's largest outlet centers. The 180 brand-name discount fashion shops include Jimmy Choo, Neiman Marcus, Versace, Saint Laurent Paris, J. Crew, Armani, Gucci, and Prada. ⊠ *48400 Seminole Rd., off I–10, Cabazon* ☎ *951/849–5018* ⊕ *www.premiumoutlets.com.*

Palm Springs is a golfer's paradise: the area is home to more than 125 courses.

SHOPPING DISTRICTS

Uptown Design District. A loose-knit collection of consignment and secondhand shops, galleries, and lively restaurants extends north of Palm Springs' downtown. The theme here is decidedly retro. Many businesses sell mid-century modern furniture and decorator items, and others carry clothing and estate jewelry. One spot definitely worth a peek is **Shag, the Store,** the gallery of fine art painter Josh Agle. For antique costume jewelry check out **Dazzles.** If you dig the mid-mod aesthetic, breeze through the furnishings at **Towne Palm Springs.** ⊠ *N. Palm Canyon Dr., between Amado Rd. and Vista Chino.*

SPAS

Estrella Spa at the Avalon Hotel Palm Springs. This spa earns top honors each year for the indoor/outdoor experience it offers with a touch of Old Hollywood ambience. You can enjoy your massage in one of four outdoor treatment cabanas in a garden, experience a sugar or salt scrub, get a facial or pedicure fireside, or receive a full-body treatment with lemon crystals. Whatever the treatment, you can use the spa's private pool, take a break for lunch, and order a drink from the hotel's bar. ⊠ *Avalon Hotel Palm Springs, 415 S. Belardo Rd.* ☎ *760/318–3000* ⊕ *www.avalonpalmsprings.com* ✄ *Salon. Services: facials, specialty massages, prenatal massages, outdoor treatments, wellness classes. $145, 60-min massage, $260, spa package.*

Feel Good Spa at the Ace Hotel. The Feel Good Spa within its own dedicated facility at the Ace Hotel reopened in 2017 after a head-to-toe renovation, and has five treatment rooms. The estheticians use local clay, mud, sea algae, and other natural ingredients, which you can purchase at the on-site shop. ✉ *701 E. Palm Canyon Dr.* ☎ *760/866–6188* ⊕ *www.acehotel.com/palmsprings* ☞ *Fully equipped gym. Services: wraps and scrubs, massage, facials, in-room treatments, salon, wellness classes, yoga. $110, 60-min massage.*

Palm Springs Yacht Club. It's all about fun at the Parker Palm Springs hotel's yacht club. Guests receive a complimentary cocktail while lounging in a poolside tent. Before spa treatments, you can choose music from a playlist and the staff will stream it to your room. When you're ready to crash, wander over to the outdoor café for a burger and Pimm's. Treatments might feature local clay or stones, or a Thai massage. ✉ *4200 E. Palm Canyon Dr.* ☎ *760/321–4606* ⊕ *www.theparkerpalmsprings.com/spa* ☞ *Sauna, steam room, indoor pool. Services: scrubs and wraps, massage, facials, manicures, pedicures, waxing, salon, fitness center with TechnoGym equipment, dining and cocktails. $195, 60-min massage.*

THE DESERT RESORTS

The term *desert resorts* refers to the communities along or just off Highway 111—Cathedral City, Rancho Mirage, Palm Desert, Indian Wells, Indio, and La Quinta—along with Desert Hot Springs *(see Along Twentynine Palms Highway)*, which is north of Palm Springs off Highway 62 and Interstate 10.

RANCHO MIRAGE

8

4 miles southeast of Cathedral City.

The rich and famous of Rancho Mirage live in beautiful estates and patronize elegant resorts and expensive restaurants. Although many mansions here are concealed behind the walls of gated communities and country clubs, the grandest of them all, Sunnylands, the Annenberg residence, is open to the public as a museum and public garden.

The city's golf courses host many high-profile tournaments. You'll find some of the desert's fanciest resorts in Rancho Mirage, and plenty of peace and quiet.

GETTING HERE AND AROUND
Due east of Cathedral City, Rancho Mirage stretches from Ramon Road on the north to the hills south of Highway 111. The western border is Da Vall Drive, the eastern one Monterey Avenue. Major east–west cross streets are Frank Sinatra Drive and Country Club Drive. Most shopping and dining spots are on Highway 111.

EXPLORING
The Annenberg Retreat at Sunnylands. The stunning 25,000-square-foot winter home and retreat of the late Ambassador Walter H. and Leonore Annenberg opened to the public in 2012. You can spend a whole day enjoying the 9 glorious acres of gardens (see website schedule of free guided walks, classes, and other programs), or take a guided 90-minute tour of the residence (reservations essential), a striking mid-century modern edifice designed by A. Quincy Jones. Floor-to-ceiling windows

The Desert
Resorts

frame views of the gardens and Mount San Jacinto, and the expansive rooms hold furnishings from the 1960s and later, along with impressionist art (some original, some replicas). The history made here is as captivating as the surroundings. Eight U.S. presidents—from Dwight Eisenhower to Barack Obama—and their First Ladies have visited Sunnylands; Ronald and Nancy Reagan were frequent guests. Britain's Queen Elizabeth and Prince Philip also relaxed here, as did Princess Grace of Monaco and Japanese Prime Minister Toshiki Kaifu. Photos, art, letters, journals, and mementos provide insight into some of the history that unfolded here. ⊠ *37–977 Bob Hope Dr., south of Gerald Ford Dr.* ☏ *760/202–2222* ⊕ *www.sunnylands.org* ⊠ *House tours $45, tickets available online 2 wks in advance; guided bird tour $35; open-air shuttle tour of grounds, $20; visitor center and gardens free* ☯ *Closed Mon.–Wed. Closed July and Aug. and during retreats.*

FAMILY **Children's Discovery Museum of the Desert.** This museum features a number of hands-on exhibits, including a miniature rock-climbing area, a magnetic sculpture wall, make-it-and-take-it-apart projects, a rope maze, and an area for toddlers. Kids can paint a VW Bug, work as chefs in the museum's pizza parlor, assemble their own cars on a racetrack, and build pies out of arts and crafts supplies. ⊠ *71–701 Gerald Ford Dr., at Bob Hope Dr.* ☏ *760/321–0602* ⊕ *www.cdmod.org* ⊠ *$10* ☯ *Closed Mon. May–Dec.*

Koffi. Locals often hit this chain to get their caffeine fix, and it's a fine pit stop for pastries, pre-made sandwiches, and bagels. This outpost is the roasting facility, so the beans here are as fresh as they come. ✉ *71–380 Hwy. 111* ☎ *760/340–2444* ⊕ *www.kofficoffee.com.*

WHERE TO EAT AND STAY

$$$

MEDITERRANEAN

✕ **Catalan.** At this restaurant known for its beautifully prepared Mediterranean cuisine you can dine inside or under the stars in the atrium. The service here is attentive, and the menu roams Spain, Italy, California and beyond. **Known for:** attentive service; delicious paella with clams; happy hour with inventive cocktails. $ *Average main: $27* ✉ *70026 Hwy. 111* ☎ *760/770–9508* ⊕ *www.catalanrestaurant.com* ☾ *Closed Mon.*

$

MEXICAN

FAMILY

✕ **Las Casuelas Nuevas.** Hundreds of artifacts from Guadalajara, Mexico, lend festive charm to this casual restaurant, which has an expansive garden patio. Tamales and shellfish dishes are among the specialties—expect more traditional Mexican fare, rather than California-influenced creations. **Known for:** vast tequila menu; weekend live entertainment; lively happy hour. $ *Average main: $15* ✉ *70–050 Hwy. 111* ☎ *760/328–8844* ⊕ *www.lascasuelasnuevas.com.*

$$$

RESORT

Agua Caliente Casino, Resort, Spa. As in Las Vegas, the Agua Caliente casino is in the lobby, but once you get into the spacious, beautifully appointed rooms of the resort, all of the cacophony at the entrance is forgotten. **Pros:** poolside cabanas outfitted with TV and Wi-Fi; package deals include access to Indian Canyons Golf Course; on-site Sunstone Spa. **Cons:** casino ambience; not appropriate for kids. $ *Rooms from: $250* ✉ *32–250 Bob Hope Dr.* ☎ *888/999–1995* ⊕ *www.hotwatercasino.com* ⤴ *366 rooms* ⦿ *No meals.*

$$$$

RESORT

FAMILY

Omni Rancho Las Palmas Resort & Spa. The desert's most family-friendly resort, this large venue holds Splashtopia, a huge water-play zone. **Pros:** rooms come with private balconies or patios; trails for hiking and jogging; nightly entertainment. **Cons:** second-floor rooms accessed by very steep stairs; golf course surrounds rooms; resort hosts conventions. $ *Rooms from: $299* ✉ *41-000 Bob Hope Dr.* ☎ *760/568–2727, 888/444–6664* ⊕ *www.rancholaspalmas.com* ⤴ *444 rooms* ⦿ *No meals.*

$$$$

RESORT

FAMILY

Fodor'sChoice

★

The Ritz Carlton, Rancho Mirage. On a hilltop perch overlooking the Coachella Valley, this luxury resort spoils guests with exemplary service and comforts that include a trio of pools, access to the desert's finest spa, and private outdoor sitting areas for each room. **Pros:** fire pit overlooking Coachella Valley; access to Mission Hills golf courses and tennis; spa that's a destination in itself. **Cons:** hefty rates; some airport noise; resort and parking fees ($30 each). $ *Rooms from: $489* ✉ *68900 Frank Sinatra Dr.* ☎ *760/321–8282* ⊕ *www.ritzcarlton.com* ⤴ *244 rooms* ⦿ *No meals.*

$$$$

RESORT

FAMILY

The Westin Mission Hills Golf Resort & Spa. A sprawling resort on 360 acres, the Westin offers a slew of activities for all ages and is surrounded by fairways and putting greens, two family-friendly pools (one lagoon-style with a 75-foot waterslide) and an adults-only pool. **Pros:** gorgeous grounds; first-class golf facilities; daily activity programs for kids and adults. **Cons:** rooms are spread out; pricey. $ *Rooms from: $369* ✉ *71333 Dinah Shore Dr.* ☎ *760/328–5955, 800/937–8461* ⊕ *www.westinmissionhills.com* ⤴ *552 rooms* ⦿ *No meals.*

8

NIGHTLIFE

Agua Caliente Casino. This elegant and surprisingly quiet casino contains 1,300 slot machines, 36 table games, an 18-table poker room, a high-limit room, a no-smoking area, and six restaurants. The Show, the resort's concert theater, presents acts such as The Moody Blues, Joe Bonamassa, and Sophia Loren, as well as live sporting events. ⊠ *32–250 Bob Hope Dr., at E. Ramon Rd.* ☎ *760/321–2000* ⊕ *www. hotwatercasino.com.*

SPORTS AND THE OUTDOORS

GOLF

ANA Inspiration Championship. The best female golfers in the world compete in this championship held in late March or early April. ⊠ *Mission Hills Country Club* ☎ *760/834–8872* ⊕ *www.anainspiration.com.*

Fodor's Choice ★ **Westin Mission Hills Resort Golf Club.** Golfers at the Westin Mission Hills have two courses to choose from, the Pete Dye and the Gary Player Signature. They're both great, with amazing mountain views and wide fairways, but if you've only got time to play one, choose the Dye. The club is a member of the Troon Golf Institute, and has several teaching facilities, including the Westin Mission Hills Resort Golf Academy and the *Golf Digest* Golf School. ■TIP➜ The resort's Best Available Rate program guarantees golfers (with a few conditions) the best Internet rate possible. ⊠ *71333 Dinah Shore Dr.* ☎ *760/328–3198* ⊕ *www. playmissionhills.com* ⌨ *Gary Player, $74–$180; Pete Dye, $114–$172* ⚑ *Pete Dye Resort: 18 holes, 5525 yards, par 72; Gary Player Signature: 18 holes, 5327 yards, par 70.*

SHOPPING

MALL

The River at Rancho Mirage. This shopping-dining-entertainment complex holds 20 high-end shops, including the SoCal darling Diane's Beachwear, all fronting a faux river with cascading waterfalls. Also here are a 12-screen cinema, an outdoor amphitheater, and many restaurants including Fleming's Prime Steakhouse and Babe's Bar-B-Que and Brewery. ⊠ *71–800 Hwy. 111, at Bob Hope Dr.* ☎ *760/341–2711* ⊕ *www. theriveratranchomirage.com.*

SPAS

Fodor's Choice ★ **The Ritz Carlton Spa, Rancho Mirage.** Two hundred–plus suspended quartz crystals guard the entrance of the desert's premier spa. With private men's and women's areas, a co-ed outdoor soaking tub, food service, and some of the kindest spa technicians around, guests can expect pampering par excellence. The signature Spirit of the Mountains treatment, which starts with a full-body exfoliation, includes a massage, and ends with a body wrap and a scalp massage with lavender oil, is a blissful experience. The gym, equipped with state-of-the-art machines, is open 24/7. Private trainers are available to guide your workout; wellness classes are also available. ⊠ *68900 Frank Sinatra Drive* ☎ *760/202–6170* ⊕ *www.ritzcarlton.com* ⌔ *Fully equipped gym. Salon. Services: body wraps, body scrubs, facials, mineral baths, specialty massages, outdoor treatments, waxing, wellness classes. $165, 50-min massage; $330, signature package.*

The Spa at Mission Hills. The emphasis at this spa in a quiet corner of the Weston Mission Hills Resort is on comfort rather than glitz and glamour. Attentive therapists incorporate coconut milk, lemon balm, mint, thyme, red algae, hydrating honey, and other botanicals into their treatments. Yoga and other wellness classes are also available. ⊠ *71333 Dinah Shore Dr.* ☎ *760/770–2134* ⊕ *www.spaatmissionhills. com* ☞ *Steam room. Gym with: machines, cardio, pool. Services: rubs and scrubs, massages, facials, nail services. $125, 50-min massage.*

PALM DESERT

2 miles southeast of Rancho Mirage.

Palm Desert is a thriving retail and business community with popular restaurants, private and public golf courses, and premium shopping along the main commercial drag, El Paseo. Each October, the Palm Desert Golf Cart Parade launches "the season" with a procession of 80 golf carts decked out as floats buzzing up and down El Paseo. The town's stellar sight to see is the Living Desert complex.

GETTING HERE AND AROUND

Palm Desert stretches from north of Interstate 10 to the hills south of Highway 111. West–east cross streets north to south are Frank Sinatra Drive, Country Club Drive (lined on both sides with gated golfing communities), and Fred Waring Drive. Monterey Avenue marks the western boundary, and Washington Street forms the eastern edge.

EXPLORING

Fodor'sChoice ★ **El Paseo.** West of and parallel to Highway 111, this mile-long Mediterranean-style shopper's paradise is lined with fountains, courtyards, and upscale boutiques. You'll find shoe salons, jewelry stores, children's shops, two dozen restaurants, and nearly as many art galleries. The strip is a pleasant place to stroll, window-shop, people-watch, and exercise your credit cards. ■ TIP→ In winter and spring a free bright-yellow shuttle ferries shoppers from store to store and back to their cars. ⊠ *Between Monterey and Portola Aves.* ☎ *877/735–7273* ⊕ *www.elpaseo.com.*

FAMILY Fodor'sChoice ★ **Living Desert.** Come eye-to-eye with wolves, coyotes, mountain lions, cheetahs, bighorn sheep, golden eagles, warthogs, and owls at the 1,800-acre Living Desert. Easy to challenging scenic trails traverse desert terrain populated with plants of the Mojave, Colorado, and Sonoran deserts. In recent years the park has expanded its vision to include Australia and Africa. At the 3-acre African WaTuTu village you'll find a traditional marketplace as well as camels, leopards, hyenas, and other African animals. Children can pet African domesticated animals, including goats and guinea fowl, in a "petting kraal." Gecko Gulch is a children's playground with crawl-through underground tunnels, climb-on snake sculptures, a carousel, and a Discovery Center that holds ancient Pleistocene animal bones. Elsewhere, a small enclosure contains butterflies and hummingbirds, and a cool model train travels through miniatures of historic California towns. ■ TIP→ A garden center sells native desert flora, much of which is unavailable elsewhere. ⊠ *47900 Portola Ave., south from Hwy. 111* ☎ *760/346–5694* ⊕ *www. livingdesert.org* ☞ *$20.*

8

Palm Springs Art Museum in Palm Desert. A satellite branch of the Palm Springs Art Museum, this gallery space tucked into a desert garden at the west entrance to El Paseo exhibits cutting-edge works by contemporary sculptors and painters. The on-site restaurant **Cuistot** (*760/340–1000, www.cuistotrestaurant.com*) is a splendid, if pricey, place to enjoy French cuisine. ✉ *72–567 Hwy. 111* ✥ *in El Paseo* ☎ *760/346–5600* 🌐 *www.psmuseum.org/palm-desert* 🎟 *Free* 🕒 *Closed Mon.*

Santa Rosa and San Jacinto Mountains National Monument. Administered by the U.S. Bureau of Land Management, this monument protects Peninsula bighorn sheep and other wildlife on 280,000 acres of desert habitat. Stop by the visitor center for an introduction to the site and information about the natural history of the desert. A landscaped garden displays native plants and frames an impressive view. The well-informed staff can recommend hiking trails that show off the beauties of the desert. ■ **TIP→ Free guided hikes are offered on Thursday and Saturday.** ✉ *51–500 Hwy. 74* ☎ *760/862–9984* 🌐 *www.blm.gov* 🎟 *Free.*

WHERE TO EAT AND STAY

$ AMERICAN Fodor's Choice ★

🍴 **Bouchee.** Devotees of this La Quinta favorite come here for farm-to-table Euro-style meals and deli items. Order the salads or gorgeous sandwiches—the salmon salad is to die for—at the counter, then retire to the French-inspired dining area, or the shaded outdoor terrace. **Known for:** premade dinner to go; gourmet wine and cheese shop; locally sourced ingredients. [$] *Average main: $10* ✉ *72–785 Hwy. 111* ✥ *off Plaza Way near El Paseo* ☎ *442/666–3296* 🌐 *www.boucheecafe-anddeli.com* 🕒 *No dinner.*

$$ ECLECTIC Fodor's Choice ★

🍴 **Clementine's Gourmet Marketplace and Cafe.** A favorite of families, lunching ladies, and couples, Clementine's presents an artful mix of Mediterranean flavors. Diners at the café perch at long wooden communal tables to tuck into baked egg Ficelle, lamb burgers, and other specialties, but this space's nerve center is the take-out counter and kitchen that brims with pre-made salads, boulangerie-style meats and cheeses, and decadent French-inspired pastries and desserts. **Known for:** Mediterranean market vibe; cocktail bar and happy hour; regular evening special events. [$] *Average main: $18* ✉ *72990 El Paseo* ☎ *760/834–8814* 🌐 *www.clementineshop.com* 🕒 *No dinner.*

$$$$ SEAFOOD

🍴 **Pacifica Seafood.** Choice seafood, rooftop dining, and reduced prices at sunset draw locals and visitors to this busy restaurant on the second floor of the Gardens of El Paseo. Seafood that shines in dishes such as butter-poached Maine lobster tail, grilled Pacific swordfish, and barbecued sugar-spiced salmon arrives daily from San Diego; the menu also includes chicken, steaks, and meal-size salads. **Known for:** inventive sauces and glazes; bar with 150 different vodkas; lower-price sunset menu. [$] *Average main: $38* ✉ *73505 El Paseo* ☎ *760/674–8666* 🌐 *www.pacificaseafoodrestaurant.com* 🕒 *No lunch June–Aug.*

$$$ RESORT FAMILY

🏨 **Desert Springs J. W. Marriott Resort and Spa.** With a dramatic U-shape design, this sprawling hotel, which attract business travelers, couples, and families alike, is set on 450 landscaped acres and wraps around the desert's largest private lake. **Pros:** gondola rides on the lake to restaurants; popular lobby bar; wonderful spa. **Cons:** crowded in-season; high resort fee; long walk from lobby to rooms. $ *Rooms from: $259 ⊠ 74–855 Country Club Dr.* ☎ *760/341–2211, 888/538–9459* ⊕ *www.desertspringsresort.com* ⬅ *884 rooms* ⦿ *No meals.*

PERFORMING ARTS

McCallum Theatre. The principal cultural venue in the desert, this theater hosts productions from fall through spring. *Fiddler on the Roof* has played here; Lily Tomlin, Willie Nelson, and Michael Feinstein have performed, and Joffrey Ballet dancers have pirouetted across the stage. ⊠ *73–000 Fred Waring Dr.* ☎ *760/340–2787* ⊕ *www.mccallumtheatre.com.*

SPORTS AND THE OUTDOORS

BALLOONING

Fantasy Balloon Flights. Sunrise excursions over the southern end of the Coachella Valley lift off at 6 am and take from 60 to 90 minutes; a traditional champagne toast follows the landing. Afternoon excursions are timed to touch down at sunset. ⊠ *Palm Desert* ☎ *760/568–0997* ⊕ *www.fantasyballoonflight.com* ☑ *$195.*

GOLF

Desert Willow Golf Resort. Praised for its environmentally smart design, this public golf resort planted water-thrifty turf grasses and doesn't use pesticides. The Mountain View course has four configurations; Firecliff is tournament quality with five configurations. A public facility, Desert Willow is one of the country's top-rated golf courses. ⊠ *38–995 Desert Willow Dr., off Country Club Dr.* ☎ *760/346–0015* ⊕ *www.desertwillow.com* ☑ *Mountain View from $65, Firecliff from $65* ⅄ *Mountain View: 18 holes, 7079 yards, par 72; Firecliff: 18 holes, 7056 yards, par 72.*

8

INDIAN WELLS

5 miles east of Palm Desert.

For the most part a quiet and exclusive residential enclave, Indian Wells hosts major golf and tennis tournaments throughout the year, including the BNP Paribus Open tennis tournament. Three hotels share access to championship golf and tennis facilities, and there are several noteworthy resort spas and restaurants.

GETTING HERE AND AROUND

Indian Wells lies between Palm Desert and La Quinta, with most resorts, restaurants, and shopping set back from Highway 111.

WHERE TO EAT AND STAY

$$$$ ✕ **Vue Grille and Bar at the Indian Wells Golf Resort.** This not-so-private
AMERICAN restaurant at the Indian Wells Golf Resort offers a glimpse of how the country-club set lives. The service is impeccable, and the outdoor tables provide views of mountain peaks that seem close enough to touch. **Known for:** farm-to-table cuisine; grilled steaks and seafood; flatbreads and burgers. $ *Average main: $34* ⊠ *44-500 Indian Wells La.* ☎ *760/834–3800* ⊕ *www.vuegrilleandbar.com.*

$$$$ RESORT FAMILY Fodor's Choice ★ [H] **Hyatt Grand Regency Indian Wells Resort.** This stark-white resort adjacent to the Golf Resort at Indian Wells is one of the grandest in the desert. **Pros:** excellent business services; butler service in some rooms; very pet friendly. **Cons:** big and impersonal; spread out over 45 acres; noisy public areas. [$] *Rooms from: $350* ✉ *44–600 Indian Wells La.* ☎ *760/776–1234* 🌐 *indianwells.regency.hyatt.com* 🛏 *480 rooms, 40 villas* 🍴 *No meals.*

$$$$ RESORT [H] **Miramonte Resort & Spa.** A warm bit of Tuscany against a backdrop of the Santa Rosa Mountains characterizes the most intimate of the Indian Wells hotels. **Pros:** gorgeous gardens; daily wellness classes; one of the desert's best spas. **Cons:** adult-oriented; limited resort facilities on site; rooms could use some sprucing up. [$] *Rooms from: $279* ✉ *45000 Indian Wells La.* ☎ *760/341–2200* 🌐 *www.miramonteresort.com* 🛏 *215 rooms* 🍴 *Some meals.*

$$$$ RESORT FAMILY [H] **Renaissance Indian Wells Resort and Spa.** The centerpiece of this luxurious resort, adjacent to the Golf Resort at Indian Wells, is an eight-story atrium lobby, onto which most rooms open. **Pros:** adjacent to golf-tennis complex; kids club; bicycles available. **Cons:** higher noise level in rooms surrounding pool; somewhat impersonal ambience. [$] *Rooms from: $289* ✉ *44–400 Indian Wells La.* ☎ *760/773–4444* 🌐 *www.renaissancehotels.com* 🛏 *560 rooms* 🍴 *No meals.*

SPORTS AND THE OUTDOORS

GOLF

Fodor's Choice ★ **Golf Resort at Indian Wells.** Adjacent to the Hyatt Regency Indian Wells, this complex includes the Celebrity Course, designed by Clive Clark and twice a host to the PGA's Skins game (lots of water here), and the Players Course, designed by John Fought to incorporate views of the surrounding mountain ranges. Both courses consistently rank among the best public courses in California. **■TIP→ It's a good idea to book tee times well in advance, up to 60 days.** ✉ *44–500 Indian Wells La.* ☎ *760/346–4653* 🌐 *www.indianwellsgolfresort.com* 🎫 *Both courses $69–$219* ⛳ *Celebrity Course: 18 holes, 7050 yards, par 72; Players Course: 18 holes, 7376 yards, par 72.*

TENNIS

BNP Paribas Open. Drawing 200 of the world's top players, this tennis tournament takes place at Indian Wells Tennis Garden for two weeks in March. Various ticket plans are available, with some packages including stays at the adjoining Hyatt Regency Indian Wells or Renaissance Esmeralda resorts. ✉ *78200 Miles Ave.* ☎ *800/999–1585* 🌐 *www.bnpparibasopen.com.*

SPAS

Fodor's Choice ★ **The Well.** A luxurious 12,000-square-foot facility, The Well draws on international treatments and ingredients to indulge the senses and relax the body. Treatments such as hot stone and full-body massages, table yoga, and a couples' Pittura Festa experience, which involves painting each other with colorful therapeutic muds, are well worth the splurge. Sugar or salt exfoliating scrubs may well restore the soul in addition to the skin. ✉ *Miramonte Resort, 45–000 Indian Wells La.* ☎ *866/843–9355* 🌐 *www.miramonteresort.com* ☞ *Services: facials, nail care, solo and couple's massages, scrubs, and other body therapies. $165, 60-min massage.*

LA QUINTA

4 miles south of Indian Wells.

The desert became a Hollywood hideout in the 1920s, when La Quinta Hotel (now La Quinta Resort and Club) opened, introducing the Coachella Valley's first golf course. Old Town La Quinta is a popular attraction; the area holds dining spots, shops, and galleries.

GETTING HERE AND AROUND

Most of La Quinta lies south of Highway 111. The main drag through town is Washington Street.

WHERE TO EAT AND STAY

$$$$ AMERICAN

🍴 **Arnold Palmer's.** From the photos on the walls to the trophy-filled display cases to the putting green for diners awaiting a table, Arnie's essence infuses this restaurant. Families gather in the spacious restaurant for birthdays and Sunday dinners, and the service is always attentive. **Known for:** homemade meat loaf; top-notch wine list; entertainment most nights. [$] *Average main: $34* ✉ *78164 Ave. 52, near Desert Club Dr.* ☎ *760/771–4653* 🌐 *www.arnoldpalmersrestaurant.com.*

$$$$ BISTRO Fodor's Choice ★

🍴 **Lavender Bistro.** This romantic bistro makes diners feel like they've been transported to southern France. The spacious outdoor atrium is decked out with flowers, fountains, and twinkling lights. **Known for:** live music on the patio and in the fireside lounge; organic ingredients; extensive locavore menu. [$] *Average main: $34* ✉ *78073 Calle Barcelona* ☎ *760/564–5353* 🌐 *www.lavenderbistro.com* 🕒 *Closed June–Sept.*

$$$$ RESORT FAMILY

🏨 **La Quinta Resort and Club.** Opened in 1926 and now a member of the Waldorf-Astoria Collection, the desert's oldest resort is a lush green oasis set on 45 acres. **Pros:** individual swimming pools in some rooms; gorgeous gardens; pet and family friendly. **Cons:** a party atmosphere sometimes prevails; spotty housekeeping/maintenance. [$] *Rooms from: $329* ✉ *49499 Eisenhower Dr.* ☎ *760/564–4111* 🌐 *www.laquintaresort.com* 🛏 *586 rooms, 210 villas* 🍽 *No meals.*

PERFORMING ARTS

La Quinta Arts Festival. More than 200 artists participate each March in a four-day juried show that's considered one of the best in the West. The event, held at La Quinta Civic Center, includes sculptures, paintings, watercolors, fiber art, and ceramics. ✉ *78495 Calle Tampico* ☎ *760/564–1244* 🌐 *www.lqaf.com* 🎟 *$20; multiday tickets $25.*

SPORTS AND THE OUTDOORS

GOLF

Fodor's Choice ★

PGA West. A world-class golf destination where Phil Mickelson and Jack Nicklaus play, this facility includes five resort courses and four private ones. Courses meander through indigenous desert landscapes, water features, and bunkers. The Norman, Nick Tournament, and TPC Stadium courses are "shot-makers" courses made for pros. TPC highlights include its two lakes, "San Andreas Fault" bunker, and island green called "Alcatraz." The Norman course has tight fairways and small greens. ✉ *49–499 Eisenhower Dr.* ☎ *760/564–5729 for tee times* 🌐 *www.pgawest.com* 🎟 *Mountain*

Course, $159–$229; Dunes, $119–$189; Greg Norman, $159–$229; TPC Stadium, $189–$269; Jack Nicklaus Tournament, $159–$229 🏌 *Mountain Course: 18 holes, 6732 yards, par 72; Dunes: 18 holes, 6712 yards, par 72; Greg Norman: 18 holes, 7156 yards, par 72; TPC Stadium: 18 holes, 7300 yards, par 72; Jack Nicklaus Tournament: 18 holes, 7204 yards, par 72.*

SHOPPING

SPAS

Spa La Quinta. The gorgeous Spa La Quinta may be the grandest spa in the entire desert. At this huge stand-alone facility you'll find everything from massages to facials to salon services, plus a beautiful garden setting with a large fountain, flowers galore, plenty of nooks where you can hide out and enjoy the sanctuary, and a Jacuzzi with a waterfall. ✉ *49499 Eisenhower Dr.* ☎ *760/777–4800* ⊕ *www.laquintaresort.com* ☞ *Fitness center with cardio. Services: aromatherapy, body wraps and scrubs, massage, skin care, salon services, water therapies. $170, 50-min massage; $195, 30-min HydraFacial.*

INDIO

5 miles east of Indian Wells.

Indio is the home of the renowned date shake: an extremely thick and sweet milk shake made with dates. The city and surrounding countryside generate 95% of the dates grown and harvested in the United States. If you take a hot-air balloon ride, you will likely drift over the tops of date palm trees.

GETTING HERE AND AROUND

Indio is east of Indian Wells and north of La Quinta. Highway 111 runs right through Indio, and Interstate 10 skirts it to the north.

EXPLORING

FAMILY **National Date Festival and Riverside County Fair.** Indio celebrates its raison d'être each February at its date festival and county fair. The mid-month festivities include an Arabian Nights pageant, camel and ostrich races, and exhibits of local dates, plus monster truck shows, a demolition derby, a nightly musical pageant, and a rodeo. ✉ *Riverside County Fairgrounds, 82–503 Hwy. 111* ☎ *800/811–3247, 760/863–8247* ⊕ *www.datefest.org* 🎟 *$10, parking $10.*

Shields Date Garden and Café. Sample, select, and take home some of Shields's locally grown dates. Ten varieties are available, including the giant supersweet royal medjools, along with specialty date products such as date crystals, stuffed dates, confections, and local honey. At the Shields Date Garden Café you can try an iconic date shake, dig into date pancakes, or go exotic with a date tamale. Breakfast and lunch are served daily. ✉ *80–225 Hwy. 111* ☎ *760/347–0996* ⊕ *www.shieldsdategarden.com* 🕐 *No dinner.*

WHERE TO EAT

$$ ✗ **Ciro's Ristorante and Pizzeria.** Serving pizza and pasta since the 1960s, SICILIAN this popular casual restaurant has a few unusual pies on the menu, including cashew with three cheeses. The decor is classic pizza joint,

with checkered tablecloths and bentwood chairs. **Known for:** daily pasta specials; classic Italian dishes; house-made, hand-tossed pizza dough. $ *Average main: $16* ✉ *81–963 Hwy. 111* ☎ *760/347-6503* ⊕ *www.cirosofindio.com* ⊗ *No lunch Sun.*

$$$ ✗**Jackalope Ranch.** It's worth the drive to Indio to sample flavors of
AMERICAN   the Old West, 21st-century style. Inside a rambling 21,000-foot building, holding a clutch of indoor/outdoor dining spaces, you may be seated near an open kitchen, a bar, fountains, fireplaces, or waterworks. Jackalope can be a busy, noisy place; ask for a quiet corner if that's your pleasure. **Known for:** Western-style barbecue; casual, down-home locals hangout; lively vibe. $ *Average main: $30* ✉ *80–400 Hwy. 111* ☎ *760/342-1999* ⊕ *www.thejackaloperanch.com.*

NIGHTLIFE AND PERFORMING ARTS
MUSIC FESTIVALS

Fodor's Choice   **Coachella Valley Music and Arts Festival.** Among Southern California's big-
★   gest parties, the festival draws hundreds of thousands of rock music fans to Indio each April for two weekends of live concerts. Headliners include acts such as Lady Gaga, Kendrick Lamar, Lorde, Phantogram, Jack Johnson, and Radiohead. Many attendees camp on-site, but to give your ears a rest post-concert you might want to stay at a nearby hotel. ■**TIP➔ The festival sells out before the lineup is announced, so expect to pay big bucks if you haven't purchased tickets by late fall.** ✉ *Empire Polo Club, 81–800 Ave. 51* ⊕ *www.coachella.com.*

EN ROUTE   **Coachella Valley Preserve.** For a glimpse of how the desert appeared before development, head northeast from Palm Springs to this preserve. It has a system of sand dunes and several palm oases that were formed because the San Andreas Fault lines here allow water flowing underground to rise to the surface. A mile-long walk along Thousand Palms Oasis reveals pools supporting the tiny endangered desert pupfish and more than 183 bird species. Families like the relatively flat trail that is mostly shaded. The preserve has a visitor center, nature and equestrian trails, restrooms, and picnic facilities. Guided hikes are offered October–March. ■**TIP➔ Be aware that it's exceptionally hot in summer here.** ✉ *29200 Thousand Palms Canyon Rd., Thousand Palms* ☎ *760/343-2733* ⊕ *www.coachellavalleypreserve.org* ⊠*Free* ⊗ *Visitor center closed June–Aug.*

ALONG TWENTYNINE PALMS HIGHWAY

Designated a California Scenic Highway, the Twentynine Palms Highway connects two of the three entrances to Joshua Tree National Park and provides gorgeous high-desert views, especially in winter and spring when you might find yourself driving beneath snowcapped peaks or through a field of wildflowers. Park entrances are located at Joshua Tree and Twentynine Palms. Yucca Valley and Twentynine Palms have lodging and dining options, and other services. Along the way, look out for the eye-catching artwork by artists associated with the avant-garde High Desert Test Sites (⊕ *www.highdeserttestsites.com*).

DESERT HOT SPRINGS

9 miles north of Palm Springs.

Desert Hot Springs's famous hot mineral waters, thought by some to have curative powers, bubble up at temperatures of 90°F to 148°F and flow into the wells of more than 40 hotel spas.

GETTING HERE AND AROUND

Desert Hot Springs lies due north of Palm Springs. Take Gene Autry Trail north to Interstate 10, where the street name changes to Palm. Continue north to Pierson Boulevard, the town's center.

EXPLORING

Cabot's Pueblo Museum. Cabot Yerxa, the man who found the spring that made Desert Hot Springs famous, built a quirky four-story, 35-room pueblo between 1939 and his death in 1965. Now a museum run by the city of Desert Hot Springs—Yerxa was the town's first mayor—the Hopi-inspired adobe structure is filled with memorabilia of his time as a homesteader; his encounters with Hollywood celebrities at the nearby Bar-H Ranch; his expedition to the Alaskan gold rush; and many other events. The home, much of it crafted out of materials Yerxa recycled from the desert, can only be seen on hour-long tours. Outside, walk the grounds to a lookout with amazing desert views. ✉ *67–616 E. Desert View Ave., at Eliseo Rd.* ☎ *760/329–7610* 🌐 *www.cabotsmuseum.org* 🎟 *$13* 🕒 *Closed Mon. Oct.–May., closed Mon. and Tues. June–Sept.* ☞ *Tours 9:30, 10:30, 11:30, 1:30, 2:30 Oct.–May, and 9:30, 10:30, 11:30 June–Sept. Tours limited to 12 people.*

WHERE TO STAY

$$$ HOTEL 🏨 **The Spring.** Designed for those who want to detox, lose weight, or chill out in the mineral pools, The Spring delivers quiet and personal service atop a Desert Hot Springs hill. **Pros:** access to mineral pools 24 hours a day; complimentary continental breakfast; spa and lodging packages available. **Cons:** rooms lack character. [$] *Rooms from: $199* ✉ *12699 Reposo Way* ☎ *760/251–6700* 🌐 *www.the-spring.com* 🛏 *12 rooms* 🍴 *Breakfast.*

SHOPPING

SPAS

Fodor's Choice ★ **Two Bunch Palms.** This iconic retreat has long been a favorite with Los Angeles yogis for its peaceful, palm-shaded grounds and hot springs pools. Big changes occurred in 2014, with new rooms added and a fresh look for the existing ones. Guests can still purchase a day pass to soak in the grotto, attend yoga classes, lounge on the grounds, and enjoy a spa treatment or two. ■ **TIP→ This is an adults-only, whispers-only destination.** ✉ *67–425 Two Bunch Palms Tr.* ☎ *760/676–5000* 🌐 *www.twobunchpalms.com* 🎟 *Day pass $25 weekdays, $40 weekends* ☞ *Services: facials, nail care, solo and couple's massages, breath work, water, and other therapies; treatments from $135, 60-min massage.*

YUCCA VALLEY

30 miles northeast of Palm Springs.

One of the high desert's fastest-growing cities, Yucca Valley is emerging as a bedroom community for people who work as far away as Ontario, 85 miles to the west. In this suburb you can shop for necessities, get your car serviced, grab coffee or purchase vintage furnishings, and chow down at fast-food outlets. Just up Pioneertown Road you'll find the most-talked-about dining establishment in the desert, Pappy and Harriet's, the famed performance venue that hosts big-name talent.

GETTING HERE AND AROUND

The drive to Yucca Valley on Highway 62/Twentynine Palms Highway passes through the Painted Hills and drops down into a valley. Take Pioneertown Road north to the Old West outpost.

EXPLORING

FAMILY **Hi-Desert Nature Museum.** Creatures that make their homes in Joshua Tree National Park are the focus here. A small live-animal display includes scorpions, snakes, lizards, and small mammals. You'll also find rocks, minerals, and fossils from the Paleozoic era, taxidermy, and Native American artifacts. There's also a children's area and art exhibits. ✉ *Yucca Valley Community Center, 57116 Twentynine Palms Hwy.* ☎ *760/369–7212* 🌐 *hidesertnaturemuseum.org* 🎟 *Free* 🕒 *Closed Sun.–Wed.*

Pioneertown. In 1946 Roy Rogers, Gene Autry, the Sons of the Pioneers (the music group for whom the town is named), and Russ Hayden built Pioneertown, an 1880s-style Wild West movie set complete with hitching posts, saloon, and an OK Corral. You can stroll past wooden and adobe storefronts and feel like you're back in the Old West. Or not: Pappy and Harriet's Pioneertown Palace, now the town's top draw, has evolved into a hip venue for indie and mainstream performers such as Dengue Fever, Neko Case, and Robert Plant. ✉ *53688 Pioneertown Rd., Pioneertown* ✣ *4 miles north of Yucca Valley* 🌐 *pappyandharriets.com.*

8

WHERE TO EAT AND STAY

$$$ AMERICAN FAMILY Fodor's Choice ★ 🍴 **Pappy & Harriet's Pioneertown Palace.** Smack in the middle of what looks like the set of a Western is this cozy saloon where you can have dinner, relax over a drink at the bar, and catch some great indie bands or legendary artists—Leon Russell, Sonic Youth, Paul McCartney, and Robert Plant—have all played here. Pappy & Harriet's may be in the middle of nowhere, but you'll need reservations for dinner on weekends, especially on Sunday night. **Known for:** live music several days/nights a week; Tex-Mex, Santa Maria-style barbecue; fun and lively atmosphere. [$] *Average main: $25* ✉ *53688 Pioneertown Rd., Pioneertown* ☎ *760/365–5956* 🌐 *www.pappyandharriets.com* 🕒 *Closed Tues. and Wed.*

$ HOTEL 🏨 **Best Western Joshua Tree Hotel & Suites.** This hotel has spacious, nicely appointed rooms decorated in soft desert colors. **Pros:** convenient to Joshua Tree National Park; pleasant lounge; pool and hot tub. **Cons:**

on a busy highway; limited service. $ *Rooms from: $116* ✉ *56525 Twentynine Palms Hwy.* ☎ *760/365-3555* ⊕ *www.bestwestern.com* ⤷ *95 rooms* ⦿ *Breakfast.*

$ ⛶ **Rimrock Ranch Cabins.** The quiet beauty of the surrounding desert
RENTAL   attracts Hollywood writers, artists, and musicians to circa-1940s housekeeping cabins, an Airstream trailer, the Hatch House duplex, and lodge
rooms. **Pros:** quiet desert hideaway; fun vibe for music fans; rich music
heritage on site. **Cons:** rustic cabins will not appeal to resort seekers;
far from most services. $ *Rooms from: $90* ✉ *53688 Pioneertown Rd.,
Pioneertown* ☎ *760/228–0130, 818/557–6383* ⊕ *www.rimrockranch-
pioneertown.com* ⤷ *7 rental units* ⦿ *No meals.*

JOSHUA TREE

12 miles east of Yucca Valley.

Artists and renegades have long found solace in the small upcountry
desert town of Joshua Tree, home to artsy vintage shops, cafés, and
B&Bs and a gateway to Joshua Tree National Park. Those who zip
through town might wonder what all the hype is about, but if you
slow down and spend time chatting with the folks in this funky community, you'll find much to love.

GETTING HERE AND AROUND

Highway 62 is the main route to and through Joshua Tree. Most businesses are here or along Park Boulevard as it heads toward the park.

ESSENTIALS

Visitor Information Joshua Tree Visitor Center. ✉ *6554 Park Blvd.*
☎ *760/366-1855.*

EXPLORING

Fodor's Choice   **Noah Purifoy Foundation.** This vast 10-acre art installation full of
★   "assemblage art" on a sandy tract of land in the town of Joshua
Tree honors the work of artist Noah Purifoy. The sculptures blend
with the spare desert in an almost post-apocalyptic way. Purifoy lived
most of his life in this desert until his death is 2004. He used found
materials to make commentary on social issues. His art has been
showcased at LACMA, J. Paul Getty Museum, MOCA, and many
more. ✉ *63030 Blair Lane* ☎ *213/382-7516* ⊕ *www.noahpurifoy.
com* ⛶ *Free* ☉ *Closes at sunset.*

WHERE TO EAT AND STAY

$ ✗ **Crossroads Cafe.** Mexican breakfasts, chicken-cilantro soup, and
AMERICAN   hearty sandwiches are among the draws at this Joshua Tree institution for prehike breakfasts, birthday lunches, and early dinners.
Taxidermied animals and beer-can lights hint at the community's con-
sciousness, while the tattooed waitresses and slew of veggie options
make it clear the Crossroads is unlike anywhere else in San Bernardino County. **Known for:** rustic wooden interior and bar; hearty
and affordable meals; vegetarian and vegan dishes. $ *Average main:
$12* ✉ *61715 Twentynine Palms Hwy.* ☎ *760/366-5414* ⊕ *crossroad-
scafejtree.com.*

Check out the sculptures made of found materials at the Noah Purifoy Foundation in Joshua Tree.

$$$$
B&B/INN
Fodor's Choice
★

Sacred Sands. The dramatic exterior of this strawbale house, atop a mountain near Joshua Tree National Park's western entrance, hints at the design-forward intentions of the friendly owners, Scott and Steve. **Pros:** hot tubs infused with tea tree oil and Epsom salts; extravagant breakfasts; indoor and outdoor showers. **Cons:** expensive for the area; few nearby dining options. $ *Rooms from: $329* ✉ *63155 Quail Springs Rd.* ☎ *760/424–6407* ⊕ *www.sacredsands.com* ☞ *4 rooms* ❏ *Breakfast.*

TWENTYNINE PALMS

12 miles east of Joshua Tree.

The main gateway town to Joshua Tree National Park, Twentynine Palms is also the location of the U.S. Marine Air Ground Task Force Training Center. You can find services, supplies, and lodging in town.

GETTING HERE AND AROUND

Highway 62 is the main route to and through Twentynine Palms. Most businesses here center around Highway 62 and Utah Trail, 3 miles north of Joshua Tree's entrance.

ESSENTIALS

Visitor Information Twentynine Palms Visitor Center and Gallery. ✉ *73484 Twentynine Palms Hwy.* ☎ *760/367–6197* ⊕ *www.visit29.org.*

EXPLORING

Oasis of Murals. Twenty-six murals painted on the sides of buildings depict the history and current lifestyle of Twentynine Palms. If you drive around town, you can't miss the murals, but you can also pick up a free map from the Twentynine Palms Visitor Center. ✉ *Twentynine Palms* 🌐 *www.action29palmsmurals.com.*

29 Palms Art Gallery. This gallery features work by local painters, sculptors, and jewelry makers inspired by the desert landscape. If you find yourself inspired as well, sign up for one of the day-long art workshops. ✉ *74055 Cottonwood Dr.* ☎ *760/367–7819* 🌐 *www.29palmsartgallery.com* ⏲ *Closed Mon.–Wed. Also closed Thurs. in summer.*

WHERE TO STAY

$$ B&B/INN 🏨 **Campbell House.** To the wealthy pioneer who erected the stone mansion now occupied by this bed-and-breakfast, expense was no object, which is evident in the 50-foot-long planked maple floor in the great room, the intricate carpentry on the walls, and the huge stone fireplaces that warm the house on the rare cold night. **Pros:** elegant rooms and public spaces; spa services and massage room; great horned owls on property. **Cons:** somewhat isolated location; three-story main building doesn't have an elevator. [$] *Rooms from: $145* ✉ *74744 Joe Davis Dr.* ☎ *760/367–3238* 🌐 *www.campbellhouse29palms.com* 🛏 *2 rooms, 10 cottages* 🍴 *Breakfast.*

$$ B&B/INN FAMILY Fodor's Choice ★ 🏨 **29 Palms Inn.** The closest lodging to the entrance to Joshua Tree National Park, the funky 29 Palms Inn scatters a collection of adobe and wood-frame cottages, some dating back to the 1920s and 1930s, over 70 acres of grounds that include the ancient Oasis of Mara, a popular destination for birds and bird-watchers year-round. **Pros:** gracious hospitality; exceptional bird-watching; popular with artists. **Cons:** rustic accommodations; limited amenities. [$] *Rooms from: $165* ✉ *73950 Inn Ave.* ☎ *760/367–3505* 🌐 *www.29palmsinn.com* 🛏 *20 rooms, 4 guesthouses* 🍴 *Breakfast.*

ANZA-BORREGO DESERT

Largely uninhabited, the Anza-Borrego Desert is popular with those who love solitude, silence, space, starry nights, light, and sweeping mountain vistas. This desert lies south of the Palm Springs area, stretching along the western shore of the Salton Sea down toward Interstate 8 along the Mexican border. Isolated from the rest of California by mile-high mountains to the north and west, most of this desert falls within the borders of Anza-Borrego Desert State Park, which at more than 600,000 acres is the largest state park in the contiguous United States.

For thousands of years Native Americans of the Cahuilla and Kumeyaay people inhabited this area, spending their winters on the warm desert floor and their summers in the mountains. The first Europeans—a party led by the Spanish explorer Juan Baptiste de Anza—crossed this desert in 1776. Anza, for whom the desert is named, made the trip through here twice. Roadside signs along Highways 86, 78, and S2 mark the route of the Anza expedition, which spent Christmas Eve 1776 in what is now Anza-Borrego Desert State Park. Seventy-five years later thousands of immigrants on their way to the goldfields up north crossed the desert on the Southern Immigrant Trail, remnants of which remain along Highway S2. Permanent settlers arrived early in the 20th century, and by the 1930s the first adobe resort cottage had been built.

BORREGO SPRINGS

59 miles south of Indio.

The permanent population of Borrego Springs, set squarely in the middle of Anza-Borrego Desert State Park, hovers around 2,500. From September through June, when temperatures stay in the '80s and '90s, you can engage in outdoor activities such as hiking, nature study, golfing, tennis, horseback riding, and mountain biking. If winter rains cooperate, Borrego Springs puts on some of the best wildflower displays in the low desert. In some years the desert floor is carpeted with color: yellow dandelions and sunflowers, pink primrose, purple sand verbena, and blue wild heliotrope. The bloom generally lasts from late February through April. For current information on wildflowers around Borrego Springs, call Anza-Borrego Desert State Park's wildflower hotline (760/767–4684).

GETTING HERE AND AROUND

You can access Anza Borrego by taking the Highway 86 exit from Interstate 10, south of Indio. Highway 86 passes through Coachella and along the western shore of the Salton Sea. Turn west on Highway S22 at Salton City and follow it to Peg Leg Road, where you turn south until you reach Palm Canyon Drive. Turn west and the road leads to the center of Borrego Springs, Christmas Circle, where most major roads come together. Well-marked roads radiating from the circle will take you to the most popular sites in the state park. If coming from the San Diego area, drive east on Interstate 8 to the Cuyamaca Mountains, exit at Highway 79, and enjoy the lovely 23-mile drive through the mountains until you reach Julian; head east on Highway 78 and follow signs to Borrego Springs.

ESSENTIALS

Visitor Information Borrego Springs Chamber of Commerce & Visitors Bureau. ⊠ *786 Palm Canyon Dr.* ☎ *760/767–5555, 800/559–5524* ⊕ *www.borregospringschamber.com.*

EXPLORING

Fodor's Choice ★ **Anza-Borrego Desert State Park.** One of the richest living natural-history museums in the nation, this state park is a vast, nearly uninhabited wilderness where you can step through a field of wildflowers, cool off in a palm-shaded oasis, count zillions of stars in the black night sky, and listen to coyotes howl at dusk. The landscape, largely undisturbed by humans, reveals a rich natural history. There's evidence of a vast inland sea in the piles of oyster beds near Split Mountain and of the power of natural forces such as earthquakes and flash floods. In addition, recent scientific work has confirmed that the Borrego Badlands, with more than 6,000 meters of exposed fossil-bearing sediments, is likely the richest such deposit in North America, telling the story of 7 million years of climate change, upheaval, and prehistoric animals. Evidence has been unearthed of sabre-toothed cats, flamingos, zebras, and the largest flying bird in the northern hemisphere beneath the now-parched sand. Today the desert's most treasured inhabitants are the herds of elusive and endangered native bighorn sheep, or borrego, for which the park is named. Among the strange desert plants you may observe are the gnarly elephant trees. As these are endangered, rangers don't encourage visitors to seek out the secluded grove at Fish Creek, but there are a few examples at the visitor center garden. After a wet winter you can see a short-lived but stunning display of cacti, succulents, and desert wildflowers in bloom.

The park is unusually accessible to visitors. Admission to the park is free, and few areas are off-limits. There are two developed campgrounds, but you can camp anywhere; just follow the trails and pitch a tent wherever you like. There are more than 500 miles of dirt roads, two huge wilderness areas, and 110 miles of riding and hiking trails. Many sites can be seen from paved roads, but some require driving on dirt roads, for which rangers recommend you use a four-wheel-drive vehicle. When you do leave the pavement, carry the appropriate supplies: a cell phone (which may be unreliable in some areas), a shovel and other tools, flares, blankets, and plenty of water. The canyons are susceptible to flash flooding, so inquire about weather conditions (even on sunny days) before entering. ■TIP➔ Borrego resorts, restaurants, and the state park have Wi-Fi, but the service is spotty at best. If you need to talk to someone in the area, it's best to find a phone with a landline.

The sites and hikes listed below are arranged by region of the park and distance from the Visitor Center: in the valley and hills surrounding Borrego Springs, near Tamarisk Campground, along Highway S2, south of Scissors Crossing, and south of Ocotillo Wells.

Stop by the **Visitor Center** to get oriented, to pick up a park map, and to learn about weather, road, and wildlife conditions. Designed to keep cool during the desert's blazing-hot summers, the center is built underground, beneath a demonstration desert garden containing examples of most of the native flora and a little pupfish pond. Displays inside the center illustrate the natural history of the area. Picnic tables are scattered throughout, making this a good place to linger and enjoy the view.

A 1½-mile trail leads to **Borrego Palm Canyon,** one of the few native palm groves in North America. The canyon, about 1 mile west of the Visitor Center, holds a grove of more than 1,000 native fan palms, a stream, and a waterfall. Wildlife is abundant along this route. This moderate hike is the most popular in the park.

With a year-round stream and lush plant life, **Coyote Canyon,** approximately 4½ miles north of Borrego Springs, is one of the best places to see and photograph spring wildflowers. Portions of the canyon road follow a section of the old Anza Trail. This area is closed between June 15 and September 15 to allow native bighorn sheep undisturbed use of the water. The dirt road that gives access to the canyon may be sandy enough to require a four-wheel-drive vehicle.

The late-afternoon vista of the Borrego badlands from **Font's Point,** 13 miles east of Borrego Springs, is one of the most breathtaking views in the desert, especially when the setting sun casts a golden glow in high relief on the eroded mountain slopes. The road from the Font's Point turnoff can be rough enough to make using a four-wheel-drive vehicle advisable; inquire about road conditions at the Visitor Center before starting out. Even if you can't make it out on the paved road, you can see some of the view from the highway.

East of Tamarisk Grove campground (13 miles south of Borrego Springs), the **Narrows Earth Trail** is a short walk off the road. Along the way you can see evidence of the many geologic processes involved in forming the canyons of the desert, such as a contact zone between two earthquake faults, and sedimentary layers of metamorphic and igneous rock.

The 1.6-mile round trip **Yaqui Well Nature Trail** takes you along a path to a desert water hole where birds and wildlife are abundant. It's also a good place to look for wildflowers in spring. At the trailhead across from Tamarisk Campground you can pick up a brochure describing what can be seen along the trail.

Traversing a boulder-strewn trail is the easy, mostly flat **Pictograph/Smuggler's Canyon Trail.** At the end is a collection of rocks covered with muted red and yellow pictographs painted within the last hundred years or so by Native Americans. Walk about ½ mile beyond the pictures to reach Smuggler's Canyon, where an overlook provides views of the Vallecito Valley. The hike, from 2 to 3 miles round-trip, begins in Blair Valley, 6 miles southeast of Highway 78, off Highway S2, at the Scissors Crossing intersection.

Just a few steps off the paved road, **Carrizo Badlands Overlook** offers a view of eroded and twisted sedimentary rock that obscures the fossils of the mastodons, saber-tooths, zebras, and camels that roamed this region a million years ago. The route to the overlook through Earthquake Valley and Blair Valley parallels the Southern Emigrant Trail. It's off Highway S2, 40 miles south of Scissors Crossing.

Geology students from all over the world visit the Fish Creek area of Anza-Borrego to explore the canyon through Split Mountain. The narrow gorge with 600-foot walls was formed by an ancient stream. Fossils in this area indicate that a sea once covered the desert floor. From Highway 78 at Ocotillo Wells, take Split Mountain Road south 9 miles. ✉ *Visitor Center, 200 Palm Canyon Dr., Hwy. S22* ☎ *760/767–4205, 760/767–4684 wildflower hotline* ⊕ *www.parks.ca.gov* ✇ *Free; day use parking in campground areas $10* ☞ *Make a campground reservation at: reservecalifornia.com.*

FAMILY

Fodor's Choice

★

Galleta Meadows. At Galleta Meadows, camels, llamas, saber-toothed tigers, tortoises, and monumental gomphotherium (a sort of ancient elephant) appear to roam the earth again. These life-size bronze figures are of prehistoric animals whose fossils can be found in the Borrego Badlands. The collection of more than 130 sculptures created by Ricardo Breceda was commissioned by the late Dennis Avery, who installed the works of art on property he owned for the entertainment of locals and visitors. Maps are available from Borrego Springs Chamber of Commerce. ✉ *Borrego Springs Rd., from Christmas Circle to Henderson Canyon* ☎ *760/767–5555* ✇ *Free.*

8

WHERE TO EAT

$$ MODERN AMERICAN

🍴 **The Arches.** On the edge of the Borrego Springs Resort, Golf Club & Spa's golf course, set beneath a canopy of grapefruit trees, The Arches is a pleasant place to eat. For breakfast you'll find burritos alongside French toast; omelets and eggs benedict; or for lunch (best enjoyed on the patio) or dinner, the options include sandwiches, salads, and entrées such as spinach and mushroom tortellini, shrimp basted in seafood oil and simmered in a green coconut curry broth, and burgers topped with smoked bacon in a brioche bun. **Known for:** light fare; nightly specials; popular happy hour. [$] *Average main: $22* ✉ *1112 Tilting T Dr.* ☎ *760/767–5700* 🌐 *www.borregospringsresort.com/dining.asp* 🕒 *Summer hrs vary; call ahead.*

$$$ AMERICAN

🍴 **Carlee's Place.** Sooner or later most visitors to Borrego Springs wind up at Carlee's Place for a drink and a bite to eat. The extra-large menu has everything: burgers, salads, seafood, sandwiches, and prime rib. **Known for:** all-American down-home setting; martinis and classic cocktails; relatively affordable fare. [$] *Average main: $25* ✉ *660 Palm Canyon Dr.* ☎ *760/767–3262.*

$ MEXICAN

🍴 **Carmelita's Mexican Grill and Cantina.** A friendly, family-run eatery tucked into a back corner of what is called "The Mall," Carmelita's draws locals and visitors all day, whether it's for a hearty breakfast, a cooked-to-order enchilada or burrito, or to tip back a brew at the bar. The menu lists typical combination plates (enchiladas, burritos, tamales, and tacos). **Known for:** dog-friendly outdoor patio; house-made masa dough; full bar with sports TVs. [$] *Average main: $14* ✉ *575 Palm Canyon Dr.* ☎ *760/767–5666.*

$$$ MODERN AMERICAN

🍴 **Coyote Steakhouse.** The upscale Coyote Steakhouse at the Palms at Indian Head hotel caters to those who want a fancy dinner, particularly hunks of filet mignon or rack of lamb served at candlelit tables with white tablecloths overlooking the pool. Pet owners will appreciate the canine menu, whose treats include house-made peanut-butter dog cookies. **Known for:** romantic candlelit dining room; pork tenderloin and prime rib; classic mid-century setting. [$] *Average main: $30* ✉ *2220 Hoberg Rd.* ☎ *760/767–7788* 🌐 *www.thepalmsatindianhead.com* 🕒 *Coyote Steakhouse, no breakfast or lunch; Red Ocotillo, no breakfast or lunch July and Aug.*

$ MEXICAN

🍴 **Los Jilberto's Taco Shop.** A casual local favorite for affordable Mexican dishes, Jilberto's serves up big burritos and meaty enchiladas. **Known for:** authentic Mexican dishes cooked to order; all-day breakfast menu; reasonable prices. [$] *Average main: $9* ✉ *655 Palm Canyon Dr.* ☎ *760/767–1008* 🌐 *www.losjilbertostacoshop.com* 💳 *No credit cards.*

WHERE TO STAY

$$$ RESORT FAMILY Fodor's Choice ★

🏨 **La Casa Del Zorro.** The draws at this desert hideaway a short drive from Anza Borrego State Park include three guest-only pools, a hot tub, five night-lit tennis courts and two pickle ball courts, a yoga studio, a spa, a restaurant, and the lively Fox Den Bar. The 42-acre property pays tribute to its surroundings with a cactus garden, a fire pit, and two tall, welded-metal animal sculptures by local artist Ricardo Breceda. **Pros:** private pool or hot tub in many casitas; Butterfield

Room serves strawberry French toast; on-site spa, bar, and restaurant. **Cons:** service can be spotty. [$] *Rooms from: $189* ✉ *3845 Yaqui Pass Rd.* ☎ *760/767–0100* 🌐 *www.lacasadelzorro.com* 🛏 *48 rooms, 19 casitas* 🍴 *No meals.*

SPORTS AND THE OUTDOORS

GOLF

Borrego Springs Resort, Golf Club & Spa. The two 9-hole courses here, Mesquite and Desert Willow, are generally played as an 18-hole round by most golfers, starting with Mesquite. Both courses have natural desert landscaping and mature date palms. ✉ *1112 Tilting T Dr.* ☎ *760/767–3330* 🌐 *www.borregospringsresort.com* 🎟 *From $35* ⛳ *18 holes, 6760 yards, par 71* ☞ *Closed June–Sept. Closed Thurs. Oct.–May.*

SHOPPING

Anza-Borrego State Park Store. The Anza-Borrego Foundation, a land conservation group, runs this store that sells guidebooks, maps, clothing, desert art, and gifts for kids. Its enthusiastic staffers also assist with trip planning. Foundation guides organize hikes, naturalist talks, classes, research programs, and nature walks. ✉ *587 Palm Canyon Dr., No. 110* ☎ *760/767–0446* 🌐 *www.theabf.org* 🕒 *Closed weekends June–Sept., and Thurs. Oct.–May.*

Borrego Outfitters. This contemporary general store stocks high-end outdoor gear, hiking essentials, personal care items from Burt's Bees, footwear from Teva and Thymes, swimsuits, and tabletop items. You can browse through racks of clothing and piles of hats, all suited to the desert climate. ✉ *579 Palm Canyon Dr.* ☎ *760/767–3502* 🌐 *www.borregooutfitters.com.*

SALTON SEA

30 miles southeast of Indio, 29 miles east of Borrego Springs.

The Salton Sea, one of the largest inland seas on Earth, is the product of both natural and artificial forces. The sea occupies the Salton Basin, a remnant of prehistoric Lake Cahuilla. Over the centuries the Colorado River flooded the basin and the water drained into the Gulf of California. In 1905 a flood once again filled the Salton Basin, but the exit to the gulf was blocked by sediment. The floodwaters remained in the basin, creating a saline lake 228 feet below sea level, about 35 miles long and 15 miles wide, with a surface area of nearly 380 square miles. The sea, which lies along the Pacific Flyway, supports 400 species of birds. Fishing for tilapia, boating, camping, and bird-watching are popular activities year-round.

GETTING HERE AND AROUND

Salton Sea State Recreation Area includes about 14 miles of coastline on the northeastern shore of the sea, about 30 miles south of Indio via Highway 111. The Sonny Bono Salton Sea National Wildlife Refuge fills the southernmost tip of the sea's shore. To reach it from the recreation area, continue south about 60 miles to Niland; continue south to Sinclair Road, and turn west following the road to the Refuge Headquarters.

EXPLORING

FAMILY **Salton Sea State Recreation Area.** This huge recreation area on the sea's north shore draws thousands each year to its playgrounds, hiking trails, fishing spots, and boat launches. Ranger-guided bird walks take place on Saturday; you'll see migrating and native birds including Canada geese, pelicans, and shorebirds. ⊠ *100–225 State Park Rd., North Shore* ☎ *760/393–3052* ⊕ *www.parks.ca.gov* ✆ *$7.*

Sonny Bono Salton Sea National Wildlife Refuge. The 2,200-acre wildlife refuge here, on the Pacific Flyway, is a wonderful spot for viewing migratory birds. There's an observation deck where you can watch Canada geese, and along the trails you might view eared grebes, burrowing owls, great blue herons, ospreys, and yellow-footed gulls. ⚠ Though the scenery is beautiful, the waters here give off an unpleasant odor, and the New River, which empties into the sea, is quite toxic. ⊠ *906 W. Sinclair Rd., Calipatria* ☎ *760/348–5278* ⊕ *www.fws.gov/refuge/ sonny_bono_salton_sea/* ✆ *Free* ☼ *Closed weekends Mar.–Oct.*

JOSHUA TREE
NATIONAL PARK

WELCOME TO
JOSHUA TREE NATIONAL PARK

TOP REASONS
TO GO

★ **Rock climbing:** Joshua Tree is a world-class site with challenges for climbers of just about every skill level.

★ **Peace and quiet:** Roughly two hours from Los Angeles, this great wilderness is the ultimate escape from technology.

★ **Stargazing:** You'll be mesmerized by the Milky Way flowing across the summer sky. For spectacular natural fireworks, visit in mid-August during the Perseid meteor shower and watch shooting stars streak overhead.

★ **Wildflowers:** In spring, the hillsides explode in a patchwork of yellow, blue, pink, and white.

★ **Sunsets:** Twilight is a magical time here, especially during the winter, when the setting sun casts a golden glow on the mountains.

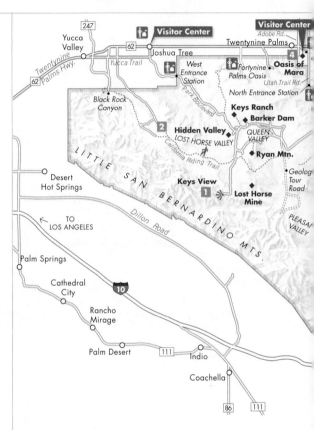

1 Keys View. This is the most dramatic overlook in the park—on clear days you can see Signal Mountain in Mexico.

2 Hidden Valley. Crawl between the big rocks and you'll understand why this boulder-strewn area was once a cattle rustlers' hideout.

3 Cholla Cactus Garden. Come here in the late afternoon, when the spiky stalks of the bigelow (jumping) cholla cactus are backlit against an intense blue sky.

4 Oasis of Mara. Walk the nature trail around this desert oasis, which the first settlers, the Serrano, dubbed "the place of little springs and much grass."

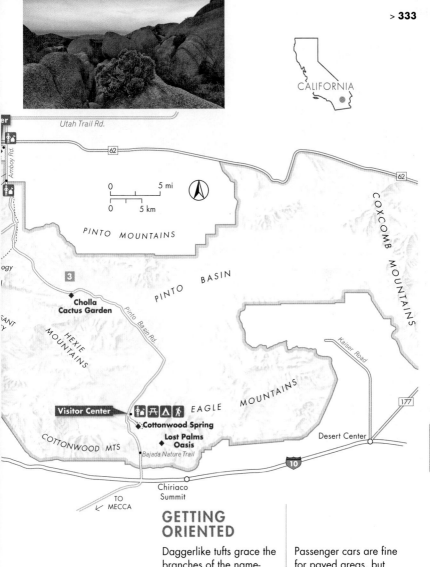

CALIFORNIA

Utah Trail Rd.

62

0   5 mi
0   5 km

PINTO MOUNTAINS

COXCOMB MOUNTAINS

62

PINTO BASIN

ogy

3

PINTO Basin Rd.

◆ **Cholla Cactus Garden**

HEXIE MOUNTAINS

SANT EY

Kaiser Road

177

MOUNTAINS

Visitor Center ▸ EAGLE

◆**Cottonwood Spring**

Lost Palms Oasis ◆

Bajada Nature Trail

COTTONWOOD MTS

Desert Center

9

10

Chiriaco Summit

TO ↙ MECCA

GETTING ORIENTED

Daggerlike tufts grace the branches of the namesake trees of Joshua Tree National Park in southeastern California, where the arid Mojave Desert meets the sparsely vegetated Colorado Desert (part of the Sonoran Desert, which lies across California, Arizona, and Northern Mexico).

Passenger cars are fine for paved areas, but you'll need four-wheel drive for many of the rugged backcountry roadways. At the park's most popular sites, parking is limited. Joshua Tree does not have public transportation.

Updated by Steve Pastorino

One of the last great wildernesses in the continental United States, Joshua Tree National Park teems with fascinating landscapes and life-forms. It attracts around 1.5 million visitors each year, yet is mysteriously quiet at dawn and dusk. The park features ruggedly beautiful desert scenery, enormous boulders and jagged rocks, natural cactus gardens, and lush oases shaded by elegant fan palms. The landscape shifts abruptly from the arid stubble of the low Sonoran Desert to vast stands of the park's namesake Joshua trees in the higher, wetter Mojave Desert. Members of the yucca family of shrubs, the plants' unruly limbs are said to have reminded Mormon pioneers of the prophet Joshua's outstretched arms reaching toward heaven.

JOSHUA TREE PLANNER

WHEN TO GO

October through May, when the desert is cooler, is when most visitors arrive. Daytime temperatures range from the mid-70s in December and January to mid-90s in October and May. Lows can dip to near freezing in midwinter, and you may even encounter snow at the higher elevations. Summers can be torrid, with daytime temperatures reaching 110°F.

PLANNING YOUR TIME
JOSHUA TREE IN ONE DAY

After stocking up on water, snacks, and lunch in Yucca Valley or Joshua Tree (you won't find any supplies inside the park), begin your visit at the **Joshua Tree Visitor Center**, where you can pick up maps and peruse exhibits to get acquainted with what awaits you. Enter the park itself at the nearby **West Entrance Station** and continue driving along the highly scenic and well-maintained **Park Boulevard.** Stop first at **Hidden Valley,** where you can relax at the picnic area or hike the easy 1-mile loop trail. After a few more miles turn left onto the spur road that takes you to the trailhead for the **Barker Dam Nature Trail.** Walk the easy 1.3-mile loop to view a water tank ranchers built to quench their cattle's thirst; along the way you'll spot birds and a handful of cactus varieties. Return to Park Boulevard and head south; you'll soon leave the main road again for the drive to **Keys View.** The easy loop trail here is only 0.25 mile, but the views extend for miles in every direction—look for the San Andreas Fault, the Salton Sea, and nearby mountains. Return to Park Boulevard, where you'll find **Cap Rock,** another short loop trail winding amid rock formations and Joshua trees.

Continuing along Park Boulevard, the start of the 18-mile self-guided **Geology Tour Road** will soon appear on your right. A brochure outlining its 16 stops is available here; note that the round-trip will take about two hours, and high-clearance vehicles are recommended after stop 9. ■TIP→ Do not attempt if it has recently rained. Back on Park Boulevard, you'll soon arrive at the aptly named **Skull Rock.** This downright spooky formation is next to the parking lot; a nearby trailhead marks the beginning of a 1.7-mile nature trail. End your day with a stop at the **Oasis Visitor Center** in Twentynine Palms, where you can stroll through the historic **Oasis of Mara,** popular with area settlers.

GETTING HERE AND AROUND
AIR TRAVEL
Palm Springs International Airport is the closest major airport to Joshua Tree National Park. It's about 45 miles from the park. The drive from Los Angeles International Airport to Joshua Tree takes about two hours.

CAR TRAVEL
An isolated island of pristine wilderness—a rarity these days—Joshua Tree National Park is within a short drive of 11 million Southern California residents. Most visitors, in fact, make the two-hour drive from the Los Angeles area to enjoy a weekend of solitude in 792,726 acres of untouched desert. The urban sprawl of Palm Springs (home to the nearest airport) is 45 miles away, but gateway towns Joshua Tree, Yucca Valley, and Twentynine Palms are just north of the park. If you're staying in the Palm Springs area, you can enjoy the highlights of the park in one day, including a stop for a picnic at a scenic spot.

■TIP→ If you'd prefer not to drive, most Palm Springs area hotels can arrange a half- or full-day tour that hits the highlights of Joshua Tree National Park. But you'll need to spend two or three days camping here to truly experience the quiet beauty of the desert.

PARK ESSENTIALS
PARK FEES AND PERMITS
Park admission is $25 per car, $12 per person on foot, bicycle, motorcycle, or horse. The Joshua Tree Pass, good for one year, is $40.

PARK HOURS

The park is open every day, around the clock, but visitor centers are staffed from approximately 8 am to 5 pm. The park is in the Pacific time zone.

CELL-PHONE RECEPTION

Cell phones don't work in most areas of the park. There are no telephones in the interior of the park.

EDUCATIONAL OFFERINGS

LECTURES

The Desert Institute at Joshua Tree National Park. The nonprofit educational partner of the park offers a full schedule of lectures, classes, and hikes. Class topics include basket making, painting, and photography, while field trips include workshops on cultural history, natural science, and how to survive in the desert. ⊠ *74485 National Park Dr., Twentynine Palms* ☎ *760/367–5525* ⊕ *www.joshuatree.org.*

Stargazing. At Joshua Tree National Park you can tour the Milky Way on summer evenings using binoculars. Rangers also offer programs on some evenings when the moon isn't visible. Pick up a schedule at a visitor center. ⊠ *Cottonwood Campground Amphitheater and Oasis Visitor Center.*

RANGER PROGRAMS

Evening Programs. Rangers present hour-long lectures, often on Friday or Saturday evening, at Black Rock Canyon Nature Center, Cottonwood Amphitheater, Indian Cove Amphitheater, and Jumbo Rocks Campground. Topics range from natural history to local lore. The schedule is posted at the visitor centers. ⊠ *Joshua Tree National Park* ☒ *Free.*

Fodor's Choice

★

Keys Ranch Tour. A guide takes you through the former home of a family that homesteaded here for 60 years. In addition to the ranch, a workshop, store, and schoolhouse are still standing, and the grounds are strewn with vehicles and mining equipment. The 90-minute tour, which begins at the Keys Ranch gate, tells the history of the family that built the ranch. Tickets are $10, and reservations are required. ⊠ *Hidden Valley Picnic Area* ☎ *760/367–5522* ⊕ *www.nps.gov/jotr.*

TOURS

Big Wheel Tours. Based in Palm Desert, Big Wheel Tours offers van excursions, Jeep tours, and hiking trips through the park. Bicycle tours (road and mountain bike) are available outside the park boundary. Pickups are available at Palm Springs area hotels. ⊠ *74850 42nd Ave., Palm Desert* ☎ *760/779–1837* ⊕ *www.bwbtours.com* ☒ *From $119.*

Trail Discovery. You can get a full day of exploring Joshua Tree with Trail Discovery, along with information on the park's plants, animals, geography, and history. Park admission, bottled water, hip packs, snacks, and fruit are included. Transportation is not provided. ☎ *760/413–1575* ⊕ *www.palmspringshiking.com* ☒ *From $95.*

VISITOR INFORMATION

Park Contact Information Joshua Tree National Park. ⊠ *74485 National Park Dr., Twentynine Palms* ☎ *760/367–5500* ⊕ *www.nps.gov/jotr.*

VISITOR CENTERS

Cottonwood Visitor Center. The south entrance is the closest to Interstate 10, the east–west highway from Los Angeles to Phoenix. Exhibits in this small center, staffed by rangers and volunteers, illustrate the region's natural history. The center also has restrooms. ⊠ *Cottonwood Spring, Pinto Basin Rd.* ⊕ *www.nps.gov/jotr.*

Joshua Tree Visitor Center. This visitor center has interesting exhibits illustrating park geology, cultural and historic sites, and hiking and rock-climbing activities. There's also a small bookstore and café. Restrooms with flush toilets are on the premises. ⊠ *6554 Park Blvd., Joshua Tree* ☎ *760/366–1855* ⊕ *www.nps.gov/jotr.*

> ### PLANTS AND WILDLIFE IN JOSHUA TREE
>
> Joshua Tree will shatter your notions of the desert as a wasteland. Life flourishes here, as flora and fauna have adapted to heat and drought. In most areas you'll be walking among native Joshua trees, ocotillos, and yuccas. One of the best spring desert wildflower displays in Southern California blooms here. You'll see plenty of animals—reptiles such as nocturnal sidewinders, birds like golden eagles or burrowing owls, and occasionally mammals like coyotes and bobcats.

Oasis Visitor Center. Exhibits here illustrate how Joshua Tree was formed, reveal the differences between the park's two types of desert, and demonstrate how plants and animals eke out an existence in this arid climate. Take the ½-mile nature walk through the nearby Oasis of Mara, which is alive with cottonwood trees, palm trees, and mesquite shrubs. Facililities include picnic tables, restrooms, and a bookstore. ⊠ *74485 National Park Dr., Twentynine Palms* ☎ *760/367–5500* ⊕ *www.nps.gov/jotr.*

EXPLORING

SCENIC DRIVES

Park Boulevard. If you have time only for a short visit, driving Park Boulevard is your best choice. Traversing the most scenic portions of Joshua Tree, this well-paved road connects the north and west entrances in the park's high desert section. Along with some sweeping desert views, you'll see jumbles of splendid boulder formations, stands of Joshua trees, and Hidden Valley and Barker Dam, remnants of the area's wild and woolly past. From the Oasis Visitor Center, drive south. After about 5 miles, the road forks; turn right and head west toward Jumbo Rocks (clearly marked with a road sign). ⊠ *Joshua Tree National Park.*

Pinto Basin Road. This paved road takes you from high Mojave desert to low Colorado desert. A long, slow drive, the route runs from the main part of the park to Interstate 10; it can add as much as an hour to and from Palm Springs (round-trip), but the views and roadside exhibits make it worth the extra time. From the Oasis Visitor Center, drive south. After about 5 miles, the road forks; take a left and continue another 9 miles to the Cholla Cactus Garden, where the sun fills the cactus needles with light. Past that is the Ocotillo Patch, filled with spindly plants bearing razor-sharp thorns and, after a rain, bright green leaves and brilliant red flowers. Side trips from this route require a 4X4. ⊠ *Joshua Tree National Park.*

HISTORIC SITES

FAMILY **Hidden Valley.** This legendary cattle-rustlers' hideout is set among big boulders along a 1-mile loop trail. Kids love to scramble on and around the rocks. There are shaded picnic tables here. ⊠ *Park Blvd.* ✛ *14 miles south of west entrance.*

Fodor'sChoice **Keys Ranch.** This 150-acre ranch, which once belonged to William and
★ Frances Keys and is now on the National Historic Register, illustrates one of the area's most successful attempts at homesteading. The couple raised five children under extreme desert conditions. Most of the original buildings, including the house, school, store, and workshop, have been restored to the way they were when William died in 1969. The only way to see the ranch is on one of the 90-minute walking tours usually offered Friday–Sunday, October–May, and weekends in summer; advance reservations required. ⊠ *Joshua Tree National Park* ✛ *2 miles north of Barker Dam Rd.* ☎ *760/367–5522* ⊕ *www.nps.gov/jotr/ planyourvisit/ranchtour.htm* ⊠ *$10, available at Joshua Tree and Oasis visitor centers.*

SCENIC STOPS

Barker Dam. Built around 1900 by ranchers and miners to hold water for cattle and mining operations, the dam now collects rainwater and is a good place to spot wildlife such as the elusive bighorn sheep. ⊠ *Barker Dam Rd.* ✛ *Off Park Blvd., 10 miles south of west entrance.*

Cholla Cactus Garden. This stand of bigelow cholla (sometimes called jumping cholla, since its hooked spines seem to jump at you) is best seen and photographed in late afternoon, when the backlit spiky stalks stand out against a colorful sky. ⊠ *Pinto Basin Rd.* ✛ *20 miles north of Cottonwood Visitor Center.*

Cottonwood Spring. Home to the native Cahuilla people for centuries, this spring provided water for travelers and early prospectors. The area, which supports a large stand of fan palms, is one of the best stops for bird-watching, as migrating birds (and bighorn sheep) rely on the water as well. A number of gold mines were located here, and the area still has some remains, including an *arrastra* (a gold ore–grinding tool) and concrete pillars. ⊠ *Cottonwood Visitor Center.*

Fortynine Palms Oasis. A short drive off Highway 62, this site is a bit of a preview of what the park's interior has to offer: stands of fan palms, interesting petroglyphs, and evidence of fires built by early American Indians. Since animals frequent this area, you may spot a coyote, bobcat, or roadrunner. ⊠ *End of Canyon Rd.* ✛ *4 miles west of Twentynine Palms.*

Fodor'sChoice **Keys View.** At 5,185 feet, this point affords a sweeping view of the Santa
★ Rosa Mountains and Coachella Valley, the San Andreas Fault, the peak
of 11,500-foot Mt. San Gorgonio, the shimmering surface of Salton
Sea, and—on a rare clear day—Signal Mountain in Mexico. Sunrise
and sunset are magical times, when the light throws rocks and trees
into high relief before bathing the hills in brilliant shades of red, orange,
and gold. ⊠ *Keys View Rd.* ⊹ *16 miles south of park's west entrance.*

Lost Palms Oasis. More than 100 fan palms comprise the largest group of
the exotic plants in the park. A spring bubbles from between the rocks,
but disappears into the sandy, boulder-strewn canyon. The 7.5-mile
round-trip hike is not for everyone. Bring plenty of water! ⊠ *Cottonwood Visitor Center.*

Ocotillo Patch. Stop here for a roadside exhibit on the dramatic display
made by the red-tipped succulent after even the shortest rain shower.
⊠ *Pinto Basin Rd.* ⊹ *About 3 miles east of Cholla Cactus Gardens.*

SPORTS AND THE OUTDOORS

HIKING

There are more than 190 miles of hiking trails in Joshua Tree, ranging
from quarter-mile nature trails to 35-mile treks. Some connect with
each other, so you can design your own desert maze. Remember that
drinking water is hard to come by—you won't find water in the park
except at the entrances. Bring along at least a gallon per person for all
but the shortest hikes, more if the weather is hot.

EASY

Cap Rock. This ½-mile wheelchair-accessible loop—named after a boulder that sits atop a huge rock formation like a cap—winds through
fascinating rock formations and has signs that explain the geology of
the Mojave Desert. *Easy.* ⊠ *Joshua Tree National Park* ⊹ *Trailhead: at
junction of Park Blvd. and Keys View Rd.*

Skull Rock Trail. The 1.7-mile loop guides hikers through boulder piles,
desert washes, and a rocky alley. It's named for what is perhaps the
park's most famous rock formation, which resembles the eye sockets
and nasal cavity of a human skull. Access the trail from within Jumbo
Rocks Campground or from a small parking area on the highway just
east of the campground. *Easy.* ⊠ *Joshua Tree National Park* ⊹ *Trailhead: at Jumbo Rocks Campground.*

MODERATE

Mastodon Peak Trail. Some boulder scrambling is required on this 3-mile
hike that loops up to the 3,371-foot Mastodon Peak, but the journey
rewards you with stunning views of the Salton Sea. The trail passes
through a region where gold was mined from 1919 to 1932, so be on
the lookout for open mines. The peak draws its name from a large rock
formation that early miners believed looked like the head of a prehistoric behemoth. *Moderate.* ⊠ *Joshua Tree National Park* ⊹ *Trailhead:
at Cottonwood Spring Oasis.*

9

Fodor's Choice   **Ryan Mountain Trail.** The payoff for hiking to the top of 5,461-foot Ryan
★   Mountain is one of the best panoramic views of Joshua Tree. From here
you can see Mt. San Jacinto, Mt. San Gorgonio, Lost Horse Valley, and
the Pinto Basin. You'll need two to three hours to complete the 3-mile
round-trip with 1,000-plus feet of elevation gain. *Moderate.* ⊠ *Joshua
Tree National Park* ⊹ *Trailhead: at Ryan Mountain parking area, 16
miles southeast of park's west entrance, or Sheep Pass, 16 miles southwest of Oasis Visitor Center.*

ROCK CLIMBING

With an abundance of weathered igneous boulder outcroppings, Joshua
Tree is one of the nation's top winter-climbing destinations. There are
more than 4,500 established routes offering a full menu of climbing
experiences—from bouldering for beginners in the Wonderland of
Rocks to multiple-pitch climbs at Echo Rock and Saddle Rock. The
best-known climb in the park is Hidden Valley's Sports Challenge Rock.
A map inside the *Joshua Tree Guide* shows locations of selected wilderness and nonwilderness climbs.

TOURS AND OUTFITTERS

Joshua Tree Rock Climbing School. The school offers several programs,
from one-day introductory classes to multiday programs for experienced climbers, and provides all needed equipment. Beginning classes,
offered year-round on most weekends, are limited to six people age eight
or older. ⊠ *Joshua Tree National Park* ☎ *760/366–4745, 800/890–4745*
⊕ *www.joshuatreerockclimbing.com* ✉ *From $195.*

Vertical Adventures Rock Climbing School. About 1,000 climbers each
year learn the sport in Joshua Tree National Park through this school.
Classes, offered September–May, meet at a designated location in the
park, and all equipment is provided. ⊠ *Joshua Tree National Park*
☎ *800/514–8785* ⊕ *www.vertical-adventures.com* ✉ *From $145.*

MOJAVE DESERT

WELCOME TO THE MOJAVE DESERT

TOP REASONS TO GO

★ **Nostalgia:** Old neon signs, historic motels, and restored (or neglected but still striking) rail stations abound across this desert landscape. Don't miss the classic eateries along the way, including Summit Inn in Oak Hills and Emma Jean's Holland Burger Cafe in Victorville.

★ **Death Valley wonders:** Visit this distinctive landscape to tour some of the most varied desert terrain in the world.

★ **Great ghost towns:** California's gold rush brought miners to the Mojave, and the towns they left behind have their own unique charms.

★ **Cool down in Sierra country:** Head up U.S. 395 toward Bishop to visit the High Sierra, home to majestic Mt. Whitney.

★ **Explore ancient history:** The Mojave Desert is replete with rare petroglyphs, some dating back almost 16,000 years.

1 The Western Mojave. Stretching from the town of Ridgecrest to the base of the San Gabriel Mountains, the western Mojave is a varied landscape of ancient Native American petroglyphs, tufa towers, and hillsides covered in bright orange poppies.

2 The Eastern Mojave. Joshua trees and cacti dot a predominantly flat landscape that is interrupted by dramatic, rock-strewn mountains. The area is largely uninhabited, so be cautious when driving the back roads, where towns and services are scarce.

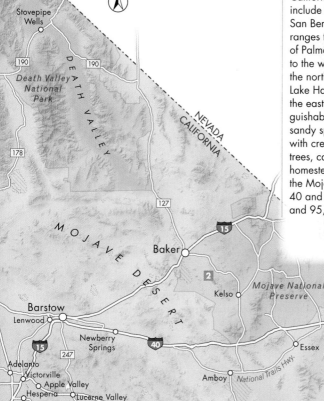

GETTING ORIENTED

The Mojave Desert, once part of an ancient inland sea, is one of the largest swaths of open land in Southern California. Its boundaries include the San Gabriel and San Bernardino mountain ranges to the south; the areas of Palmdale and Ridgecrest to the west; Death Valley to the north; and Needles and Lake Havasu in Arizona to the east. The area is distinguishable by its wide-open sandy spaces, peppered with creosote bushes, Joshua trees, cacti, and abandoned homesteads. You can access the Mojave via interstates 40 and 15, highways 14 and 95, and U.S. 395.

10

Stovepipe Wells

190

Death Valley National Park

178

127

15

Baker

2

Kelso

Mojave National Preserve

95

Needles

40

ARIZONA

Barstow

Lenwood

Newberry Springs

40

Essex

Adelanto

Victorville

Apple Valley

Hesperia

Lucerne Valley

Oak Hills Lake

Arrowhead

Big Bear Lake

Crestline

247

95

Amboy

National Trails Hwy.

18

247

215

SAN BERNARDINO MOUNTAINS

NEVADA

CALIFORNIA

DEATH VALLEY

MOJAVE DESERT

0   20 mi

0   20 km

Updated by
Joan Patterson

Dust and desolation, tumbleweeds and rattlesnakes, barren landscapes and failed dreams—these are the bleak images that come to mind when most people hear the word *desert*. Yet the remote regions east of the Sierra Nevada possess a singular beauty, the vast open spaces populated with spiky Joshua trees, undulating sand dunes, faulted mountains, and dramatic rock formations. With a few exceptions the area is not heavily peopled, providing expanses in which visitors can both lose and find themselves.

The topography is extreme; while Death Valley drops to almost 300 feet below sea level and contains the lowest (and hottest) spot in North America, the Mojave Desert, which lies to the south, has elevations ranging from 3,000 to 5,000 feet.

PLANNING

WHEN TO GO
Spring and fall are the best seasons to tour the desert. Winters are generally mild, but summers can be cruel. If you're on a budget, be aware that room rates drop as the temperatures rise.

GETTING HERE AND AROUND
AIR TRAVEL
McCarran International Airport in Las Vegas is the nearest airport to many eastern Mojave destinations. Needles Airport and Inyokern Airport serve small, private planes.

Contacts Inyokern Airport. ⊠ *1669 Airport Rd., off Hwy. 178, 9 miles west of Ridgecrest, Inyokern* ☎ *760/377–5844* ⊕ *www.inyokernairport.com.* **McCarran International Airport.** ⊠ *5757 Wayne Newton Blvd., Las Vegas* ☎ *702/261–5211* ⊕ *www.mccarran.com.* **Needles Airport.** ⊠ *711 Airport Rd., Needles* ☎ *760/247–2371* ⊕ *cms.sbcounty.gov/airports.*

BUS TRAVEL

Greyhound provides bus service to Barstow, Victorville, and Palmdale; check with the chambers of commerce about local bus service, which is generally more useful to residents than to tourists.

Contacts **Greyhound.** ☎ *800/231–2222* ⊕ *www.greyhound.com.*

CAR TRAVEL

The major north–south route through the western Mojave is U.S. 395, which intersects with Interstate 15 between Cajon Pass and Victorville. Farther west, Highway 14 runs north–south between Inyokern (near Ridgecrest) and Palmdale. Two major east–west routes travel through the Mojave: to the north, Interstate 15 to Las Vegas, Nevada; to the south, Interstate 40 to Needles. At the intersection of the two interstates, in Barstow, Interstate 15 veers south toward Victorville and Los Angeles, and Interstate 40 gives way to Highway 58 west toward Bakersfield.

■ TIP➔ **For the latest Mojave traffic and weather, tune in to the Highway Stations (98.1 FM near Barstow, 98.9 FM near Essex, and 99.7 FM near Baker).** Traffic can be especially troublesome Friday through Sunday, when thousands of Angelenos head to Las Vegas for a bit of R&R.

Contacts **Caltrans Current Highway Conditions.** ☎ *800/427–7623* ⊕ *www.dot.ca.gov.*

TRAIN TRAVEL

Amtrak trains traveling east and west stop in Victorville, Barstow, and Needles, but the stations aren't staffed, so you'll have to purchase tickets in advance and handle your own baggage. The Barstow station is served daily by Amtrak California motor coaches that stop in Los Angeles, Bakersfield, Las Vegas, and elsewhere.

Contacts **Amtrak.** ☎ *800/872–7245* ⊕ *www.amtrak.com.*

HEALTH AND SAFETY

Let someone know your trip route, destination, and estimated time of return. Before setting out, make sure your vehicle is in good condition. Carry water, a jack, tools, and towrope or chain. Keep an eye on your gas gauge and try to keep the needle above half. Stay on main roads, and watch out for wildlife, horses, and cattle.

Drink at least a gallon of water a day (more if you're hiking or otherwise exerting yourself). Dress in layered clothing and wear comfortable, sturdy shoes and a hat. Keep snacks, sunscreen, and a first-aid kit on hand. If you have a headache or feel dizzy or nauseous, you could be suffering from dehydration. Get out of the sun immediately and drink plenty of water. Dampen your clothing to lower your body temperature. Do not enter abandoned mine tunnels or shafts of which there are hundreds in the Mojave Desert. The structures may be unstable, and there may be hidden dangers such as pockets of bad air. Avoid canyons during rainstorms. Floodwaters can quickly fill up dry riverbeds and cover or wash away roads. Never place your hands or feet where you can't see them: rattlesnakes, scorpions, and black widow spiders may be hiding there.

10

Contacts **Barstow Community Hospital.** ✉ *820 E. Mountain View St., Barstow* ☎ *760/256–1761* ⊕ *www.barstowhospital.com.* **BLM Rangers.** ☎ *916/978–4400* ⊕ *www.blm.gov/ca.* **San Bernardino County Sheriff.** ☎ *760/256–4838 in Barstow, 760/733–4448 in Baker* ⊕ *cms.sbcounty.gov/sheriff.*

HOURS OF OPERATION

Early morning is the best time to visit sights and avoid crowds, but some museums and visitor centers don't open until 10. If you schedule your town arrivals for the late afternoon, you can drop by the visitor centers just before closing hours to line up an itinerary for the next day.

RESTAURANTS

Throughout the desert, dining is a fairly simple affair. There are chain establishments in Ridgecrest, Victorville, and Barstow, as well as some ethnic eateries. *Restaurant reviews have been shortened. For full information, visit Fodors.com.*

HOTELS

Chain hotel properties and roadside motels are the desert's primary lodging options. The tourist season runs from late May through September. Reservations are rarely a problem, but it's still wise to make them. *Hotel reviews have been shortened. For full information, please visit Fodors.com.*

WHAT IT COSTS			
	$	$$	$$$	$$$$
Restaurants	under $16	$16–$22	$23–$30	over $30
Hotels	under $120	$120–$175	$176–$250	over $250

Restaurant prices are the average cost of a main course at dinner or, if dinner is not served, at lunch, excluding sales tax of 7.75%. Hotel prices are the lowest cost of a standard double room in high season, excluding service charges and 7.25% tax.

TOURS

Sierra Club. The San Gorgonio Chapter of the Sierra Club and the chapter's Mojave Group conduct interesting field trips and desert excursions. Activities are often volunteer-run and free, but participants are sometimes required to cover parking and other expenses. ☎ *951/684–6203* ⊕ *sangorgonio2.sierraclub.org* ✉ *Some free; fee tour prices vary.*

VISITOR INFORMATION

Contacts **Barstow Welcome Center.** ✉ *2796 Tanger Way, Barstow* ☎ *760/253–4782* ⊕ *www.visitcalifornia.com/destination/california-welcome-centers-desert.* **Bureau of Land Management.** ✉ *California Desert District Office, 22835 Calle San Juan De Los Lagos, Moreno Valley* ☎ *951/697–5200* ⊕ *www.blm.gov/ca.* **Death Valley Chamber of Commerce.** ☎ *888/600–1844* ⊕ *www.deathvalleychamber.org.*

THE WESTERN MOJAVE

This vast area is especially beautiful along U.S. 395. From January through March, wildflowers are in bloom and temperatures are manageable. Year-round, snowcapped mountain peaks are irresistible sights.

LANCASTER

8 miles north of Palmdale.

Points of interest around Lancaster include a state poppy reserve that bursts to life in the spring and Edwards Air Force Base, which offers a fascinating tour of historical military aircraft. Lancaster was founded in 1876, when the Southern Pacific Railroad arrived. Before that, several Native American tribes, some of whose descendants still live in the surrounding mountains, inhabited it.

GETTING HERE AND AROUND

From the Los Angeles basin, take Highway 14, which proceeds north to Mojave and Highway 58, a link between Bakersfield and Barstow. Regional Metrolink trains serve Lancaster from the Los Angeles area. Local transit exists, but a car is the best way to experience this area.

ESSENTIALS

Visitor Information Destination Lancaster. ⊠ *554 W. Lancaster Blvd.* ☎ *661/948–4518* ⊕ *www.destinationlancasterca.org.*

EXPLORING
TOP ATTRACTIONS

Antelope Valley Indian Museum. This museum got its start as a private collection of American Indian antiquities gathered in the 1920s by artist and amateur naturalist Howard Arden Edwards. Today, his Swiss chalet-style home is a state museum known for one-of-a-kind artifacts from California, Southwest, and Great Basin native tribes, including ancient tools, artwork, basketry and rugs. To get here, exit north off Highway 138 at 165th Street East and follow the signs, or take the Avenue K exit off Highway 14. ⊠ *15701 E. Ave. M* ☎ *661/946–3055* ⊕ *www.avim.parks.ca.gov* ⊠ *$3.*

Antelope Valley Poppy Reserve. The California poppy, the state flower, can be spotted throughout the state, but this quiet park holds the densest concentration. Eight miles of trails wind through 1,745 acres of hills carpeted with poppies and other wildflowers, including a paved section that allows wheelchair access. Keep in mind that poppy flowers will curl up their petals if it's too windy or cold, so plan accordingly. ■ TIP➔ **Blooming season is usually March through May.** On a clear day at any time of year, you'll be treated to sweeping views of Antelope Valley. ⊠ *15101 Lancaster Rd., west off Hwy. 14, Ave. I Exit* ☎ *661/724–1180 wildflower hotline, 661/946–6092* ⊕ *www.parks.ca.gov/?page_id=627* ⊠ *$10 per vehicle.*

10

OFF THE BEATEN PATH

Exotic Feline Breeding Compound's Feline Conservation Center. About two dozen species of wild cats, from the unusual, weasel-size jaguarundi to leopards, tigers, and jaguars, inhabit this small, orderly facility. You can see the cats up close (behind barrier fences) in the parklike public zoo and research center, and docents are available to answer questions. ⊠ *Rhyolite Ave. off Mojave-Tropico Rd., Rosamond* ☎ *661/256–3793* ⊕ *www.wildcatzoo.org* ⊒ *$7* ⊘ *Closed Wed.*

WORTH NOTING

Air Force Flight Test Museum at Edwards Air Force Base. This museum, at what many consider to be the birthplace of supersonic flight, chronicles the rich history of flight testing. Numerous airplanes are on exhibit, from the first F-16B to the only remaining YF-22. While those with approved base entry have access to regular museum hours, a general-public tour takes place once a month. The 3½-hour tour includes indoor museum exhibits and driving tours of the aircraft. The tour requires a reservation and you have to provide basic information for a background check at least a week in advance (a month for non-U.S. residents), but be aware that slots fill up fast. On the base's website, click Tours for details. ⊠ *Edwards Air Force Base Visitor Control Center , 405 S. Rosamond Blvd., Edwards* ☎ *661/277–8050, 661/277–3510* ⊕ *www.afftcmuseum.org* ⊒ *Free.*

Antelope Valley Winery/Donato Family Vineyard. Cyndee and Frank Donato purchased the Los Angeles–based McLester Winery in 1990 and moved it to Lancaster, where the high-desert sun and nighttime chill work their magic on wine grapes such as Merlot, Zinfandel, and Sangiovese. In addition to tastings, the winery hosts a Saturday farmers' market (from May through November between 9 and noon) and sells grass-fed buffalo and other game and exotic meats such as venison, pheasant, and wild boar. ⊠ *42041 20th St. W, at Ave. M* ☎ *661/722–0145, 888/282–8332* ⊕ *www.avwinery.com* ⊒ *Winery free, tasting $6.50 to $15.*

OFF THE BEATEN PATH

Devil's Punchbowl Natural Area. A mile from the San Andreas Fault, the namesake of this attraction is a natural bowl-shaped depression in the earth, framed by 300-foot rock walls. At the bottom is a stream, which you can reach via a moderately strenuous 1-mile hike. You also can detour on a short nature trail; at the top an interpretive center has displays of native flora and fauna, including live animals such as snakes, lizards, and birds of prey. ⊠ *28000 Devil's Punchbowl Rd., south of Hwy. 138, Pearblossom* ☎ *661/944–2743* ⊒ *Free.*

10

OFF THE BEATEN PATH

St. Andrew's Abbey. Nestled in the foothills of the Antelope Valley, this peaceful enclave is both Benedictine monastery and restful retreat for those wanting to get away from the bustle of everyday life. Day visitors can walk the lush tree-lined grounds, including a large, shaded pond teeming with ducks and red-eared turtles, or browse the well-stocked gift shop for religious keepsakes. An extensive collection of ceramic tiles in the image of saints and angels by Father Maur van Doorslaer, a Belgian monk whose work U.S. and Canadian collectors favor, are among the items sold here to help sustain the monastery and its good works. ⊠ *31001 N. Valyermo Rd., south of Hwy. 138, Valyermo* ☎ *888/454–5411, 661/944–2178 ceramics studio* ⊕ *www. saintsandangels.org* ⊒ *Free.*

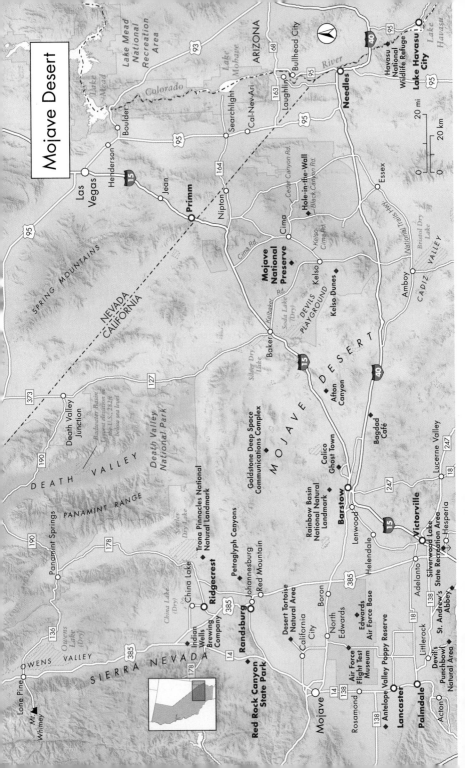

RED ROCK CANYON STATE PARK

48 miles north of Lancaster.

On the stretch of Highway 14 that slices through Red Rock Canyon State Park, it's easy to become caught up in the momentum of rushing to your "real" destination. But it would be a shame not to stop for this deeply beautiful canyon, with its rich, layered colors and Native American heritage.

GETTING HERE AND AROUND

The only practical way to get here is by car, taking Highway 14 north from the Palmdale-Lancaster area or south from Ridgecrest.

Red Rock Canyon State Park. A geological feast for the eyes with its layers of pink, white, red, and brown rock, this remote canyon is also a region of fascinating biological diversity—the ecosystems of the Sierra Nevada, the Mojave Desert, and the Basin Range all converge here. Native Americans known as the Kawaiisu lived here some 20,000 years ago; later, Mojave Indians roamed the land for centuries. You can still see remains of gold mining operations in the park, and movies such as *Jurassic Park* have been shot here. For a quiet nature trail a little off the beaten path try the 0.75-mile loop at Red Cliffs Natural Preserve on Highway 14, across from the entrance to the Ricardo Campground. ⊠ *Visitor Center, 37749 Abbott Dr., off Hwy. 14, Cantil* ☎ *661/946–6092* ⊕ *www.parks. ca.gov* ⌛ *$6 per vehicle.*

RIDGECREST

28 miles northeast of Red Rock Canyon State Park, 77 miles south of Lone Pine.

A military town that serves the U.S. Naval Weapons Center to its north, Ridgecrest has scores of stores, restaurants, and hotels. With about 25,000 residents, it's the last city of any significant size you'll encounter as you head northeast toward Death Valley National Park. It's a good base for visiting regional attractions such as the Trona Pinnacles and Petroglyph Canyons.

GETTING HERE AND AROUND

Arrive here by car via U.S. 395 or, from the Los Angeles area, Highway 14. The local bus service is of limited use to tourists.

ESSENTIALS

Transportation Contacts Ridgerunner Transit. ☎ *760/499–5040* ⊕ *ridgecrest-ca.gov/transit/transit.*

Visitor Information Ridgecrest Area Convention and Visitors Bureau. ⊠ *643 N. China Lake Blvd., Suite C* ☎ *760/375–8202, 800/847–4830* ⊕ *www.racvb.com.*

EXPLORING

TOP ATTRACTIONS

FAMILY

Fodor's Choice

★

Petroglyph Canyons. Thousands of well-preserved images of animals and humans are scratched or pecked into dark basaltic rocks at Big Petroglyph and Little Petroglyph canyons in the Coso Mountain range, the largest concentration of ancient rock art in the Northern Hemisphere. The canyons lie within the million-acre U.S. Naval Weapons Center at China Lake. Only the drawings of Little Petroglyph can be visited, and only on a guided tour arranged in advance through the Maturango Museum. Tour participants must be U.S. citizens over 10 years of age, and fill out an online application to obtain security clearance. Detailed information about the spring and fall tours, which fill up fast, is provided on the museum's website. ✉ *100 E. Las Flores Ave.* ☎ *760/375–6900* 🌐 *www.maturango.org* 🎟 *$55* 🕒 *Closed Jan. and Feb. and July and Aug.*

Trona Pinnacles National Natural Landmark. Fantastic-looking formations of calcium carbonate, known as tufa, were formed underwater along fault lines in the bed of what is now Searles Dry Lake. Some of the more than 500 spires stand as tall as 140 feet, creating a landscape so surreal that it doubled for outer-space terrain in the film *Star Trek V.*

An easy-to-walk ½-mile trail allows you to see the tufa up close, but wear sturdy shoes—tufa cuts like coral. The best road to the area can be impassable after a rainstorm. ✉ *Pinnacle Rd.* ✥ *5 miles south of Hwy. 178, 18 miles east of Ridgecrest* ☎ *760/384–5400 Ridgecrest BLM office* 🌐 *www.recreation.gov.*

OFF THE BEATEN PATH

Indian Wells Brewing Company. After driving through the hot desert, you'll surely appreciate a cold one at Indian Wells Brewing Company, where master brewer Rick Lovett lovingly crafts his Lobotomy Bock, Amnesia I.P.A., and Lunatic Lemonade, among others. If you have the kids along, grab a six-pack of his specialty root beer, black cherry, orange, or cream soda. ✉ *2565 N. Hwy. 14, 2 miles west of U.S. 395, Inyokern* ☎ *760/377–5989* 🌐 *www.mojavered.com.*

WORTH NOTING

FAMILY **Maturango Museum.** The museum contains interesting exhibits that survey the Upper Mojave Desert area's art, history, and geology, and sponsors tours of the amazing rock drawings in Petroglph Canyons. ✉ *100 E. Las Flores Ave., at Hwy. 178* ☎ *760/375–6900* 🌐 *www.maturango.org* 🎟 *$5, kids under 18 free.*

WHERE TO STAY

$$ HOTEL 🏨 **Hampton Inn & Suites Ridgecrest.** Clean and reliable, the Hampton has a well-equipped exercise room, pool, spotless Internet service, and complimentary breakfast. **Pros:** attentive, friendly service; good breakfast; big rooms. **Cons:** a rather strong chain vibe. [$] *Rooms from: $159* ✉ *104 E. Sydnor Ave.* ☎ *760/446–1968* 🛏 *93 rooms* 🍴 *Breakfast.*

$$$ HOTEL 🏨 **SpringHill Suites Ridgecrest.** The spacious rooms and contemporary feel of this all-suites Marriott brand hotel make this a welcome choice after a long drive in the desert. **Pros:** spacious rooms; good breakfast; helpful staff. **Cons:** pricey. [$] *Rooms from: $194* ✉ *113 E. Sydnor Ave.* ☎ *888/236–2427, 760/446–1630* 🌐 *www.marriott.com/hotels/travel/iyksh-springhill-suites-ridgecrest* 🛏 *93 studio suites* 🍴 *Breakfast.*

RANDSBURG

21 miles south of Ridgecrest, 26 miles east of Red Rock Canyon State Park.

Randsburg and nearby Red Mountain and Johannesburg make up the Rand Mining District, which first boomed with the discovery of gold in the Rand Mountains in 1895. Rich tungsten ore, used in World War I to make steel alloy, was discovered in 1907, and silver was found in 1919. The boom has gone bust, but the area still has some residents, a few antiques shops, and plenty of character. Butte Avenue is the main drag in Randsburg, whose tiny city jail, just off Butte, is among the original buildings still standing. An archetypal Old West cemetery perched on a hillside looms over Johannesburg.

GETTING HERE AND AROUND

Arriving by car is the best transportation option. From Red Rock Canyon, drive east on Redrock Randsburg Road. From Ridgecrest, drive south on South China Lake Road and U.S. 395.

EXPLORING

Rand Desert Museum. The colorful history of the Rand Mining District during its heyday is celebrated in this small museum, including historical mining photographs, documents, and artifacts. ⊠ *161 Butte Ave.* ☎ *760/371–0965* ⊕ *www.randdesertmuseum.com* ✉ *Free* ⊙ *Closed weekdays.*

OFF THE BEATEN PATH

Desert Tortoise Natural Area. It may not always be easy to spot the elusive desert tortoise in this peaceful protected habitat but the approximately 40-square-mile area often blazes with wildflowers in the spring and early summer. It is also a great spot to see desert kit fox, red-tailed hawks, cactus wrens, and Mojave rattlesnakes; walking paths and a small interpretive center are part of the experience. ⊠ *8 miles northeast of California City via Randsburg Mojave Rd.* ☎ *951/683–3872* ⊕ *www.tortoise-tracks.org* ✉ *Free.*

General Store. Built as Randsburg's Drug Store in 1896, the General Store is one of the area's few surviving ghost-town buildings with an original tin ceiling, light fixtures, and 1904-era marble-and-stained-glass soda fountain. You can still enjoy a phosphate soda from that same fountain, or a lunch of burgers, hot dogs, and chili. ⊠ *35 Butte Ave.* ☎ *760/374–2143* ⊕ *www.randsburggeneralstore.com* ⊙ *Closed Tues.–Thurs.*

White House Saloon. This still-surviving saloon served miners and cowboys when it was first established way back in 1897; nowadays tourists and bikers sidle up to the bar for a burger, ice-cold brew, and a giant dose of Old West nostalgia. ⊠ *168 Butte Ave.* ☎ *760/374–2464* ⊙ *Closed Mon.–Thurs.*

10

THE EASTERN MOJAVE

Majestic, wide-open spaces define this region, with the Mojave National Preserve being one of the state's most remote but rewarding destinations.

VICTORVILLE

87 miles south of Ridgecrest.

At the southwest corner of the Mojave is the sprawling town of Victorville, a town with a rich Route 66 heritage and a museum dedicated to the Mother Road. Victorville was named for Santa Fe Railroad pioneer Jacob Nash Victor, who drove the first locomotive through the Cajon Pass here in 1885. Once home to Native Americans, the town later became a rest stop for Mormons and missionaries. In 1941 George Air Force Base, now an airport and storage area, brought scores of military families to the area, many of which have stayed on to raise families of their own.

GETTING HERE AND AROUND

Drive here on Interstate 15 from Los Angeles or Las Vegas, or from the north via U.S. 395. Amtrak and Greyhound also serve the town. There are local buses, but touring by car is more practical.

ESSENTIALS

Transportation Information The Victor Valley Transit Authority. ☎ 760/948–3030 ⊕ www.vvta.org.

Visitor Information Victor Valley Chamber of Commerce. ⊠ *14174 Green Tree Blvd., at St. Andrews Dr.* ☎ *760/245–6506* ⊕ *www.vvchamber.com.*

EXPLORING

TOP ATTRACTIONS

California Route 66 Museum. Visitors from around the world still think of Historic Route 66 as one of the best ways to see the real America and this 4,500-square-foot museum is chock-full of memorabilia such as maps and postcards, photographs, paintings, and nostalgic displays that bring the iconic highway's history to life. Friendly museum volunteers are more than happy to answer questions and take your picture inside the flower-painted VW Love Bus. ⊠ *16825 S. D St., between 5th and 6th Sts.* ☎ *760/951–0436* ⊕ *www.califrt66museum.org* ▥ *Free.*

WORTH NOTING

FAMILY **Mojave Narrows Regional Park.** This 840-acre park is one of the few spots where the Mojave River flows aboveground and the result is open pastures, wetlands, and two lakes surrounded by cottonwoods and cattails. Amenities include camping, fishing, equestrian/walking trails, and a large playground with waterpark. ⊠ *18000 Yates Rd., north on Ridgecrest Rd. off Bear Valley Rd.* ☎ *760/245–2226* ⊕ *cms.sbcounty.gov/parks* ▥ *$8 weekdays, $10 weekends and holidays* ⊘ *Closed Tues. and Wed.*

WHERE TO EAT AND STAY

$
DINER

✕ **Emma Jean's Holland Burger Cafe.** The short-order cook and his grill are literally center stage in this tiny, family-owned restaurant along Historic Route 66, which has changed little since it first opened in 1947. It's the peach cobbler, Brian burger, and fried chicken that keep locals lining up at the door, but anyone wanting a glimpse of 20th-century Americana can get their kicks here, too. **Known for:** Route 66 memorabilia; historical diner. $ *Average main: $8* ⊠ *17143 N. D St., at Water Power Housing Dr.* ☎ *760/243–9938* ▭ *No credit cards* ☉ *Closed Sun. No dinner.*

$
AMERICAN
FAMILY

✕ **Molly Brown's Country Cafe.** There's no mystery why this place is a locals' favorite. The cozy eatery offers a mouthwatering breakfast menu that includes everything from chicken fried steak to a sizzling garden skillet brimming with fresh vegetables; pair it with a slice of homemade pumpkin bread. **Known for:** hearty breakfasts; locals' favorite; homemade breads. $ *Average main: $10* ⊠ *15775 Mojave Dr.* ☎ *760/241–4900* ⊕ *www.mollybrownscountrycafe.com.*

$$
HOTEL
FAMILY

▥ **Courtyard Marriott Victorville Hesperia.** Rooms are spacious and contemporary, and there is both an indoor pool and large outdoor patio and pool area ideal for large groups. **Pros:** convenient location off I–15; some rooms with desert views; two pools; free Wi-Fi. **Cons:** breakfast only with certain room rates; bistro menu options limited. $ *Rooms from: $136* ⊠ *9619 Mariposa Rd., Hesperia* ☎ *760/956–3876* ⊕ *www.marriott.com* ⇆ *123 rooms, 8 suites.*

$
HOTEL
FAMILY

▥ **La Quinta Inn and Suites Victorville.** This small hotel offers a touch more than your typical chain, with contemporary decor in cozy earth tones and spacious rooms. **Pros:** near shopping mall; helpful staff; hot breakfast; outdoor pool and Jacuzzi. **Cons:** some freeway noise. $ *Rooms from: $109* ⊠ *12000 Mariposa Rd., Hesperia* ☎ *760/949–9900* ⊕ *www.lq.com* ⇆ *53 rooms, 22 suites* ▯◯▮ *Breakfast.*

BARSTOW

32 miles northeast of Victorville.

Barstow was born in 1886, when a subsidiary of the Atchison, Topeka, and Santa Fe Railway began construction of a Harvey House depot and hotel here. The depot has been restored and includes two free museums, the family-friendly Calico Ghost Town is just north of town, and there are well-known chain motels and restaurants right off Interstate 15 if you need a rest and refuel before the next stop.

10

GETTING HERE AND AROUND

Driving here on Interstate 15 from Los Angeles or Las Vegas is the best option, although you can reach Barstow via Amtrak or Greyhound. The local bus service is helpful for sights downtown.

ESSENTIALS

Transportation Information Barstow Area Transit/Victor Valley Transit. ☎ *760/948–3030* ⊕ *vvta.org.*

Visitor Information Barstow Area Chamber of Commerce and Visitors Bureau. ⊠ *229 E. Main St.* ☎ *760/256–8617* ⊕ *www.barstowchamber.com.* **California Welcome Center.** ⊠ *2796 Tanger Way, Suite 100, off*

Many of the buildings in the popular Calico Ghost Town are authentic.

Lenwood Rd. ☎ *760/253–4782* ⊕ *www.visitcalifornia.com/attraction/california-welcome-center-barstow.*

EXPLORING
TOP ATTRACTIONS

FAMILY

Fodor'sChoice

★

Calico Ghost Town. This former silver-mining boom town was started in 1881 and within a few years boasted 500 mines and 22 saloons. Its reconstruction by Walter Knott of Knott's Berry Farm makes it more about G-rated family entertainment than the town's gritty past, but that doesn't seem to take away from the fun of panning for (fool's) gold, touring the original tunnels of Maggie Mine or taking a leisurely ride on the Calico Odessa Railroad. Five of the original buildings are still standing, such as the impressive Lane's General Store, and its setting among the stark beauty of the Calico Hills can make a stroll along this once-bustling Main Street downright peaceful. ■**TIP**➜ Calico also has ghost tours and regular events such as the yearly bluegrass festival on Mother's Day weekend. ✉ *36600 Ghost Town Rd., off I–15, Yermo* ☎ *760/254–2122* ⊕ *cms.sbcounty.gov/parks/Parks/CalicoGhostTown.aspx* 🎫 *$8.*

Casa Del Desierto Harvey House. This historic train depot was built around 1911 (the original 1885 structure was destroyed by fire) and was one of the original Harvey Houses, providing dining and lodging for weary travelers along the rail lines. Waitresses at the depots were popularized in movies such as *The Harvey Girls* with Judy Garland. It now houses offices and two museums: the Western American Railroad and Route 66 Mother Road, but you can still walk along the porticos of the impressive Spanish Renaissance Classical building, or stroll into the restored lobby where you'll find the original staircase, terrazzo floor, and copper chandeliers. ✉ *681 N. 1st Ave., near Riverside Dr.* ☎ *760/255–1890 Route 66 museum* ⊕ *www.barstowharveyhouse.com.*

FAMILY

Fodor's Choice
★

Goldstone Deep Space Communications Complex. Friendly and enthusiastic staffers conduct guided tours of this 53-square-mile complex. Tours start at the Goldstone Museum, where exhibits detail past and present space missions and Deep Space Network history. From there, you'll drive out to see the massive concave antennas, starting with those used for early manned space flights and culminating with the 24-story-tall "listening" device. This is one of only three complexes in the world that make up the Deep Space Network, tracking and communicating with spacecraft throughout our solar system. ■TIP→ Appointments are required; contact the complex to reserve a slot. ✉ *Ft. Irwin Military Base, Ft. Irwin Rd. off I–15, 35 miles north of Barstow* ☎ *760/255– 8688* ⊕ *www.gdscc.nasa.gov.*

Rainbow Basin National Natural Landmark. Many science-fiction movies set on Mars have been filmed at this landmark 8 miles north of Barstow. Huge slabs of red, orange, white, and green stone tilt at crazy angles like ships about to capsize and traces of ancient beasts such as mastodons and bear-dogs, which roamed the basin up to 16 million years ago have been discovered in its fossil beds. The dirt road around the basin is narrow and bumpy so vehicles with higher clearance are recommended and rain can quickly turn the road to mud; at times, only four-wheel-drive vehicles are permitted. ✉ *Fossil Bed Rd., 3 miles west of Fort Irwin Rd. (head north from I–15)* ☎ *760/252–6000* ⊕ *www.recreation.gov.*

Skyline Drive-In Theatre. Check out a bit of surviving Americana at this dusty drive-in, where you can watch the latest Hollywood flicks among the Joshua trees and starry night sky. Keep in mind the old-time speakers are no more; sound is tuned in via car radio. ✉ *31175 Old Hwy. 58* ☎ *760/256–3333* ⌧ *$9 per person* ⊙ *Closed in winter.*

FAMILY

Western America Railroad Museum. You can almost hear the murmur of passengers and rhythmic, metal-on-metal clatter as you stroll past the old cabooses, railcars and engines, such as Sante Fe number 95, that are on display outside the historic Barstow station where this museum is located. The next stop is the indoor portion of the collection, including a train simulator, rail equipment, model railroad display and other memorabilia. A handful of artifacts from the depot's Harvey House days are on display, as well as period dining-car china from railways around the country. ✉ *Casa Del Desierto, 685 N. 1st Ave., near Riverside Dr.* ☎ *760/256–9276* ⊕ *www.barstowrailmuseum.org* ⊙ *Closed Mon.–Thurs.*

10

WORTH NOTING
Afton Canyon. Because of its colorful, steep walls, Afton Canyon is often called the Grand Canyon of the Mojave. It was carved over thousands of years by the rushing waters of the Mojave River, which makes one of its few aboveground appearances here. The dirt road that leads to the canyon is ungraded in spots, so it is best to explore it in an all-terrain vehicle. ✉ *Off Afton Rd., 36 miles northeast of Barstow via I–15* ⊕ *www.recreation.gov.*

Bagdad Café. Tourists from all over the world flock to this Route 66 eatery where the 1987 film of the same name was shot. Built in the 1940s, the divey Bagdad Café's walls are crammed with memorabilia donated by visitors famous and otherwise. The very limited bill of fare includes the Bagdad omelet and a buffalo burger with fries, but this place is really about soaking up the Route 66-Americana vibe. ✉ *46548 National Trails Hwy., at Nopal La., Newberry Springs* ☎ *760/257–3101.*

FAMILY **Mojave River Valley Museum.** The floor-to-ceiling collection of local history, both quirky and conventional, includes Ice Age fossils such as a giant mammoth tusk dug up in 2006, Native American artifacts, 19th-century handmade quilts, and displays on early settlers. Entrance is free and there's a little gift shop with a nice collection of books about the area. **■ TIP→ The story about Possum Trot and its population of folk-art dolls is not to be missed.** ✉ *270 E. Virginia Way, at Belinda St.* ☎ *760/256–5452* 🌐 *www.mojaverivervalleymuseum.org.*

WHERE TO EAT AND STAY

$$$ STEAKHOUSE 🍴 **Idle Spurs Steakhouse.** This spacious steak-and-seafood restaurant, with its Western-style memorabilia and cheerful white fairy lights, has been a favorite among locals for decades. The menu is very basic no-frills steakhouse fare, but the service is friendly and it's a bit of cozy, mid-century charm in the middle of the Mojave. **Known for:** locals' favorite; family run; dated but cozy. [$] *Average main: $24* ✉ *690 Old Hwy. 58, at Camarillo Ave.* ☎ *760/256–8888* 🌐 *thespurs.us* 🕓 *Closed Mon.*

$ AMERICAN FAMILY 🍴 **Peggy Sue's 50s Diner.** Checkerboard floors and life-size versions of Elvis and Marilyn Monroe greet you at this funky '50s coffee shop and pizza parlor in the middle of the Mojave. Outside, kids can play by the duck pond before heading in to spin a tune on the jukebox or order from the soda fountain. **Known for:** movie, TV memorabilia; over-the-top '50s vibe; gift shop. [$] *Average main: $10* ✉ *35654 W. Yermo Rd., at Daggett-Yermo Rd., Yermo* ☎ *760/254–3370* 🌐 *www.peggysuesdiner.com.*

$ AMERICAN 🍴 **Slash X Ranch Cafe.** Known as a favorite stop for off-roaders, this rowdy Wild West-esque watering hole 8 miles south of main street Barstow is named for the cattle ranch that preceded it. Hearty fare such as burgers and giant breakfast burritos are served up here.There's a large outdoor patio area and if you've got the time, try to count the multitude of customer ball caps tacked to the ceiling. **Known for:** cold beer; good-time vibe. [$] *Average main: $10* ✉ *28040 Barstow Rd., at Powerline Rd.* ☎ *760/252–1197* 🌐 *slashxoffroad.com* 🕓 *Closed Mon.–Wed.*

$$ HOTEL 🏨 **Ayres Hotel Barstow.** In a sea of chain hotels this one has a few homespun touches up its sleeves, such as the free on-site dinner on Tuesday and Thursday evening. **Pros:** clean rooms, engaged management; entirely nonsmoking. **Cons:** pricey for Barstow. [$] *Rooms from: $139* ✉ *2812 Lenwood Rd.* ☎ *760/307–3121* 🌐 *www.ayreshotels.com/ayres-hotel-barstow* 🛏 *92 rooms* 🍽 *Breakfast.*

MOJAVE NATIONAL PRESERVE

Visitor center 118 miles east of Barstow, 58 miles west of Needles.

The 1.6 million acres of the Mojave National Preserve hold a surprising abundance of plant and animal life—especially considering their elevation (nearly 8,000 feet in some areas). There are traces of human history here as well, including abandoned army posts and vestiges of mining and ranching towns.

GETTING HERE AND AROUND

A car is the best way to access the preserve, which lies between interstates 15 and 40. Kelbaker Road bisects the park from north to south; northbound from I–40, Essex Road gets you to Hole-in-the-Wall on pavement but is graveled beyond there.

EXPLORING

Hole-in-the-Wall. Created millions of years ago by volcanic activity, Hole-in-the-Wall formed when gases were trapped between layers of deposited ash, rock, and lava; the gas bubbles left holes in the solidified material.

You will encounter one of California's most distinctive hiking experiences here. Proceeding clockwise from a small visitor center, you walk gently down and around a craggy hill, past cacti and fading petroglyphs to Banshee Canyon, whose pockmarked walls resemble Swiss cheese. From there you head back out of the canyon, supporting yourself with widely spaced iron rings (some of which wiggle precariously from their rock moorings) as you ascend a 50-foot incline that deposits you back near the visitor center. The one-hour adventure can be challenging but wholly entertaining. ■ TIP➔ There are no services (gas or food) nearby; be sure to fill your tank and pack some snacks before heading out here. ✉ *Mojave National Preserve* ☎ *760/252–6104* ⊕ *www.nps.gov/moja* ✉ *Free.*

Fodor'sChoice
★
Kelso Dunes. As you enter the preserve from the south, you'll pass miles of open scrub brush, Joshua trees, and beautiful red-black cinder cones before encountering the Kelso Dunes. These golden, fine-sand slopes cover 70 square miles, reaching heights of 600 feet. You can reach them via a short walk from the main parking area, but be prepared for a serious workout. When you reach the top of a dune, kick a little bit of sand down the lee side and listen to the sand "sing." North of the dunes, in the town of Kelso, is the Mission revival–style **Kelso Depot Visitor Center.** The striking building, which dates to 1923, contains several rooms of desert- and train-themed exhibits. ✉ *For Kelso Depot Visitor Center, take Kelbaker Rd. exit from I–15 (head south 34 miles) or I–40 (head north 22 miles)* ☎ *760/252–6100, 760/252–6108* ⊕ *www.nps.gov/moja* ✉ *Free.*

10

NEEDLES

150 miles east of Barstow.

Along Route 66 and the Colorado River, Needles is a decent base for exploring Mojave National Preserve and other desert attractions. Founded in 1883, the town, named for the jagged mountain peaks that overlook the city, served as a stop along the Santa Fe railroad line.

GETTING HERE AND AROUND

Greyhound and Amtrak both pass through town daily, though most travelers arrive by car, either via Interstate 40 (east–west) or Highway 95 (north–south). Needles Area Transit is the local bus service.

ESSENTIALS

Bus Information Needles Area Transit. ☎ *866/669–6309* ⊕ *www.cityofneedles.com.*

Visitor Information Needles Chamber of Commerce. ✉ *100 G St., at Front St.* ☎ *760/326–2050* ⊕ *www.needleschamber.com.*

EXPLORING

FAMILY

Fodor's Choice

★

Havasu National Wildlife Refuge. In 1941, after the construction of Parker Dam, President Franklin D. Roosevelt set aside Havasu National Wildlife Refuge, a 30-mile stretch of land along the Colorado River between Needles and Lake Havasu City. Best seen by boat, this beautiful waterway is punctuated with isolated coves, sandy beaches, and Topock Marsh, a favorite nesting site of herons, egrets, and other waterbirds. You can see wonderful petroglyphs on the rocky red canyon cliffs of Topock Gorge. The refuge has three points that provide boat access to Topock Marsh, though not to the lower Colorado River. ■ TIP➔ Spring is by far the best time to visit, as the river is more likely to be robust and wildflowers in bloom. ✉ *Off I–40, 13 miles southeast of Needles* ☎ *760/326–3853* ⊕ *www.fws.gov/refuge/havasu.*

OFF THE
BEATEN
PATH

London Bridge. London Bridge dates back to the 1830s when it spanned the River Thames in London, England, then was taken apart in the late 1960s and reconstructed piece-by-piece in, of all places, the planned community of Lake Havasu City, AZ. Today, it is a draw for curious tourists (even Brits who remember it at the original location) and connects the city to a small island. Riverbanks on both sides have numerous restaurants, hotels, and RV parks. ✉ *Lake Havasu City* ☎ *928/855–4115* ⊕ *www.havasuchamber.com.*

WHERE TO EAT AND STAY

$

PIZZA

✕ River City Pizza. This inexpensive pizza place off Interstate 40 is a local favorite and offers a range of specialty pies, hearty appetizers, subs and pasta. Top it off with a mug of cold lager, or a glass of wine out on the small patio. **Known for:** locals' favorite; unique pizza menu. $ *Average main: $12* ✉ *1901 Needles Hwy.* ☎ *760/326–9191* ⊕ *www.rivercitypizzaco.com.*

$

HOTEL

⌑ Best Western Colorado River Inn. One of the best hotels in town, this Best Western offers a handful of larger rooms with pull-out couches, a voucher for a free breakfast at the cafe next door, and an attractive pool area that offers some precious shade. **Pros:** good rates; clean rooms; nice pool. **Cons:** town's dead at night (and not much livelier during the day); occasional train noise. $ *Rooms from: $90* ✉ *2371 Needles Hwy.* ☎ *760/326–4552, 800/780–7234* ⊕ *www.bestwestern.com* ⤴ *63 rooms* ⎟◉⎮ *Breakfast.*

$

RESORT

FAMILY

⌑ Fender's River Road Resort. On a calm section of the Colorado River, this funky little 1960s-era Route 66 motel-resort is off the beaten path in a town that's in the proverbial middle of nowhere. **Pros:** on the river; friendly staff; peaceful. **Cons:** several minutes from the freeway; rooms could use refreshing. $ *Rooms from: $66* ✉ *3396 Needles Hwy.* ☎ *760/326–3423* ⊕ *www.fendersresort.com* ⤴ *10 rooms, 31 RV sites, 10 campsites.*

DEATH VALLEY NATIONAL PARK

WELCOME TO DEATH VALLEY NATIONAL PARK

TOP REASONS TO GO

★ **Roving rocks:** Death Valley's Racetrack is home to moving boulders, an unexplained phenomenon that has scientists baffled.

★ **Lowest spot on the continent:** Stand on the lowest spot on the continent at Badwater, 282 feet below sea level.

★ **Wildflower explosion:** During the spring, this desert landscape is ablaze with greenery and colorful flowers, especially between Badwater and Ashford Mill.

★ **Ghost towns:** Death Valley is renowned for its Wild West heritage and is home to dozens of crumbling settlements including Ballarat, Cerro Gordo, Chloride City, Greenwater, Harrisburg, Keeler, Leadfield, Panamint City, Rhyolite, and Skidoo.

★ **Naturally amazing:** From canyons to sand dunes to salt flats and dry lake beds, Death Valley serves up plenty of geological treasures.

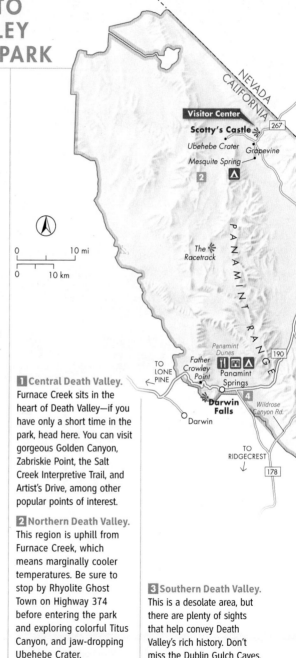

1 Central Death Valley. Furnace Creek sits in the heart of Death Valley—if you have only a short time in the park, head here. You can visit gorgeous Golden Canyon, Zabriskie Point, the Salt Creek Interpretive Trail, and Artist's Drive, among other popular points of interest.

2 Northern Death Valley. This region is uphill from Furnace Creek, which means marginally cooler temperatures. Be sure to stop by Rhyolite Ghost Town on Highway 374 before entering the park and exploring colorful Titus Canyon, and jaw-dropping Ubehebe Crater.

3 Southern Death Valley. This is a desolate area, but there are plenty of sights that help convey Death Valley's rich history. Don't miss the Dublin Gulch Caves.

11

4 **Western Death Valley.**
Panamint Springs Resort is
a nice place to grab a meal
and get your bearings
before moving on to quaint
Darwin Falls, smooth rolling
sand dunes, beehive-
shaped Wildrose Charcoal
Kilns, and historic Stovepipe
Wells Village.

CALIFORNIA

GETTING ORIENTED

Death Valley National Park
covers 5,310 square miles,
ranges from 6 to 60 miles
wide, and measures 140
miles north to south. Within
the park, the Panamint
Range parallels Death Valley
to the west, the Amargosa
Range to the east. Nearly
the entire park lies in southeastern California, with a
small eastern portion crossing over into Nevada.

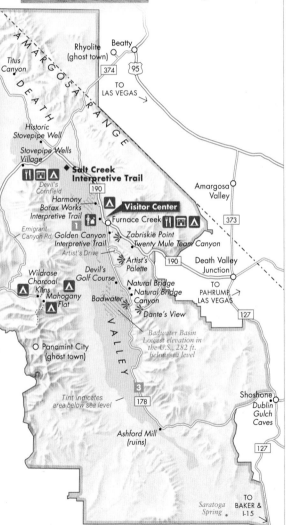

Titus Canyon

AMARGOSA RANGE

DEATH

Rhyolite (ghost town)   Beatty

374   95

TO
LAS VEGAS

Historic Stovepipe Well

Stovepipe Wells Village

◆ **Salt Creek Interpretive Trail**

Devil's Cornfield   190

Harmony Borax Works Interpretive Trail

Visitor Center

Emigrant Canyon Rd.   Furnace Creek   373

Golden Canyon Interpretive Trail

Artist's Drive

Zabriskie Point

Twenty Mule Team Canyon

Artist's Palette

Amargosa Valley

190   Death Valley Junction

Wildrose Charcoal Kilns

Devil's Golf Course

Mahogany Flat

Natural Bridge

Natural Bridge Canyon

Badwater

Dante's View

TO
PAHRUMP
LAS VEGAS

127

Panamint City (ghost town)

VALLEY

*Badwater Basin
Lowest elevation in
the U.S., 282 ft.
below sea level*

*Tint indicates
area below sea level*

3

178

Shoshone

Dublin Gulch Caves

Ashford Mill (ruins)

127

Saratoga Spring

TO
BAKER &
I-15

Updated by
Steve Pastorino

The desert is no Disneyland. With its scorching summer heat and vast, sparsely populated tracts of land, it's not often at the top of the list when most people plan their California vacations. But the natural riches of Death Valley—the largest national park outside Alaska—are overwhelming: rolling waves of sand dunes, black cinder cones thrusting up hundreds of feet from a blistered desert floor, riotous sheets of wildflowers, bizarrely shaped Joshua trees basking in the orange glow of a sunset, tiny pupfish that enthrall youngsters, and a silence that is both dramatic and startling.

DEATH VALLEY PLANNER

WHEN TO GO

Most of the park's one million annual visitors come between late fall and early spring, taking advantage of moderate temperatures and the lack of rainfall. During these cooler months you will need to book a room in advance, but don't worry: the park never feels crowded. If you visit in summer, believe everything you've ever heard about desert heat—it can be brutal, with temperatures often topping 120°F. The dry air wicks moisture from the body without causing a sweat, so drink plenty of water. Bring sunglasses, a hat, and sufficient clothing to block the sun's rays and the wind. Flash floods are fairly common; sections of roadway can be flooded or washed away, as they were after a major flood in 2015. The wettest month is February, when the park receives an average of 0.3 inch of rain.

FESTIVALS AND EVENTS
MAY
Bishop Mule Days. Entertainment at this five-day festival over the Memorial Day weekend includes top country-music stars, an arts-and-crafts fair, barbecues, country dances, the longest-running nonmotorized parade in the U.S., and more than 700 mules competing in 181 events. Admission is free. ⊠ *1141 N. Main St., Bishop* ☎ *760/872–4263* ⊕ *www.muledays.org.*

PLANNING YOUR TIME
DEATH VALLEY IN ONE DAY
If you begin the day in Furnace Creek, you can see several sights without doing much driving. Bring plenty of water with you, and some food, too. Get up early and drive the 20 miles on Badwater Road to **Badwater,** which looks out on the lowest point in the Western Hemisphere and is a dramatic place to watch the sunrise. Returning north, stop at **Natural Bridge,** a medium-size conglomerate rock formation that has been hollowed at its base to form a span across the canyon, and then at the **Devil's Golf Course,** so named because of the large pinnacles of salt present here. Detour to the right onto **Artist's Drive,** a 9-mile one-way, northbound route that passes **Artist's Palette.** The reds, yellows, oranges, and greens come from minerals in the rocks and the earth. Four miles north of Artist's Drive you will come to the **Golden Canyon Interpretive Trail,** a 2-mile round-trip that winds through a canyon with colorful rock walls. Just before Furnace Creek, take Highway 190 3 miles east to **Zabriskie Point,** overlooking dramatic, furrowed red-brown hills and the **Twenty Mule Team Canyon.** Return to Furnace Creek, where you can grab a meal and visit the museum at the Furnace Creek Visitor Center. Heading north from Furnace Creek, pull off the highway and take a look at the **Harmony Borax Works.**

GETTING HERE AND AROUND
AIR TRAVEL
The closest airport to the park with commercial service, Las Vegas McCarren International Airport, is 130 miles away, so you'll still need to drive a couple of hours to reach the park. Roughly 160 miles to the west, Burbank's Bob Hope Airport is the second-closest airport.

CAR TRAVEL
It can take more than three hours to cross from one side of the park to another, so it's important to choose an entrance point that makes sense for what you want to see. If you're driving from Los Angeles, enter through the western portion along Highway 395; if you're coming from Las Vegas, enter from the north at Beatty, Nevada, or via the central entrance at Death Valley Junction. Travelers from Orange County, San Diego, and the Inland Empire should access the park via Interstate 15 North at Baker.

Distances can be deceiving within the park: what seems close can be very far away. Much of the park can be viewed on regularly scheduled bus tours, but these often don't allow time for hikes to sites not seen from the road, such as Salt Creek, Golden Canyon, and Natural Bridge. The best option is to drive to a number of the sites, get out of the car, and walk.

When driving in Death Valley, reliable maps are important, as signage is often limited or, in a few places, nonexistent. Bring a phone but don't rely on cell coverage exclusively in every remote area, and pack plenty of food and water (3 gallons per person per day is recommended). Cars, especially in summer, should be prepared for the hot, dry weather too. Some of the park's most spectacular canyons are only accessible via four-wheel-drive vehicles but if this is the way you want to travel, make sure the trip is well-planned and use a backcountry map. Be aware of possible winter closures or driving restrictions because of snow. The National Park Service's website (⊕ *nps.gov/deva*) stays up-to-date on road closures during the wet (and popular) months. ⚠ One of the park's signature landmarks, Scotty's Castle, and the eight-mile road connecting it to the park border may be closed until 2019 due to damage from a 2015 flood.

Driving Information California Highway Patrol. ☏ *800/427–7623 recorded info from CalTrans, 760/872–5900 live dispatcher at Bishop Communications Center* ⊕ *www.chp.ca.gov.* **California State Department of Transportation Hotline.** ☏ *800/427–7623* ⊕ *www.dot.ca.gov.*

PARK ESSENTIALS

PARK FEES AND PERMITS

The entrance fee is $25 per vehicle and $12 for those entering on foot or bike. The payment, valid for seven consecutive days, is collected at the park's ranger stations, self-serve fee stations, and the visitor center at Furnace Creek. Annual park passes, valid only at Death Valley, are $50.

A permit is not required for groups of 14 or fewer, but if you're planning an overnight visit to the backcountry, complete a registration form at the Furnace Creek Visitor Center. Backcountry camping is allowed in areas that are at least 2 miles from maintained campgrounds and the main paved or unpaved roads and ¼ mile from water sources. Most abandoned mining areas are restricted to day use.

PARK HOURS

The park is open year-round, and can be visited day or night. Most facilities within the park remain open year-round, daily 8–6.

CELL-PHONE RECEPTION

Results vary, but in general you should be able to get fairly good cell-phone reception on the valley floor. In the surrounding mountains, however, don't count on it.

EDUCATIONAL OFFERINGS

RANGER PROGRAMS

FAMILY **Junior Ranger Program.** Children can join this program at any of the three visitor centers, where they can pick up a workbook and complete up to 15 projects (based on their age) to earn a souvenir badge. ✉ *Death Valley National Park.*

RESTAURANTS

Inside the park, if you're looking for a special evening out in Death Valley, head to the Inn at Death Valley Dining Room, where you'll be spoiled with fine wines and juicy steaks. It's also a great spot to start the day with a hearty gourmet breakfast. Most other eateries within the park are mom-and-pop-type places with basic American fare. Outside the park, dining choices are much the same, with little cafés and homey diners serving up coffee shop–style burgers, chicken, and steaks. If you're vegetarian or vegan, BYOB (bring your own beans). *Restaurant reviews have been shortened. For full information, visit Fodors.com.*

HOTELS

It's difficult to find lodging anywhere in Death Valley that doesn't have breathtaking views of the park and surrounding mountains. Most accommodations, aside from the Inn at Death Valley, are homey and rustic. Rooms fill up quickly during the fall and spring seasons, and reservations are required about three months in advance for the prime weekends.

Outside the park, head to Beatty or Amargosa Valley in Nevada for a bit of nightlife and casino action. The western side of Death Valley, along the eastern Sierra Nevada, is a gorgeous setting, though it's quite a distance from Furnace Creek. Here, you can stay in the historic Dow Villa Motel, where John Wayne spent many a night, or head farther south to the ghost towns of Randsburg or Cerro Gordo for a true Wild West experience. *Hotel reviews have been shortened. For full information, visit Fodors.com.*

WHAT IT COSTS				
	$	**$$**	**$$$**	**$$$$**
Restaurants	under $12	$12–$20	$21–$30	over $30
Hotels	under $100	$100–$150	$151–$200	over $200

Restaurant prices are the average cost of a main course at dinner, or if dinner is not served, at lunch. Hotel prices are the lowest cost of a standard double room in high season.

TOURS

Death Valley Adventure Tour (*Adventure Motorcycle [AdMo] Tours*). Motorcycle enthusiasts can sign up for a guided Death Valley Adventure Tour that starts and ends in Las Vegas. The five-day tour through Death Valley covers 800 miles. The tours, which run October through May, include hotel accommodations, gasoline, breakfasts, two dinners, snacks, a support vehicle, and a professional guide. To join, you'll need a motorcycle driver's license and experience with off-road and all-terrain riding. ⊠ *Death Valley* ☎ *760/249–1105* ⊕ *www.admotours.com* 🖃 *From $3,568.*

Furnace Creek Visitor Center programs. This center has many programs, including ranger-led hikes that explore natural wonders such as Golden Canyon, nighttime stargazing parties with telescopes, and evening ranger talks. There are also occasional programs at the Borax Museum at Furnace Creek Ranch and the historic Harmony Borax Works mining site, first established in 1883. Visit the website for a complete list. ⊠ *Furnace Creek Visitor Center, Rte. 190, 30 miles northwest of Death Valley Junction, Death Valley* ☎ *760/786–2331* ⊕ *www.nps.gov/deva/planyourvisit/tours.htm* 🖃 *Free.*

Pink Jeep Tours Las Vegas. A 10-passenger luxury vehicle with oversized viewing windows will pick you up at most Strip hotels for visits to landmarks such as Dante's Peak, Furnace Creek, Devil's Golf Course, and Zabriskie Point. The tours run from about 7 am to 4 pm from September through May, are professionally narrated, and include lunch and bottled water. ⊠ *3629 W. Hacienda Ave., Las Vegas* ☎ *888/900–4480* ⊕ *pinkjeeptourslasvegas.com* ✉ *From $275.*

VISITOR INFORMATION

Park Contact Information Death Valley National Park. ☎ *760/786–3200* ⊕ *www.nps.gov/deva.*

VISITOR CENTERS

⚠ **The popular visitor center at Scotty's Castle is closed until at least 2019 as a result of a major flash flood in 2015 that damaged the structure and destroyed the access road.**

Furnace Creek Visitor Center and Museum. The exhibits and artifacts here provide a broad overview of how Death Valley formed; you can pick up maps at the bookstore run by the Death Valley Natural History Association. This is also the place to sign up for ranger-led walks (available November through April) or check out a live presentation about the valley's cultural and natural history. The helpful center offers regular showings of a 20-minute film about the park and children can get their free Junior Ranger booklet here, packed with games and information about the park and its critters. ⊠ *Hwy. 190, Death Valley* ✛ *30 miles northwest of Death Valley Junction* ☎ *760/786–3200* ⊕ *www.nps.gov/ deva.*

EXPLORING

SCENIC DRIVE

Artist's Drive. This 9-mile, one-way route skirts the foothills of the Black Mountains and provides intimate views of the changing landscape. Once inside the palette, the huge expanses of the valley are replaced by the small-scale natural beauty of pigments created by volcanic deposits or sedimentary layers. It's a quiet, lonely drive, and shouldn't be rushed. Reach Artist's Palette by heading south on Badwater Road from its intersection with Route 190. ⊠ *Death Valley National Park.*

HISTORIC SITES

Charcoal Kilns. Ten well-preserved stone kilns, each 25 feet high and 30 feet wide, stand as if on parade. The kilns, built by Chinese laborers for a mining company in 1877, were used to burn wood from pinyon pines to turn it into charcoal. The charcoal was then transported over the mountains into Death Valley, where it was used to extract lead and silver from the ore mined there. If you hike nearby Wildrose Peak, you will be rewarded with terrific views of the kilns. ⊠ *Wildrose Canyon Rd., Death Valley* ✛ *37 miles south of Stovepipe Wells.*

Plants and Wildlife in Death Valley

CLOSE UP

There's a general misconception that Death Valley National Park consists of mile upon endless mile of flat desert sands, scattered cacti, and an occasional cow skull. Many people don't realize that across the valley floor from Badwater—the lowest point in the Western Hemisphere—Telescope Peak towers at 11,049 feet above sea level. The extreme topography of Death Valley is a lesson in geology. Two hundred million years ago seas covered the area, depositing layers of sediment and fossils. Between 3.5 million and 5 million years ago faults in the Earth's crust and volcanic activity pushed and folded the ground, causing mountain ranges to rise and the valley floor to drop. The valley was then filled periodically by lakes, which eroded the surrounding rocks into fantastic formations and deposited the salts that now cover the floor of the basin.

Most animal life in Death Valley (51 mammal, 36 reptile, 307 bird, and 3 amphibian species) is found near the limited sources of water. The bighorn sheep spend most of their time in the secluded upper reaches of the park's rugged canyons and ridges. Coyotes often can be seen lazing in the shade next to the golf course and have been known to run onto the fairways to steal a golf ball. The only native fish in the park is the pupfish, which grows to slightly longer than an inch. In winter, when the water is cold, the fish lie dormant in the bottom mud, becoming active again in spring. Because they are wary of large moving shapes, you must stand quietly over a pool at Salt Creek to see them.

Botanists say there are more than 1,000 species of plants here (21 exist nowhere else in the world), though many annual plants lie dormant as seeds for all but a few months in spring, when rains trigger a bloom. The rest congregate around the few water sources. Most of the low-elevation vegetation grows around the oases at Furnace Creek and Scotty's Castle, where oleanders, palms, and salt cedar grow. At higher elevations you will find pinyon, juniper, and bristlecone pine.

Harmony Borax Works. Death Valley's mule teams hauled borax from here to the railroad town of Mojave, 165 miles away. The teams plied the route until 1889, when the railroad finally arrived in Zabriskie. Constructed in 1883, one of the oldest buildings in Death Valley houses the Borax Museum, 2 miles south of the borax works at the Inn at Furnace Creek (between the restaurants and the post office). Originally a miners' bunkhouse, the building once stood in Twenty Mule Team Canyon. Now it displays mining machinery and historical exhibits. The adjacent structure is the original mule-team barn. ⊠ *Harmony Borax Works Rd., west of Hwy. 190, 2 miles north of Furnace Creek* ⊕ *www. nps.gov/deva/historyculture/harmony.htm.*

FAMILY

Fodor's Choice

★

Scotty's Castle. This Moorish-style mansion, begun in 1924 and never completed, takes its name from Walter Scott, better known as Death Valley Scotty. An ex-cowboy, prospector, and performer in Buffalo Bill's Wild West Show, Scotty always told people the castle was his, financed by gold from a secret mine. In reality, there was no mine, and the house belonged to a Chicago millionaire named Albert Johnson, whom Scott had finagled into investing in the fictitious mine. Despite the con, Johnson and Scott became great friends. The house functioned for a while as a hotel and still contains works of art, imported carpets, handmade European furniture, and a tremendous pipe organ. ⚠ **The structure and its access road were significantly damaged during a flash flood in 2015 and are closed to the public until at least 2019.** ⊠ *Scotty's Castle Rd. (Hwy. 267), Death Valley* ✛ *53 miles north of Salt Creek Interpretive Trail* ☎ *760/786–2392* ⊕ *www.nps.gov/deva* ⊠ *$15.*

SCENIC STOPS

Artist's Palette. So called for the contrasting colors of its volcanic deposits and sedimentary layers, this is one of the signature sights of Death Valley. Artist's Drive, the approach to the area, is one-way heading north off Badwater Road, so if you're visiting Badwater from Furnace Creek, come here on the way back. The drive winds through foothills of sedimentary and volcanic rocks. About 4 miles into the drive, a short side road veers right to a parking lot that's a few hundred feet before the "palette," whose natural colors include shades of green, gold, and pink. ⊠ *Off Badwater Rd., Death Valley* ✛ *11 miles south of Furnace Creek.*

Badwater. At 282 feet below sea level, Badwater is the lowest spot on land in North America—and also one of the hottest. Stairs and wheelchair ramps descend from the parking lot to a wooden platform that overlooks a sodium chloride pool, a small but remarkably persistent reminder that the valley floor used to contain a lake. You can continue past the platform on a broad, white path that peters out after a half mile or so. Badwater is one of the most popular and easily accessible sites within the park. From this lowest point, be sure to look across to Telescope Peak, which towers more than 2 miles above the valley floor. ⊠ *Badwater Rd., Death Valley* ✛ *19 miles south of Furnace Creek.*

Fodor'sChoice
★
Dante's View. This lookout is 5,450 feet above sea level in the Black Mountains. In the dry desert air you can see across most of 160-mile-long Death Valley. The view is astounding. Take a 10-minute, mildly strenuous walk from the parking lot toward a series of rocky overlooks, where with binoculars you can spot some of Death Valley's signature sites. A few interpretive signs point out the highlights below in the valley and across, in the Sierra. Getting here from Furnace Creek takes about an hour—time well invested. ⊠ *Dante's View Rd., Death Valley* ✛ *Off Hwy. 190, 35 miles from Badwater, 20 miles south of Twenty Mule Team Canyon.*

Devil's Golf Course. Thousands of miniature salt pinnacles carved into surreal shapes by the desert wind dot this wildly varied landscape. The salt was pushed up to the earth's surface by pressure created as underground salt- and water-bearing gravel crystallized. Get out of your vehicle and take a closer look; you'll see perfectly round holes descending into the ground. ⊠ *Badwater Rd., Death Valley* ✛ *13 miles south of Furnace Creek. Turn right onto dirt road and drive 1 mile.*

11

Golden Canyon. Just South of Furnace Creek, these glimmering mountains are perhaps best known for their role in the original *Star Wars*. The canyon is also a fine hiking spot, with gorgeous views of the Panamint Mountains, ancient dry lake beds, and alluvial fans. ⊠ *Hwy. 178, Death Valley* ⊹ *From the Furnace Creek Visitor Center, drive 2 miles south on Hwy. 190, then 2 miles south on Hwy. 178 to the parking area. The lot has a kiosk with trail guides.*

Racetrack. Getting here involves a 28-mile journey over a rough dirt road, but the reward is well worth the trip. Where else in the world do rocks move on their own? This phenomenon has baffled scientists for years and is perhaps one of the last great natural mysteries. The best research on the rocks shows the movement requires a rare confluence of conditions: rain and then cold to create a layer of ice that becomes a sail for gusty winds that push the rocks along—sometimes for several hundred yards. When the mud dries, a telltale trail remains. The trek to the Racetrack can be made in a sedan, but beware—sharp rocks can slash tires; a truck or SUV with thick tires, high clearance, and a spare tire are suggested. ⊠ *Death Valley* ⊹ *27 miles west of Ubehebe Crater via dirt road.*

Sand Dunes at Mesquite Flat. These dunes, made up of minute pieces of quartz and other rock, are ever-changing products of the wind-rippled hills, with curving crests and a sun-bleached hue. The dunes are the most photographed destination in the park, and you can see them at their best at sunrise and sunset. Keep your eyes open for animal tracks—you may even spot a coyote or fox. Bring plenty of water, and note where you parked your car: It's easy to become disoriented in this ocean of sand. If you lose your bearings, climb to the top of a dune and scan the horizon for the parking lot. ⊠ *Death Valley* ⊹ *19 miles north of Hwy. 190, northeast of Stovepipe Wells Village.*

Stovepipe Wells Village. This tiny 1926 town, the first resort in Death Valley, takes its name from the stovepipe that an early prospector left to indicate where he found water. The area contains a motel, restaurant, convenience store, RV hookups, swimming pool, and landing strip, though first-time park visitors are better off staying in Furnace Creek, which is more central. Off Highway 190, on a 3-mile gravel road immediately southwest, are the multicolor walls of Mosaic Canyon. ⊠ *Hwy. 190, Death Valley* ⊹ *2 miles from Sand Dunes, 77 miles east of Lone Pine* ☎ *760/786–2387* ⊕ *www.deathvalleyhotels.com.*

Titus Canyon. This popular one-way, 27-mile drive starts at Nevada Highway 374 (Daylight Pass Road), 2 miles from the park's boundary. Along the way you'll see Leadville Ghost Town and finally the spectacular limestone and dolomite narrows. Toward the end, a two-way section of gravel road leads you into the mouth of the canyon from Scotty's Castle Road. This drive is steep, bumpy, and narrow. High-clearance vehicles are strongly recommended. ⊠ *Death Valley National Park* ⊹ *Access road off Nevada Hwy. 374, 6 miles west of Beatty, NV.*

DID YOU KNOW?

One of the best ways to experience Artist's Palette—a beautiful landscape of colorful mineral deposits—is by following Artist's Drive, a 9-mile one-way road through the area.

Twenty Mule Team Canyon. This canyon was named in honor of the 20-mule teams that, between 1883 and 1889, carried 10-ton loads of borax through the burning desert (though they didn't actually pass through this canyon). Along the 2.7-mile, one-way loop road off Highway 190, you'll find the soft rock walls reach high on both sides, making it seem like you're on an amusement-park ride. Remains of prospectors' tunnels are visible here, along with some brilliant rock formations. ⊠ *20 Mule Team Rd.* ✛ *Off Hwy. 190, 4 miles south of Furnace Creek, 20 miles west of Death Valley Junction.*

Ubehebe Crater. At 500 feet deep and ½ mile across, this crater resulted from underground steam and gas explosions about 3,000 years ago. Volcanic ash spreads out over most of the area, and the cinders lie as deep as 150 feet, near the crater's rim. Trek down to the crater's floor or walk around it on a fairly level path. Either way, you need about an hour and will be treated to fantastic views. The hike from the floor can be strenuous. ⊠ *N. Death Valley Hwy., Death Valley* ✛ *8 miles northwest of Scotty's Castle.*

Zabriskie Point. Although only about 710 feet in elevation, this is one of Death Valley National Park's most scenic spots, overlooking a striking panorama of wrinkled, multicolor hills. It's a great place to watch the sunrise, but it can be bustling any time of day. Pair it with a drive out to magnificent Dante's View. ⊠ *Hwy. 190, Death Valley* ✛ *5 miles south of Furnace Creek.*

SPORTS AND THE OUTDOORS

BICYCLING

Mountain biking is permitted on any of the back roads and roadways open to the public (bikes aren't permitted on hiking trails). Visit ⊕ *www. nps.gov/deva/planyourvisit/bikingandmtbiking.htm* for a list of suggested routes for all levels of ability. Bicycle Path, a 4-mile round-trip trek from the visitor center to Mustard Canyon, is a good place to start. Bike rentals are available at the Oasis at Death Valley, by the hour or by the day.

TOURS AND OUTFITTERS

Escape Adventures (*Escape Adventures*). Mountain bike into the heart of Death Valley on the Spirit of the Mojave Mountain Bike Adventure, a six-day trip through the national park. The 110-mile journey (on single-track trails) includes accommodations (both camping and inns). Bikes, tents, sleeping bags, helmets, and other gear may be rented for an additional price. Tours are available February–April and October only. ⊠ *Death Valley National Park* ☎ *800/596–2953, 702/838–6966* ⊕ *www.escapeadventures.com* ✉ *From $1,190.*

BIRD-WATCHING

Approximately 350 bird species have been identified in Death Valley. The best place to see the park's birds is along the Salt Creek Interpretive Trail, where you can spot ravens, common snipes, killdeer, spotted sandpipers, and great blue herons. Along the fairways at Furnace Creek Golf Course, you can see kingfishers, peregrine falcons, hawks, Canada geese, yellow warblers, and the occasional golden eagle. Scotty's Castle, closed until at least 2019, draws wintering birds from around the globe that are attracted to its running water, shady trees, and shrubs. Other good spots to find birds are at Saratoga Springs, Mesquite Springs, Travertine Springs, and Grimshaw Lake near Tecopa.

You can download a complete park bird checklist, divided by season, at ⊕ *www.nps.gov/deva/learn/nature/upload/death-valley-bird-checklist. pdf.* Rangers at Furnace Creek Visitor Center often lead birding walks through various locations between November and March.

FOUR-WHEELING

Maps and SUV guidebooks for four-wheel-drive and other backcountry roads (including the popular Cottonwood/Marble canyons, Racetrack, Eureka Dunes, Saratoga Springs, and Warm Springs Canyon) are offered at the Furnace Creek Visitor Center. Remember: never travel alone and be sure to pack plenty of water and snacks. The park recommends checking ⊕ *www.nps.gov/deva/planyourvisit/backcountryroads. htm* for back-road conditions before setting out. Driving off established roads is strictly prohibited in the park.

ROADS

Butte Valley. This 21-mile road in the southwest part of the park climbs from 200 feet below sea level to an elevation of 4,700 feet. The geological formations along the drive reveal the development of Death Valley. ⊠ *Trailhead on Warm Spring Canyon Rd., Death Valley ⊹ 50 miles south of Furnace Creek Visitor Center.*

Warm Springs Canyon. If you have a four-wheel-drive vehicle and nerves of steel, this route takes you past Warm Springs talc mine and through Butte Valley, over Mengel Pass and toward **Geologists Cabin,** a charming and cheery little cabin where you can spend the night, if nobody else beats you to it. The park suggests checking their website or asking a ranger to check current conditions on all backcountry roads. The cabin, which sits under a cottonwood tree, has a fireplace, table and chairs, and a sink. Farther up the road, the cabins at Mengel's Home and Russell Camp are also open for public use. Keep the historic cabins clean and restock any items that you use. ⊠ *Warm Springs Canyon Rd., off Hwy. 190/Badwater Rd., Death Valley.*

GOLF

Furnace Creek Golf Course. Golfers rave about how their drives carry at altitude, so what happens on the lowest golf course in the world (214 feet below sea level)? Its improbably green fairways are lined with date palms and tamarisk trees, and its level of difficulty is rated surprisingly high. You can rent clubs and carts, and there are golf packages available for The Oasis at Death Valley guests. In winter, reservations are essential. ⊠ *Hwy. 190, Furnace Creek* ☎ *760/786–2301* ⊕ *www. oasisatdeathvalley.com* ✉ *From $35* ⛳ *18 holes, 6215 yards, par 70.*

HIKING

Plan to hike before or after midday in the spring, summer, or fall, unless you're in the mood for a masochistic baking. Carry plenty of water, wear protective clothing, and keep an eye out for black widows, scorpions, snakes, and other potentially dangerous creatures. Some of the best trails are unmarked; if the opportunity arises, ask for directions.

EASY

FAMILY
Fodor'sChoice
★
Darwin Falls. This lovely 2-mile round-trip hike rewards you with a refreshing year-round waterfall surrounded by thick vegetation and a rocky gorge. No swimming or bathing is allowed, but it's a beautiful place for a picnic. Adventurous hikers can scramble higher toward more rewarding views of the falls. *Easy.* ⊠ *Death Valley National Park* ⊹ *Trailhead: access the 2-mile graded dirt road and parking area off Hwy. 190, 1 mile west of Panamint Springs Resort.*

Natural Bridge Canyon. A rough 2-mile access road from Badwater Road leads to a trailhead. From there, set off to see interesting geological features in addition to the bridge, which is ¼ mile away. The one-way trail continues for a few hundred meters, but scenic returns diminish quickly and eventually you're confronted with climbing boulders. *Easy.* ⊠ *Death Valley* ⊹ *Trailhead: access road off Badwater Rd., 15 miles south of Furnace Creek.*

FAMILY
Salt Creek Interpretive Trail. This trail, a ½-mile boardwalk circuit, loops through a spring-fed wash. The nearby hills are brown and gray, but the floor of the wash is alive with aquatic plants such as pickleweed and salt grass. The stream and ponds here are among the few places in the park to see the rare pupfish, the only native fish species in Death Valley. Animals such as bobcats, fox, coyotes, and snakes visit the spring, and you may also see ravens, common snipes, killdeer, and great blue herons. *Easy.* ⊠ *Death Valley* ⊹ *Trailhead: off Hwy. 190, 14 miles north of Furnace Creek.*

MODERATE

Fall Canyon. This is a 3-mile, one-way hike from the Titus canyon parking area. First, walk ½ mile north along the base of the mountains to a large wash, then go 2½ miles up the canyon to a 35-foot dry fall. You can continue by climbing around to the falls on the south side. *Moderate.* ⊠ *Death Valley National Park* ⊹ *Trailhead: access road off Scotty's Castle Rd., 33 miles northwest of Furnace Creek.*

FAMILY **Mosaic Canyon.** A gradual uphill trail (4 miles round-trip) winds through the smoothly polished, marbleized limestone walls of this narrow canyon. There are dry falls to climb at the upper end. *Moderate.* ✉ *Death Valley* ✥ *Trailhead: access road off Hwy. 190, ½ mile west of Stovepipe Wells Village.*

DIFFICULT

Fodor's Choice ★ **Telescope Peak Trail.** The 14-mile round-trip (with 3,000 feet of elevation gain) begins at Mahogany Flat Campground, which is accessible by a rough dirt road. The steep and at some points treacherous trail winds through pinyon, juniper, and bristlecone pines, with excellent views of Death Valley and Panamint Valley. Ice axes and crampons may be necessary in winter—check at the Furnace Creek Visitor Center. It takes a minimum of six grueling hours to hike to the top of the 11,049-foot peak and then return. Getting to the peak is a strenuous endeavor; take plenty of water and only attempt it in fall unless you're an experienced hiker. *Difficult.* ✉ *Death Valley* ✥ *Trailhead: off Wildrose Rd., south of Charcoal Kilns.*

HORSEBACK AND CARRIAGE RIDES

TOURS AND OUTFITTERS

FAMILY **Furnace Creek Stables.** Set off on a one- or two-hour guided horseback, carriage, or haywagon ride from Furnace Creek Stables. The rides traverse trails with views of the surrounding mountains, where multicolor volcanic rock and alluvial fans form a background for date palms and other vegetation. Evening carriage rides take passengers around the golf course and The Ranch at Death Valley. The stables are open October–May only. ✉ *Hwy. 190, Furnace Creek* ☎ *760/614–1018* 🌐 *www.furnacecreekstables.net* 🎫 *From $55.*

SHOPPING

Experienced desert travelers carry a cooler stocked with food and beverages. You're best off replenishing your food stash in Ridgecrest, Barstow, or Pahrump, larger towns that have a better selection and nontourist prices.

Ranch General Store. This convenience store carries groceries, souvenirs, camping supplies, and other basics. ✉ *Hwy. 190, Furnace Creek* ☎ *760/786–2345* 🌐 *www.oasisatdeathvalley.com/activities/shopping/.*

WHERE TO EAT

$ AMERICAN 🍴 **19th Hole.** Next to the clubhouse of the world's lowest golf course, this open-air spot serves hamburgers, hot dogs, chicken, and sandwiches. The full-service bar has a drive-through service for golfers in carts. **Known for:** kielbasa dog; breakfast burrito; golf cart drive-through. [$] *Average main: $8* ✉ *Furnace Creek Golf Course, Hwy. 190, Furnace Creek* ☎ *760/786–2345* 🌐 *www.oasisatdeathvalley.com/dining/* 🕓 *Closed mid-May–mid-Oct. No dinner.*

$$$$ AMERICAN Fodor's Choice ★ 🍴 **Inn at Death Valley Dining Room.** Fireplaces, beamed ceilings, and spectacular views provide a visual feast to match this fine-dining restaurant's ambitious menu. Dinner entrées include fare such as salmon, free-range chicken, and filet mignon, and there's a seasonal menu of vegetarian dishes. **Known for:** views of surrounding desert; old-school charm; can be pricey. [$] *Average main: $38* ✉ *Inn at Death Valley, Hwy. 190, Furnace Creek* ☎ *760/786–3385* 🌐 *www.furnacecreekresort.com* 🕒 *Closed mid-May–mid-Oct.*

$$ AMERICAN 🍴 **Panamint Springs Resort Restaurant.** This is a great place for steak and a beer—choose from more than 150 different beers and ales—or pasta and a salad. In summer, evening meals are served outdoors on the porch, which has spectacular views of Panamint Valley. **Known for:** good burgers; extensive beer selection. [$] *Average main: $15* ✉ *Hwy. 190, Death Valley* ✢ *31 miles west of Stovepipe Wells* ☎ *775/482–7680* 🌐 *www.panamintsprings.com/services/dining-bar.*

WHERE TO STAY

For the busy season (November–March) you should make reservations for lodgings within the park several months in advance.

$$$$ HOTEL Fodor's Choice ★ 🏨 **The Inn at Death Valley.** Built in 1927, and currently undergoing an extensive renovation, this adobe-brick-and-stone lodge in one of the park's greenest oases offers Death Valley's most luxurious accommodations. **Pros:** refined; comfortable; great views. **Cons:** services reduced during low season (July and August); expensive; annoying resort fee. [$] *Rooms from: $499* ✉ *Furnace Creek Village, near intersection of Hwy. 190 and Badwater Rd., Death Valley* ☎ *760/786–2345* 🌐 *www.oasisatdeathvalley.com* 🕒 *Closed mid-May–June and Sept.–mid-Oct.* 🛏 *66 rooms* 🍽 *No meals.*

$ B&B/INN 🏨 **Panamint Springs Resort.** Ten miles inside the west entrance of the park, this low-key resort overlooks the sand dunes and peculiar geological formations of the Panamint Valley. **Pros:** slow-paced; friendly; peaceful and quiet after sundown. **Cons:** far from the park's main attractions; Internet very limited; most rooms don't have TV. [$] *Rooms from: $94* ✉ *Hwy. 190, Death Valley* ✢ *28 miles west of Stovepipe Wells* ☎ *775/482–7680* 🌐 *www.panamintsprings.com* 🛏 *15 rooms, 5 cabins* 🍽 *No meals.*

$$$$ RESORT 🏨 **The Ranch at Death Valley.** Originally the crew headquarters for the Pacific Coast Borax Company, the four buildings here have motel-style rooms that are good for families. **Pros:** good family atmosphere; central location. **Cons:** rooms can get hot despite air-conditioning; parking near your room can be problematic. [$] *Rooms from: $279* ✉ *Hwy. 190, Furnace Creek* ☎ *760/786–2345, 800/236-7916* 🌐 *www.oasisatdeathvalley.com* 🛏 *224 rooms* 🍽 *No meals.*

$$ HOTEL 🏨 **Stovepipe Wells Village.** If you prefer quiet nights and an unfettered view of the night sky and nearby sand dunes and Mosaic Canyon, this property is for you. **Pros:** intimate, relaxed; no big-time partying; authentic desert-community ambience. **Cons:** isolated; cheapest patio rooms very small; limited Wi-Fi access. [$] *Rooms from: $140* ✉ *Hwy. 190, Stovepipe Wells* ☎ *760/786–2387* 🌐 *www.escapetodeathvalley.com* 🛏 *83 rooms* 🍽 *No meals.*

SEQUOIA AND KINGS CANYON NATIONAL PARKS

WELCOME TO SEQUOIA AND KINGS CANYON NATIONAL PARKS

TOP REASONS TO GO

★ **Gentle giants:** You'll feel small—in a good way—walking among some of the world's largest living things in Sequoia's Giant Forest and Kings Canyon's Grant Grove.

★ **Because it's there:** You can't even glimpse it from the main part of Sequoia, but the sight of majestic Mount Whitney is worth the trip to the eastern face of the High Sierra.

★ **Underground explora- tion:** Far older even than the giant sequoias, the gleaming limestone for- mations in Crystal Cave will draw you along dark, marble passages.

★ **A grander-than-Grand Canyon:** Drive the twist- ing Kings Canyon Scenic Byway down into the jag- ged, granite Kings River Canyon, deeper in parts than the Grand Canyon.

★ **Regal solitude:** To spend a day or two hiking in a subalpine world of your own, pick one of the many trailheads at Mineral King.

1 Giant Forest–Lodge- pole Village. One of the most heavily visited areas of Sequoia contains major sights such as Giant Forest, General Sherman Tree, Crystal Cave, and Moro Rock.

2 Grant Grove Village– Redwood Canyon. The "thumb" of Kings Canyon National Park is its busiest section, where Grant Grove, General Grant Tree, Panoramic Point, and Big Stump are the main attractions.

3 Cedar Grove. The drive through the high-country portion of Kings Canyon National Park to Cedar Grove Village, on the canyon floor, reveals magnificent granite formations of varied hues. Rock meets river in breathtaking fashion at Zumwalt Meadow.

4 Mineral King. In the southeast section of Sequoia, the highest road- accessible part of the park is a good place to hike, camp, and soak up the unspoiled grandeur of the Sierra Nevada.

5 Mount Whitney. The highest peak in the Lower 48 stands on the eastern edge of Sequoia; to get there from Giant Forest you must either backpack eight days through the mountains or drive nearly 400 miles around the park to its other side.

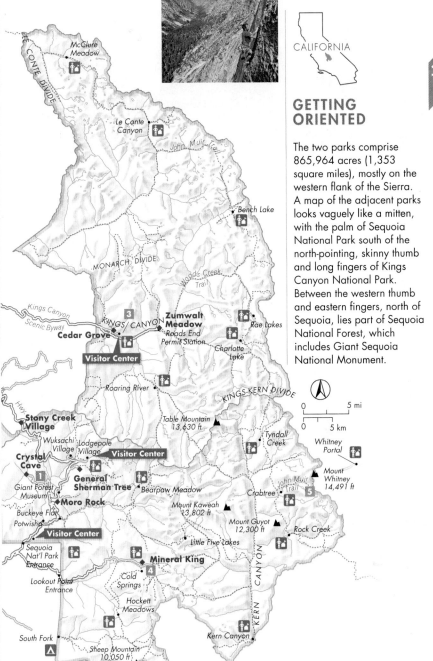

CALIFORNIA

12

GETTING ORIENTED

The two parks comprise 865,964 acres (1,353 square miles), mostly on the western flank of the Sierra. A map of the adjacent parks looks vaguely like a mitten, with the palm of Sequoia National Park south of the north-pointing, skinny thumb and long fingers of Kings Canyon National Park. Between the western thumb and eastern fingers, north of Sequoia, lies part of Sequoia National Forest, which includes Giant Sequoia National Monument.

McClure Meadow

LE CONTE DIVIDE

Le Conte Canyon

John Muir Trail

Bench Lake

MONARCH DIVIDE

Woods Creek Trail

Kings Canyon Scenic Byway

KINGS CANYON

Zumwalt Meadow

Cedar Grove

Roads End Permit Station

Rae Lakes

Charlotte Lake

Visitor Center

Roaring River

KINGS-KERN DIVIDE

0   5 mi
0   5 km

Stony Creek Village

Table Mountain 13,630 ft

Tyndall Creek

Whitney Portal

Wuksachi Village   Lodgepole Village

Visitor Center

Crystal Cave

Mount Whitney 14,491 ft

Giant Forest Museum

General Sherman Tree   Bearpaw Meadow

Crabtree

John Muir Trail

Moro Rock

Buckeye Flat

Mount Kaweah 13,802 ft

Rock Creek

Potwisha

Mount Guyot 12,300 ft

Visitor Center

Little Five Lakes

Sequoia Nat'l Park Entrance

KERN CANYON

Mineral King

Lookout Point Entrance

Cold Springs

Hockett Meadows

South Fork

Kern Canyon

Sheep Mountain 10,050 ft

Updated by Cheryl Crabtree

Although *Sequoiadendron giganteum* is the formal name for the redwoods that grow here, everyone outside the classroom calls them sequoias, big trees, or Sierra redwoods. Their monstrously thick trunks and branches, remarkably shallow root systems, and neck-craning heights are almost impossible to believe, as is the fact they can live for more than 2,500 years. Many of these towering marvels are in the Giant Forest stretch of Generals Highway, which connects Sequoia and Kings Canyon national parks.

Next to or a few miles off the 46-mile Generals Highway are most of Sequoia National Park's main attractions and Grant Grove Village, the orientation hub for Kings Canyon National Park. The two parks share a boundary that runs from the Central Valley in the west, where the Sierra Nevada foothills begin, to the range's dramatic eastern ridges. Kings Canyon has two portions: the smaller is shaped like a bent finger and encompasses Grant Grove Village and Redwood Mountain Grove (two of the parks' largest concentration of sequoias), and the larger is home to stunning Kings River Canyon, whose vast, unspoiled peaks and valleys are a backpacker's dream. Sequoia is in one piece and includes Mount Whitney, the highest point in the lower 48 states (although it is impossible to see from the western part of the park and is a chore to ascend from either side).

PLANNING

WHEN TO GO

The best times to visit are late spring and early fall, when temperatures are moderate and crowds thin. Summertime can draw hordes of tourists to see the giant sequoias, and the few, narrow roads mean congestion at peak holiday times. If you must visit in summer, go during the week. By contrast, in wintertime you may feel as though you have the parks all to yourself. But because of heavy snows, sections of the main park roads can be closed without warning, and low-hanging clouds can move in and obscure mountains and valleys for days. From early October to late April, check road and weather conditions before venturing out. ■TIP➔ **Even in summer, you can escape hordes of people just walking ¼ to ½ mile off the beaten path on a less-used trail.**

PLANNING YOUR TIME

SEQUOIA NATIONAL PARK IN ONE DAY

After spending the night in Visalia or Three Rivers—and provided your vehicle's length does not exceed 22 feet—shove off early on Route 198 to the **Sequoia National Park entrance.** Pull over at the **Hospital Rock** picnic area to gaze up at the imposing granite formation of Moro Rock, which you later will climb. Heed signs that advise "10 mph" around tight turns as you climb 3,500 feet on **Generals Highway** to the **Giant Forest Museum.** Spend a half hour here, then examine trees firsthand by circling the lovely **Round Meadow** on the **Big Trees Trail,** to which you must walk from the museum or from its parking lot across the road.

Get back in your car and continue a few miles north on Generals Highway to see the jaw-dropping **General Sherman Tree.** Then set off on the **Congress Trail** so that you can be further awed by the Senate and House big-tree clusters. Buy lunch at the **Lodgepole** complex, 2 miles to the north, and eat at the nearby **Pinewood** picnic area. Now you're ready for the day's big exercise, the mounting of **Moro Rock.**

You can drive there or, if it is summer, park at the museum lot and take the free shuttle. Count on spending at least an hour for the 350-step ascent and descent, with a pause on top to appreciate the 360-degree view. Get back in the car, or on the shuttle, and proceed past the **Tunnel Log** to **Crescent Meadow.** Spend a relaxing hour or two strolling on the trails that pass by, among other things, **Tharp's Log.** By now you've probably renewed your appetite; head to **Sequoia Barbequeat Wuksachi Lodge** (summer evenings only) or the restaurant at **Wuksachi Lodge.**

KINGS CANYON NATIONAL PARK IN ONE DAY

Enter the park via the **Kings Canyon Scenic Byway** (Route 180), having spent the night in Fresno or Visalia. Better yet, wake up already in **Grant Grove Village,** perhaps in the **John Muir Lodge.** Stock up for a picnic with takeout food from the **Grant Grove Restaurant,** or purchase prepackaged food from the nearby market. Drive east a mile to see the **General Grant Tree** and compact **Grant Grove's** other sequoias. If it's no later than midmorning, walk up the short trail at **Panoramic Point,** for a great view of Hume Lake and the High Sierra. Either way, return to Route 180 and continue east. Stop at Junction View to take in several noteworthy peaks that tower over Kings Canyon. From here, visit **Boyden Cavern** or continue to **Cedar Grove Village,** pausing along the way for a gander at **Grizzly Falls.** Eat at a table by the **South Fork of the Kings River,** or on the deck off the Cedar Grove Snack Bar. Now you are ready for the day's highlight, strolling **Zumwalt Meadow,** which lies a few miles past the village.

After you have enjoyed that short trail and the views it offers of **Grand Sentinel** and **North Dome,** you might as well go the extra mile to **Roads End,** where backpackers embark for the High Sierra wilderness. Make the return trip—with a quick stop at **Roaring River Falls**—past Grant

Grove and briefly onto southbound **Generals Highway.** Pull over at the **Redwood Mountain Overlook** and use binoculars to look down upon the world's largest sequoia grove, then drive another couple of miles to the **Kings Canyon Overlook,** where you can survey some of what you have done today. If you've made reservations and have time, have a late dinner at **Wuksachi Lodge.**

GETTING HERE AND AROUND
AIR TRAVEL
The closest airport to Sequoia and Kings Canyon national parks is Fresno Yosemite International Airport (FAT).

Airport Contacts Fresno Yosemite International Airport (*FAT*). ⊠ *5175 E. Clinton Way, Fresno* ☎ *800/244-2359 automated info, 559/454-2052 terminal info desk* ⊕ *www.flyfresno.com.*

CAR TRAVEL
Sequoia is 36 miles east of Visalia on Route 198; Grant Grove Village in Kings Canyon is 56 miles east of Fresno on Route 180. There is no automobile entrance on the eastern side of the Sierra. Routes 180 and 198 are connected by Generals Highway, a paved two-lane road that sometimes sees delays at peak times due to ongoing improvements. The road is extremely narrow and steep from Route 198 to Giant Forest, so keep an eye on your engine temperature gauge, as the incline and congestion can cause vehicles to overheat; to avoid overheated brakes, use low gears on downgrades.

If you are traveling in an RV or with a trailer, study the restrictions on these vehicles. Do not travel beyond Potwisha Campground on Route 198 with an RV longer than 22 feet; take straighter, easier Route 180 instead. Maximum vehicle length on Generals Highway is 40 feet, or 50 feet combined length for vehicles with trailers.

Generals Highway between Lodgepole and Grant Grove is sometimes closed by snow. The Mineral King Road from Route 198 into southern Sequoia National Park is closed 2 miles below Atwell Mill either on November 1 or after the first heavy snow. The Buckeye Flat–Middle Fork Trailhead road is closed from mid-October to mid-April when the Buckeye Flat Campground closes. The lower Crystal Cave Road is closed when the cave closes (typically in November). Its upper 2 miles, as well as the Panoramic Point and Moro Rock–Crescent Meadow roads, close with the first heavy snow. Because of the danger of rockfall, the portion of Kings Canyon Scenic Byway east of Grant Grove closes in winter. For current road and weather conditions, call ☎ *559/565-3341.*

■TIP➔ Snowstorms are common from late October through April. Unless you have a four-wheel-drive vehicle with snow tires, you should carry chains and know how to install them.

PARK ESSENTIALS
PARK FEES AND PERMITS
The admission fee is $30 per vehicle, $25 per motorcycle, and $15 per person for those who enter by bus, on foot, bicycle, horse, or any other mode of transportation; it is valid for seven days in both parks. U.S.

residents over the age of 62 pay $10 for a lifetime pass, and permanently disabled U.S. residents are admitted free.

If you plan to camp in the backcountry, you need a permit, which costs $15 for hikers or $30 for stock users (e.g., horseback riders). One permit covers the group. Availability of permits depends upon trailhead quotas. Reservations are accepted by mail or email for a $15 processing fee, beginning March 1, and must be made at least 14 days in advance (☏ 559/565–3766). Without a reservation, you may still get a permit on a first-come, first-served basis starting at 1 pm the day before you plan to hike. For more information on backcountry camping or travel with pack animals (horses, mules, burros, or llamas), contact the Wilderness Permit Office (☏ 530/565–3766).

PARK HOURS
The parks are open 24/7 year-round. They are in the Pacific time zone.

EDUCATIONAL OFFERINGS
Educational programs at the parks include museum-style exhibits, ranger- and naturalist-led talks and walks, film and other programs, and sightseeing tours, most of them conducted by either the park service or the nonprofit Sequoia Natural History Association. Exhibits at the visitor centers and the Giant Forest Museum focus on different aspects of the park: its history, wildlife, geology, climate, and vegetation—most notably the giant sequoias. Weekly notices about programs are posted at the visitor centers and elsewhere.

Grant Grove Visitor Center at Kings Canyon National Park has maps of self-guided park tours. Ranger-led walks and programs take place throughout the year in Grant Grove. Cedar Grove and Forest Service campgrounds have activities from Memorial Day to Labor Day. Check bulletin boards or visitor centers for schedules.

EXHIBITS
Giant Forest Museum. Well-imagined and interactive displays at this worthwhile stop provide the basics about sequoias, of which there are 2,161 with diameters exceeding 10 feet in the approximately 2,000-acre Giant Forest. ⊠ *Sequoia National Park* ✛ *Generals Hwy., 4 miles south of Lodgepole Visitor Center* ☏ *559/565–4480* ▱ *Free* ⊂ *Shuttle: Giant Forest or Moro Rock–Crescent Meadow.*

PROGRAMS AND SEMINARS
Evening Programs. The Sequoia Parks Conservancy presents films, hikes, and evening lectures during the summer and winter. From May through October the popular Wonders of the Night Sky programs celebrate the often stunning views of the heavens experienced at both parks. ⊠ *Sequoia National Park* ☏ *559/565–4251* ⊕ *www.exploresequoiakingscanyon.com.*

Free Nature Programs. Almost any summer day, ½-hour to 1½-hour ranger talks and walks explore subjects such as the life of the sequoia, the geology of the park, and the habits of bears. Giant Forest, Lodgepole Visitor Center, and Wuksachi Village are frequent starting points. Look for less frequent tours in the winter from Grant Grove. Check bulletin boards throughout the park for the week's offerings. ⊕ *www.exploresequoiakingscanyon.com.*

Seminars. Expert naturalists lead seminars on a range of topics, including birds, wildflowers, geology, botany, photography, park history, backpacking, and pathfinding. Reservations are required. Information about times and prices is available at the visitor centers or through the Sequoia Parks Conservancy. ⊠ *Sequoia National Park* ☎ *559/565–4251* ⊕ *www. exploresequoiakingscanyon.com.*

TOURS

Fodor's Choice ★ **Sequoia Field Institute.** The Sequoia Parks Conservancy's highly regarded educational division conducts single-day and multiday "EdVenture" tours that include backpacking hikes, natural-history walks, cross-country skiing, kayaking excursions, and motorcoach tours. ⊠ *47050 Generals Hwy., Unit 10, Three Rivers* ☎ *559/565–4251* ⊕ *www.exploresequoia-kingscanyon.com* 🖃 *From $275 for a ½-day guided tour.*

Sequoia Sightseeing Tours. This locally owned operator's friendly, knowledgeable guides conduct daily interpretive sightseeing tours in Sequoia and Kings Canyon. Reservations are essential. The company also offers private tours. ⊠ *Three Rivers* ☎ *559/561–4189* ⊕ *www.sequoiatours. com* 🖃 *From $69 tour of Sequoia; from $139 tour of Kings Canyon.*

RESTAURANTS

In Sequoia and Kings Canyon national parks, you can treat yourself (and the family) to a high-quality meal in a wonderful setting in the Peaks restaurant at Wuksachi Lodge, but otherwise you should keep your expectations modest. A good strategy is to embrace outdoor eating. You can grab bread, spreads, drinks, and fresh produce at one of several small grocery stores, or get take-out food from the Grant Grove Restaurant, the Cedar Grove snack bar, or one of the two small Lodgepole eateries. The summertime Sequoia Barbeque at Wuksachi Lodgeue is a hybrid experience between dining in and picnicking out. Between the parks and just off Generals Highway, the Montecito Sequoia Lodge has a year-round buffet. *Restaurant reviews have been shortened. For full information, visit Fodors.com.*

HOTELS

Hotel accommodations in Sequoia and Kings Canyon are limited, and—although they are clean and comfortable—tend to lack much in-room character. Keep in mind, however, that the extra money you spend on lodging here is offset by the time you'll save by being inside the parks. You won't be faced with a 60- to 90-minute commute from the less-expensive motels in Three Rivers (by far the most charming option), Visalia, and Fresno. Reserve as far in advance as you can, especially for summertime stays. *Hotel reviews have been shortened. For full information, visit Fodors.com.*

WHAT IT COSTS			
$	**$$**	**$$$**	**$$$$**
Restaurants	under $12	$12–$20	$21–$30	over $30

	$	**$$**	**$$$**	**$$$$**
Restaurants	under $12	$12–$20	$21–$30	over $30
Hotels	under $100	$100–$150	$151–$200	over $200

Restaurant prices in the reviews are the average cost of a main course at dinner, or if dinner is not served, at lunch. Hotel prices are the lowest cost of a standard double room in high season, excluding taxes and service charges.

VISITOR INFORMATION

National Park Service Sequoia and Kings Canyon National Parks. ⊠ *47050 Generals Hwy. (Rte. 198), Three Rivers* 🕾 *559/565–3341* ⊕ *nps.gov/seki.*

SEQUOIA VISITOR CENTERS

Foothills Visitor Center. Exhibits here focus on the foothills and resource issues facing the parks. You can pick up books, maps, and a list of ranger-led walks, and get wilderness permits. ⊠ *47050 Generals Hwy., Rte. 198, 1 mile north of Ash Mountain entrance, Sequoia National Park* 🕾 *559/565–3341.*

Lodgepole Visitor Center. Along with exhibits on the area's history, geology, and wildlife, the center screens an outstanding 22-minute film about bears. You can buy books, maps, and tickets to cave tours and the Wolverton barbecue here. ⊠ *Sequoia National Park ✛ Generals Hwy. (Rte. 198), 21 miles north of Ash Mountain entrance* 🕾 *559/565–3341* ⊗ *Closed Oct.–Apr.* ⊂ *Shuttle: Giant Forest or Wuksachi-Lodgepole-Dorst.*

KINGS CANYON VISITOR CENTERS

Cedar Grove Visitor Center. Off the main road and behind the Sentinel Campground, this small ranger station has books and maps, plus information about hikes and other activities. ⊠ *Kings Canyon National Park ✛ Kings Canyon Scenic Byway, 30 miles east of Rte. 180/198 junction* 🕾 *559/565–3341* ⊗ *Closed mid-Sept.–mid-May.*

Kings Canyon Park Visitor Center. The center's 15-minute film and various exhibits provide an overview of the park's canyon, sequoias, and human history. Books, maps, and weather advice are dispensed here, as are (if available) free wilderness permits. ⊠ *Kings Canyon National Park ✛ Grant Grove Village, Generals Hwy. (Rte. 198), 3 miles northeast of Rte. 180, Big Stump entrance* 🕾 *559/565–3341.*

SEQUOIA NATIONAL PARK

EXPLORING

SCENIC DRIVES

Fodor's Choice ★ **Generals Highway.** One of California's most scenic drives, this 46-mile road is the main asphalt artery between Sequoia and Kings Canyon national parks. Some portions are also signed as Route 180, others as Route 198. Named after the landmark Grant and Sherman trees that leave so many visitors awestruck, Generals Highway runs from Sequoia's Foothills Visitor Center north to Kings Canyon's Grant Grove Village. Along the way, it passes the turnoff to Crystal Cave, the Giant Forest Museum, Lodgepole Village, and other popular attractions. The lower portion, from Hospital Rock to the Giant Forest, is especially steep and winding. If your vehicle is 22 feet or longer, avoid that stretch by entering the parks via Route 180 (from Fresno) rather than Route 198 (from Visalia or Three Rivers). Take your time on this road—there's a lot to see, and wildlife can scamper across at any time. ⊠ *Sequoia National Park.*

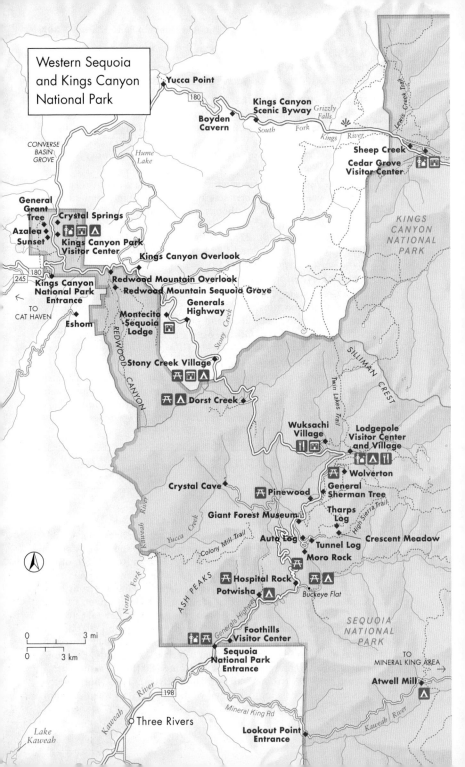

Western Sequoia
and Kings Canyon
National Park

Yucca Point

180

Kings Canyon
Scenic Byway
Boyden
Cavern

*Grizzly
Falls*

South   Fork

Kings   River

Sheep Creek

Cedar Grove
Visitor Center

Lewis Creek Trail

CONVERSE
BASIN
GROVE

*Hume
Lake*

KINGS
CANYON
NATIONAL
PARK

General
Grant
Tree

Crystal Springs

Azalea
Sunset

Kings Canyon Park
Visitor Center

Kings Canyon Overlook

180

245

Kings Canyon
National Park
Entrance

TO
CAT HAVEN

Eshom

Redwood Mountain Overlook
Redwood Mountain Sequoia Grove

Montecito
Sequoia
Lodge

Generals
Highway

Stony   Creek

Stony Creek Village

Dorst Creek

SILLIMAN   CREST

Twin Lakes Trail

Wuksachi
Village

Lodgepole
Visitor Center
and Village

REDWOOD   CANYON

Crystal Cave

Pinewood

Wolverton

General
Sherman Tree

Kaweah   River

Yucca   Creek

Colony Mill Trail

Giant Forest Museum

Auto Log

Tunnel Log

Moro Rock

Tharps
Log

High Sierra Trail

Crescent Meadow

0   3 mi
0   3 km

ASH   PEAKS

Hospital Rock

Potwisha

Buckeye Flat

SEQUOIA
NATIONAL
PARK

TO
MINERAL KING AREA

North   Fork

Foothills
Visitor Center

Sequoia
National Park
Entrance

Generals Highway

River

198

Three Rivers

Mineral King Rd

Kaweah   River

Atwell Mill

*Lake
Kaweah*

Lookout Point
Entrance

SCENIC STOPS

Sequoia National Park is all about the trees, and to understand the scale of these giants you must walk among them. If you do nothing else, get out of the car for a short stroll through one of the groves. But there is much more to the park than the trees. Try to access one of the vista points that provide a panoramic view over the forested mountains. Generals Highway (on Routes 198 and 180) will be your route to most of the park's sights. A few short spur roads lead from the highway to some sights, and Mineral King Road branches off Route 198 to enter the park at Lookout Point, winding east from there to the park's southernmost section.

Auto Log. Before its wood showed signs of severe rot, cars drove right on top of this giant fallen sequoia. Now it's a great place to pose for pictures or shoot a video. ⊠ *Sequoia National Park* ⊕ *Moro Rock–Crescent Meadow Rd., 1 mile south of Giant Forest.*

Crescent Meadow. A sea of ferns signals your arrival at what John Muir called the "gem of the Sierra." Walk around for an hour or two and you might decide that the Scotland-born naturalist was exaggerating a wee bit, but the verdant meadow is quite pleasant and you just might see a bear. Wildflowers bloom here throughout the summer. ⊠ *Sequoia National Park* ⊕ *End of Moro Rock–Crescent Meadow Rd., 2.6 miles east off Generals Hwy.* ☞ *Shuttle: Moro Rock–Crescent Meadow.*

Fodor's Choice ★ **Crystal Cave.** One of more than 200 caves in Sequoia and Kings Canyon, Crystal Cave is composed largely of marble, the result of limestone being hardened under heat and pressure. It contains several eye-popping formations. There used to be more, but some were damaged or obliterated by early-20th-century dynamite blasting. You can only see the cave on a tour. The Daily Tour ($16), a great overview, takes about 50 minutes. To immerse yourself in the cave experience—at times you'll be crawling on your belly—book the exhilarating Wild Cave Tour ($135). Purchase Daily Tour tickets at either the Foothills or Lodgepole visitor center; they're not sold at the cave itself. ⊠ *Crystal Cave Rd., off Generals Hwy.* ☎ *877/444-6777* ⊕ *www.explorecrystalcave.com* 🖼 *$16* ☉ *Closed Oct.–late May.*

Fodor's Choice ★ **General Sherman Tree.** The 274.9-foot-tall General Sherman is one of the world's tallest and oldest sequoias, and it ranks No. 1 in volume, adding the equivalent of a 60-foot-tall tree every year to its approximately 52,500 cubic feet of mass. The tree doesn't grow taller, though—it's dead at the top. A short, wheelchair-accessible trail leads to the tree from Generals Highway, but the main trail (½ mile) winds down from a parking lot off Wolverton Road. The walk back up the main trail is steep, but benches along the way provide rest for the short of breath. ⊠ *Sequoia National Park* ⊕ *Main trail Wolverton Rd. off Generals Hwy. (Rte. 198)* ☞ *Shuttle: Giant Forest or Wolverton–Sherman Tree.*

Mineral King Area. A subalpine valley of fir, pine, and sequoia trees, Mineral King sits at 7,500 feet at the end of a steep, winding road. This is the highest point to which you can drive in the park. It is open only from Memorial Day through late October. ⊠ *Sequoia National Park* ⊕ *Mineral King Rd., 25 miles east of Generals Hwy. (Rte. 198)* ☉ *Closed late Oct.–May.*

12

Fodor's Choice   **Moro Rock.** Sequoia National Park's best nontree attraction offers pan-
★   oramic views to those fit and determined enough to mount its 350 or
so steps. In a case where the journey rivals the destination, Moro's
stone stairway is so impressive in its twisty inventiveness that it's on
the National Register of Historic Places. The rock's 6,725-foot summit
overlooks the Middle Fork Canyon, sculpted by the Kaweah River and
approaching the depth of Arizona's Grand Canyon, although smoggy,
hazy air often compromises the view. ⊠ *Sequoia National Park* ✛ *Moro
Rock–Crescent Meadow Rd., 2 miles east off Generals Hwy. (Rte. 198)
to parking area* ☞ *Shuttle: Moro Rock–Crescent Meadow.*

Tunnel Log. This 275-foot tree fell in 1937, and soon a 17-foot-wide,
8-foot-high hole was cut through it for vehicular passage (not to mention the irresistible photograph) that continues today. Large vehicles
take the nearby bypass. ⊠ *Sequoia National Park* ✛ *Moro Rock–Crescent Meadow Rd., 2 miles east of Generals Hwy. (Rte. 198)* ☞ *Shuttle:
Moro Rock–Crescent Meadow.*

SPORTS AND THE OUTDOORS

The best way to see Sequoia is to take a hike. Unless you do so, you'll
miss out on the up-close grandeur of mist wafting between deeply scored,
red-orange tree trunks bigger than you've ever seen. If it's winter, put on
some snowshoes or cross-country skis and plunge into the snow-swaddled
woodland. There are not too many other outdoor options: no off-road
driving is allowed in the parks, and no special provisions have been made
for bicycles. Boating, rafting, and snowmobiling are also prohibited.

BIRD-WATCHING

More than 200 species of birds inhabit Sequoia and Kings Canyon
national parks. Not seen in most parts of the United States, the white-
headed woodpecker and the pileated woodpecker are common in most
mid-elevation areas here. There are also many hawks and owls, including the renowned spotted owl. Species are diverse in both parks due to
the changes in elevation, and range from warblers, kingbirds, thrushes,
and sparrows in the foothills to goshawk, blue grouse, red-breasted nut-
hatch, and brown creeper at the highest elevations. The Sequoia Parks
Conservancy (☎ *559/565–4251* ⊕ *www.sequoiaparksconservancy.org*)
has information about bird-watching in the southern Sierra.

CROSS-COUNTRY SKIING

For a one-of-a-kind experience, cut through the groves of mammoth
sequoias in Giant Forest. Some of the Crescent Meadow trails are suitable for skiing as well; none of the trails is groomed. You can park at
Giant Forest. Note that roads can be precarious in bad weather. Some
advanced trails begin at Wolverton.

Alta Market and Ski Shop. Rent cross-country skis and snowshoes here.
Depending on snowfall amounts, instruction may also be available.
Reservations are recommended. Marked trails cut through Giant Forest,
about 5 miles south of Wuksachi Lodge. ⊠ *Sequoia National Park* ✛ *At
Lodgepole, off Generals Hwy. (Rte. 198)* ☎ *559/565–3301* ☞ *Shuttle:
Wuksachi-Lodgepole-Dorst.*

12

FISHING

There's limited trout fishing in the creeks and rivers from late April to mid-November. The Kaweah River is a popular spot; check at visitor centers for open and closed waters. Some of the park's secluded back-country lakes have good fishing. A California fishing license, required for persons 16 and older, costs about $15 for one day, $24 for two days, and $47 for 10 days (discounts are available for state residents and others). For park regulations, closures, and restrictions, call the parks at ☎ *559/565–3341* or stop at a visitor center. Licenses and fishing tackle are usually available at Hume Lake.

California Department of Fish and Game. The department supplies fishing licenses and provides a full listing of regulations. ☎ *916/928–5805* ⊕ *www.wildlife.ca.gov.*

HIKING

The best way to see the park is to hike it. The grandeur and majesty of the Sierra is best seen up close. Carry a hiking map and plenty of water. Visitor center gift shops sell maps and trail books and pamphlets. Check with rangers for current trail conditions, and be aware of rapidly changing weather. As a rule of thumb, plan on covering about a mile per hour.

EASY

Fodor's Choice ★ **Big Trees Trail.** This hike is a must, as it does not take long and the setting is spectacular: beautiful Round Meadow surrounded by many mature sequoias, with well-thought-out interpretive signs along the path that explain the ecology on display. The 0.7-mile Big Trees Trail is wheelchair accessible. Parking at the trailhead lot off Generals Highway is for cars with handicap placards only. The round-trip loop from the Giant Forest Museum is about a mile long. *Easy.* ⊠ *Sequoia National Park* ⊹ *Trailhead: off Generals Hwy. (Rte. 198), near the Giant Forest Museum* ☞ *Shuttle: Giant Forest.*

Fodor's Choice ★ **Congress Trail.** This 2-mile trail, arguably the best hike in the parks in terms of natural beauty, is a paved loop that begins near General Sherman Tree. You'll get close-up views of more big trees here than on any other Sequoia hike. Watch for the clusters known as the House and Senate. The President Tree, also on the trail, supplanted the General Grant Tree in 2012 as the world's second largest in volume (behind the General Sherman). An offshoot of the Congress Trail leads to Crescent Meadow, where in summer you can catch a free shuttle back to the Sherman parking lot. *Easy.* ⊠ *Sequoia National Park* ⊹ *Trailhead: off Generals Hwy. (Rte. 198), 2 miles north of Giant Forest* ☞ *Shuttle: Giant Forest.*

Crescent Meadow Trails. A 1-mile trail loops around lush Crescent Meadow to Tharp's Log, a cabin built from a fire-hollowed sequoia. From there you can embark on a 60-mile trek to Mount Whitney, if you're prepared and have the time. Brilliant wildflowers bloom here in midsummer. *Easy.* ⊠ *Sequoia National Park* ⊹ *Trailhead: the end of Moro Rock–Crescent Meadow Rd., 2.6 miles east off Generals Hwy. (Rte. 198)* ☞ *Shuttle: Moro Rock–Crescent Meadow.*

MODERATE

Tokopah Falls Trail. This trail with a 500-foot elevation gain follows the Marble Fork of the Kaweah River for 1.75 miles one-way and dead-ends below the impressive granite cliffs and cascading waterfall of Tokopah Canyon. The trail passes through a mixed-conifer forest. It takes 2½ to 4 hours to make the round-trip journey. *Moderate.* ⊠ *Sequoia National Park* ✛ *Trailhead: off Generals Hwy. (Rte. 198), ¼ mile north of Lodgepole Campground* ⌗ *Shuttle: Lodgepole-Wuksachi-Dorst.*

DIFFICULT

Mineral King Trails. Many trails to the high country begin at Mineral King. Two popular day hikes are Eagle Lake (6.8 miles round-trip) and Timber Gap (4.4 miles round-trip). At the Mineral King Ranger Station (559/565–3768) you can pick up maps and check about conditions from late May to late September. *Difficult.* ⊠ *Sequoia National Park* ✛ *Trailheads: at end of Mineral King Rd., 25 miles east of Generals Hwy. (Rte. 198).*

HORSEBACK RIDING

Trips take you through forests and flowering meadows and up mountain slopes.

TOURS AND OUTFITTERS

Grant Grove Stables. Grant Grove Stables isn't too far from parts of Sequoia National Park, and is perfect for short rides from June to September. Reservations are recommended. ☎ *559/335–9292 summer, 559/799–7247 off-season* ⊕ *www.visitsequoia.com/grant-grove-stables. aspx* ⊠ *From $40.*

KINGS CANYON NATIONAL PARK

EXPLORING

SCENIC DRIVES

Fodor's Choice
★

Kings Canyon Scenic Byway. The 30-mile stretch of Route 180 between Grant Grove Village and Zumwalt Meadow delivers eye-popping scenery—granite cliffs, a roaring river, waterfalls, and Kings River Canyon itself—much of which you can experience at vista points or on easy walks. The canyon comes into view about 10 miles east of the village at **Junction View.** Five miles beyond, at **Yucca Point,** the canyon is thousands of feet deeper than the more famous Grand Canyon. **Canyon View,** a special spot 1 mile east of the Cedar Grove Village turnoff, showcases evidence of the area's glacial history. Here, perhaps more than anywhere else, you'll understand why John Muir compared Kings Canyon vistas with those in Yosemite. Driving the byway takes about an hour each way without stops. ⊠ *Kings Canyon National Park* ✛ *Rte. 180 north and east of Grant Grove village.*

HISTORIC SITES

Fallen Monarch. This toppled sequoia's hollow base was used in the second half of the 19th century as a home for settlers, a saloon, and even to stable U.S. Cavalry horses. As you walk through it (assuming entry is permitted, which is not always possible), notice how little the wood has decayed, and imagine yourself tucked safely inside, sheltered from a storm or protected from the searing heat. ⊠ *Kings Canyon National Park ✛ Grant Grove Trail, 1 mile north of Kings Canyon Park Visitor Center.*

SCENIC STOPS

Kings Canyon National Park consists of two sections that adjoin the northern boundary of Sequoia National Park. The western portion, covered with sequoia and pine forest, contains the park's most visited sights, such as Grant Grove. The vast eastern portion is remote high country, slashed across half its southern breadth by the deep, rugged Kings River Canyon. Separating the two is Sequoia National Forest, which encompasses Giant Sequoia National Monument. The Kings Canyon Scenic Byway (Route 180) links the major sights within and between the park's two sections.

General Grant Tree. President Coolidge proclaimed this to be the "nation's Christmas tree," and 30 years later President Eisenhower designated it as a living shrine to all Americans who have died in wars. Bigger at its base than the General Sherman Tree, it tapers more quickly. It's estimated to be the world's third-largest sequoia by volume. A spur trail winds behind the tree, where scars from a long-ago fire remain visible. ⊠ *Kings Canyon National Park ✛ Trailhead: 1 mile north of Grant Grove Visitor Center.*

Redwood Mountain Sequoia Grove. One of the world's largest sequoia groves, Redwood contains within its 2,078 acres nearly 2,200 sequoias whose diameters exceed 10 feet. You can view the grove from afar at an overlook or hike 6 to 10 miles down into the richest regions, which include two of the world's 25 heaviest trees. ⊠ *Kings Canyon National Park ✛ Drive 6 miles south of Grant Grove on Generals Hwy. (Rte. 198), then turn right at Quail Flat; follow it 2 miles to the Redwood Canyon trailhead.*

SPORTS AND THE OUTDOORS

The siren song of beauty, challenge, and relative solitude (by national parks standards) draws hard-core outdoors enthusiasts to the Kings River Canyon and the backcountry of the park's eastern section. Backpacking, rock-climbing, and extreme-kayaking opportunities abound, but the park also has day hikes for all ability levels. Winter brings sledding, skiing, and snowshoeing fun. No off-road driving or bicycling is allowed in the park, and snowmobiling is also prohibited.

CROSS-COUNTRY SKIING

Roads to Grant Grove are accessible even during heavy snowfall, making the trails here a good choice over Sequoia's Giant Forest when harsh weather hits.

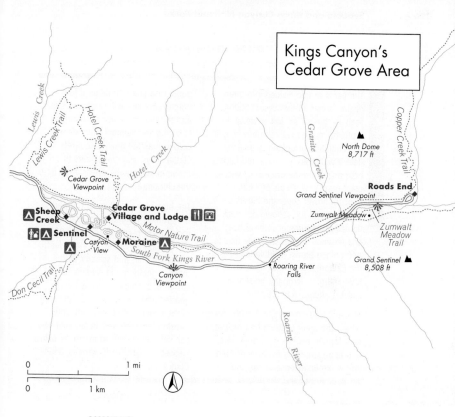

Kings Canyon's
Cedar Grove Area

North Dome
8,717 ft

Cedar Grove
Viewpoint

Roads End

Grand Sentinel Viewpoint

Sheep
Creek

Cedar Grove
Village and Lodge

Zumwalt Meadow

Zumwalt
Meadow
Trail

Sentinel

Motor Nature Trail

Canyon
View

Moraine

South Fork Kings River

Grand Sentinel
8,508 ft

Canyon
Viewpoint

Roaring River
Falls

0   1 mi

0   1 km

HIKING

You can enjoy many of Kings Canyon's sights from your car, but the giant gorge of the Kings River Canyon and the sweeping vistas of some of the highest mountains in the United States are best seen on foot. Carry a hiking map—available at any visitor center—and plenty of water. Check with rangers for current trail conditions, and be aware of rapidly changing weather. Except for one trail to Mount Whitney, permits are not required for day hikes.

Roads End Permit Station. You can obtain wilderness permits, maps, and information about the backcountry at this station, where bear canisters, a must for campers, can be rented or purchased. When the station is closed (typically October–mid-May), complete a self-service permit form. ⊠ *Kings Canyon National Park ✛ Eastern end of Kings Canyon Scenic Byway, 6 miles east of Cedar Grove Visitor Center.*

EASY

Big Stump Trail. From 1883 until 1890, logging was done here, complete with a mill. The 1-mile loop trail, whose unmarked beginning is a few yards west of the Big Stump entrance, passes by many enormous stumps. *Easy.* ⊠ *Kings Canyon National Park ✛ Trailhead: near Big Stump Entrance, Generals Hwy. (Rte. 180).*

CLOSE UP

Plants and Wildlife in Sequoia and Kings Canyon

The parks can be divided into three distinct zones. In the west (1,500–4,500 feet) are the rolling, lower-elevation foothills, covered with shrubby chaparral vegetation or golden grasslands dotted with oaks. Chamise, red-barked manzanita, and the occasional yucca plant grow here. Fields of white popcorn flower cover the hillsides in spring, and the yellow fiddleneck flourishes. In summer, intense heat and absence of rain cause the hills to turn golden brown. Wildlife includes the California ground squirrel, noisy blue-and-gray scrub jay, black bears, coyotes, skunks, and gray fox.

At middle elevation (5,000–9,000 feet), where the giant sequoia belt resides, rock formations mix with meadows and huge stands of evergreens—red and white fir, incense cedar, and

ponderosa pines, to name a few. Wildflowers like yellow blazing star and red Indian paintbrush bloom in spring and summer. Mule deer, golden-mantled ground squirrels, Steller's jays, and black bears (most active in fall) inhabit the area, as does the chickaree.

The high alpine section of the parks is extremely rugged, with a string of rocky peaks reaching above 13,000 feet to Mount Whitney's 14,494 feet. Fierce weather and scarcity of soil make vegetation and wildlife sparse. Foxtail and whitebark pines have gnarled and twisted trunks, the result of high wind, heavy snowfall, and freezing temperatures. In summer you can see yellow-bellied marmots, pikas, weasels, mountain chickadees, and Clark's nutcrackers.

Fodor's Choice ★ **Grant Grove Trail.** Grant Grove is only 128 acres, but it's a big deal. More than 120 sequoias here have a base diameter that exceeds 10 feet, and the **General Grant Tree** is the world's third-largest sequoia by volume. Nearby, the Confederacy is represented by the **Robert E. Lee Tree,** recognized as the world's 11th-largest sequoia. Also along the easy-to-walk trail are the **Fallen Monarch** and the **Gamlin Cabin,** built by 19th-century pioneers. *Easy.* ⊠ *Kings Canyon National Park* ⊹ *Trailhead: off Generals Hwy. (Rte. 180), 1 mile north of Kings Canyon Park Visitor Center.*

Roaring River Falls Walk. Take a shady five-minute walk to this forceful waterfall that rushes through a narrow granite chute. The trail is paved and mostly accessible. *Easy.* ⊠ *Kings Canyon National Park* ⊹ *Trailhead: 3 miles east of Cedar Grove Village turnoff from Kings Canyon Scenic Byway.*

Fodor's Choice ★ **Zumwalt Meadow Trail.** Rangers say this is the best (and most popular) day hike in the Cedar Grove area. Just 1.5 miles long, it offers three visual treats: the South Fork of the Kings River, the lush meadow, and the high granite walls above, including those of Grand Sentinel and North Dome. *Easy.* ⊠ *Kings Canyon National Park* ⊹ *Trailhead: 4½ miles east of Cedar Grove Village turnoff from Kings Canyon Scenic Byway.*

12

MODERATE

Big Baldy. This hike climbs 600 feet and 2 miles up to the 8,209-foot summit of Big Baldy. Your reward is the view of Redwood Canyon. Round-trip the hike is 4 miles. *Moderate.* ⊠ *Kings Canyon National Park* ⊹ *Trailhead: 8 miles south of Grant Grove on Generals Hwy. (Rte. 198).*

Redwood Canyon Trails. Two main trails lead into Redwood Canyon Grove, the world's largest sequoia grove. The 6.5-mile **Hart Tree and Fallen Goliath Loop** passes by a 19th-century logging site, pristine Hart Meadow, and the hollowed-out Tunnel Tree before accessing a side trail to the grove's largest sequoia, the 277.9-foot-tall Hart Tree. The 6.4-mile **Sugar Bowl Loop** provides views of Redwood Mountain and Big Baldy before winding down into its namesake, a thick grove of mature and young sequoias. *Moderate.* ⊠ *Kings Canyon National Park* ⊹ *Trailhead: off Quail Flat. Drive 5 miles south of Grant Grove on Generals Hwy. (Rte. 198), turn right at Quail Flat and proceed 1½ miles to trailhead.*

DIFFICULT

Hotel Creek Trail. For gorgeous canyon views, take this trail from Cedar Grove up a series of switchbacks until it splits. Follow the route left through chaparral to the forested ridge and rocky outcrop known as Cedar Grove Overlook, where you can see the Kings River Canyon stretching below. This strenuous 5-mile round-trip hike gains 1,200 feet and takes three to four hours to complete. *Difficult.* ⊠ *Kings Canyon National Park* ⊹ *Trailhead: at Cedar Grove Pack Station, 1 mile east of Cedar Grove Village.*

HORSEBACK RIDING

One-day destinations by horseback out of Cedar Grove include Mist Falls and Upper Bubb's Creek. In the backcountry, many equestrians head for Volcanic Lakes or Granite Basin, ascending trails that reach elevations of 10,000 feet. Costs per person range from $35 for a one-hour guided ride to around $250 per day for fully guided trips for which the packers do all the cooking and camp chores.

TOURS AND OUTFITTERS

Cedar Grove Pack Station. Take a day ride or plan a multiday adventure along the Kings River Canyon with Cedar Grove Pack Station. Popular routes include the Rae Lakes Loop and Monarch Divide. Closed early September–late May. ⊠ *Kings Canyon National Park* ⊹ *Kings Canyon Scenic Byway, 1 mile east of Cedar Grove Village* ☎ *559/565–3464* ⊕ *www.nps.gov/seki/planyourvisit/horseride.htm* 🖃 *From $40 per hr or $100 per day.*

Grant Grove Stables. A one- or two-hour trip through Grant Grove leaving from the stables provides a taste of horseback riding in Kings Canyon. Closed October–early June. ⊠ *Kings Canyon National Park* ⊹ *Rte. 180, ½ mile north of Grant Grove Visitor Center* ☎ *559/335–9292 mid-June–Sept.* ⊕ *www.nps.gov/seki/planyourvisit/horseride.htm* 🖃 *From $45.*

SLEDDING AND SNOWSHOEING

In winter, Kings Canyon has a few great places to play in the snow. Sleds, inner tubes, and platters are allowed at both the Azalea Campground area on Grant Tree Road, ¼ mile north of Grant Grove Visitor Center, and at the Big Stump picnic area, 2 miles north of the lower Route 180 entrance to the park.

Snowshoeing is good around Grant Grove, where you can take occasional naturalist-guided snowshoe walks from mid-December through mid-March as conditions permit. Grant Grove Market rents sleds and snowshoes.

NEARBY TOWNS

Numerous towns and cities tout themselves as "gateways" to the parks, with some more deserving of the title than others. One that certainly merits the name is frisky **Three Rivers,** a Sierra foothills hamlet (population 2,200) along the Kaweah River. Close to Sequoia's Ash Mountain and Lookout Point entrances, Three Rivers is a good spot to find a room when park lodgings are full. Either because Three Rivers residents appreciate their idyllic setting or because they know that tourists are their bread and butter, you'll find them almost uniformly pleasant and eager to share tips about the best spots for "Sierra surfing" the Kaweah's smooth, moss-covered rocks or where to find the best cell-phone reception (it's off to the cemetery for Verizon customers).

Visalia, a Central Valley city of about 128,000 people, lies 58 miles southwest of Sequoia's Wuksachi Village and 56 miles southwest of the Kings Canyon Park Visitor Center. Its vibrant downtown contains several good restaurants. If you're into Victorian and other old houses, drop by the visitor center and pick up a free map of them. A clear day's view of the Sierra from Main Street is spectacular, and even Sunday night can find the streets bustling with pedestrians. Visalia provides easy access to grand Sequoia National Park and the serene Kaweah Oaks Preserve.

Closest to Kings Canyon's Big Stump entrance, **Fresno,** the main gateway to the southern Sierra region, is about 55 miles west of Kings Canyon and about 85 miles northwest of Wuksachi Village. This Central Valley city of nearly a half-million people is sprawling and unglamorous, but it has all the cultural and other amenities you'd expect of a major crossroads.

GETTING HERE AND AROUND

Sequoia Shuttle. In summer the Sequoia Shuttle connects Three Rivers to Visalia and Sequoia National Park. ☎ 877/287–4453 ⊕ www.sequoiashuttle.com ✉ $15 round-trip.

Visitor Information Fresno/Clovis Convention & Visitors Bureau. ✉ 1550 E. Shaw Ave., Suite 101, Fresno ☎ 559/981–5500, 800/788–0836 ⊕ www.playfresno.org. **Sequoia Foothills Chamber of Commerce.** ✉ 42268 Sierra Dr., Three Rivers ☎ 559/561–3300 ⊕ www.threerivers.com. **Visalia Convention & Visitors Bureau.** ✉ Kiosk, 303 E. Acequia Ave., at S. Bridge St., Visalia ☎ 559/334–0141, 800/524–0303 ⊕ www.visitvisalia.org.

CLOSE UP

Mount Whitney

At 14,494 feet, Mount Whitney is the highest point in the contiguous United States and the crown jewel of Sequoia National Park's wild eastern side. The peak looms high above the tiny, high-mountain desert community of Lone Pine, where numerous Hollywood Westerns have been filmed. The high mountain ranges, arid landscape, and scrubby brush of the eastern Sierra are beautiful in their vastness and austerity.

Despite the mountain's scale, you can't see it from the more traveled west side of the park because it is hidden behind the Great Western Divide. The only way to access Mount Whitney from the main part of the park is to circumnavigate the Sierra Nevada via a 10-hour, nearly 400-mile drive outside the park. No road ascends the peak; the best vantage point from which to catch a glimpse of the mountain is at the end of Whitney Portal Road. The 13 miles of winding road leads from U.S. 395 at Lone Pine to the trailhead for the hiking route to the top of the mountain. Whitney Portal Road is closed in winter.

Mt. Whitney Trail. The most popular route to the summit, the Mt. Whitney Trail can be conquered by very fit and experienced hikers. If there's snow on the mountain, this is a challenge for expert mountaineers only. All overnighters must have a permit, as must day hikers on the trail beyond Lone Pine Lake, about 2½ miles from the trailhead. From May through October, permits are distributed via a lottery run each February by Recreation.gov. The Eastern Sierra Interagency Visitor Center (*760/876–6222*), on Route 136 at U.S. 395 about a mile south of Lone Pine, is a good resource for information about permits and hiking. ⊠ *Kings Canyon National Park* ☎ *760/873–2483 trail reservations* ⊕ *www.fs.usda.gov/inyo*.

NEARBY ATTRACTIONS

OFF THE BEATEN PATH

Exeter Murals. More than two dozen murals in the Central Valley city of Exeter's cute-as-a-button downtown make it worth a quick detour if you're traveling on Route 198. Several of the murals, which depict the area's agricultural and social history, are quite good. All adorn buildings within a few blocks of the intersection of Pine and E streets. If you're hungry, the **Wildflower Cafe**, at 121 South E Street, serves inventive salads and sandwiches. Shortly after entering Exeter head west on Pine Street (it's just before the water tower) to reach downtown. ⊠ *Exeter* ✚ *Rte. 65, 2 miles south of Rte. 198, about 11 miles east of Visalia* ⊕ *cityofexeter.com/about-8187/gallery/murals*.

OFF THE BEATEN PATH

Colonel Allensworth State Historic Park. It's worth the slight detour off Highway 99 to learn about and pay homage to the dream of Allen Allensworth and other black pioneers who in 1908 founded Allensworth, the only California town settled, governed, and financed by African Americans. At its height, the town prospered as a key railroad transfer point, but after cars and trucks reduced railroad traffic and water was diverted for Central Valley agriculture, the town declined and was eventually deserted. Today the restored and rebuilt schoolhouse, library, and other structures commemorate Allensworth's heyday, as do festivities that take place each October. ⊠ *4129 Palmer Ave., off Hwy. 43; from Hwy. 99 at Delano, take Garces Hwy. west to Hwy. 43 north; from Earlimart, take County Rd. J22 west to Hwy. 43 south, Allensworth* ☎ *661/849–3433* ⊕ *www.parks.ca.gov* ⊠ *$6 per car.*

FAMILY   **Forestiere Underground Gardens.** Sicilian immigrant Baldassare Forest-
Fodor's Choice   iere spent four decades (1906–46) carving out an odd, subterranean
★   realm of rooms, tunnels, grottoes, alcoves, and arched passageways that once extended for more than 10 acres between Highway 99 and busy, mall-pocked Shaw Avenue. Though not an engineer, Forestiere called on his memories of the ancient Roman structures he saw as a youth and on techniques he learned digging subways in New York and Boston. Only a fraction of his prodigious output is on view, but you can tour his underground living quarters, including bedrooms (one with a fireplace), the kitchen, living room, and bath, as well as a fishpond and auto tunnel. Skylights allow exotic full-grown fruit trees to flourish more than 20 feet belowground. ⊠ *5021 W. Shaw Ave., 2 blocks east of Hwy. 99, Fresno* ☎ *559/271–0734* ⊕ *www. undergroundgardens.com* ⊠ *$17* ۞ *Closed Dec.–Feb.*

Kaweah Oaks Preserve. Trails at this 344-acre wildlife sanctuary off the main road to Sequoia National Park lead past majestic valley oak, sycamore, cottonwood, and willow trees. Among the 134 bird species you might spot are hawks, hummingbirds, and great blue herons. Bobcats, lizards, coyotes, and cottontails also live here. The Sycamore Trail has digital signage with QR codes you can scan with your smartphone to access plant and animal information. ⊠ *Follow Hwy. 198 for 7 miles east of Visalia, turn north on Rd. 182, and proceed ½ mile to gate on left side, Visalia* ☎ *559/738–0211* ⊕ *www. sequoiariverlands.org* ⊠ *Free.*

Project Survival's Cat Haven. Take the rare opportunity to glimpse a Siberian lynx, a clouded leopard, a Bengal tiger, and other endangered wild cats at this conservation facility that shelters more than 30 big cats. A guided hour-long tour along a quarter mile of walkway leads to fenced habitat areas shaded by trees and overlooking the Central Valley. ⊠ *38257 E. Kings Canyon Rd. (Rte. 180), 15 miles west of Kings Canyon National Park, Dunlap* ☎ *559/338–3216* ⊕ *www.cathaven. com* ⊠ *$15.*

Sequoia National Forest and Giant Sequoia National Monument. Delicate spring wildflowers, cool summer campgrounds, and varied winter-sports opportunities—not to mention more than half of the world's giant sequoia groves—draw outdoorsy types year-round to this sprawling district surrounding the national parks. Together, the forest and monument cover nearly 1,700 square miles, south from the Kings River and east from the foothills along the San Joaquin Valley. The monument's groves are both north and south of Sequoia National Park. One of the most popular is the **Converse Basin Grove,** home of the Boole Tree, the forest's largest sequoia. The grove is accessible by car on an unpaved road.

The Hume Lake Forest Service District Office, at 35860 Kings Canyon Scenic Byway (Route 180), has information about the groves, along with details about recreational activities. In springtime, diversions include hiking among the wildflowers that brighten the foothills. The floral display rises with the heat as the mountain elevations warm up in summer, when hikers, campers, and picnickers become more plentiful. The abundant trout supply attracts anglers to area waters, including 87-acre **Hume Lake,** which is also ideal for swimming and nonmotorized boating. By fall the turning leaves provide the visual delights, particularly in the Western Divide, Indian Basin, and the Kern Plateau. Winter activities include downhill and cross-country skiing, snowshoeing, and snowmobiling. ⊠ *Sequoia National Park ✛ Northern Entrances: Generals Hwy. (Rte. 198), 7 miles southeast of Grant Grove; Hume Lake Rd. between Generals Hwy. (Rte. 198) and Kings Canyon Scenic Byway (Rte. 180); Kings Canyon Scenic Byway (Rte. 180) between Grant Grove and Cedar Grove. Southern Entrances: Rte. 190 east of Springville; Rte. 178 east of Bakersfield* ☎ *559/784–1500 forest and monument, 559/338–2251 Hume Lake* ⊕ *www.fs.usda.gov/sequoia.*

AREA ACTIVITIES

SPORTS AND THE OUTDOORS

BOATING AND RAFTING

Hume Lake. This reservoir, built by loggers in the early 1900s, is now the site of several church-affiliated camps, a gas station, and a public campground. Outside Kings Canyon's borders, Hume Lake offers intimate views of the mountains. Summer lodge room rentals start at $150. ⊠ *Hume Lake Rd., off Kings Canyon Hwy., 8 miles northeast of Grant Grove, 64144 Hume Lake Rd., Hume* ☎ *559/305-7770* ⊕ *www.humelake.org.*

Kaweah White Water Adventures. Kaweah's trips include a two-hour excursion (good for families) through Class III rapids, a longer paddle through Class IV rapids, and an extended trip (typically Class IV and V rapids). ⊠ *40443 Sierra Dr., Three Rivers* ☎ *559/740–8251* ⊕ *www. kaweah-whitewater.com* ✑ *$50–$120 per person.*

Kings River Expeditions. This outfit arranges one- and two-day whitewater rafting trips on the Kings River. ⊠ *1840 W. Shaw Ave., Clovis* ☎ *559/233–4881, 800/846–3674* ⊕ *www.kingsriver.com* ✑ *From $145.*

HORSEBACK RIDING

Wood 'n' Horse Training Stables. For hourly horseback rides or riding lessons, contact this outfit. ⊠ *42846 N. Fork Dr., Three Rivers* ☎ *559/561–4268* ⊕ *www.wdnhorse.com.*

WHERE TO EAT

IN THE PARKS

SEQUOIA

$
CAFÉ
✕ **Lodgepole Market, Deli, and Snack Bar.** The choices here run the gamut from simple to very simple, with the three counters only a few strides apart in a central eating complex. For hot food, including burgers, hot dogs, and pizzas, venture into the snack bar. **Known for:** quick and convenient dining; many healthful options. $ *Average main: $10 ⊠ Next to Lodgepole Visitor Center, Sequoia National Park ☎ 559/565–3301.*

$$$
MODERN
AMERICAN
✕ **The Peaks.** Huge windows run the length of the Wuksachi Lodge's high-ceilinged dining room, and a large fireplace on the far wall warms both body and soul. The diverse dinner menu—by far the best at both parks—reflects a commitment to locally sourced and sustainable products. **Known for:** seasonal menus with fresh local ingredients; great views of sequoia grove; box lunches. $ *Average main: $28 ⊠ Wuksachi Lodge, 64740 Wuksachi Way, Wuksachi Village ☎ 559/565–4070 ⊕ www.visitsequoia.com/the-peaks-restaurant.aspx.*

$$$
BARBECUE
✕ **Sequoia Barbeque at Wuksachi Lodge.** Weather permitting, diners congregate nightly for traditional Old West barbecue. After the meal, listen to a naturalist talk, join in an interactive living history presentation, and clear your throat for a campfire sing-along. **Known for:** authentic Old West grilling; entertaining living history talks. $ *Average main: $25 ⊠ Sequoia National Park ✛ Wolverton Rd., 1½ mile northeast off Generals Hwy. (Rte. 198) ☎ 559/565–4070 ⊙ No lunch. Closed early Sept.–mid-June.*

KINGS CANYON

$$
AMERICAN
✕ **Cedar Grove Snack Bar.** The menu here is surprisingly extensive, with dinner entrées such as pasta, pork chops, trout, and steak. For breakfast, try the biscuits and gravy, French toast, pancakes, or cold cereal. **Known for:** scenic river views; extensive options. $ *Average main: $15 ⊠ Cedar Grove Village, Kings Canyon National Park ☎ 559/565–0100 ⊙ Closed Oct.–May.*

OUTSIDE THE PARKS

$
CAFÉ
✕ **Antoinette's Coffee and Goodies.** For smoothies, well-crafted espresso drinks, breakfast bowls, and pumpkin chocolate-chip muffins and other homemade baked goods, stop for a spell at this convivial coffee shop. Antoinette's is known as the town's hub for vegan and gluten-free items. **Known for:** plentiful vegan and gluten-free items; Wi-Fi on site. $ *Average main: $7 ⊠ 41727 Sierra Dr., Three Rivers ☎ 559/561–2253 ⊕ www.antoinettescoffeeandgoodies.com ⊙ Closed Tues. No dinner.*

$$
AMERICAN
✕ **Buckaroo Diner.** Set on a bluff overlooking the Kaweah River, the boho-chic Buckaroo serves fresh, house-made dishes made with seasonal organic ingredients. A local couple started the restaurant in 2014, first operating out of a food truck and later expanding into a building that housed the original 'ol Buckaroo restaurant for decades. **Known for:** lemon ricotta pancakes for brunch; fried organic chicken; daily specials. $ *Average main: $14 ⊠ 41695 Sierra*

Dr., Three Rivers ☎ *559/465–5088* 🌐 *theolbuckaroo.com* 🕑 *No lunch weekdays. Closed Tues.–Weds.*

$$ MODERN AMERICAN 🍴 **Café 225.** High ceilings and contemporary decor contribute to the relaxed and sophisticated atmosphere at this popular downtown restaurant. Chef-owner Karl Merten can often be spotted at area markets seeking out locally grown ingredients for his seasonally changing dishes. **Known for:** wood-fired rotisserie menu items; fresh local ingredients; sophisticated vibe. [$] *Average main: $19* ✉ *225 W. Main St., Visalia* ☎ *559/733–2967* 🌐 *www.cafe225.com* 🕑 *Closed Sun.*

$$$ AMERICAN 🍴 **Gateway Restaurant and Lodge.** The view's the draw at this roadhouse that overlooks the Kaweah River as it plunges out of the high country. The Gateway serves everything from osso buco and steaks to shrimp in Thai chili sauce. **Known for:** scenic riverside setting; fine dining in otherwise casual town; popular bar. [$] *Average main: $29* ✉ *45978 Sierra Dr., Three Rivers* ☎ *559/561–4133* 🌐 *www.gateway-sequoia.com.*

$ AMERICAN 🍴 **The Lunch Box.** A casual downtown café and bakery, the Lunch Box serves healthful meals at reasonable prices. Choose from nearly 50 types of hot and cold sandwiches and wraps, more than 20 different salads, and soups such as chicken noodle and Tuscan tomato. **Known for:** fresh, healthful local ingredients; quick service; many menu option and combinations. [$] *Average main: $10* ✉ *112 N. Court St., at Main St., Visalia* ☎ *559/635–8624* 🌐 *lunchboxcateringcompany.com* 🕑 *Closed Sun.*

$$$ MODERN AMERICAN 🍴 **School House Restaurant & Tavern.** A Wine Country–style establishment that sources ingredients from the on-site gardens and surrounding farms and orchards, this popular restaurant occupies a redbrick 1921 schoolhouse in the town of Sanger. Chef Ryan Jackson, who grew up on local fruit farms, returned home after stints cooking at prestigious Napa Valley restaurants to create seasonal menus from the bounty of familiar backyards. **Known for:** fresh ingredients from neighboring farms and orchards; historic country setting; convenient stop between Kings Canyon and Fresno. [$] *Average main: $27* ✉ *1018 S. Frankwood Ave., at Hwy. 180 (King's Canyon Rd.), 20 miles east of Fresno, Sanger* ☎ *559/787–3271* 🌐 *schoolhousesanger.com* 🕑 *Closed Mon. and Tues.*

$ AMERICAN 🍴 **Sierra Subs and Salads.** This well-run sandwich joint satisfies carnivores and vegetarians alike with crispy-fresh ingredients prepared with panache. Depending on your preference, the centerpiece of the Bull's Eye sandwich, for instance, will be roast beef or a portobello mushroom, but whichever you choose, the accompanying flavors—of ciabatta bread, horseradish-and-garlic mayonnaise, roasted red peppers, Havarti cheese, and spinach—will delight your palate. **Known for:** many vegetarian, vegan, and gluten-free options; weekly specials. [$] *Average main: $8* ✉ *41717 Sierra Dr., Three Rivers* ☎ *559/561–4810* 🌐 *www.sierrasubsandsalads.com* 🕑 *Closed Mon. No dinner.*

$$$$ EUROPEAN Fodor's Choice ★ 🍴 **The Vintage Press.** Built in 1966, this is the best restaurant in the Central Valley. The California–Continental cuisine includes dishes such as crispy veal sweetbreads with a port-wine sauce and filet mignon with a cognac-mustard sauce. **Known for:** wine list with more than 900 selections; chocolate Grand Marnier cake and other homemade desserts and ice creams. [$] *Average main: $32* ✉ *216 N. Willis St., Visalia* ☎ *559/733–3033* 🌐 *www.thevintagepress.com.*

WHERE TO STAY

IN THE PARKS

SEQUOIA

$$
RESORT

⊞ **Silver City Mountain Resort.** High on Mineral King Road, this privately owned resort has rustic cabins and Swiss-style chalets, all with at least a stove, refrigerator, and sink. **Pros:** rustic setting; friendly staff; "off the grid" ambience. **Cons:** electricity (by generator) available only between noon and 10 pm. $ *Rooms from: $120* ⊠ *Sequoia National Park* ✛ *Mineral King Rd., 21 miles southeast of Rte. 198* ☎ *559/561–3223* ⊕ *www.silvercityresort.com* ⊘ *Closed Nov.–late May* ⇖ *11 units, 6 with shared bath* ⦿⊙ *No meals.*

$$$$
HOTEL
Fodor's Choice
★

⊞ **Wuksachi Lodge.** The striking cedar-and-stone main building is a fine example of how a structure can blend effectively with lovely mountain scenery. **Pros:** best place to stay in the parks; lots of wildlife. **Cons:** rooms can be small; main lodge is a few-minutes' walk from guest rooms; slow Wi-Fi. $ *Rooms from: $229* ⊠ *64740 Wuksachi Way, Wuksachi Village* ☎ *559/565–4070, 888/252–5757* ⊕ *www.visitsequoia.com/lodging.aspx* ⇖ *102 rooms* ⦿⊙ *No meals.*

KINGS CANYON

$$
HOTEL

⊞ **Cedar Grove Lodge.** Backpackers like to stay here on the eve of long treks into the High Sierra wilderness, so bedtimes tend to be early. **Pros:** a definite step up from camping in terms of comfort. **Cons:** impersonal; not everybody agrees it's clean enough. $ *Rooms from: $141* ⊠ *Kings Canyon Scenic Byway, Kings Canyon National Park* ☎ *866/807–3598* ⊕ *www.visitsequoia.com/Cedar-Grove-Lodge.aspx* ⊘ *Closed mid-Oct.–mid-May* ⇖ *21 rooms* ⦿⊙ *No meals.*

$
HOTEL

⊞ **Grant Grove Cabins.** Some of the wood-panel cabins here have heaters, electric lights, and private baths, but most have woodstoves, battery lamps, and shared baths. **Pros:** warm, woodsy feel; clean. **Cons:** can be difficult to walk up to if you're not in decent physical shape; costly for what you get. $ *Rooms from: $94* ⊠ *Kings Canyon Scenic Byway in Grant Grove Village, Kings Canyon National Park* ☎ *866/807–3598* ⊕ *www.visitsequoia.com/Grant-Grove-Cabins.aspx* ⇖ *33 cabins, 9 with bath; 17 tent cabins* ⦿⊙ *No meals.*

$$$
HOTEL

⊞ **John Muir Lodge.** In a wooded area in the hills above Grant Grove Village, this modern, timber-sided lodge has rooms and suites with queen- or king-size beds and private baths. **Pros:** open year-round; common room stays warm; quiet. **Cons:** check-in is down in the village. $ *Rooms from: $200* ⊠ *Kings Canyon Scenic Byway, ¼ mile north of Grant Grove Village, 86728 Highway 180, Kings Canyon National Park* ☎ *866/807–3598* ⊕ *www.visitsequoia.com/john-muir-lodge.aspx* ⇖ *36 rooms* ⦿⊙ *No meals.*

CLOSE UP

Best Campgrounds in Sequoia and Kings Canyon

12

Campgrounds in Sequoia and Kings Canyon occupy wonderful settings, with lots of shade and nearby hiking trails. Some campgrounds are open year-round, others only seasonally. Except for Bearpaw (around $350 a night including meals), fees at the campgrounds range from $12 to $35, depending on location and size. There are no RV hookups at any of the campgrounds; expect a table and a fire ring with a grill at standard sites. Only Bearpaw, Lodgepole, Dorst Creek, Potwisha, and Buckeye Flat accept reservations, and for all of these you'll need to book well ahead. The rest are first come, first served. Campgrounds around Lodgepole and Grant Grove get busy in summer with vacationing families. Keep in mind that this is black-bear country and carefully follow posted instructions about storing food. Bear-proof metal containers are provided at many campgrounds.

IN SEQUOIA

Atwell Mill Campground. At 6,650 feet, this peaceful, tent-only campground is just south of the Western Divide. ⊠ *Mineral King Rd., 20 miles east of Rte. 198* ☎ *559/565–3341.*

Bearpaw High Sierra Camp. Classy camping is the order of the day at this tent hotel and restaurant. Make reservations starting on January 2. ⊠ *High Sierra Trail, 11.5 miles from Lodgepole Village* ☎ *888/252–5757* ⊕ *www.visitsequoia.com.*

Dorst Creek Campground. Wildlife sightings are common at this large campground at elevation 6,700 feet. ⊠ *Generals Hwy., 8 miles north of*

Lodgepole Visitor Center ☎ *559/565–3341 or 877/444–6777.*

Lodgepole Campground. The largest Lodgepole-area campground is also the noisiest, though things quiet down at night. ⊠ *Off Generals Hwy. beyond Lodgepole Village* ☎ *559/565–3341 or 877/444–6777.*

Potwisha Campground. On the Marble Fork of the Kaweah River, this midsize campground, open year-round, at elevation 2,100 feet gets no snow in winter and can be hot in summer. ⊠ *Generals Hwy., 4 miles north of Foothills Visitor Center* ☎ *559/565–3341 or 877/444–6777.*

IN KINGS CANYON

Azalea Campground. Of the three campgrounds in the Grant Grove area, Azalea is the only one open year-round. It sits at 6,500 feet amid giant sequoias. ⊠ *Kings Canyon Scenic Byway, ¼ mile north of Grant Grove Village* ☎ *559/565–3341.*

Sentinel Campground. At 4,600 feet and within walking distance of Cedar Grove Village, Sentinel fills up fast in summer. ⊠ *Kings Canyon Scenic Byway, ¼ mile west of Cedar Grove Village* ☎ *559/565–3341.*

Sheep Creek Campground. Of the overflow campgrounds, this is one of the prettiest. ⊠ *Off Kings Canyon Scenic Byway, 1 mile west of Cedar Grove Village* ☎ *No phone.*

Sunset Campground. Many of the easiest trails through Grant Grove are adjacent to this large camp, near the giant sequoias at 6,500 feet. ⊠ *Off Generals Hwy., near Grant Grove Visitor Center* ☎ *No phone.*

OUTSIDE THE PARKS

The only lodging immediately outside the parks is in Three Rivers. Options include inns, chain and mom-and-pop motels, and riverside cabins. Numerous chain properties operate in Visalia or Fresno (your favorite is likely represented in one or both cities), about an hour from the south and north entrances, respectively.

$$$ HOTEL FAMILY

🏨 **Montecito-Sequoia Lodge.** Outdoor activities are what this year-round family resort is all about, including many that are geared toward teenagers and small children. **Pros:** friendly staff; great for kids; lots of fresh air and planned activities. **Cons:** can be noisy with all the activity; some complaints about cleanliness; not within national park. [$] *Rooms from: $179* ✉ *63410 Generals Hwy., 11 miles south of Grant Grove, Sequoia National Forest* ☎ *559/565–3388, 800/227–9900* 🌐 *www.montecitosequoia.com* 🕒 *Closed 1st 2 wks of Dec.* 🛏 *37 rooms, 13 cabins* 🍴 *All meals.*

$$ B&B/INN Fodor's Choice ★

🏨 **Rio Sierra Riverhouse.** Guests at Rio Sierra come for the river views, the sandy beach, and the proximity to Sequoia National Park (6 miles away), but invariably end up raving equally about the warm, laid-back hospitality of proprietress Mars Roberts. **Pros:** seductive beach; winning hostess; river views from all rooms; contemporary ambience. **Cons:** books up quickly in summer; some road noise audible in rooms. [$] *Rooms from: $185* ✉ *41997 Sierra Dr., Hwy. 198, Three Rivers* ☎ *559/561–4720* 🌐 *www.rio-sierra.com* 🛏 *5 rooms* 🍴 *No meals* ☞ *2-night min stay on summer weekends.*

$ B&B/INN

🏨 **The Spalding House.** This restored Colonial Revival inn is decked out with antiques, oriental rugs, handcrafted woodwork, and glass doors. **Pros:** warm feel; old-time atmosphere; great place for a twilight stroll. **Cons:** no TVs in rooms. [$] *Rooms from: $95* ✉ *631 N. Encina St., Visalia* ☎ *559/739–7877* 🌐 *www.thespaldinghouse.com* 🛏 *3 suites* 🍴 *Breakfast.*

TRAVEL SMART SOUTHERN CALIFORNIA

GETTING HERE AND AROUND

▌ AIR TRAVEL

Flying time to California is about 6½ hours from New York and 4¾ hours from Chicago. Travel from London to either Los Angeles or San Francisco is 11 hours and from Sydney approximately 15. Flying between San Francisco and Los Angeles takes about 90 minutes.

AIRPORTS

Southern California Hollywood Burbank Airport (*Bob Hope Airport*). ☎ *818/840–8840* ⊕ *www.hollywoodburbankairport.com.* **John Wayne Airport.** ☎ *949/252–5200* ⊕ *www. ocair.com.* **Long Beach Airport.** ☎ *562/570– 2600* ⊕ *www.lgb.org.* **Los Angeles International Airport.** ☎ *310/641–5700* ⊕ *www.lawa. org/welcomelax.aspx.* **Ontario International Airport.** ☎ *909/937–2700* ⊕ *www.flyontario. com.* **San Diego International Airport.** ☎ *619/400–2404* ⊕ *www.san.org.*

FROM LOS ANGELES TO:	BY AIR	BY CAR
San Diego	55 mins	2 hrs
Death Valley	No flights	5 hrs
San Francisco	1 hr 30 mins	5 hrs 40 mins
Monterey	1 hr 10 mins	5 hrs
Santa Barbara	50 mins	1 hr 40 mins
Big Sur	No flights	5 hrs 40 mins
Sacramento	1 hr 30 mins	5 hrs 30 mins

▌ BUS TRAVEL

Greyhound is the major bus carrier in California. Regional bus service is available in metropolitan areas.

Bus Information Greyhound. ☎ *800/231– 2222* ⊕ *www.greyhound.com.*

▌ CAR TRAVEL

Two main north–south routes run through California: Interstate 5 through the middle of the state, and U.S. 101, a parallel route closer to the coast. Slower but more scenic is Highway 1, which winds along much of the coast.

From north to south, the state's main east–west routes are Interstate 80, Interstate 15, Interstate 10, and Interstate 8. Much of California is mountainous, and you may encounter winding roads and steep mountain grades.

FROM LOS ANGELES TO:	ROUTE	DISTANCE
San Diego	I-5 or I-405	127 miles
Las Vegas	I-10 to I-15	270 miles
Death Valley	I-10 to I-15 to Hwy. 127 to Hwy. 190	290 miles
San Francisco	I-5 to I-580 to I-80	382 miles
Monterey	U.S. 101 to Salinas, Hwy. 68 to Hwy. 1	320 miles
Santa Barbara	U.S. 101	95 miles
Big Sur	U.S. 101 to Hwy. 1	349 miles
Sacramento	I-5	391 miles

GASOLINE

Gas stations are plentiful throughout the state. Many stay open late, except in rural areas, where Sunday hours are limited and where you may drive long stretches without a chance to refuel.

ROAD CONDITIONS

Rainy weather can make driving along the coast or in the mountains treacherous. Some smaller routes over mountain ranges and in the deserts are prone to flash flooding. When the weather is particularly bad, Highway 1 may be closed due to mud and rock slides.

Road Conditions Caltrans Current Highway Conditions. ☎ *800/427-7623* ⊕ *www.dot. ca.gov.*

Weather Conditions National Weather Service. ☎ *707/443-6484 northernmost California, 831/656-1710 San Francisco Bay area and central California, 775/673-8100 Reno, Lake Tahoe, and northern Sierra, 805/988-6615 Los Angeles area, 858/675-8700 San Diego area, 916/979-3041 Sacramento area* ⊕ *www.weather.gov.*

ROADSIDE EMERGENCIES

Dial 911 to report accidents and to reach the police, the California Highway Patrol (CHP), or the fire department. On some rural highways and on most interstates, look for emergency phones on the side of the road.

In Los Angeles, the Metro Freeway Service Patrol provides assistance to stranded motorists under nonemergency conditions. Dial 511 from a cell phone and choose the "motorist aid" option to reach them 24 hours a day.

RULES OF THE ROAD

All passengers must wear a seat belt at all times. A child must be secured in a federally approved child passenger restraint system and ride in the back seat until at least eight years of age or until the child is at least 4 feet 9 inches tall. Children who are eight but don't meet the height requirement must ride in a booster seat or a car seat. It is illegal to leave a child six years of age or younger unattended in a motor vehicle. Unless indicated, right turns are allowed at red lights after you've come to a full stop. Left turns between two one-way streets are allowed at red lights after you've come to a full stop. Drivers with a blood-alcohol level higher than 0.08 who are stopped by police are subject to arrest.

The speed limit on some interstate highways is 70 mph; unlimited-access roads are usually 55 mph. In cities, freeway speed limits are between 55 mph and 65 mph. Many city routes have commuter lanes during rush hour.

You must turn on your headlights whenever weather conditions require the use of windshield wipers. Texting on a wireless device is illegal for all drivers. If using a mobile phone while driving it must be hands-free and mounted (i.e., it's not legal having it loose on the seat or your lap). For more driving rules, refer to the Department of Motor Vehicles driver's handbook at ⊕ *www.dmv.ca.gov.*

CAR RENTAL

When you reserve a car, ask about cancellation penalties, taxes, drop-off charges (if you're planning to pick up the car in one city and leave it in another), and surcharges (for being under or over a certain age, for additional drivers, or for driving across state or country borders or beyond a specific distance from your point of rental). All these things can add substantially to your costs. Request car seats and extras such as GPS when you book.

Rates are sometimes—but not always—better if you book in advance or reserve through a rental agency's website. There are other reasons to book ahead, though: for popular destinations, during busy times of the year, or to ensure that you get certain types of cars (vans, SUVs, exotic sports cars).

■**TIP**➔ Make sure that a confirmed reservation guarantees you a car. Agencies sometimes overbook, particularly for busy weekends and holiday periods.

A car is essential in most parts of California. In sprawling cities such as Los Angeles and San Diego, you'll have to take the freeways to get just about anywhere.

Rates statewide for the least expensive vehicle begin as low as $30 a day, usually on weekends, and less than $200 a week. This does not include additional fees or the tax on car rentals (8%–10%). Be sure to shop around—you can get a decent deal by shopping the major car-rental companies' websites. A few companies rent specialty cars such as convertibles or sport-utility vehicles.

In California you must have a valid driver's license and be 21 to rent a car; rates may be higher if you're under 25. Some agencies will not rent to those under 25; check when you book. Non-U.S. residents must have a license, valid for the entire rental period, with text in the Roman alphabet that clearly identifies it as a driver's license. In addition, most companies also require an international license; check in advance.

Specialty Car Agencies Beverly Hills Rent a Car. ☎ 310/923–7833 ⊕ www.bhrenta-car.com. **Enterprise Exotic Car Rentals.** ☎ 866/458–9227 ⊕ exoticcars.enterprise.com. **MCar** (Midway Car Rental). ☎ 866/717–6802 ⊕ www.midwaycarrental.com.

▌TRAIN TRAVEL

Amtrak provides rail service within California. On some trips—to Yosemite National Park, for example—passengers board motor coaches part of the way. The rail service's scenic *Coast Starlight* trip begins in Los Angeles and hugs the Pacific Coast to San Luis Obispo before it turns inland for the rest of its journey to Portland and Seattle.

Information Amtrak. ☎ 800/872–7245 ⊕ www.amtrak.com.

ESSENTIALS

▌ ACCOMMODATIONS

The lodgings we review are the top choices in each price category. *For an expanded review of each property, please see www. fodors.com.* We don't specify whether the facilities cost extra; when pricing accommodations, ask what's included and what costs extra. *For price information, see the planner in each chapter.*

Be sure you understand the hotel's cancellation policy. Some places allow you to cancel without any kind of penalty— even if you prepaid to secure a discounted rate—if you cancel at least 24 hours in advance. Others require you to cancel a week in advance or penalize you the cost of one night. Small inns and B&Bs are most likely to require you to cancel far in advance. Most hotels allow children under a certain age to stay in their parents' room at no extra charge, but others charge for them as extra adults; find out the cutoff age for discounts.

BED-AND-BREAKFASTS

California has more than 1,000 bed-and-breakfasts. You'll find everything from simple homestays to lavish luxury lodgings, many in historic hotels and homes. The California Association of Boutique and Breakfast Inns has about 300 member properties that you can locate and book through its website.

Reservation Services California Association of Boutique and Breakfast Inns. ☎ *800/373–9251* ⊕ *www.cabbi.com.*

▌ COMMUNICATIONS

INTERNET

Internet access is widely available in urban areas, but it can be difficult to get online in rural communities. Most hotels offer some kind of connection—usually broadband or Wi-Fi. Many hotels charge a daily fee ($10– $15) for Internet access. Cafés with free Wi-Fi are common throughout California.

▌ EATING OUT

California has led the pack in bringing natural and organic foods to the forefront of American dining. Though rooted in European cuisine, California cooking sometimes has strong Asian and Latin influences. Wherever you go, you're likely to find that dishes are made with fresh produce and other local ingredients.

The restaurants we list are the cream of the crop in each price category. *For price information, see the planner in each chapter.*

CUTTING COSTS

The better grocery and specialty-food stores have grab-and-go sections, with prepared foods on a par with restaurant cooking, perfect for picnicking (remember, it infrequently rains between May and October). At resort areas in the off-season you can often find two-for-one dinner specials at upper-end restaurants; check coupon apps or local papers or with visitor bureaus.

RESERVATIONS AND DRESS

Regardless of where you are, it's a good idea to make a reservation if you can. For popular restaurants, book as far ahead as you can (often 30 days), and reconfirm as soon as you arrive in California. (Large parties should always call ahead to check the reservations policy.)

Online reservation services make it easy to book a table. OpenTable covers many California cities.

Contacts OpenTable. ⊕ *www.opentable.com.*

▌ HEALTH

Smoking is illegal in all California bars and restaurants, including on outdoor dining patios in some cities. If you have an existing medical condition that may require emergency treatment, be aware that many rural and mountain communities have only daytime clinics, not hospitals with 24-hour emergency rooms.

Outdoor sports are a huge draw in California's moderate climate, but caution, especially in unfamiliar areas, is key. Drownings occur each year because beach lovers don't heed warnings about high surfs with their deadly rogue waves. Do not fly within 24 hours of scuba diving.

If you're spending time in the national parks or forests, be sure to follow posted instructions that outline how to avoid encounters with bears (e.g., store your food in bear lockers) and how to prevent exposure to hantavirus, carried in deer mouse droppings in remote areas.

▌ HOURS OF OPERATION

Banks in California are typically open weekdays 9–6; most are open on Saturday but close on Sunday and most holidays. Smaller shops usually operate 10 or 11–6, with larger stores remaining open until 8 or later. Hours vary for museums, historical sites, and state parks, and many are closed one or more days a week, or for extended periods during off-season months.

▌ MONEY

Los Angeles and San Diego are expensive cities to visit, and rates at coastal and desert resorts are also high. A day's admission to a major theme park is more than $100 per person, though you may be able to get discounts by purchasing tickets in advance online. Hotel rates average $150 to $250 a night (though you can find cheaper places), and dinners at even moderately priced restaurants often cost $20 to $40 per person. Costs in Death Valley/Mojave Desert region are considerably less—some motels in the Mojave charge less than $100.

CREDIT CARDS

It's a good idea to inform your credit-card company before you travel. Otherwise, unusual activity might prompt the company to put a hold on your card.

Record all your credit-card numbers—as well as the phone numbers to call if your cards are lost or stolen—so you're prepared should something go wrong.

▌ SAFETY

California is a safe place to visit, as long as you take the usual precautions. In large cities ask the concierge or desk clerk to point out areas on your map that you should avoid. Lock valuables in a hotel safe when you're not using them. Keep an eye on your handbag when you're out in public. Security is high (but mostly invisible) at theme parks and resorts.

When hiking, stay on trails—rangers say that the majority of hikers needing to be rescued have gone off trail—and heed signs at trailheads about dangerous situations such as cliffs with loose rocks and how to react if you encounter predatory animals that live in the area. Bring plenty of water, hike with a companion if possible, and learn to identify and avoid contact with poison oak, a ubiquitous plant in California that causes a severe rash.

▌ TAXES

Sales tax in the state of California is 7.25%, but local taxes vary and may be as much as an additional 2.5%. Sales tax applies to all purchases except for food bought in a grocery store; food consumed in a restaurant is taxed, but take-out food is not. Hotel taxes vary widely by region, from about 8% to 16.5%.

▌ TIME

California is in the Pacific time zone. Pacific daylight time (PDT) is in effect from mid-March through early November; the rest of the year the clock is set to Pacific standard time (PST).

TIPPING

TIPPING GUIDELINES FOR CALIFORNIA	
Bartender	$1–$3 per drink, or 15%–20% per round
Bellhop	$2–$3 per bag, depending on the level of the hotel
Hotel Concierge	$5–$10 for advice and reservations, more for difficult tasks
Hotel Doorman	$2–$3 for hailing a cab
Valet Parking Attendant	$3–$5 when you get your car
Hotel Maid	$3–$5 per day; more in high-end hotels
Waiter	18%–22% (20%–25% is standard in upscale restaurants); nothing additional if a service charge is added to the bill
Skycap at Airport	$1–$2 per bag
Hotel Room-Service Waiter	15%–20% per delivery, even if a service charge was added since that fee goes to the hotel, not the waiter
Taxi Driver	15%–20%, but round up the fare to the next dollar amount
Tour Guide	15% of the cost of the tour, more depending on quality

TOURS

Guided tours are a good option when you don't want to do it all yourself. You travel along with a group (sometimes large, sometimes small), stay in prebooked hotels, eat with your fellow travelers (the cost of meals is sometimes included in the price of your tour, sometimes not), and follow a schedule.

But not all guided tours are an if-it's-Tuesday-this-must-be-Yosemite experience. A knowledgeable guide can take you places that you might never discover on your own, and you may be pushed to see more than you would have otherwise.

Tours aren't for everyone, but they can be just the thing for trips to places where making travel arrangements is difficult or time-consuming.

Whenever you book a guided tour, find out what's included and what isn't. A "land-only" tour includes all your travel (by bus, in most cases) in the destination, but not necessarily your flights to and from or even within it. Also, in most cases prices in tour brochures don't include fees and taxes. And remember that you'll be expected to tip your guide (in cash) at the end of the tour.

GENERAL TOURS

Trafalgar. A dependable tour operator whose guides know California well, Trafalgar conducts nearly a dozen excursions around the state. One takes in San Francisco, Monterey, Big Sur, Yosemite, and Lake Tahoe, and another surveys the Northern California Wine Country. ☎ 866/513–1995 ⊕ www.trafalgar.com/usa 🖂 From $1695.

VISITOR INFORMATION

The California Travel and Tourism Commission's website takes you to each region of California, with digital visitor guides in multiple languages, driving tours, maps, welcome center locations, information on local tours, links to bed-and-breakfasts, and a complete booking center. It also links you—via the Destinations menu—to the websites of city and regional tourism offices and attractions. *For the numbers and websites of regional and city visitor bureaus and chambers of commerce, see the Planning section in each chapter.*

Contacts California Travel and Tourism Commission. ☎ 800/462–2543 ⊕ www.visitcalifornia.com.

INDEX

PHOTO CREDITS

NOTES

NOTES

NOTES

NOTES

NOTES

NOTES

NOTES

NOTES

ABOUT OUR WRITERS

Native Californian Cheryl Crabtree has worked as a freelance writer since 1987 and regularly travels up, down, and around California for work and fun. She has contributed to *Fodor's California* since 2003 and also contributes to the *Fodor's National Parks of the West* guide. Cheryl is editor of *Montecito Magazine* and co-authors *The California Directory of Fine Wineries* book series, Central Coast and Napa, Sonoma, Mendocino editions. Her articles have appeared in many regional and national magazines. Cheryl updated the Central Coast, Palm Springs, and Sequoia & Kings Canyon National Park chapters this edition.

Daniel Mangin returned to California, where he's maintained a home for three decades, after two stints at the Fodor's editorial offices in New York City, the second one as the editorial director of Fodors.com and the Compass American Guides. With several-dozen wineries less than a half-hour's drive from home, he often finds himself transported as if by magic to a tasting room bar, communing with a sophisticated Cabernet or savoring the finish of a smooth Pinot Noir. Daniel updated the Inland Empire and Travel Smart chapters.

Steve Pastorino has visited nearly a dozen national parks on behalf of Fodor's and has favorite spots in all of them. In the summer, the longtime sports marketer and his family of five are often found at baseball diamonds. He updated the Joshua Tree National Park and Death Valley National Park chapters.

Joan Patterson is a freelance writer and editor based in southern Nevada who contributed to the Mojave Desert chapter for this edition and has worked on chapters in both *Fodor's Las Vegas* and *Fodor's Complete Guide to National Parks of the West*. She has worked in small-town newspaper production as a reporter, photographer, and news editor, and has been a features writer covering Las Vegas for the *Las Vegas Review-Journal* as both staff member and freelancer.

A veteran traveler, Claire Deeks van der Lee feels lucky to call San Diego home. Claire loves road-tripping around her adopted state of California, so it was a perfect fit for her to work on the Experience and Southern California's Best Road Trips chapters of this book. Claire has traveled to more than 40 countries, and has contributed to *Everywhere* magazine and several Fodor's guides.

Updating our Los Angeles chapter was a team of writers from Fodor's Los Angeles: Michele Bigley, Alene Dawson, Paul Feinstein, Kathy A. McDonald, Ashley Tibbits, and Clarissa Wei. *The following Fodor's staff members contributed to the Nightlife section of the Los Angeles chapter:* Meg Butler, Audrey Farnsworth, Rachael Levitt, Rachael Roth, Jesse Tabit, and Jeremy Tarr.

Updating our San Diego chapter was a team of writers from Fodor's San Diego: Marlise Kast-Myers, Kai Oliver-Kurtain, Archana Ram, Juliana Shallcross, Jeff Terich, and Claire Deeks van der Lee.